Beyond Paradise

HOLLYWOOD LEGENDS SERIES

Carl Rollyson, General Editor

Ramon Novarro, ca. 1928

Beyond Paradise

THE LIFE OF RAMON NOVARRO

André Soares

UNIVERSITY PRESS OF MISSISSIPPI • JACKSON

www.upress.state.ms.us

The University Press of Mississippi is a member of the
Association of American University Presses.

Unless otherwise credited, photographs are from the collection of the author.

Paperback edition published 2010 by University Press of Mississippi
Copyright © 2002 by André Soares
Foreword copyright © 2002 by Anthony Slide
All rights reserved
Manufactured in the United States of America

First printing 2010
∞
Library of Congress Cataloging-in-Publication Data

Soares, André.
Beyond paradise : the life of Ramon Novarro / André Soares. — Paperback ed.
p. cm. — (Hollywood legends series)
Includes bibliographical references and index.
Includes filmography.
ISBN 978-1-60473-457-7 (pbk. : alk. paper) 1. Novarro, Ramon, 1899–1968.
2. Motion picture actors and actresses—United States—Biography. 3. Hispanic
American motion picture actors and actresses—Biography. I. Title.
PN2287.N6S66 2010
791.4302′8092—dc22
[B]   2009037526

British Library Cataloging-in-Publication Data available

To Frank Carothers

CONTENTS

I have long thought that Ramon Novarro's finest performance on screen is in the title role of the 1927 Ernst Lubitsch production *The Student Prince in Old Heidelberg*. When first seen he is rather gauche, not exactly aloof but somewhat withdrawn from the all-male student company around him. As he discovers romance for the first time in the quite lovely form of Norma Shearer, he blossoms. Here, we have what Sigmund Romberg described in his original-source operetta as "the sunshine of our happy youth." Of course, it all fades away as the demands of society intervene. Life changes so seldom for the better, as Ramon Novarro himself was to discover.

Once the prince becomes a king, once the actor becomes a star, he must, if not withdraw from the all-male companionship, at least keep it securely hidden from the prying eyes of society. The establishment, be it the studio system or the Catholic Church, makes demands on public figures, and those demands can lead to tragic consequences. In *The Student Prince*, Ramon Novarro loses the one love of his life. In real life, the actor lost the majority of those whom he had loved through the years, along with the ability to cope, and, ultimately, his life.

This story of human frailty is recounted here in carefully considered and well-documented style by André Soares. It might perhaps be regarded as the gay version of *An American Tragedy*—or, in view of Novarro's roots, *A Pan-American Tragedy*.

I never met Ramon Novarro. He died three years before I came to the United States and began interviewing and socializing with the last members of the silent film community. When I was a young man in London in the

1960s, my interest in silent film was such that I did belong to both the Rudolph Valentino Memorial Guild and the Ramon Novarro Film Club. The guild was a somewhat more formal group, with monthly film screenings at the elegant home of direct-voice medium Leslie Flint, who would converse on a regular basis with Valentino (busy in the other world, appearing in new musicals composed by Ivor Novello and speaking English better than he ever did in this life). The Ramon Novarro Film Club was distinctly more homey, and its members, I realize in hindsight, less affected. It would meet at the homes of the various members, including John Lanchbery, then principal conductor of the Royal Ballet at Covent Garden. When Novarro was killed, John worried how his film club members would react to news of his homosexuality, of which we were both aware. He need not have been concerned; the ladies of the fan club simply ignored it, preferring to believe that their hero had been murdered by a couple of thugs who had invaded his property.

On one occasion, I invited the Ramon Novarro Film Club to my apartment to view a 16mm print of a ten-minute interview with Novarro conducted for the BBC by Philip Jenkinson. My projector failed to work, and Leslie Flint, who lived in the same building, graciously invited the film club to watch the film in a minitheater previously dedicated only to the productions of Rudolph Valentino. Thus, for the first time since Novarro was an extra and Valentino was the star of *The Four Horsemen of the Apocalypse* in 1921, the two actors shared a screen—and afternoon tea was also served.

In retrospect, I feel great affection for Audrey Homan, who ran the Ramon Novarro Film Club, and for the members whose names I no longer remember. They were a fine group of ordinary individuals, devoted to Novarro's memory. In many ways, Novarro was as decent and as caring as his fan club members. I can still recall his telephoning Audrey, and all of us gathering around to sing "Happy Birthday" to him on what turned out to be the last birthday celebration of his life.

When I did make it to Hollywood, one of the first stars to invite me to her home on a regular basis was Novarro's (and Valentino's) leading lady Alice Terry. Somewhat plump, and far from being as reclusive as one would be led to believe, Alice was full of good humor and funny stories relating to her career and that of her director husband, Rex Ingram. She had been a close friend to Novarro from the 1920s until his death, and he was the one individual of whom she said little and never joked.

· · ·

Alice Terry once remarked to me that the biggest thing Valentino ever did was to die. His early death gave him immortality, which a continuing career and a likely disastrous debut in talkies would not have done. Strangely, Novarro's death also gave him a form of immortality. He is remembered not as one of the best leading men of silent films, who made an easy transition to sound, but rather because of the brutal circumstances of his death.

With this biography, André Soares sets the record straight. He provides a full account of Novarro's early years in Mexico and the United States, his close ties to his family, and his first efforts to enter the world of entertainment. Through meticulous research in the payroll records of Metro and MGM, through a viewing of Novarro's extant films, a reading of the trade and fan publications, and conversations with those from the period still alive, André Soares offers the definitive record of Ramon Novarro's rise from extra to Hollywood star.

That image is never obscured by fan worship. The author notes both Novarro's strengths and faults as an actor. I have always felt that under Rex Ingram's direction, Novarro proves his worth as a performer. He is not bad in the title role of *Ben-Hur*, but, one has to admit, he is a little flabby in the seminude scenes. He lacks the muscular definition of George Walsh, the first actor assigned to the role. To his credit, Novarro can, and does, play sailors and football players at MGM despite his obvious failings in the physicality of the roles and his lack of sympathy with the characterizations. Ramon Novarro is a star, but he is also a leading man to some of the finest actresses of the period, from his most frequent (and best), Alice Terry, to Greta Garbo.

Novarro's career aside, André Soares has also managed to provide as definitive as possible a record of the actor's private life. He does not stoop to cheap gossip or innuendo, but documents what can be proven, having talked to Novarro's family, former costars, and others—including, for the first time, the convicted killers. Incredibly, the author has also unearthed parts of Novarro's unpublished memoirs (with the assistance of the actor's literary executor, Leonard Shannon) and his personal correspondence in libraries and in private hands. These sources provide the reader with a unique account of Ramon Novarro's thoughts and deeds.

Because he was a public figure, Novarro's problems as a gay man were greater than those of other homosexual men during that period. A visit to a gay bar or a casual pickup on Hollywood Boulevard was out of the question. He could only be seen at gay nightspots if he was in the company of a woman, usually the accommodating Alice Terry. (Alice served as a beard so often that when another gay actor, Barry Norton, was seen escorting her around town, a gossip columnist in *The Hollywood Reporter* asked whom Norton was trying to fool.) Aside from one long-term relationship with publicist and entertainment journalist Herbert Howe, Novarro enjoyed no lasting affairs; in later years, his only solace lay in young men obtained through a male escort agency.

Two of those young men were found guilty in Ramon Novarro's death. It was a tragedy for all concerned—not just Novarro—and it was so unnecessary. His killing is symbolic of the danger that gay men of his generation faced. It is not accused killers Paul and Tom Ferguson who should have been on trial in 1969 but American society.

It is all here in *Beyond Paradise*. Read it and weep for a man and a generation. And thank André Soares for providing us with the opportunity to understand, to sympathize with, and perhaps to chastise the Mexican film star of the 1920s and 1930s, the closeted gay man, the guilt-ridden human being who was Ramon Novarro.

On Halloween morning 1968, radio and television newscasts announced the discovery of actor Ramon Novarro's badly beaten, bloodied corpse in his Spanish-style Hollywood Hills home. The grisly news shocked those who knew Novarro personally as well as the millions of older moviegoers who decades earlier had admired the star of *Ben-Hur, Scaramouche,* and *The Student Prince.* At the time of his death a half-forgotten figure of another era, the sixty-nine-year-old Novarro had been one of the most popular film performers of the 1920s and early 1930s—and filmdom's first Latin American star.

By the late 1960s, however, Novarro's acting career consisted mainly of guest spots in television series. If it were not for the horrendous manner in which he was killed, his passing would have received scant notice. As it was, Novarro's death made front-page news the world over. More than a thousand mourners passed by his bier while his body lay in state in a downtown Los Angeles mortuary.

In the days that followed, two young brothers were arrested and charged with Novarro's murder. Each told the police that he was not responsible for Novarro's death, and that they had gone to the actor's house to "hustle" him. Shortly thereafter, news reports about the police investigation disclosed that the romantic hero who on-screen had made love to some of Hollywood's most glamorous stars—from Alice Terry and Barbara La Marr to Greta Garbo, Myrna Loy, Joan Crawford, and Norma Shearer—was offscreen sexually attracted to men. This revelation, at a time when homosexuality was still considered either a serious psychological disorder or a form of sexual perversion, came as another shock to many, including some who *thought* they had known Novarro intimately. Although the actor had frequently asserted in the press that he would never marry and in later years had openly declared that marriage was "one mistake I did not make," fans and some friends were aghast that the deeply religious man described in the *Variety* obituary as a "gentle, gentlemanly version" of Valentino had been a homosexual.

Granted, Novarro's reputation had not been spotless. In the last three decades of his life, several encounters with the law for drunken driving had been widely reported. Even so, the Novarro image ingrained in the public's mind was a composite of respectability: the consummate and well-liked professional; the generous son and brother who had supported his large Mexican family after becoming a Hollywood star in the early 1920s; and especially the ardent Catholic who during his life had more than once seriously considered the priesthood or the monastery.

A series of lurid revelations during the trial of the two accused killers further shattered Novarro's old public image as a paragon of virtue. In the months and years to come, those disclosures would lead to outlandish rumors about the manner of Novarro's death and to distortions about Novarro's life and character. These fables have overshadowed his professional accomplishments and his historical importance as the first Latin American performer to succeed in Hollywood.

MGM's top male star at the dawn of the sound era and one of the biggest international box-office attractions of his day, Novarro was also a darling of the critics of the 1920s and 1930s. The *New York Herald Tribune*'s highly respected Richard Watts, Jr., expressing the opinion of most of his colleagues, once declared the Mexican star "one of the most charming, intelligent, tasteful and generally expert of screen players, and he is so attractive a performer that he seems competent even in the midst of an atrocity." Despite Novarro's highly successful transition to sound films, aided by a fine singing voice, serious miscasting and formulaic roles in several "atrocities" eventually cooled the ardor of film audiences.

Since his best work has generally been unavailable until fairly recently, Novarro has largely been forgotten by modern film audiences and film historians alike. Yet the truth remains that no other Latin American performer—from Gilbert Roland and Dolores del Río to Ricardo Montalbán and Anthony Quinn—has ever reached the prominence held by Ramon Novarro at the peak of his career.

Beyond Paradise

Mexican Roots

Get Out Your Maps! And look up Buango [*sic*]," proclaimed a geographically challenged fan magazine writer in the January 1923 issue of *Photoplay*. "Never heard of it? Neither did we. But it's destined for immortality." That city—actually Durango, Mexico—was the birthplace of Ramon Novarro (born Samaniego), Metro Pictures' fast-ascending romantic star. According to Metro's publicity department, in the veins of the handsome young Mexican heartthrob ran the blood of the earliest Spanish conquistadores mingled with that of Aztec royalty, a studio-created myth that only partly matched Novarro's actual family history.

In the ninth century, a half-Moorish prince of the Iberian kingdom of Navarra erected a castle near the village of Samaniego (possibly of Celtic origin), a few miles north of the Ebro River in modern Spain's Basque country. In time, his descendants, who became one of the most renowned noble families in the region, adopted the village designation as their own surname, thus giving birth to the Samaniego lineage. Through intermarriages with other blue-blooded families, the Samaniegos spread across the northern section of the Iberian Peninsula, where the Samaniego men often held high offices reserved for the nobility. Ramon Novarro's direct ancestors came from the small Castilian town of Burgos, from which two brothers emigrated to the New World in the early seventeenth century.

The Samaniegos' long journey from Europe to New Spain, a territory that encompassed all the land under Spanish rule north of the Isthmus of Panama, occurred approximately one century after the arrival of the first Spanish conquistadores. Eduardo Samaniego, Ramon Novarro's youngest brother, recounted in his memoirs that his ancestors settled in the town of Querétaro, about 160 miles northwest of Mexico City. There, Eduardo asserts, they helped in the fight against the Otomí Indians, for which service the Samaniegos were awarded the title of counts.

By the time of Mexico's independence from Spanish rule in 1821, Novarro's branch of the Samaniegos had settled in Bavispe, a small, desolate village in the northwestern Sonora Province. Don Florentino Samaniego served as commander of the local presidio, while his wife, María Josefa Delgado, of the influential Ortíz family of Santa Fé de Nuevo México, tended their five children—one of whom was to become Novarro's paternal grandfather, Mariano Samaniego Delgado (in Mexico, following the Spanish custom, the mother's maiden name is placed after the father's surname).

In 1838, after Don Florentino was killed during an Apache raid, six-year-old Mariano traveled two hundred miles northeast with his widowed mother and his siblings to El Paso del Norte (known today as Ciudad Juárez, or simply Juárez), in the neighboring state of Chihuahua. Their final destination was the home of Mariano's maternal grandmother, then living with her brother, the revered Father Ramón Ortíz.

As one of the most important and influential personages in the region, Mariano's great-uncle was at the center of the social life of El Paso del Norte. Throughout the years, Father Ortíz shared his spacious house—surrounded by seven acres of orchards, vineyards, and corrals—with two older sisters, several nephews and nieces, his personal servants, and numerous guests. Besides his religious and social duties, the padre was actively involved in political affairs, even organizing an armed resistance to the invading American armies during the Mexican War in the mid-1840s.

One consequence of that war that was to directly affect the Samaniegos was the forfeiture of Mexican territory to the United States. After losing Alta California and Nuevo México to American forces, Mexico ceded all territories north of both the Rio Grande and the Gila River to its northern neighbor. This border shift, certified by the Treaty of Guadalupe Hidalgo in 1848, would haunt the Samaniegos for generations as a later change in the course of the Rio Grande resulted in the loss of their land in the Juárez–El Paso area to the American government.

With the financial assistance of his great-uncle Father Ortíz, the young Mariano Samaniego received his education at a seminary in Durango, located approximately four hundred miles south of El Paso del Norte. He also studied in Mexico City, and a few years later left for Europe to attend medical school at the University of Paris. While in France, he befriended Felipe Pérez Gavilán (his was a composite surname), with whom he shared the same nationality, professional interests, and upper-class background.

In 1860, Mariano—now Dr. Samaniego—and Felipe returned together to Mexico, finding their native country again embroiled in warfare. A three-year civil war, which pitted the clerical-military institutions against those who sought to break the establishment's political grip, was nearing its end. One year later, France's interventionist army and the puppet government of Ferdinand Maximilian became the new foes. Throughout that crisis, Dr. Samaniego served as a surgeon in the Republican Army of the North under the command of General Luis Terrazas, one of Chihuahua's most powerful men and the state's governor for several terms. Dr. Samaniego married María Carmen Siqueiros during that time, settling his wife in El Paso del Norte, whereas Felipe settled in Durango after his marriage to Rosa Guerrero, an alleged descendant of Aztec nobility.

Following the withdrawal of the last French troops from Mexico in March 1867 and the execution of Maximilian in June of that year, peace was finally declared. Once relieved of active duty, Dr. Samaniego returned to El Paso del Norte, where, for the next three decades, he was to practice medicine and dentistry on both sides of the Mexican-American border. During that period, he would also serve in the Chihuahua legislature, function three times as interim state governor, act as the state representative in the Mexican National Congress, and serve as the Mexican vice-consul in Franklin, Texas, just across the Rio Grande from El Paso del Norte. In addition, he fathered six children, one of whom was to become Ramon Novarro's father—Mariano Nicolás Samaniego, born in 1871.

Growing up near the U.S. border, the young Mariano spoke fluent English. He attended high school in Las Cruces, New Mexico, and later studied at the University of Pennsylvania's Dental School. In that period, Mariano paid a visit to the Pérez Gavilán household while on a business trip to Durango. He was then introduced to Felipe's daughter, the petite brunette María Leonor, one year his junior.

Gifted with a dramatic soprano voice, Leonor had begun taking voice-training lessons at the age of seven. She occasionally sang at family parties, but the Pérez Gaviláns were a traditional well-to-do Mexican family, and a career—especially one onstage—was unthinkable for a respectable woman. Yet, Leonor would never completely abandon singing. At times, she would sit at the piano and sing arias from *Tosca* or *Aida*, and in later years she and Novarro would spend hours singing together.

Leonor soon established a close rapport with Mariano, a development that must have pleased both patriarchs of those two prominent families. The courtship resulted in marriage on October 24, 1892, at about the time of Mariano's graduation from the dental school; after the wedding, the couple settled in Durango, quite possibly so Leonor could remain close to her family.

Lying in a fertile valley of the Sierra Madre almost seven thousand feet above sea level, Durango, known as *la Perla del Guadiana*—the Pearl of the Guadiana Valley—had its origins in the exploitation of iron ore in the surrounding mountains. The riches acquired from the mines were lavishly spent on exquisite colonial edifices, many of which exhibited decorated portals, elaborate arches, and carefully landscaped courtyards and gardens. Some, such as the Juan José Zambrano residence—which even housed the millionaire's own private theater—were magnificent palaces that reflected the wealth and power of Durango's elite.

In the mid-1890s, Dr. Mariano Samaniego opened a dental office in his new home at 39 de la Septima Calle de Negrete, and according to family lore, he quickly earned a reputation as one of the best dentists in that town of nearly thirty thousand inhabitants. Besides housing Dr. Samaniego's busy practice, the residence consisted of a kitchen, a vestibule, a bathroom, a living room, and several bedrooms. Corridors of polished tiles led to three inner courts, each centered on a *pileta*, a small water receptacle surrounded by pots of flowers, beside which a shade tree grew. In the back, a mirador—a wide, sheltered terrace—overlooked an orchard of orange, cherry, peach, and other fruit trees. Along the perimeter, vine-covered walls, iron-bound doors, and shuttered windows kept the house cool and secluded.

Emilio, the Samaniegos' first child, was born in 1895. He was followed by twelve siblings: Guadalupe, Rosa, Ramón, Leonor, Mariano, María de la Luz, Antonio, José, Felipe, Carmen, Angel, and Eduardo, born in 1911, when Señora Samaniego was thirty-nine years old. Like most nations of the time, Mexico had high birth rates *and* high infant- and child-mortality rates. Unsanitary conditions and inadequate medical care made childhood deaths commonplace even in wealthier households. Emilio died of scarlet fever before his fifth birthday, while diphtheria was the likely cause of Felipe's death at the age of three. Since Emilio had been the firstborn and Felipe the tenth, Señora Samaniego referred to their early deaths as "tithes" she had paid—*diezmos y primicias,* the first of the crop and a tenth of the remainder given to the Church.

Ramón, who became the oldest surviving male child by the time he was one year old, was born at the family home on the Calle de Negrete on the morning of February 6, 1899. Numerous sources state that he was baptized with fourteen names but used only José Ramón Gil Samaniego after reaching adulthood. Such a profusion of names may conceivably have been given him at his christening, though his birth certificate shows only three names: Ramón Gil Samaniego.

While the older girls at the Samaniego household helped in the care of their younger siblings, Ramón was cared for by Señora Samaniego herself. The boy, for his part, endeavored to please his mother, whether performing odd jobs to buy her an engraved gold medal as a memento of a rare singing performance, or developing an appreciation for the things she liked. Mother and son's close bond was made even stronger by those shared interests, one of which was a fondness for music and theater. Ramón was six years old when his mother began teaching him piano, as she envisioned her eldest son becoming a concert pianist. A few years later, his musical education was extended to include voice, and soon he was singing in church choirs.

Also at the age of six, a cotton-wigged Ramón performed his first acting piece with sister Guadalupe at their grandmother's birthday party: a recitation of Spanish poet Ramón Campoamor's "Quién supiera escribir" ("If Only I Could Write"), the tale of an illiterate peasant girl who begs a priest to compose a letter to her sweetheart. Inspired by the warm applause, Ramón later presented a series of puppet shows in a marionette theater, a gift from his mother on his eighth birthday. In those early theatrical endeavors, he was frequently joined by his cousin and fellow theater enthusiast Rafael Pérez Gavilán, while the Samaniego girls helped to set the stage by embroidering the minitheater's curtains.

Holidays and weekends were often spent at one of the Pérez Gaviláns' haciendas. The main property was La Hacienda de Navacoyán, on the outskirts of Durango, though Señora Samaniego's La Ochoa and her brother Luis's La Sauceda, which was surrounded by the imposing Sierra Madre range, were also frequent holiday destinations. Years later, Novarro nostalgically recalled "wonderful summers . . . on the family ranch, where we lived out of doors, swam, and rode horseback." Although the Samaniego children did not actually live outdoors while at the family haciendas—La Sauceda, for example, possessed a spacious main house, its own church, and cottages for the workers—in those relatively isolated days in rural Mexico (the country's population in 1910 was a little more than fifteen million), it probably *felt* as though they did.

For the children, simple things left lasting impressions. The sighting of African Americans was a thrilling event, as blacks were practically nonexistent in that part of Mexico. In order to glimpse the unusual-looking foreigners, the children would ride on horseback to the train station to wave at the black porters aboard American trains. (Years later, blacks still held a distinct interest for at least one Samaniego. When Novarro met architect Paul Williams at a small cocktail party, he rose to his feet, saying, "You're the first of your race that I have had the pleasure of meeting. May I shake the hand of so distinguished a member?" Williams politely obliged.)

As was the custom in Mexico—especially among the upper classes, which were both spiritually and politically associated with the Catholic Church—religion played a central role in the upbringing of the Samaniego children. Daily mass was an obligation, not a choice. At the haciendas, if the children failed to attend mass in the morning, they were not allowed to go horseback riding in the afternoon. As would be expected, they went to mass assiduously. Following Mexican tradition, Christmas letters were written to the Holy Child, not to Santa Claus; during Easter, the emphasis was not on bunnies and chocolate eggs, but on burning an effigy of Judas. Birthdays were celebrated twice: on the day of one's birth and on the day of one's patron saint (Ramón's other birthday celebration was held on August 31).

In accordance with its preeminence as an archdiocese, early-twentieth-century Durango boasted a vast array of Catholic structures, including the majestic baroque Catedral Basilica Menor, the Church of Santa Ana also in the baroque style, the sanctuaries of Guadalupe and Our Lady of the Angels, and the Church of the Compañia. These shrines were not merely tourist attractions or relics of another era; they were real places of worship. Growing up surrounded by those sumptuous examples of religious reverence and by his family's traditional beliefs, Ramón found Catholicism an almost tangible part of his existence.

In the Samaniego household, religious devotion was closely intertwined with familial devotion. Each night before going to bed, the children dropped to one knee to receive their mother's blessing, a Catholic ritual suggesting the saintliness of parents. Señora Samaniego, in particular, represented the bastion of faith and tradition in the family, as she was responsible for instilling in her offspring the proper cultural and social mores. According to Herbert Howe, Novarro's future publicist and companion, there was little demonstration of affection in the home. "Compliments were never paid," Howe observed. "Whatever came, came as a gift of God and to Him only thanks was rendered." Howe theorized that such restraint in the expression of tenderness during his formative years might explain Novarro's own lack of warmth in his adult years.

The Samaniegos' untroubled days were abruptly shattered by a double blow in the early 1910s. Still in his early forties, Dr. Samaniego developed facial neuralgia, a disease that caused sudden, strong shocks in the nerves on the right side of his face. Each time he underwent surgery, some facial nerves had to be removed, which eventually resulted in a severe impairment of his optical nerves. Physically unable to continue his dental practice, Dr. Samaniego had to resort to other sorts of work. He began teaching English at the Instituto Juárez, but without the dental office, his income was substantially curtailed. Ramón, the eldest son, was barely in his teens and still too young to find a job. Income from the La Ochoa hacienda surely helped, though in all likelihood the Samaniegos managed to stay financially afloat through the help of their relatives. Another sort of crisis, however, could not be remedied by family intervention.

By 1910, President Porfirio Díaz had dominated Mexican politics for more than three decades. But with the passing of the years, Mexicans had become increasingly resentful of the regime's disregard of citizens' rights and the blatant political favoritism shown for Díaz's cronies and foreign interests. Exacerbating the general dissatisfaction, the country's economy had foundered during the first decade of the twentieth century. High inflation and unemployment led to unrest, and as protests mounted, repression intensified. Thus the groundwork was laid for the revolution, which exploded in 1910 after the defeat of landowner and industrialist Francisco E. Madero in that summer's fraudulent presidential election. In November, Madero, who had fled to the United States, led an uprising against the Díaz government, which was brought down several months later. Díaz resigned and left for Paris, but the fighting continued unabated. In their struggle for power, divergent groups of revolutionaries and counterrevolutionaries battled one another, while fighting also erupted within the disparate groups themselves.

Durango soon became enmeshed in the turmoil. In May 1911, bandits and rebels, many of whom were displaced peasants, attacked the town, while federal soldiers erected barricades throughout the area. The situation briefly improved in the aftermath of Madero's victorious entry into Mexico City, but after Victoriano Huerta, commandant of the federal forces, seized control of the capital from Madero in February 1913, the second phase of the revolution began. Following a siege of forty days in late spring, Durango became one of the first state capitals to fall into the hands of anti-Huerta revolutionaries. Learning establishments were closed, including Our Lady of Guadalupe, the school Ramón was attending. A state of anarchy prevailed as rival rebel leaders fought to take control of the city. Houses, stores, and businesses were ransacked, and entire districts went up in flames. Durango's citizens lived in perpetual fear. Stray bullets killed innocent bystanders even inside their homes. A knock at the door in the middle of the night could mean death to anyone who was identified with the wrong political faction.

To escape the danger, which was especially grave for a family belonging to the urban elite, the Samaniegos left for Mexico City, where conditions had been somewhat normalized. Once the family was settled with some wealthy relatives, the children started school again. Ramón was sent to the prestigious Instituto Científico de México, which had been founded by Jesuit priests. This one-story, late-eighteenth-century building was popularly known as the Colegio de los Mascarones, or School of the Big Figureheads, because the effigies atop its portals looked like the sculpted figures on the prows of boats. Fan magazines would later assert that at Mascarones fourteen-year-old Ramón went through military training, developed into an accomplished athlete and track champion, and during breaks from those strenuous physical activities studied music, French, and English. Those probably exaggerated claims can be neither confirmed nor disproved, for the school's records for that tumultuous period have long since disappeared.

Months after the Samaniegos' arrival in Mexico City, another counter-revolution broke out. This latest uprising led to Huerta's ouster by Venustiano Carranza and his Constitutionalist Army. Following this latest change in government, news arrived that conditions in Durango had improved. Dr. Samaniego, who was probably excused from military service because of his poor health, decided to return home to check on the family possessions, taking with him Ramón, Angel, and Eduardo. Soon after their arrival in Durango, more fighting erupted, severing all communications between that city and the capital for eleven agonizing months.

In the spring of 1915, the family was finally reunited in Durango. Shortly thereafter, Guadalupe and Rosa announced their desire to enter a convent, and they were soon followed by the young Leonor, who felt quite lost after the departure of her two older sisters. Ramón, then sixteen years old, had developed into a rebellious teenager, poking fun at the local townspeople and putting "questionable ideas" into the heads of children who had been entrusted to him. But influenced by his sisters' decision, Ramón too began considering the religious life. Years later, he jokingly recalled his wish "to die a martyr and be canonized." He began fasting, sleeping on the floor without covering, performing servants' duties, rising daily at five in the morning, and walking around with eyes downcast. Other children started singing "Ave Maria" whenever they saw him, "but I was rapt to Heaven, and did not mind."

Exaggerated as such a story may be, the young Ramón conceivably decided that only certain types of behavior were appropriate for those truly serious about the teachings of the Church. Catholicism was not something reserved only for morning mass. Faith was to be lived at every moment of one's existence. As an upper-class youth, Ramón may also have been attracted to the high social status of the priesthood. The clergy had lost some of its power since the government of nineteenth-century statesman Benito Juárez, but it was still a wealthy and influential social force in Mexico. Thus, belonging to so revered and respected an institution could be not only an answer to a spiritual call, but also an affirmation of one's social standing. Likewise, the call of the priesthood could also be seen as Ramón's attempt to cling to an older and more traditional social order, an understandable view for a young man who was witnessing the destruction of his way of life. Whatever the underlying motivations may have been at that time, Novarro's faith was to remain constant throughout the years—though his devoutness did vary according to his emotional state.

But dreams of martyrdom and sainthood were brushed aside once Ramón became enthralled by the operatic stage. He gave up the idea of becoming a priest, at least temporarily, after seeing an old Metropolitan Opera advertisement for Enrico Caruso and Geraldine Farrar in *Manon*. Additionally, the youngster had been greatly impressed by the (then still unfinished) Palacio de Bellas Artes while in the capital. "In Mexico City the Opera is a beautiful place," Novarro recalled for *Screenland* magazine in 1929. "[It's] a wonderful temple of music comparable only to the Paris Opera in grandeur." The elaborate costumes and decor, the social prestige, and the overall glamorous atmosphere of the opera world thus charmed him away from a stark life inside a Mexican monastery. "Perhaps it was the devil tempting me," Novarro remarked years later. "I'm still not so sure it wasn't." To eradicate any sense of guilt for his defection, Ramón consulted the local priest, who granted him sanction to make music his life's work.

In the mid-1910s, Dr. Samaniego was again working as a night school English teacher at the Instituto Juárez, one of the few educational establishments that remained open in Durango. But despite periods of tranquillity, the Samaniegos realized they could not remain in town with the constant threat of attacks by marauders from either side of the ongoing conflict. Furthermore, with most schools closed, they would be unable to provide an education for their children. The couple eventually decided they should send the children to the United States, where they could stay with Dr. Samaniego's relatives in El Paso or Los Angeles. This venture appealed to Ramón, for even though his English was spotty—and to some extent would remain so for the rest of his life—there were markedly better opportunities for an artistic career north of the Rio Grande than he could possibly find in revolution-plagued Mexico. After much haggling, he finally persuaded his mother to allow him to travel north ahead of everyone else.

In September 1916, seventeen-year-old Ramón, accompanied by fifteen-year-old Mariano, headed north to Texas by train. About one-third of the way into the trip, in the small town of Escalón, the train stopped. The bridge ahead of them had been destroyed. Then word came that the bridge leading back to Durango had also been blown up. For two days, the two Durango travelers survived on tortillas, beans, and dirty water, while Ramón fretted that the rebel Pancho Villa might invade the town and have his ears cut off—an unqualified disaster for an aspirant to a music career. Finally, a train arrived from Torreón bearing bridge-building personnel; but since Ramón was unsure about the quality of their work, he decided to walk back to Durango with his brother.

Upon the two brothers' return, Señora Samaniego insisted that it was God's will that they stay home, to which Ramón countered, "Maybe he was just testing us." Determined to prove to both God and his mother that his destiny lay on the northern side of the border, Ramón, carrying $100 (approximately $1,350 today) in gold coins and now accompanied by both Mariano and a local friend, once more attempted the perilous journey north, but this time via Monterrey and Piedras Negras. A few days later, after going through immigration procedures that included a physical examination, bathing, and disinfecting, Ramón and Mariano were safe in Eagle Pass, Texas. They proceeded to El Paso to meet with their relatives, but shortly afterward—without notifying their parents—the duo headed farther west, as Ramón was intent on pursuing a show business career in Los Angeles.

In the fall of 1917, the rest of the family followed. For them, too, it was a dismal train ride from Durango to El Paso. Corpses hanging from telephone poles along the tracks across northern Mexico's desolate landscape were a constant reminder of the danger posed by rebels, renegade government forces, and common thieves. The many potential hazards notwithstanding, the Samaniegos reached the safety of El Paso in November 1917.

Guadalupe, Rosa, and the young Leonor were the only family members who remained behind. Guadalupe had become a novice in the Order of the Sisters of the Cross and was eventually sent to the Church of San Juan Bautista in Coyoacán, a suburb of Mexico City, where she was to manage the sisterhood's business affairs. Rosa had joined the Order of the Sisters of Charity, adopting the name of her older sister Guadalupe (which must have caused some confusion in the family). After her novitiate in Havana, she was assigned to nurse leprosy sufferers in the Canary Islands. From there, she was relocated to Madrid and later to Teruel, in northeastern Spain. The young Leonor followed in Rosa's footsteps, also being sent to Cuba, then to the Canary Islands, and later to Spain, where she remained until the early 1930s.

To attend to business interests, the Samaniegos stayed in El Paso for nearly a year. But the promise of the milder Southern California weather, coupled with the desire to see Ramón and Mariano, motivated the family to move west. In August 1918, they were finally reunited in Los Angeles.

TWO

Arrival in Paradise

My mother thought it was the closest place to paradise," recalled Carmen Gavilán, and for a family recently arrived from a country torn by a bloody revolution, Los Angeles probably did seem like paradise. In the late 1910s, the city was surrounded by open spaces and green hillsides with rows of flowery pepper trees, while its streets were lined with date and fan palms. Near-constant sunshine, pure air, and a leisurely pace further contributed to the city's paradisiacal allure.

But for all its apparent serenity, the sleepy Mexican town of several decades earlier had been transformed into a fast-growing American city. Los Angeles County's population almost doubled from 500,000 in 1910 to more than 930,000 by the end of the decade. Along with the thousands of new residents arriving from the American Midwest, two other forces helped spur this colossal growth: Mexican immigration and the booming film industry, which had relocated en masse from the East Coast.

The first local film studios had been makeshift affairs, but once the industry achieved a sense of security, permanent facilities were built in an area stretching from Culver City, just a few miles from the Pacific Ocean, to the eastern end of the San Fernando Valley and East Los Angeles, approximately fifteen miles away. Before the 1910s were over, motion pictures had become the county's leading industry.

In the meantime, Mexican immigrants were settling primarily in the downtown Plaza area, then known as Sonoratown, so they could easily get to work in the nearby railroads. Main Street between Sixth and Macy Streets was the heart of the community, with restaurants, theaters, barbershops, pool halls, and numerous other businesses catering to Mexican nationals. By far the fastest-growing national group in California during the 1910s, Mexicans began spreading eastward from the Plaza into Alhambra and East Los Angeles.

Some of this great influx from south of the border coincided with the United States' entry into World War I in April 1917, which resulted in widespread labor shortages. Mexicans were especially welcome as cheap and hard workers, but, paradoxically, the war also brought on a surge of anti-foreign sentiment. In parts of the American Southwest, including the then largely WASP city of Los Angeles, the seething xenophobia took the form of a "Brown Scare," as locals feared the invasion of poor, uneducated, brown-skinned Catholics into their communities.

During that same period, Mexicans also became one of the main targets of a "scare" of another color—red—after federal agents launched a hunt for alleged Communists and anarchists, an operation supported by merchants and manufacturers whose main objective was to prevent labor organizing. Since many Mexicans worked in crucial sectors of the economy, such as railroad construction and agriculture, they were perceived as a particularly serious threat. This association of Mexicans with Communism would continue for years, and later was to affect Novarro directly.

To avoid being targeted by the several scares—and as a sign of their own ethnic prejudices—the small minority of upper-class Mexicans (even if they had Indian blood) and Mexicans of European ancestry often referred to themselves as "Spanish." Despite their dark brown hair and eyes, the Samaniegos were lighter skinned than most of their fellow nationals, but they too must have had to deal with anti-Mexican discrimination—whether or not they called themselves Spanish. Mexican children, for example, were often segregated into schools of inferior quality, while their parents frequently had to pay higher rents than white Americans for comparable dwellings.

Ramón and Mariano arrived in Los Angeles on Thanksgiving Day, 1916. At first, they stayed with their physician uncle, Dr. José Samaniego, and his family at 420 South Serrano Avenue, about two miles west of downtown. The two young brothers remained at their uncle's home until sometime in 1917, when their names first appear in the Los Angeles city directory (Ramón is listed as "Raymond") as residents of a boardinghouse on 852 South Main Street, in the heart of the downtown district.

In spite of their uncle's assistance, Ramón and Mariano faced severe financial hardships during their first two years in Los Angeles. Lured by the glamour of Hollywood—and disregarding his parents' disapproval—shortly after his arrival Ramón temporarily set opera to the side to try his luck in the film business. With only minimal security at the studios, he had little difficulty walking through the gates and into casting offices, but actually landing a job was a different matter. The dark-haired, brown-eyed, handsome young Mexican was competing daily with thousands of other applicants. "I almost lost hope," he later told *Picture-Play*'s Margaret Ettinger. "Finally one day, I was given an extra part. Then I thought my days of hardship were over. But they weren't. It was months before I was cast as an extra again, and in the meantime I nearly starved."

In those preunion times, for a daily salary ranging from $3 to $5 (approximately $30 to $50 today), extras had to be on the set by early morning and sometimes work until late at night, without the benefit of overtime pay or any of today's amenities. It was hard and irregular work that rarely led to larger roles, but for the inexperienced Ramón, working as an extra was the only way to break into the business. His first bit part was that of a Mexican bandit in the 1917 Famous Players–Lasky release *The Jaguar's Claws*, for which he traveled with the company to the Mojave Desert. Believing this to be his big chance—"my motto was, Anything to Attract the Attention of Your Boss"—Ramón began "acting" during a pivotal scene. Unimpressed, director Marshall Neilan immediately ordered him out.

Ramón's other bit roles that year included a German soldier in *The Little American*, starring Mary Pickford, and an Aztec warrior in Cecil B. DeMille's *The Woman God Forgot*. According to Herbert Howe, the determined young Mexican once again tried to attract some attention by displaying his piano virtuosity to the film's star, opera diva Geraldine Farrar—feeling insulted when she acknowledged his playing with a mere "pretty good." Thrilled with his first $5 (instead of the usual $3) extra role, Ramón also appeared as a shepherd in *The Hostage*, allegedly through the influence of the picture's star, matinee idol Wallace Reid, who had taken a liking to the struggling extra after meeting him on the set of *The Woman God Forgot*.

Since extra and bit player work remained sporadic, Ramón supplemented his income with a variety of odd jobs, such as grocery clerk and busboy at the celebrity-packed Victor Hugo Restaurant, and made good use of his childhood music lessons by tutoring in piano. But his most surprising moneymaking activity during that lean period was posing nude for students at the J. Francis Smith School of Illustration and Painting (future film star Leatrice Joy was a fellow model).

In the late 1910s, baring one's body even for art's sake was perceived in most circles as a form of depravity. Nude modeling was thus a peculiar choice of work for a youngster who not long before had considered becoming a priest. Ramón likely saw nothing wrong with that activity for *himself*, though he would certainly have forbidden any of his siblings from doing the same. He was an artist, and in his view, artists were exempt from the traditional moral code. In later years, he would accept, even admire, the unorthodox behavior of many of his female costars, while frowning upon the same in his sisters. This moral compartmentalization—or double standard—would remain a constant element in Novarro's life: he would embrace or reject the conservative cultural values he was raised with according to the circumstances.

Ramón obtained a steadier source of income working as an usher at Tally's Theater and Clune's Auditorium, jobs that also gave him the chance to rub elbows with stars of the theater and music worlds. Now a firm believer in French psychotherapist Émile Coué's motto, "Every day in every way I'm getting better and better," Ramón was confident that others would soon recognize his multifarious talents. Hence, he began scattering seeds wherever he could, from the film studios to the stage and the opera, with the hope that at least one of them would bear fruit. He later claimed to have tried auditioning for Geraldine Farrar, dance diva Anna Pavlova, stage grand dame Minnie Maddern Fiske, and opera singer Mary Garden, who was allegedly impressed by the young usher's boldness but, like the other celebrities, quietly ignored his pleas.

Another way Ramón found to make himself visible to both celebrities and talent scouts was working for $10 a week as a combination usher and bit player at the Majestic Theater in downtown Los Angeles. The stock company, which had been set up to showcase the talents of established stage performers Edward Everett Horton, Evelyn Varden, and Franklin Pangborn, would allow Ramón to encounter influential show business figures both onstage and in the audience.

As a put-down of Method actors, Novarro would later affirm that he neither required nor sought dramatic-school training, but his time with the Majestic company (and later at the Hollywood Community Theater) served as a hands-on apprenticeship. His first role with the company was that of a Japanese bird seller in J. H. Benrimo's *The Willow Tree*, which was followed by numerous other parts that, however small, exposed him to the techniques and expertise of the Majestic's stage veterans.

After Novarro had become a star, columnist Louella Parsons described how he had learned every part in every play presented at the Majestic with a determination—or perhaps obsessiveness—that surprised both directors and fellow actors. Even if such dedication was exaggerated for publicity purposes, the young immigrant *was* consumed with the idea of success in the new country. Film actress Betty Blythe, who later appeared with a bearded and heavily made-up Ramón (as Herod) in a production of Oscar Wilde's *Salome* at the Hollywood Community Theater, remembered seeing him play three different parts in one production, and "doing each one with equal skill."

In the summer of 1918, around the time his family arrived in Los Angeles, Ramón's professional fortunes took a turn for the better with the appearance of choreographer Marion Morgan. Since the mid-1910s, this former director of summer dance programs at the University of California at Berkeley had been touring the country with her own ballet company. Inspired by history and classical legends, Morgan's modernistic dances were performed at upscale vaudeville theaters and as prologues to feature films at the more prestigious movie palaces. In the summer of 1918, while looking for a male dancer who would not be drafted and sent to the battlefields of Europe, Morgan spotted Ramón in a production at the Majestic. She allegedly picked him for the ballet *Attila and the Huns* because she liked his physique, though the actual reason for her choosing the five-foot-six-inch, slightly pudgy bit player with no dance experience was most probably his Mexican citizenship.

In August, Ramón left his family house and headed to New York, where *Attila* rehearsals would be held. He rented a room in a boardinghouse on Forty-ninth Street, and, since he was not getting paid during rehearsals, worked nights as a pastry boy at the Horn and Hardart Automat on Broadway for $1.60 a night. Obsessed with pursuing a show business career during the day and forced to earn a living at night, an exhausted Ramón developed sore feet, which slowed him down on the dance stage. He was summarily fired, but had to be rehired when his replacement proved to be even less adequate. Despite his exhaustion, Ramón must have been a quick study, for in early fall he left New York with the *Attila and the Huns* troupe for a tour of the Orpheum theater circuit in the northern United States and Canada.

Morgan's latest routine, described by an enthralled Milwaukee reviewer as "quite the most beautiful thing of the year," depicted a sinuous Attila and his fellow serpentine Huns as they battled and pillaged their way through Italy. Despite the acclaim, Ramón felt homesick after months on the road. "I was anxious to get back to the West Coast," he later recalled, "and, though I almost expected to go through the same hardships I had endured before, even then the call was too strong to resist. There was that inner desire to suffer, I believe." Melodramatics aside, Ramón missed his family and perhaps felt he should do more to help in their support. Also, touring theaters in Wisconsin or Ontario would not do as much for his career as appearing at the Majestic in Los Angeles, where he could be seen by talent scouts.

In June 1919, Morgan's troupe finally returned to Los Angeles. After two more weeks with the company, Ramón decided he had had enough of vaudeville and opted instead to once again haunt the casting offices of film studios. He resumed his work as an usher at the Majestic and began taking dance lessons from Ernest Belcher, a long-faced, impeccably groomed Englishman who owned the renowned Celeste School of Dancing in Hollywood.

Belcher's thirteen-year-old stepdaughter, actress Lina Basquette (then the child star of the Lena Baskette Featurettes), later recalled having had her first crush on the twenty-year-old Mexican dance student. She was not alone. Fellow Belcher alumna Derelys Perdue, a slender brunette who became Novarro's frequent dance partner, was also infatuated with the handsome young Mexican. Ramón's interests, however, lay elsewhere.

During his stint at the Majestic and with Morgan's troupe, Ramón learned more than acting techniques and dance steps. Having been raised in an environment in which rules of conduct for both genders were precise, narrow, and strictly enforced, he was likely both terrified and fascinated by the relative freedom from societal mores enjoyed—at least on the surface—by artists. If Ramón was not fully aware of his sexual orientation by the late 1910s, his contact with show people opened his eyes to manifestations of human sexuality taught neither by church nor by family. Marion Morgan, for instance, preferred the company of women to that of men, and would in later years become film director Dorothy Arzner's life partner. The Majestic players Edward Everett Horton and Franklin Pangborn were both "prissy" types—a characteristic they would use to good advantage in films of the 1930s and 1940s—whose sexual orientation was no secret among their coworkers.

In sharp contrast, Ramón quite possibly had had little—if any—understanding of homosexuality while growing up in Durango. The institution of the Code of Napoleon during Emperor Maximilian's rule had decriminalized same-sex relations, but these continued to be frowned on by the Mexican government. Effeminate men were frequently harassed by the police, and those accused of having engaged in homosexual acts could be sent to jail. De facto prejudice against gays was so pervasive that many—perhaps most—Mexicans remained unaware that sex with a partner of the same gender was actually legal.

Thus, despite Ramón's recent exposure to a wider spectrum of human sexuality and his own personal views about artists like himself, he still had to cope with his cultural constraints. Certain kinds of activities were deemed unfit for a man, and even though Ramón rebelled against such arbitrary rules, he remained susceptible to self-doubt. "I didn't take the work seriously," he would later confess to *Photoplay* about his dancing with Morgan's troupe. "...I was afraid of being thought a sis." In reality, the struggling actor and dancer had good reason to believe he lacked a strong virile image, for his delicate features, slight stature, and mild manner could be—and sometimes were—perceived as effeminate.

Lina Basquette remembered that her mother, much to the teenager's chagrin, used to refer to Ramón as a "sissy." Such a derisive remark may have stemmed from Mrs. Belcher's prejudices against soft-mannered male dancers, though she may have been aware of an intimate attachment between Ramón and a fellow dance student. While at Belcher's studio, Ramón had met Louis Samuel, a small, dark ballet dancer three years his junior. The two quickly became close friends in spite of their different temperaments and backgrounds—while the Mexican Catholic Ramón was lively and carefree, the Hungarian Jewish Samuel was taciturn and distrustful. Years later, Basquette would recall that Samuel watched over Ramón the way "Damon guarded Pythias," asserting that he "saw to it that Ramón was well protected—especially from females." In a letter to author Allan Ellenberger, Basquette remembered Samuel as "insanely jealous of man, woman or child that Ramon felt a friendship or affection for. He had a sullen disposition and seldom did his eyes stray from Ramon."

The exact type of relationship Ramón and Samuel shared has never been made clear, though Basquette's remarks suggest that it was more than a simple friendship. The two Belcher alumni were to remain intimate—though not necessarily involved—until their association was abruptly shattered in the early 1930s.

Meanwhile, Ramón persevered in his efforts to make his mark in Hollywood. In the summer of 1919, while working as a busboy at the Alexandria Hotel, the main hub of the film community's social life, Ramón heard that the legendary director D. W. Griffith was searching for a new leading man for his next production. Years later, Novarro would remember, "When D. W. used to come in to lunch at the Alexandria, I always made sure that I cleared his table. He always said that he discovered me. Actually, I discovered him."

At the Los Angeles premiere of *Broken Blossoms*, Ramón approached the venerated director of *The Birth of a Nation*, asking him for a chance in films. Probably trying to get rid of him, Griffith consented to see the eager youth at his studio the following day. The next day and every day for the ensuing two weeks, Ramón expectantly waited at the studio's reception bench for hours. When Griffith finally decided to see him, the young actor was ready with a short scene he himself had written.

According to "On the Road with Ramon," Herbert Howe's humorous version of Novarro's life for *Motion Picture*, Ramón's acting piece concerned a neurotic murderer who, while on his way to a prison cell, is throttled by the ghost of his victim. While Ramón choked himself, Griffith abruptly interrupted the drama to inquire, "But who is the victim?"

"That," came the reply, "is left to the imagination."

Intrigued, Griffith ordered a test. A report was promised for the following day, but when Ramón heard nothing, he wrote a pleading letter and rushed to the director's turf at the Alexandria. After bribing a bellhop, Ramón headed for the director's room. When the door opened, he handed the letter to a disheveled, pajama-clad Griffith and blurted out, "My future is in your hands, Mr. Griffith."

As it turned out, Ramón's professional future lay elsewhere. Griffith returned to his Long Island studio and never bothered calling the spirited Mexican. "I sometimes wonder," Novarro later observed, "if there was really any film in that camera."

While Ramón was working at the Alexandria (off and on in the late 1910s), another young Latin was making the rounds at the hotel. An Italian immigrant who had been earning his living as a small-time actor, tea dancer, and escort, Rodolfo Guglielmi—later to be known as Rudolph Valentino—was trying to make himself visible to talent scouts. Legend has it that around this time a romance developed between the two future Latin Lovers, as nothing could be more ironic to Hollywood gossipmongers than an affair between two male film stars known as heterosexual sex symbols.

Novarro and Valentino were ideal targets. Despite his circumspection, Novarro was known in certain Hollywood circles to be gay, and his death made that knowledge public, whereas rumors questioning the androgynous Valentino's masculinity abounded during his reign as Hollywood's supreme screen lover.

Those tales were created largely by resentful and xenophobic male members of the press who derisively referred to Valentino as a "wop," a "he-vamp," and, most infamously, a "pink powder puff." Valentino's overly ornamented screen appearances and passionate displays of love, which were deemed unmasculine by conservative American men and a threat to impressionable young male filmgoers, helped fuel the anti-Valentino rhetoric. Stories about the star's habit of using women's beauty products (which he firmly denied) and his problematic first marriage to Jean Acker, a lesbian who locked him out of the bedroom on their wedding night, did nothing to still the rumors. A second marriage to the willful (and oft-rumored bisexual) Natacha Rambova only led to more tales about Valentino's unmanliness, as word spread that Rambova was the one who wore the pants in the Valentino household.

Claims that Valentino had homosexual inclinations have so far been unfounded, but even if they had been true, that in itself would be no indication that he and Novarro were ever lovers. In a 1962 interview, Novarro stated that he had met his fellow Latin Lover only once, while the struggling Mexican was eking out a living as an usher at Clune's Auditorium. Actually, he saw Valentino at least one more time, during the filming of Rex Ingram's *The Four Horsemen of the Apocalypse,* in which Valentino stars and Ramón appears as an extra. Nonetheless, there is no evidence that they ever socialized, nor that any sort of more intimate relationship—platonic or otherwise—ever developed between them.

If the Valentino-Novarro rumors began while Novarro was still alive, he surely was not embarrassed by them. In later years, he would make jokes about having his name tied to that of the more popular Latin Lover, once referring to himself as the devoted "woman in black," a perennial visitor to Valentino's grave.

Since his return to Los Angeles with Marion Morgan's troupe, Ramón had been living with his family in a rented two-story house at 2323 Hope Street, several blocks south of the boardinghouse where he had previously stayed. Señora Samaniego had wanted to buy the Hope Street property, but her husband concluded they could not afford the $6,000 price and refused to borrow the required amount from his relatives.

Though Los Angeles initially seemed like paradise compared to war-torn Durango, life in the new land was anything but paradisiacal for the Samaniegos. Their sole income was the dwindling inheritance left by Dr. Samaniego's father and the little money Ramón and Mariano earned at odd jobs. Except for Ramón (and perhaps Mariano, then working as a bottler in a dairy), whose English had improved since his arrival, the only family member who spoke fluent English was the semi-invalid Dr. Samaniego. The lack of a good command of English reduced the other family members' chances for employment and made their struggle in that period of high inflation even more daunting. Even so, in the close-knit Mexican community, they were no doubt helped in their search for jobs by Dr. Samaniego's relatives and assorted *comadres* and *compadres*.

The children were sent to school, and eventually most family members began working at odd jobs. José became a soda jerk at a local drugstore, Angel and Eduardo sold the *Los Angeles Times* at the corner of Pico and Union, Antonio delivered furniture, Luz and Carmen worked as part-time stock-girls at the Broadway department store, and Señora Samaniego gave singing lessons. Unable to hold a job, Dr. Samaniego kept busy taking chiropractic lessons. As a conservative man with conventional ideas about his duties as husband and father, Dr. Samaniego's male ego must have been seriously bruised by his inability to support his family. Worst of all, he was the one being supported by them.

With his father semi-incapacitated, Ramón, as the eldest male child, had to assume most of the responsibility for the family's support. Such responsibility, however, clashed with his artistic ambitions. Traditional families like the Samaniegos regarded film actors—with the exception of Hollywood royalty such as Mary Pickford and Lillian Gish—as only slightly more respectable than thieves and prostitutes. According to Novarro, his mother, who still envisioned him as a venerated concert pianist, staunchly opposed his acting pursuits, while Dr. Samaniego was particularly disdainful of his oldest son's chosen career path, often declaring he had "a first-class nut in the family that would never amount to anything." But no amount of scolding, protesting, or ridicule from his parents was to prevent the relentlessly ambitious young man from pursuing his professional goal.

While Ramón doggedly pursued a show business career, an unexpected disaster threatened his family's—and his own—chances for remaining in Los Angeles. One night, eleven-year-old Carmen stopped playing with her dolls in the attic to go have dinner downstairs, leaving a lighted candle behind. After the meal, José went upstairs and immediately darted back down yelling, "The house is on fire!" All ten Samaniegos ran about trying to salvage what they could, but, as the fire rapidly spread, all they could do was stand in front of the house and watch it burn. The firemen eventually managed to extinguish the flames, but the water caused more damage than the fire itself, and many family possessions were lost to looters.

The Samaniegos had nowhere to go. A return to Durango would have been unwise. Whatever the political climate in Mexico, the Samaniegos had no guarantee that they would be able to rebuild their lives with the Mexican economy and social fabric nearly destroyed by almost a decade of warfare. A move back to El Paso to stay with relatives was a possibility, but the harsher climate would have been detrimental to Dr. Samaniego's health. Ultimately, the family opted to stay in Los Angeles, counting on the assistance of Dr. Samaniego's brother and of the local Mexican community.

A few months after the fire the family found a new home: a two-story Craftsman house at 1340 Constance Street, just southwest of downtown and only a short distance from their previous residence. At that time, Constance Street lay in a mostly middle-class white neighborhood, and only blocks away from the Bonnie Brae and Alvarado mansions, where several Hollywood celebrities lived. This was a preferred residential area for upper-class Mexican émigrés. They could hobnob with some of the city's elite while remaining conveniently close to Spanish-speaking merchants and the flavor of Mexican culture.

Despite the house fire, the search for another residence, and the Samaniegos' ever-unstable financial situation—even with outside assistance, most of them had to earn a living—Ramón was unstoppable in his quest for success. While dancing with Derelys Perdue in a prologue at the Kinema Theater he met actor Richard Dix, then working for Goldwyn Pictures during the day and dating Perdue at night. Dix was so impressed by a bit Ramón had done in a Mabel Normand picture that he tried to induce his studio to give the dancing Mexican a chance, but, as Dix would later remember, "No one seemed especially interested."

Unable to secure a substantial part, Ramón continued laboring as an extra in films. Sometimes he also appeared on-screen in highly stylized dance sequences choreographed by Marion Morgan; among them were an ancient Roman bacchanal in Allen Holubar's *Man—Woman—Marriage*, in which he and Derelys Perdue danced seminaked atop a mirrored table (a week's work at $25 a day), and the dagger dance in the Mack Sennett feature *A Small Town Idol*. In the latter sequence, also with Perdue, Ramón is nearly unrecognizable garbed in a glittering loincloth and under heavy faunlike makeup.

In late 1920, Ramón finally landed an actual screen role in Goldwyn's *Mr. Barnes of New York*, receiving billing for the first time, as the Corsican youth Antonio Paoli. Though still a minor part—Paoli gets killed in a duel a few minutes into the picture—Ramón's role is crucial, as his death sets the vendetta plot in motion. Paoli's sister vows revenge for her brother's death but must first identify his killer, who might well be her new husband. Director Victor Schertzinger gave the young hopeful a chance in this Tom Moore vehicle after watching Ramón portray a lovestruck dancing shepherd in *The Concert*. Novarro later said that Schertzinger was so impressed with his work that he had Paoli's role enlarged (additional takes were shot by future MGM producer Paul Bern).

Around that time, Ramón altered his family name by adding an *s* at the end of "Samaniego." ("Ramón" had already been changed to "Ramon" in print ads for his dance routines.) The ardently Catholic twenty-one-year-old was an equally ardent believer in seers, palm readers, and numerology, which assigns different values to letters of the alphabet. The extra *s* was supposed to give his name the cosmic vibrations of the "master number" eleven, a number especially conducive to success in artistic endeavors. But regardless of the name change, any hopes Ramón had for immediate recognition were dashed when Goldwyn shelved *Mr. Barnes of New York*, possibly because of a backlog in the studio's output.

Only several months later, in the summer of 1921, did Ramón's professional luck change, with the appearance of artist and poet Ferdinand Pinney Earle. The burly, handsome forty-three-year-old Earle (nicknamed "Affinity Earle" after stating in court during a divorce lawsuit that he felt only "affinity" for his mistress) had been working for the studios as a designer of ornate dialogue intertitles since the mid-1910s. His ultimate goal was to transpose great operas onto film, but after considering *Aida*, *Faust*, *Tristan and Isolde*, and *The Ring of the Niebelungen* for his directorial debut, Earle settled on the poems of Omar Khayyam, "the astronomer poet of Persia."

Earle later explained that he was "determined not to launch the production of my Opus No. 1 until I had adequately protected myself against all the usual evils of the way, especially as I was to make an entirely new type of picture." Probably because no major studio was interested in the project, Earle signed with impresario Theodore Ahrens, who then formed the Rubaiyat Company with Earle as acting president. Earle's contract also stipulated that he was to be the picture's author, director, editor, production manager, and art director, and that no changes could be made without his written consent. He was thus assured that his depiction of *The Rubaiyat of Omar Khayyam*, "might be produced under ideal conditions and safeguarded from intolerable interferences and outside worries."

In early June 1921, production began at the Hollywood Studios and at a lot on Earle's two-and-a-half-acre estate at 2140 North Highland Avenue, which had been temporarily converted into a studio. (The sand dune scenes were filmed in Oxnard, a coastal town approximately sixty miles northwest of Los Angeles.) Celebrated Shakespearean actor Frederick Warde was selected for the part of Omar Khayyam, and high-culture stage actress and director Hedwiga Reicher was chosen as the second female lead, while Earle cast himself in the role of Destiny. (Future *King Kong* screamer Fay Wray, then a guest at Earle's house, was cast as an extra.)

The leading lady was found in late June in the person of eighteen-year-old beauty-contest winner Kathleen Key. Earle had placed ads in search of a "girl of oriental beauty," and found her in this pert, dark-eyed brunette. The director also found the romantic male lead through an ad in the trades. According to Earle's son Eyvind, "Ramón came to the front door one day and was hired." Ramón's looks, which could pass as Middle Eastern, and the poise and grace of movement he had acquired as a dancer were the likely reasons for his landing the role of Omar Khayyam's nephew, Ben-Ali. In addition to acting in the picture, Ramón was to choreograph its dance sequences.

Earle's version of *The Rubaiyat* dealt with Khayyam and Ben-Ali's struggles against a desert bandit, a simplistic storyline that would be offset by the production's sets, cinematography, and special effects. Through multiple exposures, Earle melded elaborate paintings and miniatures to the built sets, a creative way to save money while also giving the picture a magical grandeur. Describing the effect as "motion painting," Earle explained, "My object has been to create a dream world so convincing...as to baffle the beholder and at the same time to achieve many times richer and vaster sets—without wrecking the finances of a Rockefeller." When asked if the picture might be too artistic for the average moviegoer, Earle replied, "The privilege of enjoying beauty is not confined to the upper classes. It is a universal thing. ...I have not attempted to make it a picture for the few." The moneymen, however, disagreed.

Earle would later refer to the making of *The Rubaiyat* as a "bloody venture," for besides abhorring his juvenile's performance—Earle "just thought I was terrible," Novarro recalled in the 1950s—the director had to persevere with his production "in spite of continual and infernal interferences." After the picture was completed, Theodore Ahrens confiscated several reels of the film without Earle's knowledge and, complaining that "there was too much artistic aroma" in the $65,000 production (the average cost for a studio picture at the time), ordered that the film be reassembled without the director's input. In response, Earle filed a lawsuit in federal court demanding an injunction against the release of the film.

For the moment, Earle triumphed. Exhibition of *The Rubaiyat*, which was scheduled to preview in New York on January 14, 1922, was barred by the courts. Later that year, Ramón lamented, "It may never be shown to the public, but such a beautiful screen poem it is, so sensual." In September 1922, more than one year after filming had been completed, a truncated version of *The Rubaiyat* was shown to a private audience of studio chiefs, financiers, artists, critics, and socialites. "Two solid hours vanished as but a minute, so fascinating did the production prove," wrote an enthralled reviewer. The audience was so enthusiastic that they burst into applause at the mere sight of Earle's sets. Earle himself was satisfied with the visual qualities of the picture, and had by then (after seeing the rough cut) changed his mind about Ramón's work.

United Artists offered to distribute *The Rubaiyat*, but several months later handed the still-unreleased film back to Earle. (In his autobiography, Eyvind Earle asserts that the makers of UA's *The Thief of Bagdad* stole the decor and numerous scenes from *The Rubaiyat*.) Ultimately, Earle's "motion painting" was shelved for lack of a distributor. Without the benefit of a marquee name, the picture was deemed too artistic to be commercially viable, while the December 1922 release of First National's *Omar the Tentmaker*—about the same Persian poet—further hindered its box-office prospects.

Long before the New York special screening of *The Rubaiyat*, Ramón had been desperately looking for more acting parts. Since he was presumably "terrible" in that picture, the still-unknown actor feared that unless he landed another role before the release of Earle's "motion painting," he would never work again. Yet, when director J. Emmett Flynn saw a *Rubaiyat* sequence in the fall of 1921 for the purpose of evaluating Kathleen Key, he completely ignored Key and instead asked Ramón to test for a part in his prestigious costume drama *Monte Cristo*. But despite Flynn's enthusiasm and his careful direction of Ramón's tests, Fox ultimately opted for a name actor, Gaston Glass, forcing the luckless Ramón to continue his seemingly futile struggles.

Ramón then joined the Hollywood Community Theater, a one-hundred-seat playhouse in the heart of Hollywood that served both as a showcase for budding talent and as a means for established stars such as Wallace Reid, Conrad Nagel, and Henry B. Walthall to demonstrate their versatility. None of the talent involved received payment, but that disadvantage was offset by the guaranteed success of the shows, which were performed for sold-out audiences packed with film industry professionals.

The appeal of the Community Theater notwithstanding, Ramón was most probably disheartened to return to minor parts on the semiprofessional stage after having savored an important role in a feature film. But a man for whom he had briefly worked in the recent past was unexpectedly to show up again and dramatically change the aspiring actor's fortunes. Enter Rex Ingram.

THREE

Ramon's Columbus

After watching Rex Ingram's 1921 adaptation of Vicente Blasco Ibáñez's *The Four Horsemen of the Apocalypse*, playwright and film critic Robert E. Sherwood remarked that the picture "will be hailed as a great dramatic achievement; one which deserves—more than any other picture play that the war inspired—to be handed down to generations yet unborn. . . . [It] is a living, breathing answer to those who still refuse to take motion pictures seriously. Its production lifts the silent drama to an artistic plane that it has never touched before."

The nearly bankrupt Metro Pictures had a large financial stake in *The Four Horsemen*. The production costs had reached an astounding $608,000, at a time when the average budget for feature films was $60,000. Ingram himself had much to lose if the film failed to ignite at the box office. As his first superproduction, *The Four Horsemen* could either propel him to the forefront of Hollywood directors or destroy his chances of ever achieving that status.

To the relief of all involved, *The Four Horsemen of the Apocalypse*, which premiered in New York on March 6, 1921, proved to be a phenomenal hit. At the end of its run, *The Four Horsemen* had reportedly earned more than $4 million in box-office rentals, perhaps surpassed only by D. W. Griffith's 1915 *The Birth of a Nation* (box-office numbers for the Griffith picture are unreliable). The picture catapulted twenty-four-year-old Rudolph Valentino to international superstardom and turned Ingram into one of the top film directors of the time, second in prestige only to Griffith.

In *The Four Horsemen*'s famous tango scene, shot sometime in the second half of 1920, Ramón danced in the background with his sister Luz (often misidentified as the much younger Carmen), though they cannot be discerned on screen. Ramón, however, can be briefly glimpsed in the Call to Arms sequence—in which a woman wrapped in the French flag sings "La Marseillaise"—looking outraged at a man who refuses to stand up while the anthem is sung. But for Ingram, Ramón was just one among the hundreds of extras used in the picture. The director paid him scant notice during filming and later remarked he had no recollection of the Mexican extra on *The Four Horsemen* set.

Yet, *The Four Horsemen* is, even if indirectly, an important picture in the career of the unnoticed Mexican extra, for it brought together figures who were to loom large in his professional future. Kathleen Key, who had a small part in the film, a few months later became his love interest in *The Rubaiyat*. June Mathis, *The Four Horsemen*'s scenarist and unofficial producer, was to become the creative force behind *Ben-Hur*. Alice Terry, the picture's leading lady, would be Ramón's leading lady in four films. And, finally, there was Rex Ingram.

Rex Ingram—not to be confused with the 1940s character actor of the same name—was the man Erich von Stroheim called "the world's greatest director." His work inspired Japanese director Yasujiro Ozu to pursue a film career. *The Red Shoes* codirector Michael Powell, who got his first job working for Ingram, once referred to him as "the greatest stylist of his time," while filmmaker David Lean acknowledged an indebtedness to Ingram's cinematic vision. When future MGM head Dore Schary was asked to name the top creative people in the early days of film, his choices were D. W. Griffith, Rex Ingram, Cecil B. DeMille, and Erich von Stroheim—in that order.

Born Reginald Ingram Montgomery Hitchcock in Dublin on January 15, 1893, Ingram spent most of his childhood in the several Irish towns to which his clergyman father was assigned. He later attended St. Columba's College in Dublin County, and in 1911, two years after his mother's death, he emigrated to the United States, where he worked at rail yards in New Haven and studied sculpture at Yale.

After watching the 1911 Vitagraph film version of *A Tale of Two Cities*, the handsome young Irishman became fascinated with the artistic possibilities offered by motion pictures. In 1913, he joined the Edison Company in the Bronx as actor, scriptwriter, and general handyman, moving to Vitagraph's Brooklyn studios the following year as a contract actor under the name Rex Hitchcock. By 1915, he had settled behind the cameras as Rex Ingram, writing vehicles for Theda Bara and other major Fox stars.

One year later, the twenty-three-year-old Ingram began his career as a director at the Universal lot in Los Angeles. His first film, the underworld melodrama *The Great Problem*, was followed by nine other pictures at that studio, nearly all of them set in exotic locales. According to Ingram biographer Liam O'Leary, the director gradually gained a reputation for his "fine pictorial sense, relentless pursuit of atmosphere," and, being highly superstitious, for his "use of deformed actors, especially dwarfs and hunchbacks."

Ingram's unquestionable talent was matched only by his arrogance, fiery temperament, and lack of respect for authority. "He had a bad temper," one of his assistants, Jean Comte de Limur, would later remark. "He didn't like people very much. . . . He was not friendly at all with anybody. And he was peculiar." The first serious consequence of his short temper came about in late 1917, when he was fired by Universal after disagreements with the studio bosses.

Following a two-year professional lull, a stint with the Royal Canadian Air Force, an unsuccessful marriage to actress Doris Pawn, a successful return to Universal, and two popular pictures for Metro, Ingram was selected for the plum job of directing *The Four Horsemen of the Apocalypse*. June Mathis, one of the most powerful women in Hollywood at that time, had persuaded Metro officials to give the twenty-seven-year-old Irishman a chance after working with him in *Hearts Are Trumps*. In spite of the solid craftsmanship of Ingram's earlier work, the masterful care and attention to pictorial detail he brought to *The Four Horsemen* came as a surprise.

Much like Stroheim, Ingram wanted total control over his films and tirelessly strove for realism in every aspect of their production. In *The Four Horsemen*, for example, he demanded that Rudolph Valentino and Alice Terry speak their (inaudible) lines in French so as to give greater authenticity to their characters. Ingram's obsessive care paid off once again with the July 1921 release of *The Conquering Power*—also starring Terry and Valentino, and with more inaudible French dialogue. Critics and audiences alike were captivated by the picture's painstaking detail, despite a production environment fraught with problems.

During the making of *The Conquering Power*, Valentino—pushed by then lover Natacha Rambova—fought Metro for a steeper raise than the extra $50 a week the studio had given him after *The Four Horsemen*. Metro would go only as high as another $50 (for a total of $400). Feeling exploited, the angry star refused to cooperate with Ingram throughout the production, an attitude that led to volcanic fights with the pugnacious director. Upon the picture's completion, Valentino moved to Famous Players–Lasky, where, for $500 a week, he starred that same year in another blockbuster, *The Sheik*— thus confirming his reputation as *the* great screen lover of the era.

A more serious professional loss for Ingram was the departure of June Mathis, who also left Metro for Famous Players. According to cinematographer John F. Seitz, Mathis already resented Ingram's getting too much credit for *The Four Horsemen* and was infuriated by both the director's and the studio's treatment of her beloved Valentino. Due to Mathis's abrupt departure, her unfinished screenplay for Ingram's next project, the bucolic *Turn to the Right,* had to be completed by Mary O'Hara (the future author of *My Friend Flicka*). Two years later, Ingram's falling-out with Mathis would prove tremendously costly to him; but for now, Metro retained enough confidence in the director to entrust him with the studio's most distinguished production for the following year: an elaborate screen adaptation of Sir Anthony Hope's 1894 swashbuckling novel *The Prisoner of Zenda.*

In the early 1920s, the success of the German import *Madame Dubarry* and of the Douglas Fairbanks swashbucklers *The Mark of Zorro* and *The Three Musketeers* led to a vogue for costume spectacles. Cosmopolitan produced *When Knighthood Was in Flower,* Famous Players–Lasky came up with *To Have and to Hold,* Griffith filmed *Orphans of the Storm,* First National starred Richard Barthelmess in *The Fighting Blade,* and Fairbanks himself got busy again working on his screen version of *Robin Hood.* Cecil B. DeMille wanted to produce *The Prisoner of Zenda* with Wallace Reid in the lead, but DeMille had a formidable rival to contend with. *Zenda* was said to be the first novel Ingram had ever read, and the Metro contract director was determined to translate it into film.

Set in the mythical kingdom of Ruritania, *The Prisoner of Zenda* is a tale of love and betrayal, honor and greed, exchanged identities and rousing swordfighting: the weakling King Rudolf is kidnapped by his villainous half brother's gang, led by the suave Rupert of Hentzau, and must be temporarily replaced by a vacationing Englishman. Metro's extravagant adaptation was to be based both on the Hope novel and on the Edward Rose play that had opened in London in 1896.

The story goes that while directing *The Conquering Power,* Ingram picked Ramón out of the ranks of extras as a potential threat to an increasingly difficult Valentino. Ingram vowed that he would turn the young unknown into a star, and thus demonstrate to the temperamental Italian that he was not indispensable. "That was studio publicity—the usual bunk," Novarro, who did not even work in that Ingram picture, would inform writer DeWitt Bodeen years later. "It didn't happen like that at all."

In all probability, Ingram first noticed Ramón when Ferdinand Earle showed him a cut of the as yet unreleased *Rubaiyat*. (Ingram had developed such a fascination with the poems of Omar Khayyam that he had once worked on his own translation.) Not long afterward, Ingram saw Ramón perform at the Hollywood Community Theater, at the suggestion of Margaret Loomis, a dancer and actress then playing a supporting role in the director's *Turn to the Right* and Ramón's partner in a Spanish pantomime called *The Royal Fandango*.

Liam O'Leary asserts that "Ingram was impressed with the boy, and felt that here was the substitute for Valentino. There were the good looks, grace of movement, the Latin temperament, all allied to real acting ability." Margaret Ettinger concurred in *Picture-Play*: "Mr. Ingram was looking for a 'Rupert [of Hentzau],' and Ramón was the type he desired." According to Novarro, however, it took more than dancing the fandango for him to land the role of the debonair Ruritanian schemer.

Margaret Loomis, probably aware that Ramón had lost the *Monte Cristo* role because of his lack of public recognition, urged him to see Ingram, as the director was not averse to hiring an unknown. Following his *Fandango* partner's advice, Ramón headed for 1721 Romaine Avenue, near downtown Hollywood, where, in the words of columnist Adela Rogers St. Johns, Metro Pictures stood "so prettily, all shining white and bright green shutters and well-kept lawns, clipped hedges and little flower beds." Reaching Ingram amid these well-tended confines, however, turned out to be more difficult than the aspiring actor had expected.

"When I went to the Metro casting office and asked to see Mr. Ingram," Novarro told Bodeen, "I got exactly nowhere." After leaving Metro, the dejected Ramón headed to the nearby Hollywood Studios, where Ferdinand Earle was editing *The Rubaiyat*. Once there, he persuaded Earle to write him a personal letter of introduction to Ingram, which read: "My dear Mr. Ingram: Columbus discovered America today [October 12], a few hundred years ago, and you may date today as your discovery of Ramon. He has walked away with *The Rubaiyat*. I take the liberty of introducing him to you."

With Earle's letter in hand, Ramón bypassed the casting director and headed straight to Ingram's set. The director received the short, dark twenty-two-year-old with courtesy, but remarked that he envisioned Rupert of Hentzau as a mature, six-foot-tall, Teutonic-looking actor. "I had my make-up kit with me," Novarro later recalled, "and asked him to describe exactly what type he had in mind." Ingram drew four sketches of his mental image of Rupert of Hentzau's face on the back of Earle's letter. "My heart sank when I saw mustaches and a short Prussian beard," continued Novarro. "I was very young then and my own beard took months to become even scraggly."

Ingram, impressed by Ramón's eagerness, let him test for the part the following day. He liked the youth's performance, but still thought him too young. Even after a second test, for which the makeup man provided Ramón with a false mustache and goatee, Ingram still considered the young Mexican too immature for the role—until he came up with the idea of having Ramón sport a monocle.

"When Mr. Ingram ran that [third] test off, he was pleased," Novarro later remembered. Metro immediately put the ecstatic actor on its payroll for $100 a week (approximately $1,000 today), while Ingram promised that "I would be his new leading man and that he would groom me for stardom. I was deliriously happy, and didn't dare believe it. But that's exactly what he did."

Had Ramón been hired to play the small role in *Monte Cristo*, which was in production at the time of *The Prisoner of Zenda* casting, he would have missed his chance of being discovered by one of the most prominent directors in the industry. A fervent believer in the "All's for the best" philosophy, whenever Novarro reminisced about this stroke of luck that had completely changed the course of his life, he would invariably marvel, "It's just wonderful how fate works."

Production on *The Prisoner of Zenda* began early in November 1921, with Lewis Stone, one of the rare actors Ingram respected, top-billed in the dual roles of King Rudolf of Ruritania and the Englishman Rudolf Rassendyll; Ingram's fiancée, Alice Terry, as Princess Flavia; and Barbara La Marr, known as "the girl who was too beautiful," as Antoinette de Mauban, the object of Rupert of Hentzau's lust. With Ingram's exacting guidance, Ramón succeeded in appearing as skilled on-screen as his more seasoned fellow performers, and later remembered his experiences during filming as "a lot of fencing, a lot of hard work, very happy."

Despite the close friendship that steadily developed between them, Novarro always saw Ingram as a figure to be deferred to. The director, for his part, felt paternalistic toward the young Mexican six years his junior. Even years later, Novarro would often refer to his early mentor as "Mr. Ingram." On the other hand, there was never such formality between Ramón and Ingram's lovely wife-to-be.

Born in Vincennes, Indiana, on July 24, 1899, Alice Frances Taaffe moved with her family to Southern California in the early 1910s, where she began working as an extra at the Thomas Ince Studio in Culver City. Like Novarro, Alice went through a long and arduous apprenticeship, appearing in numerous bits and a few small supporting parts, until landing her first major role in Ingram's *Hearts Are Trumps* in 1920. To look acceptable on-screen, the chocolate eclair–loving actress had to go on a strict diet, have her teeth straightened, and don a blond wig. The look matched her cool aloofness so well that the auburn-haired Alice Taaffe, now renamed Alice Terry, became a (near) permanent film blonde.

Terry achieved top leading-lady status in her next picture, *The Four Horsemen of the Apocalypse*, though she was never to reach true stardom. That was partly due to her own lack of ambition, and partly because the cool screen persona projected by the warm, witty, and extroverted real-life Terry was too aloof for most filmgoers. Even critics felt she was *too* reserved, and frequently remarked upon her chilly demeanor. Ironically, Terry's performances remain effective because of that very restraint, especially when compared to those of her overly emotive costars.

Ingram and Terry first met in 1917 while she was working as an extra in the director's *Humdrum Brown*. They became more closely acquainted two years later, after Terry, still working as an extra, fled in tears from the set of *The Day She Paid*. Ingram had screamed at her during filming, but later apologized and asked her to accept a small role in *Shore Acres*, which he was going to direct at Metro. From then on, Terry played the female lead in all but two of Ingram's films.

What began as a brother-sister relationship eventually developed into a romance of sorts. Ingram was often too deeply immersed in his work to give much attention to Terry, though he did find time for their wedding on Saturday, November 5, 1921. Even then, the director would not allow marriage to disrupt his work. The couple were back on *The Prisoner of Zenda* set the following Monday.

As *Zenda* was to be one of the major Hollywood productions of the year, Ramón realized that this was his chance to prove himself as star material. If he failed, another opportunity might not be forthcoming. Luckily, he could count on both the director and the leading lady for absolute support.

During a location shoot in the San Bernardino Mountains, when all members of the *Zenda* company were required to share rooms, Ramón was paired with Malcolm McGregor, a handsome young actor who had known Ingram at Yale. The morning after their first night at the inn, a shaky and white-faced McGregor approached Terry and declared he would not spend another night in the same room with Ramón. McGregor refused to elaborate, but Terry assumed that Ramón had made unwanted advances toward him.

Terry's—and surely Ingram's—discovery of Ramón's sexual orientation made no difference to them. The subject was probably left undiscussed, but Ramón knew that he had been accepted as he was. Regardless of his sexuality, he was to have the lead in all four of Ingram's productions in the next two years.

In late March 1922, a little more than one month after production had ended on *The Prisoner of Zenda*, shooting began on Ingram's next project, a remake of *Black Orchids*, one of the director's own 1917 Universal releases. According to film editor Grant Whytock, the previous version had been "murdered by the front office for being too erotic," so Ingram had decided to tackle the same story again, making it "twice as erotic."

The director himself wrote the scenario, which was inspired by *Vendetta*, English fantasist Marie Corelli's Gothic tale of lust, murder, and revenge: A novelist reads to his capricious daughter his latest story about an alluring Parisian fortune-teller who wreaks havoc in the lives of men—one is poisoned, another is mortally wounded in a duel, and a third is stabbed. The vamp gets her comeuppance when she is locked in a dungeon by one of the betrayed lovers and left to starve to death. The writer's daughter is understandably impressed by the story and decides that instead of a life of fanciful dalliances, she will accept the love of her faithful suitor. It would be a challenge to Ingram's trademark visual flair to turn this cheaply lurid tale into a major Metro production.

After a brief return to the Hollywood Community Theater, where he played a small role as an Italian doctor in *Enter Madame*, Ramón was given two roles in *Black Orchids*. He was to portray the vamp's true love, Ivan de Maupin, and the young suitor Henri in the wraparound story. Alice Terry wanted to play the killer-vamp Zareda, and was actually announced for the role in early reports, but Ingram felt she could not project a sufficiently wicked persona. Instead, he chose fellow *Zenda* player Barbara La Marr, who would also play the writer's frivolous daughter. Others in the production included *Zenda* cast members Lewis Stone as the man who ultimately destroys Zareda and her lover; Ingram regular Edward Connelly; and an orangutan named Joe Martin, a holdover from the 1917 film and the star of *A Monkey*

Hero and other two-reelers. Stone, demoted to second lead, still received the picture's highest salary, $1,000 a week, compared with Ramón's $150 (a hefty 50 percent increase) and La Marr's $200.

The dark-haired, green-eyed Barbara La Marr was often presented as another Ingram discovery, despite her several film credits prior to *Zenda*. Born on July 28, 1896, as Reatha Dale Watson in either Richmond, Virginia (according to herself), or North Yakima, Washington (according to her foster family), La Marr began her show business career as a child—she played Little Eva in *Uncle Tom's Cabin*—and later danced in vaudeville. By her early twenties, she had reportedly been kidnapped, gang-raped, once divorced, and twice widowed. One of her (by then) three husbands was found to be a bigamist, and another was jailed after forging checks to buy gifts for his wife.

By the late 1910s, she had adopted the mellifluous name Barbara La Marr and was working as a scenario writer for Fox and United Artists, when she was selected to play vamps in Douglas Fairbanks's *The Nut* and in the Louis B. Mayer production *Harriet and the Piper*. Both Fairbanks and Mayer became enthralled by the looks of the young brunette. According to Adela Rogers St. Johns, so did future MGM producer Paul Bern, who fell so profoundly under La Marr's spell that he tried to commit suicide over her.

Writing about the 1920s siren, columnist Edwin Schallert rhapsodized, "Her radiance is that of moonlight in the heavy shadows of the night.... Calypso she is, burning with a flame of subtle ecstasy." Although immune to La Marr's "Calypso" charms, Ramón developed a close friendship with his costar. La Marr, after having been pursued, betrayed, and abused so often by heterosexual men (and by some alleged bisexuals), was not only tolerant of but quite welcoming to gay men. Perhaps she felt they would not take advantage of her or become obsessed with her, as had the other men in her life. Besides Ramón, La Marr would also become a close friend of gay actors William Haines and Clifton Webb.

Joining Bern, Mayer, Fairbanks, and Schallert as victim of La Marr's charms was the orangutan Joe Martin, who jealously guarded the actress wherever she went. In one scene, Edward Connelly had to put a necklace around La Marr's delicate neck, a gesture that enraged the lovestruck ape. In a fit of overprotective zeal, Joe bit Connelly on the arm so severely that he started bleeding. "It took three of us twisting [Joe's] balls to make him let go," Grant Whytock later remembered. As a result of the incident, Connelly refused to work again with the orangutan, a problem solved by cinematographer John Seitz's clever use of matte technique, which enhanced the film's visual splendor and allowed the two foes to appear together on-screen without actually having been present on the set at the same time.

For Ramón, however, the shooting of *Black Orchids* proceeded smoothly. Ingram was intent on turning his newest male discovery into as big a star as his previous one—he even asked Ramón to dress like Valentino and comb his hair in the same way as the Italian lover. "Very soon you will be seeing in print that you are a genius and the reincarnation of Apollo," the director told his protégé. "Don't believe either statement, as I am paying good money to have that published." According to Herbert Howe, Ingram took great pains to make the slightly chubby and acne-prone actor look flawless on-screen with appropriate lighting, and saw to it that Ramón had the right publicity stills, said the right things at interviews, and met the right people. In the meantime, the director relegated his wife's career to a secondary position. "Alice really was remarkable," Novarro later remembered, "because she was never jealous; any other woman in her place would have been very jealous and very nasty to me. I have never in my life [received] even an ugly look from Alice."

Terry's indifference to her husband's obsession with Ramón was mainly a result of her lack of concern for her own acting career. As for Ingram, his drive to turn Ramón into a superstar was at least partly due to spite, for he remained hostile toward Valentino long after the latter's departure from Metro. "He's all right," Ingram said condescendingly of the supreme Latin Lover in the February 1923 issue of *Picture-Play*. "When he worked in *The Four Horsemen* he was glad to be told what he didn't know, and willing to be directed. I photographed him from only two angles, even in long shots, because his lips are rather thick. . . . Valentino has changed a good deal. I'd have liked to see Tony Moreno do *Blood and Sand*—he's bigger than Valentino, and so would have looked the part a little more."

A more pragmatic reason for Ingram's desire to elevate Ramón to stardom was that Metro itself was in dire need of a major box-office name. In the early 1920s, Bert Lytell, Alice Lake, and Viola Dana were the studio's most important stars, but none of them was in the same league as Gloria Swanson or Wallace Reid. (Alla Nazimova had been the studio's biggest name, but she was gone by 1922, while Mae Murray's films were released by Metro but produced by Tiffany.) Valentino would have become Metro's only real superstar, but his defection to Famous Players left the spot open for another new type. Ramón, with his youthful, dark good looks, was the obvious choice to fit the bill.

One important step in Ramón's road to stardom was to make his name more appealing to American filmgoers, as most Anglophones found "Samaniegos" unpronounceable—and, according to *Photoplay*, "the few who could pronounce it didn't have time." Consequently, during the production of *Black Orchids* a somewhat reluctant Ramon Samaniegos was rechristened Ramon Novarro (Rodolfo Guglielmi di Valentina d'Antonguolla had become Rudolph Valentino for the same practical reason). When Novarro legally adopted his screen name as part of his own in April 1924—he would sign as Ramón Novarro Samaniegos—he told the judge that he was tired of being called "salmon eggs."

Since as far back as the 1920s, numerous reports have stated that "Novarro" was a surname on his mother's side of the family. In reality, "Novarro" was suggested by the Iberian kingdom of Navarra, the cradle of the Samaniegos. The choice of Novarro, an unusual variation of the common Spanish surname Navarro, occurred for the same reason Ramón had added an *s* to Samaniego—by changing the *a* to an *o*, the numerologist Ramón achieved the cosmic vibration of the "master number" eleven.

"Novarro" was certainly easier to pronounce than "Samaniegos," but that did not prevent further misspellings, as evidenced by Metro's and later MGM's spelling inconsistencies in both their advertising and internal correspondence. Much to his annoyance, Ramón would see his name in print as "Navarro" almost as often as "Novarro." Even his first name was not immune to careless spellings. "Ramón," after losing its accent for good in the English-language press, studio ads, and film credits, was misspelled at times as "Roman" or "Raymond." At any rate, the choice of a surname other than Samaniego must have ultimately appealed to Ramón, as it carried the necessary "cosmic vibes" for artistic success, and should he become truly famous, the new name would distance his show business career from his family life.

As with *The Four Horsemen*, both Metro and Ingram had much at stake on *The Prisoner of Zenda*, which was to be released on July 31 at the Astor Theater in New York (only several weeks after the release of Goldwyn's *Mr. Barnes of New York*, in which Ramón was totally ignored by the critics). Metro's arrangements for the rights to Ingram's previous film, *Turn to the Right*, had made it difficult for that picture to earn a profit—the film rights had cost the studio $250,000 plus 50 percent of the box-office receipts, a deal that was second in cost only to Goldwyn's acquisition of the *Ben-Hur* rights. Bankruptcy was thus a possibility for the still financially shaky studio if *Zenda*, Metro's only early 1922 production, failed to recoup its hefty

$323,000 investment. As for Ingram, *The Prisoner of Zenda* was his chance to prove he could deliver another major hit without the help of either Rudolph Valentino or June Mathis.

Luckily for all involved, *The Prisoner of Zenda* opened to wide acclaim, with the *Moving Picture World* review summing up the compliments of most critics: "The moving-picture going public knows that 'A Rex Ingram Production'... means screen entertainment of the highest caliber—artistic in the extreme, intelligent in conception, appealing in content and, above all, showman-like in general." At the end of the year, *The Prisoner of Zenda* was listed in fourth place among the best films of 1922 in the influential *Film Daily* poll of film reviewers, and though no official numbers are available, reports in the trades indicate that the picture grossed more than enough to justify the studio's financial risk.

Despite highly publicized accounts of Ramón's looks and talents, including his mastery of the art of monocle flipping, many reviewers failed to remark upon the fifth-billed Ramon Novarro—though in the instances when he was mentioned, the notices were generally positive. *Photoplay*, for one, commended his "fine bit of acting" and stated that the newcomer "seems a decided find and an entirely new type." Strangely, no major reviewer remarked that Novarro's monocle flipping could have profited from a bit more practice. In the picture, Rupert flips his monocle so it will land precisely on his eye. It does—only to immediately fall off. An abrupt cut then shows the monocle miraculously in place.

Apart from too much eye-rolling and his less than consummate monocle-flipping skill, Novarro's work in *The Prisoner of Zenda*, a solid and gorgeously photographed piece of filmmaking, ranks as some of the best in his career. His arrogant and cynical—but immensely charming—Rupert totally eclipses the weak and dull hero as portrayed by Lewis Stone (an imbalance absent in the 1937 remake, which pitted Douglas Fairbanks, Jr., against Ronald Colman). Also, Novarro's dark good looks fit the Central European Rupert surprisingly well, and since there is no audible dialogue, his Mexican accent does not detract from the performance. Unfortunately, after being molded into a romantic hero, Novarro would never be allowed to play another sleek villain during his years as a star.

With its critical and financial success, *Zenda* fully compensated those with high stakes in its production. Metro executives recouped their monetary investment and added another major prestige production to their company's roster; Ingram proved to himself and everyone else that he could stand on his own without either Valentino or Mathis; and Novarro, after more than half a decade of struggle, found himself finally headed to film stardom.

. . .

"I want to tell you that he is all you might expect, and more," Margaret Ettinger asserted in *Picture-Play*, "and yet I hate to rob you of any of the thrill of surprise of seeing him for the first time. So, I am not going to rave about him as I would like to; I am not going to tell you of his amazing charm and good looks; I am just going to tell you the story of his struggles for recognition as he told it to me. . . ." The piece, called "To the Ladies— Ramon the Romantic," consisted mainly of studio-generated fluff—"I will tell you that he is twenty-one years old [he was twenty-three]; a little over medium height [he was five feet six inches]; lithe and slender, as most dancers are [in spite of his fandango dancing, he was more on the pudgy side]"— but Ettinger was right in her assertion that one of the newcomer's main assets was "his decided newness of type."

Throughout most of the 1910s, male matinee idols in American motion pictures had almost invariably been the "all-American" type. WASP-looking men such as Maurice Costello, J. Warren Kerrigan, Francis X. Bushman, Wallace Reid, and Thomas Meighan were the period's top male romantic stars. These performers, with the possible exception of the more lively Reid, fit the Victorian image of manliness: dependable, no-nonsense, stoic, unsensual. Douglas Fairbanks was the only swarthy all-American star of that time—and by far the most dynamic. He can hardly be considered a romantic star, though, for the love interests in his films were of less importance than Fairbanks's own over-the-top exuberance.

In the aftermath of World War I, Victorian tradition was shattered in the United States. Women began to vigorously challenge gender roles in the rapidly urbanizing nation, and, as symbols of emancipation, began bobbing their hair, wearing skirts above the calves, and dancing the Charleston. On the political front, American women finally gained the right to vote in 1920. At least in the major urban centers, it was a period of rebelliousness against the old norms. Foreignness and exoticism were no longer dangerous, but alluring. On film, this shift in mores and tastes was manifested in the Latin Lover craze.

Since the early days of film—and especially after the 1915 advent of Theda Bara as the vamp in *A Fool There Was*—American male filmgoers had been allowed to lust after bewitching dark-haired, dark-eyed women whose main appeal was their exotic and forbidden allure. Despite the devastating consequences to the vamps' screen victims, millions of men secretly desired to succumb to them. Following the war, changes in mores allowed women to secretly lust after their own he-vamps, though there would be a marked difference between the female and the male of the species. While the she-vamp was an irredeemable source of evil and destruction, her male counterpart was merely a man of unbridled, though genuine, passion. Enter the Latin Lover.

The first official Latin Lover, Madrid-born Antonio Moreno, came to the fore in a string of serials in the late 1910s, but in those days, despite Moreno's popularity, men with darker looks were normally relegated to playing villains devoid of sensuality. Lew Cody, *the* he-vamp of the decade, could hardly be considered sexually enticing. With his black penciled mustache and equally black oily hair, Cody was little more than the stereotypical serial villain of the period. Even Valentino, at first, played mostly villainous supporting roles. When Dorothy Gish suggested the future sex symbol for the lead in the 1919 release *Scarlet Days,* a Griffith picture set in Mexico, the director turned her down, opting instead for all-American Richard Barthelmess in heavy makeup. Griffith believed that audiences would not warm to a swarthy, foreign actor.

In 1921, Valentino's explosion on the screen in both *The Four Horsemen of the Apocalypse* and *The Sheik* changed Griffith's—and the industry's—concept for good. Valentino was soon followed by a series of dark-eyed, dark-haired types who often had little in common but swarthy good looks. Those included Novarro, Don Alvarado, Gilbert Roland, and Ricardo Cortez (born Jacob Krantz in Vienna). Antonio Moreno, even if technically a predecessor of Valentino's, graduated to grade-A features only in the early 1920s and emerged as a first-rank star. Rod La Rocque was repackaged to fit the mold, while Ronald Colman, Warner Baxter, and John Gilbert, though not labeled as Latins, possessed the same type of dark looks.

Of course, the old Hollywood male ideal did not disappear from the screen completely. Milton Sills, Richard Dix, and the ultraserious Richard Barthelmess, actors with looks and personae similar to their Victorian predecessors', also became major stars at the turn of the decade, while Thomas Meighan and Wallace Reid remained big box-office names. Yet, the indisputable lovemaking heroes of the 1920s were the Arabs, Cossacks, Frenchmen, Spaniards, Argentinians, and Pacific Islanders incarnated by, as one contemporary put it, the "black-eyed brigade."

The "Latin" way of lovemaking became known for its seductive looks, passionate kisses, and exaggerated declarations of love, even though not every Latin Lover followed that style (while some non-Latins, such as John Gilbert, did). Novarro was a clear exception. Throughout the 1920s, apart from a few roles such as Rupert in *The Prisoner of Zenda* or the womanizing Lord Brinsley in *A Certain Young Man,* he was cast either as an intense and serious-minded hero, among them André-Louis Moreau in *Scaramouche* and Judah Ben-Hur, or, most often, as a tender, earnest, and unthreatening boy in love. Only his characters' names and settings, which were almost invariably foreign, differentiated his screen persona from that of a lighter-hearted version of Richard Barthelmess.

In contrast, neither subtlety nor restraint was to be found in Valentino's acting lexicon. His eyes rolled in ecstasy at the sight of the woman of his dreams. His nostrils flared with desire or anger—or both. His seductive leer made his female costars (and many of his fans) recoil in a mixture of horror and sexual arousal. Whereas some of the two Latin Lovers' roles, such as Novarro's Jamil Abdullah in *The Arab* and Valentino's Juan Gallardo in *Blood and Sand,* could have been played by either actor, the resulting characterizations and pictures would have been markedly different.

Although not exactly subtle by today's standards, Novarro's acting, in comparison to Valentino's, is a model of understatement. More often than not, there was an impishness to Novarro's look that suggested fun, not danger. A perfect example is his whimsical lovemaking with Dorothy Janis in the 1929 romantic melodrama of the South Seas, *The Pagan.* When Novarro sees Janis lying by a pond, he lies by her side and tries to entertain her by making his biceps vibrate. He tries to teach Janis to do the same, but she cannot. Feeling the softness of her arm, he caresses her gently. While Valentino's stormy lovemaking is laughable when watched today, Novarro's tender moments, as in this scene, are still touching. When the Mexican Latin Lover displayed intense passion, as in the finale of the 1930 melodrama *Call of the Flesh,* romantic yearning—not sensuality—was the driving force.

Ultimately, Novarro's more conventional persona gave him an edge over Valentino in terms of casting, allowing him to tackle "regular guy" roles that completely eluded the Italian Lover—the Sheik would have been unthinkable as Dick Randall, the Naval Academy student in *The Midshipman;* or as Karl Heinrich, the boyish monarch in *The Student Prince;* or as Tommy Winslow, the navy flier in *The Flying Fleet.* On the downside, Novarro's milder screen image prevented him from reaching the heights achieved by the more erotically charged Valentino, though it still carried enough appeal and freshness—plus a touch of "exotica"—to turn him into one of the top three romantic idols of the 1920s, and filmdom's first Latin American star.

Ascendant Star

Ingram knew he had in Novarro a star in the making, but despite the director's care in grooming and promoting his newest male discovery, others remained skeptical. "It is generally felt in Hollywood that Rex has made Barbara Le [sic] Marr a star by the work she did in *The Prisoner of Zenda*," read a December 1922 *Classic* article by Harry Carr, "but that his 'find,' Ramon Novarro, is something of a disappointment. It is hard to say just what Rodolph [a temporary alternate spelling] Valentino's appeal is; but apparently Novarro hasn't it." Ironically, Carr would become one of Novarro's staunchest champions in the near future, but in late 1922, his impression of the ascending star was matched by that of a number of film critics.

Novarro's notices were at best lukewarm when *Trifling Women*—as *Black Orchids* came to be called against Ingram's will—opened on October 2 at New York's Astor Theater. The *New York Times* may have found his romantic hero appealing, but others thought him ineffectual, with *Variety* observing that "Mr. Nevarre's [sic] part could...have been assumed by almost any juvenile of pictures," and sneering that his Ivan de Maupin would have worked better as "Ivan the Terrible" instead of "Ivan the Sap." As for Ingram, some reviewers were able to appreciate his idiosyncratic vision, while others were not.

"Moonlight on tiger skins and blood dripping onto white faces, while sinister apes, poison, and lust kept the plot rolling," is how filmmaker Michael Powell later described *Trifling Women*, perhaps Ingram's most personal film. It contained a minimum of intertitles, relying instead on its Gothic atmosphere to convey the appropriate mood. "An unquestionable masterpiece," raved the exhibitors' magazine *Harrison's Report*. Other reviewers were less enthusiastic. The *New York Times*, even if impressed by Ingram's directorial touch, called the story line of *Trifling Women* "an impossible rigmarole," while *Variety* thought the picture was a poor follow-up to *The Prisoner of Zenda*.

Since *Trifling Women* is now lost, it is impossible to judge how this bizarre piece of Hollywood Gothic would have stood the test of time. Its influence, however, may be felt in a later piece of Hollywood Gothic, Billy Wilder's *Sunset Boulevard*. The atmospheric, shadowy lighting of Wilder's masterpiece, courtesy of *Trifling Women*'s cinematographer John Seitz; Norma Desmond's mascara-eyed, tragic femme fatale, an aged version of the characters Barbara La Marr had played; and even the dead chimp are all eerily reminiscent of Ingram's 1922 film. Judging by the stills, a series of ultrastylized tableaux, *Trifling Women* must have been, if nothing else, a gaudy feast for the eyes.

Once again, much had been at stake in a Rex Ingram production, especially since *Trifling Women* had been the only picture since *The Prisoner of Zenda* to be shot at Metro in the first half of 1922. The box-office returns of Ingram's latest production are unknown, but it is quite possible that it turned out to be a financial disappointment. The picture was likely too personal to appeal to the general public, and it had gone nearly 50 percent over budget (its total cost was more than $270,000).

Despite the widespread doubts about Novarro's potential as a film star, and even if *Trifling Women* was not the hit Metro and Ingram had expected it to be, some in the industry were beginning to take notice of the director's protégé. According to Novarro, Samuel Goldwyn thought his performance in *The Prisoner of Zenda* "was the finest thing he had seen," and offered him a two-year contract at $2,500 a week.

When Ingram heard of Goldwyn's offer, Novarro recalled, "he looked very sad and said I probably should accept it since he couldn't afford to pay such a salary." Instead, the young actor rejected the offer, declaring, "Mr. Ingram is the one that believed in me.... If anyone is going to cash in on me it's Rex Ingram." Although Ingram's initial response was "You have no business being grateful in this business. Get your money when you can," the director was clearly touched by Novarro's gratitude—even while insisting that his use of the dutiful actor in subsequent pictures had nothing to do with personal feelings. "You are capable of doing the work that I want to be done," he told his protégé, "and that's why I'm hiring you."

Novarro, for his part, also knew that Ingram was capable of doing the best possible work to assure his pupil his long-sought film stardom. More than sheer loyalty to the director, Novarro's refusal of the Goldwyn offer was thus a pragmatic one. "If Goldwyn didn't have anything for me, he'd have to lend me out," Novarro later explained, "and loan-outs were then more often disastrous than helpful. In all my career as a contract actor, I've never once gone on loan-out." Additionally, Goldwyn's financial offer was probably far less tempting than Novarro's recollection of it. Although a January 1923 *New York Morning Telegraph* article did state that the "Goldwyn Company" (Samuel Goldwyn, Inc.; Goldwyn had been ousted from Goldwyn Pictures in early 1922) had made the ascending Metro actor a generous offer, the $2,500 a week claimed by Novarro sounds much too generous. That was the amount Ingram himself was making, and many of the industry's foremost stars did not earn as much.

Modesty was hardly a Novarro trait, and he may well have colored some of his memories, including Goldwyn's offer, in rosy tones. Except for Ferdinand Earle, who Novarro admitted found him "terrible" in *The Rubaiyat* (though Earle later changed his mind), every other director or producer he remembered meeting he also remembered as marveling at his talent and offering to sign him on the spot. He reported high praise from Allen Holubar and Victor Schertzinger; Marshall Neilan, he recalled, described him as the "most promising young man of the year" after watching *The Rubaiyat*; Paul Bern thought him so handsome that he told him, "When you get rid of that face, if you're not too tired, you might become a great actor"; and Mary Pickford, the most powerful woman in pictures at the time, invited him to be her leading man in *Rosita*.

Even though the Pickford offer—like Goldwyn's—is conceivably based on fact, only Parisian sensation Maurice Chevalier was consistently mentioned as a prospective lead for *Rosita*. If Novarro was at all considered, he was surely a minor contender for the part that eventually went to George Walsh. Yet, exaggerations aside, Novarro's status in the industry *was* increasing because of his decision to remain associated with his powerful mentor. His next two pictures for Ingram would solidify his standing as a major ascendant star.

While shooting *Trifling Women*, Ingram had signed a new contract with Metro to make six pictures in the next two years. After his Gothic melodrama was completed, he was scheduled to leave for New York to begin preparations for his next project, an adaptation of Victor Hugo's *Toilers of the Sea* to be shot off the coast of Maine with Terry, Novarro, and Edward Connelly. Perhaps owing to its high cost, estimated at more than $250,000, the picture was postponed for months and then finally discarded. (Another reason might be that director Roy William Neill had his own version in the works.) Ingram thus chose another subject, an interethnic love story to be filmed in the South Pacific.

The scenario, written by Ingram, was based on one of the narratives found in *The Red Mark and Other Stories,* a collection of South Seas tales by the "American Kipling," John Russell. In the picture, initially called *The Passion Vine* but released as *Where the Pavement Ends,* Novarro plays Motauri, a carefree Pacific Islander in love with a white missionary's daughter, portrayed by Alice Terry—the two stars' first romantic pairing. In order to take the role of Motauri, Novarro, much to his chagrin, had to turn down an offer to work with Lillian Gish in *The White Sister.*

Shooting of the South Seas love story began in late September 1922 at the Hialeah Studios near Miami, which, because of budget constraints, had to pass for a South Pacific island. Mountain scenes were shot in Cuba, and some additional footage was filmed at Metro's New York facilities. As in *Trifling Women,* the plot was not the strongest element of *Where the Pavement Ends.* Ingram, with the help of John Seitz's lenses and Grant Whytock's editing, used images to depict the freedom and innocence of the natural world being destroyed by the zeal and prejudices of European culture. An underwater sequence showing Motauri diving for pearls in close proximity to a man-size shark was considered particularly striking.

Despite the serenity of the on-screen scenery, the production was a difficult one. The relentless heat scorched actors and crew alike. Novarro, who perspired easily, had to have his makeup retouched every few minutes. He also recalled having his legs and feet badly bruised after carrying Alice Terry down a weedy slope barefoot, as Ingram would not allow him to wear any protection for fear of destroying authenticity. When Novarro refused to reshoot the scene—one leg was swollen and covered with ugly sores—Ingram exploded, threatening that he would never work with the "difficult" actor again. Novarro was devastated. "I worshiped the man," he lamented. He need not have worried. In the end, the director always forgave him.

Before the national release of *Where the Pavement Ends,* the studio demanded that Ingram film an alternative happy ending (exhibitors could then select the one they preferred). In the original ending, Motauri throws himself off a waterfall because his love for the white woman cannot be consummated (in deference to the Bible, miscegenation was a film taboo). In the alternate story, there is a prologue explaining that Motauri is in reality a nicely tanned white boy who grew up on the island unaware of his ethnicity. All is revealed at the end so the lovers can return to New England together for a life of blissful racial purity.

Novarro preferred the tragic ending, "if it is the logical thing." One assumes that by "the logical thing" he meant an ending that was true to the tone of the story, and not the "logical" ending for an interethnic romance. In his case, though, the happy ending actually *looks* more plausible. In the film's stills, the Mediterranean-looking Mexican does not in anyway resemble a Pacific Islander. Yet, Novarro was adamant. In his public complaint, he added that too many happy endings made motion pictures predictable, and that producers were "making a mistake in trying to put out pictures that everyone will see ... [for] they seldom really satisfy anyone."

The *New York Times* agreed with Novarro's judgment. At the film's opening on April 1, 1923, at New York City's 5,230-seat Capitol Theater, the *Times* reviewer hailed *Where the Pavement Ends* as "a picture without hokum, without the lovers embracing in the last scene." (Obviously, reviewers had seen Ingram's original version.) Other comments ranged from *Photoplay's* finding *Where the Pavement Ends* Ingram's best picture yet to critics who, though mesmerized by the film's look, thought the story too contrived, happy ending or not.

The role of Motauri brought Novarro's best notices to date. *Variety* declared that he "would be rather too conventionally and spiritually good-looking for a regular hero, but in these surroundings he is a picturesque figure." In fact, *Where the Pavement Ends* gave Novarro his first chance to put the boy-in-love persona to full use (in *Trifling Women* his role was smaller and subordinate to La Marr's). The loss of *The Rubaiyat of Omar Khayyam* and *Trifling Women* is lamentable because of the unique visual quality of those pictures, but the loss of *Where the Pavement Ends* is made worse by what may have been one of Novarro's best performances—in view of his outstanding work in the considerably lighter but similarly themed *The Pagan*. One can only speculate how his youth (he was twenty-three when the picture was shot) and lack of film experience were reflected in his depiction of Motauri's own innocence and earnestness.

Novarro was certainly pleased with his first successful full-fledged lead, despite the tacked-on happy ending in one version. "I say to a man who criticizes Mr. Ingram," he told Louella Parsons, "if you have never liked his pictures, you will love this, it is so different, and I say to you who like Mr. Ingram you will love this because it is his finest." Even if these remarks carried a whiff of self-promotion—after all, *he* was the leading man of Ingram's "finest" film—Novarro genuinely admired his mentor. He knew he could not have been any more fortunate than to be professionally attached to the man who was one of the most respected and commercially successful filmmakers in the world.

The interview with Louella Parsons was supposedly scheduled after she had learned about Metro's rising contract player and had "decided to talk with the young man and see how his sudden rise to affluence had affected him." In reality, Metro was now pushing Novarro at full force toward stardom. To demonstrate his importance, Louella explained in her piece that the interview had been arranged by Marcus Loew, the head of Metro Pictures' parent company, Loew's Incorporated.

Unlike fellow interviewer Margaret Ettinger, Louella did report Novarro's age accurately, though she managed to botch his family name ("Samanegas"), the title of his latest film ("The End of the Pavement"), and his nationality ("Spaniard"). Furthermore, she strangely remarked that Novarro's voice "should be worth his fortune if Spanish accents are being used this year," even though movies were silent and would remain so for five more years. Novarro's salary was also inflated by the studio to an astronomical $1,250 a week, with the possibility of an increase to $5,000 the following year. Marcus Loew went along with the farce—typical of those days—claiming, "I paid him an unheard of salary for a beginner. But he could get it elsewhere and I wanted to meet the bids."

Actually, Metro had by then raised Novarro's salary to $250, and would give him another $100 raise in March 1923. Still, despite a considerably more modest increase in earnings than that reported in the press, Novarro's career was rapidly progressing. Although the young Mexican did not experience Valentino's meteoric rise to fame, his professional advance was significant when compared to that of Metro's other budding star of the early 1920s, fellow *Prisoner of Zenda* alumnus Malcolm McGregor. Like Novarro, McGregor had worked as an extra and bit player until his *Zenda* appearance as the dashing Count Von Tarlenheim; unlike Novarro's, McGregor's early promise failed to materialize. He remained a second-rate leading man until his career fizzled out in 1930, not for lack of Novarro's star charisma, but for lack of Novarro's close professional liaison with a master builder of talent like Rex Ingram.

The steady rise of Novarro's career began at a time when Hollywood's "moral decadence" was making headlines all over the country. In September

1921, comedian Fatty Arbuckle was accused of sexually assaulting and ultimately killing a starlet at a booze-soaked party in San Francisco. Five months later, William Desmond Taylor, the director of several Mary Pickford films, was shot to death at his home. The press played up the involvement in the Taylor case of comedienne Mabel Normand and screen gamine Mary Miles Minter.

Arbuckle, one of the most popular comedians of the time, saw his acting career destroyed by the scandal. His films were banned and withdrawn from circulation, even though he was eventually acquitted of the charges. Meanwhile, Mary Miles Minter, the Pickford-like star of wholesome films such as *Lovely Mary* and *Anne of Green Gables*, and Arbuckle's frequent costar Mabel Normand had to cope with considerable unwelcome publicity and media scrutiny.

The notoriety of the Hollywood scandals was compounded by their sheer number. In the early 1920s, the public was shocked to learn of the possible suicides of Griffith's leading man Robert Harron and of actress Olive Thomas, the wife of Jack Pickford and sister-in-law of Mary. Serial star Juanita Hansen was admitted to a drug-rehabilitation clinic, thirty-two-year-old superstar Wallace Reid died suddenly while trying to break his morphine addiction, and Rudolph Valentino was on trial for bigamy (he had married Natacha Rambova before his divorce from Jean Acker had become official under California law).

Church, civil, and government leaders were outraged by the perceived moral and social degradation of the film colony. "Hollywood . . . a community of dissolute actors and actresses and others of the movie industry," was how journalist Thoreau Cronyn summarized the public's image of the film capital for the *New York Herald*. "The worst of them unspeakably vile, the best suspicionable; a colony of unregenerates and narcotic addicts; given to wild night parties commonly known as 'orgies;' heroes of the screen by day and vicious roisterers by night; a section of civilization gone rottenly to smash."

Obviously, drunken parties, drug addiction, murders, and suicides did not occur only in Hollywood, but few cases outside Hollywood created countrywide headlines. Thoreau Cronyn, who was sent to Los Angeles with the explicit purpose of uncovering the truth, felt the hysteria was unjustified. In his series of articles about the film colony, he concluded that most tales about Hollywood's depravity were either exaggerated or blatantly false. But the offended bastions of morality did not care for *that* sort of Hollywood tale. Along with members of the press avid for a sensational story, they accused the film capital of being a source of smut both in life and on the country's screens.

In an attempt to clean up its image and to avoid tougher censorship laws by state and county boards, in 1922 the studios created a self-regulatory board, the Motion Picture Producers and Distributors of America. Will Hays, chairman of the Republican National Committee and U.S. postmaster general, was chosen as head of the organization, which became known simply as the Hays Office. As an extra measure, the studios also began placing controls on the stars' private lives. In the aftermath of the Arbuckle scandal, both Universal and Paramount (the Famous Players–Lasky distributing arm) announced that they would bind their contract performers to "morality clauses" in an attempt to safeguard their investments. "Members of the Paramount Stock Company," read one such clause, "are expected to avoid places, circumstances, and conduct which might in any way bring themselves and the motion picture profession into disrepute. Any member failing strictly to observe this rule is liable to instant dismissal from the company." By the end of the decade, morality clauses would be in effect in most major Hollywood studios.

Another safeguard against negative publicity was the usually sympathetic film press. Studios made sure that fan magazines portrayed their contract players in a favorable light, with the threat that important forthcoming stories would be sent to more cooperative publications. Seriously damaging information, such as a star's homosexuality, was to remain taboo (even in the regular press) unless the star was deemed overly contentious by either the magazine or the studio. Even then, such articles were composed of innuendos that only the very sophisticated or those already in the know were able to understand—though the threat to the targeted star was evident.

In May 1924, *Photoplay* published an innuendo-laden article about Nita Naldi's "sister act" with a woman called Mary Rinaldi, whose surname Nita had adopted in altered form. The piece was topped by a picture of the popular film vamp holding the other woman's shoulder as they stood face-to-face. For the average reader the article just meant that Naldi was truly a woman of mysterious and exotic ways, but for the more sophisticated, the implications were clear. (In an earlier *Photoplay* issue Naldi had been referred to as Lilyan Tashman's "chum and most intimate friend." Tashman was well known in Hollywood and New York circles for preferring sexual partners of her own gender.) Alla Nazimova was also the target of sly insinuations after her breakup with Metro in 1921. According to Nazimova's biographer, Gavin Lambert, the studio itself planted negative stories in the fan magazines about its former star, including a reference to her illuminated swimming pool "crowded with Hollywood ingenues."

Novarro could ill afford such public embarrassments, regardless of their subtlety. His career was finally moving forward, and the ambitious young actor was not going to allow rumors about his sexuality to jeopardize his chances for success. Metro would also do its best to ensure that any "wrong-doing" was kept hidden from public view—the incident between Novarro and Malcolm McGregor during the filming of *Zenda*, for instance, would never have become public in those days. Still, there was always the chance that a news outlet beyond the studio's control could get hold of a story. Homosexual acts were illegal in California, and sting operations entrapping gays occurred regularly. A whiff of scandal with regard to Novarro's sexual orientation could easily have meant the end of his budding career. Likewise, even though his professional and family names were now distinct, those closer to him and his family knew he was a Samaniego. Widespread rumors would be demoralizing not only to Novarro, but also to every member of his traditional Mexican family.

Despite Novarro's circumspection about his sexuality, some at Metro presumably knew that the studio's biggest heartthrob was "temperamental." He had been a modernistic dancer, after all, and he was never seen with women on the town. Those were inconvenient facts, but studio publicists had to guarantee that Novarro was perceived by the public as being as conventionally masculine as possible. In fact, throughout his career, pictures of Novarro performing such "manly activities" as playing tennis, rowing, and jogging would be mass-produced for public consumption.

In an April 1923 interview for *Photoplay*, Novarro admitted to Herbert Howe, "They don't like me to say it, but I like dancing." The "They" Novarro referred to clearly stood for Metro's publicity department, which would rather have Novarro discussing baseball or boxing matches. But regardless of what "They" wanted, Novarro *did* say what he thought. This rebelliousness against excessive studio control over his private life would later be manifested by Novarro's refusal to get married for the sake of publicity. He was surely aware that being gay and single, per se, was not an impediment to Hollywood success. J. Warren Kerrigan and Eugene O'Brien were two other stars of the period facing the same potential problem, and both had been highly successful. The barrel-chested, hawk-nosed Kerrigan had been one of the biggest—possibly *the* biggest—romantic male lead of the 1910s despite asserting that "it doesn't seem quite fair to me for a picture hero to be married, besides I have my Mother." The big, burly O'Brien, once described as "the screen's perennial bachelor," was superstar Norma Talmadge's most popular leading man. He was said to be favored in that role by Talmadge's husband, producer Joseph Schenck, who knew that O'Brien posed no threat to his marriage.

The most important public-image strategy for a gay actor—or for any performer—was to establish and maintain positive relations with the press. First having Ingram as his mentor, and later counting on Herbert Howe as his guide and publicist, Novarro was always gracious and receptive to the press. In return, stories about him were almost invariably positive. "Ramon Novarro has made a personal friend of almost every writer who has ever talked to him and I don't ever recall having read anything unflattering about Ramon in all the time he's been on the screen," *Screen Book* asserted in 1934. "When he sees writers on the lot whom he knows, he makes a point of asking them to visit him in his dressing room or on his set. That's why the same writers do stories over and over again on him."

The article in which Novarro admitted he liked dancing carried no "sissy" innuendos. To the contrary, Herbert Howe implied that the young actor was courageous, honest, and had a mind of his own ("They" could not tell *him* what to do); in the future, the press would continually justify Novarro's perpetual bachelorhood by referring to his unflagging devotion to his large family. Since his relations with the studio's front office were also generally cordial in spite of several contractual disputes, Novarro never had to fear damaging stories being planted in the press. To the contrary, he could fully rely on Metro, and later on the all-powerful MGM, to shield him from any damaging revelations.

At that moment, Novarro's private life was not having any negative effect on the progress of his career. All his energies were concentrated on one objective: to become a successful film actor. More than simply a professional goal, success in Hollywood meant the end of his family's financial difficulties. And Novarro knew that his efforts were being rewarded—his next project for Ingram would be their most spectacular to date.

With the success of *Where the Pavement Ends*, Metro had allowed Ingram to make another expensive production, a film version of Rafael Sabatini's 1921 bestselling novel *Scaramouche: A Romance of the French Revolution*. For this project, bigger and more complex than either *Trifling Women* or *Where the Pavement Ends*, Ingram left the writing to others so that he could concentrate on the period reconstruction and other preproduction technicalities. Former journalist Willis Goldbeck, Ingram's press agent (soon to be replaced by Herbert Howe), was brought in to turn Sabatini's sweeping novel into a viable motion picture script.

Preproduction work on *Scaramouche* began in January 1923. An eighteenth-century French village was built on a sixty-acre lot in the Hollywood foot-hills, and another major set was erected at Metro. Novarro, playing the dashing avenger André-Louis Moreau, and Alice Terry, as the love interest, would be supported by an enormous cast, including Lewis Stone one more time playing Novarro's foe. Following Ingram's instructions, historical char-acters were cast with actors—professionals or not—who resembled paintings of the real-life figures.

Shooting was to have begun on St. Patrick's Day, 1923, but, according to legend, production was halted for the first ten days because the Dublin-born director would not stop celebrating. Ingram's idiosyncratic ways made good copy for the film press, but they were at least partly responsible for *Scaramouche* going over schedule. The picture, which was set to be completed by midsummer, was still being edited in September. Its then-staggering $858,000 cost concerned some Metro executives, who believed that Ingram's latest effort could never possibly recover the studio's investment. Yet, they feared confronting the temperamental director. Ingram did not tolerate front-office interference, and, in fact, *Scaramouche* was to be his last film made under any supervision other than his own.

The picture finally opened on September 30 at New York's Forty-fourth Street Theater to exuberant audiences. The *New York Times* hailed it as "an en-grossing and charming film," while several other reviewers considered *Scara-mouche* to be the director's best work. At the end of the year, Ingram's epic of the French Revolution was listed as the sixth best film in the annual *Film Daily* poll of film critics, and upon its wide release in February 1924, it became one of the most successful box-office hits of the year. Although billed after Alice Terry—but now ahead of Lewis Stone—Novarro was the indisputable star of the picture, Ingram's biggest success since *The Four Horsemen of the Apocalypse*. The *New York Times* complimented the dashing leading man for proving himself "an accomplished actor," the *Los Angeles Times* praised André-Louis Moreau as "his best and most convincing work," and *Variety* asserted that *Scaramouche* "will do for him what *The Four Horsemen* did for Valentino."

Variety's assertion proved to be somewhat of an overstatement, though *Scaramouche* did turn Novarro into a star—in popularity, if not yet in the credits. Boasting better pacing and a charismatic performance by the gor-geously photographed leading man—well matched by Lewis Stone's suave villain—*Scaramouche* is a far more compelling spectacle than *The Prisoner of Zenda*. A few years later, Novarro would understandably refer to the French Revolution epic as his favorite picture and his most enjoyable filming ex-perience.

. . .

At the time of the *Scaramouche* premiere, Novarro had just returned to Los Angeles from a brief New York vacation. While Ingram prepared his next project, Novarro was getting ready to appear in the Louis B. Mayer production *Thy Name Is Woman*, the first time he would be directed by someone other than his mentor since the *Rubaiyat* fiasco more than two years earlier. Forty-nine-year-old Fred Niblo, a gregarious former vaudevillian and ex–brother-in-law of Broadway celebrity George M. Cohan, had been chosen to guide the proceedings.

Though not in the same league as Rex Ingram, Niblo was a respected figure in the industry. *Photoplay* had dubbed him "a directorial knight of the screen" after the release of *The Famous Mrs. Fair* in 1923, a time when Niblo was rapidly solidifying his name as a stylish and versatile director of glossy star vehicles. Those included Douglas Fairbanks's rousing *The Mark of Zorro* and *The Three Musketeers*, Valentino's melodramatic *Blood and Sand*, and the pirate adventure *Strangers of the Night* with Barbara La Marr and Niblo's Australian-born wife Enid Bennett. Since 1922, Niblo had been attached to Louis B. Mayer Productions, an association that would shortly lead him to his—and Novarro's—most acclaimed project. *Thy Name Is Woman*, however, was *not* to be that project.

With a scenario by Bess Meredyth based on Austrian playwright Karl Schönherr's *The She-Devil*, *Thy Name Is Woman* is the type of over-the-top melodrama so often associated with silent films. The plot, set in Spain's mountainous northeast, grows out of a love triangle involving the chief of a smuggling ring (mean-looking character actor William V. Mong), the chief's wife (Barbara La Marr), and a youthful carabinero (Novarro), who must seduce the smuggler's wife so she will betray her husband to the police. Mayer had acquired the rights to both the story and Novarro's services through a distribution deal with Metro.

Shooting at Mayer's Mission Road studio near downtown Los Angeles proceeded at an even more hectic pace than was normal for a programmer like *Thy Name Is Woman*. Novarro was forced to work literally day and night in order to be free in time to play the lead in Ingram's next ambitious project: a remake of Edgar Selwyn's *The Arab*, which had been a hit both onstage and on-screen—directed by Cecil B. DeMille—in the previous decade.

Rex Ingram had decided to tackle Selwyn's tale of cultural clashes for several reasons. According to his biographer, Liam O'Leary, "Ingram felt a strange affinity with the Arab people, approving of their rather passive attitude to life, contrasting it with the rush and bustle of American habits." Ingram also held DeMille's work in low esteem and believed he could more accurately portray Arab culture on-screen. Finally, this desert tale mixing adventure, comedy, and romance would be another excellent vehicle to showcase his protégé and would provide a convenient excuse for the director to distance himself from Hollywood. Following the success of *Where the Pavement Ends* and *Scaramouche*, Ingram was in a position to insist on location shooting. After some haggling, Metro grudgingly agreed.

Set in a Turkish province, *The Arab* relates the efforts of a Bedouin leader's impish son, Jamil Abdullah Azam, to charm the American daughter of a Christian missionary. She is initially wary of him, but her attitude changes when the bratty Bedouin rescues a group of Christian children from an evil Muslim governor. Comparisons between the Bedouin Jamil and Valentino's Sheik seemed inevitable, but even if Novarro was concerned about that possibility, he trusted his mentor's judgment. Modesty was not one of Ingram's qualities, and the director may well have convinced his leading man that under his guidance Jamil would be *incomparable*. Indeed, despite Ingram's early efforts to turn Novarro into another Valentino, the Mexican lover had by now created his very own distinctive persona.

In late 1923, about two years after his rise from the ranks of extras and bit players, Ramon Novarro had reached the first echelon of Hollywood fame (even though his name still appeared below the title). Besides his association with one of the industry's foremost directors, Novarro was aided by the fact that he faced little competition in the young-heartthrob field. Another salary dispute, this time with Famous Players–Lasky, had kept Valentino off the country's screens since *The Young Rajah* in November 1922. Wallace Reid had died early in 1923; John Gilbert was working for Fox, then a second-rank studio; Ricardo Cortez was just getting started; Warner Baxter, Edmund Lowe, and Ronald Colman, though all more than thirty years old, were still waiting for their star-making break; and John Barrymore, Milton Sills, J. Warren Kerrigan, Eugene O'Brien, and Thomas Meighan were already past forty.

By 1923, Ingram and Metro had realized that to promote Novarro as a Latin Lover was not only inappropriate to his persona, but would also relegate him forever to the status of a second-rank Valentino. Director and studio publicists may have reasoned that if Novarro was portrayed as a south-of-the-border version of apple-pie "Americanness," then once the Latin Lover craze faded, their newest investment would still have a career. This strategy could be seen as early as the Louella Parsons interview. "The world to Ramon Novarro is a wonderful place," Louella mused, "filled with kind, thoughtful people and generous critics who write beautiful stories and think only good thoughts in the world. At 23 Ramon is like the little boy who believes so thoroughly in fairies and Santa Claus his family can not bear to disillusion him. It would be a pity to tell this trusting youth that there are any wolves grazing in the motion picture pasture."

Despite Louella's embellishments and simplifications, Novarro's public image actually resembled the real Novarro at that time. In 1923, Novarro was young, handsome, and on his way to becoming very wealthy; moreover, he could count on the support and guidance of one of the film capital's top directors. At this stage in his life Ramón Samaniego was experiencing as reality the things he had dreamed of since he was a little boy, and he could easily afford to see the world as a thoroughly benign place. Regard-ess of the suffering and horror he had witnessed during the Mexican Revolution, Los Angeles was a universe away from that past. As a devout Catholic, Ramón conceivably saw the difficulties he and his family had encountered in their native land as a test from God. Since the Samaniegos' faith had remained solid, they were now being compensated in the success of their oldest male child. Even so, success would prove to have its incon-veniences.

As Ramon Novarro became a household name, public curiosity about his private life greatly increased. The two most common questions were "How tall is he?" and "Is he married?" The answer to the first one was easy. Metro needed only to add a few inches to Novarro's height (his official height in the early 1920s was five feet ten inches; later in the decade, he mysteriously shrank to five eight). As for the second question, the obvious answer was a resounding "No," but the studio knew that, whether factual or fabricated, the aura of Hollywood romance had to be kept alive in the public imagi-nation. Fan magazines were filled with reports of "engagements" between young and beautiful performers that would quickly be denied in the next issue, only to resurface again in the next.

Novarro, however, was reluctant to play the part of a ladies' man off-screen, preferring to spend his private moments with his family at their Constance Street residence. In order to counterbalance the reticence of its leading star, Metro (and later MGM) came up with its own series of "Rav-ishing Ramon" romances. For the rest of Novarro's career as a star, he would be romantically linked to numerous actresses, from the tomboyish Elsie Janis to the glamorous Greta Garbo—Alice Terry, his most frequent costar, escaped this fate only because she was already married to Ingram. Such fictitious pairings usually occurred when the two stars were seen regularly socializing, as in the late-1920s Novarro-Janis "romance," or when they had appeared in the same film, as in the post–*Mata Hari* Novarro-Garbo "affair." During Novarro's early days as a star, Metro attached him to Barbara La Marr and Edith Allen, the second female lead in *Scaramouche*.

The round-faced, dark-haired Allen had originally been spotted by Ingram at a New York café, and had returned east soon after her part in the film was completed. A note in the September 1923 issue of *Photoplay* reported that Allen seemed smitten with Novarro, who had also left for New York after finishing his role in *Scaramouche*. As *Photoplay* speculated, could that be because the dashing star was equally smitten with the petite brunette? No. Before the year was over, someone other than Edith Allen would become seriously smitten with Novarro. The star, for his part, would fully return the attention—and not for publicity purposes.

On November 18, Novarro sailed aboard the *Majestic* to France, in what was his first trip outside North America—and during which the seasick actor remained locked in his cabin. Also aboard was one of Hollywood's top journalists and the best fan magazine writer of the time—arguably of all time—Herbert Howe. Howe was sailing under Rex Ingram's auspices to publicize the making of *The Arab*, but succeeded in spending time with the picture's star only on the day before the ship docked in Cherbourg. On their belated encounter, the writer "touched a secret spring to [Ramon's] confidence, for that evening was one of charmed revelation." By the time production on *The Arab* was over, Herbert Howe had become a fixture in both Novarro's professional and personal lives.

Herbert Riley Howe was born on September 28, 1893, in Sioux Falls, South Dakota, the older of two sons of a New York teacher turned civil engineer and his Illinois-born wife. Howe's interest in the film industry began as a child, when he would spend hours watching flickers at his uncle's nickelodeon in South Dakota. He was said to have graduated from the "State University" (which state is not clear; he did not graduate from the University of South Dakota); and following graduation, he left for New York City, where he worked as a publicist for several film companies. His career was interrupted by World War I, during which he served in the U.S. Tank Corps after spending one night in a French dungeon for "trying to see France without first asking nursey if I might play around."

Howe returned to New York upon his discharge, was hired as a reporter for the *New York Telegraph,* and began doubling as a fan magazine writer. In 1921 he was named western representative of Brewster Publications, which included fan magazines *Shadowland, Motion Picture,* and *Motion Picture Classic.* During that time, he also worked as a publicist for Vitagraph Pictures, and not long thereafter began acting as Rex Ingram and Alice Terry's press agent. The following year, Howe started writing for *Photoplay,* then the most popular of all film publications. In addition to writing pieces about specific film stars, he was given his own highly entertaining special section, "Close-Ups and Long-Shots."

A literary critic once remarked that Howe's was "the most polished form of wit," which well describes his perceptive insights, intelligent and irreverent humor, pointed jabs at the film community, and surprisingly modern sensibility. "Close-Ups and Long-Shots" served as an antidote for readers nauseated by the typical mushiness cranked out by most fan magazine writers. Decades after they were written, Howe's articles have lost none of their amusing edge.

"The secret of Herbert Howe's success as an interviewer," fellow *Photoplay* writer Adela Rogers St. Johns noted, "is that he knows everybody worth knowing in pictures—and he doesn't care what he says about them." Indeed, Howe's facetious observations about film notables were not exactly a publicist's dream. "It seems that no one," he quipped about the oft-married Barbara La Marr, "not even Barbara, knows exactly how many husbands she's had. At this writing a recount is on." In the article "An Evolution Trial at the Zoo," Howe offended apes everywhere by comparing the behavior of movie stars to that of orangutans. To a man whose daughter wanted to go into pictures, he caustically wrote, "My advice concerning your daughter is—shoot her, as painlessly but as definitely as possible." He also suggested that F. Scott Fitzgerald's play *The Vegetable* should be retitled *Vegetables* so a possible film adaptation could boast an all-star cast.

Howe's jabs could also be serious. He condemned his fellow journalists for dirtying the image of Mabel Normand, one of his closest friends, and chastised the film industry for ignoring the plight of Anna Q. Nilsson, a popular actress who lay ailing in bed after a serious back injury. Nonetheless, in spite of referring to the film capital as "Mr. Dante's Hollywood" and as an "enlarged Cabinet of Dr. Caligari," Howe clearly loved being a member of that community and relished his job as one of its foremost commentators.

The popular image of this average-looking, heavy-drinking intellectual from Sioux Falls was that of the Hollywood Boulevardier: a sophisticated man-about-town, a reader of Nietzsche and Schopenhauer, a European—in spirit, if not in birth—lost among the sunshine and palm trees of Southern California. Howe, who always insisted that he hated work as much as he loved booze, at times threatened to leave his Hollywood Hills home for the fashionable south of France, though he ended up remaining in Los Angeles for several more years. While in town, he could be spotted dining with Pola Negri, dancing with Corinne Griffith, and attending concerts with Florence Vidor.

Initially, Howe feigned indignation at "pretty" types like Novarro (whom he had briefly interviewed in late 1922) and Valentino (whose *Photoplay* "autobiography" he ghostwrote)—most probably because he was then promoting the rugged, all-American Malcolm McGregor. Additionally, Howe had not been too impressed by the Mexican newcomer at the time of their first interview, finding him "a pallid personality... restrained, secretive, not a little wary [Novarro had admittedly been leery of Howe's reputation as a cynical sophisticate]...There was no warmth or resiliency about him."

But beginning with *The Arab*, Howe's columns became filled with praise for Novarro's gallantry, kindness, looks, poise, wit, and whatever other traits the writer could conjure up. "At first thought," Howe later observed, "it would seem there could be little in common between a Mexican devoutly religious and an American devoutly pagan; one a budding go-getter and the other a [self-proclaimed] descendant of Sitting Bull, who wasn't named that way for his love of work." Howe, of course, was not merely a reporter expressing his opinions of a movie star: by then he had also become Novarro's publicist. Yet, his adulation of Novarro was not just for the sake of publicity. Howe had become truly captivated by the heartthrob from Durango. "He made me think of one of those bounding bright-eyed fox terriers," Howe remarked, "which at first annoy you, then get your affection and finally have you worrying lest they get run over." Furthermore, Howe, like Ingram, had "a predilection for the gents of sepia finish."

Before working with Novarro and the Ingrams, Howe had acted as a publicist for another "gent of sepia finish," Antonio Moreno, whom the writer admitted to seeing nearly every day throughout 1920—as buddies. "Tony introduced me to Hollywood and the flowery path long ago," he wrote in 1925, "and for several years I was closely associated with him." Whether or not theirs was more than a professional relationship, Moreno's notorious temper tantrums doubtlessly contributed to their split, an eventuality the equally short-tempered Howe did not have to fear from the (almost) invariably courteous Novarro. In fact, the young Mexican's civil demeanor was an added attraction to Howe. According to author Lawrence Quirk, a nephew of *Photoplay*'s editor in chief, James R. Quirk, "the devoutly pagan" Howe was so enamored of Novarro that he converted to Catholicism (or at least pretended to for a short while).

James Quirk knew of Howe's dual duties, a not uncommon occurrence at fan magazines, and believed that Howe's close association with Novarro made his writings about Metro's popular star more intimate and insightful. Fan magazine readers were also aware that the star and the journalist shared a very close relationship. "Herb Howe is Ramon Novarro's best friend," remarked *Photoplay's* own Answer Man. "If you read Herb's pages you will often find little things about Ramon that none of the rest of us know." *Motion Picture* agreed that Novarro and Howe's friendship was special, asserting that "no one outside of [Novarro's] family knows him as Herbert Howe does." Years later, at the dawn of talking pictures, Howe expressed his surprise that "an old friend" with no talent for singing could now be seen—and heard—emitting melodious tones from the screen. His readers immediately mistook the untalented singer (probably Corinne Griffith in First National's *The Divine Lady*) for Novarro. "Imagine more my surprise," Howe remarked, "at a downpour of letters asking if Ramon Novarro really had a double for his voice in *The Pagan*, the assumption being, I suppose, that I never had another friend."

Still, Howe was safe even when admitting in print that Novarro's "eyes so mesmerize a mood that you forget to listen," since most of his readership was composed of females who felt exactly as he did, and would accept his adoration unquestioningly. Also, Howe was a well-known ladies' man—in print. He frequently mused in his columns about the incredible beauty of Corinne Griffith, declared himself enthralled by the allure of Pola Negri, and even dared to select the ten most beautiful women in motion pictures. And finally, the mere concept of homosexuality in most of the United States, even in the Roaring Twenties, was practically nonexistent. An unholy relationship between Howe and Novarro was thus unimaginable for most readers.

Upon their arrival in Paris in midfall 1923, Novarro and Howe were joined by Alice Terry, with whom they proceeded to the French Riviera and then on to Tunisia, where exterior scenes of *The Arab* were to be shot at the oasis of Gabès and the medieval city Sidi-bou-Zaid. Interiors would be filmed later at the Joinville studios, when the company returned to Paris.

In *The Arab*, as he had previously done in *Where the Pavement Ends* and would later do in *The Pagan*, the devoutly Catholic Novarro played a non-Christian hero in a picture that either mocked or questioned rigid Christian mores and rules of conduct. In *Where the Pavement Ends*, the Christian missionary is a racist bigot with little concern for the happiness of his daughter. In *The Pagan*, Novarro's carefree Henry Shoesmith wonders why, to reach God, Christians must be crammed inside an enclosed, oppressively hot church when the divine is everywhere in the island's glorious landscape. Likewise, in *Call of the Flesh*, intractable religiosity—in the form of the heroine's brother, who insists she must leave Novarro's high-spirited hero for convent life— is seen as an evil that nearly destroys the lives of both protagonists. In *The Arab*, Jamil adopts a breezy attitude toward religion that only enhances his likableness. Whenever he wants to learn a new European language, he joins the appropriate mission and "converts" to Christianity, only to return to his old ways after achieving his linguistic objective.

Obviously, the unorthodox view of Christianity displayed by Novarro's characters did not necessarily reflect the opinions of Novarro the individual, but the actor was close enough to Ingram to have comfortably expressed his concern should anything in *The Arab* offend his Catholic sensibility. During that time, Ingram, the rebellious son of a Protestant pastor, probably influenced Novarro's religious views, which were further challenged by the nonbeliever Herbert Howe (not surprisingly, certain Samaniegos thought him a bad influence on Novarro). Yet, Novarro's tolerance had quite possibly developed before he met them, perhaps through his exposure to theater people early in his career, or maybe even earlier, as a reaction against his ultraconservative religious background—after all, for years he had been an ardent believer in the very un-Catholic "sciences" of palm reading and numerology.

At this point in his life, Novarro's ardent faith apparently did not prevent him from being accepting of either unconventional approaches to religion or unconventional manifestations of human sexuality, including his own. His relationship with Herbert Howe could thus flourish in its own secure compartment.

Shooting in North Africa and Europe lasted nearly four months. Rex Ingram's immersion in the culture he prized so dearly deepened his "strange affinity" for the Arab people. He competed with local riders in one of the film's spectacular horse-riding sequences; became friends with the bey of Tunis; was presented with his own private court jester; and after returning to France, even took the trouble of rescuing a North African boy, Kada-

Abd-el-Kader, who, according to Howe, was being held in "virtual slavery" by a Parisian. The Ingrams, who never had children of their own, eventually adopted the boy.

Novarro, on whose performance *The Arab* rested, was considerably less impressed by his surroundings. "The desert—also the South Sea islands— are very lovely to look at in pictures," he later observed, "but [when] you go there, you lose all that romantic feeling." He suffered under both the relentless heat of the Tunisian desert and Ingram's rigorous command. According to Howe, Novarro's "carelessness at times was exasperating to Rex Ingram. And the alibi Ramon would offer was still more exasperating." One such occasion was the Mexican Bedouin's lack of poise while walking on the dunes, a problem he blamed on the softness of the sand. Ingram was "disgusted" by the excuse. He wanted his protégé to obey to the letter his most minute instructions: in order for Novarro to *be* the Arab Jamil, he had to walk on the sand like a man of the desert, sit on a horse like an expert horseman, and ogle women like an ardently heterosexual man. During the shooting of one scene, after telling his leading man to look in the direction of a woman seductively standing at a doorway, Ingram begged him, "For God's sake, try to look interested!"

Despite Ingram's meticulous demands and the overall lack of infrastructure, *The Arab* proceeded on schedule. Christmas 1923 was spent at a hotel in Tunis. Novarro had requested that no gift be given him because, in Howe's words, "he was embarrassed by direct demonstrations"—though he felt no qualms about occupying center stage at the party. Besides impersonating, among others, comedian Ed Wynn and stage star Minnie Maddern Fiske, Novarro entertained his friends by singing Mexican songs and playing "Ave Maria" at the piano. Once the year-end festivities were over, the company resumed work for several more weeks in both Tunisia and Joinville.

Novarro finally returned to the United States on March 8. Howe arrived with the Ingrams three days later, possibly because he had served as an accessory in the surreptitious departure of Kada-Abd-el-Kader from France.

While Novarro was overseas, *Thy Name Is Woman* had its Los Angeles gala premiere on February 4 at the Mission Theater. The event, attended by a star-studded audience, was followed by a dinner party at the fashionable Biltmore Hotel in honor of Fred Niblo. The evening was a great success, but the picture itself was an artistic letdown. As a result of Niblo's heavy-handed direction, Novarro's carabinero in love suffers from an acute case of earnestness that seems both forced and coy, and despite his off-screen friendship with Barbara La Marr, the couple exude precious little chemistry in their love scenes. Only William V. Mong's solid performance, praised by *Variety* as "a work of art," makes this turgid melodrama (barely) watchable.

Reviews were mixed to negative. The *New York Times* may have found *Thy Name Is Woman* "not nearly as disappointing as one might infer from the title," but *Life* (probably Robert E. Sherwood) summed up the opinions of many by describing the picture as "a pretty sorry mess," its "thrills... phony and its tragic moments no more than laughable." The three leads, however, generally managed good notices of their own. And in spite of the picture's tragic ending—La Marr gets stabbed to death by Mong, who then dies of a heart attack, while Novarro is sentenced to death for having really fallen in love with La Marr (he is pardoned at the last minute)—*Thy Name Is Woman* did brisk business on the strength of the stars' names. Even then, solid box-office receipts could not hide the film's numerous flaws. After such an artistic disappointment, the actor was eager to resume his association with his mentor. But Novarro and Ingram would never work together again.

By the time he made *The Arab*, Rex Ingram had decided to leave Hollywood permanently for Europe. As early as 1921, Ingram had expressed an interest in filming *Ivanhoe* in England and several other pictures in Paris. This desire to distance himself from the film capital had intensified after a bitter professional disappointment and a monumental change in the Hollywood power structure.

Ingram, like almost everyone else in Hollywood, was certain that he would be chosen as director of what promised to become the greatest motion picture of its time, *Ben-Hur*. But while making *Where the Pavement Ends*, the director was notified that he had been rejected for the job. June Mathis, the main force behind the *Ben-Hur* juggernaut, was the person most probably responsible for Ingram's rejection. More than two years after their rift, she still had not forgiven him. According to Adela Rogers St. Johns, during the time *The Four Horsemen of the Apocalypse* and *The Conquering Power* were made, Mathis had been in love with Ingram, not, as rumors had it, with Valentino (for whom she felt a sisterly devotion). If St. Johns was correct, this revelation adds a new dimension to Mathis's dogged antagonism toward Ingram since their quarrel.

Ingram was devastated by the rejection. *Ben-Hur* was such an important project to him that his contract stipulated that Metro would loan him out in case another company was to produce it. According to John Seitz, when

Ingram was notified that *Ben-Hur* was going to be made without him, he suffered "a sudden change in personality. Everything had been going so well and he was having his way in almost everything. This came as a great shock."

Compounding the problem, the thirty-one-year-old maverick director was unhappy with the changes occurring in the film industry. In early 1924, negotiations began for the merger of three producing companies, Goldwyn Pictures, Metro Pictures, and Louis B. Mayer Productions. Goldwyn had the talent and top-notch production facilities; Metro had an extensive distribution arm through its parent company, Loew's; and Louis B. Mayer had the required managerial skills to preside over the gigantic new studio. Also, Mayer could rely on the assistance of twenty-four-year-old Irving G. Thalberg, a talented producer who had joined Mayer Productions after leaving Universal in February of the previous year.

The merger of the Metro, Goldwyn, and Mayer companies—with the side addition of publishing magnate William Randolph Hearst's Cosmopolitan Pictures—officially took place during a ceremony at the Goldwyn studios on April 26, 1924. The amalgamation of the three studios led to a consolidation of power in the hands of Mayer, who was named studio chief, and Thalberg, who became supervisor of production.

Ingram had always dreaded having studio executives meddling in his productions. In an August 1921 article for *Photoplay*, he had complained, "My sympathies are all with those directors who stand or fall on their own merits. I have too often seen a good picture, and the career of a promising director, ruined by so-called *supervision*." His distrust of the new company's front office was reciprocated.

Mayer disliked Ingram's style, and demanded that *The Arab*'s footage be shipped to Los Angeles so the film could be assembled far from the director's control. Ingram was so enraged that he insisted on the incorporation of a clause into his contract stating that his pictures should be billed as "A Rex Ingram Production for Metro-Goldwyn," instead of the usual "Louis B. Mayer Presents . . . A Metro-Goldwyn Picture." Ingram refused to speak to the new studio head, and reported only to Marcus Loew and his second-in-command, Nicholas Schenck in New York.

Reflecting his anger and frustration over both the *Ben-Hur* debacle and the merger, Ingram gave an interview to a French newspaper avowing that he would never make another picture in Hollywood—an assertion that proved to be prophetic. Mayer felt that Ingram and others like him were ingrates who had profited from the system and were now badmouthing it. Ingram, on the other hand, felt that he had managed to make artistic films *despite* the system, not because of it. The future would prove him both right and wrong.

For now, Ingram had one more laurel in the form of *The Arab*, which was his, and Novarro's, first film to be released by the new company. On July 13, 1924, Ingram's latest effort premiered at New York's Capitol Theater to mostly positive reviews—*Variety* proclaimed the picture "the finest sheik film of them all," while the *New York Times* called it "entertainment which begets thought." Novarro and Terry (minus blond wig) were also hailed for their acting, with Novarro commended for his "manliness" and his "youth and personal magnetism." Curiously, none of the major reviewers compared him to Valentino.

The success of *The Arab* was a bittersweet achievement for Ingram. Upon his return to the United States in early 1924, he suffered a nervous breakdown, spending most of his time in New York while Alice Terry headed West to appear in a number of films. In late fall, Ingram finally sailed for the French Riviera city of Nice, where he leased (and later bought) his own production facilities. At the time of his departure, Rex Ingram was one of the highest-paid directors in Hollywood and had just been named one of the top three motion picture directors by both the *Film Daily* and *Photoplay* film exhibitor polls.

Novarro's professional relationship with Ingram had been extremely beneficial to the young actor. Theirs was a remarkable five-film collaboration, one that had taken the young actor from a professional dead end to the forefront of Hollywood stardom. Now that the break with Ingram was inevitable— Novarro was not going to leave Hollywood and his family to pursue a career in Europe—the twenty-five-year-old must have felt insecure about his future. Novarro knew he owed his present success to Ingram. He was also aware that there would never be anyone else like Ingram to guide his professional steps. With the myriad changes taking place in Hollywood, how would he deal with the new studio power structure without his mentor? Who would choose the vehicles that best suited his abilities?

On a personal level, Ingram's departure was also a major blow to Novarro. They were intimate friends, even if the exact type of relationship they shared remains unclear. In Novarro's interviews, he frequently discussed his admiration for Ingram as an artist, but hardly ever mentioned their friendship. Their professional association as mentor-protégé and Novarro's regular use of "Mr. Ingram" throughout his life imply that they developed something akin to a father-son rapport. Although there was only a six-year difference between them, Ingram was assured, worldly, and sophisticated in ways that Novarro would never become.

Ingram's distinct appreciation of male beauty—evidenced by his grooming of Valentino, Novarro, and later, Iván Petrovich and Novarro look-alike Pierre Batcheff, and by his many drawings of young North African men— has led to speculation not only that Ingram was gay, but also that a sexual liaison developed between Irish mentor and Mexican protégé. Those conjectures have gained some credence because Ingram and Terry often spent months (sometimes years) at a time away from each other, and because they lived in separate quarters both in Nice and after their return to Los Angeles in the mid-1930s. Terry, in fact, was the lover of British actor Gerald Fielding while still married to Ingram, and one of Terry's friends has asserted that Ingram had been sharing his quarters with a young man at the time of his death. Still, Ingram may have preferred his own private quarters so he could work and study in tranquillity, for those were the two passions that occupied most of his time; the young man, if he really existed, may well have been just a houseboy.

By all accounts, Ingram was completely open-minded about sexual matters. He was both aware and accepting of Novarro's sexual orientation, and according to Terry's longtime friends film historian Anthony Slide and agent Alan Brock, he was always fascinated by other people's sexual activities, regardless of gender. Such curiosity does not imply that Ingram *practiced* different sorts of sexual behavior, or even that he wished to. His only known affairs were with women, many of those after his marriage to Terry—and with her knowledge—including a romantic liaison with his discovery Rosita García.

Ultimately, there is no evidence that Ingram had homosexual inclinations, or that any kind of sexual intimacy occurred between him and Novarro. Whether or not there ever was any sexual attraction between them—platonic or consummated, one-sided or mutual—their relationship endured for decades because of their mutual admiration. "Isn't that boy a wonder?" Ingram had exclaimed while watching Novarro play a scene in *Scaramouche*. "He's the greatest actor on the screen—I've never seen anyone like him."

Publicity (and the director's flare-ups) aside, Ingram was sincerely enthusiastic about Novarro. "Rex had an eliciting faith in Ramon," Herbert Howe later explained, "and he worked with furious determination to justify it to the world." That is why the director featured the then unknown Mexican in no fewer than five consecutive pictures. Novarro also had never seen anyone like Ingram, nor would he ever again. Despite their professional and physical separation, Novarro's gratitude remained undiminished. In the introduction of his first independent production, the 1936 Spanish-language feature *Contra la corriente*, he dedicates the picture *"A mis padres, a mi Patria, al hombre a quién debo lo que soy y lo que sé: Rex Ingram"* [To my parents, to my Country, to the man to whom I owe what I am and what I know: Rex Ingram].

After Ingram's departure, Novarro could rely on the intelligent and experienced industry insider Herbert Howe for advice and constant positive publicity. But that was different from having a mentor who had chosen stories and roles specifically to suit his talents, who had guided him through the filming process, who had acted like a father to him in a manner that his own ailing father could not. Before his departure, Ingram advised his protégé to work only for well-established directors in carefully selected vehicles, but for the remainder of his career Novarro would usually heed only the first half of Ingram's advice. Oftentimes, to the detriment of both his career and himself, he would ignore it altogether.

FIVE

"How Fate Works"

In April 1924, Novarro's contract with the newly formed Metro-Goldwyn came up for renewal. Exaggerated reports stated that his weekly earnings skyrocketed from the $500 he had been receiving to an exorbitant $10,000, but the MGM payroll ledger shows a raise of only $500. Even then, $1,000 a week (approximately $10,000 today) was enough for him to begin enjoying a distinctly more lavish lifestyle. Upon his return from Europe, Novarro bought a Lincoln coupé for himself and a $5,500 mansion for his family.

The new Samaniego home, at 2265 West Twenty-second Street at Gramercy Place, lay in the West Adams district, which until the late 1910s had been the most prestigious residential section of Los Angeles. Only two miles east of their Constance Street house, this considerably more upscale—and mostly WASP—neighborhood of sumptuous Victorian and Craftsman mansions was still conveniently located near the Mexican district. The two-story, "Main Street" American-style house boasted a spacious living room, several bedrooms, and servants' quarters, but since all ten Samaniegos had to share that space, rear wings were added to provide sufficient bedrooms for the male siblings.

Novarro himself designed his bedroom, dressing room, and bath. The bedroom, which was as large as a living room, had two beds, one in the main area and the other in an alcove, and was furnished to Novarro's eclectic taste—a mixture of modern and traditional Mexican furniture decorated with religious artifacts, among them a crown of thorns. In an arched recess stood the centerpiece of the room, a grand piano covered with a Roman cope.

Novarro also bought the adjacent lots on both sides of the house, where he built a swimming pool and a tennis court. Through the years he added a solarium and an upstairs porch to the main house, and had his brother Eduardo, an architecture student, oversee the construction of a sauna. When all the additions were completed, the property presented a façade of opulence, though the interior of the house remained unpretentious. More than a gift to himself and to his family, Novarro's West Adams residence represented a bridge between past and present: it was both Novarro's deference to the revered Samaniego name and a proud, concrete symbol of his achievements in the new country.

Now that their days of financial hardships were over, the Samaniegos faced a quite different problem. According to Novarro, his family were unable to grasp his film stardom, and were eager to continue living a "normal" life even though one in their midst was a world-famous actor. One means to achieve "normality" was to maintain old family rules, such as demanding that everyone be prompt, in the proper attire, at dinnertime; another was to discourage Novarro's younger siblings from being spoiled by their older brother's money. On one occasion, Señora Samaniego prevented Novarro from buying fur coats for his sisters lest they become accustomed to luxuries their future husbands could not afford. Indeed, there was a particular emphasis on inculcating the girls with traditional Mexican views of womanhood. Unlike the boys, who were sent to American universities with Novarro's financial help, Luz and Carmen had to learn to cook, sew, and keep a home. In typical Mexican fashion, the Samaniegos believed that it was not only unnecessary but even undesirable for women to have "too much" education. Such rationale placed the Samaniego women in a difficult position: they were not given the necessary education and training, but were criticized by their brothers when they were unable to care for their own needs.

Dr. Samaniego remained, for all purposes, a semi-invalid (*Picture-Play* melodramatically exaggerated the extent of his illness by describing him as a blind man who could never see his son either on-screen or off). He kept his chiropractic equipment in the attic, and practiced his acquired skills only as a hobby. His facial neuralgia remained such a severe problem that at one point morphine was prescribed to soothe the pain, but the solution developed into an even more serious problem when Dr. Samaniego started becoming addicted to the drug. Against the advice of his physician brother José, he stopped taking it, and, despite an agonizing withdrawal, managed to overcome the dependence.

. . .

Following his contract renewal, Novarro started work on *The Red Lily*, his first picture to be produced by the new studio. This project reunited him with *Thy Name Is Woman* director Fred Niblo, whose wife, the blond and round-faced Enid Bennett (a type similar to Alice Terry), was cast as the female lead—her fifteenth role under her husband's guidance. The story, created by Niblo and adapted by Bess Meredyth for the screen, concerns two young lovers who leave their French village for Paris to begin a new life away from small-town intolerance. In spite of the young couple's high hopes, a series of mishaps turn life in the big city into an urban nightmare— the boy becomes a thief, and the girl a prostitute known as the Red Lily— but all ends (absurdly) well at the final fade-out.

When Niblo was unable to find a boy to play Novarro's character as a child, the actor suggested his thirteen-year-old brother Eduardo, who was reportedly hired for the part (if so, his scenes were cut from the final continuity). This was a rare incursion of a Samaniego into a Novarro picture. Mariano, the brother who had come to Los Angeles with Novarro in the mid-1910s, also attempted an acting career of his own, though with no luck and with no apparent help from Novarro, who felt he had the right and responsibility to steer his younger siblings away from Hollywood. "They shall go to school," he told Herbert Howe—though concern for the education of his brothers and sisters was conceivably matched by a desire to maintain his ascendancy at home. Except for Eduardo, only two other Samaniegos are known to have worked in Novarro's MGM films: Carmen, as an extra in the 1929 release *Devil-May-Care*; and, in the following year, Señora Samaniego, in a supporting role in *La Sevillana*, the Spanish-language version of *Call of the Flesh*. (Novarro, however, did help some of his siblings find jobs at MGM during the Depression. Antonio and Eduardo worked behind the cameras in the 1934 production *Viva Villa!*, and Leonor was a seamstress at the studio.)

Four months after wrapping up, *The Red Lily* opened at the Capitol Theater on September 28 to mostly negative reviews. Critics described the picture as "sordid" and "hackneyed," and its characters as "revolting" and "prime specimens of degraded humanity." Only Enid Bennett's small-town girl turned prostitute was singled out for praise, with the *New York Times* declaring that the actress "gives one of the most remarkable performances ever seen on the screen." Novarro was generally panned for his immature and contrived performance, which is especially unsettling when compared to Bennett's subtler and more complex portrayal. Without Ingram to tone him down, Novarro's pantomime in this heavy-handed melodrama seems exaggerated even by silent-film standards. Nonetheless, the actor was pleased with the results, later referring to *The Red Lily* as "quite a good picture."

Variety predicted that *The Red Lily* would wither once word spread of its downbeat tone, but even though final numbers are unavailable, according to trade magazine reports *The Red Lily* performed quite well in the fall of 1924. *Scaramouche* was Novarro's biggest blockbuster of the year, followed by three medium-range successes: *The Arab, Thy Name Is Woman,* and *The Red Lily.* Yet, his four pictures notwithstanding, Novarro failed to be included among the top ten box-office stars in the 1924 *Film Daily* poll of exhibitors—an especially puzzling omission, since Rex Ingram, with only *Scaramouche* and *The Arab* to his credit, was ranked in third place in the directors' list.

Obviously, such polls should not be taken as an absolute measure of a star's box-office pull. William Haines, the country's official top male box-office attraction of 1930, was surely very popular, but at MGM alone, both Lon Chaney's and Novarro's most successful 1930 pictures outgrossed Haines's in the domestic market. Yet, despite their shortcomings, those polls did reflect the exhibitors' estimates of the prime attractions in the industry. Those listed near the top could thus use their ranking as leverage when renewing their contracts, even if the ultimate bargaining chip remained the revenues their films brought the studios.

Financially, Novarro was doing quite well in mid-1924, though at $1,000 a week he still trailed fellow Metro-Goldwyn contract players Lon Chaney at $2,500, Alice Terry at $2,000, John Gilbert at $1,500, and both Conrad Nagel and Lew Cody at $1,250. But even if Novarro's salary did not match his rising popularity, the studio knew that his name meant solid box-office receipts. When Metro-Goldwyn urgently needed a replacement for the lead in the studio's biggest and most problem-plagued project of the year, Novarro was the chosen one.

In September 1876, forty-nine-year-old former general, failed lawyer, and minor essayist Lew Wallace was inspired to write his most successful novel after debating religion with Robert G. Ingersoll, the controversial author of *Some Mistakes of Moses* and *Why I Am an Agnostic.* During a train ride, Ingersoll had deeply disturbed the Christian Wallace by pointing out his ignorance about even the most basic Christian theology. As a result of this discussion, the embarrassed dilettante devoted the next three years to studying the Bible and concocting a novel in which a first-century Jewish prince is enslaved by Romans, battles pirates, defeats his vile Roman enemy in a bloody chariot race, and emerges triumphant as a Christian convert at the finale.

Ben-Hur: A Tale of the Christ did not become a bestseller when first published in the fall of 1880, but after two years the novel exploded into one of the top-selling literary works in history, outselling every book in the United States except the Bible. Inevitably, show business impresarios were eager to transform this literary phenomenon into a box-office bonanza. Wallace refused several offers until 1899, when theater entrepreneurs Marc Klaw and Abraham Erlanger persuaded him to sell the *Ben-Hur* dramatic rights for a percentage of the gross income of the stage production.

Klaw and Erlanger's theatrical adaptation was to be no ordinary stage show. They wanted *Ben-Hur* to become *the* Broadway superspectacle of all time. The production opened at the Broadway Theater on November 29, 1899, with matinee idol Edward J. Morgan in the title role, and future film cowboy star William S. Hart as his nemesis, Messala. This theatrical extravaganza boasted huge onstage crowds, a series of choruses, spectacular lighting effects, and, for its climactic sequence, two horse-drawn chariots darting at full speed on parallel treadmills, with a Circus Maximus backdrop revolving behind them. Nearly half a million theatergoers saw *Ben-Hur* during its first season, and close to twenty million more saw it in the following years, as touring companies spread over the United States, Canada, Great Britain, the Netherlands, and Australia.

In 1907, two years after Wallace's death, the Kalem film company released a one-reel version of *Ben-Hur* without having bothered to acquire the rights for the story. Kalem was sued by the copyright holders and, after nearly four years of legal maneuvering, lost the case when the United States Supreme Court declared that the fledgling motion picture industry must abide by existing copyright laws. Several motion picture producers then tried to buy the film rights to the literary and theatrical sensation, but Wallace's son, Henry, had a very low opinion of films and refused to sell the rights for the book until 1920, when he was offered $600,000 by the Classical Cinematograph Corporation—a business entity Abraham Erlanger had recently formed with fellow theatrical impresarios Charles Dillingham and Florenz Ziegfeld. Erlanger then declared that Classical Cinematograph would sell the film rights for an unprecedented $1 million.

After a deal with Famous Players–Lasky fell through, on June 14, 1922, Goldwyn Pictures (then no longer associated with Samuel Goldwyn) announced that it had won the bid to film *Ben-Hur*. Instead of paying the $1 million up front, Goldwyn Pictures was to cover the production costs and give half of its take of the box office to Erlanger and his fellow Classical Cinematograph partners. The projected cost for the epic was $1.25 million, which meant that *Ben-Hur* would have to earn Goldwyn Pictures at least $2.5 million if the studio was to recover its investment (not including distribution and advertising expenses), at a time when only three films (Griffith's *The Birth of a Nation*, Ingram's *The Four Horsemen of the Apocalypse*, and Charles Chaplin's *The Kid*) had brought in as much.

Despite the inordinate financial risk for a company on the verge of bankruptcy, Goldwyn's ambitious and extravagant president, F. J. Godsol, was betting on the success of *Ben-Hur*. After all, the story had a presold audience; it was a superspectacle that would look infinitely more impressive on film than on stage; and it boasted both violence and carnal passion—with a touch of popular spirituality—to enthrall the millions who enjoy their sex and savagery wrapped in a message from the divine.

At first, Erlanger demanded control over every aspect of the film production, including approval of the final release print, until he was dissuaded by June Mathis. The dynamic and aggressive Mathis, who had recently moved from Famous Players to Goldwyn, had remained one of the most powerful women in the industry. "She fairly lives and breathes motion pictures," reported the *New York Morning Telegraph* in February 1924, "and if ever a woman had her hand on the pulse of the film industry, it is this indefatigable worker, who not only knows what she wants, but knows how to get it." As Goldwyn's editorial director, Mathis headed the scenario department and acted as a de facto production supervisor, ruling over her own autonomous unit. For her efforts she was reported to have been paid $1,500 a week, the same salary Louis B. Mayer would make as the production chief at MGM. With Erlanger's consent, Mathis was assigned as the *Ben-Hur* scenarist, and she rapidly turned into the driving force of the project.

More than a motion picture production, *Ben-Hur* became Mathis's all-consuming passion. While presiding over a reunion of former *Ben-Hur* stage performers at the Goldwyn studios, Mathis declared, "Success for *Ben-Hur* is already written on the heights . . . and it now rests with the screen to give that immense scope of which it is capable, to make *Ben-Hur* immortal." One of her first decrees was that the film be shot in Italy, a demand welcomed by the studio, as filming in that country might eliminate more than half the budget through favorable exchange rates and lower labor costs (at 55¢ a day, Italian extras cost one-tenth as much as Hollywood extras). As usual, Mathis was getting exactly what she wanted.

Next on the agenda was the selection of director and cast. Soon after Goldwyn announced its plans to produce *Ben-Hur*, the press began speculating on the potential candidates. "The questions of the hour are," observed the *New York Morning Telegraph* in January 1923, " 'who's going to play *Ben-Hur*? Who is to direct *Ben-Hur*?' " D. W. Griffith, Cecil B. DeMille, Marshall

Neilan, King Vidor, and Erich von Stroheim were among those considered for the director's chair. The extravagant von Stroheim, a recent Goldwyn acquisition after he had been fired by Universal, was rumored to be the top contender in the fall of 1923—"we wouldn't be surprised if he went to Europe and rebuilt Palestine and the Roman Empire with all their ancient glory," sneered *Photoplay*. As for Judah Ben-Hur, the search for the perfect actor was the 1920s equivalent of the later search for Scarlett O'Hara.

In Mathis's *Ben-Hur* scenario, the Italian Valentino is mentioned as her choice to play the Jewish hero, while the Jewish stage actor Jacob Ben-Ami was her choice to portray the Roman Messala. But here even the obstinate Mathis found an immovable obstacle. After a salary dispute with Famous Players–Lasky in September 1922, Valentino had refused to appear in any more pictures for that studio. Famous Players, in turn, obtained an injunction preventing the recalcitrant star from working for any other film company. Mathis may have hoped for some kind of compromise, but she needed to start looking at the other possibilities.

After Valentino—the clear favorite among the public—the strongest contenders were Thomas Meighan, another established star who would also have to be borrowed from Famous Players; Antonio Moreno, who, according to Francis X. Bushman, was Valentino's personal choice; and George Walsh and James Kirkwood, both of whom had the advantage of being under long-term contracts with Goldwyn. Among the leading men tested for the part were Richard Dix, Edmund Lowe, J. Warren Kerrigan, and George O'Brien, as well as Moreno and Walsh. Other candidates ranged from cowboy star Buck Jones to English theater favorite Ivor Novello, and included John Gilbert, Richard Barthelmess, Conrad Nagel, Warner Baxter, and Ronald Colman.

Even before *The Prisoner of Zenda* had been released, Novarro, then still known as Samaniegos, had been mentioned by Margaret Ettinger as the strongest contender for the role of Ben-Hur—*if* Rex Ingram was hired as director. "I want you to know if I am fortunate enough to be given *Ben-Hur* to direct," Ingram had told Ettinger, "Mr. Samanegos [*sic*] will be cast in the title role."

Ettinger was exultant. "Ben-Hur, the most coveted of all! The one play each screen actor, no matter how great or small, has dreamed of some day immortalizing on the screen," she rhapsodized. "Ramon Samanegos [*sic*] indeed must have real ability to inspire Director Ingram's confidence to such a degree as that." Once Ingram's name was scratched off the list of possible directors in late 1922, Novarro's chances dimmed considerably—though there was still *some* hope. The Goldwyn decision makers might overrule

Mathis and opt for Ingram to direct, or, in case another director was selected, they might still want the fast-rising Metro heartthrob for the lead.

Months of indecision and wild rumors about the mammoth project followed. Even the Goldwyn front office did not seem to know where *Ben-Hur* was headed. Inevitably, this confusion led to ridicule in the press, with Herbert Howe, for one, joking in *Photoplay* that Ben-Hur would be played by *The Kid*'s child star, Jackie Coogan, and become "the best picture of 1940." Both the rumors and the ridicule continued until September 28, 1923, when Goldwyn announced the name of the man who was to direct *Ben-Hur*. To nearly unanimous astonishment, the chosen one was Charles J. Brabin, a forty-year-old Englishman better known as Theda Bara's husband.

According to Goldwyn's announcement, Brabin was picked because he "has been a student of Bible history for many years, knows Europe and the continent [which continent was not made clear], and is an accomplished linguist." In reality, Brabin came ahead of more prominent names because of *Driven*, his independently made, low-budget picture that had been released to considerable acclaim earlier that year. June Mathis, who had worked with Brabin during his stint at Metro in the late 1910s, and the other Goldwyn executives probably figured the director was well qualified to keep down the *Ben-Hur* production costs.

When the press questioned the wisdom of the studio's choice, especially since the renowned Rex Ingram had been eager to tackle the job, Mathis retorted that Ingram had been chosen to direct *The Four Horsemen* merely because of the work he had done under Brabin's supervision. (Ingram had acted in a couple of films directed by Brabin in their days at Edison; he may also have written scenarios for him.) Mathis's—and by extension, the studio's—decision was set. The day after his announcement, Brabin sailed for Europe to make a preliminary survey of film locations.

Three months later, on December 28, F. J. Godsol heralded the names of three *Ben-Hur* principals. Kathleen Key, Novarro's leading lady in *The Rubaiyat*, was selected to play Ben-Hur's sister, Tirzah; beauty contest winner and horse-opera leading lady Gertrude Olmsted was cast as the love interest, Esther; and thirty-four-year-old Goldwyn contract player George Walsh had won the coveted role of Ben-Hur. In the next few days, the casting was completed: film vamp Carmel Myers was to play the seductive Iras, while dethroned screen idol Francis X. Bushman, who had previously worked with Brabin in five films, was selected as Messala.

June Mathis was instrumental in the selection of most of the picture's chief performers. Kathleen Key was chosen by Mathis, who remembered the young actress from *The Four Horsemen*. Gertrude Olmsted was also Mathis's personal choice, and Carmel Myers was picked after Mathis saw pictures of the brunette actress in her *Dancer of the Nile* costumes. As for Francis X. Bushman, Mathis explained that he "was the only one of the screen players considered for the role of Messala who passed the photographic test." Godsol informed the press that George Walsh, Mathis's choice for the title role after she had failed to get Valentino, was picked "not only because of his ability as an actor, but for his physical attainments as well."

Novarro was on location in Tunisia when he heard of Walsh's selection. Despite knowing his chances had been slim, the *Ben-Hur* hopeful was surely disappointed by the news—though he would later claim otherwise. Even if Novarro accepted his loss without protesting, others did not hesitate to voice their dismay at the selections. "The cast would discourage me completely," complained *Photoplay's* James Quirk, "if it weren't for the fact that Charles Brabin is to direct, and he is a good director, and June Mathis is a good scenario writer."

The selections of Bushman and Walsh were particularly surprising. Bushman, said to have been the first film star in Hollywood history to have his name appear above the title, had not acted in a supporting or a villain's role since achieving stardom in the early 1910s. He later claimed that he had objected to playing the villain on this occasion but had been convinced by William S. Hart that Messala was "the best goddamned part in the picture." In any case, the forty-year-old former King of the Movies could not afford to be choosy. His thriving film career had come to an abrupt halt in 1918, after several mediocre pictures and the revelation that "the most handsome man in the world" and one of the screen's "most eligible bachelors" was being sued for divorce by the mother of his five children, who accused him of being a wife beater and child abuser.

As for George Walsh, his lackluster film career made him an odd choice to play Ben-Hur. This New York–born Georgetown graduate and younger brother of director Raoul Walsh had begun working in films in the mid-1910s, after a bout with typhoid fever prevented him from pursuing a career in baseball. By the end of the decade, the beefy and handsome Walsh had become a Fox star in a series of lowbrow, action-packed programmers that gave the actor ample opportunity to display his athletic abilities. Walsh's success, however, was quickly undermined by too many formulaic vehicles. Making matters worse, he received some unwelcome publicity when his wife, actress Seena Owen, sued for divorce, naming fellow performer Estelle Taylor as correspondent. (According to Walsh, Owen also tried to kill him.) With his film career in the doldrums, Walsh took refuge in vaudeville in the early

1920s, until he was brought back to Hollywood by two notable 1923 releases, Goldwyn Pictures' *Vanity Fair* and Mary Pickford's *Rosita*.

"It was no doubt Mr. Walsh's work and appearance opposite Mary Pickford in *Rosita* which helped win the role for him," reasoned Louella Parsons in the *New York Morning Telegraph*. In reality, it was not Walsh's performance as Don Diego that seduced Mathis and the powers that be at Goldwyn, but his bulging physique. Parsons herself admitted that she at first had misgivings about Walsh, but asserted that the actor's stills for the role "immediately converted us to the wisdom of the Goldwyn selection." The big, athletic Walsh looked impressive in a toga (or less) and would be the perfect match for the equally brawny Bushman.

Walsh accepted a pay cut in order to play the title role in the most highly anticipated Hollywood production ever. At $400 a week, he was making $100 less than supporting players Bushman and Myers. After signing the required six-month contract, Walsh departed for Rome on February 20, 1924. By then, most of the crew members had already been at the Italian capital for several months. Mathis had sailed on February 6, carrying with her the 1,722-scene *Ben-Hur* screenplay she had written. While aboard the *City of Paris*, she sent a wire to Goldwyn's second-in-command, Abraham Lehr: "Many thanks. Shall do all in my power to make you proud of me."

American filmmaking in Europe had become relatively common in the early 1920s. Ingram's *The Arab* was partly shot in France; Griffith filmed *Isn't Life Wonderful* in Germany; Famous Players had a subsidiary studio built in England; and *The Eternal City, Nero,* and *The White Sister* were all filmed at least partially in Italy.

Those countries, still recovering from the destruction of World War I, had economies that were in disarray, and their once-extensive film-production facilities had become obsolete after being abandoned or underutilized for years. At this relatively early stage of motion picture development, a few years meant tremendous technical advances, a situation that placed Europe's filmmaking infrastructure and personnel at a considerable disadvantage in relation to Hollywood.

Italy, in particular, was a notorious case. The country had been the birthplace of historical spectacles, among them *The Last Days of Pompeii, Quo Vadis,* and *Cabiria,* pictures that had inspired Griffith, DeMille, and other American directors to attempt longer and even more spectacular films. Nevertheless, the destruction and disruptions brought on by the war had ruined the local film industry. The battered postwar Italian economy and the country's con-voluted political climate—a series of weak coalition governments that had finally collapsed when Benito Mussolini seized power in October 1922—further discouraged native film entrepreneurs from investing in modern pro-duction facilities.

Mussolini had been of "great assistance" to director George Fitzmaurice during the making of the romantic melodrama *The Eternal City* and had promised to provide facilities and every sort of service required by the *Ben-Hur* production company. But Il Duce's promises notwithstanding, the local infrastructure was incapable of handling the demands of a spectacle on the scale of *Ben-Hur*. Compounding problems, the American crew had to cope with strikes and labor disputes caused by socialists who were constantly seeking to demoralize the Fascist regime. Those ubiquitous and seemingly unending hassles affected all involved in the production.

After having suffered the ignominy of crossing the Atlantic in second-class accommodations, George Walsh arrived in Rome in early March 1924 to receive the type of treatment normally accorded extras. The star of *Ben-Hur* was shoved into the background, and there he stayed throughout his four months in Italy. June Mathis, for her part, was dismayed by the slow progress of production and was furious at Brabin's orders that she was not to talk to him on the set. *Ben-Hur's* editorial director was earning $1,000 a week without any say in the development of the picture, except to approve or disapprove of scenes after they had been shot. (Mathis's wages were 50 percent lower than her reported salary at Goldwyn. Either the figures released to the press had been inflated, or she had accepted a salary cut to keep production costs down on her pet project.) Soon, two antagonistic factions formed: one behind Mathis and the other backing Brabin.

As working conditions at Rome's Cines studio remained chaotic, Brabin headed for Anzio, thirty miles south of the Italian capital, to begin work on the film's monumental sea battle, in which pirate ships attack a fleet of Roman galleys. The production was allowed to build only thirty of the requested seventy Roman galleys, and those had to be docked after they were deemed unseaworthy by the Anzio port authorities. Eventually the vessels were allowed out to sea as long as they remained anchored. Thus, the cameramen were challenged to create a fast-paced sea battle with mo-tionless boats.

Those types of complications, which seemed to beset every aspect of the production, badly damaged morale. By midspring it was clear that *Ben-Hur* was headed for disaster. Partly due to the spiraling costs of the film, Goldwyn Pictures had ceased to exist as an independent corporation and was now part of the Loew's subsidiary Metro-Goldwyn.

Marcus Loew placed the responsibility for averting the potential disaster he had just acquired into the hands of studio chief Louis B. Mayer and second-in-command Irving Thalberg, who immediately ordered that Mathis, Brabin, and Walsh be fired, and the script rewritten. In a May 2 telegram, Loew's friend and adviser Joseph Schenck tried to reassure him about Abraham Erlanger's possible reaction to the dismissals, especially that of Mathis. "The worst Erlanger could do," Schenck's cable read in part, "would be to cancel the contract for producing *Ben-Hur,* which probably would be the very best thing for you notwithstanding the loss you will incur in production costs already invested."

After receiving the go-ahead from Loew, Mayer approached Fred Niblo about taking over the directorship from Brabin. At first, Niblo was reluctant. "Personally I will be more than pleased if you will count me out entirely," he wrote Mayer. "It is not too big a job for me but if I can't do it right I don't want to do it at all." He also complained about Mathis's adaptation, "twice as long a continuity as it should be," and her selection of the cast, "the most uninteresting and colorless that I have ever seen in a big picture." In his cable to Loew, Schenck had also criticized Mathis for the *Ben-Hur* fiasco, noting that she had also been responsible for the scenario of the interminable *Greed,* and for the adaptations of *In the Palace of the King* and *Day of Faith,* two of Goldwyn's biggest flops that year.

In a few months, Mathis had fallen from being Goldwyn's "million-dollar girl"—her life had been insured for that amount by the studio—to being the woman partly responsible for the studio's downfall. Certainly her time in Rome had not been productive. While *Ben-Hur* was foundering, Mathis was spending most of her Italian season bickering with Brabin, trying to finish the picture's endless screenplay, and denying rumors about her engagement to George Walsh. Once Niblo was persuaded to accept the job (at $2,500 per week), Mathis, with whom he had clashed during the making of *Blood and Sand* at Famous Players, truly had to go. To replace her, the studio hired scenarists Carey Wilson and Bess Meredyth.

Since Walsh had appeared only once before the cameras—to do a test with an Italian actor—he could easily be discarded. Metro-Goldwyn wanted a bigger name for the role, and the two obvious candidates among its contract players were Novarro and John Gilbert. According to DeWitt Bodeen, Louis B. Mayer favored Novarro as the studio's potential leading star, and that may well have been true. The conservative Mayer must have appreciated

Novarro's reputation as a religious family man with impeccable manners, and conceivably was then unaware of his star's sexual orientation. Even if Mayer knew of it, Novarro was so circumspect about his homosexuality that the studio chief possibly found it a minor flaw when compared to Gilbert's drinking and generally boisterous demeanor.

Practical considerations also made Novarro the most expedient choice. He had worked well with Niblo in both *Thy Name Is Woman* and *The Red Lily;* moreover, Gilbert was then working on *His Hour,* which was scheduled to remain in production into the second week of June. Immediately afterward he was to begin work on *He Who Gets Slapped.*

On Sunday, June 8, 1924, Novarro was interrupted at lunch by a call from Irving Thalberg requesting his presence at the studio. Upon his arrival at Thalberg's office, Novarro was informed that he had been selected for the role of Ben-Hur. The news surprised him, despite rumors that drastic measures were being planned to salvage the out-of-control epic. Yet, there were two conditions to Thalberg's offer. First, he wanted Novarro to test for the part that same day. Risking his professional future, Novarro refused. "You'll make the test in a hurry," he protested, "...I won't have a chance." If Thalberg wanted to see his physique, Novarro recommended he watch *Where the Pavement Ends.* The young executive relented. Second, Thalberg asked Novarro to waive his contract with the studio for the duration of the production, which was scheduled to last three months. He was not to receive a raise while working in *Ben-Hur* and would have to pay his living expenses while abroad. Novarro consented, though he demanded that Herbert Howe come with him to handle his publicity (he would cover Howe's expenses). By then, Novarro's initial shock had turned to glee. He went directly to Howe to tell him they were leaving for New York the following morning, then headed home to announce to his family his imminent departure for Italy to star in *Ben-Hur.*

The next day, under a veil of secrecy, Novarro was taken by a studio limousine to the Pasadena train station, where he met Mayer, Carey Wilson, Bess Meredyth, Fred Niblo and Enid Bennett, and Herbert Howe. In New York, the group was received by Marcus Loew and his legal adviser, J. Robert Rubin, who were to sail with them to Europe while Mayer returned to California. Loew instructed Novarro to tell reporters at the docks that he was going to Europe on vacation, since June Mathis, Charles Brabin, and George Walsh were still unaware that they had been fired.

Before boarding the *Leviathan* on June 14, Novarro dutifully told reporters about his "vacation," while Niblo claimed to be on his way to France to film exteriors for the as yet unreleased *The Red Lily*. He would then head for Monte Carlo to shoot his next picture with Norma Talmadge. Aware of the problems facing *Ben-Hur* in Italy, the press was suspicious. Since Marshall Neilan had also left for Europe the night before with his wife, actress Blanche Sweet, to film *The Sporting Venus*, rumors soon surfaced that either director—or perhaps both—would replace Brabin in Rome.

As the *Leviathan* sailed for Europe, one important piece was missing from the *Ben-Hur* saga to make Novarro's elation complete. Rex Ingram biographer Liam O'Leary claimed that Mayer, in an act of desperation, had invited Ingram to take over the reins of *Ben-Hur*, but the director, out of pride or pettiness, made so many demands that Mayer looked elsewhere. DeWitt Bodeen offered a different version, in which Ingram was once again passed over because Mayer would neither forgive nor forget, while Thalberg thought him simply inadequate for the job. However it happened, Ingram was not to direct *Ben-Hur*. According to editor Grant Whytock, it was from then on (and not after the dispute over *The Arab*) that Ingram refused to have Mayer's name in his pictures.

In spite of his excitement, Novarro must have approached the project with mixed feelings. *Ben-Hur* was a unique opportunity for him to attain superstardom, but would Niblo be capable of bringing out the best in him? Their previous pictures together had been minor compared to *The Prisoner of Zenda*, *Scaramouche*, or *The Arab*, and critics had deemed Novarro's acting in Niblo's films inferior to his work for Ingram. Now Niblo was supposed to guide Novarro in a project that was considerably bigger than anything he had ever done for his former mentor. The twenty-five-year-old actor knew who his ideal director would have been, as he would state shortly before his death. "I do not mean to deprecate Mr. Niblo, who was always a meticulous craftsman," he told Bodeen in 1967, "but I do think that Rex Ingram would have brought more artistry and sophistication to *Ben-Hur*."

In addition to missing Ingram's directorial touch, Novarro also had to face a loyalty issue. Ingram, after all, had been the first to envision him as the Jewish prince, and had promised to give him the role if he, Ingram, was chosen to direct it. Now that Novarro had been selected as the star, he was powerless to reciprocate. Novarro was in, but the man who had transformed him into a name big enough to win that most coveted of roles was out.

Finally, Novarro had to face another moral issue: the displacement of George Walsh. Although extremely ambitious, Novarro, by all accounts, was also a considerate person. He was sailing for Europe in secrecy to replace an actor who was unaware he had been fired. Walsh was inevitably going to be publicly humiliated, even though he was in no way responsible for the *Ben-Hur* fiasco. Unfortunately, no mention can be found of Novarro's true feelings about getting a role he had craved so ardently, under such ambivalent circumstances. (He would later state that he found Walsh "a very attractive man" whose acting "never was much good.")

In an interview with fan magazine writer Gladys Hall, Novarro claimed knowing since his days as an extra that the role of Ben-Hur would one day be his. Sometime in 1918, while still living on Hope Street, he was practicing facial expressions before a mirror in his mother's room when the mirror suddenly grew out of proportion and the room disappeared in a blur. At that moment, he saw another figure next to him in the mirror, a bigger and stronger man wearing a toga. In a flash, Novarro realized that the man was himself—as Ben-Hur. Once the mirror returned to its normal size and his mother's bedroom rematerialized, Novarro ran downstairs screaming that he was going to be a successful motion picture actor. "Not for one tiny instant did I feel a doubt, a qualm or a misapprehension," he recalled. Even after production had started with George Walsh in the lead, Novarro avowedly remained confident. "I knew that I was going to play that part. *I knew it.*"

This fantastic tale apparently originated with Novarro himself. He had been from the very beginning highly enthusiastic about the part of Judah Ben-Hur, for besides its obvious career advantages, the story also held a personal allure for him. Granted, Ben-Hur is a proud Jew, but the high point of Lew Wallace's tale is his hero's acceptance of Jesus as savior. Whatever the big man in the mirror was—a vivid dream, a hallucination, or some inexplicable precognitive vision—Novarro clearly trusted that it was God's will that he be given the role. "Success does not rest with us," he would later say, "it does not come from our own efforts even, it is sent by God." What Novarro did not realize was that this "gift from God" would come at a hefty price.

SIX

Harrowing Triumph

Despite Metro-Goldwyn's attempt to keep the turmoil in Italy out of the news, it became widely known that *Ben-Hur* would soon undergo a major overhaul. "The *Ben-Hur* expeditions to Italy bid fair to become as numerous as the crusades," quipped the *Los Angeles Times* in late June 1924. "There is still a rumor that the original company may finish the picture, but this seems to be mere camouflage."

While the new group was en route to Europe, the studio finally announced that Charles Brabin would be replaced because of ill health, though no mention was made of either June Mathis or George Walsh. A few days later, Francis X. Bushman learned about Walsh's fate by reading the *New York Morning Telegraph* in Rome. He approached Walsh, who said he had been expecting that outcome, but not one effected so brutally. "The great injury I incurred, was in their not announcing publicly the full facts," Walsh wrote to film historian Kevin Brownlow in 1966. "Unfortunately for me, the public figured I had failed to fill the bill."

In the meantime, Marcus Loew was hosting dinner parties every evening aboard the *Leviathan*, while Novarro, according to Herbert Howe, tried to elude eager female fans. After their arrival in Cherbourg, the group headed to Paris, where Novarro and Howe spent a night on the town, and then traveled on to Rome. On July 4, 1924, they arrived in the Italian capital during a violent thunderstorm.

In the next few days, Loew officially announced to the company the various changes in personnel, while at home the press was abuzz with news of the upheaval. "If a bad beginning makes a good ending," remarked *Photoplay*, "*Ben-Hur* will be the greatest picture of all time."

. . .

Charles Brabin soon returned to Hollywood, where he made sure everyone knew his health was just fine by suing the studio for $583,000—$23,000 for unpaid salary and $560,000 for damages to his reputation. The suit, which contended that he had not been provided with the necessary equipment to perform his job, was settled for $33,000. Brabin was then hired by Colleen Moore to direct her in *So Big*, a well-received drama that helped restore his prestige within the industry.

George Walsh was not as lucky. After his return to Hollywood, he was relegated to playing leads at poverty-row studio Chadwick Pictures. In late 1924, when Metro-Goldwyn-Mayer (as Metro-Goldwyn had become known) issued a statement rationalizing the dismissals, James Quirk remarked in *Photoplay*, "Mr. Loew explains why they felt constrained to annihilate Walsh, and then wishes him good luck. But what we wonder is—will Mr. Walsh deposit the good wishes in his bank?" There was no mention of a financial settlement between the studio and the replaced actor, and Loew's "good wishes" notwithstanding, Walsh's career would never recover from the *Ben-Hur* debacle.

June Mathis openly blamed Brabin for the fiasco, adding, "Despite my own disappointment, my chief regret has been the treatment of Mr. Walsh. I had complete faith in his ability to play *Ben-Hur*. I realize that many other people did not believe in him. But the same thing occurred when I selected Rudolph Valentino for the role of Julio in *The Four Horsemen*. Valentino justified himself and I am confident Mr. Walsh would have done the same thing. Actually, Mr. Walsh was given no opportunity to succeed or fail. He was withdrawn without a chance. Indeed, Mr. Novarro was in Rome for three days before Mr. Walsh was notified that he had been succeeded in the leading role." Mathis remained in Rome for a few more days with her fiancé, cameraman Silvano Balboni, who had also been fired, and left the Italian capital on July 15.

Now that Mathis was returning home, the *New York Morning Telegraph* reported that she was "happier than she has been in six months." But her happiness was short-lived. Upon arriving in Hollywood, Mathis discovered that there was no room for her at MGM. She attempted to reestablish her old position in the industry by becoming a producer-scenarist at First National, but despite writing and supervising a handful of films, including Colleen Moore's successful *Irene*, Mathis was never to attain the power and prestige she had enjoyed before *Ben-Hur*. On July 26, 1927, Mathis, age thirty-five, died of a heart attack while watching a theater performance of

The Squall. Her remains were laid beside those of Rudolph Valentino, who had died the previous year.

In Rome, the new company began preparing to resume work at the Cines studio. "Niblo now has everything in hand," a buoyant J. Robert Rubin wired Mayer on June 30. "Believe things will go satisfactorily.... Made adjustment with Walsh; took tests of Novarro looks wonderful.... Feel very hopeful for success." Ensuing events, however, would prove Rubin much too optimistic.

A few days after Rubin's telegram, Fred Niblo wired Louis B. Mayer, "Condition serious. Must rush work before November rains; no sets or lights available before August 1st. 200 reels of film wasted; bad photography; terrible action." The director decided that production was going to start from scratch, as nearly all of Brabin's footage was deemed worthless. When Mayer and Thalberg saw Brabin's rushes several weeks later, they heartily agreed with Niblo. "I inwardly breathe a prayer of relief that we have taken the hysterical action that was necessary to make a change," Thalberg wrote Niblo."... It is almost beyond my conception that such stuff could have been passed by people of even moderate intelligence."

Niblo, of course, was not the only one feeling the intense pressure to perform. Next in line was Novarro, whose choice as a substitute for Walsh had been greeted by the press courteously, though unenthusiastically. One reason for the general coolness was the way MGM handled the exchange of talent; another was that many doubted that the small-framed and relatively inexperienced Novarro, who had barely established himself as a box-office name with *Scaramouche* only a few months earlier, could live up to the larger-than-life role of Ben-Hur.

Earlier in the year, when the dismissal of George Walsh had seemed like a distinct possibility, Herbert Howe had kept his influential *Photoplay* column abuzz with hints about his companion's prodigious talents. "Think of any great role," he urged in May 1924, "and you'll think of Novarro: *Romeo, Ben Hur, Galahad, Dorian Grey.*" But now that Ben-Hur was his, Novarro had to prove himself equal to the task. Scenarist Bess Meredyth wrote Mayer that Novarro felt "more enthusiastic than ever" about his role, but the actor must have been aware that if he failed to meet the high expectations, Walsh's fate could well become his own. His earlier "vision" had promised that he would get the part, not that he would keep it.

To prepare himself for the physical demands of the role, Novarro woke up at six every morning to work out for thirty minutes at a gym, and from there headed for some outdoor exercising with a trainer. Some days he also practiced rowing and swimming in the Tiber River. By August 14, when shooting finally commenced, Novarro was in fine physical condition, though hardly as well developed as his costar Francis X. Bushman. The extra muscle tone needed had to be provided by the makeup department, while sandals with heels and padding were used to compensate for another of Novarro's physical handicaps for the part, his height. Whenever he shared the frame with Bushman, the camera had to be carefully positioned—or Bushman had to stand in a small trench—so the villain would not tower over the hero.

So that the production might proceed smoothly and any further complications be reported to Culver City, Mayer delegated Harry Edington, Brabin's production manager, to assist Niblo with the shoot. The director was certainly in need of help, as labor and technical problems continued endlessly throughout the oppressive Roman summer.

Meanwhile, the American press and the film community were whirring with rumors that all *still* was not well for the problem-plagued spectacle. In September, the *New York Morning Telegraph* reported that "Hollywood is still juggling the rumor that the ill-fated production of *Ben-Hur* is to be finished on California soil and not under the handicaps of Italy." Yet, Niblo was determined to finish the production abroad. "They say Mr. Loew had a headache over the *Ben-Hur* troubles before," continued the *Telegraph* article. "By this time he is probably having nightmares." It would have been understandable if he was. By mid-1924, the cost of the film had skyrocketed from the projected $1.25 million to close to an unprecedented $2 million. If expenses continued mounting, the new studio could suffer a fate similar to Goldwyn's. In spite of the enormous gamble, MGM persevered. The studio and its parent company, Loew's, were bound by a contractual commitment to Abraham Erlanger and his partners.

Niblo and the MGM executives placed most of the blame for *Ben-Hur's* woes on the Italian workers, but others felt that the never-ending chaos was the result of mismanagement at the top. "The Italians are the hardest-working people I ever saw," director Henry King, who shot both *Romola* and *The White Sister* in Italy in the early 1920s, reminisced years later. "They *want* to get the right effect. They *want* to please you. . . . I think that a great deal of the trouble the *Ben-Hur* people had in Italy was due to a lack of understanding for the people." Although Niblo initially managed a resurgence of goodwill among the Italians, a few weeks later morale had sunk to a new low.

Meanwhile, new cast members continued to arrive. The new leading lady appeared in early October. Gertrude Olmsted, who had waited without pay for eight months and was never even sent to Rome, had been replaced by May McAvoy in the role of Esther. "Ramon Novarro wasn't any taller than I was, now I couldn't play with [him] because he was too small," Olmsted later told film historian Anthony Slide. "I was simply out.... There was nothing to be said." The studio felt that the small, wide-eyed McAvoy, who had made a name for herself by playing sweet-natured heroines, would be ideal as the love interest. McAvoy signed for five weeks, but having little to do once in Rome, filled her time by sight-seeing with her mother.

On October 12, Mayer arrived with his wife and two daughters in Rome to check on the production. Niblo was then preparing to shoot the sea battle, which had been a disaster under Brabin, though this time, newer, bigger, and safer ships had been built. As an extra advantage, Niblo had recently handled a similar sequence in the swashbuckler *Strangers of the Night*.

The launching of the ships off the coast of Livorno, about 150 miles northwest of Rome, was an auspicious one, with Italian officials and diplomatic representatives participating in the elaborate ceremony. The weather, however, turned stormy; the seas became too rough for the technical crew to control camera setups, and shooting had to be delayed. Later in October, despite persisting rough seas and heavy winds, filming finally began. Because an oil-drenched galley was supposed to go up in flames, extras were offered hazard bonuses to remain on board for as long as physically possible. But when the fire was set, the strong winds quickly fanned the flames. The Italian extras panicked. Forgetting their safety instructions, they dashed to the edge of the ship and jumped overboard. Dinghies had been stationed nearby in case of an emergency, but they were hard-pressed to cope with the dozens of men struggling in the turbulent seas, some of them weighed down by heavy armor, others unable to swim.

Fred Niblo's wife, Enid Bennett, recalled watching helplessly as the galley caught fire. With one man reported missing, MGM at once ordered Bennett and her husband back to Rome, for fear that Italian authorities would arrest the director. "It was a scary journey," Bennett told Kevin Brownlow in 1967. "Every time a carabiniere appeared on the train we thought it was the end. I've heard it said that three [extras] were missing, but I remember one. And I remember the wardrobe man, to protect Fred, did away with his clothes and effects. When he turned up, he had to make them up to him."

Following the catastrophic sea battle, the production continued limping along. Crumbling under the immense pressure, Niblo became increasingly edgy, going so far as to yell and throw things at the extras, most of whom were inexperienced and understood no English. Enid Bennett, who acted as the company's unofficial pacifier, later persuaded her husband to apologize, but friction worsened when Alexander Aronson, the head of the MGM Paris office, was summoned to the Italian capital to supervise Niblo. Hostilities between director and supervisor began immediately, and were to continue throughout the company's stay in Rome.

> *Ben-Hur* has been in production two years and fresh players are still arriving. The *Three Wise Men* arrived from Hollywood recently. A studio official brutally refused to meet them at the train. He said he had met enough Wise Men from Hollywood. Unfortunately the *Wise Men* arrived just as the *Madonna* quit. She had been brought from Paris two months previous to enact the role of the *Virgin*. In departing she said she didn't mind living her part for a couple of months, but when it dragged into years ... *Mon Dieu! Je suis une parisienne!* (Herbert Howe discussing the *Ben-Hur* tribulations in Europe in his March 1925 *Photoplay* column)

While Niblo struggled with the production, B. Reeves Eason, a director of B Westerns and an expert horseman, was brought in to handle the training for the climactic chariot race. Here, too, problems abounded because of the poor conditions of the track. At one point, Novarro, who never quite achieved dexterity in chariot riding, made a wrong move, which resulted in his chariot being trampled by Bushman's. The spectators were certain that Novarro had been killed, but he came out from underneath the debris unscathed.

The actor, already frustrated with the slow pace of filming, was now angry at his perceived mistreatment by both Niblo and the production executives. Prior to the life-threatening chariot-riding exercises, Novarro had already performed another hazardous stunt in late September, for the scene in which Ben-Hur and his future Roman mentor, Quintus Arrius, find themselves adrift on a partially submerged fragment of wreckage. Novarro, wearing a skimpy loincloth, and seventy-five-year-old Frank Currier suffered agonizing cold during the three-day shoot in the Mediterranean. The doubles who were supposed to stand in for them during camera setups and long shots yelled for help after twenty minutes on the freezing float. Thus, Novarro and Currier had to go back on the raft and double for the doubles for the rest of the shoot.

For the desert sequence, when Judah Ben-Hur is taken as a slave by the Romans, Novarro had to spend one hour every day covering himself with collodion—a potentially toxic substance that gave the appearance of parched skin—and one hour each evening removing the collodion with kerosene, soap, and water. In the hot summer days the body makeup melted, and in the cold fall days it froze. "Sometimes when I cracked the stuff my skin would go with it," Novarro later recalled. "It is a wonder I didn't get poisoning." Additionally, the star of the picture had to suffer the ignominy of being pulled by the hair thirty-six times, as assistant director Al Raboch ordered take after take for the sequence in which Roman soldiers torture a dehydrated Ben-Hur. When Raboch requested a thirty-seventh take, Novarro, who complained that his hair was beginning to fall off, rebelled. "Nothing doing," he protested. "You are going to take your three best and just be happy with it." Novarro's "gift from God" was rapidly turning into the present from hell.

By mid-December, production had so deteriorated that Alexander Aronson urged the corporate heads to fire Niblo. "Have definitely decided picture will never be made under present management," Aronson stated in a wire to Thalberg. "Nothing that [Niblo] can do will change my opinion. . . . [I] will remove him from picture definitely and without reservation." The California and New York decision makers refused to go along with Aronson, though Mayer did urge the director to speed things up. "Great danger. Cast, organization again becoming restless," Mayer cabled Niblo after the studio head had returned to Culver City. "Remember we promised them quick work with three directors [Al Raboch and Christy Cabanne were the other two] so they can get home early. Am so worried. Please cable every other day."

Christmas was spent at the Excelsior Hotel, where the company, except for Novarro and Herbert Howe (Howe had demanded that they find another hotel for themselves), was staying in Rome. Howe later wrote that he—dressed as Santa Claus—and Novarro spent Christmas morning distributing candy to poor Italian children in the Trastevere quarter, "or somewhere spelled something like that and smelling worse." This experience in Christian goodwill was marred by the children's kicking and shoving the unsteady Santa, who had celebrated much too enthusiastically the night before.

When the new year arrived, Novarro was ready to do some kicking and shoving himself. On January 2, after another grueling chariot-riding session, he left word for Aronson that he was sick and, accompanied by Howe, left town for the French Riviera. He had lost faith in Niblo, and was tired of both the director's abuse and the overall mismanagement.

Howe later recounted in *Photoplay* his and Novarro's misadventures following their sudden departure from Rome. Their trip got off to an unpromising start when Novarro discovered he had left his passport at the hotel, and Howe discovered that his French visa had expired. At customs, they tried to convince French authorities to let the famous movie star and the important *Photoplay* correspondent into the country by showing them a turkey gravy recipe that Carmel Myers's mother had written on official-looking stationery. (Why they had that with them Howe did not make clear.) The border guards remained unconvinced. In an act of desperation, Novarro and Howe contacted Aronson, who vainly demanded that they return to Rome. The local French consul was equally unsympathetic.

While plotting their next move, they checked into a hotel on the Italian side of the border. The hotel clerk suggested that they might get a rowboat and try to sneak into France by sea, adding, "Of course, they might shoot at you." Not wanting to be shot at, they decided to cross the border at a sand strip along the shore. Since Novarro and Howe were carrying no luggage, the border officer at the beach believed their story that they were guests at a French hotel, and let the two illegal border-crossers pass. After accomplishing their goal, the pair headed for the Hotel de Paris in Monte Carlo, where they spent a couple of evenings losing all their cash at casinos.

Once Aronson had located them, he wired Novarro and commanded that the actor return immediately to Rome. The star ignored the command, preferring instead to go with Howe to Rex Ingram's villa near Nice. When Aronson found Novarro again, he angrily threatened the truant star with serious consequences unless he returned at once. At Ingram's insistence, Novarro and his companion headed back to Rome. Upon his return on January 7, Novarro received a cable from Marcus Loew asking him to be more cooperative in the future.

That same day, Novarro learned that the company would finish filming in Italy in two weeks. Although almost no usable footage had been shot, Aronson, with the assistance of scenarist Carey Wilson, had persuaded Mayer to bring the production back to Culver City. "He [Niblo] has met his Waterloo," Aronson cabled Mayer. "He is licked here and knows it." According to the plan, the company would return to Rome in the spring when weather conditions had improved.

The day after Novarro's return to Rome, the company was assembled to meet the Italian royal family on the Circus Maximus set. Cast, crew, and assorted visitors, among them superstar Norma Talmadge, were all instructed to remain silent, with the exception of Niblo, whose duty it was to introduce the other Hollywood celebrities present. "It was the coldest day I ever lived through," remembered Carmel Myers, who, like the rest of the crowd, stood for more than one hour in the chilly wind only to see the royal family come and go without a single handshake. Niblo, because of either clumsiness or arrogance, had failed to introduce his troupe. (Aronson, who was with him, was also partly to blame.) Irritated by one more blunder, Novarro remarked that he would demand pay as an extra for his crowd scene appearance, but relented after a princess smiled at him from her car. It was later reported that the royals were as disappointed at not meeting the stars as the stars were at not meeting the royals.

Incidents such as the royal fiasco were a consequence of Niblo's increasing alienation from his coworkers, a problem cast and crew perceived as outright disrespect. Granted, Niblo was under heavy pressure from the studio—he and Mayer had had a serious feud during the studio chief's stay in Rome—but so was everyone else, including the star of the picture. In the recent past, Novarro had worked well with Niblo, but by the time their Italian stay neared its end, star and director had become actively antagonistic toward each other.

According to Aronson, Novarro began displaying "considerable temperament, and to a point where he has been unreasonable." Novarro became indignant when told he would not have time to tour Europe before heading back to MGM's Culver City studios to resume work on *Ben-Hur*, demanding that he sail with Howe on a ship with no other company member aboard, and insisting on leaving Rome as soon as possible. Counting on Novarro's promise of "faithful cooperation and unlimited time" to fulfill all his duties, Aronson consented. Following the terms of their agreement, Novarro would leave for France on January 17 and spend one week in that country before returning to the United States.

Novarro, however, failed to live up to his side of the bargain. He refused to do the necessary close-up shots at the Circus Maximus, and on the evening before his departure, he refused to obey Niblo's request to do a series of interior shots of the Roman galley, even though Aronson had ordered lights and heaters transferred from assistant director Christy Cabanne's set to Niblo's. (There was sufficient lighting for only one unit at a time.) Novarro alleged he was too tired to work that evening, but promised to be on the set at 9:30 the following morning and work until noon. "Although I rebelled at taking dictation from an actor," Aronson wrote to legal counsel J. Robert Rubin, "realizing the importance of getting this stuff, I swallowed my indignation, knowing that in two and a half hours we could get what we wanted, and hence the quarrel was not needed."

The next morning, Novarro arrived on the set at 10:45. At noon, having finished only two shots, he refused to proceed any further, insisting he had to leave for France immediately. "Whether he has a girl in Nice, or whether he wanted to see Rex Ingram and spend a few days with him, I do not know," Aronson commented. "... I am just citing this to you showing his utter lack of responsibility and lack of cooperation."

Despite Aronson's angry—and not entirely unjustified—complaints, Novarro's attitude at the end of the Italian shoot was *not* an example of a star's ego spinning out of control. By all accounts, Niblo had been a ruthless taskmaster, making life miserable for his actors, extras, and crew members. "Man after man came to me definitely stating that they had no faith in Niblo since he could not produce on the screen," Aronson wrote Mayer, "and that his harsh personality and biting sarcastic abuse forced them into a desire to be fired and go home!" The studio, for its part, was generally unresponsive to the needs of players and crew members. Its main concern was to keep the budget from skyrocketing even further—from September to December, nearly $650,000 had been added to the cost of the picture.

Novarro had waived his previous contract, had to cope with interminable delays, had to perform hazardous stunts, and, since the picture revolved around his character, also had to deal more frequently than anyone else with Niblo's brutal and sarcastic attacks. (Not surprisingly, he much preferred working under Cabanne's guidance.) In his letter to Rubin, Aronson asserted that Novarro "repeatedly stated to me ... pictures have been a grief to him, he has had every disappointment, none of his dreams have come true, and that so far as he is concerned he is through with pictures. He cares neither for fame nor for money." Novarro's anger and frustration may have given the usually docile actor the yearning to rebel, but Howe was the likely force behind Novarro's sudden display of star power. As an experienced Hollywood insider, Howe knew that, at this stage, MGM could hardly afford to fire the star of their $3 million picture.

"He has not been the only one of our problems," Aronson added in his letter to Rubin. (Francis X. Bushman had threatened to leave for Egypt unless he received a $1,000-a-week raise. To appease the defiant second lead—at this stage, Bushman could not have been replaced either—Mayer loaned him some money.) "It seems to me that many of our actors feel that with the tremendous investment of money that we have in this picture they can run us! If this picture had cost one tenth of what it actually has, I would have put Novarro on the carpet." Instead, Novarro left with Howe for France and, probably to taunt the studio, posed as a producer of *Ben-Hur* for a reporter of the *Paris Herald*, freely giving out information about the costs of the film, and declaring that in the future he would divide his time between Hollywood and Nice.

As planned, on January 17 Novarro and Howe left on the *La France* for

New York. Novarro avoided any social activity aboard the ship, spending all his time with his cabin mate, singing Mexican ballads and recounting Mexican legends. *Ben-Hur* had been left behind—for now.

On January 28, the *Ben-Hur* company returned on the *Berengaria* to the United States. Soon afterward, the *American Film Gazette* reported that political unrest had been the reason for the unit's abrupt departure from Italy, a claim that incensed Italian authorities. As a rebuttal to the *Gazette's* accusation, the Italian newspaper *Epoca* headlined a report that was quickly picked up by the *Chicago Daily News* and soon circulated throughout the United States. It asserted that the American film company had been expelled from Italy because of the drunken and lewd behavior of its stars and production team, who, "after having made scandalous tests of nude supers [bit players] indiscriminately, after having profited generously from good Italian wine and liquors and after having spent enormous sums of money, realized that they were incapable of completing the film."

To avoid trouble for future MGM productions filmed in Italy or for the distribution of the studio's films in that country—and to combat the negative publicity at home—Niblo asserted in every interview he gave that there had been no labor problems in Italy, the company had done "everything we set out to do in Italy and Africa," the Italian authorities had been "most cordial," and the Italian people had been "charming." Bad weather, not bad politics, was to blame for the company's departure. Eventually, the negative *Ben-Hur* rumors subsided.

The problems in Italy, however, continued. In late February, a fire consumed the property warehouse, while the Joppa Gate, a gigantic set that had taken months to build, was partially destroyed by a storm. Moreover, MGM had lost its lease on the Roman studio facilities and was facing a lawsuit from the owner of the lumber used in the Circus Maximus. The lumber had been rented, not bought, and its owner wanted it back. At that point, the front office ordered the tearing down of all sets, with the exception of the Circus Maximus, though even that one was later discarded. Thalberg, who had always opposed filming in Italy, persuaded Mayer to have the arena built in Culver City, ensuring that *Ben-Hur* would remain under their close supervision until the last scene was shot.

But despite Thalberg and Mayer's watchful eye, more problems ensued. The plan to build the Circus in a lot adjacent to the studio had to be scrapped a few days after construction had begun, for the city council of Culver City had decided to build a storm drain on the site. City workers unceremoniously razed all the sets that studio workers had erected. The Circus was then relocated to the corner of Venice Boulevard and Brice Road (now La Cienega Boulevard), one mile northeast of MGM. For three months, eight hundred men worked on the construction of the mammoth set, the largest ever built for a motion picture up to that time.

Far more problematic than building the Circus Maximus was Niblo's handling of his directorial duties. When production was resumed on the MGM lot on February 18, 1925, nearly 600 scenes (out of 774) still remained to be filmed, along with a considerable number of retakes of scenes previously shot in Rome, since Thalberg and Mayer deemed much of Niblo's Italian footage to be of inferior quality. (According to Novarro, the Italian film lab technicians were high on dope while developing the film.) Though now on his home turf, Niblo remained unsure how to proceed. "After carefully working with Niblo and giving him every aid and getting his best effort," Mayer wired Loew's second-in-command Nicholas Schenck, "we are convinced that he can never get the quality of stuff that is expected of *Ben-Hur.* . . . This picture has cost so much that we feel unless it is greatest picture ever made no chance of getting our money back or even great part of it and Niblo apparantly [*sic*] has lost himself. Actors like Novarro and Macavoy [*sic*] [are] not barrymores and gishes [*sic*] and need great help, which Niblo doesn't seem able [to] give them. Consequently performances [are] ordinary where [they] should be inspired."

Mayer asked Schenck to borrow Warner Bros.' contract director Ernst Lubitsch, whose German historical spectacles had been received to wide acclaim around the world, but that attempted deal fell through. Whether the proposal was turned down by Lubitsch himself or by Warner Bros. head Harry Warner, Niblo was to keep his job until the end.

Construction of the various sets and other logistical problems so delayed progress that the principals were able to work in other productions during their long interludes of inactivity. In between *Ben-Hur* filming schedules, MGM paired Francis X. Bushman with Mae Murray in *The Masked Bride*, May McAvoy was loaned to Warners to play in *Lady Windermere's Fan*, and Novarro was starred in *The Midshipman*.

A run-of-the-mill programmer, *The Midshipman* revolves around the training of cadets at the Annapolis Naval Academy, with a little drama stirred up when the cadet played by Novarro chooses to resign from the academy rather than denounce the alleged misconduct of his sweetheart's brother. All ends well when a lowly civilian proves to be the real culprit. Naval Academy graduate Christy Cabanne, now relieved of his *Ben-Hur* duties, was chosen to direct this MGM homage to the American navy and the studio's response to *Classmates*, a highly popular Richard Barthelmess vehicle for First National. Ex–Mack Sennett beauty Harriet Hammond was the romantic interest, while freckle-faced former child star Wesley Barry provided comic relief as her callow brother (the best moment in the picture occurs when Novarro imagines Barry's sister to look like him in drag). For this innocuous piece of propaganda, the studio received the full cooperation of the United States Navy, which loaned the production two destroyers and a plane for its climactic scenes, and allowed the company to film that year's graduation ceremony at Annapolis.

An overlong flag-waver whose chief interest today is the presence of Joan Crawford in a bit part, *The Midshipman* was nevertheless an important milestone in Novarro's career. The picture was his first film as a full-fledged star, a status symbolized on screen and in publicity material by his name appearing above the title; it was Novarro's first lead in a "man's picture"; and it was the Mexican actor's first all-American role.

In fact, the casting of Novarro as an American navy cadet was a calculated attempt by MGM to expand its star's audience. Novarro's previous roles as a leading man had been either too exotic or too foppish for the taste of many American male moviegoers. Unlike John Gilbert, who appealed to both sexes, Novarro's core audience was mostly female. Additionally, the Latin Lover craze appeared to be waning. Valentino's last two pictures, *Cobra* and *A Sainted Devil*, had been box-office disappointments, while no other so-called Latin Lover had made a strong mark with the public since Novarro's emergence three years earlier. Although Duncan Renaldo and Don Alvarado—neither of whom ever achieved star status—were beginning their careers at that time, most male performers with "foreign-sounding" names were now changing them to "American" ones. Thus, Novarro's fellow Mexican and former co-usher at the Pantages, Luis Antonio Damaso de Alonso, became Gilbert Roland (in honor of his two favorite screen performers, John Gilbert and Ruth Roland), Romanian-born Nicholas Pratza was renamed Nick Stuart, and Argentinian Alfredo Carlos de Birben was rechristened Barry Norton.

Besides sounding all-American, Novarro's Cadet Dick Randall was a character most American males could relate to more easily than to *Where the Pavement Ends'* Motauri, *Scaramouche's* André-Louis Moreau, or *Thy Name Is Woman's* Spanish carabinero. The carabinero, like the young hero in *Trifling Women*, was too weak to garner much empathy from most men. Motauri was too exotic, while André-Louis looked much too foppish in tights and with a little ponytail. (Douglas Fairbanks starred in numerous costume pictures, but his makeup and clothes, unlike Novarro's, always made him look conventionally masculine; the same would be true of Errol Flynn.) Dick Randall, on the other hand, wore military uniforms, sported a crew cut, fought one of his classmates, rescued the leading lady, and graduated as a member of the United States Navy before the final fade-out, while the magic of silent films spared audiences the distraction of hearing all-American Cadet Randall's thick Mexican accent.

MGM's tactic worked beautifully. When *The Midshipman* opened on October 11, 1925, it was greeted by generally amiable reviews and an enthusiastic reception by the public. "Not a picture that will stop your heart from beating," read the trade publication *Harrison's Report*, "but one that will make you leave the theater fully conscious that you have had more than your money's worth of entertainment." The picture, one of the biggest hits of the year for the studio, was to become the third most profitable of all of Novarro's MGM films because of its relatively low cost. It also served as a welcome boost to the actor's popularity just a few months prior to the release of the infinitely costlier *Ben-Hur*. Surprisingly, Novarro's routine performance, which displays little of the charm he had exuded in his Ingram films, was praised by most critics, even if some did complain of the actor's stiffness in the more dramatic moments. The Navy Department had no such qualms. It was so pleased with both the film and its star that it is said to have used Novarro's likeness in some of its recruiting posters.

On September 29, only a few days before the premiere of *The Midshipman*, a ghost from Novarro's past unexpectedly materialized. Ferdinand Pinney Earle's *The Rubaiyat of Omar Khayyam*, after languishing for almost four years for lack of distribution, finally surfaced as *A Lover's Oath* via the Astor Company, a small distributor with the habit of reediting old films to focus the story on the star of the moment. Astor, in fact, wanted Novarro to work nights for them—without MGM's knowledge—to shoot a few close-ups under the direction of film star Milton Sills. Since Novarro refused to cooperate, Astor, determined to enlarge his role, resorted to editing in the same scenes Earle had shot of Novarro four years earlier—but inserted in reverse.

Despite Novarro's rising box-office pull, *A Lover's Oath* failed to catch the public fancy. Generally negative reviews, such as *Variety's* remark that the picture's action was "jerky and disconnected" and its titles "rather sickeningly gushy," were part of the problem. Since *A Lover's Oath* had been fully reedited at the time of its release (at least in part by Milton Sills, who worked on it without pay) and is now lost, it is impossible to judge if Earle's original vision was truly artistic and innovative, or just pretentious and ponderous. However, both the 1925 reviews and the public's indifference clearly showed that Astor's tactics to improve the picture's accessibility and commercial potential were a dismal failure.

Ferdinand Earle himself also surfaced that year as an assistant to art director Cedric Gibbons in the creation of sets and visual effects for *Ben-Hur*, including the design of the Star of Bethlehem, the Valley of the Lepers, and the flight into Egypt. Some reports have also credited him with the direction of the Nativity Scene with Betty Bronson of *Peter Pan* fame as the Virgin Mary, though studio files list Christy Cabanne as the man responsible.

After experiencing the relatively easy production of *The Midshipman*, Novarro found himself back on the *Ben-Hur* grind in late summer, getting ready for the climactic chariot race, which became a major Hollywood event. For the filming of the master shot, MGM invited stars, directors, writers, publicists, and local dignitaries, many of whom were free to come because other studios had declared that Saturday, October 3, an unofficial holiday. Douglas Fairbanks, Mary Pickford, Betty Bronson, Colleen Moore, Lillian Gish, and others were on hand along with three thousand extras to cheer Novarro—insured by the studio for $3 million—Bushman, ten stuntmen charioteers, and their forty-eight horses.

Perched atop a one-hundred-foot platform, Niblo was officially present to supervise the filming, though the actual direction was the work of B. Reeves Eason and his sixty-two assistants, including then-unknowns Henry Hathaway and William Wyler (the director of the 1959 remake). To cover every possible angle, a record forty-two cameras were strategically placed throughout the set. There were cameras in a car driven in front of the galloping horses, inside a pit in the racetrack, behind soldiers' shields, and even on an airplane circling the stadium.

The morning was foggy, but shortly before noon the fog lifted. Huge tapestries were flung back, and the twelve chariots dashed forward. The riders circled the racetrack, lap after lap, with no major incidents until the sixth lap, when stuntman Mickey Millerick's chariot caught the inner rail at the south turn. Millerick lost control as his chariot careened toward the middle of the track. Sensing disaster, assistant director Henry Hathaway ran onto the track frantically waving his arms to warn the approaching charioteers, but to no avail. In a matter of seconds, three chariots crashed into Millerick's, while a fourth leaped over it. "Through a miracle," *Variety* marveled years later, "no one was hurt." No one person perhaps, but, according to Novarro, seven horses were injured so badly that they had to be put down.

Niblo often told reporters that Novarro himself performed all the stunts, though that was mere publicity. Stuntman Buster Gallagher took over from Novarro in all the dangerous stunts, and rode Novarro's chariot on October 3. MGM's $3 million insurance on Novarro notwithstanding, Mayer and Thalberg wanted Judah Ben-Hur to survive intact until the last shot of the picture had been taken.

Eason continued working in the Circus for weeks, shooting close-ups of details—Novarro and Bushman's faces, racing wheels, lashing whips—that would add excitement to the race on-screen. From a total of more than 200,000 feet of film (53,000 of which were shot on October 3), editor Lloyd Nosler and his assistants cut a 750-foot, seven-and-a-half-minute sequence that is one of the most exhilarating ever recorded on film. All in all, *Ben-Hur*'s editors had to create a coherent story out of 1 million feet of film, of which 12,000 were used for the final cut.

In the fall, Thalberg suffered a heart attack that some attributed to his *Ben-Hur* travails. The doctors were uncertain whether he would recover, but in a few weeks the bedridden producer was supervising the editing of the chariot race, which was projected on the ceiling of his bedroom. Once the rough cut was assembled, a preview was held on December 2 at the Criterion Theater in Pasadena. Audience comments were generally positive, though some felt the picture was overlong.

While Lloyd Nosler worked on the final cut, Thalberg ordered retakes and additional shots that continued until December 16. Then—more than two years after Charles Brabin had sailed to Europe—the saga ended. "All of a sudden, smoke bombs went off, pistols were fired, and all hell broke loose," Bushman later recalled. "It was our farewell. We shook hands all around, and do you know?—there were tears in our eyes. We had been through so much for so long...." Novarro, for his part, was happy it was all over. "Things can be a little too long" he would later remark, "and this was just too long."

On December 18, Novarro, accompanied by Herbert Howe, Fred Niblo, Enid Bennett, Francis X. Bushman, and May McAvoy, boarded a train for New York. On December 30—a mere two weeks after the last shot had been taken—*Ben-Hur* was premiered at Broadway's George M. Cohan Theater, an illustrious legitimate stage house.

Metro-Goldwyn-Mayer's future rested on the public reception of its epic. Despite the enormous success of the studio's *The Merry Widow* and *The Big Parade*, MGM would suffer a severe blow, perhaps even a fatal one, if *Ben-Hur* proved to be a commercial failure. The price tag of the picture had reached almost $4 million—at a time when the average cost of an MGM picture was $160,000—turning this historical spectacle into the most expensive motion picture ever produced. (It would remain the costliest film until *Gone with the Wind* fourteen years later.) If adjusted for inflation, *Ben-Hur*'s cost would be a little above $40 million today, but considering that film production costs have increased much more steeply than the general inflation index, if made in 2002, *Ben-Hur* would surely turn into a nine-figure-plus production.

The $4 million cost, the studio's contract with the Classical Cinematograph Corporation, and distribution and advertising expenses required that *Ben-Hur* earn MGM approximately $11 million if the studio was to break even—when in the mid-1920s, worldwide blockbusters, with rare exceptions, meant $3 million in rentals. "Not only every Christian, but every Mohammedan, every Hebrew, every Buddhist and every Sun Worshiper in America will have to buy a ticket for it," observed *Photoplay*'s James Quirk, "if General Lew Wallace's classic is to make any money for the producers."

Expectations were high at the packed theater before the two-hour-and-thirty-minute feature began rolling. Would the inordinate amounts of time, money, effort, and anguish that had gone into the making of this monumental epic be reflected in the finished film? After the lights went down, there was respectful applause when the title *Ben-Hur: A Tale of the Christ* flashed on the screen. As the picture progressed, the sophisticated Broadway audience grew increasingly enthralled until they lost themselves in excitement, cheering and clapping during the chariot race. The exhilaration lasted until the final fade-out, when *Ben-Hur* and its makers were rewarded with a thundering ovation. "Well kid, you were repaid last night for all the hard work you put in on *Ben-Hur*," Nicholas Schenck wired Thalberg in Hollywood. "It was the most magnificent opening I ever witnessed."

Absent from the triumphant gala premiere was the star of the picture. Either a severe cold (the official version) or uncontrollable stage fright (the rumored version) kept Novarro away from the opening of the most important film of his career—though another possibility for his absence may have been Herbert Howe's recommendation that the actor who played the larger-than-life Judah Ben-Hur *not* go to the premiere. In the days of silent films, when film stars were genuinely worshiped by their audiences, Howe believed that personal appearances would dim a star's brilliance. Novarro concurred.

"We are an illusion," he would later say. "The audience does not look at us as real. We are just an image on a giant screen that can never live up to their expectations in person." At the opening night of *Ben-Hur,* Novarro (following Howe's advice) may well have felt that the mythical Judah Ben-Hur would become even more resplendent if the flesh-and-bone mortal who had portrayed him was absent from the theater.

The next day, New York newspapers carried mostly ecstatic reviews of what the *New York Times* called "probably the most comprehensive and important spectacular subject that has ever been filmed." The trade publications were even more enthusiastic. *Photoplay* called *Ben-Hur* "a thing of beauty ... a truly great picture. No one, no matter what his age or religion, should miss it." For *Variety's* critics (there were two reviews occupying nearly a full page), the latest multimillion-dollar Hollywood epic was next in importance only to the Second Coming. One of them wrote:

> *Ben-Hur* in film form has been years in coming to the screen. ... And it was well worth waiting all these years for! ... As the industry today stands, so *Ben-Hur* stands: the greatest achievement that has been accomplished on the screen for not only the screen itself, but for all motion picturedom. You can scrap all the 'epics' that have been shown prior to the arrival of *Ben-Hur* and start a new book. It isn't a picture! It's the Bible! ... No matter what happens to others, *Ben-Hur* will remain, as the Bible remains. ... *Ben-Hur* will go down the ages of the picture industry to mark an epoch in its progress. An event that swung the tidal wave of humanity to the screen. The miracle picture that will convert the most skeptical. To say that it is colossal, tremendous, terrific, magnificent, awe-inspiring, all means nothing. *Ben-Hur* on the screen must be seen.

Niblo, who received sole credit for the direction, must have felt vindicated by the unbridled praise bestowed upon him. "*Ben-Hur* immediately places Fred Niblo ... in the class of the immortals among the directors of the screen," decreed *Variety.* "... [His work] surpasses anything that Griffith ever did." Ironically, B. Reeves Eason, the man responsible for the most exciting sequence in the picture, was ignored in most major reviews.

Notices for the supporting cast were mixed. Claire McDowell as Ben-Hur's mother and Betty Bronson as the Virgin Mary were invariably praised, but some reviewers complained that Carmel Myers's Iras—wearing a wig taken from ZaSu Pitts in *Greed*—was too much of a film vamp and that

Francis X. Bushman's acting consisted of too much posturing. May McAvoy and her curly blond wig were particularly singled out for critical scorn.

As for Novarro, *Ben-Hur* brought him the best reviews of his career. *Variety* predicted that he would be "made for all time by his performance here." The *New York Times* lauded him as "a sturdy, handsome young chap, with an excellent figure. His performance is all that one could wish, for he is fervent and earnest throughout, and restrained in his display of affection." Novarro "is magnificent," raved the *New York Herald Tribune*. "Of course," the reviewer added, "Mr. Novarro is conceded to be one of the most sincere, the most convincing and the most versatile of the screen actors, but even his faithful followers said, 'I wonder,' when he was chosen to play Ben-Hur. Their argument was 'he isn't big enough.' All one can say is go and see him play Ben Hur."

Other reviewers praised Novarro's "manly, handsome, heroic" performance, his ability to make Judah Ben-Hur "strikingly vivid," and "the maturity and authority . . . to say nothing of physical fitness" that he brought to the role (the reviewer was obviously unaware that Novarro's muscles had been plastered on him by the makeup department). Abraham Erlanger, promoting the picture in which he held a solid financial interest, publicly stated, "I have employed a dozen or more Ben-Hur's, including some very distinguished names in theater history. But to my mind, Ramon Novarro is the greatest of them all." On a more personal level, Novarro was rewarded with a telegram from Rex Ingram that read, "You give a great performance, Ramon. I am very proud of you."

Advertised as a "reverent rendering of History's mightiest events," *Ben-Hur* became the biggest hit of 1926. Though nearly absent on-screen, the sex angle that helped sell Cecil B. DeMille's biblical spectacles did find its way into MGM's promotion of this "exquisite Romance of Sacred and Profane Love." A photograph of a naked Novarro—with his genitals barely out of view—was used in the film's publicity as an enticement to those drawn more to the profane than to the sacred. The caption read, "This picture proves rather conclusively that he has no intention of entering a monastery or taking up the profession of concert pianist."

As an "event" motion picture, *Ben-Hur* was shown in limited release for the first two years. Initial prices, ranging from 50¢ to $1.50, were commensurate with those of stage shows. The star-studded Los Angeles premiere was held on August 2, 1926, at the Biltmore Theater, which, not coincidentally, was owned by Abraham Erlanger. Local reviews were as exuberant as those in New York, with the *Los Angeles Times* raving that *Ben-Hur* "will, without doubt or reservation, prove to be the greatest attraction ever seen in the theater. . . . Ramon Novarro rises to a plane unsurpassed in his performance."

On October 8, 1927, *Ben-Hur* finally opened nationwide to capacity audiences. The picture also became an international sensation, setting attendance records in cities throughout the world for months after its overseas opening in London in late 1926. More than a decade after the original release of the film, French poet and playwright Jean Cocteau contended that its appeal remained undiminished, calling *Ben-Hur* "the epic *par excellence.*"

In its first four years of release, *Ben-Hur* earned MGM more than $4.3 million domestically and $5 million internationally, for a worldwide total of nearly $9.4 million—equivalent to approximately $95 million today. Although reliable figures are unavailable for *The Birth of a Nation* and *The Four Horsemen of the Apocalypse*, *Ben-Hur* in all likelihood far surpassed the worldwide box-office take of both of those films, becoming the most successful motion picture of the silent era. Even then, the production left MGM $700,000 in the red. A considerable share of the rentals covered publicity and distribution expenses, while the rest was equally split between the studio and the Classical Cinematograph Corporation.

Despite *Ben-Hur's* failure to recoup its exorbitant cost, the film was by any standards a stupendous box-office success. Equally important, it was a highly respected production that, coming out in MGM's second year, brought enormous prestige to the studio. *Ben-Hur* was listed as one of the top ten films of 1925 by the *New York Times* and figured in second place, behind the German-made *Varieté*, on *Film Daily's* yearly national poll of film critics—the first Novarro picture not directed by Ingram to be featured on the list. Two years later, after its nationwide release in 1927, the MGM epic could still be found in fifth place on the *Film Daily* poll.

More than three-quarters of a century after its original release, *Ben-Hur* remains an impressive example of grandiose filmmaking. Granted, certain backdrops are obviously painted, the sea battle is overlong and poorly edited, and the special effects are primitive when compared to today's computer-generated product. On the other hand, the plot moves at a steady pace, while the brilliantly edited chariot race has lost none of its excitement. More surprisingly, the quasi-religious epic remains not only thrilling, but also touching. In spite of its heavy-handed religiosity—even in the 1920s, certain reviewers thought it lacked finesse—moments of beauty, as when Ben-Hur's leprous mother, not daring to touch him, kneels down to kiss the stone slab on which he sleeps, still retain their emotional charge. Unlike most of Cecil B. DeMille's religious epics, *Ben-Hur* does not spend much time on assorted orgies and temptations of the flesh—though modern audiences are surprised to find male nudity and bare female breasts in a 1925 picture. The nonexploitative and reverential tone of the film surely appealed to its star.

"A less experienced actor would have been swayed by his emotions," remarked Louella Parsons about the picture's leading man, "but Mr. Novarro exercises an admirable restraint." Although "restraint" is hardly the word to describe Novarro's showy, charismatic, and grandiloquent performance, the praise he received from Louella and other reviewers is perfectly understandable. Those qualities passed for great acting then—and, with certain concessions to modern tastes, still do—and could well have won him an Academy Award had the Academy of Motion Picture Arts and Sciences existed. But there is more to Novarro's portrayal than mere glitz. Underneath the histrionics lie charm and honesty, attributes that a director with a finer touch, such as Rex Ingram or King Vidor, would have relied on for a more nuanced performance. Still, Novarro does shine in several key moments, whether expressing a mixture of anger, triumph, and pain after the climactic chariot race, or looking majestic in two-strip Technicolor while feted in the streets of Rome as "the greatest athlete of his day."

With the possible exception of Twentieth Century–Fox's 1963 *Cleopatra*, no other motion picture has had as tortuous a history as MGM's 1925 epic. However, unlike Fox's historical pageant, *Ben-Hur* ultimately turned into a remarkable triumph for all involved. With *Ben-Hur*, *The Big Parade*, and *The Merry Widow*, the newly formed MGM consolidated its status as a major Hollywood powerhouse. Fred Niblo followed the gigantic epic with high-profile vehicles for Greta Garbo, Lillian Gish, and Norma Talmadge (he never worked with Novarro again). Francis X. Bushman had a brief resurgence in popularity and might have gone further had he not antagonized Mayer with his threat to quit *Ben-Hur* in midproduction. Despite her negative reviews, May McAvoy went on to play leads in several important films, including the historical milestone *The Jazz Singer*. But no one realized more professional recognition from the *Ben-Hur* experience than did the picture's star. In fact, Novarro became so closely associated with the part of this most un–Latin Lover of roles that for years afterward he received fan mail addressed to "Mr. Ben-Hur."

In late 1918, while nineteen-year-old Ramón Samaniego was in New York rehearsing with Marion Morgan's troupe during the day and working as a pastry boy at night, he would sometimes sit on the steps of a church off Broadway to rest between job assignments.

"As I sat there," Novarro later reminisced to Herbert Howe, "I would look up at the signs in the sky and read the names that were written there in electric lights. And do you know, I could always see my own name up there?"

"And how did you feel when you saw it there—actually?" Howe inquired.

"Well, you see," came the reply, "I had always seen it there—actually."

Through a twist of fate, Ramon Novarro's name was now shining brighter than those of most performers in film history ever had or ever would. Yet, never again was Novarro to appear in a motion picture nearly as monumental, as successful, or as highly acclaimed as *Ben-Hur*.

SEVEN

A Certain Young Man

By early 1926, Novarro and Herbert Howe had been together for more than two years. Since Howe had had a new house built for himself in Beverly Hills in mid-1925, he and Novarro had been able to spend time together in town without interruptions from either Howe's brother Milton, with whom Herbert had been living in the Hollywood Hills, or the numerous Samaniegos. Louis Samuel, Novarro's fellow dance student at Ernest Belcher's school, still played a part in the actor's life, but now as his personal assistant. Whatever Samuel felt about Novarro's relationship with Howe, there was little he could do to keep Howe away from his boss. Officially in the role of publicist, Howe was Novarro's inseparable companion both in Southern California and elsewhere.

"There's no better way of learning a fellow's character than by knocking around the world with him when soul and stomach are tried by bad food and good licker [sic], sleepless nights in Paris and sleepy days in Sahara deserts, to say nothing of the trial of constant association," Howe declared in his column. "I've traveled nearly fifty thousand miles with Ramon Novarro, to Africa with Ingram and to Rome with *Ben-Hur,* and I am convinced that there is at least one idol in the movie realm who is worthy of all the public worship given him." At home, Howe used his writing skills to promote Novarro's image, making sure that his lover-client's name appeared in almost every "Close-Ups and Long-Shots" column. No letters exchanged between the two are known to survive, but Howe's columns, even when his role as a publicist is taken into account, are a clear indication of his feelings for Novarro.

In his 1925 holiday column, for instance, Howe had named those deserving "a Merrie Christmas and a Happy New Year in the name of humanity," including D. W. Griffith, Charles Chaplin, Mary Pickford, and Rex Ingram ("because he discovered the finest actor, married the wittiest woman and made the most beautiful pictures"). In Howe's words, Novarro was listed "because he has genius as an actor and musician, and with it the character of a shining knight, but especially because he supplies me with copy, is the best traveling companion since D'Artagnan and does Ed Wynn, [entertainer Miss] Patricola, Fanny Brice, Harold Lloyd, Alice Terry, Rex Ingram and Ramon Novarro better than they do themselves." To balance his effusiveness, on a few occasions Howe would criticize certain elements of Novarro's personality, stating once that beneath Novarro's "gentle courtly mien you soon strike bronze. Indeed, the very qualities of tenderness and sympathy are the ones in which Novarro's nature is most wanting." Once Howe had squeezed his criticism in, he would continue discussing Novarro with further praise.

In late January, Howe and his "best traveling companion" had planned to sail for Europe on vacation, but the unexpected death of Novarro's friend and frequent costar Barbara La Marr led to a change in those plans. Soon after finishing *The Girl from Montmartre* for First National, La Marr had suffered a complete breakdown, partly compounded by a disastrous diet that had ravaged her body already weakened by drugs, alcohol, and a bout with tuberculosis. Seriously ill with nephritis, a chronic kidney ailment, the twenty-nine-year-old actress was being treated at a rest home in the Los Angeles suburb of Altadena when she died on January 30. Her burial was scheduled for the following Friday, so Novarro, then on his way to New York, could be present. Upon hearing the news, he and Howe canceled their European trip and returned to California to attend funeral services at a Culver City chapel.

Shortly thereafter, Novarro and Howe left for Quebec City, where they spent one week at the luxurious Château Frontenac overlooking the St. Lawrence River. Coming after the grueling *Ben-Hur* production and La Marr's untimely death, the Quebec sojourn was supposed to help Novarro calm his nerves with adequate rest. Music, of course, played a part in the relaxation. Although there was no piano in the hotel rooms, Novarro would go down to the ballroom in the after hours to play the grand piano onstage to Howe, the hotel janitor, and the scrub ladies. Upon their return to Los Angeles, Novarro was ready to resume work at MGM—now as an established superstar.

· · ·

"Lyric charm, poetical charm, plus the beauty of a Greek boy," Adela Rogers St. Johns rhapsodized in the January 1926 issue of *Photoplay*, selecting Novarro as one of the ten best-looking men in motion pictures. "Think of him when you read of Keats, when you read of Byron, when you read *Romeo and Juliet*." Keats, Byron, and Shakespeare may have been outside the realm of most filmgoers, but millions of them around the world did think of Novarro as *The Midshipman*'s Cadet Randall and as Judah Ben-Hur. With two major hits in less than a year, for the time being Novarro had shown himself capable of enhancing his star status without Rex Ingram's guidance.

Still, Novarro was not regarded as *the* number one male attraction at MGM. That distinction was shared by two rather disparate performers: the creepy Lon Chaney and the amorous John Gilbert. The forty-two-year-old Chaney was highly successful with both critics and audiences as an interpreter of doomed men who, whether good or evil, were invariably ugly. But despite his seniority in the studio's ranking of stars, Chaney was clearly no competition for Novarro in the romantic leading man arena. Gilbert, also included in Adela St. Johns's top ten list, was another matter.

Five months younger than Novarro, John Gilbert was born John Cecil Pringle into a family of strolling players in Logan, Utah, on July 10, 1899. He began getting bit parts in films in 1915 and by the end of the decade had progressed to important supporting roles. In the early 1920s, two lead roles at Fox—the dashing heroes of *Monte Cristo* and *Cameo Kirby*—gave Gilbert's career the necessary momentum to earn him a lucrative $1,500-a-week contract at MGM. With his oft-mustached dark good looks, piercing brown eyes, and passionate lovemaking, Gilbert was touted in mid-decade as the most likely candidate to take over Valentino's title as *the* Great Screen Lover. Gilbert, in fact, had one major advantage over the Latin Lover. While Valentino's exotic, elflike features possessed an androgynous quality that alienated a large segment of the male audience, Gilbert's more conventional looks made him the ideal model of the passionate lover for both sexes.

Novarro's pretty-boy looks were no more exotic than Gilbert's, but his gentle lovemaking appealed more to the maternal than to the sensual female instinct. "When I kissed a lady," Novarro later recalled, "it was a kiss—not a bite." Gilbert, on the other hand, devoured his leading ladies without even touching them. Indeed, the German-English Gilbert was a much more fitting incarnation of the Latin Lover than was the Mexican Novarro. Gilbert eschewed Valentino's gimmicks of eye rolling and nostril flaring, but his eyes forcefully spelled out the urgency of sexual desire in a way that Novarro's never did. Not surprisingly, audiences reacted more readily to Gilbert.

In the mid-1920s, Novarro had one colossal hit in *Ben-Hur*, but Gilbert had two in that same period: *The Merry Widow* and the war drama *The Big Parade*, which made even more money domestically than *Ben-Hur*. And unlike Novarro's blockbuster, the two Gilbert pictures were not only popular and prestigious, but also highly profitable. *The Big Parade*, made at a cost of $380,000, earned the studio more than $3.5 million, the largest profit margin of an in-house MGM production until *Mrs. Miniver* seventeen years later. The profits of those two Gilbert films were vital in helping the new studio offset its *Ben-Hur* losses.

Although Gilbert's salary was more than 50 percent higher than Novarro's during their first two years at MGM, there is no evidence that the relationship between the two potential rivals was anything less than cordial. The same, however, could not be said of Gilbert's rapport with his boss. Louis B. Mayer so abhorred Gilbert's rowdy demeanor that he allegedly punched the studio's top male romantic star after hearing him call his own mother "a whore."

Mayer may have preferred Novarro's more restrained manners, but the public had clearly been captivated by Gilbert's ardor. As a result, it was Gilbert who followed his two 1925 successes with the Rafael Sabatini swashbuckler *Bardelys the Magnificent*; with a costarring role in *La Bohème* next to the studio's highest-paid star, Lillian Gish; and with *Flesh and the Devil*, in which he was paired for the first time with MGM's sensational Swedish import, Greta Garbo.

Regardless of a 140 percent raise—to $3,000 a week—in mid-1926 that placed Novarro on the same wage level as Gilbert and Chaney, MGM seemed unsure how to exploit either Novarro's talents or his skyrocketing popularity. As a follow-up to his *Ben-Hur* triumph, the boyish Novarro was incongruously assigned a slight comedy of manners in which he was to portray a dapper, middle-aged English lord.

By 1926, Novarro had played a wide variety of nationalities and ethnic types: Persian, Bedouin, Spaniard, Frenchman, Anglo-American, Central European, Middle Eastern Jew, and Pacific Islander (in at least some prints of *Where the Pavement Ends*). His Mexican accent went unheard in silent films, and his looks, neither too dark nor too fair, allowed him to pass for any of those types, with the exception of the Pacific Islander. Yet, the upper-class English roué in *Bellamy the Magnificent* was an incomprehensible case of miscasting. It was not just a matter of looks, but even more of manner. Novarro, after all, had become a star by capitalizing on his boyishness, a quality that would be completely lacking in this next assignment.

Even another role as an Anglo-Saxon military cadet would have been more fitting: a Mexican in uniform looks much the same as an American or a Finn, and moreover, those roles carried a guaranteed box-office appeal. Equally baffling was the studio's inability to develop an interesting Mexican character for its Mexican star, who never played a character of his own nationality during his years of stardom. This missed opportunity is especially puzzling because both the studio and Herbert Howe made good use of the Mexican angle in their publicity materials.

One fan magazine article asserted that Novarro had "more real American blood than George Washington [for] in him flows the blood of the Aztec, the original American noble." Another, inaccurately titled "Ramon's Ancestors Greeted the Mayflower" and written by a certain Manuel Reyes (possibly a Herbert Howe pseudonym, as the style is similar to Howe's), tried to justify the selection of Novarro as *The Midshipman*'s all-American Cadet Randall by detailing the star's patrician American origins.

"Your ancestors came over on the Mayflower I suppose," Reyes quoted an unnamed (and likely fictitious) interviewer.

"No," Novarro supposedly replied, "they were here to meet it."

Reyes then explained that on his mother's side, Novarro was descended from the native inhabitants of the Americas, and challenged the erroneous assumption that all those south of the Rio Grande belong to a single ethnic and cultural group. "Against this romantic background of Aztec splendor," he observed, "Novarro has suffered the appellation of 'Latin' in silence. . . . As the facts stand, he is more genuinely American than the descendants of those who suffered *mal de mer* on the Mayflower; their ancestors, compared to his are *nouveau*." According to the piece, inaccurate publicity was responsible for Novarro's being identified as "Spanish," though the Mexican star had since "insisted upon the truth of his American birth." One obvious problem with this dramatic revelation was that Aztecs and all-American military cadets with a last name like Randall had little in common. Another was that Novarro, as his looks clearly attested, *was* predominantly of Spanish blood. And finally, such emphasis on Novarro's partially non-European lineage could backfire.

In those days, non-Germanic or Catholic Europeans were often perceived as less than white by WASP Americans. Those with Indian blood, such as most Mexicans, ranked considerably further down the ethnic scale. The studio gambled that despite Novarro's actual ethnic background, the Mexican star's popularity and Mediterranean looks would continue to make him worthy of his fair-skinned leading ladies—as long as he played Caucasian characters. Otherwise, as in *The Arab* or in the Ingram cut of *Where the Pavement Ends*, love could not be consummated unless the heroine was of a similar ethnicity. Hence Novarro's half-white Pacific Islander in *The Pagan* is allowed to find romantic bliss with a half-white heroine, and to ensure a happy ending for the 1933 Novarro release *The Barbarian*, Myrna Loy's character reveals that she is part Egyptian. (Ethnic mixing could play a positive role in American films as long as that mixing occurred *before* the story began.)

Strangely, for someone who took pride in his national background ("don't ask him if he's Spanish; he's Mexican, and proud of it!" asserted a film publication in 1930), Novarro paid only lip service to the idea of playing a character of his own nationality, and kept silent about Hollywood's negative portrayals of Mexicans during his years as a star. His silence on the latter point is particularly curious, as American films frequently depicted those from south of the border as dirty, ugly, and vicious. *Patria*, a 1916 serial showing Japanese and Mexican hordes pillaging American homes and kidnapping American women, was found so offensive that Japan issued a formal protest to the American government. Mexico remained silent about *Patria* because diplomatic ties with its northern neighbor had been broken, but in 1922, when the political climate had begun to settle, the Mexican government issued a temporary ban on *all* films from any American company that produced "anti-Mexican" motion pictures.

Even offscreen, Mexicans were perceived as a threat to the Anglo-Saxon civilization of North America, most especially as a menace to the purity of white women. Cowboy star Tom Mix could thus brag in print that he had hunted "any greaser that had insulted a white woman" during his (fictionalized) pre-Hollywood days. Nor were Mexicans the only targets of insensitive national or ethnic slurs in the press. Blacks were frequently referred to as "darkies" in mainstream magazines, while jokes about the Chinese and their laundries were deemed funny. Even a sophisticate like Herbert Howe referred to the Japanese as "Japs" and joked about "colored folk" who ate chicken every day. The problem was not a general lack of political correctness, but pervasive racism and xenophobia in mainstream American society.

Throughout his life, Novarro was to keep silent on the issue. In contrast, his cousin and fellow Durango native Dolores del Río was quite vocal. "I would like to play in stories concerning my native people, the Mexican race," she stated in the early 1930s, after having played French, Acadian, Russian, and Spanish women. "It is my dearest wish to make fans realize their real beauty, their wonder, their greatness as a people. As I see it, the vast majority today regard Mexicans as either a race of bandits or laborers, dirty, unkempt and uneducated. That is quite erroneous. Hence my big ambition to show to all, the best that's in my nation."

MGM also wanted Novarro to show what was "best in his nation," but with a radically different intent than del Río's. Studio executives were concerned not with portraying better Mexicans on-screen, but with portraying Novarro as a better kind of Mexican in print. (The same tactic was used with del Río, whose publicity emphasized her family's wealth and the fact that she had been educated in Europe.) That was how the MGM matinee idol could be distinguished from both his mostly poor and uneducated countrymen who had fled north during the revolution and the greasy villains of the screen. Consequently, whether true or not—no evidence can be found either way—Novarro's Indian ancestors had to be noble.

Another approach to making Novarro's "Mexicanness" more palatable was to depict the star as an all-American boy trapped in a Mexican body. This strategy emphasized Novarro's dedication to his family, his devotion to his Church, and his aversion to the Hollywood social scene ("He keeps as aloof as Pola Negri. And, like her, he would rather endure the plague than a party"). Besides downplaying his foreignness, this sort of publicity matched Novarro's unpretentious screen persona and helped conceal his sexual orientation. "It is hard to write about one of these upstanding, whole-wheat boys," Howe had asserted in his first Novarro article for *Photoplay*. "My sympathies are all with the criminal classes. And Ramon is not one of these, even though he is a Hollywood resident and a Mexican. Not that I mean any disparagement of Mexicans." Perhaps not, but Howe's point was that Novarro was *different* from the American public's perception of Mexicans—so different that he could be an American. During the pre-talkie era, no one would hear the difference.

MGM's contradictory approaches to Novarro's image, the foreign and the homespun, melded into one in both the public mind and on-screen: Ramon Novarro became Hollywood's exotic boy next door. In real life, he was well known to be a Mexican, but one who personified the "American" qualities of gallantry, piety, and familial devotion. On-screen, he may not have looked exactly like Johnny Iowa or Billy Alabama, but he certainly behaved like them—or at least the way they were supposed to behave. This hybrid image, livelier and warmer than most of his early film characters, turned out to be highly effective. Until he outgrew his youthful persona, Novarro thrived as the boyish and spirited hero, whether an American navy cadet, a Teutonic prince, or a Spanish heartbreaker. His turn as the English lord in *Bellamy the Magnificent* was one of the rare instances during his stardom when he strayed from that image.

In Roy Horniman's novel *Bellamy the Magnificent*, Lord Bellamy is described as a fortyish man "of imposing appearance" whose motto is "If one can be constantly falling in love, one will remain young indefinitely." Somehow, someone at MGM thought that Lord Bellamy was a role for Ramon Novarro. Mustached and monocled, with white powder on his hair, Novarro was supported by recent MGM acquisition Sally O'Neil, *Ben-Hur* vamp Carmel Myers, and Renée Adorée of *The Big Parade* fame. Hobart Henley, fresh from two well-received Norma Shearer comedies, *His Secretary* and *A Slave of Fashion*, was set to direct.

The plot of *Bellamy the Magnificent* revolves around Bellamy's many amorous conquests, and climaxes with his being unfairly accused of cheating at cards. When Bellamy, as a ruse, threatens to kill himself, his jealous valet confesses to the misdeed. Filming of this comedy of manners began in mid-March 1926, three months after Novarro had finished his participation in *Ben-Hur*. What should have been obvious from the start, that the star lacked the poise and maturity essential for the part, became painfully clear once the rushes were screened—the dailies were so poor that all the existing footage had to be scrapped. Over the next several months, various writers struggled to come up with solutions for the troubled picture.

Filming restarted later in the year, some of it under the direction of Edmund Goulding, but the new footage proved to be no better than the earlier one. Novarro "somehow seemed to be unconsciously conscious of the inconsistency in playing the love-sick awkward boy in the grand manner of a sophisticated man of the world and conqueror of women's hearts," scenarist Bela Sekely wrote in a studio memo. "Consequently, his acting was constrained, he seemed to be ill at ease and his face in the attempt of drawing his features into an expression of sophistication . . . looked very unnatural and out of atmosphere." By that time, the story had lost most of Horniman's plot and characters and had suffered several title changes, with the studio finally settling on *A Certain Young Man*. The lead character—now a considerably tamer and younger philanderer—had been renamed Lord Gerald Brinsley.

It was surely disheartening for Novarro to find himself entangled in another problematic picture immediately after his *Ben-Hur* travails, especially in a programmer clearly designed to cash in on his surging popularity. Despite the phenomenal success of *Ben-Hur*, which was still holding strong in selected theaters, an inappropriate follow-up vehicle could seriously damage Novarro's star status and belie Howe's prediction that he was the "artist who would one day wear a halo of higher watt than any other."

On August 23, during the time Novarro was working on retakes for the frustrating *A Certain Young Man*, thirty-one-year-old Rudolph Valentino, the star who at one point had worn "a halo of higher watt than any other," died at the Polyclinic Hospital in New York, where he was being treated for a ruptured ulcer. After lying in state at Campbell's Funeral Parlor, mourned by a crowd estimated at one hundred thousand, the body of the Latin Lover was transported to Los Angeles, where it was buried in a crypt loaned by a devastated June Mathis. Novarro escorted Alice Terry to the September 14 funeral at the Hollywood Memorial Park Cemetery, a rite attended by more than ten thousand mourners. Novarro, who barely knew Valentino, declared at the time that his death had "robbed art of a true son. His work and his personality were inspirations to all who knew him."

A few weeks earlier, an unsigned editorial in the *Chicago Tribune* had called the Italian-born screen idol a "pink powder puff" and had accused him of leading real American men on the road to effeminacy. "Why didn't someone quietly drown Rudolph Guglielmo [sic], alias Valentino, years ago?" read the article. "... Hollywood is the nation's school of masculinity. Rudy, the beautiful gardener's boy, is the prototype of the American male. Hell's bells. Oh, sugar."

Earlier in the decade, Valentino had already been criticized for playing such unmanly roles as the bejeweled hero in *The Young Rajah* and the effete dandy in *Monsieur Beaucaire*. "Something has happened to the Valentino of *The Sheik* and *Blood and Sand*," complained *Photoplay* about the latter screen role. "... He doesn't look a bit dangerous to women." Neither did he look "dangerous" in real life while wearing a slave bracelet his wife and acting manager Natacha Rambova had given him. Yet, none of the previous attacks had exhibited the viciousness of the *Chicago Tribune* article. Valentino was so incensed that he wrote a letter to the *Chicago Herald Examiner* challenging the *Tribune*'s anonymous writer to a boxing match (the challenge went unanswered). The Latin Lover then asserted his manliness in interviews, posed in boxer shorts for photographers, and even fought one round with a sportswriter—but the damage had been done.

Besides poking fun at Valentino, the *Chicago Tribune* piece served as a warning to Novarro and all other gay performers, since the shocking aspect of the editorial was that Valentino's star status and prestige had failed to protect him from public ridicule. Unlike Valentino, who at the time was working independently through United Artists, Novarro was an MGM contract player and could fully count on the studio's powerful influence on the press, but even then, the almighty MGM was unable to control every news item published in the country. Accusations of effeminacy or innuendos about a star's "unmanly behavior" could well destroy the career of any screen heartthrob. In Valentino's case, his sudden death turned *The Son of the Sheik* into a major hit and the star into a lasting film icon, but for those who would rather avoid the death option, an expedient marriage followed by a child or two could suffice to stifle unwelcome rumors. Novarro, if caught up in such rumors, might have to relinquish either his bachelorhood or his career.

Even though he was more talked about than ever after *Ben-Hur*, Novarro persisted in his refusal to play the studio publicity game using trumped-up girlfriends and prospective wives. When a report stated that Novarro had taken out a marriage license in New York to wed Katherine Wilson, a minor stage actress, Novarro simply replied, "As Mark Twain once said, 'the report of my death is grossly exaggerated.'" (Wilson herself had apparently concocted the marriage story.) The most he would do for his heterosexual image was endorse a perfume called Ben-Hur by declaring, "We must admit the seductive sway of perfume when combined with the beauty of woman," or remark about Lillian Gish, an actress hardly known for her sex appeal, "I cannot resist any one whose eyes are set far apart like hers." Howe did not urge him to go on dates with starlets or escort actresses to parties, as the savvy publicist recognized that the devout family-man image fit Novarro's persona better than that of a man-about-town.

Accordingly, the young star's withdrawn and carefully guarded private life further enhanced and protected his image. In fact, Novarro remembered living nearly like a recluse during the height of his stardom. "The stars of my day enjoyed a certain privacy," he told DeWitt Bodeen in later years. "We lived two lives: our film life, and our own private one. It wasn't only Garbo who lived as a recluse—almost all of us did. I don't know if we actually had better taste, or it was forced upon us. But the intimate details of our personal lives were never publicized unless we deliberately allowed them to be. And it wasn't all a desire for privacy. Some of us realized it was necessary in order to sustain the public illusion that made us stars."

But in spite of Novarro's assertion, most stars of the 1920s and 1930s kept at least some of their private affairs wide open to public view, especially when convenient for their image. Thus, stories about Pola Negri's temper tantrums, John Gilbert's affairs, Clara Bow's love scandals, and even Bebe Daniels's arrest for speeding were turned into fodder for the press. Home photo sessions with Corinne Griffith, Joan Crawford, and others stars posing with their respective spouses, children, parents, in-laws, pets, and/or furniture were a frequent staple of fan magazines.

Novarro, of course, was disingenuous in claiming not to know the reasons for his desire for privacy. Although his cultural background would have made privacy imperative regardless of his sexual orientation, it was personal and professional survival, not better taste or a desire to maintain his screen mystique, that led to his seclusion. Moreover, a desire to protect his family impelled Novarro to go further in that respect. "I know that not until late in my MGM career was I photographed with my mother or any of my brothers or sisters," he told Bodeen. "I lived one life—my professional one—at MGM when I was busy making films. When I left the studio, I took up my life as Ramón Samaniego."

Novarro's longing for privacy notwithstanding, Howe made sure his readers knew about his client's "normal" manhood. He once wrote that he had watched Novarro "knock a fellow in the general direction of Heaven" (adding, "with an apologetic grace"), and and in his columns Howe generously dropped hints about Novarro's heterosexuality—whether a lighthearted mention that the Mexican heartthrob might be interested in becoming "one of the future Messrs. La Marr" or a remark about his dizzying effect on the opposite sex. Those demonstrations of Novarro's boundless heterosexual appeal had to be accompanied by an explanation as to why the lady-killer remained not only unmarried, but also unpaired. "The Italian girls went wild over Ramon Novarro, but he came back as fancy free as ever," Howe had reported in the April 1925 issue of *Photoplay*. "The romantic young actor never gave them a tumble, having other matters on hand. He was too busy trying to make a success of his role of Ben Hur." Other accounts had him too busy trying to care for his large family. Even so, some were not deceived.

In the sardonic mid-1920s publication *Who's Whose in Hollywood*, author B. W. Sayres—probably a pseudonym for a film publicist or columnist—cattily discussed Hollywood celebrities with the knowledge and cynicism of an insider. Sayres's surprisingly modern bite spared neither Novarro nor Howe. Novarro is described as "the *Galahad* of pictures, but alas, a sawed off sheik! ... Boy Scout trying to look like a hard guy ... Too refined to even live in Hollywood. Thinks party is something politicians have. Should be drowned or get his eyes opened ... Natural, easy worker. But if he *must* play grown-ups, get him a director, a highchair and a footstool. He's too fine to be made *rediculous* [*sic*]." Howe, for his part, is presented as "Sir Galahad's admiring audience and Greek chorus. Clean and clever. Anyhow, clever." The most revealing section came near the end of the booklet, where the author parodied the Q&A sections of fan magazines. In a reply to an imaginary letter writer, Sayres explained, "As for your other hero, yes, dear, it is indeed true. Mr. Howe says he is not married at ALL. Mr. Howe says he is too *refined,* and Mr. Howe is the positively only person who is refined enough to know him."

This caustic take on Hollywood personalities received little exposure outside film circles, as the booklet was apparently self-published, but the potential damage of such publications was obvious. If *Who's Whose in Hollywood* could find its way to the presses, so could other books or news articles with perhaps even more explicit commentary. Some of those might be picked up by magazines or newspapers beyond studio control and become national stories along the lines of the *Chicago Tribune*—originated "pink powder puff" editorial. The major studios of the day had to ensure that their voices would cut through any static created by negative publicity, while stars, most of whom were bound by morality clauses in their contracts, had to be careful to preserve a clean public image. MGM thus flooded news outlets with stories of Novarro's churchgoing habits and familial devotion, while Howe's columns served as the star's public certification of both decency and manliness.

Despite Howe's best promotional efforts, filmmaking and motion picture stardom had lost some of their allure for Novarro after Ingram's departure for Europe. Novarro had no one at MGM to guide him through difficult productions, as he had discovered during the torturous making of *Ben-Hur,* nor was there anyone at the studio to carefully craft scenarios that best showcased his star quality, as demonstrated by the *A Certain Young Man* misfire. Finally, Barbara La Marr's and Rudolph Valentino's deaths had clearly shown that film stardom was no guarantee of a long and contented life. Now twenty-seven, Novarro decided he should start focusing on his old dreams while he still had time.

Singing—glamorous opera singing in particular—had been Novarro's passion since boyhood. "As a little boy, I used to envision myself as the opera singers we saw in Mexico," he would reminisce. "I hummed the airs and saw myself enacting their parts. Of course we of the Latin races feel far differently about opera than do perhaps you colder-blooded Americans." Besides offering Novarro "the glamour of costumes, of scenery, of the drama that goes with it all," opera was considered a much loftier manifestation of artistic expression by traditional upper-class Mexicans than motion picture acting.

As it was, Novarro's film star status could be both an aid and a hindrance to his operatic ambitions. Theaters might be thronged with fans curious to hear the star of *Ben-Hur* sing, but opera purists might automatically dismiss the efforts of the actor who had played in *Thy Name Is Woman*. Therefore, Novarro planned to stage his opera debut abroad, assuming that "over there I will be judged as a singer only; here I would first be regarded as 'a movie actor,' and then a singer." Meanwhile, in order to avoid ridicule either at home or overseas as an unrefined Hollywood personality toying with high art, Novarro began voice training at his home with "Belgian" concert singer Louis Graveure (born Wilfred Douthitt in London), then billed as "the Favorite Baritone of the Day."

Always impeccably attired and accustomed to riding around town in a chauffeured limousine, the gray-haired, goateed Graveure—who consistently denied that he had ever been named Douthitt—avidly encouraged Novarro to resume his musical aspirations. "In addition to possessing a tenore robusto voice of exceptional quality," Graveure proclaimed, "Mr. Novarro is a thorough musician and an accomplished pianist. He is the coming great tenor."

Graveure's hyperboles aside, Novarro did have a talent for music. He had been familiar with musical rhythms since early childhood, when he would listen to his mother sing and practice at the piano, and as a silent film actor, he had learned to move and act on the set to the tempo of musical accompaniment (which was supposed to create the necessary mood for a scene). "It is so easy," he later remarked, "for everyone is born with a certain amount of rhythm. One talks, reads, walks and sleeps in rhythm." Yet, hard work would be necessary if he was going to master those rhythms and achieve true vocal excellence.

Sundays and stretches between film projects were thus spent studying music. "We worked six days a week making pictures in those days," Novarro told DeWitt Bodeen, "and often on Saturday evenings I was driven directly from the studio to the railroad station and rode up to San Francisco on the overnight *Lark*, studied there on Sunday with my favorite vocal coach [Graveure, who taught a voice class in that city], and took the overnight train back to Los Angeles, arriving just in time to be driven directly to the Culver City lot for Monday's shooting." Apart from his practice with Louis Graveure, Novarro used his own "intimate theater" as a testing ground for his vocal progress.

· · ·

Possibly inspired by millionaire Juan José Zambrano's addition of a private theater to his Durango residence, which Ramón Samaniego had seen as a boy, Novarro built as an annex to the Gramercy house his own sixty-five-seat theater, El Teatro Intimo. Within its cream-tinted plaster walls, the theater boasted an orchestra pit for twelve musicians, a stage for a company of thirty, overhead lighting, electrically controlled curtains, and underground dressing rooms. Lettered in crimson and gold on parchment scrolls, Novarro's Spanish-language invitations for the inauguration of his theater read:

> I am honored in inviting you to the inauguration of my little theater with the first edition of the Novarro revue, which is given to celebrate the thirty-fourth wedding anniversary of the beloved authors of my days, Señor Doctor don Mariano N. Samaniego and Señora doña Leonor Gavilán de Samaniego; presented on the twenty-fourth of the current October [1926] at eight-thirty (prompt).

The first "Novarro revue" consisted of one-act plays and musical numbers directed by Novarro, and performed in Spanish by the star and by young members of the local Mexican community. Besides Herbert Howe and a select few, the guests were restricted to the Mexican social and business elite of Los Angeles, including representatives of Mexican president Plutarco Elías Calles. After the revue was over, Novarro took Howe to a secluded roof garden, where, seated along the parapet overlooking the lighted city, the "Novarro revue" star-director asked his companion for his thoughts about the presentation. "The direction was too good," Howe predictably exclaimed. "Several of the company all but equaled the star." Whether or not Howe's praise was justified, more "Novarro revues" would be forthcoming, though on a less sumptuous scale.

After its elegant premiere, the Teatro Intimo was mainly used for smaller productions attended only by Spanish-speaking close friends and relatives— as Herbert Howe once observed, the Samaniegos, like most traditional upper-class Mexican families, "cling to the adage that there are no friends like the old friends, and thru the habit of living *en famille* they find the companionship of home sufficient." Novarro usually limited his efforts to organizing the productions of one-act playlets he himself had adapted from Spanish plays and novels, while friends and family members took part as performers. Because of the limited seating capacity, the invitations were strictly personal. Motion pictures, in Novarro's own words, would "never enter this theater," while film celebrities were invited only for special events, such as a night in honor of Louis Graveure in the summer of 1927.

Graveure's evening also marked Novarro's public debut as a singer. "Out of the darkness came the glory chant of the Ave Maria," described *Photoplay.* "Then slowly the light of a vagrant moon found the face of the troubadour as kneeling, hand on heart, he sang his praise of the Queen of Heaven." Dressed in "striking costumes" and surrounded by sets created by light effects and drapery, Novarro sang "and visualized dramatically" a program of ten chants, lyrical ballads, and folk songs—six of them in Spanish, three in Italian, and one in French. After the presentation, dinner was served on the grounds. On exceptional occasions, such as the Graveure evening, Spanish-speaking friends of the family and Hollywood personalities, such as Irving Thalberg and wife Norma Shearer, ate at the same table, though family and film people did not usually mingle.

Novarro segregated areas of his life—professional, family, and sexual— in the same manner that he compartmentalized his morals. Just as he kept his homosexuality in a sealed compartment protected from his religious beliefs, he, for the most part, also maintained his show business life apart from his family, whereas gay friends, whether or not in the film business, occupied their own private realm. Sometimes those disparate groups shared the same space, as during a special Teatro Intimo celebration, but there would be only superficial contact between them. At such times, Novarro made little effort beyond the politely necessary to acquaint family members with Hollywood or gay friends, or vice versa. In the mid-1920s, the only frequent American guest and sole Hollywood personality Novarro allowed to cross over was Herbert Howe.

Novarro's parents and his more mature siblings conceivably knew the type of relationship he had with his publicist, though Novarro may have justified Howe's constant presence as a career requirement. Even so, explanations and justifications were likely unnecessary. Novarro, after all, was the de facto head of the household and the source of the family's material well-being. Every Samaniego was fully aware of that, and those siblings who momentarily forgot the fact were quickly reminded of it by Novarro himself. In addition, neither Novarro's parents nor his siblings would have spoken out about such a private issue.

Discretion was a cherished Samaniego trait; it would be exercised in matters professional as well as personal. "When any of my family like my pictures, they tell me so very sanely and quietly," Novarro told *Modern Screen* in 1931. As an example, he recalled the Los Angeles opening of *Ben-Hur,* when, instead of going to the premiere, he had dinner with Howe and then returned home while his family was at the show. Dressed in his best pair of silk lounging pajamas, Novarro "waited, so excited I could hardly sustain my imitation of a bored star awaiting expected praise"—though none was forthcoming that evening. After arriving home, instead of barging into his bedroom to finally declare their realization that Ramón Gil Samaniego had become a bona fide superstar, his parents and siblings went straight to bed. The next morning, they commended both the picture and his work in it in a cordial but unobtrusive manner.

Likewise, if some of the Samaniegos speculated about why the twenty-seven-year-old heartthrob in their midst spent most of his free time with his "devoutly pagan" publicist instead of with a nice Catholic Mexican girl, they kept their reservations to themselves.

In the early fall of 1926, while *A Certain Young Man* lay temporarily shelved, Novarro began work on *The Great Galeoto*, an adaptation of the 1881 play *El Gran Galeoto* by the Nobel Prize–winning Spanish playwright José Echegaray y Eizaguirre. For this film, Novarro and his favorite actress, Alice Terry, were reunited on-screen for the last time.

Terry had spent the latter half of 1924 and part of 1925 in California, appearing in four productions, including the highly successful outdoors romance *The Great Divide*. She had fought for a salary increase that, at $2,000 a week, placed her among the highest-paid MGM performers of the mid-1920s, even though the studio did not officially "star" her in its productions. During that busy period, Terry's marriage to Rex Ingram nearly came to an end. The director's nervous breakdown after *The Arab* and the couple's long-term separation—Ingram refused to come to Hollywood—placed a heavy strain on their union. Eventually, the marital turmoil subsided, and, with her Hollywood film commitments ended, Terry returned to France to work for her husband in *Mare Nostrum* and *The Magician*.

While Ingram prepared their next production, *The Garden of Allah*, Terry sailed back to the United States to appear in *The Great Galeoto*—for which her salary had been raised to $3,000 a week, plus miscellaneous personal expenses. Before filming began, however, she had to go on one of her perennial diets. Upon her return, *Photoplay* had sneered that "it looks as though Alice were headed for the circus," but by the time the cameras were ready to roll, Terry was, once again, back to her normal on-screen weight.

John M. Stahl, a hard taskmaster who liked to shoot a single scene numerous times using different angles, was assigned to direct *The Great Gal-*

eoto—the first (and only) time Novarro and Terry worked together under the guidance of someone other than Ingram. Thalberg believed that Stahl, renowned for his deft handling of domestic melodramas, possessed the right touch to bring to life this story about a Spanish family destroyed by malicious gossip. (In the Arthurian legends, Galeoto, or Galahalt was the go-between for Lancelot and Guinevere.) Set in modern Madrid, *The Great Galeoto* tells the story of an old diplomat (veteran character actor Edward Martindel) who loses his trust in both his young second wife (Terry) and his son (Novarro) after gossip spreads that the young man and his stepmother have fallen in love.

Not long after production began, filming was halted after Novarro collapsed at the studio. The first reports had him suffering from the flu, but his illness turned out to be a serious case of food poisoning. Novarro's temperature reached 105 degrees that night, but despite the ordeal, he was back on the set in a week. From then on, the making of *The Great Galeoto* proceeded uneventfully.

In later years, Terry asserted that her favorite screen lovers had been the Latins, for when it came to Anglo-Saxons, "I'd as soon have a chair as the typical man." Of those she had worked with, Novarro was

the best actor of all. I think there was no picture that you could've put him in that he couldn't have reached to every scene and I think the others couldn't have. I think that Valentino was so much a type that he couldn't have played certain scenes. . . . [Lewis] Stone was an actor. . . . He played every scene well, but there was never any height to it. Tony Moreno was a good actor, but . . . I couldn't have seen him in certain parts. Ramon, I could have seen in almost any part outside of an American boy. And I think he had more ham in him— I don't like to use the word ham. Maybe it's nerve or maybe confidence . . . to get up and try something where someone like [Ronald] Colman, for instance, wouldn't try because he'd feel silly. But Ramon would attempt anything—comedy, drama, crazy scenes, anything, and he could do it. I always thought he was capable of doing better than almost anyone possibly besides [John] Barrymore, who I think had the same thing.

During the filming of *The Great Galeoto*, it was rumored that the versatile Novarro was to star as Romeo, a role that had been announced for both Valentino and Douglas Fairbanks a few years earlier. Ernst Lubitsch was reportedly offered the directorial job, while Juliet would be played by Norma

Shearer. At about the same time, other rumors had Novarro and *The Phantom of the Opera* heroine Mary Philbin appearing in another version of *Romeo and Juliet* for Universal. Neither production materialized. "The [MGM] Eastern office had to be consulted, and they consulted their salesmen, who consulted the exhibitors, who consulted I don't know who," an unhappy Novarro remarked. "Anyway, *Romeo and Juliet* is not being produced. You begin to feel, after a few adventures in this maze, that you are up against a monster without a head." As for the Universal version, Louis B. Mayer refused to loan Novarro.

Besides losing Romeo, Novarro also lost Jesus. Mayer refused to loan out his prized star for the title role in Cecil B. DeMille's independently made *The King of Kings,* as Novarro was set to start work on *Old Heidelberg* shortly after finishing *The Great Galeoto.* The timing was unfortunate. *The King of Kings* might have become the professional boost Novarro needed after the disastrous *A Certain Young Man* and the small-scale *The Great Galeoto.* Ultimately, the role of Jesus went to veteran stage and screen actor H. B. Warner.

Following the enormous success of Erich von Stroheim's *The Merry Widow,* Irving Thalberg was said to have offered the director another operetta to be translated to the silent screen, Sigmund Romberg's *The Student Prince in Heidelberg* (officially, the MGM picture—named *Old Heidelberg*—was to be an adaptation of Wilhelm Meyer-Förster's novel *Karl Heinrich,* the original source of the tale). The iconoclastic von Stroheim, however, declined this project about a prince torn between his love for a commoner and his duty to his country, opting instead to direct the similarly themed *The Wedding March* for independent producer Pat Powers—and thus away from Thalberg's close supervision.

After failing to secure recent German import E. A. Dupont and MGM contract director John S. Robertson (who preferred directing Lillian Gish in *Annie Laurie*), Thalberg settled on the thirty-four-year-old, Berlin-born Ernst Lubitsch—an odd choice for the assignment despite his German background. Although in 1919 Lubitsch had directed the successful *Die Austernprinzessin,* inspired by Leo Fall's operetta *Die Dollarprinzessin,* the reputation of Lubitsch's German period rested on his historical pageants, whereas in Hollywood he was known for his sophisticated boudoir comedies. That may well have been Thalberg's intention: to bring in a sophisticated "alien" talent to refine and revitalize an old genre. As the assigned star, Novarro must have been pleased. While shooting *Ben-Hur* in Rome, he had expressed his "earnest ambition to work under the direction of Mr. Lubitsch, who is unquestionably a genius of the new art, the supreme master in the reincarnating of history."

Lubitsch had been brought to the United States by Mary Pickford, whom he directed in *Rosita*. He then moved to Warner Bros., where his relatively expensive films garnered much prestige but little profits. After reaching an agreement with Warners to cancel the remainder of his contract, the director accepted MGM's offer, bringing in his frequent collaborator Hans Kräly to write the adaptation.

Filming began in December 1926 with Jean Hersholt as the young prince's kind professor and Norma Shearer, Thalberg's then girlfriend and future wife, as the leading lady. In five years, the Canadian-born, highly ambitious Shearer had risen from the ranks of bit players to become one of MGM's top performers, generally portraying either naive young maidens or sophisticated women of the world in a series of popular moderate-budget productions. By the time filming began on *Old Heidelberg*, the twenty-five-year-old star was making $2,000 a week and was well on her way to being crowned Queen of the Lot.

Novarro's and Shearer's previous credits notwithstanding, Lubitsch was dissatisfied with their choices. Editor Andrew Marton later noted that Lubitsch "never thought that Ramon Novarro or Norma Shearer was the right casting for the film, but the studio insisted and he was stuck with them." It remains a mystery why the director thought the capable and charming Shearer lacked the necessary qualities to play the enamored barmaid Kathi, but to his mind, Novarro lacked the Teutonic looks the role demanded. MGM disagreed.

If Mary Pickford and Greta Garbo could play Spanish señoritas in *Rosita* and *The Torrent* respectively, and Austrian-born Ricardo Cortez could become known as a Latin Lover, then Novarro certainly could play a Germanic character. He had already convincingly portrayed the Central European Rupert of Hentzau, and though his hair and eyes were dark, his skin was quite fair. Especially after Lord Brinsley of *A Certain Young Man*, the boyish and earnest Prince Karl Heinrich must have seemed ideal casting.

In spite of the story's light touch, filming was at times tense. *Old Heidelberg* was Lubitsch's first picture for MGM, Novarro's first major production since *Ben-Hur*, and Shearer's first prestige assignment personally supervised by Thalberg since the beginning of their romantic involvement. It was crucial for director and stars that *Old Heidelberg* be a success.

One problem during shooting was that neither performer was used to the director's methods. Novarro remembered that if the desired result was not achieved, Lubitsch would announce, "I'll do it again—and again." According to Novarro, Lubitsch once shot one take 102 times until he was completely satisfied. Other Lubitsch methods that disturbed the two leads included reducing rehearsal time to enhance spontaneity, and explaining scenes by acting them out in his thick German accent. (Mary Pickford, who felt an intense dislike for Lubitsch, called him a "frustrated actor.")

Lubitsch also displeased MGM because of his Stroheim-like expenditures. Costume designer Ali Hubert arrived from Europe with thirty-two trunks of apparel and accessories to comply with the director's demand for authenticity. Once the studio scenes were finished, Lubitsch traveled to Germany to shoot exteriors, though, according to Andrew Marton, none of that footage was used in the final edit. After 108 production days, costs had soared to $1,205,000, an amount well above the studio average even for a prestige picture. Retitled *The Student Prince in Old Heidelberg*, Novarro's latest became MGM's costliest picture since *Ben-Hur*. (As a comparison, the 1924 release *Three Women*, Lubitsch's most expensive Warners production, had cost a relatively paltry $329,000.)

Another—alleged—problem was that Lubitsch exasperated Novarro by subtly needling him about his homosexuality. In Lawrence Quirk's biography of Norma Shearer, the author quotes director King Vidor as saying that Lubitsch shot several takes of an uncomfortable Novarro performing a buddy scene with an effeminate extra, a sequence that was later cut by Thalberg. Quirk also asserts that during a 1960 interview he conducted with Novarro, the actor's face "darkened" when he mentioned Lubitsch and *The Student Prince*. "It was not one of my favorite films," Novarro is quoted as saying, "and Lubitsch certainly wasn't my kind of director. I know he did well with others, but he was wrong for me. We just didn't have simpatico, and I was glad when it was over with." These harsh remarks are not corroborated elsewhere; in fact, Novarro stated in the late 1950s that working with Lubitsch had been "grand, perfect," naming the director as the most influential figure in his career after Rex Ingram.

At the time *The Student Prince* wrapped up in April 1927, *The Great Galeoto*, now renamed *Lovers?*, opened in New York on April 9 to mixed reviews. Whereas Mordaunt Hall of the *New York Times* called it "an absorbing picture," *Motion Picture News* thought it "too dull, spiritless . . . [and] overbalanced with its romance." *Variety* praised the picture's look but panned the director and the script. Novarro and Alice Terry, however, received generally positive notices. Indeed, this first post–*Ben-Hur* Novarro release, now a lost film, set a pattern that would last, with few exceptions, for the rest of his career as a star: the picture would receive either mixed or negative reviews, while Novarro's notices remained overwhelmingly positive.

Shortly after finishing *The Student Prince*, Novarro—whose weekly salary had recently been raised to $5,000—embarked on another picture, *Romance*, from the 1903 adventure novel by Joseph Conrad and Ford Maddox Hueffer (later Ford Maddox Ford). Dorothy Farnum, who had written the screen adaptation of Rafael Sabatini's swashbuckler *Bardelys the Magnificent*, was assigned to transpose to the screen the adventures of a dashing Englishman who rescues a young heiress from the hands of a cunning pirate.

From the start, *Romance* had been intended as a Novarro vehicle. In view of the *A Certain Young Man* fiasco, Dorothy Farnum noted that "it has been difficult for the adapter to think of Mr. Novarro as an English gentleman. He has seemed to be more—the Mexican Caballera [*sic*] of Mystery, a vagabond soul, Adventurer of high degree in search of romance." Thus, the English hero was transformed into a Spaniard, while the story itself developed more than a passing resemblance to *Zorro*.

Josephine Lovett later took over screenwriting duties from Farnum (a common procedure, as scripts went through numerous uncredited hands before achieving their final versions), while her husband and frequent collaborator, John S. Robertson, was hired as director. Robertson, who had been responsible for several Richard Barthelmess hits, was an appropriate choice, given his previous experience with swashbucklers (*The Fighting Blade, Annie Laurie*) and seafaring tales (*Captain Salvation*). As the romantic interest, King Vidor's wife and ascending MGM player Eleanor Boardman was the initial choice, but the studio finally opted for Marceline Day, a delicate, brown-haired, blue-eyed beauty fresh from the popular *Captain Salvation* and from being named one of the Baby Stars of 1926 by the Western Associated Motion Picture Advertisers (Wampas).

The Road to Romance—MGM's fancier title for its adaptation of Conrad and Hueffer's novel—opened shortly after the September 21 release of *The Student Prince in Old Heidelberg*. Although notices for the seafaring melodrama were considerably worse than those for *The Student Prince*, the unkind reviews of the latter film were especially disheartening. After all, *The Student Prince* was not only the studio's costliest picture that year, but it had also been handled by one of the industry's foremost directors.

Variety bluntly complained that Lubitsch had been "miscast" in his first MGM production, taking "any kick right out of the picture, if any were there in the script for him." On the positive side, Mordaunt Hall called *The Student Prince* a "splendid shadow story," and Richard Watts, Jr., contended that "the picture does for wistful romance what Stroheim's *The Merry Widow* did for that of a more earthly type." *Photoplay* opted for a curious middle ground, praising the leading man and the picture while panning the leading lady and the director.

The best-acting honors went to Jean Hersholt's kindly Dr. Jüttner. Shearer's notices ranged from "she has never done better work in her life" to complaints that she was completely out of her element. As for Novarro, some critics remarked that he was too Latin-looking for the role, and *Variety* criticized his "ghastly" makeup, but even then, the star's notices were almost invariably positive. "This is the best work that Ramon Novarro has ever done," *Life's* Robert E. Sherwood observed. "It is comparable with the best work that any one has ever done on the screen."

Shortly before his death, Lubitsch declared in a letter to biographer Herman Weinberg that his "essential" American silent films were *The Marriage Circle*, *Lady Windermere's Fan*, *The Patriot*, and *Kiss Me Again*. His exclusion of *The Student Prince* is bewildering, as that film remains one of his finest, silent or not. The plot is slight, but Lubitsch's delicate touch results in a series of lyrical moments made particularly affecting by the wistful finale (luckily, Lubitsch, backed by Shearer, retained the original ending against MGM's wishes). Despite his misgivings, the director also succeeded with his stars, for Novarro and Shearer give poignant and fully believable characterizations in roles that could easily have turned coy and saccharine. Ironically, this silent film version of the operetta remains far more compelling than the flat 1954 remake.

On October 8—the date of the general release of the acclaimed *Ben-Hur*—*The Road to Romance* premiered to mostly mediocre notices. "One must like Novarro a lot to like the picture," commented *Variety*, "but those who do, will. Otherwise it's too grossly exaggerated [and] . . . has too many holes in the tale." Novarro, as usual, fared better than the picture, which he himself thought "inconsequential." And since *The Road to Romance* is another lost film, modern audiences cannot witness the star doing "a neat bit as a nance" to deceive the scheming pirate in a court scene akin to the Zorro/Don Diego masquerade. Novarro, who in his later films sometimes seemed slightly effeminate without trying, must have been amusing as a masculine hero pretending to be an effete weakling.

Novarro's first year on screen since *Ben-Hur* (he had had no releases in 1926) had proven to be a disappointing one. Meanwhile, his MGM competitors had brought the studio huge box-office receipts. Lon Chaney's *Mr. Wu* and *Tell It to the Marines* earned MGM more than $1 million each worldwide, while John Gilbert sizzled in his two pairings with Greta Garbo, *Flesh and the Devil* and *Love*, both of which, along with *La Bohème*, also surpassed the million-dollar mark internationally. In addition, the MGM roster now had a fourth male star, William Haines, the wisecracking romantic lead of *Tell It to the Marines*.

Novarro's films, on the other hand, had failed to live up to the studio's— and his own—expectations. In spite of its popularity (nearly $1.6 million in worldwide rentals), *The Student Prince* ended $307,000 in the red because of its high cost. In contrast, all of Chaney's and Gilbert's million-dollar-plus grossers resulted in hefty profits for the studio. *Lovers?* showed a relatively minor profit of $104,000, which left *The Road to Romance* as Novarro's only solidly profitable 1927 release, though, at $202,000, it was still well below the numbers for Chaney's and Gilbert's most lucrative efforts.

Novarro's career was not falling into a downward spiral, but neither was it advancing as he might have expected following his *Ben-Hur* triumph. Creating further concern for his professional future, the sound revolution was fast overtaking the industry. Novarro had a fine and well-trained voice, but there was widespread fear that performers who spoke English with a pronounced accent would be doomed if sound pictures became the norm. Compounding problems, as the decade neared its end, Novarro was to find himself enmeshed in a series of personal tragedies. These not only would lead him to reconsider his life choices, but would also bring about a profound change in the lighthearted young man from Durango that was to last until his death.

EIGHT

Crossroads

Following the October 6, 1927, release of Warner Bros.' part-talkie *The Jazz Singer*, industry insiders gradually realized that silent films were doomed. In the next two years, sound was to represent either a blessing or a curse to motion picture performers, depending on their ability to deal with the microphone. For Novarro, it could represent both. Sound would allow him to display his singing skills on film, but the new technology would also make his Mexican accent clearly apparent, and thus seriously limit his choice of roles.

Even before the sound revolution, Novarro had considered giving up Hollywood for a musical career. Besides the desire to fulfill a long-cherished childhood dream to appear in opera, he had grown increasingly disillusioned with his post–*Ben-Hur* film career. While he (and Herbert Howe) talked in print about his desire to play in a life story of Leonardo da Vinci, to portray thirteenth-century Catalan mystic Ramón Llull, and to star in a film version of André Maurois's *Ariel—Life of Shelley*, the studio (with the exception of *The Student Prince*) repeatedly cast him in mundane roles in equally mundane pictures. "Disappointments only came after I had achieved what then I considered as a success," Novarro told Howe in 1927. "I always looked forward to the time—which is now—when I could be free to do great things. But I am no freer to do them now than I was then."

Thus, Novarro continued with his vocal training, which would improve his elocution and diction if talking pictures became a reality, and, most important, would give him the necessary tools to pursue a career in opera, or at least on the concert stage. In fact, by the late 1920s his interest in music had become so dominant that acting was relegated to a distinctly subordinate status. "I am grateful to motion pictures," he told *Vanity Fair*, "because they have made it possible for me to study singing, which is about to open up a new career for me. Compared to music, the screen is so dissatisfying." For now, music seemed to offer Novarro his best professional possibilities, but the partial neglect of his film career was to prove costly.

In mid-December 1927, shortly after returning from a three-week New York vacation with his family, Novarro began working on his next picture, a new version of Ben Ames Williams's seafaring novel *All the Brothers Were Valiant*. Veteran William Nigh, who oscillated between high- and low-budget productions, was assigned to direct this high-end programmer initially called *China Bound* (later retitled *Across to Singapore*). Novarro was to portray Joel Shore, the youngest and best-looking of four sailor brothers (a part played by his old Metro rival Malcolm McGregor in that studio's 1923 version), while bulky character actor Ernest Torrence landed the role of the oldest and ugliest Shore brother. As the romantic interest, the studio cast producer Harry Rapf's discovery Joan Crawford, an ambitious young actress who had gone from bit player to leading lady in a year's time. Still several months prior to *Our Dancing Daughters* and film stardom, Crawford's role was merely decorative, but she and her leading man—who thought her "very endearing, sincere, buoyant"—worked well together.

Soon after production on the uneventful *Across to Singapore* ended in late January 1928, Novarro embarked on more retakes for *A Certain Young Man*, which had remained shelved since the fall of 1926. Those were done with a virtually new company because leading lady Sally O'Neil, director Hobart Henley, and key supporting player Carmel Myers were no longer with MGM. Of the original main cast, only Novarro and Renée Adorée were still at the studio. Joan Crawford was initially suggested as a replacement for O'Neil, but Marceline Day was awarded the part, while former actor George O'Hara took over directorial duties. The sections with Myers had to be reedited to match the retakes and revised story line, which now had Lord Gerald Brinsley as a womanizer tamed by his love for an American girl.

While *A Certain Young Man* was being reassembled, Novarro began working on the costume melodrama *The Loves of Louis*, later renamed *Forbidden Hours*. This had begun as a convoluted version of *The Man in the Iron Mask*, but after considerable rewriting, it was transformed into a rehash of *The Student Prince*—with a happy ending to enhance the picture's box-office appeal. Director Harry Beaumont, a recent MGM acquisition from Fox, was selected to handle this second pairing of Novarro with Renée Adorée, an actress

Novarro liked and respected. The lovely and gifted Adorée, who had been playing top supporting roles in major pictures and leads in programmers, was now receiving a major push to stardom as the feminine lead for the top male stars at the studio. In *Forbidden Hours,* she was to play a commoner for whom Novarro's King Michael IV of Balanca abdicates his crown—until plot machinations by scenarist A. P. Younger abruptly lead him back to the throne with the pretty plebeian at his side.

Since the fall of 1926, Novarro had worked on six films while continuing with his singing lessons and directing plays at the Teatro Intimo. With such a demanding schedule, he had little time or inclination to take part in Hollywood's social scene. "On a few occasions," he later recalled, "I was a guest at a dinner party at Pickfair [the royal residence of Mary Pickford and Douglas Fairbanks]—that was about it as far as parties went. I socialized with my mother, my brothers, and sisters." (Dr. Samaniego's health allowed for little socializing.) Left unmentioned were a few film personalities, such as a visiting Alice Terry, and Herbert Howe, with whom Novarro would spend nights at the Hollywood Bowl or at traditional Mexican restaurants in the downtown area. But despite Novarro's many professional commitments and his until then somewhat reclusive behavior, his constricted social circle expanded considerably after the effervescent Elsie Janis came onto the scene.

"What Bernhardt is to the stage, Elsie Janis is to vaudeville," proclaimed *Variety* about the slight, homely entertainer born Elsie Bierbower in Columbus, Ohio, on March 16, 1889. Goaded by a ferocious stage mother who once remarked, "There are Elsie Janises born every day, but not mothers to give up their whole lives for them," Janis began her show business career at an early age. She rapidly acquired a reputation as a celebrity impersonator, and by her midteens had developed into a major vaudeville star.

During World War I, Janis traveled overseas to entertain American troops at the front, becoming known as the "American Expeditionary Forces Sweetheart." Upon her return to the United States, she was decorated by General John Pershing, appeared in a couple of films, and toured with a cast of exservicemen in the highly successful revue *Elsie and Her Gang.* As her stage career slowed down in the late 1920s, Janis, now approaching forty, came to Hollywood to work as a screenwriter. After watching Novarro's performance in *Ben-Hur,* she arranged for an introduction, and quickly became his frequent social companion. "It was Elsie Janis who brought me out of my shell," Novarro later recalled. "She kept after me until I was almost forced to go out escorting her. She introduced me to [actress] Ruth Chatterton, and when I did go to parties, it was usually to escort Miss Janis, Miss

Chatterton, or Beth Fairbanks, the first wife of Doug Senior, whom I liked."

Despite Novarro's newfound duty as a party escort to sundry females, Janis remained his premier social partner. Not surprisingly, rumors—probably fanned by MGM—soon surfaced that the couple were more than just good chums, with one article asserting that Novarro thought the pert entertainer "one of the world's ideal women." Novarro, as usual, either ignored or discredited those stories, but Janis's private reaction to the rumors and her personal feelings for Novarro are unclear. In her interviews, she stressed their friendship and nothing else, while Novarro is barely mentioned in her 1932 autobiography *So Far So Good!*

Recent rumors that Janis was a lesbian, which would imply that she and Novarro used each other as beards, are apparently based on the fact that the tomboyish performer (in *A Girl Like I,* screenwriter Anita Loos quipped that boys' clothes "always suited [Janis] better than girls'") married only in her forties. However, no evidence can be found that Janis had homosexual inclinations. Though hardly the most reliable of Hollywood chroniclers, Anita Loos remembered that Janis "was always romantically involved with whatever leading man happened to be playing opposite her," including actor Walter Pidgeon. Janis herself recalled in her autobiography having fallen in love with numerous men—some platonically, some not—among them British stage heartthrobs Owen Nares and Basil Hallam. Janis's prolonged unmarried state was most likely the result of her mother's overbearingness, not lesbianism—according to Helen Hayes, Mrs. Bierbower "did everything but take her daughter's bows." Janis, in fact, was married shortly after her mother's death.

Perhaps not coincidentally, Elsie Janis entered Novarro's life as Herbert Howe withdrew from it. Howe and Novarro would still see each other sporadically throughout the years, but by early 1928 the closeness of their personal and professional relationship had come to an end. Howe had stopped working for *Photoplay* in the summer of 1926, and from then on worked as a freelancer for publications such as the *Los Angeles Times* and *Motion Picture,* which in the first half of 1927 published the adulatory but insightful five-part piece "On the Road with Ramon." Later that year, Howe sold his Beverly Hills home to Joan Crawford and moved to a beach house in Ventura. He returned to *Photoplay* as a freelancer in 1928, but by then Novarro's name was conspicuously absent from his columns—a full-length article Howe wrote about a trip to Mexico, for instance, failed to include a single mention of his former companion. From then on, encomiums were replaced by jabs at Novarro's expense. One quiet disparagement, in *The New Movie Magazine*, referred to "a favorite of the fair [who] has never fallen for one of them" as one of the ironies of Hollywood.

The reasons for the Novarro-Howe split—in all likelihood an acrimonious one—remain cloudy. Howe's departure from *Photoplay* was surely unrelated to the end of his relationship with Novarro: the writer remained a respected Hollywood commentator and continued to promote his client in other venues, including the lengthy *Motion Picture* piece—later referred to by Novarro as "the finest write up a star could have had." Therefore, personal incompatibility seems the cause for the professional split, not vice versa, especially since Howe's liaison with Novarro was *first* personal and *then* professional. Or perhaps it was a mixture of both. Howe had definite ideas about Novarro's talents, and those did not match his client's—Howe would later criticize Novarro's choice of roles and say that Novarro's voice was inadequate for opera.

The relationship was thus quite possibly strained to the breaking point by disagreements about Novarro's career steps, coupled with Howe's temper, Novarro's (in Howe's words) "cool, detached, unsentimental" character, and his hectic schedule. Novarro would not allow anything or anyone to get in the way of his work, or, especially, in the way of his music. In an August 1931 article for *The New Movie Magazine*, Howe remembered how he "would become exasperated" when, during his European travels with Novarro, his companion would break up the party because it was time for his vocal training. Howe also observed, not without resentment, that "all Ramon requires of people is that they be a good audience. When he attends a party he looks for the piano, and before you know it he is singing and playing. Such a resourceful person makes a friend seem superfluous. Ramon craves music as most men crave love. That is why he is happier and more detached; he can always have music."

In that same *New Movie Magazine* article, Howe makes it clear that he wanted more from Novarro than Novarro could ever give him. "All of his emotions are adolescent," Howe wrote. "He never hates because he never loves too much," adding, "He is not a particularly good companion. As he often said: 'I have so little to give.' His life is expressed in acting, not in thought or conversation. You get the essence of him seeing him on the screen. Off the screen he is . . . a theater with the lights out."

Placing further strain on the Novarro-Howe relationship, the actor had to cope with serious family difficulties. Sometime in 1927, Señora Samaniego had noticed an anomalous growth on her son José's left side. José, then a twenty-one-year-old agronomy student at the California Agricultural College at Davis, assured her that the lump was just a temporary result of injuries he had suffered while playing football. But when the growth did not heal, the family urged him to consult with a doctor cousin. After a biopsy revealed a malignant tumor, José was forced to undergo surgery. In time, he recovered and returned to Davis, but his health drastically deteriorated in the winter of 1928.

In the spring, Novarro sailed for Europe on the French liner *DeGrasse* to meet his parents, two siblings, and his uncle Ramón Guerrero, a close family relative. At the last minute, Novarro had decided to bring José along with him because the young man was upset about an upcoming physical checkup. Most of the family had already crossed the Atlantic in late 1927, having planned their trip so they could spend extra time visiting with the Samaniego nuns, Sisters Guadalupe (née Rosa) and Leonor, both of whom were working at a Madrid hospital.

When the two brothers met up with the other family members, José looked so emaciated that some of the Samaniegos at first failed to recognize him. In fact, José had become so ill during the voyage that he was admitted to a hospital for an operation the day after their arrival in Spain. Further difficulties arose when the incision failed to mend, prompting Señora Samaniego to travel to Lourdes to ask the Virgin Mary for help. Soon afterward, the wound began healing, but the relief would prove only temporary. X-ray treatments José later received in Paris further weakened him.

Before returning with his family to the United States in the early summer, Novarro traveled on his own to Rex Ingram and Alice Terry's villa in the south of France. Their reunion must have been a bittersweet one. José's illness was casting a pall over Novarro's spirits, and the three old partners were equally dissatisfied with their professional paths. Long-term film commitments—*Ben-Hur* and *The Student Prince*—and myriad other (unfulfilling) endeavors at Culver City had prevented Novarro from collaborating with his mentor and his favorite screen partner in any of their European projects.

As for Ingram, despite reports in the American press that he was too busy in Nice to return to Hollywood, the truth was that the thirty-five-year-old director's career had suffered a downturn after his move to Europe. Ingram's 1926 release *Mare Nostrum* was considerably reedited before its American premiere and, according to *Photoplay,* did not receive the strong push the studio had given King Vidor's *The Big Parade.* Indeed, by the late 1920s Vidor had replaced Ingram as MGM's foremost director. Not surprisingly, *The Garden of Allah,* which opened in 1927, turned out to be Ingram's last venture for MGM despite the picture's robust profits. The director refused to return to Hollywood, and MGM refused to deal with a contract talent living and working six thousand miles from the studio gates. As a result of his shakier professional ground, Ingram's notorious short temper worsened, which led to the desertion of numerous old friends and professional partners.

Alice Terry was also unwilling to remain attached to MGM or any other studio, but for different reasons than her husband's. The twenty-nine-year-old actress was simply tired of both filmmaking and having to worry about her figure. Burdened by rigorous diets whenever she had to face the camera, Terry was ready to quit acting and devote herself to a life of epicurean pleasures. Additionally, she was keeping herself occupied with eighteen-year-old Gerald Fielding, a British actor who had a small part in *The Garden of Allah*. Motion pictures had long lost their importance to her.

Now that neither Ingram nor Terry was associated with MGM, chances of a professional reunion with Novarro—to his regret—no longer existed.

Upon his return to California in mid-July, Novarro continued to brood over his film career. *Across to Singapore* had opened on April 29 to mostly mediocre reviews. Calling the seafaring picture "six or seven reels of highly dramatic violence," *Variety* complained that it lacked a coherent plot and character development, an opinion seconded by the *New York Times*'s Mordaunt Hall, who stated that "the story as a whole is frequently artificial and forced, and therefore unconvincing." Ernest Torrence stole the acting honors, while Novarro received some of his worst reviews to date. Although Mordaunt Hall considered him "quite good," numerous publications, including *Variety* and *Film Daily*, thought him badly miscast. In reality, though not believable as the younger brother of the big, Anglo-Saxon Torrence, Novarro has some good moments in this programmer, especially in the early comic scenes. If his performance is below the standard of some of his previous efforts, it is because this disjointed tale provides little opportunity for well-rounded acting. Unfortunately, he would not fare any better with his next picture.

On June 9, a drastically reedited *A Certain Young Man* finally reached the screen. It was well known within Hollywood that this latest Novarro vehicle had been beset by complications, but MGM seemed to have a talent for successfully rescuing problematic productions—*Ben-Hur* being the most notable example. Nevertheless, in the case of Novarro and *A Certain Young Man*, the studio was not nearly as successful.

"The result is not bad, although plenty of details give a hint of what a palooka it probably was when first turned out," remarked *Variety*, whereas Mordaunt Hall found *A Certain Young Man* "very amusing and very shallow." Inevitably, Novarro was adversely compared to Adolphe Menjou, Hollywood's idea of the sophisticated man-of-the-world, whose *A Gentleman of Paris* (a more faithful adaptation of *Bellamy the Magnificent*) had opened the previous October. *Variety* commended the changes made to Lord Brinsley, as Novarro was too "boyish in type, stature and personality to make much of an impression attempting a Menjou," but even then, many critics thought the star seriously miscast.

Novarro himself abhorred his—now lost—womanizing Englishman. "In acting, in directing, in everything—I want to be *definite*," he told *Modern Screen* in April 1931. "Even when I am later proven wrong—it will at least have been so definite that I myself know it. I am responsible for the worst performance that has ever been given on the screen. It was in *A Certain Young Man* and it was terrible. I am mortally ashamed of it—yet I'd rather have been that bad than just fair."

Audiences, however, thought that "that bad" was much worse than "just fair." Ads captioned "HE LOVED the ladies!" showed a mustached Novarro exploding heart-shaped balloons with a cigarillo and removing women from his top hat, but they failed to lure filmgoers in the United States and abroad. Ultimately, *A Certain Young Man* made less money domestically than any other Novarro vehicle for MGM, excepting the 1934 release *Laughing Boy*, and it earned Novarro's fourth weakest rentals abroad. The picture lost only $50,000 because of its relatively low cost.

Forbidden Hours, the last 1928 Novarro release, opened on July 22 to even worse notices than those for *Across to Singapore* and *A Certain Young Man*. "A comic opera kingdom," blasted the *New York World*. "Lame vehicle limps along slowly through rehash of *Student Prince* and *Merry Widow* themes, lacks action and acting," panned *Film Daily*. "If you are one of those who can believe anything when the eyes of Renée Adorée become misty," commented the *New York Morning Telegraph*, "you are going to thoroughly enjoy *Forbidden Hours* . . . [but if you] can retain logic and sense through a close-up of [Adorée's teary eyes] you will find the story very trite, very unoriginal, and perhaps so improbable that it will verge on burlesque."

Even though Novarro received several good notices, including one from the *New York Times*, many critics felt that the star sank with the film, with the *New York Morning Telegraph* complaining that his "talents are totally lost" and the *New York Herald Tribune* asserting that his "acting lacked conviction." Even his appearance was panned. The *World* snidely remarked that Novarro wears a "uniform two sizes too tight for him," while the *New York Morning*

Telegraph quipped that he "runs around in the sauciest of uniforms and an air of surpassing ennui." In truth, Novarro's characterization suffers because of the absence of a plot. His attempts at being cute and likable initially work, but they soon become tiresome because that is all both Balanca's King Michael IV and *Forbidden Hours* have to offer.

Despite the mostly poor reviews, both *Across to Singapore* and *Forbidden Hours* did brisk business in the United States, though the latter was unexplainably one of Novarro's most disappointing releases overseas. The profits brought in by *Across to Singapore*, more than $300,000, were Novarro's highest since *The Midshipman*, but that was offset by the flop of *A Certain Young Man* and the disappointing returns of *Forbidden Hours*, especially in view of its low cost. In the meantime, Lon Chaney's and John Gilbert's vehicles continued to earn the studio considerable sums. Chaney's lowest profit that year was $387,000 for *Big City*, while Gilbert's lowest was $174,000 for *The Cossacks*, a picture that had cost nearly two and a half times more than either *Singapore* or *Forbidden Hours*.

The problem was not with Novarro, but with the studio's choice of roles, which had one of its top stars playing against type in both *A Certain Young Man* and *Forbidden Hours*. As one reviewer remarked, Novarro had "for a long while been seen as a good little boy, the sort you like to introduce to mother. But Ramon, like the leopard, is changing his cinematic spots and is turning out to be a lounge roué—in a 'ruffined' [*sic*] way, of course." MGM, however, was uncertain how to present the new Novarro. In *A Certain Young Man*, he starts the film as a lady-killer only to revert to his old persona after falling in love halfway through the film, while his king Michael IV in *Forbidden Hours* begs his beloved's forgiveness immediately after attempting to rape her. "They made me play two or three characters in a picture instead of one," Novarro later complained. "I might be a nasty boy, but if I fell in love it could not be in a nasty way; I must be noble." After this series of disappointing films, Novarro was now certain that Louis B. Mayer and Irving Thalberg, unlike Rex Ingram, had no idea how best to use his talents.

Unable to work again for his mentor and with his favorite actress, frustrated with MGM's choice of roles, depressed over his brother's illness, anxious about his uncertain future in opera, and now without Herbert Howe by his side, Novarro suffered a marked change in attitude. Even as he intensified his socializing—the private young man of bygone days now relished being the life of any party—Novarro considered renouncing not just the screen, but also music, fame, wealth, friends, and family to join a Catholic brotherhood.

· · ·

Rumors about Novarro's yearning to enter a monastery had often circulated in the press, including Herbert Howe's columns. Such suggestions added an aura of mystery to the handsome film star, made him seem more like his larger-than-life screen characters, and helped explain his long-standing bachelorhood. "I have a theory of my own about Novarro," wrote Novarro's friend and columnist Harry Carr. "At first it seemed so strange and outlandish, I have hesitated to tell it to anyone. I am firmly convinced that this boy is the window through which the light and the learning of a people long since vanished from the earth shines again." In a 1930 *Motion Picture* article, columnist Gladys Hall seconded Carr's inflated, solemn tones. "One can perceive about this dark, young head the cowl of the monk, the background of stained glass, the dim odors of sanctuary, organ pipes—a crucifix," Hall contemplated. "Music and solitude—these are the passions of him who knows no earthly passions and never has."

Purple prose notwithstanding, Novarro's devotion to his church and to spirituality in general was genuine. Despite fame and material success, his spiritual aspirations had remained an intrinsic part of his life. Soon after the foundation of El Retiro San Iñigo in 1925, Novarro had begun visiting this Jesuit retreat in Northern California, where, at first, he sought time away from professional and personal demands, conversed with the priests, and practiced the spiritual exercises that were meant to expand his responsiveness to himself, to his God, and to others. "Oh, that place up there," he told *Screen Play*, "I love it very much. There is always trouble during the making of a picture. There are always things happening unexpectedly which are upsetting. When I come home from there, everything seems so much more beautiful."

Tormented by the present and apprehensive of the future, in mid-1928 Novarro considered taking holy orders at El Retiro, but his inquiries were rebuffed. "Ramón was a very complicated person," remembered his sister Carmen. "He had a spiritual yearning of some kind, but he was told he didn't have a vocation." His rejection was plausibly a result of his fame and Hollywood background, though those in charge of the retreat perhaps felt that Novarro, in his attempt to escape from the outside world, was simply unqualified for Jesuit life.

According to Carmen, Novarro accepted the refusal with little grief. "After all, life is nothing without religion," he told *Photoplay*, "but doing your work and your duty *is* religion. No one goes free. Even though I entered this monastery I should probably find something which would prevent me from the absolute freedom I have been seeking. To go into the priesthood in order to avoid the worries of the world would make me a coward rather than a helper for my religion."

Novarro later illustrated his understanding about his place in life with a parable Señora Samaniego had told him during his childhood: "A priest went to the Sacred Heart and pleaded for a new cross, claiming that the one which he carried was too heavy. The Sacred Heart took him to a room which contained all of Life's crosses. 'Choose!' he instructed. The priest looked at each one. Huge crosses, small crosses, medium-sized crosses. In one corner, far away by itself, a cross so small it could scarcely be distinguished. 'I will take this one,' he offered. 'And that is the one you are already bearing,' the Sacred Heart responded."

"And I knew that my cross was like that," Novarro observed. "I knew that I should give of whatever talents I have through the motion pictures which have helped to develop them for me. In them I can sing as well as act and, when I can no longer sing or act, I can direct singing pictures. I will secure a contract which allows me to work six months and study languages and my religion during the others. I shall no longer long for the one thing or the other. I shall blend them all by remaining in motion pictures. . . . I'll still be under orders. I'll still have to do things which are unpleasant. But every song I sing will be perfect, every setting as beautiful as the best experts can make it."

Although he was never to take holy orders, religion and spirituality remained indispensable to Novarro for the rest of his life. His interest in religious and metaphysical literature continued undiminished, he donated money and artifacts to churches and Catholic causes, he continued attending spiritual retreats well into his fifties, and he periodically thought of joining a monastery. But in spite of his monastic aspirations, Novarro would have had a difficult time if he had joined a religious order, for his devoutness vacillated according to his emotional and psychological states. For some periods he would attend daily mass, and then he would not go at all; after alcohol had become a problem, he would remain sober during a spiritual retreat, but afterward go on a drinking binge. With the passing of the years, changes in Novarro's personality would also lead to a shift in his conception of religion and spirituality. The young man who had talked to Herbert Howe "about himself and God, not as the kaiser did, but more like [the simpleton stage character] Merton" would turn his "joyful illusioned" religious beliefs into increasingly onerous and oppressive dogmas.

. . .

With an existence behind monastery walls no longer an option, Novarro's interests returned to things of this world. If his film career had been generally disappointing in the last two years, sound promised expanded possibilities for a musical career on film. "I am very proud of the industry to which I belong," Novarro asserted. "There has been so much advancement, and even greater development to come. The people who are willing to learn, to work and prepare themselves for talking pictures will last, the others will disappear. I'm very glad now that I studied voice." The old "All's for the best" adage had resurfaced, at least in regard to his profession—thus, his rejection from El Retiro could mean only that greater opportunities awaited him on the talking screen. Still, MGM was far behind Warner Bros. and other studios in sound-recording technology because both Thalberg and Mayer had initially thought that sound pictures would be merely a passing novelty.

Instead of being cast in a musical (or in a previously announced adaptation of Thornton Wilder's *The Bridge of San Luis Rey*), Novarro began work on *Gold Braid*, a flag-waving action melodrama clearly intended to lift his box-office standing as *The Midshipman* had three years earlier. In fact, *Gold Braid* was a sequel of sorts to the earlier film, as the story begins the day before the midshipmen's graduation ceremony. The plot, a trifling excuse for the spectacular aerial sequences, focuses on the friendship and rivalry of navy pilots Tommy Winslow—Novarro's second "manly" American role—and Steve Randall, portrayed by the tall and handsome former Griffith leading man Ralph Graves. The object of the affections of both fliers was pretty eighteen-year-old newcomer Anita Page. George W. Hill, who had gained a reputation as an action director with the highly successful *Tell It to the Marines*, was assigned to handle this "silent" film with synchronized music score and sound effects.

Much of *Gold Braid* was filmed in late summer 1928 in the San Diego area, mostly at the Hotel del Coronado and at the local naval base. According to reports of the time, Novarro took flying lessons for his role, but that was undoubtedly studio publicity. His character's flying stunts were all performed by expert pilots, and all of Novarro's shots inside the cockpit were clearly filmed on the ground.

During those two months of filming, Novarro developed a solid rapport with Anita Page. Despite her Northern European looks—alabaster skin, blond hair, and blue eyes—Page was of mixed Spanish, English, and French ancestry, born Anita Pomares in Queens, New York. Like Joan Crawford,

Page was a Harry Rapf protégée who quickly graduated from bits to leading-lady status, and who was now being pushed to stardom by being cast opposite the studio's top male stars. Besides being young, pretty, and of Spanish heritage, Page was Catholic. Not surprisingly, rumors began circulating during the production of *Gold Braid* that she and Novarro were becoming more than just "good friends." The sweet-looking blonde certainly seemed a better aesthetic and cultural match for him than the older, plainer, and bouncier Elsie Janis. Page herself has stated that Novarro often announced to the crew that she was "the most beautiful girl in the world," and that during one love scene, they continued kissing long after director George Hill had yelled "Cut!" She has also asserted that Novarro went so far as proposing marriage to her while they were performing a romantic scene on the last day of filming. "We had this scene coming up," she recalled, "and he told me to play it like I really meant it. That's when he said, 'I love you, will you marry me?'" Page recalled that she jokingly brushed the offer aside, deeply disappointing Novarro. However, Page herself may have taken both Novarro's "marriage proposal" and his "disappointment" much too seriously.

Page has told film historian Michael Ankerich that on the first day of filming, Novarro invited her out on a date. But the attractive pair did not go alone. They were chaperoned by a young naval officer, who continued to accompany them in their meetings throughout the making of the picture. In this account, Page is merely a front for Novarro to go on dates with another man without incurring the curiosity of crew members and other production personnel. Being only eighteen, Page quite possibly mistook Novarro's friendliness and attention for true romantic interest. Hence, Novarro's "proposal" was in all likelihood nothing more than a joke related to the scene they were performing, or perhaps a way for the star to bring out from his inexperienced leading lady the emotional response the scene required.

According to Page, Novarro was not the only gay star at MGM who proposed to her. In William J. Mann's biography of William Haines, Page asserts that Haines asked for her hand in marriage during the filming of *Are You Listening?* in 1932. One day during production, she and Haines were "standing outside when all of a sudden he grabbed me and gave me a big kiss—I mean, he *really* kissed me." Haines then proposed to her, but she turned him down. Mann reasons that "it's quite possible, perhaps even likely" that the marriage proposal took place, even though Haines had a lover at the time and had never before played the studio's heterosexual game. By 1932, Haines's career had nosedived, and the former star may have thought that by playing by the rules he had once ignored he could persuade the

MGM front office to give him another chance. After the wedding, Anita Page's naïveté would help him maintain his sexual independence.

Such a solution would have been impossible for Novarro. He could use Page as a cover for his dates with the naval officer in San Diego, but for a devout Catholic man, the sacrament of marriage was to be taken seriously. Moreover, Novarro was under no pressure from the studio to marry Page or anyone else. Even if his recent vehicles had not been spectacularly profitable, Novarro *was* a major star—*Ben-Hur* was still playing to full houses—and would remain one for several more years. Haines's stardom, on the other hand, was considerably more ephemeral.

Born in Staunton, Virginia, on January 1, 1900, Haines had come to Hollywood in 1922 after winning a "New Faces" contest sponsored by Goldwyn Pictures. After a slow start, he became a star in 1926 with two of his archetypal performances: as the cocky and self-centered ballplayer who redeems himself at the end in *Brown of Harvard*, and later in the year, as the cocky and self-centered private who redeems himself at the end in *Tell It to the Marines*. Subsequently, he was cast in a series of cheaply made, lightweight programmers that earned considerable profits for MGM—the earnings of his vehicles actually surpassed Novarro's in 1928. But Haines's solid box-office record notwithstanding, the wisecracking star was not cast in prestige productions, possibly because his juvenile all-American appeal was stronger in suburbs and smaller towns. During his four years as an official MGM star, his only "event" picture was King Vidor's *Show People*, in which Haines played second fiddle to Marion Davies.

In private, Haines was relatively open about his sexual orientation in an era when the mere concept of homosexuality was almost invariably neither discussed nor understood. He made campy jokes and unceremoniously brought his lover Jimmie Shields, an ex-sailor five years his junior, both to the studio and to parties. (Shields was referred to in the press as "Billy Haines' best friend.") Publicity reports had Haines linked to screen sirens Barbara La Marr and Pola Negri, but when asked about girlfriends, Haines would reply that he was enamored of his friend Polly Moran, a parrot-nosed, bucktoothed comedienne seventeen years his senior.

One major problem with Haines's openness was that not everyone was accepting. Louis B. Mayer, for instance, disliked Haines's manner—his breeziness could come across as brashness—and the studio chief often tried to restrain the actor's offscreen behavior. In Mayer's view, MGM was a family unit that would be stigmatized if one of its members became enmeshed in scandal. The unlawfulness of homosexual acts in California made even cruising in public places a risky pastime, one that could potentially result in unwelcome lurid headlines.

One frequently repeated rumor had Haines involved in a sex scandal in 1925 that almost ruined his career. Worse yet for the studio, Novarro was also implicated. According to one version of the story, Lew Cody, MGM's he-vamp of the 1920s, upon hearing that Haines had called him "a stuffed shirt," went to Mayer and told the studio chief that Haines and Novarro were patronizing a male bordello on Wilshire Boulevard. Haines's career was only beginning at that time, and could easily have been terminated without heavy losses for the studio. Novarro, on the other hand, represented a hefty $4 million investment in the form of the as yet unreleased *Ben-Hur*. Thus, while Novarro was severely reprimanded by Mayer, Haines was to have his contract revoked. He was rescued by Marion Davies, who persuaded her lover, William Randolph Hearst, to intercede on Haines's behalf.

This tale, which is supposed to have been related in Anita Loos's auto-biographical *A Girl Like I*, has been retold as fact in several publications, even though the account is filled with inaccuracies and inconsistencies. Novarro was involved with Herbert Howe at the time and rarely socialized, as he was still enmeshed in the arduous *Ben-Hur* shoot; William Haines had not yet become friends with Marion Davies; Anita Loos began working at MGM only in the early 1930s; and, most conclusively, there is no mention of the male brothel incident in *A Girl Like I*.

Other rumors, those concerning a romantic liaison between Novarro and Haines in the mid-1920s, also seem farfetched. They would certainly have made an odd pair. While Haines was brassy and boisterous, Novarro was mild-mannered and discreet, especially regarding his sexuality. Opposite temperaments may sometimes attract, but not when one was as conscious about his public image as Novarro. Publicist Frank Lieberman later remembered Haines affirming that he and Novarro had never been close, as Novarro preferred to stick to himself. In fact, Haines and Novarro were never referred to as friends in reports of that time, nor was there any mention of their socializing together.

While Novarro worked on *Gold Braid*, MGM was drafting a new contract for him—he had already stipulated his demands, including a hefty salary raise and the guarantee of three consecutive vacation months each year during which he could perform onstage and make phonograph records. In early fall, he was called to Mayer's office and shown the new contract. He was told to read the document quickly, as the studio chief was leaving in half an hour for New York. Thalberg then walked in through a secret panel that connected his and Mayer's offices and immediately began playing with his key and chains "as was his wont when a little distraction was needed." Mayer, for his part, kept interrupting Novarro's reading with questions about his family. The star tried to ignore Mayer's and Thalberg's annoying behavior while endeavoring to finish reading the contract as rapidly as possible. Everything seemed to be in order until he encountered a provision that was not exactly to his liking: a clause that permitted him to do stage work and make records, but that did not allow him to promote these non-MGM undertakings by using his name, likeness, poses, or sounds.

Novarro stopped reading and glared at Mayer. "Does this also include farting?" he inquired. Mayer was shocked. Thalberg stopped fiddling with his keys. "How can I do anything if I am not allowed to advertise *me*, or what I can do besides act?" he continued. "No, Mr. Mayer, you just go to New York and have a good time. This contract needs revising, and I am sure that Mr. Thalberg and I will get together during your absence." Novarro then turned to Thalberg. He reminded the executive of the contract he had waived back in 1924, before leaving for Rome to appear for three months in *Ben-Hur*—a three-month production that took nineteen months to complete. He finished his contention by demanding a $100,000 bonus to make up for his wage loss during the *Ben-Hur* saga. Hearing this, Mayer rushed out of the room.

Novarro eventually received a $50,000 bonus, but he claimed, "I didn't mind, as I had a very profitable contract to counteract my loss." His October 5, 1928, agreement with MGM stipulated that he was to appear in five features for the studio from June 1929 to December 1930, with his salary starting at $75,000 for the first film and ending with $150,000 for the fifth. Other perks included the studio's commitment to "consult and cooperate with Novarro so far as is practical" in regard to material, players, and directors; to pay for his expenses whenever the star worked on a production away from Los Angeles; and to guarantee that Novarro's name appear in larger print than any other in ads and in the pictures themselves, except with his consent. Finally, MGM also granted him the right to make records and to appear onstage, in concerts, and on the radio without any restrictions regarding his promotion, apart from the demand that he always be billed as an MGM star.

On October 31, three weeks after signing the new contract, Novarro sailed for French Polynesia to appear in his last picture under the old contract, *The Pagan*, in which once again he was to play an innocent Pacific Islander created by author John Russell. Renée Adorée, eighteen-year-old newcomer Dorothy Janis, and frequent film villain (and sometimes director) Donald Crisp were the other principals in the cast. The assigned director was thirty-nine-year-old W. S. Van Dyke, an ex-lumberjack, prospector, and gold miner who had begun his film career as an assistant to D. W. Griffith on *Intolerance.* Edmund Goulding had been the studio's first choice, but Van Dyke's experience the year before with *White Shadows in the South Seas,* which he had taken over after the dismissal of documentarian Robert Flaherty, made him the more logical option.

Similar in theme to *White Shadows in the South Seas, The Pagan* presents European civilization as indisputably the villian—an uncommon approach in films of the period. On the surface, the story is about a carefree but wealthy half-caste, Henry Shoesmith, Jr., who attempts to please a ruthless white trader so he can romance the man's "Christian duty," a pretty half-caste girl. On a deeper level, *The Pagan* deals with the subversion of the island's way of life by white invaders, from their belief that the value of nature lies only in pounds and dollars to their imposition of an alien and unsuitable religion. Although both Novarro's and Janis's characters are part European, their behavior is all idealized Pacific Islander: playful and innocent. Renée Adorée's Madge is the only good white character, though, significantly, she is a prostitute and an outcast in her own Euro-Christian society. Frances Marion and Novarro himself wrote the initial treatments—he expressly wanted to emphasize that the "pagan" Henry Shoesmith behaved more like a Christian than the intolerant followers of Jesus—though Dorothy Farnum received the final adaptation credit. John Howard Lawson, one of the future Hollywood Ten, was responsible for the perceptive intertitles.

Van Dyke had promised to return from the South Pacific by Christmas so Novarro could prepare for a scheduled spring 1929 European opera debut. *White Shadows in the South Seas,* which had been shot in French Polynesia's Marquesas Islands, had shown the director the pitfalls of location shooting in that part of the globe, so Van Dyke felt confident that those same mistakes would be avoided while filming in the Paumotu (now Tuamotu) Archipelago farther south. Additionally, his background as a director of cheap quickies, mostly Westerns, had taught him how to work rapidly and efficiently, a practice he maintained even after being entrusted with bigger budgets. Yet, "One Take Woody" was unable to shoot *The Pagan* as planned, for incessant rains forced the company to stay idle for a full month. While waiting for the weather to clear, Novarro attended church, visited the local art colony, and practiced his music. "Give him any sort of stringed instrument and a crowd of natives," Van Dyke later recalled, "and he was a native himself."

Managing to compensate for the long stretch of bad weather with twelve-hour working days, seven days a week, the company returned home on December 23. "It was quite a pleasant trip, nevertheless," Novarro told reporters upon his arrival, "but California looks mighty good just the same." At the Gramercy household, however, things looked anything but "mighty good."

Novarro's ailing brother José had been bedridden since midsummer. Despite intervals when he seemed to be improving, his health had taken a serious downturn. Shortly after the new year, a doctor was brought in to care for him full-time, but to little avail. José, age twenty-three, died the evening of February 22, 1929. "Injuries suffered in a football game at Berkeley two years earlier" was the cause of death given to the press. After services at the neighboring St. Agnes Church, José's body was buried at the family's new plot in the Calvary Cemetery in East Los Angeles.

In sharp contrast to the current pain and turmoil in his personal life, Novarro's film career had just gone through a sudden resurgence with the February 9, 1929, release of *Gold Braid*, now rechristened *The Flying Fleet*. Dedicated "to the officers and men of NAVAL AVIATION," the picture became the most-praised Novarro vehicle since *Ben-Hur* more than three years earlier.

"The ace of air epics," cheered *Photoplay;* "the most successful technically and dramatically of all the navy pictures," proclaimed *Variety;* "a vigorous melodrama...nothing quite as stirring or as beautiful as some of these [aerial stunt] scenes has so far been pictured in animated photography," raved Mordaunt Hall in the *New York Times.* Most reviewers also lauded Novarro, with *Variety* referring to him as "likeable, natural and clean-cut" and *Motion Picture* praising his "sincere and convincing" performance, even though many agreed with the *Chicago Tribune* that the star had "the picture taken right away from him" by the much taller and brawnier Ralph Graves.

The *Top Gun* of its day—one reviewer referred to it as a cinematic "male Follies"—*The Flying Fleet* stands the test of time better than most so-called adult dramas of the period. The aerial sequences, including a dogfight between the two protagonists, remain thrilling, while George Hill adroitly handled the actors on the ground. Both Novarro and Graves give remarkably natural performances, even though the cardboard characters and juvenile situations leave little room for solid characterizations. Graves may have had the showier role, but *The Flying Fleet* was a Ramon Novarro vehicle. It became the box-office remedy its star needed by netting MGM more than $1.2

million worldwide. The $443,000 in profits were close to those of *The Midshipman*, Novarro's most profitable MGM picture to date, a particularly impressive feat considering that the earlier film had cost less than half as much as the more recent production.

Still, the public and critical reception of Novarro's latest release could not cure his emotional anguish. "I was absorbed by my work," he later recalled. "I thought success was everything. And then I came to the realization that it was about the least important thing in my life." Signaling his despair, he wrote to his friend and patron of the arts Noël Sullivan, "Now I fear life more than death!" He thought of canceling his European opera debut, but was persuaded by Elsie Janis to proceed.

On March 20, 1929, Novarro—under the name Samaniego—accompanied by his parents and two siblings sailed aboard the *Leviathan* to Spain. Upon their arrival, Novarro left his family in Madrid and traveled to Berlin, where he was scheduled to sing arias from *La Tosca* at the Berlin Philharmonic Hall. He had reportedly paid the Berlin Philharmonic to perform on their stage, and had asserted to the press that he was determined to do his utmost in this first step toward a new career. "I'm just standing on the threshold of a new venture," he was quoted in *Screenland*, "and hoping I'll succeed in it. It all depends on whether I make good—none of us can ever tell until we try!" But despite Novarro's apparent self-confidence and his (by now much battered) motto "All's for the best," his eagerly anticipated opera debut failed to materialize.

"My trip to Europe started to be quite a disappointing one," Novarro wrote Noël Sullivan. Upon his arrival in Berlin, Novarro was "hoping that hard work and the change of environment would do me good, but under the circumstances...it proved to be nearly fatal. I was quite ill all of the time. I don't think I have ever been nearer to a complete nervous breakdown as I was then. I was nearly out of my mind and all I could stand of it was three weeks."

One day Novarro collapsed in his hotel room. He later wandered aimlessly through the streets of Berlin. Finally, he decided to leave for the south of France (probably to stay with Rex Ingram and Alice Terry) to recuperate. One afternoon he walked into a small concert hall in the French Riviera and sat in a back-row seat. "A boy in his early 20s was the artist of the recital," Novarro later recalled. "An unknown boy fighting his way to success. He played light, lilting melodies. There was so much youth, hope and eagerness in him and his music, that suddenly I felt a new wave of peace coming over me. I wanted to meet him and thank him, but I didn't because

I was afraid he might think I was a sentimental fool. I don't even know his name, but I shall always remember that hour."

In the previous two years, Novarro's relationship with Herbert Howe had ended, he had been rejected by El Retiro, his long-awaited operatic debut had failed to take place, he had worked in films he did not care for, and he had lost one of his brothers to cancer. Meanwhile, he had to cope with the pressures of being a superstar. One way to allay his anxiety was to travel to El Retiro to meditate. Another was to drown his angst in alcohol.

It is impossible to pinpoint precisely when Novarro's drinking got out of control, but his alcohol addiction surely began during this tense period. A self-admitted heavy drinker, Herbert Howe once reported reading in one column "that Ramon had just been educated to his first cocktail," adding that he happened to know "that Ramon knew more about wine and cocktails than the hosts who were educating him." As the decade came to a close, Novarro's personal and professional problems, combined with a more active social life, quite probably led to ever more frequent drinking. Soon he was no longer drinking only to forget his troubles. Although there would be sober stretches—usually when he was involved in a project—alcohol was to remain a constant problem literally until the end.

NINE

The Singer of Durango

While Novarro lay sunk in depression in Europe, his mellow *The Pagan,* referred to by the *New York Times*'s Mordaunt Hall as "a tale as languid as a Summer's breeze...gloriously photographed," opened on May 11, 1929, to excellent reviews and outstanding business. Released with a synchronized score, the picture allowed film audiences to hear Novarro's voice for the first time—singing "The Pagan Love Song" on the sound track. The star, for his second film in a row, gathered glowing personal reviews. *Variety* praised his "capital bit of acting," Mordaunt Hall his "especially good" performance, and *Photoplay* his bringing "profound understanding and pagan grace to his characterization of a half-caste youth whose only god is nature, and whose only law is love."

Surprisingly, many reviewers paid scant notice to Novarro's light tenor singing, which had been heavily promoted by MGM. Nonetheless, "The Pagan Love Song," with lyrics by future producer Arthur Freed and music by Nacio Herb Brown (whose most famous composition, "Singin' in the Rain," also came out that same year), became a phenomenal hit and emerged as Novarro's trademark song. Ironically, the MGM front office is said to have hated the tune, but kept it because new lyrics would not have matched Novarro's lip movements in close-up.

Boasting a score that well matches its idyllic locale, beautifully captured by cinematographer Clyde de Vinna's lenses, *The Pagan* also presents Novarro in one of the best performances of his career. Though Henry Shoesmith, Jr., is not a demanding role in terms of heavy dramatics, few actors have ever been able to portray innocence and goodness with such grace and effortlessness—a particularly notable feat considering the harrowing personal problems the star was experiencing at the time. Herbert Howe later observed that "no other man of thirty-one [Novarro was actually twenty-nine during filming] could waggle his toes at the camera as he did in *The Pagan* and seem quite all right," and indeed, Novarro's acting seems wondrously natural perhaps because it is *not* acting. As Howe also asserted, the Henry Shoesmith, Jr., of *The Pagan* and the Ramon Novarro of the 1920s were the same type of person, "joyful, childlike, primitive, serene. No one could really dislike him." Still, director W. S. Van Dyke must be given some of the credit for the star's work, as he also brought out solid portrayals by the other cast members.

Years later, Novarro referred to Henry Shoesmith, Jr., as one of his favorite roles because, in contrast to Lord Gerald Brinsley or Prince Michael IV, Henry was consistent in his motivations. Henry also became one of Novarro's most well-liked characters among the filmgoing public, partly because of his endearing charm, but mostly because of the star's pleasant singing. *The Pagan* turned into MGM's second-biggest success of the year among the studio's nontalking pictures, right behind the Greta Garbo–John Gilbert powerhouse *A Woman of Affairs*. With $1,352,000 in worldwide rentals—at a time when the average global earnings of MGM nontalking films was $700,000—*The Pagan* became Novarro's third-highest box-office success to date, after *Ben-Hur* and *The Student Prince*. But unlike these two previous hits, the lyrical South Seas tale generated considerable profits for the studio— the largest figure yet for a Novarro vehicle.

Pleased with the success of *The Pagan*, MGM wanted Novarro back in Culver City to begin work on his next project. Mayer wired the actor in Europe, asking for his return to California to star in a property the studio had just bought for him, a musical adaptation of the French play *La Bataille des dames*. Realizing he had to continue with his life in Los Angeles, in mid-May, a more self-possessed Novarro sailed on the *Empress Scotland* by way of Quebec to the United States. While in New York, he sang on a national broadcast and then headed for Lansing, Michigan, to spend a few days studying under Louis Graveure, who was then teaching voice at the Michigan State University. Novarro was back in Los Angeles on June 21, telling reporters it had been "worth going to Europe just for the thrill of getting home again," and predicting that talking pictures would create a boom year for films all over the world.

To prime himself for the cameras, Novarro spent a weekend at a Jesuit retreat at Loyola College, a short distance from his West Adams home. "I enjoyed it more than ever, and it has done me a great deal of good, both physically and spiritually," he wrote Noël Sullivan, with whom he shared an ardent devotion to the Catholic Church. Reinvigorated, Novarro was now ready to tackle his first talking picture.

Adapted for the screen by Richard Schayer and Lubitsch collaborator Hans Kräly, *The Battle of the Ladies* relates the romantic misadventures of a follower of Napoleon Bonaparte who is condemned to death by King Louis XVIII for conspiring against the French throne. The director was the meticulous Sidney Franklin, who, in sharp contrast to W. S. Van Dyke, was known for his slow pace, while "the Queen of Blues Singers," Marion Harris, and pretty, petite, twenty-two-year-old Dorothy Jordan were cast in the featured roles. *The Battle of the Ladies* was also to have songs by Clifford Grey and Herbert Stothart, and a two-strip Technicolor ballet number directed by Albertina Rasch, with music by her husband, Dimitri Tiomkin.

In spite of his emotional problems, Novarro fulfilled his professional obligations without any snags (unlike Marion Harris, whose frequent tardiness was duly noticed in production reports). The fact that he was pleased with the songs certainly helped, for the production was a difficult one. Problems with the new technology slowed the pace of filming, since extra care had to be taken to prevent minor noises, such as the rustling of clothes, from being picked up by the microphone. Additionally, musical numbers were still being recorded live take after take because of the technical difficulties in editing sound and image together (with rare exceptions, lip-synching to prerecorded performances was still a few years away). Novarro, although confident in his singing and acting ability, had to adjust himself to the new sound techniques. Adjustments included modulating his voice so it could be properly registered by the microphone, and acting in an atmosphere of the utmost silence. Gone were the musicians who had created the appropriate mood during the now all but vanished silent era. He later credited Ruth Chatterton, who had recently arrived in Hollywood from Broadway, for helping him with his line delivery.

On October 20, several weeks after filming of *The Battle of the Ladies* had been completed, MGM had a series of photographic studies of Novarro published in the *Los Angeles Times* under the title "Novarro with Impressions." These glossy shots—for which Novarro had paid $1,000 earlier in the year—had been taken outside MGM by a freelance photographer, George Hurrell, because the star wanted to have full control over which of his pictures would reach news outlets. (He would sometimes order the studio *not* to use a certain print, only to see it later in the press.) As captured by Hurrell's camera, Novarro looks exquisitely glamorous in a series of costumes, from Mexican peasant to Spanish grandee. An instant success, these pictures helped launch George Hurrell's Hollywood career.

Novarro had been introduced to Hurrell by aviatrix Florence Barnes, better known as "Pancho," whom the actor had met at a party in Laguna Beach two years earlier. Born to a wealthy Southern California family, the twenty-eight-year-old Barnes had left her Episcopalian pastor husband and her son in the mid-1920s and, disguised as a man, had sailed away on a freighter containing a cargo of bananas and contraband weapons for Mexico. Dubbed "Pancho" during her Mexican foray, Barnes so liked the nickname that she kept it for the rest of her life. Later renowned for breaking aviatrix Amelia Earhart's world speed record for women in 1930, Pancho was also notorious for wearing unkempt men's clothes, and for both her abrasive demeanor and her unabashedly coarse language. "She would never use a five- or six-letter word when a four-letter word would do," remembered fellow aviator Chuck Yeager. "She had the filthiest mouth that any of us fighter jocks had ever heard."

Though an unlikely pair, the brash Pancho romped with the courteous Novarro for a few years. "Ramon Novarro was a real Latin heartbreaker," she later recalled. "Everywhere he went the women trailed him like a bunch of dogs chasing a bitch in heat." Apparently, Pancho herself led others to believe not only that she was one of those women, but also that her interest was reciprocated. "He did everything for me," she told Hurrell, "bought clothes, flowers, jewelry and all the romantic stuff." That notion seems to have been wishful thinking. Novarro was always an admirer of beautiful and sophisticated women like Alice Terry, Myrna Loy, and Greta Garbo. Barnes may have been a good party companion, but she did not fit the stylish pattern. Even MGM did not attempt to create a fictionalized romance between the film star and the aviatrix, for a mannish, pudgy, foulmouthed, cigar-chomping woman with a nickname like "Pancho" hardly met the public image of Novarro's ideal paramour. (She was also still officially married to the pastor.)

The Wall Street crash in late October 1929 seems not to have seriously affected Novarro. However he had invested his money until then, any loss he may have incurred because of the crash failed to affect his lifestyle. He had just been paid $75,000 for *The Battle of the Ladies* and would soon be earning $100,000 for his next project, *The House of Troy*, an adaptation of Spanish novelist Alejandro Pérez Lugin's *La Casa de la Troya*. Production on this tale about the tribulations of a handsome, philandering student in the small Spanish town of Santiago de Compostella began on November 13, with Robert Z. Leonard, chiefly known for a series of sophisticated vehicles starring his (then) wife Mae Murray, as director, and Dorothy Jordan again cast as the object of Novarro's affections. To make full use of Novarro's talents, this star vehicle was to give the hero the opportunity to sing several romantic ballads throughout his courtship of the young señorita.

As was the case with *The Battle of the Ladies*—which had by now been retitled *Devil-May-Care*—shooting was marred by the technicians' inexperience with sound. Uncharacteristically, Novarro was often several minutes late on the set, though his tardiness was probably related to delays at the studio, not to personal problems. Nevertheless, he *was* anxious about the upcoming release of *Devil-May-Care*, which would be the test of his future as a talking star.

By late 1929, talkies had rendered silent films all but obsolete. Most Hollywood performers as well as numerous Broadway imports had already made their microphone debuts either in part-talkies, those mostly silent films with last-minute additions of talking scenes, or all-talking pictures, the first of which, Warner Bros.' crime melodrama *Lights of New York*, had opened in July 1928.

Those performers who had failed the microphone test were rapidly on their way out of the American film industry. Foreigners were particularly affected. The respected Emil Jannings, who had come from Germany in 1927 to become the first Academy Award–winning actor, headed back home two years later without making a single talking picture. Norwegian-born Greta Nissen, a rising star in the late 1920s, was summarily dropped from the superproduction *Hell's Angels* because of her accent, while Vilma Banky, a beautiful Hungarian who had created a stir in her romantic pairings with Ronald Colman, found her once flourishing career abruptly halted for the same reason.

MGM hoped that presenting Novarro as a lilting foreigner in *Devil-May-Care* would smooth his transition to talking roles. His singing had already been heard to considerable public acclaim in *The Pagan*, and it was emphasized in the publicity for *Devil-May-Care*, with Novarro proclaimed as "the Golden Voice of the Silver Screen." Audiences were thus reminded that they would receive a double treat: they would hear Novarro talk for the first time and they would hear him sing once again with his *own* voice (unlike performers whose singing voices had to be dubbed, such as Richard Barthelmess in *Weary River* and Alice White in *Show Girl*). Novarro's speaking voice, however, remained an unknown quantity.

The major concern at the time was not so much what a performer sounded like in real life, but how he or she would record. Despite the rapid progress in recording and mixing technology during that crucial period, sound equipment still tended to alter the actors' voices. "My dear," exclaimed Ethel Barrymore upon hearing herself after a screen and voice test, "I consider that an excellent imitation of Elsie Janis giving an imitation of Barrymore." Rose Hobart, one of the many talents recently imported from Broadway, later remembered going to a showing of *Liliom*, in which she appeared with Fox star Charles Farrell. As Hobart approached the auditorium, she was startled to hear a strong, masculine voice emanating from the screen. She marveled at what the microphone had done for Farrell's high-pitched tones, which she thought sounded too effeminate, until she looked up at the screen and realized that the "strong, masculine voice" was not Farrell's, but her own.

The fact that Hobart's voice recorded at a low key did not affect her burgeoning film career, but had she been a silent film star whose voice had been heard for years inside the audiences' heads, the outcome might have been different. The classy Florence Vidor quit films after only one talkie, *Chinatown Nights*, because her voice recorded poorly. Bebe Daniels bought out her Paramount contract because the studio believed she had no future in talking pictures. And May McAvoy, Novarro's leading lady in *Ben-Hur* and the female lead in the first part-talkie, *The Jazz Singer*, was discarded by Warner Bros. because of an alleged lisp.

Among the many tales of performers whose careers were destroyed by talking pictures, the fate of John Gilbert has become legendary. Even though the causes of his downfall were more complex than just the way he sounded, Gilbert, the heir to Valentino as Hollywood's Great Lover, possessed a light tenor voice that clashed with his dashing on-screen image. Worse yet, early microphones made his voice sound more high-pitched than it actually was. In one single year, Gilbert, who had just signed a $250,000-per-picture contract, would free-fall from his status as MGM's top romantic male star to that of a has-been. Novarro's singing voice, so far, had gone over well, but would his speaking voice match the expectations of his audience?

Labeled "the first dramatic operetta of talking pictures," *Devil-May-Care* premiered on December 22, 1929, at the Astor Theater in New York. Novarro's Lieutenant Armand first appears nearly two minutes into the picture, with his back to the camera. After Napoleon finishes a long farewell speech to his troops, he asks Armand if he is crying. In close-up, a dewy-eyed Novarro utters his first spoken words on screen: "No, sir." These two words hardly seem eventful, but at the time they were a revelation to the millions of filmgoers who had known Novarro's face for seven years without ever having heard his speaking voice on-screen. Another revelation occurred a few seconds later, when Armand replies to Napoleon's question about his lack of gaiety, "It will return, sire, when you comb [*sic*] back from Elba!" Oddly, the French officer had a Mexican accent. Novarro and MGM were fervently hoping that filmgoers would shrug off this minor detail.

Devil-May-Care was greeted by generally positive though unenthusiastic reviews. The *New York Times*'s Mordaunt Hall casually referred to the picture as "pleasant entertainment," whereas *Variety* regarded it as just "an average good talker." The trivial story line and several slow-moving sequences were the most frequently cited problems with the film. Those tepid notices were especially disappointing when compared to the accolades conferred on Ernst Lubitsch's sophisticated operetta *The Love Parade*, but at least the star was given a far warmer reception than was given his vehicle.

If Novarro fan Mordaunt Hall (surprisingly) felt him unimpressive as a singing Frenchman with a Mexican accent, most other reviewers were eloquent in their praise of Novarro's first speaking role. *Film Daily* judged that the star used "his excellent voice to advantage," *Photoplay* praised him for "the finest performance of his career," the *New York Telegram* cheered his "finished and expert" performance, and the *New York Sun* rated him "the most talented foreigner casting his lot in Hollywood." The *New York Mirror* summed it up with, "The movies may go to Broadway, to grand opera, even to France and Ireland, for singing movie stars, but they'll not produce an entertainer like the little movie-boy, Ramon Novarro."

Novarro's accent, which had been a source of concern, was praised by most reviewers regardless of its incongruity with the character's nationality. In fact, the thirty-year-old Mexican star was often compared to the forty-one-year-old French import Maurice Chevalier, who had created a sensation as Count Alfred in *The Love Parade*. "In comparing the Novarro screen technique with that of Chevalier," wrote Harry Evans in *Life*, "we would say that the big difference is in the range of feminine appeal. Ramon is certain to increase the blood pressure of most ladies between the ages of sixteen and forty-six. Chevalier, with his added sophistication, must...sacrifice many adolescents in order to attract the more comprehensive group that includes all the fair sex from twenty-four on." Even those who felt that Novarro's talents were not as fully developed as those of the Frenchman predicted that his star turn in *Devil-May-Care* would guarantee him a solid place in talking pictures. "He is hardly a Chevalier in quality," remarked the *New York Herald Tribune*'s Richard Watts, Jr., "but with his admirable singing voice, his expert comedy manner and his thoroughly engaging sincerity, he proves so attractive a performer that he must now be definitely set down as one of the triumphant personages of the new cinema."

It is not difficult to understand why Novarro's performance in *Devil-May-Care* was so well received. Despite the slow pace of the action and the uninspired quality of most of the songs, his acting, when compared to that of other film performers of the period, is remarkably restrained. His singing is pleasant enough, and, even more important, his voice perfectly matches his still youthful good looks. His heavy but intelligible Mexican accent was not a problem for 1929 American filmgoers—Novarro sounded like a foreigner; Armand was foreigner. Whether Mexicans and Frenchmen sounded the same was apparently of little concern. What truly mattered was Novarro's charm, which, even if calculated at times, remains notably effective in the humorous episodes.

Sheer star charisma turned *Devil-May-Care* into Novarro's third 1929 release to surpass the $1 million mark in international rentals, and turned it into his third most successful picture to date. Its success, Novarro's first chance to fulfill his dream of incorporating music to film, was both a personal and a professional relief for him. He thus began preparing for his third consecutive musical, *The Singer of Seville*, with high expectations.

Set in Spain, Novarro's latest vehicle was to be the story of a carefree and arrogant grand opera hopeful who learns he must suffer from a broken heart before he can sing from the soul. Before the final fade-out, the young *sevillano's* lack is supplied by ex–convent girl Dorothy Jordan, in her third and last pairing with Novarro. *The Singer of Seville* was also to mark Novarro's fourth appearance with Renée Adorée, and his second with Ernest Torrence, his rival brother in *Across to Singapore*. Charles Brabin, the man MGM had fired from *Ben-Hur* eight years earlier, was set to direct. But most important, this light musical was to offer Novarro his first on-screen opportunity to display his years of operatic practice with a rendition of Jules Massenet's "Ah! fuyez, douce image" from *Manon* and an aria from Ruggero Leoncavallo's *Pagliacci*. (The *Pagliacci* sequence, filmed in two-strip Technicolor, cannot be found in current prints and is possibly lost.)

"The success of sound experiments has made screen work doubly attractive to me and my sole ambition now is to tie up my voice with the screen in the best possible manner," Novarro was quoted in the picture's pressbook, "for I have become convinced that motion pictures are an excellent medium for light opera. Not heavy grand opera, for which the average person is musically unprepared, but the light, lilting arias which are to be found in so many operatic works and which are enjoyed fully as much by the mov-

iegoer as the ardent student of music." But despite the "musical unprepar-
edness" of the average person, Novarro was determined to meld his métier
with his passion—he was the one who urged the studio to add operatic
aspirations to his *Singer of Seville* character. As a precaution against too much
high culture, he was also to sing two "accessible" numbers composed by
Herbert Stothart and lyricist Clifford Grey, and a third for which he is
credited on the sheet music—though not on-screen—as Stothart's collaborator, "Lonely," the picture's love theme and most memorable composition.

Production on *The Singer of Seville* began January 27, 1930—Novarro's
third picture in six months. Although this hectic film schedule was set by
the studio, Novarro probably preferred to keep busy at work, for he could
then set aside his personal problems and keep his drinking under control.
For him, *The Singer of Seville* was an unusually intense production, as he had
to act, sing, dance, and assist Charles Brabin in the direction—in fact, Novarro later claimed *he* directed the picture, though Brabin's contract precluded
him from receiving codirector credit. In addition to those myriad chores,
Novarro had to cope with a life-threatening problem during filming: Renée
Adorée was seriously ill with tuberculosis.

One night, Adorée began hemorrhaging on the set. While the actress
rested in his dressing room, Novarro called *The Singer of Seville* supervisor
Hunt Stromberg and asked him to immediately relieve her of duty, offering
to redo all his scenes with another actress at no charge to the company.
Stromberg was unmoved. He felt the delay would be too costly and yelled
that the ailing actress had to finish all her scenes that night. After being
treated by a doctor, Adorée returned to the set against the physician's orders.
While shooting her last scene, she began hemorrhaging again and lost consciousness. She was finally rushed to a hospital, and from there was removed
to a sanatorium in La Crescenta, east of Los Angeles.

According to some reports, Novarro had insisted on having Adorée cast
in *The Singer of Seville* because he knew she was ill and in need of money. If
that is true, he must have been unaware of the seriousness of her illness, for
Adorée would have needed rest, not long working hours, six days a week,
in a role that had her dancing onstage and running around the Seville sets.
Novarro would surely not have allowed his fellow performer to undergo
such strenuous physical effort knowing she was suffering from a potentially
deadly—and highly contagious—disease.

In April 1930, approximately one month after finishing *The Singer of Seville*,
Novarro relocated with his family to Santa Monica on the coast to escape

another highly contagious disease, polio, which was spreading panic in large sections of Los Angeles. He signed a four-month lease for $600 a month on a fourteen-room Craftsman-style residence at 130 Adelaide Drive, overlooking the Santa Monica Canyon, with the option to purchase the house for $125,000. His stay in Santa Monica during the spring and early summer was also supposed to be a vacation away from home even while he remained in the Los Angeles area, for he was not required to report to the studio until July 31. As he had in years past, Novarro spent his free time practicing his singing both at home and with Louis Graveure in Lansing. On May 13, he also sang on an NBC radio broadcast from New York, and from there returned to Lansing for more lessons with Graveure.

It was probably while in Michigan that Novarro decided to buy a new car. He wrote a check for the vehicle and drove away. A few days later, apparently after his return to the Santa Monica house, he received a call from the car dealer. The check had bounced. The star who had made $248,000 in 1928, $170,000 in 1929, and $125,000 for his latest picture immediately called his bank. He was informed he had a total of $160 in his account.

Novarro had had such complete trust in his personal assistant (and former dance classmate) Louis Samuel that he had given Samuel power of attorney over his financial affairs. In the late 1920s, while Novarro was busy making films and feeling depressed over his brother José's fatal illness, Samuel used that power of attorney to transfer funds from his boss's accounts to those of his own brother, a stock market investor. Some of the transfer likely occurred after the October 1929 stock market collapse, as Novarro had remained solvent throughout early 1930. At that time, many investors— quite possibly Samuel's brother among them—were buying cheap securities in the hopes that the market had bottomed out, but after a rally in April 1930, the market resumed its slide.

An investigation of Novarro's accounts later revealed that Samuel had also been embezzling his boss's money to pay the mortgage of his luxurious new residence in the Hollywood Hills. The house, which had been designed in 1928 by Frank Lloyd Wright, Jr. (known as Lloyd Wright), was initially supposed to have been a small one-bedroom dwelling for the bachelor Samuel, but the layout was considerably expanded after he decided to end his bachelor lifestyle in 1929. That same year, Samuel and his wife, Grace, finally moved into the striking 5609 Valley Oak Drive residence. Novarro, of course, knew of the Valley Oak house—he presumably had introduced Lloyd Wright to Samuel, since the architect had also been responsible for Herbert Howe's Beverly Hills house—but the revelations about his friend's duplicity came as a horrific shock.

Besides having to deal with the unexpected financial disaster, a devastated Novarro had to come to terms with the betrayal of a longtime and trusted friend. Instead of pressing charges against his former companion, which could have led to unpleasant headlines, Novarro opted to take over the Valley Oak house. Two years later, when Novarro received $30,000 (most of it in credit) from the Internal Revenue Service for "overassessment of income tax and interest" due to his embezzlement losses, he still refused to reveal Samuel's identity to the press.

For the time being, Novarro had to borrow $10,000 to meet his lease payments on the Santa Monica house and to cover the normal living expenses for himself and his family. The Samaniegos and probably a few close friends were aware of his problem, but the public would learn of the seriousness of Novarro's financial debacle only on July 30, 1937, when he revealed it in an interview at New York's WHN radio station.

Meanwhile, Novarro had suffered a professional setback when *The House of Troy*—renamed *In Gay Madrid*—opened on June 7 to mostly dismal notices. "Many is the time when an eager spectator might wish the picture were correctly titled, assuming that life in the Spanish capital to be more interesting than in the chosen locale," remarked one reviewer. "Unreal story, poor acting, ditto direction and general lack of popular appeal," panned *Variety*. "Badly produced, confusedly told, and a most unfortunate occurrence," decreed the *New York Sun*. The *New York Herald Tribune*'s Richard Watts, Jr., dismissed Novarro's latest effort as an "incredibly inept film," lacking both gaiety and Madrid. "Were it not for the ugly things that the film does to its star," Watts, Jr., lamented, ". . . *In Gay Madrid* would seem one of the most hilarious of burlesques." Ramon Novarro "deserves more humane treatment," summed up the *New York Post*.

Those negative reviews are surprising, considering that *In Gay Madrid* is much superior to the more favorably received *Devil-May-Care*. Undeniably, *In Gay Madrid* creaks at times, and the happy ending is particularly abrupt, but for the most part it is a pleasant light romance. Both the script and Robert Z. Leonard's direction allow Novarro ample opportunity to display his comedic talents, which had been only sporadically employed in his previous effort. The picture also presents his most effective pairing with Dorothy Jordan, whom Novarro thought a "delightful" leading lady. Overall, *In Gay Madrid* is one of the best Novarro showcases of all his talking pictures. Indeed, even those critics who hated the picture were nearly unanimous in their enthusiastic praise of Novarro's star turn.

On the strength of Novarro's name, *In Gay Madrid* performed fairly well at the international box office, though the picture failed to duplicate the success of its predecessor. At home, the lower box-office receipts were probably due in part to the poor reviews accorded the film, but there was another even more daunting obstacle to its success: the rapidly fading popularity of film musicals in the American market.

Initially, musicals, such as the 1929 MGM releases *The Broadway Melody* and *The Hollywood Revue of 1929*, had brought huge earnings to the studios. Even as many silent-film stars were being dethroned by the talkie revolution, musicals were resurrecting the careers of Hollywood has-beens who were able to sing and dance. RKO's *Rio Rita* gave a much needed lift to the career of Bebe Daniels after she had left Paramount, while *The Broadway Melody* brought former star Bessie Love back from vaudeville. "Today, in the midst of the microphone panic," *Photoplay* had reported in April 1929, "Bessie is one of the few stars who know where their next Rolls-Royce is coming from." Before 1930 was over, Bessie's "next Rolls-Royce" was no longer such a sure thing. By that time, MGM had canceled her contract—musicals and the stars associated with them had become box-office poison.

Such rapid decline in popularity was largely a result of both the repetitive nature of most musicals—either lifeless operettas or endless rehashes of backstage stories—and their sheer number. Additionally, musicals were a greater financial risk for the studios: the more elaborate sets and the extra rehearsal time required made them costlier than the average picture. By mid-1930, song-and-dance spectacles were either making a minuscule profit or losing money. Universal's expensive *The King of Jazz* was reported to have lost $1 million, while MGM lost more than $300,000 on *New Moon* and *The Rogue Song*, two operettas starring Metropolitan baritone Lawrence Tibbett. The only 1930 musical to bring MGM solid profits was *Chasing Rainbows*, which had an early January release.

One major victim of the musical bust was MGM's *The Hollywood Revue of 1930*, directed by Charles Reisner, the man responsible for the highly successful *Revue* of the previous year. During production, the picture was renamed *The March of Time*, apparently because most of the featured performers were not Hollywood personalities, but veteran stage and vaudeville notables, including DeWolf Hopper, comedians Weber and Fields, and former stage and silent-screen actress Marie Dressler, who, at age sixty-two, was in the midst of a sensational film career renaissance. To make the picture more alluring to 1930 audiences, the studio inserted numbers with rising songster Bing Crosby crooning "Poor Little G String" and, in two-strip Technicolor, a sailor-garbed Novarro (who had been absent from the previous *Revue* because of his ill-fated European trip) singing French composer André Messager's "Long Ago in Alcala."

After many of the *March of Time* musical numbers had been shot, including Crosby's, Novarro's (probably shortly after he finished work on *The Singer of Seville*), and another featuring cavemen, Indians, and a chorus of five hundred, the picture was abruptly scrapped. With the diminished interest in film musicals, the studio preferred to cut its losses rather than to invest more money on a project clearly doomed to box-office failure. Some of the sketches later surfaced in short films, and three years later, after musicals were resurrected by Warner Bros.' cheaply made and highly successful *42nd Street*, a few *March of Time* numbers were incorporated into the MGM feature *Broadway to Hollywood*. Novarro's "Long Ago in Alcala," however, was never shown commercially in the United States, though it did surface in MGM's German-language production *Wir schalten um auf Hollywood* (We tune in to Hollywood), which was released in Germany in June 1931.

After recovering from the shock of the Louis Samuel affair, Novarro resumed a more active social life, whether spending weekends at Noël Sullivan's always busy Hyde Park mansion in San Francisco or carousing with Elsie Janis at Hollywood parties. By then, rumors linking Novarro to the chipper entertainer had subsided; "between Elsie Janis and Ramon Novarro," remarked *Photoplay* in October 1928, "—yes, you heard me—it's just a big, beautiful and sincere friendship." Also by that time, Novarro's partying had become heavily fueled by alcohol. Anita Page later recalled that her last date with Novarro, sometime in 1930, was ruined by the actor's drunkenness. While at Marion Davies's Santa Monica beach house, Novarro, after several drinks, asked Page to dance—nearly falling as they staggered across the floor. On another occasion, while actor Crauford Kent and his wife were driving an intoxicated Novarro home from a party, he became sick and threw up in their car.

The "new" Novarro had even become sufficiently daring—probably with the aid of alcohol—to go to speakeasies that catered mainly to a gay clientele. Granted, to prevent suspicions he would invariably be accompanied by a woman, whether Elsie Janis or Alice Terry when she was in town. That way, if Novarro's true interest lay in a man across the table, Janis's or Terry's presence shielded him from unwelcome rumors. He was just another star, like many others whatever their sexual orientation, enjoying a drag show in the company of friends. This was a strategy similar to the one Novarro had resorted to during the making of *The Flying Fleet*, though unlike Anita Page, Janis and Terry were surely aware of their role. The strategy worked so well that Novarro continued to use it long after his stardom had faded. "Old MGM training," he would call it.

Novarro's increased sociability coincided with MGM's attempt to replace his image as a recluse having ecclesiastical aspirations with that of "someone made out of common clay." This new tactic was a result of both Novarro's most recent screen roles, which had transformed him from the usually sweet-natured boy of his latter silent films into a ladies' man, and his having turned thirty-one in February 1930. Now that Novarro was past thirty and was no longer threatening to enter a monastery, his being "woman-proof," as one columnist had put it, had become less easily explainable.

"It seems that the most popular portrait of me is that of a saint-like individual who wants to leave all worldly pleasures behind in favor of a secluded life in a monastery," Novarro was quoted in the *Singer of Seville* pressbook. "And the universal impression seems to be that I am a confirmed bachelor with a horror of women and anything approaching domesticity." Novarro, or an MGM publicist writing for him, then went on to explain that he preferred not to discuss his ideal woman because he had not yet met her. Once he did, "then whoever she is will become my ideal."

Still, since Novarro remained uncooperative in the romantic arena, the studio continued to push the Mexican-accented boy-next-door image: Novarro was a family man—that was why he remained unmarried and unattached. As if the numerous Samaniegos were not enough evidence of Novarro's familial devotion, in 1929 the MGM publicity department made a story out of a certain Grandma Baker of Oak Park, Illinois, one of the star's most ardent fan-letter writers. According to press reports, this grandma from the country's heartland had become obsessed with the young Mexican actor after seeing one of his photographs in a magazine; she was struck by how closely the alleged descendant of Aztec royalty resembled her deceased son. "To her Ramon is not a star—but her own son, her very own son," explained Katherine Albert in *Photoplay*. Seizing the chance for a wholesome photo op, the studio had Novarro meet with the Oak Park grandma in her hometown. During the visit, they went to a second-run house to watch *The Pagan*, so the eighty-five-year-old grandma could see her "son" frolic seminaked for the seventeenth time. Later that year, more photographs of grandma and son were taken at the Samaniegos' home during Christmastime.

During that period, Grandma Baker was the only woman closely associated with Novarro in the press. The studio seemed to feel that publicity about its romantic star's ever elusive "ideal woman" would suffice to appease the curiosity of the fans. Novarro's popularity, after all, was at its highest in 1930: he was now an established star with nineteen pictures to his credit, including the colossal *Ben-Hur* and no fewer than three million-dollar-plus hits during the pivotal transition to sound. Even though *In Gay Madrid* failed to bring profits as high as Novarro's previous three efforts, its worldwide rentals were also close to the million-dollar mark. This impressive record protected Novarro from any meddling by the studio in his private life. There was nothing Loew's and MGM respected more than a solid profit-maker.

Luckily for Novarro, *The Singer of Seville*—renamed *Call of the Flesh* to make it sound less like a musical—continued his box-office hold despite opening to mixed reviews on September 12, 1930. *Variety* thought the picture uneven, the *New York Morning Telegraph* criticized the "banal" story line, and the *New York Times*'s Mordaunt Hall complained about the "lethargic" plot while praising Brabin's direction. (Novarro must have found that ironic.) The star's personal reviews, as usual, were markedly better than those of the picture, with the *New York Morning Telegraph*, for instance, declaring that Novarro, "who happens to be one of the most finished and graceful performers in the cinema, and who has a voice of real charm...emerges every bit as subtle, graceful and finished as he ever was." Curiously, the respected Richard Watts, Jr., one of Novarro's staunchest admirers, disagreed. "The appalling apparition of Mr. Ramon Novarro of all people," Watts complained, "trying to be a sort of Spanish William Haines makes the first part of *Call of the Flesh* more than a bit difficult to bear....The quiet, rather gentle charm of Mr. Novarro is his most attractive feature, and when you see him acting away at being a bumptious Latin Fresh Guy you may admire his versatility but you are hardly likely to be pleased with the result."

Indeed, Novarro's portrayal of the troubadour Juan de Dios now seems, for the most part, insufferable, as Juan's haughty behavior makes him come across like an obnoxious brat instead of an alluring heartbreaker. His rudeness and abusiveness toward Adorée's beautifully played Lola is anything but amusing, though *Call of the Flesh* (a title Novarro abhorred) is not a total misuse of the star's talents. Even Watts observed that Novarro improves as the picture progresses "to remind us—after his early lapse—that he is one of the screen's most distinguished performers." In fact, two moments in *Call of the Flesh* rank among the most memorable in Novarro's career. The first occurs at the picture's climax, when Juan pretends to be involved with fellow dancer Lola, so his true love, María Consuelo, will return to the convent from which she has fled. The second takes place at the picture's unabashedly romantic finale, when Juan, dying in his bed, is brought back to life by his reunion with María. Those two scenes could easily have become pathetically contrived had Novarro's performance been anything short of totally honest.

Instead, they demonstrate what an outstanding dramatic actor Novarro could be when given the chance.

Unfortunately, honesty is sorely lacking in Novarro's rendition of Massenet's "Ah! fuyez, douce image." His on-screen operatic debut is marked by grandiose gestures and expressions akin to some of his earlier, unsubtle silent-film performances. "Being identified with dramatic roles," Novarro had told *Screenland* in 1929, "I may be permitted to inject more of the drama of the story into the [aria] presentation than otherwise." Such an approach would have worked had his gestures been modulated to his singing, but they were not. Although Novarro's voice is perfectly acceptable for light melodies, his high-opera rendition carries too little power to justify his melodramatic posturing. Two years later, Herbert Howe would criticize Novarro for his wanting "to be operatic, when his genius is for folk songs. He can sing the ballads of Mexico as no one can sing them... But he wants to bellow like Tibbett. He wants to be the clown with the breaking heart, whereas he was born to be a gay troubadour—like Francis of Assisi." It would take Novarro a few more years to learn that lesson.

Yet, filmgoers around the world clearly enjoyed both Novarro's new "Latin Fresh Guy" image and the bathos accompanying his opera singing—which fans saw as proof of their idol's long-discussed operatic talents. *Call of the Flesh* became Novarro's biggest box-office hit since *Ben-Hur* and MGM's fourth most successful 1930 release internationally.

At the time of the *Call of the Flesh* premiere, Novarro was earning some badly needed money—$25,000—by working on that picture's Spanish-language version, *La Sevillana*. This production was one of the dozens of foreign-language adaptations of American films being made at that time, as the studios feared that subtitles and primitive dubbing techniques would drive non-English speakers away from their products. At MGM, Novarro was the obvious choice to bridge the sound-generated gap between Hollywood and the not inconsiderable Spanish-language market.

La Sevillana marked the first time Novarro acted in his native tongue on-screen and his first official directorial effort (he also wrote the Spanish-language lyrics). He was, of course, the only option to play Juan de Dios, but his landing on the director's chair may have been a form of compensation for his uncredited directorial work on *Call of the Flesh*. Furthermore, earlier in the year Novarro had offered to help in the direction of the Spanish version of *Mr. Wu*, whose leading man was uncomfortable with American filming methods. Irving Thalberg had declined the offer, but suggested

Novarro direct the upcoming Spanish-language version of *Call of the Flesh*. Novarro readily accepted the challenge. "I want to work in a medium where the quality of what I do won't be judged by my appearance," he told *Modern Screen*. "I want to direct because it is a wider and more comprehensive field. Also because I can't go on acting when I am maybe bald and fat—the public demands youth to look at, but directors can direct, no matter what their girth is. And then, I think one should always be moving forward—always one step ahead and up."

Guiding actors was hardly a novelty for the experienced Teatro Intimo director, but despite his *Call of the Flesh* training, Novarro was still not fully familiar with camera techniques. In an ironic role reversal, he was to receive solo directing credit for *La Sevillana*, though rumors suggest that the more skilled Chilean-born Carlos F. Borcosque, credited only as assistant director, handled many of the directorial responsibilities. But even if Novarro was not solely responsible for the results, and despite his inexperience behind the camera and the long hours of work that often stretched into the night, the film star enjoyed playing the role of director. "At last I am doing what I've wanted to do for years—ever since I have been in pictures," he remarked. "This is the real thrill—directing. In acting, our accomplishments belong, partly, to the director. But a director's achievement is genuine—it's something he himself has done."

Two of Novarro's family members played key roles in the making of *La Sevillana:* his uncle Ramón Guerrero adapted the English-language script to Spanish, and Señora Samaniego, billed as Sra. L. G. de Samaniego, played the Mother Superior—an appropriate role for a devoutly Catholic woman who went to mass daily. Señora Samaniego and Novarro were the only two Mexicans in the principal cast, which was composed mostly of Spanish performers, including Conchita Montenegro, whom the director-star called "a spontaneous, lively, impulsive creature," and Rosita Ballesteros in, respectively, Dorothy Jordan's and Renée Adorée's roles.

The four-week shooting of *La Sevillana* lasted until September 18, one day over schedule. Six weeks later, after having practiced his French for several weeks with two French-speaking valets, Novarro was back at the studio to direct and star in *Le Chanteur de Séville* (for another $25,000). Pretty, wide-eyed Suzy Vernon took over Jordan's role, while Pierrette Caillol replaced fellow Francophone Renée Adorée, who remained too ill to work. Filming proceeded without any major complications, and the picture was wrapped in a mere two weeks.

La Sevillana premiered in Los Angeles on December 5, 1930, at the Teatro Califórnia Internacional, then the only local first-run movie house for

Spanish-language films. The picture was well received by the local Spanish-language press and was also praised when it later opened in Spain and Spanish-speaking Latin America. *Le Chanteur de Séville* premiered at the Théâtre de la Madeleine in Paris on February 21, 1931, with *Variety* remarking that Novarro's French was "entirely satisfactory" and that the actor played the French-speaking Juan "exceedingly well."

Following those two consecutive directorial efforts, fan magazines began wondering if Ramon Novarro was poised to become the next Ernst Lubitsch or Josef von Sternberg. "I want to do simple stories that are concerned less with the physical side of life than what goes on in people's hearts and heads," Novarro told *Motion Picture*. "Spectacle bores me. It is human beings I love—I've always watched them, tried to find out what went on inside, why they did thus and so. If I can put some of that on the screen, accurately and beautifully, I shall be satisfied." Despite Novarro's high hopes, his directorial future was abruptly halted when a planned German version of *Call of the Flesh* was scrapped, and MGM discontinued its production of foreign-language adaptations. By late 1930, most studios had decided that the more cost-effective techniques of dubbing and subtitling should be employed for the overseas market. Novarro still hoped for more behind-the-camera opportunities in the studio's regular productions, and would insist on adding a supplement to his next contract allowing him to direct.

With his financial state now greatly improved, Novarro spent much of his time in late 1930 in the company of thirty-year-old adventurer Richard Halliburton, whom he had probably met through Pancho Barnes. Born to a wealthy Tennessee family, Halliburton was a Princeton graduate whose favorite pastime was to roam the world in search of adventure, whether swimming across the Panama Canal, carousing aboard his plane *The Flying Carpet*, or climbing the Matterhorn. He had become a popular figure with the success of his 1925 book *The Royal Road of Romance*, in which he narrates some of his notorious capers—though carefully omitting any mention of his sexual orientation and frequent libidinous escapades.

Some reports have contended that Novarro and Halliburton were more than just pals, but there is no indication of an affair in Halliburton's letters to their common gay friend Noël Sullivan, even though the adventurer was generally quite open about his romantic and sexual romps in his correspondence. Yet, if an affair really took place—which is not impossible—Novarro may have asked that Halliburton not allude to their relationship. That would have been a typical Novarro attitude. Though he and Sullivan must have talked about their private lives when visiting with each other, not once does either of them mention anything related to sexuality in the surviving letters of their twenty-seven-year correspondence. In all probability, Novarro deemed letters to be unsafe vehicles for broaching such private matters. A humorous thank-you letter for pajamas Sullivan had given him, "I've tested it [sic] already and [they] structured around most arrogantly, which proves that you are provoking me to the lowest of all fleshly sins," was Novarro's closest allusion to the subject of sex.

In the last week of 1930, Novarro returned to MGM to star in an adaptation of Viennese writer Arthur Schnitzler's bleak novel *Daybreak*. Initially, the picture was supposed to be a musical version of Schnitzler's story, with music by Oscar Straus, but with the apparent demise of the genre, the studio eliminated all the songs. The story itself was heavily altered by numerous hands to satisfy audiences' (and Mayer's) yearning for a happy ending, resulting in a mishmash of styles that had broad comic scenes interspersed with light romance, Old World cynicism, and an unfulfilled sense of doom. In Schnitzler's novel the Austrian army lieutenant kills himself because of his inability to pay his debts as an officer and a gentleman; in MGM's final version, he lives and is reunited with his girl for a long kiss at the final fade-out.

Originally intended for John Gilbert, Novarro's *Daybreak* role—the suave, cynical, and womanizing Austrian lieutenant Willi Kasda—was the most atypical Novarro character since Lord Brinsley of *A Certain Young Man*. He was to be supported by the mousy Helen Chandler as the love interest, and Jean Hersholt, the kindly mentor in *The Student Prince*, as the ruthless man who nearly forces Willi to commit suicide. The designated director was Belgian-born Jacques Feyder, renowned for his French silent classics *L'Atlantide* and *Thérèse Raquin*.

Feyder had come to Hollywood with his wife, actress Françoise Rosay, after finding himself in disfavor with the French government because of his 1928 satire *Les Nouveaux Messieurs*, which shows a member of the French parliament imagining his colleagues as tutu-garbed beauties. Feyder, however, was no happier in Hollywood. He found it difficult to communicate in English and to work within the confines of the studio system—though he and Novarro worked well together, as the actor was fluent in French. Even so, *Daybreak* turned out to be taxing for all involved. Feyder was taken ill, and at various times Novarro and production supervisor Bernard Hyman found themselves directing scenes. Additionally, Novarro was irritated by the constant retakes ordered by studio executives and by MGM's indecision as to which ending to choose—according to columnist Dorothy Spensley, both Schnitzler's tragic ending and the studio's happy one were filmed. It was even reported that Novarro wanted to buy the film and shelve it, fearing it would damage his artistic reputation. The result was such serious friction between the star and the front office that Spensley announced that MGM might not take up Novarro's option after his next picture was completed.

On March 11, while working on the endless retakes for *Daybreak*, Novarro once again had to cope with tragic news: his friend F. W. Murnau, the highly respected director of *Nosferatu*, *Faust*, and *Sunrise*, had died of injuries suffered in a car crash near Santa Barbara. Novarro had become friends with Murnau three years earlier, shortly before the director invited him to play the male lead in the circus drama *Four Devils*. Their friendship had endured even though Novarro's MGM contract precluded his appearing in that Fox production.

Four Devils was Novarro's second missed opportunity to work with Murnau. Two years earlier, he had declined an offer to appear in *Faust* because he had been unwilling to work abroad so soon after the *Ben-Hur* production nightmare. At the time of *Four Devils*, however, Novarro was so keen on working with the German director that he was ready to postpone his European trip with his family just to appear in the picture. But although Novarro was never to work in a Murnau project, the director remained a strong professional influence, often coaching him privately. Murnau "proved to me," Novarro later recalled, "how an actor might take a role to a certain peak, but then let the audience finish the scene, so to speak." The director—who Novarro unabashedly asserted "was an admirer of mine"—went so far as to suggest which George Hurrell pictures the star should use for publicity. Recognizing that Novarro's value at the time rested largely in his looks, Murnau selected the photographs that showed the actor's face unaltered by makeup. Novarro considered Murnau's advice so important that in later years he rated the German expatriate as the third most influential director in his career, after Ingram and Lubitsch. (According to Novarro, in a taped remark that may have carried a hint of anti-Semitism, "Lubitsch and a certain group of those people [other Jewish directors and writers] were very jealous of Murnau because Murnau was not [lowering his voice after a brief pause] Jewish.")

An introspective, shy person who avoided big parties and rarely gave interviews, Murnau was quite affable in small gatherings that often included *Sunrise* leading man George O'Brien and actor Larry Kent. Even though both Novarro and Murnau were circumspect about their homosexuality, the subject was probably acceptable between themselves. Nonetheless, stories about star and director procuring men for each other are most probably false, as such actions would have been quite uncharacteristic of either of them.

Murnau, however, did bring into Novarro's life one important person, Frank Hansen. The Scandinavian-looking Hansen had been working as Murnau's assistant for about two years (he even helped in the direction of *Four Devils*), but when the director left on a small boat for the South Pacific to shoot *Tabu*, he suggested that Novarro—no longer with Louis Samuel—might like to have "the best secretary in the world." Hansen, in fact, soon made himself indispensable to Novarro, becoming a composite of chauffeur, bodyguard, companion, and nursemaid. He drove the actor around town, protected him from impassioned fans, played Chinese checkers with him, socialized with his gay friends, and provided for his every need, going so far as to underline newspaper articles about Novarro's acquaintances to save his boss the trouble of having to look for relevant news items. Not surprisingly, Novarro later recalled Frank Hansen as "the finest person that has ever worked for me."

Hansen, whose political views leaned heavily to the right, also acted as Novarro's "adviser." The star, once called "plastic" by Herbert Howe because he was so easily influenced by the opinions and ideas of others, would at times let himself be swayed by Hansen's worldview, including his conception of Jews (which may explain Novarro's remark about Lubitsch and the other German Jews in the film colony). Throughout the years, Hansen would continue to be an influential figure in Novarro's life.

On April 7, three weeks after completing the *Daybreak* retakes, Novarro began working on the last film under his 1928 contract, *The Son of the Rajah*, later renamed *Son of India*. A modernized adaptation of F. Marion Crawford's 1882 novel *Mr. Isaacs*, this tale of an unconsummated love affair between a wealthy Indian merchant and a white American girl—a "never the twain shall meet" theme that was dear to Hollywood in the 1920s and 1930s—was set to be a major production. Novarro was to make $150,000, the most he would ever earn for a single picture; the scenario boasted a classy team of writers, including Lubitsch collaborator Ernest Vajda; and the star was to be supported by a solid cast: MGM stalwart Conrad Nagel, a handsome silent-era leading man who had been reduced to playing second leads in talking pictures; screen and stage veteran Marjorie Rambeau; and, as the love interest, former child star Madge Evans, now an attractive Broadway ingenue. Novarro was also given the option to direct, but turned it down, asking instead to be reunited with the more experienced Jacques Feyder.

Shooting of *Son of India* proceeded smoothly, despite three handicaps. First, Feyder had to film around Madge Evans's character, as the leading lady was still appearing in the Broadway play *Philip Goes Forth*. Evans arrived at the set on the day Feyder shot the last scene without her. Second, Novarro was angry because MGM had reneged on its promise to give him a week's rest during production. And third, the star of the picture became unwittingly embroiled in a legal case during filming when he was subpoenaed on behalf of a first cousin, twenty-year-old murder suspect Jacques Samaniego.

Jacques and a friend, twenty-two-year-old Wilbur Mossberg—both drug addicts—were on trial for murdering university student Ralph O. Trump during an attempted holdup. Both men were being retried after an initial mistrial, and Jacques's defense attorney wanted Novarro as a character witness. Despite the subpoena, Novarro did not attend the trial—possibly through the maneuvering of either MGM or his powerful attorney, Stanley Barnes (Pancho's brother-in-law). Samaniego and Mossberg were eventually convicted and sentenced to life plus five years on July 4, 1931. Mayer allegedly used his influence to keep Novarro's name out of the papers throughout the proceedings, but the studio head probably did not spend too much energy shielding Novarro in a case that would have led to little damaging publicity, since the star was well liked by the press and could hardly be blamed for a cousin's misdeeds.

More worrisome was the dismal critical reception accorded *Daybreak*, which had premiered on May 29. *Variety* called the picture "flat all the way," the *New York Morning Telegraph* criticized Jacques Feyder's "tedious" direction, and the *New York Post* remarked that the bowdlerization of the plot depleted it of "the vitality of the drama, the intensity of its romance and the entire Viennese spirit." Frequent Novarro supporter Mordaunt Hall of the *New York Times* was one of the few dissenting voices, praising *Daybreak* as "a most compelling talking picture."

As usual, after trashing the film, most reviewers found generous words for the star. "Never has Mr. Novarro played more dextrously or with more charm and humor," declared Richard Watts, Jr., in the *New York Herald Tribune*, while Mordaunt Hall praised his "pleasingly light characterization"; and the *New York Morning Telegraph* commended him for "keeping with his splendid record as a screen luminary." In fact, except for some unfunny broad comedy in the beginning, Novarro's performance in *Daybreak* is a beautifully modulated mixture of worldliness and sensitivity, a sort of gentler version of his Rupert of Hentzau. His only liability as a talking Austrian officer is his obviously non-Germanic accent, which becomes distracting during his character's more excitable moments. Even so, *Daybreak* is one of those rare films that improve with age. Feyder's sophisticated European touch and highly mobile camera have led to comparisons with Max Ophüls's *Letter from an Unknown Woman*, with which *Daybreak* shares a wistful quality that even its tacked-on happy ending fails to dispel.

Partly because of the avalanche of negative reviews, *Daybreak* was doing disappointing business, though an even bigger handicap was that Novarro's coolly detached, nonsinging Austrian officer, like his English lord in *A Certain Young Man*, was not the romantic Ramon Novarro audiences wanted to see. The prospects for *Son of India*, which opened on July 24, did not seem any healthier. "An overly romantic and ponderously treated rewrite on the ... inter-racial love theme," blasted *Variety*. "... The sad ending fits a pretty sad picture that might be just sad enough for the women and moderate business at best." Most reviewers concurred.

This time, even Novarro did not escape unscathed. Some critics, such as the *New York Sun*'s John Cohen, Jr., still felt he was his "ever-charming, ever-guileful" self, but others understandably thought him unimpressive as the wealthy trader Karim—Novarro's worst ever talking performance. Buried under horrific makeup, he tries to convey India's mystery by means of grimaces and stilted line delivery. Making matters worse, the rest of the talent involved in *Son of India* is as miscast as the leading man. The absurd situations and dialogue, and Feyder's unsure handling of the melodramatic plot are on a level with Novarro's immature performance.

Although neither of the Feyder-Novarro collaborations was well received at the time, director and star enjoyed their experiences together. Feyder later recalled Novarro as "happy, charming, carefree, extremely optimistic, obliging, and eager to please. He was full of laughter, continually leaping from one idea to the next, and for his director, pretty difficult to pin down." As for Novarro, he later asserted that of all his talking pictures, he was pleased only with sections of the two Feyder films (he made a special point of dismissing the happy ending imposed on *Daybreak*), and named Feyder as one of the most important directors of his career, after fellow Europeans Ingram, Lubitsch, and Murnau.

In spite of their mutual admiration, Novarro and Feyder would never work together again. Unhappy with the constraints of the American studios, the director returned to France soon after completing *Son of India*. His acclaimed French films, among them the three consecutive mid-1930s classics

Le Grand jeu, Pension Mimosas, and *La Kermesse héroïque,* have obscured his American work. As a result, the stylish *Daybreak* has been unjustly ignored by film historians.

Both *Daybreak* and *Son of India* turned out to be box-office disappointments, the former a downright fiasco. *Daybreak* lost the studio more than $100,000, becoming Novarro's first talking picture to lose money and his first box-office failure since *A Certain Young Man. Son of India* nearly broke the $1 million mark in worldwide rentals—with particularly solid earnings overseas—but its high cost left a relatively paltry $84,000 in profits. (In good part due to Novarro's salary, each Feyder picture cost more than $500,000.)

Yet, MGM knew that they had in Novarro a solid box-office star—as long as he was cast in the right vehicle. Despite the rumors that the studio was unwilling to pick up his option, MGM actually wanted Novarro to renew his contract for three more years. The star was the one reluctant to commit himself for such a long period. His operatic ambitions continued undimmed, and he was fully aware that his dream of bringing opera to the screen had perished along with the film musical. If he truly desired to sing, he would have to do it away from Hollywood. With his finances now stabilized, Novarro could well afford to be absent from the Culver City studio for several months at a time to pursue his other artistic goals.

On July 24, shortly after turning down an offer from Rex Ingram to star in a picture in Europe, Novarro signed a contract with MGM for only one picture: *Mata Hari,* in which he would costar with Greta Garbo. Needing another major hit, Novarro had insisted that he be paired with Garbo, MGM's top international box-office star. (Marie Dressler had unexpectedly become the leading domestic star with a series of lowbrow comedies.) The studio, intent on keeping Novarro's services, agreed, dropping relative newcomer Robert Montgomery from the project. Novarro, for his part, had to make several concessions to appear opposite the prestigious Swede. He consented to be costarred (he had shared star billing only once before, with Norma Shearer in *The Student Prince*), accepted second billing for the first time since attaining stardom, and even took a drastic salary cut. After receiving $5,000 at the signing of the agreement, he was to make $5,000 a week during production—a reduction of nearly two-thirds of his weekly salary for *Son of India.*

At the time of Garbo's arrival at MGM in 1925, Novarro was the star of *Ben-Hur* and one of the studio's top assets. Two years later, Novarro's career was stalled while Garbo's continued its extraordinary rise, partly because of three highly successful pairings with John Gilbert. Before the silent era was over, the alluring Garbo had become one of the biggest box-office attractions in the world. She was the last MGM star to attempt her luck in talking pictures, but despite her heavy Swedish accent, she made a successful transition to sound, playing a Swedish prostitute in *Anna Christie*. Novarro had also been fortunate with sound, but his vehicles could not boast the artistic pretensions of the Garbo productions. Consequently, even though Novarro was Garbo's (slightly lesser) male equivalent at MGM in terms of popularity, he lacked the distinction the cool Swede possessed. It was not a matter of Garbo's being considered the superior performer, for Novarro's personal reviews were almost invariably outstanding, but the perception that her mysterious persona exuded *art*, while his lighthearted portrayals did not. Having the name Greta Garbo next to his thus ensured Novarro not only solid box-office receipts, but also an equally essential requirement for an actor—prestige.

MGM came up with its own version of the life of World War I German spy Margaretha Zelle, better known as Mata Hari ("Sun" or, literally, "Eye of Dawn" in Malay), after Paramount and RKO had shelved their plans to film the story. The highly fictionalized scenario, which revolved around Mata Hari's love for a young Russian flier, was filled with risqué touches that alarmed the censors at the Hays Office. Since another three years would pass before that organization attained enough power to veto scripts, the studio moved forward with the project without making any concessions. One more erotic scene was even added during filming, showing Mata Hari and her lover, Lieutenant Alexis Rosanoff, together in her darkened bedroom, with only the tip of their cigarettes aglow.

After considering Edmund Goulding for the direction of this steamy melodrama, the studio opted for French-born (of Irish stock) veteran George Fitzmaurice, well known for his ability to create highly charged love scenes on-screen. Rounding out the main cast were veterans Lionel Barrymore and Lewis Stone (in his third and last picture with Novarro, though they have no scenes together).

Shooting began on October 1. Novarro, with more than ten years of experience as an actor and fifteen films to his credit as a star, was actually anxious about having to perform next to the forbidding twenty-six-year-old Swede. "I felt very strange," he told *Photoplay*, "and I imagine Miss Garbo also felt some restraint at the time." One possible complication was that Garbo did not like to rehearse, whereas Novarro did. He felt it necessary to go through the motions with the lights, camera, and microphones, "just as it will be when it is actually filmed." Either in deference to Novarro's seniority at the studio, or just out of consideration for an actor she respected,

Garbo offered to rehearse. In order to solve another potential complication—Garbo's concern that she might appear too tall—Novarro had to wear boots with internal lifts.

After the first scene was shot on the Mata Hari apartment set, the still photographer prepared for a picture of the two stars together. Following directions, Garbo and Novarro stood facing each other in the bedroom doorway, but there was no chemistry between them. "In a way, it was a test," Novarro later recalled. "Perhaps she felt I was watching to see if she would 'upstage' me. Or possibly she was waiting to see if I would try it on her." Once they realized there would be no hogging for the best camera angle, the tension was dispelled. Though Novarro later remembered Garbo being "offstandish [sic]" at first, she seems to have rapidly opened up to him, even telling her costar how she had missed his company on the days when he was not needed on the set.

Each day, filming began at nine in the morning and finished promptly at five in the afternoon, when Garbo's maid would hold up a makeup mirror toward the actress as a signal that the day's work was over. "She smiled graciously, said good night, and said she would see us at nine o'clock in the morning," Novarro told *Photoplay*. "No word of complaint or apology. That's all there was to it. No 'I go home!' as I heard so much about. Just an independence and courage to do what she believes is the right thing." One afternoon, when Novarro asked her to spend an extra hour on the set at George Fitzmaurice's urging, Garbo smilingly acceded, but arrived two hours late the next morning. The director never asked any more favors of either of them.

Despite Fitzmaurice's extensive use of storyboarding—detailed drawings of the sets, the positioning of the performers, and specifications for lighting and camera angles—the director left room for impromptu creativity, as in the cigarettes-aglow-in-the-dark scene. "It was not in the script," Novarro reminisced years later, "and yet I am remembered as much for that scene as I am for the chariot race in *Ben-Hur*." At the request of the Hays Office, that sequence was cut from the 1940 *Mata Hari* reissue, and has never been seen since the picture's original release. The cigarette scene, and others deleted from the reissue, are now lost.

While starring in *Mata Hari*, Novarro became enmeshed in another court case, but this time one in which he was directly concerned. On Saturday night, September 13, 1930, during the period when he was working on *La*

Sevillana, he had been involved in an automobile accident. While traveling at fifty miles an hour on Rimpau Boulevard, his car crashed into the vehicle of Southern Pacific employee Harold B. Wisdom at the Wilshire Boulevard intersection, approximately five miles west of downtown Los Angeles. Five people were in Novarro's car at the time of the accident: the actor and two other men in the rumble seat, and Frank Hansen and a woman in the front seat. The identity of the three passengers was never revealed. They fled the scene, and Novarro later claimed he had just met them at a party and could not remember their names.

One week after the collision, Novarro was served at the MGM gate with a $50,500 lawsuit on Wisdom's behalf (approximately $585,000 today). The suit alleged that Hansen's reckless driving and the ensuing crash had resulted in such severe back injuries for Wisdom that he was unable to make the long rides necessary for his job. Novarro contested the action, which was taken to court in early November of the following year.

During the brief trial, Novarro's attorney, Stanley Barnes, introduced as evidence a film made secretly—with the help of MGM—that showed the plaintiff blithely enjoying horseback riding, playing baseball, and rowing a boat, all well after the collision. Wisdom was called to the stand, where he attempted to explain that his doctor had ordered him to perform those strenuous exercises, but he was cut short by the judge's warning that his testimony could be used against him. "It is apparent the plaintiff has made an effort to mislead the court and jury as to the extent of his injuries," the judge declared, and awarded the Southern Pacific collector only $700 to cover damages to his car.

At one point in the trial, when Novarro took the stand in his defense, he avowed that before the accident he had had "only one drink with friends" and that Hansen had not consumed any alcohol. Indeed, Hansen was quite possibly sober, but Novarro's "only one drink" excuse sounds hollow when put in the context of both his early 1930s partying and his future drunken-driving problems. Since by all accounts Hansen had been at the wheel at the time of the accident, Novarro, this time, came out of the reckless-driving accusations unscathed.

On December 3, approximately two weeks after finishing work on *Mata Hari,* Novarro signed a one-year contract with MGM for two pictures. He was to make $75,000 per picture, half of what he had made for *Son of India,* but approximately 50 percent more than he had just received for *Mata Hari.* (At that time, MGM and other studios were cutting their stars' salaries because of a downturn in cinema attendance that threatened to become even more acute.) Other provisions in Novarro's new contract stipulated that he was to earn $25,000 as director of one motion picture—to be presented as "A Ramon Novarro Production"—and that he would have six months out of the year to pursue professional commitments onstage or on the radio, though he would now have to obtain MGM's written consent before doing so.

Two weeks after signing the contract, Novarro left with Frank Hansen for New York on an extended vacation. On Christmas day, while Novarro was having a turkey dinner in his hotel room with Hansen, a bouquet of roses was delivered to his door. The sender's card read only "M. H." Not recognizing the initials, Novarro was momentarily puzzled until Hansen suggested, "Mata Hari." The screen's Rosanoff was ecstatic. "Oh, my heart stopped," he would remember years later. "It was wonderful!" Within the hour, Ms. M. H. was on the phone with him, and the next evening they went out on the town to the Ritz and other fashionable nightspots.

One week later, on December 31, *Mata Hari* had its premiere at New York City's Capitol Theater, garnering the best reviews of any Novarro talkie in spite of complaints about the artificiality of the plot and its numerous historical inaccuracies (a problem Paramount had avoided earlier that year when it released a disguised version of Mata Hari's life, *Dishonored*, starring Marlene Dietrich). The two stars also received enthusiastic notices, with the *New York Times*'s Mordaunt Hall thrilled by Garbo's "flawless portrayal" and Novarro's "capital" performance.

The overwhelmingly positive reviews for *Mata Hari* are as surprising as the negative response to the much superior *Daybreak*. It should be noted that nowhere in the picture does Novarro deliver the notorious line "What's the matter, Mata?" but there are a good many other inane bits of dialogue and situations that are equally laughable. Except for Garbo, who is a mannered but intriguing Mata Hari, the rest of the cast flounders in this muddle. Novarro had been forewarned not to let Garbo's allure ruin his acting ability—as it had supposedly done with Robert Montgomery in *Inspiration* earlier in the year—but to no avail. Whether or not Garbo's charms were to blame, Novarro is particularly disappointing in the innocent-boy-in-love role he had done so well before. In contrast with Garbo's, his acting seems amateurish and insincere.

State and local censors were much less receptive to the seductiveness of *Mata Hari* than film critics had been. Cuts were ordered in several states, including the elimination of a sequence that clearly implied a sexual relationship between the two unmarried leads. Upon giving *Mata Hari* a "not recommended" rating, the representative of the Atlanta Better Film Committee stated, "I wish this picture could be destroyed. It is not fit to be shown anywhere." The public disagreed. The combination of two major stars and the promise of torrid romance (ads blasted, "When Mata Hari danced—brave men forgot honor, loyalty and country!") turned *Mata Hari* into a gigantic hit, with more than $2 million in worldwide rentals. This suggestive melodrama was, by a large margin, Garbo's biggest international success to date, and Novarro's highest-grossing picture after *Ben-Hur*. It was also one of the top fifteen moneymakers of 1932 in the domestic market, and certainly occupied a much higher ranking overseas, where it made nearly 60 percent of its revenues. Among MGM's 1932 releases—*Mata Hari* was screened on one single day in 1931—only the all-star *Grand Hotel* (also with Garbo) and *Tarzan, the Ape Man* surpassed the global earnings of the Garbo-Novarro team.

Besides providing an enormous boost to Novarro's career, *Mata Hari* also evoked, for the first time, strong rumors about a love affair between the perennial Mexican bachelor and one of his leading ladies. Those stories surely originated, as they often did, with the MGM publicity department—a Novarro-Garbo pairing would be an excellent opportunity for the studio to recapture the box-office fire stirred by the Gilbert-Garbo romance of the late silent era. The setup seemed ideal: Novarro was one of Hollywood's most eligible bachelors and Garbo its undisputable most eligible bachelorette (and one rumored to prefer the company of her own gender); the two stars had developed a solid rapport during filming; and Novarro, MGM's foremost male star of the early 1930s, not only had requested that he work with the Swedish star, but shockingly had also accepted second billing to her.

Curiously, in an early 1932 telegram to Noël Sullivan, Novarro wrote, "Garbo was magnificent—I am so much in love with her . . . that I am liable to do something rash!—For the first time in my life! I am so happy—rejoice with me!" This peculiar wire raises an interesting possibility: had Novarro *really* fallen in love with Garbo, or was Novarro's cable merely an ironic message to a gay friend who knew better than to believe studio-concocted rumors? The latter possibility seems the more logical.

In a May 1932 *New Movie Magazine* article titled "The Most Eligible Couple Will Never Marry," Novarro fully expressed his admiration for Garbo, but with a diplomatic dismissal of the romance stories. "Greta Garbo is marvelous. No other woman has ever impressed me so much; not even poor beautiful Barbara La Marr," he asserted. "Greta is everything that man desires. She has beauty, lure, mystery and an aloofness that only men understand, for it is a quality which is usually to be found only in men." Nevertheless, marriage, in those days the final step of all serious romance, was not in store for either one of them. "I think everyone should marry. That is, everyone except the artist," Novarro explained. "And he cannot serve two masters—Matrimony and Art. . . . Greta Garbo is first and always the artist and I hope I am that, too. She has promised never to marry and I know that I never shall. . . . An actor has no *right* to marry. . . . He is public property."

In that same *New Movie Magazine* issue, Herbert Howe, in his new column "The Hollywood Boulevardier," subtly, but unambiguously, quashed the gossip. Howe reported that while lunching with Novarro in the studio's cafeteria, they were frequently interrupted by inquirers wanting to know about the "affair." According to Howe, "Ramon, more concerned with sausage than romance just then, replied, 'That's what I'm trying to find out.'" Howe claimed he "didn't ask, because I knew that if there was anything to it Ramon would lie like a gentleman; if there wasn't, he might be tempted to lie also—as what gentleman wouldn't?" (Left unsaid was the fact that Howe did not *need* to ask, for he already knew the answer.) After discussing other subjects—and without bringing up Novarro's name—Howe made clear his thoughts about the matter: "Greta has friends, does attend parties, does not fall in love with leading men, never says 'I, Garbo.'" The Novarro-Garbo stories quickly died out, as both stars had sufficient clout at the studio to demand an end to them.

Over the next few years, the two *Mata Hari* costars would occasionally meet at the studio and at social gatherings, but even though they shared a heartfelt fondness for each other, there is no evidence indicating a long-lasting, close friendship.

With the worldwide success of *Mata Hari*, Novarro was once again at the top of the MGM male star roster. This was quite a reversal from his standing in 1928, when he was in fourth place—after Lon Chaney, John Gilbert, and William Haines—in average revenues per picture. From early 1929 to mid-1932—or from *The Flying Fleet* to *Mata Hari*—Novarro's average worldwide revenues, at $1,314,000, were markedly higher than those of any of his MGM competitors. (There are no figures for Chaney in 1931 or 1932; he had died in August 1930.)

Oddly, Novarro's stiffest competitor for the top male spot at the studio during the early talkie era was the ugly, slovenly, bigmouthed Wallace Beery.

This recent MGM acquisition from Paramount had proven himself a formidable box-office lure when featured with another name, whether Marie Dressler in *Min and Bill* or Chester Morris in *The Big House*, but he could not vie with the Mexican heartthrob in the romance arena. In Novarro's realm of lovemaking, the real challenges were two fast-rising newcomers: Robert Montgomery, who was being groomed for stardom by being cast opposite the studio's top female stars, and Clark Gable, who began receiving that same star-forming treatment after pushing Norma Shearer around in *A Free Soul*. Even so, both Montgomery and Gable were a couple of years away from *real* stardom. They were successful—like Beery to a certain extent—as long as they were paired with a big name. In spite of a few lapses throughout his career, Novarro was deemed a real star because he could fill movie houses with his name *alone*.

"This is magnificent!" the then-unknown Ray Milland marveled upon gazing at the lights of the mammoth Los Angeles Basin, which spreads from the western beach cities to downtown and beyond, and from Long Beach to Hollywood. "And just think that it all belongs to Ramon Novarro!" replied MGM talent scout Robert Lisman. That was in early 1930. And perhaps the world's film capital did indeed belong to Novarro that evening and hundreds of other evenings during his reign as MGM's—and Hollywood's—top male romantic star. Nonetheless, the film capital was not to remain his very much longer.

Ramon Novarro, ca. 1923

Rudolph Valentino looks contrite while Rose Dione proudly holds the French flag in Rex Ingram's 1921 blockbuster *The Four Horsemen of the Apocalypse*. Novarro (third from right), then a mere extra, looks on.

Lewis Stone drags a very dead Ramon Novarro in Rex Ingram's now lost *Trifling Women* (1922), which has a few elements in common with Billy Wilder's masterpiece *Sunset Blvd*. Among those is the work of cinematographer John F. Seitz.

Ramon Novarro (with cigarette holder) plays the scheming Rupert of Hentzau, his first important role, in Rex Ingram's 1922 Ruritanian drama *The Prisoner of Zenda*.

Standing, from left to right: Wallace MacDonald, William V. Mong, Barbara La Marr, Ramon Novarro, and Robert Edeson. Director Fred Niblo is on the right, with his arm around actress Edith Roberts on the set of the 1924 melodrama *Thy Name Is Woman*.

Rex Ingram, Herbert Howe, Alice Terry (minus blond wig), and Ramon Novarro in full Bedouin regalia while shooting *The Arab* (1924). Courtesy of the Matias Bombal Collection.

Despite popular lore, Novarro and fellow Mexicans Dolores del Río and Lupe Velez played characters of various nationalities during their heyday. Here's Novarro as all-American Naval Academy student Dick Randall in *The Midshipman*.

Ramon Novarro suffered both on-screen and off-screen in *Ben-Hur*, Hollywood's biggest worldwide blockbuster until *Gone with the Wind* fourteen years later. *Ben-Hur* also turned out to be a monumentally difficult production.

Ramon Novarro with Gilbert Roland, at the time Novarro was starring in the ill-fated *A Certain Young Man*, ca. 1927.

Student prince Ramon Novarro, barmaid Norma Shearer, and mentor Jean Hersholt in Ernst Lubitsch's silent classic *The Student Prince in Old Heidelberg*.

Ramon Novarro opens a hole in John Miljan's abdomen in *Lovers?*, one of Novarro's lost films.

Ramon Novarro in a publicity shot for another king-in-love-with-commoner saga, the poorly received *Forbidden Hours*. In this one, Renée Adorée was the object of his affections.

Ramon Novarro in a publicity shot for the popular adventure drama *Across to Singapore*.

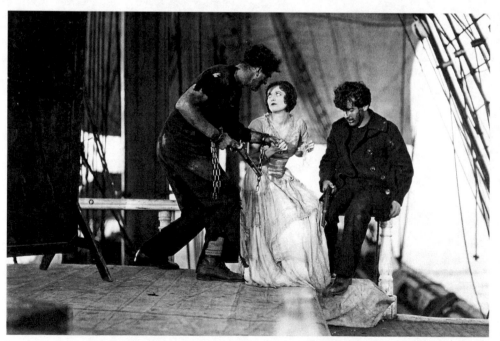

Ramon Novarro and Joan Crawford in *Across to Singapore*. Crawford would become a star later that year, following the release of *Our Dancing Daughters*.

Ramon Novarro in *The Pagan*, in which audiences got to hear his synchronized singing of "The Pagan Love Song."

The Samuel-Novarro House, designed by Lloyd Wright. The house is located atop the Los Feliz Hills, on the eastern side of the Hollywood Hills. Diane Keaton owned it for a while. Courtesy of the Matias Bombal Collection.

Ramon Novarro and singer-turned-actress Marion Harris in *Devil-May-Care*, Novarro's first talkie.

Ramon Novarro in *Manon*, the opera sequence in the highly popular melodrama *Call of the Flesh*.

Ramon Novarro and Greta Garbo in *Mata Hari*, Novarro's biggest box-office hit of the 1930s. The spy melodrama was one of Garbo's biggest hits as well. Courtesy of the Matias Bombal Collection.

Ramon Novarro and Helen Hayes in *The Son-Daughter*, in which neither one looks all that convincing as Chinese. Louise Closser Hale's makeup looks even phonier.

Ramon Novarro and Myrna Loy on the set of *The Barbarian*, Novarro's last successful film at MGM. At the time, the studio's publicity department tried to come up with a make-believe Novarro-Loy romance.

Among those present at Novarro's Teatro Intimo are Norma Shearer, Irving Thalberg, Jeanette MacDonald, Myrna Loy, Ray Milland, Dolores del Río, Cary Grant, and Randolph Scott. (Full list of guests on page 350.) Courtesy of the Matías Bombal Collection.

Ramon Novarro made a brief Hollywood comeback in the late 1940s and early 1950s. Here he's with John Garfield in John Huston's political thriller *We Were Strangers*.

Producer Sol C. Siegel, Ramon Novarro, Charlton Heston, and director William Wyler at the *Ben-Hur* premiere in 1959. Courtesy of the Matias Bombal Collection.

Ramon Novarro in the late 1920s

Fade-Out

By early 1932, less than five years since *The Jazz Singer*, the Hollywood landscape had been radically altered. The early-1930s reissues of two of the biggest hits of the previous decade, *Ben-Hur* (in abridged form) and *The Big Parade*, had generated little interest despite the addition of sound effects and a synchronized score (though *Ben-Hur* remained a strong box-office pull abroad). A mere six years old, the style and technique of those epoch-making films were regarded as badly outdated.

In addition, numerous stars of the silent era had retired, been relegated to minor roles, or moved to third-rank studios. First National superstar Colleen Moore saw her weekly salary drop from $10,000 in 1929 to less than $1,000 when she signed with MGM three years later (a contract that never resulted in a picture). Corinne Griffith was dropped by Warner Bros. in 1930 and made only one more film, in England, before retiring. Norma Talmadge, one of the top stars of silent pictures, left the screen after two talking box-office disappointments.

Sound was not the only—and often not even the main—reason for the upheaval. Causes ranged from the stars' personal problems to their being at the wrong studio at the wrong time. Novarro might well have suffered the fate of Colleen Moore or Corinne Griffith had he not been an MGM contract player. While nearly every studio was suffering heavy losses because of the deepening Depression, MGM continued profitable—albeit less so. Thus, Novarro's, Norma Shearer's, and Greta Garbo's salaries and perks, even if reduced, continued, while cost cuttings elsewhere meant the dismissal of top talent. Eventually, even MGM would resort to that tactic, though in a less drastic manner.

With the success of *Mata Hari*, Novarro's position at the top seemed secure—except that these were highly volatile times. His career could easily take a sudden downturn were he cast in the wrong vehicle. Despite numerous tales about the security and the nurturing of the studio system, major talents such as Pola Negri at Paramount and Renée Adorée at MGM had frequently been wasted in inferior productions, and often found their careers damaged by a lack of front-office vision. Unfortunately for Novarro, this was to prove the case with the first picture under his new contract.

Huddle, taken from Francis Wallace's *Saturday Evening Post* story of college life (adapted from his 1930 novel), absurdly cast thirty-three-year-old Novarro as Tony Amatto, a cocky college football player who discovers the meaning of love, honor, and teamwork before the final fade-out. The screen adaptation made a point of changing the locale from Notre Dame to Yale (Universal had recently released the similarly themed *Spirit of Notre Dame*), but the one element in the picture that most clearly needed to be changed— the star—remained.

"A singing star gets odd assignments sometimes," observed one columnist about Novarro's *Huddle* casting. Indeed, the insolent Tony Amatto, with the appropriate surname change, would have been a more fitting role for either Robert Montgomery or ex–college football player Johnny Mack Brown, both of whom had been mentioned for the part before Novarro was selected. Even William Haines, though too old at thirty-two to play a college student, would have been a better pick, for at least he possessed the required physique and screen persona. (Amatto is quite similar to Haines's football players in *Brown of Harvard* and *West Point*.) Novarro, however, was not only too old, but also too small, too well-mannered, and displayed too heavy a Mexican accent to be convincing as the tough postadolescent mill worker from Indiana who becomes a Yale football star. When Garbo learned that her *Mata Hari* costar was practicing football moves for his next picture, she could only say, "Oh, they'll never learn."

As a further professional letdown, Novarro went from Garbo's arms to those of *Son of India*'s Madge Evans, who, despite her beauty and talent, remained a minor, misused leading lady. (On the positive side, Novarro and Evans became good friends; in fact, Madge Evans, Greta Garbo, and Myrna Loy were his favorite leading ladies in talking pictures.) *Huddle* also reunited the star with another former coplayer, *The Flying Fleet*'s Ralph Graves, who was cast as the tough but fatherly coach modeled after Knute Rockne. Sam Wood, who three years earlier had delivered the successful *So This Is College* for MGM, was the assigned director.

The unusually lengthy nine-week shooting schedule began on February 12, 1932, shortly after Novarro's return from a New York trip. Not surprisingly, he dreaded the assignment. After the celebrated *Mata Hari*, he had once again been relegated to a programmer—though an expensive one at $514,000. Compounding the problem, Novarro, hardly an avid sportsman, had to learn and practice both football and soccer moves (American football was replaced by soccer in the foreign market prints). Astronomer Edwin Hubbell's visit to the set may have excited MGM's publicity department, but not the despondent star of the picture. "I am working so very hard in something I don't particularly like and my nerves are not under perfect control as yet," he wrote to Noël Sullivan in late February. One month later, Novarro would complain again, "*Huddle* seems interminable."

Many critics felt that same way when *Huddle* opened on June 16, 1932. As for Novarro, the consensus was that, though still a fine actor, he was clearly out of his element. "Cast as a shy, gentle and plaintively romantic youth," remarked one reviewer, "Mr. Novarro isn't always gentle or shy. Still, when handing out a sock or lining up in football formation, one feels that neither is his favorite sport."

Surely, Novarro had played strong characters before *Huddle*, including the seaman in *Across to Singapore*, André-Louis Moreau in *Scaramouche*, and the biggest he-man of the 1920s, Judah Ben-Hur; but Amatto was a conventional tough guy, a type that had become highly popular in the early 1930s with the rapid ascendancy of he-men like Clark Gable and James Cagney. Although Novarro is not a total failure in the role, such miscasting was a foolish move on MGM's part, one akin to Paramount casting Maurice Chevalier as a roughneck baseball player from Iowa, or to the studio's own earlier decision to star Novarro as an English lord in *A Certain Young Man*. Mayer and Thalberg had obviously not learned from their past mistakes— nor from their successes.

Novarro had excelled at the box-office in both *The Midshipman* and *The Flying Fleet*. He was not a stereotypical tough guy in either picture (despite a fistfight in the former film), but there was no need for him to be one; these were traditional manly roles with guaranteed worldwide appeal. If Novarro's accent was a problem, he could easily have portrayed the son of a Spanish or Mexican diplomat enlisted in the American armed forces. Instead, the studio cast Gable and Montgomery in, respectively, *Hell Divers* and *Shipmates*, two successful military-themed pictures that helped advance their careers.

The poor reviews notwithstanding, *Huddle* garnered a not inconsiderable $476,000 domestically on the strength of its star, but Novarro's usually reliable foreign market failed to respond to a film about American college life. With less-than-stellar returns from abroad, *Huddle* ended $28,000 in the red—an especially disheartening outcome following so soon after the wildly popular *Mata Hari*. As had happened after *Ben-Hur*, which was succeeded by *A Certain Young Man*, MGM was at a loss as to how to showcase the talents of its top male star. Consequently, Novarro's fall during this highly unstable period would be as rapid as it was inevitable.

After the unpleasant *Huddle* production, Novarro took time off to study music and to rest. Later that summer, he moved to Louis Samuel's former Hollywood Hills house, on which he had invested $5,800 in property improvements, including the additions of a pergola, a music room, and a walled garden. Lloyd Wright had been responsible for the extensive remodeling, though studio publicity claimed that Novarro himself had designed and planned the house "during his spare moments when not appearing in front of a camera."

On the outside, the Valley Oak house was an imposing structure. Located on a slope overlooking one of the Hollywood Hills canyons, it extended from its lower level on Verde Oak Road to its uppermost level and main gateway on Valley Oak. The outside walls were white concrete partially shielded by patterned copper bands reminiscent of Mesoamerican temples, with a hollow block within the reinforced concrete that theoretically made the house earthquake-proof. From the gateway, a flight of Nile green steps led down the terraced gardens to a blue-toned guest room immediately above the main house, which could be reached by a further staircase.

With the assistance of MGM art director Cedric Gibbons, Novarro devised the modernistic (and gaudy) interior, most of it furnished with pieces from the luxurious Bullock's Wilshire. The centrally located beige library boasted a panoramic view of the canyons and was used as a drawing room for cocktails served on metal tables set before futuristic loungers. The dining room, on a slightly lower level to one side of the library, had black walls which set off strands of dull silver chains; the dining table was of frosted metal with a black satin cover, an onyx-glass tabletop, and aluminum legs. To the other side of the library was the bedroom, with pale green walls and dark green furniture that included a built-in dressing table and desk. At the end of the room, French doors opened to a swimming pool lined with Nile green tiles and surrounded by white concrete walls.

The music room, where Novarro sang accompanied by friends at the piano, was underneath the dining room. Dull gold and bronze furniture and walls were covered by a rose brocade with a design akin to the copper motif found on the outside walls. This color scheme was contrasted by the whiteness of a polar bear rug and several light-colored pieces of woodwork. Adjoining the music room was a cocktail bar, and on the same floor, but reached through a separate entrance, were the servant's quarters and a passage leading down to the garage.

"I had to get away from home, to live alone in a house of my own," Novarro explained. "I had to cater to whims and notions of my own that would be impossible for others to live with. For instance, I am frequently seized with a sudden desire to play my piano when I am somewhere en route between my bath and my bedroom, clad as God made me. Now, living alone, I can gratify this desire." At his new home, Novarro also attained the freedom to entertain his friends from the film and music worlds as he wished, since family members were not invited to such gatherings. Through-out the years, guests included Myrna Loy, Lawrence Tibbett, pianist Lester Donahue, and fellow *Daybreak* performer Douglass Montgomery. Obviously, there was no mention in the press of boyfriends at Valley Oak, though Novarro undoubtedly used his newfound freedom to bring home whomever he wished.

The move to Valley Oak marked the first time in his life that Novarro planned to live alone. Frank Hansen would have moved in with him, but Hansen, for unknown reasons, left Novarro's employ at that time and moved to New York. Having relied on Hansen for nearly all his day-to-day needs, Novarro was badly upset by his departure and rapidly set about finding a substitute. The replacement turned out to be Philip Moreland, a young New Englander who shortly after being hired moved in with the star.

In August 1932, Louis B. Mayer asked Novarro to accept a salary cut because of the perilous economic times—MGM's profits had dwindled to their lowest level since 1925, a drop that meant less compensation for Mayer and Thalberg, both of whom received a percentage of the studio's net income. A similar request was sent to many other MGM players, including Colleen Moore, Walter Huston, Jean Hersholt, and Diana Wynyard, though no appeals directed to Gable, Garbo, or Shearer are known. If Mayer was asking such financial sacrifice only from those with lesser box-office value, then Novarro's reign as MGM's top male star was officially over.

Like most other performers, Novarro refused Mayer's request. In a letter dated August 26, he wrote:

> You will never know how much it grieves me to find myself in a
> position where I must turn a deaf ear to your plea. If you remember
> when I signed my contract last year, you told me almost exactly the

same thing you have now written me.... As you know, my last year's income was quite good, and consequently, my salary this year represents my income tax for this and the next year. Practically nothing is left for all the obligations I still have, mainly, my numerous family and the education of my brothers.... I should like to call your attention to the fact that this is the first and only time that I have not been able to comply with your wishes. I have tried my best this year more than ever to help people in need, and I think you know me well enough to know that, if I were able to do what you ask, I should not hesitate for a second.

A compromise of sorts was reached when Novarro signed a special contract to appear in one picture for the studio, *The Son-Daughter*, at $5,000 a week—or $2,500 less per week than he had made for *Huddle*. His previous contract, for which one picture remained, was to be resumed after the completion of this adaptation of George M. Scarborough and David Belasco's 1919 play about a Chinese maiden in love with a Chinese prince disguised as a student.

Unlike *Huddle*, *The Son-Daughter* was intended to be a major motion picture. Illustrious stage star Helen Hayes, in her second year in Hollywood, was set to costar—with top billing—as the shy but determined Chinese damsel. Though not an established box-office attraction, Hayes, like Garbo, meant prestige, a quality Novarro sorely needed after his most recent picture. The designation of three-time Academy Award nominee Clarence Brown as director was further indication that *The Son-Daughter* was planned as an important production, but even so, it was hardly the appropriate vehicle to showcase Novarro's talents. First, the story focuses on the leading female character, and second, Novarro would be buried under heavy makeup that was supposed to make him look Chinese.

Since becoming a star, Novarro had already played one secondary role, in *Mata Hari*, but at least his Lieutenant Alexis Rosanoff is a dashing aviator who makes passionate love to the sensual leading lady. *The Son-Daughter's* shaved-headed Tom Lee, on the other hand, is a shy, fragile character completely lacking in erotic charge. As for the East Asian makeup, it may have worked for Lon Chaney and Warner Oland—a Swedish-born actor who made a career playing Asians—but Novarro, as Murnau had pointed out when discussing his George Hurrell photographs, was not a character actor. His value as a film star rested on his natural looks.

Why Novarro consented to appear in *The Son-Daughter* remains a mystery. He may have believed the role of Tom Lee would expand his range as an actor, or perhaps he thought a pairing with the celebrated Helen Hayes would restore luster to his career after the inane *Huddle*. Or maybe he just wanted some extra money. Even though Novarro had made $340,000 in 1931, his most profitable year ever, he had begun that year with his finances still in disarray because of the Louis Samuel debacle. As he had mentioned in the August letter to Mayer, a considerable percentage of his 1931 wages had gone to taxes, and additionally, Novarro now had two households to maintain, Gramercy and Valley Oak.

During the production of *The Son-Daughter*, which began on September 28, both stars were courteous to each other, though Novarro did not enjoy working with Helen Hayes. In spite of reports that he greatly admired Hayes's talent, he later dismissed his renowned leading lady as "the opposite of Garbo. She's a very fine technician, but from an artistic point of view . . ." Hayes, however, (undeservedly) garnered most of the acting honors, whereas Novarro earned only scant good notices when *The Son-Daughter* opened on December 30, 1932. The picture itself received overwhelmingly negative reviews. "An ancient and slightly lethargic melodrama," panned Richard Watts, Jr. "It's old time stuff, moving slowly and laboriously toward a sad climax," complained *Variety*. "Stock situations, not for a moment believable, wholly artificial dialogue, and a clumsy, heavy plot, lacking the element of suspense," declared the *New York Sun*.

The *New York Morning Telegraph* was one of the few publications that commended Novarro for his "sympathetic appreciation [for the character] that distinguishes the true artist from the routine player." Actually, Novarro is hopelessly miscast despite a few good attempts to convey Tom Lee's humorous shyness. "I've often complained against casting Caucasians in important roles with real Chinese," observed the magazine *Script*, "as the contrast is cruel to Caucasians. Clarence Brown gets around this by using no Chinese in the cast at all (that is, none but Warner Oland, if you know what I mean). Very smart." Smart perhaps, but ineffective. The performances—with the exception of H. B. Warner's creepy nationalist—come across as vacuous stereotypes.

In spite of the Hayes-Novarro combination—Hayes was fresh from her Academy Award win for *The Sin of Madelon Claudet* the previous month—and the care given the production, *The Son-Daughter* turned out to be a financial disappointment. Poor reviews and a film attendance slump in early 1933 caused by the worsening depression diminished the stars' box-office appeal. Once the overseas rentals were added, the picture managed a minuscule $6,000 profit, hardly enough to justify the studio's monetary gamble on a grade-A production.

As a Helen Hayes picture—Novarro, after all, had what amounted to a supporting role in which he was nearly unrecognizable—*The Son-Daughter* would not have fared much worse financially had the actress been paired with Robert Montgomery, Robert Young, or Richard Cromwell, the previously announced candidates to play Tom Lee. The casting of Novarro, in fact, was both a budgetary mistake—he was much costlier than any of the other three actors—and a waste of one of the studio's top assets. Novarro had remained an important name thus far, but the continual misuse of his talents was beginning to erode his popularity. Despite MGM's insistence that his vehicles were judiciously selected, the opposite was the case. Even though it was common practice to announce a star for a particular role only to cast someone else in the part (for example, Gable replacing John Gilbert in *Red Dust* or Garbo replacing Joan Crawford in *The Single Standard*), the fact that Robert Montgomery had been the original choice for Novarro's last three roles clearly indicates that the studio was not choosing projects tailored for the persona of its Mexican heartthrob.

Novarro, of course, was also responsible for his professional doldrums. As in the late 1920s, he seemed to be more concerned with music than with film. Although his contract did not grant him choice of roles, he had enough clout at the studio to ask for—if not demand—projects that would befit his screen image. The one time he had actively requested a specific part, Lieutenant Alexis in *Mata Hari*, had resulted in his most successful talking picture. Another second lead to Garbo would have been preferable to a sole starring part in *Huddle*, but instead of fighting for better vehicles, soon after *The Son-Daughter* began its mediocre run, Novarro announced he was preparing for concert engagements in Paris and London.

But before leaving for Europe, Novarro had one more picture to make to fulfill his recently extended contract. That picture—*Man of the Nile*—turned out to be, like *Son of India*, another attempt by MGM to recapture the flavor of *The Sheik*, *The Arab*, and other "Easterns" of the previous decade.

"Every woman's dream of heaven in the twenties was to be carried off to an oasis by Valentino, Ramon Novarro, or any reasonable facsimile," declared Myrna Loy, Novarro's *Man of the Nile* leading lady. MGM was now doing its best to persuade women in the thirties to feel the same way. The studio employed numerous major scenarists (including Lenore Coffee, Anita Loos, and *Grand Hotel* writer Vicki Baum) to work on the script about a flirtatious Egyptian guide in amorous pursuit of a white tourist, with Mayer insisting on a happy ending that would please both the public and the racial purity–conscious censors. (Hence, the "white" tourist turns out to be part

Egyptian.) The studio also assembled a strong supporting cast, including former silent star Reginald Denny, Edward Arnold, and stage veteran Louise Closser Hale; hired Harold Rosson, fresh from *Red Dust* and *Tarzan the Ape Man*, as the cinematographer; and had "Pagan Love Song" composers Nacio Herb Brown and Arthur Freed contribute the picture's romantic ballad, "Love Songs of the Nile." The only questionable choice for the project was that of director Sam Wood, since his previous collaboration with Novarro had not been a successful one.

Unlike *The Arab*, which had been shot in North Africa, *Man of the Nile* was decidedly a studio-bound production. Some of the exteriors were filmed in Yuma, Arizona, but most of the picture was shot on soundstages, with stone blocks made of plaster and a desert only half an inch thick. Yet, despite Culver City's lack of exotic glamour, the production of *Man of the Nile* offered several unusual experiences for cast and crew, including coping with a temperamental camel named Rosie and enduring a 6.4-magnitude earthquake, which struck in the late afternoon of March 10.

Myrna Loy later recalled her leading man as a "gentle, quiet man," and quickly developed a solid friendship with him—one that would soon give rise to rumors of romance. Once again, MGM tried to enhance the box-office performance of one of its films by adding an offscreen romance to the publicity mix. Even if the alleged Garbo-Novarro affair had not been responsible for *Mata Hari*'s extraordinary box-office success, it surely had not hindered it. A Novarro-Loy romance could do no harm to *The Barbarian*, as *Man of the Nile* was finally called—to the contrary, it might add to Novarro's fading romantic image and heighten Loy's star status in her first important lead at the studio.

Loy learned about the affair through the papers. Three days before Novarro was to sail for Europe—the rumors were possibly so timed to avoid quick rebuttals from the star—a news article proclaimed, "Chatter in Hollywood: Only a few intimate friends know that Ramon Novarro and Myrna Loy have a tremendous yen for each other. Ramon, heretofore impervious to women with the exception of Greta Garbo, for whom he admitted a worshipful adoration, has fallen hard for the red-headed actress. Myrna returns Ramon's feeling and they have been seeing each other every day. No one has ever associated the thought of marriage with Ramon, who has frequently talked of going into a monastery. But it may be marriage in this case, for it is his greatest romance." As an illustration of the "romance," the studio released a photograph taken at the Pasadena train station upon Novarro's departure for New York. The picture shows a fur-coated Loy and a distinguished-looking Novarro—carefully placed atop a boarding step while the five-foot-six-inch actress remained on the ground—holding hands and smiling at each other while saying good-bye.

Novarro, busy in New York with preparations for his first European concert tour, did not have a chance to protest immediately to the studio. Loy, however, was in Los Angeles. After discovering she was having a "torrid romance" with her *Barbarian* leading man, she, in her own words, "raised hell" at MGM. "It was preposterous," she later recalled. "Ramon wasn't even interested in the ladies, and I was seeing [producer] Arthur [Hornblow, Jr.] exclusively, so the publicity department had chosen a most unlikely pair." Still, the rumors persisted.

On March 24, 1933, Novarro sailed for France aboard the *Paris*. He was accompanied by his brother Eduardo, who had recently graduated as an architect; his cousin Jorge Gavilán, now working as his chauffeur; current assistant Philip Moreland; and former assistant Frank Hansen, who, out of a job because of the Depression, was brought over to share Moreland's duties during the trip. As he crossed the Atlantic, Novarro was leaving behind the Loy love rumors, his shaky stardom, and, seemingly, his directorial career. His December 1931 contract had elapsed with *The Barbarian*, and Novarro had not directed any pictures for the studio as that contract had stipulated. The European trip was quite possibly the reason Novarro gave up his option to direct one picture for MGM, though no record of his decision is known to exist.

Before his departure, Novarro made a point of telling the press he was going to continue his music studies while abroad, but *without* a teacher— even though Louis Graveure was then living in Germany. Sometime in 1931, not long before Graveure left the United States, Novarro's friendship and professional association with his singing teacher had abruptly ended because Graveure's strenuous voice exercises had damaged his pupil's voice. This break in their relationship, until then marked by effusive mutual admiration, was apparently never mended. When Novarro resumed voice lessons later in the decade, he chose the famed Spanish bass and Deanna Durbin's singing coach, Andrés de Segurola.

Even without a teacher, Novarro was determined to succeed on the concert stage, a venture he had contemptuously dismissed only a few years before. In 1929, he had told *Screenland* that concerts did not interest him because they were too stiff, but now that a career in opera had become an increasingly forlorn hope, the concert stage had grown considerably more alluring. Robert Ritchie, Jeanette MacDonald's manager and fiancé, had arranged for Novarro's European appearances.

Although not as sensational as MacDonald's 1931 Parisian performances, Novarro's shows in France at the Casino Théâtre in Biarritz and at the Alhambra in Paris were warmly received—a major relief for him after the disastrous 1929 trip. Shortly after the Paris engagement, the star and his entourage, which now also included musical accompanist Jack King and his wife, headed for the Mediterranean resort Juan-les-Pins, where they met with Alice Terry. Rex Ingram did not join the group because he was busy in North Africa drawing sketches of the locals and studying Islam (he was reported to have become a convert, signing his name Bin Aliq Nasr el-Din, the Son of the Union of Victory and Religion).

Ingram had by then involuntarily retired from filmmaking. His last American film, the 1929 United Artists release *The Three Passions*, had been both a critical and a financial disappointment. ("Rex Ingram remains in Europe living as he pleases and working when the spirit moves," observed *Photoplay*. "Personally he has a great time. Professionally, he stands still.") Worse yet, Ingram had lost control of his French Riviera studio allegedly because of a scheme concocted by an associate, attorney Edouard Corniglion-Molinier (Ingram sued but lost the case). Without either Nice or Hollywood, Ingram struggled to find private financing for his next—and last—film, the talkie *Baroud*. After spending two years working on the picture, in which he also starred, he saw the million-dollar project receive only limited release in Europe and in the United States, where it opened to tepid notices as *Love in Morocco*. In six years, Ingram had fallen from star director to unemployable has-been.

From France, Novarro and his troupe headed to London, where he sang to wildly enthusiastic audiences at the Palladium. At the theater's stage door, he was attacked by hysterical fans, who grabbed buttons off his coat and tore pieces from his scarf and handkerchiefs. Novarro reacted to the assault by doing some grabbing and tearing of his own, eventually bringing home some of his rabid fans' belongings as souvenirs. Following extensive traveling through Spain, Switzerland, and Belgium, Novarro returned aboard the *Olympic* to the United States after being gone for four months. He disembarked in New York on August 1, arriving in Los Angeles ten days later to promptly deny rumors of a romantic liaison with Myrna Loy.

Novarro was as upset by the studio's maneuver as Loy had been. Decades later, he would still express indignation when the subject was broached. Betty Lasky, daughter of Paramount production executive Jesse L. Lasky, recalled that Novarro "became very angry" when she mentioned his reported romance with Loy during a 1965 interview, a strange reaction to three-decade-old gossip. Perhaps the rumors temporarily affected his friendship with Loy, for, unlike the Garbo "romance," the Loy rumors lingered for months despite Novarro's frequent public denials.

The Novarro-Loy rumors may have been good fodder for the press, but they failed to help *The Barbarian* after the picture opened on May 12, 1933. (Instead of promoting *The Barbarian* in the United States, Novarro was then singing in Europe.) "Our good old movie friend, that swarthy sheik of the desert sands, is with us again," remarked the *New York Morning Telegraph*, though not everyone was welcoming. Reviews were widely divergent, ranging from the *World Telegraph's* "a mediocre rewrite of a lot of stale desert situations" to Mordaunt Hall's observation that *The Barbarian* displayed "brightness and originality."

As usual, Novarro's notices were mostly positive, with reviewers bestowing special praise for his comedic abilities. In fact, the first hour of *The Barbarian* gives Novarro his best light moments on-screen since *In Gay Madrid* three years earlier. His is so charming a performance that not even his obviously non-Arabic accent can detract from it. The film itself, described by the equally outstanding Loy as "a wild, crazy picture," is surprisingly entertaining, despite (or because of) a frenzied and illogical second half involving lust, betrayal, death, rape, revenge, a couple of whippings, and Mayer's tacked-on serene finale.

Unlike *Daybreak*, which is marred by severe bowdlerization, *The Barbarian* remains unapologetically raunchy. From the heroine's revealing rose-petal bath (Loy later affirmed that she wore a flesh-toned garment for the scene) to the rape sequence, the picture makes no concessions to the censors. The rape, of course, is not graphic, but the look in Novarro's eyes is explicit. The old playful twinkle of the "gentle, gentlemanly Valentino" is nowhere evident. It would be another year before the Hays Office would muster enough power—through the support of vocal Catholic groups threatening a general boycott of motion pictures—to order such a scene eliminated.

In several states, however, local censors butchered *The Barbarian*. These cuts may help explain the picture's somewhat disappointing domestic box office despite the presence of two stars in excellent form, the lovely melody "Love Songs of the Nile," and the widely publicized love affair rumors. Because of its medium-to-low cost and a good, though not outstanding, run overseas, *The Barbarian* managed $100,000 in profits—the highest figure for a Novarro vehicle in which he starred alone (Loy was featured below the title) since *Call of the Flesh* three years earlier. Even so, that amount was hardly impressive, especially considering that *The Barbarian* brought in Novarro's lowest domestic rentals since *A Certain Young Man*. Whether the censors were to blame or not, Novarro had definitely been demoted in the domestic market to second-rank status.

In the mid-1920s, when Metro-Goldwyn-Mayer initiated its slogan "More stars than there are in Heaven," the brightest celestial bodies in the MGM firmament were Ramon Novarro, Lillian Gish, Marion Davies, Lon Chaney, John Gilbert, Norma Shearer, Buster Keaton, Mae Murray, and Jackie Coogan. In the following three years, Greta Garbo, William Haines, Joan Crawford, and—on a lesser scale—Tim McCoy also climbed up to official stardom. Additionally, the MGM of the 1920s boasted a wide array of top featured players, among them Conrad Nagel, Renée Adorée, Eleanor Boardman, Lionel Barrymore, and Nils Asther. By late 1933, the studio's only surviving major names of the silent era were Novarro, Shearer, Garbo, Davies, Crawford, and Barrymore.

Some, like Mae Murray, had left films. Lillian Gish had returned to the stage. Lon Chaney and Renée Adorée had died (thirty-five-year-old Adorée finally succumbed to tuberculosis in October 1933; Novarro was one of the pallbearers at the funeral). Others, like Conrad Nagel, were struggling with unimportant supporting roles or with minor leads at Poverty Row studios.

Some historians have blamed Mayer for the unexpected and spectacular decline of Novarro's two main rivals at MGM, John Gilbert and William Haines, both of whom the studio head found boisterous and unmanageable. But reality was far more complex than a series of petty vendettas. In fact, circumstances unrelated to studio politics were decisive in Gilbert's and Haines's rapid falls from public grace. Those circumstances help explain why Novarro was able to maintain his standing at MGM while the studio's other two major silent-era male stars floundered.

One major problem for both Gilbert and Haines was that they looked well beyond their years soon after they reached thirty: Gilbert because of alcohol abuse and Haines because of a fast-receding hairline matched by a fast-increasing waistline. At thirty but looking forty, Haines was too old to keep playing the same wisecracking, fast-talking young men of the silent days—and he had to cope with competitors Lee Tracy at MGM and Jack Oakie at Paramount. Another problem was financial: Gilbert's exorbitant $250,000-per-picture salary had made it nearly impossible for the studio to pair him with a costly leading lady or director in the talking era. Without the backup of an important female lead or an expensive production, Gilbert's films did not perform as well at home or, especially, abroad. Thus, as the costs of all but two of Gilbert's talkies skyrocketed to more than $500,000 (only three of his silent films had reached that mark), his formerly profitable pictures suddenly became huge money-losers. The rising costs of Haines's pictures also imperiled his star status. While his cheaply made silent vehicles had usually brought in solid profits above the $200,000 mark, all but two of his talkies showed mediocre profits of less than $90,000. (Perhaps not coincidentally, the most profitable of all, the 1930 release *The Girl Said No*, had the increasingly popular Marie Dressler in the supporting cast.)

Novarro's professional trajectory during the early talkie period differed from those of his two MGM competitors for a number of reasons. First, Novarro's boyish good looks began fading only in the mid-1930s, as he approached thirty-five. Second, unlike Gilbert, Novarro had almost invariably carried a film on his own since becoming a star, whether in silent pictures or in talkies. With the exception of *The Student Prince* and *Mata Hari*, it was his name *alone* that had turned a film into a box-office hit. Furthermore, the musical vogue that had propelled Novarro to new heights of popularity had left Haines and Gilbert untouched, since neither could sing. Finally, despite the higher costs of Novarro's talking pictures, the Mexican star had a crucial advantage over the homegrown MGM male stars, including Lon Chaney and Buster Keaton: his immense popularity abroad.

Novarro reigned as MGM's top international male star from 1925 to 1932. During his years as a contract player, eleven of his pictures made more than $450,000 abroad, compared to seven of Gilbert's (three of which costarred Greta Garbo), two of Keaton's, one of Chaney's, and none of Haines's. Haines may have been too American to travel well, but the relatively minor international appeal of Gilbert, Keaton, and Chaney is difficult to comprehend. On the other hand, Novarro's large following can be explained by both the monumental success of *Ben-Hur* and the popularity of film musicals overseas.

Partly for lack of data, foreign revenues have usually been ignored in historical accounts of the American motion picture industry, in spite of their sometimes crucial importance to a picture's profitability. As an example, *Ben-Hur* would never have recouped its production costs—which it finally did with the early-1930s reissue—without the foreign market, since nearly 60 percent of its earnings originated abroad. In Novarro's case, the overseas revenues, which represented more than half of his box-office proceeds, helped turn eight of his MGM releases, including the *Ben-Hur* reissue, into million-dollar-plus hits—second only to Clark Gable among his male contemporaries at the studio. (And unlike Novarro, Gable was then costarred with a big name in every one of his pictures.) In addition, eight of Novarro's MGM pictures made more money abroad than in the domestic market, a record matched in those days only by Garbo. Capping it all, the figures of the overseas *Ben-Hur* rerelease turned that historical spectacle into the sole motion picture of the 1920s to break the $10 million mark in worldwide rentals—a feat unsurpassed until *Gone with the Wind*.

During the early talkie era, Novarro's films from *Devil-May-Care* to *The Barbarian* brought in an average of $187,000 in profits largely because of overseas rentals. If the 1931 *Ben-Hur* reissue is included, his average jumps to $246,000. Without the receipts from foreign shores, Novarro's salary would have been too high and his dwindling domestic box office too low to render his services worthwhile for MGM. As a comparison, Haines's talkies averaged a paltry $70,000 in net income, while Gilbert's showed a catastrophic average loss of $256,000. Less than one-third of Gilbert's and less than one-fourth of Haines's revenues originated abroad.

It is true that foreign revenues comparable to Novarro's would not have been enough to help Gilbert. His pictures would still have lost money because of his enormous salary, and his drinking would have continued to be a serious problem. Haines, however, might have lasted several more years at MGM had he enjoyed Novarro's international popularity. Haines's vehicles, considerably cheaper than Gilbert's, were still profitable—a strong overseas market would have made them *highly* profitable.

During those difficult years, a performer without a record of solid profitability would need an influential patron like William Randolph Hearst to remain employed at the studio (which explains Marion Davies's endurance in spite of a series of box-office flops). Not surprisingly, MGM dropped Gilbert after his appearance in the March 1933 release *Fast Workers*, the last picture made under his "millionaire" contract. Despite a successful return to the studio later that year in Garbo's *Queen Christina*—at the star's insistence, but with his name now below the title—Gilbert appeared in only one more picture. Less than three years after departing MGM, the thirty-six-year-old former superstar was dead of a heart attack.

Haines and MGM officially parted ways in September 1933, though he had not made any pictures since the fall of the previous year. According to the always creative Anita Loos, Mayer had earlier called Haines to his office and issued an ultimatum: "You're either to give up that boyfriend of yours, or I'll cancel your contract!" In Loos's words, "without even a hesitation, Bill opted for love and told L.B. to tear up his contract."

Actually, whether or not Haines had decided to play the heterosexual game at that point would have made no difference to Mayer. What mattered to the studio head was the minuscule $28,000 average profits of Haines's last six films. If homophobia had truly been an issue, the unmarried Garbo, whose escapades at lesbian bars in Europe were reported in the early 1930s, should also have faced Mayer's wrath. But she did not. Her pictures were among MGM's most profitable. Likewise, Novarro should have headed the same route as Haines. His box office had been erratic the previous two years, he partied around town, continued denying his engagement to Myrna Loy, and maintained his stand that he would *never* marry. "Women—phooey! Marry? Not me," he was telling reporters. Instead of firing him, the studio spent lavishly on his next three pictures—because Novarro had shown that his vehicles *could* bring in gratifying profits.

In the second half of 1933, Novarro's future seemed bright. Musicals, which had given his career a major boost in the early talkie period, were back in vogue after the phenomenal success of Warner's *42nd Street* and *Gold Diggers of 1933*. Since early spring, MGM had been preparing for Novarro's first musical in three years: *The Cat and the Fiddle*, a film version of Jerome Kern and Otto Harbach's 1931 operetta about love found, lost, and regained in the European music world. His costar would be Mayer's recently acquired $4,000-a-week protégée, Jeanette MacDonald. (Novarro, for his part, was to receive $100,000 in a two-picture deal, plus $1,000 a day for retakes and additional scenes.)

Unlike the tight-budgeted *42nd Street*, *The Cat and the Fiddle* would ultimately cost an extravagant $843,000. The excess indulged by MGM on this production—the third most expensive picture of Novarro's career and the studio's fifth-costliest production that season—is particularly curious, considering that Novarro had not had a single major hit since *Mata Hari*, MacDonald had come to the studio after several box-office disappointments at Paramount and Fox, and MGM was having its worst year to date. The studio was clearly determined to lift the sagging fortunes of its former top male star, and, of even more importance to *The Cat and the Fiddle*, Mayer was intent on turning his protégée into a major star. (Mayer, who wanted MacDonald to see him as a "friend, counselor, and guide," was probably the one who had MacDonald billed above the title, as Novarro's original contract—later modified—had stipulated solo star billing.)

Veteran director William K. Howard, fresh from his well-received Fox melodrama *The Power and the Glory* and a fan of German film expressionism, was MGM's strange choice to handle this lavish musical. Myrna Loy, who had been featured in Howard's *Transatlantic* in 1931, described him as "a wonderful director"; but despite his extensive credentials and his previous handling of MacDonald in the Fox programmer *Don't Bet on Women,* the maverick Howard had no experience with film musicals, nor was he the type of contract director Mayer appreciated. (Thalberg had by then been demoted to producer status.) Like Ingram, Howard did not tolerate interference from the front office—which makes his selection by MGM, that most controlling of Hollywood studios, even more incomprehensible.

The script, meddled with by numerous hands including Anita Loos's, was finally credited to the husband-and-wife team of Bella and Sam Spewack (who would later write the stage musical *Kiss Me, Kate* with Jeanette Mac-Donald in mind). MacDonald, dissatisfied with sections of the story about two struggling songwriters whose relationship is temporarily destroyed by the girl's sudden rise to fame, was partially responsible for some of the alterations. According to operetta star Vivienne Segal, who played the picture's vamp, the leading lady was influential in other aspects of the production as well. She accused MacDonald of plotting with Mayer to trim her role and to have her photographed to look as ugly as possible (if Segal's story is true, MacDonald succeeded on both counts).

Soon after wrapping *The Cat and the Fiddle,* Novarro began working on *Laughing Boy,* the second film under his new contract. MGM had bought the rights to anthropologist Oliver La Farge's Pulitzer Prize–winning novel of Navajo life at the suggestion of screenwriter John Lee Mahin, who was assigned with John Colton to adapt this story of a young Navajo brave who marries a prostitute. Novarro, who thought he would "be foolish" to turn down the part of Laughing Boy, had signed for it in July.

For the role of Slim Girl, the kindhearted Navajo prostitute, the studio cast Lupe Velez, lesser known for her film career than for her tempestuous romances with, among others, Gary Cooper (whom Novarro had introduced to her at a 1928 party at Pickfair) and Johnny Weissmuller (whom she had married in 1933). Velez, a good friend of Novarro's offscreen, became the actor's first—and last—Mexican leading lady.

W. S. Van Dyke, for whom Novarro had done some of his best and most successful work in *The Pagan,* was designated director. Van Dyke seemed an ideal choice, not only because of his previous collaboration with Novarro, but also because he had a flair for bringing to life non-European cultures and exotic settings. After *The Pagan* and *White Shadows in the South Seas,* he had directed two highly successful adventure pictures set in Africa, *Trader Horn* and *Tarzan the Ape Man,* and the semidocumentary *Eskimo.*

As it had in the production of *Eskimo,* MGM insisted that "fidelity to detail and the authenticity of the background and the race ... should be carefully observed" in *Laughing Boy.* Except for the two leads, most of the cast was composed of Native Americans, a casting choice that made the supporting characters look more realistic—but Novarro and Velez less so. The casting of Navajos also detracted from the performance of the star of the picture, who later complained that "it was really disconcerting to work with people like that." By "people like that," Novarro probably meant amateurs who spoke their lines without feeling—the Navajos had learned English phonetically and had no idea of what they were saying.

Most of the *Laughing Boy* exteriors were filmed at the Navajo reservation near Cameron, in northern Arizona, where the harsh winter forced "One-Take Woody" to live up to his nickname. The hectic pace of filming coupled with Van Dyke's distress over his involvement in a recent fatal car accident and Novarro's unhappiness with his fellow players made the production a difficult one. Back in Culver City, the pace of filming slowed considerably, but by then Novarro had lost faith in the picture.

In early January 1934, after completing work on *Laughing Boy*, Novarro was called back for a series of retakes for *The Cat and the Fiddle*, which had an unusually long—even for a musical—seventy-four-day filming schedule. When the picture finally opened on February 16, 1934, it was greeted by widely divergent reviews, ranging from *Variety*'s categorical dismissal of all elements of the film adaptation, except its music, to the *New York Times*'s praise for its "original charm and spontaneity." Critics were more consistent in their praise of the stars, especially MacDonald for her dynamic singing. *Variety* had little to say about Novarro's performance but remarked at length on his oscillating height throughout the film—sometimes he is as tall as his costar, other times a little taller, and at other times much taller. After pairing Novarro with the spindly Garbo, MGM had lost its fear that tall leading ladies would tower over the five-foot six-inch Mexican star. As in *Ben-Hur*, careful camera placement, high-heeled boots, and shoes with lifts allowed Novarro to play opposite taller-than-average women such as MacDonald and Loy, even though, as evidenced by *Variety*'s observation, the deception was hardly consistent.

In addition to its historical importance as the first live-action feature film to utilize the three-strip Technicolor system (at the finale), *The Cat and the Fiddle* is chiefly known today for being MacDonald's first MGM film. Unjustly dismissed as an artistic and a commercial flop, the picture is superior to any of her revered pairings with Nelson Eddy, with the possible exception of *Maytime*. MacDonald and Novarro, whom she considered a "safe" partner, unlike her overpowering Paramount costar Maurice Chevalier, have an excellent on-screen rapport that is aided in the picture's lively first half by witty lines and William K. Howard's surprisingly deft, Lubitsch-like touch.

Moreover, unlike the invariably wooden Eddy or the showstopping ham Chevalier, Novarro could *act* a part. He is effervescent as the temperamental struggling composer Victor Florescu and makes good use of his dramatic moments. Novarro loses ground to Eddy only in his duets with MacDonald. Lacking Eddy's powerful baritone voice, Novarro's gentler singing is all but drowned out by MacDonald's forceful soprano.

To MGM's disappointment, *The Cat and the Fiddle* did only moderate business domestically. Despite its significant foreign revenues, the largest for a Novarro vehicle since *Mata Hari*, the picture ultimately lost $142,000. These results were especially disheartening when compared with the enormous profits amassed during this same period by the even more expensive *Dancing Lady*, a routine musical showcasing the highly popular Joan Crawford–Clark Gable team. If *The Barbarian* marked Novarro's slide into second-rank status in the United States, *The Cat and the Fiddle* confirmed it.

Apart from enabling Novarro to display his comedy flair and pleasant crooning, *The Cat and the Fiddle* presents a disturbing image of the fading star. He looks considerably older and heavier than ever before, though his disheveled hair helps disguise his deteriorating looks in the film's first half. In the second half, when Novarro's hair is combed straight back, his face looks so artificial as to be eerie. Not even as the white-powdered Prince Karl Heinrich in *The Student Prince* or the mascaraed football player in *Huddle* had he appeared so unnatural. Worse yet, the Technicolor in the finale is uncharitable to him, and so is his ungainly tight uniform, which emphasizes his chubbiness. At thirty-four, Novarro looks like an out-of-shape man of forty-five trying to pass for a slim man of thirty.

Novarro's rapidly fading looks were probably the first exterior manifestation of his drinking, which remained a severe problem. In the spring of 1933, *Silver Screen* had reported that at a party at actress Una Merkel's Hollywood Hills home—a gathering that included Ginger Rogers, Howard Hughes, Jean Harlow, and Helen Hayes—Novarro had reminisced about working with Garbo in *Mata Hari* and had done "his famous impersonations of Queen Victoria." The report, understandably, omitted the details of Novarro's Queen Victoria "impersonations."

Party guest William Bakewell, a screen juvenile who had appeared with Novarro in *Daybreak*, later recalled that some time into the party, a scream was heard from upstairs. Merkel and a few of the guests hurried up to a room, where they found a stark naked Novarro, with only a bandanna wrapped around his head, bouncing up and down on a bed, screaming, "I'm

Queen Victoria on her deathbed! I'm Queen Victoria on her deathbed!"
Some of the startled guests brought Novarro down, dressed him, and helped
him sober up. Before leaving, Novarro apologized to Merkel, who remarked
he had been the highlight of an otherwise dull party.

Such social embarrassments notwithstanding, Novarro's drinking continued. Actress Barbara Barondess, a close friend of Douglass Montgomery's,
recalled that during the location shoot of Paramount's 1934 release *Eight
Girls in a Boat,* "Douglass, Kay Johnson and I used to sneak off from Lake
Arrowhead at night to meet Ramon Novarro and all the other boys at their
parties. After three or four times of doing that, I stopped going, because I
couldn't stand all that drinking."

But in spite of Novarro's uncontrolled drinking at social occasions, there
is no evidence that it ever interfered with his work. Unlike John Barrymore
and Buster Keaton, whose alcoholism led to shooting delays, Novarro was
apparently abstemious during his acting and singing stints. Yet, even if alcohol did not affect his behavior while at the studio, it did affect his looks—
which had always been a chief reason for his popularity. Like Gilbert and
Haines several years earlier, Novarro, now in his mid-thirties, was beginning
to look too old to portray youthful heroes.

Novarro's aging looks, in fact, were only one of the myriad problems
affecting his next release. Another was censorship. Joseph Breen, a top representative of the Hays Office, had called *Laughing Boy* "a sordid, vile and
dirty story that is definitely not suited for screen entertainment," and had
insisted on changes, including the elimination of several references to prostitution and of sequences indicating "illicit" sexual activities. MGM acqui-
esced in part. Bits of dialogue were changed, and there is no *direct* mention
of prostitution in the picture, though the means by which Slim Girl helps
her husband buy livestock is quite obvious. Still, dissatisfied with the final
product and perhaps realizing that boycotts by religious groups had become
a strong possibility, MGM opted to give *Laughing Boy* a low-key release.

Advertised as the story "up to now believed too daring to film," the
picture opened on May 11, 1934, at the Metropolitan Theater in Brooklyn—the first time ever that a Novarro vehicle did not have a Broadway
premiere. The *New York Times* did not even bother to review the film, while
those publications that did were nearly unanimous in their scorn for the
script, the direction, and, this time, the star (only Lupe Velez was singled
out for praise). The awful notices, combined with MGM's indifference and
drastic cuts demanded by local censor boards—the New York board had
initially rejected the picture, which was then hurriedly reedited—turned
Laughing Boy into an abysmal financial failure. With a mere $264,000 in

worldwide revenues, the picture marked Novarro's box-office nadir both domestically and abroad, and resulted in the most severe loss for a Novarro picture since the original *Ben-Hur* run.

Novarro so abhorred *Laughing Boy* that he never sat through it. Considering the damage it caused his career, Novarro's negative feelings about the film are understandable—even though it is no worse than *The Son-Daughter, Son of India,* or *Huddle.* What sets *Laughing Boy* apart from those other vehicles is its near-amateurish feel (despite being the fourth-costliest Novarro talkie), totally unlike the glossy MGM productions of the studio era. Van Dyke clearly strove to mix the documentary style of *Eskimo* with Hollywood melodrama, but the resulting mishmash fails to blend. Oliver La Farge was so angered by the bastardization of his novel that when he met with screenwriter John Lee Mahin after the picture's release, he threw his drink (glass included) in Mahin's face.

Besides the script flaws, the picture is irreparably compromised by central miscasting. "Ramon Novarro as Laughing Boy!" sneered Mahin years later. "The poor guy was a fag; and he was an old fag then, so it was coming out. And he looked like an old whore, with his hair hanging down and a blanket on.... They should have had some virile young guy, Tyrone Power or somebody." Despite Mahin's meanness—and his absurd suggestion of Tyrone Power as the lead—Novarro, too old and ridiculously made up as a lipsticked Navajo, looks so out of his element when sharing the screen with real Native Americans that his mere presence is jarring. His performance, though sympathetic, is nothing but that of a Hollywood star playing Indian.

"Novarro, keenly sensitive, feels quite deeply the whispered gossip that he was 'on the skids,'" reported Al Sherman in *Screen Book* shortly after the *Laughing Boy* opening. Although that interview had been conducted before the film's release, the horrific reception given the Navajo melodrama made Sherman's remark quite topical. Still, MGM believed in Novarro's drawing power. Mayer surely knew that the problematic *Laughing Boy* was going to tank at the box office, but he trusted that his Mexican star could still pull in crowds in the appropriate vehicle. Thus, one month prior to the *Laughing Boy* opening, MGM signed Novarro for two more pictures to be made in late 1934 and early 1935, and for which Novarro would earn a total of $125,000 ($50,000 for the first picture and $75,000 for the second), a 25 percent increase in salary since his last two-picture deal. Having signed the new agreement, Novarro opted to forget *Laughing Boy*—a picture that might have benefited from heavy promotion by its star—and left with his sister Carmen for the concert stages of Brazil, Uruguay, and Argentina. This successful South American tour was to become the culmination of Novarro's numerous live performances since his return from Europe in August 1933.

The first of those presentations had occurred in September of that year, when Novarro hosted a special Teatro Intimo revue for a celebrity-packed audience that included Gloria Swanson, Myrna Loy, Cary Grant, Randolph Scott, Jeanette MacDonald, Alice Terry, John Gilbert, Irving Thalberg, and Norma Shearer. Besides exhibiting his own singing and comedic skills ("There is nothing more difficult than trying to sing for one's friends," he later admitted), Novarro showcased French singer Jean Sablon, whom he had met in Paris, and pianist André Renaud (one of the music students in *The Cat and the Fiddle*), who awed the spectators by playing two grand pianos at the same time. One columnist raved that Novarro "sang with new surety and beauty of tone; his comedy was delicious, untouchable by any singer I know of today."

Energized by the enthusiasm accorded his revue, Novarro followed it with a performance at the Los Angeles Philharmonic Auditorium, where he head-lined a benefit sponsored by the Mexican consulate for the victims of a catastrophic storm in Tampico. Accompanied by Juan Aguilar's orchestra, and supported by Carmen, dancing professionally with her brother for the first time, Novarro sang in English, French, and Spanish. Another important musical engagement took place on the premiere weekend of *The Cat and the Fiddle* at the Capitol, for which Novarro was paid $3,950, plus 50 percent of that week's box-office take above $50,000. During one presentation, a commotion erupted when female spectators began slugging each other to get a glimpse of their idol—Clark Gable, who was sitting in the audience. Novarro followed the Capitol assignment with a personal appearance at the premiere of *The Cat and the Fiddle* in Washington, D.C.

The success of those ventures prompted Novarro to arrange for a series of concerts in South America, where he was still a first-rank star. In early April 1934, after leasing his Valley Oak house to Douglass Montgomery, Novarro left with Carmen and his tour manager, *La Sevillana*'s assistant di-rector, Carlos F. Borcosque, aboard the *Northern Prince* for Rio de Janeiro. To escape the crowds gathered at the dock in Rio, the star left the ship in a launch at the suggestion of the local police, landing several miles from downtown Rio and then heading by car to the hotel. During his Brazilian stay, Novarro was showered with anonymous gifts. Fans waited patiently at the entrance of the hotel to get a glimpse of the Hollywood film star, with the more audacious eluding security to reach his room. According to Bor-cosque, once face-to-face with their idol, the fans would act as if "they regarded themselves in the presence of a being in every sense superior," falling into a catatonic trance until Novarro helped them recover their emotional balance. While in town, Novarro also talked to the press, reiterating that he was having "no romance with [Myrna Loy] or any other woman," and was serenaded by Carmen Miranda at a reception in his honor. On the day he left for Montevideo, a crowd of admirers gathered at the pier to wish him bon voyage.

Shortly after the ship docked at the Uruguayan capital on April 24, the fans broke through security and invaded the deck. Finding Novarro in a salon talking to reporters, they threw themselves at him so ardently that the startled actor fled in a panic. Borcosque later found a shaky Novarro hiding in a small passageway, his necktie undone, his clothes in disarray, and his face smeared with rouge and lipstick. His arrival in Buenos Aires the next day was greeted by ships blowing their sirens, three airplanes flying overhead at low altitude, and three thousand hysterical fans. Despite police protection, some of the more avid devotees followed the star to his hotel, which was forced to close its doors that day.

While in Buenos Aires, Novarro expressed his admiration for the country, but complained that "on all sides one must suffer the assaults of the people which are enough to exhaust an athlete." At his last performance at the Teatro Monumental, in which he sang Spanish ballads while Carmen danced to them, every available space was occupied, with no dividing line between the orchestra and the box seats. At the end of the show, fans stormed the stage to bid him farewell. "Ramon ceased to be the man and even the artist," wrote a local reporter. "He became an object—a sort of gem which it was necessary to see closely, to touch and to value." Before departing, Novarro wrote a thank-you letter to the Argentinian people and added two more personages to his entourage: Argentinian swimmer José Caraballo, whom Novarro was intent on bringing to Hollywood for a film career, and a life-size bust of himself sculpted by Chilean artist María Carmen Portela de Araoz Alsaro.

On the return home, Novarro's ship stopped once again in Rio, where he stayed for several days, and in Trinidad, where a local theater manager had announced the star—without his knowledge—as an upcoming attraction. Novarro refused even to get near the theater, but despite being too tired and too sunburned, he did tour the island with the local customs officer. One thousand fans were at the dock to wave him good-bye as his boat sailed north. Novarro then declared, "Now, I am going to rest."

· · ·

Novarro's rest was neither as soothing nor as lengthy as he might have hoped. Upon his return to the United States, he had to come to terms with the disastrous failure of *Laughing Boy*, and shortly after his arrival with José Caraballo in California in mid-August, he found himself involved in an unexpected political hubbub.

In late July, a police raid at the Sacramento headquarters of the Communist-dominated Cannery and Agricultural Workers Industrial Union (CAWIU) had found the names of Novarro, Dolores del Río, Lupe Velez, and James Cagney among the papers of CAWIU secretary Caroline Decker, one of seventeen "radicals" arrested under charges of criminal syndicalism. The three Mexican film stars and James Cagney were then labeled suspected Communist sympathizers by Sacramento district attorney Neil McAllister, who had declared himself determined to quell the right to advocate or contribute to "any subversive policy threatening established government." McAllister had also proposed a new injunction for the state of California that would render violators in contempt of court and subject to punishment without jury trial, and asked for injunctions against the stars if they were proven to be Communist sympathizers. He counted on the assistance of Los Angeles chief of police James E. Davis, who, the previous year, had deployed a "Red Squad" to "investigate and control radical activities, strikes, and riots." Davis had recently told the press that he intended to lead "a quiet investigation into reports that Communistic tendencies have been displayed in Hollywood."

It was no coincidence that three of the four accused film stars were of Mexican origin. In a replay of the events of the late 1910s, Mexicans were once again being targeted by law enforcement agencies for alleged Communist activities. They were a strong force in the fight to unionize the state's agricultural workers and comprised a large segment of the CAWIU, which had been working closely with the Confederación de Uniones Obreras Mexicanas (Federation of Mexican Workers Union) in California's Imperial Valley. (In October 1933, the CAWIU had encouraged a mammoth strike by 1,800 cotton workers, 75 percent of whom were Mexicans.) Additionally, both the Mexican government—through its consulates—and some influential Mexican nationals residing in California had been supporting the struggles of Mexican workers with advice and financial aid.

The accused actors quickly denounced the charges. "I deny ever giving Communists any aid or that I ever intended to," Cagney declared. "It appears to me that McAllister's actions are a bid for personal publicity at the expense of my reputation." Fully living up to her brainless "hot tamale" offscreen image, Velez stated, "Me a Communist? Ho, I don't even know what the blazes a Communist is!" adding, "I don't give my money to anybody. I need my own dough. What is the matter with this Sacramento man, anyway? I think maybe they should put him in the lockup tight." An outraged Cedric Gibbons asserted that his wife, Dolores del Río, was not interested in radical activities, whereas del Río herself announced, "It's ridiculous. I never had anything to do with Communists. I don't even know any Communists and I've never contributed a cent to anything but worthy charities."

Through his attorney, Stanley Barnes, Novarro "emphatically denied" the allegations, stating, "I belong to no Communistic organization or any similar organization, and in fact I belong to no political organization. I have in no way, directly or indirectly, aided either financially or otherwise any Communistic organization or political organization. My sole contribution to any organization for the past two years has been to the motion picture actors' relief fund, the Los Angeles Community Chest and the various charities of the Catholic Church."

Confronted by the stars' indignant demand for proof—and quite possibly by the intervention of MGM (Novarro's and Cedric Gibbons's studio) and Warner Bros. (del Río's and Cagney's studio)—McAllister decided against subpoenaing "the Hollywood four." It was later reported that Cagney's alleged Communist ties were a result of his having donated money to alleviate the suffering of the striking cotton workers. As for the three Mexican stars, it was never made clear exactly what McAllister had found in Decker's papers that might have implicated them. Their names may have been included in a list of potential donors to the cause of Mexican workers, or perhaps McAllister's accusations were simply a self-promotional scare tactic to intimidate all wealthy Mexicans by using Novarro, del Río, and Velez as scapegoats.

Novarro's rebuttal of McAllister's accusation seems perfectly honest. Always a charitable man, Novarro had frequently donated money and artifacts to churches and Catholic humanitarian organizations in the United States and Mexico, and would continue to do so until his death. But politics was beyond his sphere of interest. Friends cannot remember him addressing the subject, and he never publicly discussed social or political issues. If the Mexican Revolution, the treatment of Mexicans in American films, the 1930s raids on Mexican neighborhoods in Los Angeles, and, later, the 1950s raids and repatriations during Operation Wetback were of concern to Novarro, he kept his thoughts to himself.

.   .   .

One month after their Red Scare, Novarro and del Río were invited to their native country for the opening of Mexico City's art nouveau theater, the Palacio de Bellas Artes. Earlier in the year, Novarro had canceled a planned concert tour of Mexico because of the extensive retakes for *The Cat and the Fiddle*, but this time, free of commitments until mid-October, he accepted the invitation. This late–September 1934 visit—as the MGM representative to the inaugural—was to mark his first trip south of the border since he had fled north eighteen years earlier.

Accompanied by his brother Angel, Douglas Fairbanks, and United Artists president Joseph Schenck (José Caraballo apparently stayed at Valley Oak), Novarro arrived at the Mexican capital on September 25. While in town, he was mobbed by thousands of fans, donated money to an orphanage, posed for pictures with a 104-year-old man at a rest home, and prayed at the Basilica of Guadalupe. After two hectic weeks in his native land, Novarro returned to the United States to begin preparations for his next film assignment.

Smarting over the *Laughing Boy* fiasco, MGM had picked a vehicle that better suited Novarro's talents (though not his accent): *Tiptoes*, a bittersweet operetta taken from an original story by Vicki Baum about the romance between an Austrian archduke and a ballet dancer in 1890s Vienna. According to the *Hollywood Reporter*, the final screenplay, written by Edgar Allan Woolf and Franz Schulz, was "so completely wedded to the music, the entire script was mimeographed on special music paper, with the action and dialogue inserted between the staves and timed to each measure." But however promising on paper, *Tiptoes* would become another Novarro project irreparably marred by miscasting, inept direction, and censorship problems.

After two box-office disappointments, Novarro was in desperate need of a prominent leading lady to help restore his tattered star status at home and abroad. Surely aware of this, he had consented to be costarred as long as he was billed first in the credits (unless he was paired with Garbo). For *Tiptoes*, Jeanette MacDonald would have been an ideal costar, as she had displayed good chemistry with Novarro in *The Cat and Fiddle*, and her *The Merry Widow* had been amassing solid earnings domestically. (The picture would be even more successful overseas, though, like *The Cat and the Fiddle*, it still lost money because of its high cost.) Instead, MGM opted for British musical comedy performer Evelyn Laye, a highly popular entertainer in her native country, but not the international celebrity Novarro needed as box-office support. In addition, Laye had already proven herself a failure with American audiences in her first Hollywood tryout, the 1931 Samuel Goldwyn production *One Heavenly Night*.

Further complicating matters, the studio's pick for director was an even stranger choice than William K. Howard had been for *The Cat and the Fiddle*: Dudley Murphy, whose chief claim to fame was having codirected the 1924 experimental silent short *Le Ballet Mécanique*. Since then, Murphy had had a sporadic film career restricted to shorts and B movies until being assigned to the lavish *Tiptoes*.

Although it may seem that Louis B. Mayer was trying to sabotage Novarro's career, that was clearly not the case. MGM invested nearly $600,000 in *Tiptoes*, a medium-high budget that was the fourth-costliest ever for a Novarro vehicle. Also, the studio assigned top talent in all fields, including James Wong Howe as cinematographer, Oscar Hammerstein II as librettist, Sigmund Romberg as composer, and Herbert Stothart as musical director. Supporting the two leads were reliable players Una Merkel, Edward Everett Horton (the first time he and Novarro worked together since the old Majestic Theater days), and fast-rising newcomer Rosalind Russell. Nonetheless, MGM's unwise choices of director and leading lady doomed the picture artistically and commercially from the start.

Furthermore, since MGM had recently ratified the Production Code—a lengthy and restrictive set of rules that were supposed to make American motion pictures "clean"—it now had to handle the risqué plot with unaccustomed caution. In the original story by Vicki Baum, the hero is a monarch who must abide by the Hapsburg tradition of testing his reproductive abilities before marriage, for which purpose he chooses a ballet dancer. In the expurgated final screenplay, an archduke uses a ballet dancer as a romantic decoy only to actually fall in love with her. Despite the sophisticated Viennese setting, there were no witty double entendres or daring boudoir scenes to offend censors anywhere; but as so often happened in post-Code Hollywood films, the bowdlerization of *Tiptoes* also resulted in a picture nearly devoid of humor and wit.

Unhappy with the picture, unable to sleep because of worries about his performance, and aware that his days at MGM might be numbered if *Tiptoes* failed to please the front office, the usually placid Novarro directed temper tantrums at Dudley Murphy. His worst explosion occurred when the director refused to let him come down from a Ferris wheel seat, where he had spent most of the day, until the desired love scene was satisfactorily shot. Such contretemps notwithstanding, Novarro and Evelyn Laye (who married *David Copperfield* leading man Frank Lawton during filming) developed a solid friendship that was to last until his death. "I loved Ramon; he was one of my dearest friends," Laye wrote in *The Silent Picture* soon after his passing. "Whenever he came to London, we would walk arm in arm in Regent's

Park, perhaps have a cup of coffee together. He would always come and see me in whatever I was doing."

But in spite of the stars' excellent offscreen rapport, there were no on-screen sparks—one of the critics' chief complaints when the picture, now renamed *The Night Is Young,* opened at the Capitol on January 11, 1935. Lacking "romantic fire," as *Variety* had it, *The Night Is Young* was regarded as a beautiful but hollow accomplishment. "Invincibly correct," observed the *New York Times.* "If you want to be rude about it, you can add that it is likewise without any single distinguishing virtue except for its appalling competence in every department of its manufacture." The picture fared no better in Laye's native Britain, where the *Sunday Times* described it as "a naive and novelettish musical." The stars generally managed better notices than the film, though some reviewers thought their lack of chemistry harmed the performances.

Laye, who soon afterward returned to England permanently, is a poor match to Novarro in this pale rehash of *The Student Prince* and Erik Charell's *Congress Dances.* Their lackluster rapport creates a hole in the picture's emotional core that is mended only in the unexpectedly wistful finale. Yet, aside from some distracting effeminate mannerisms, Novarro's characterization is quite good. When the star is allowed to display his dramatic or comedic capabilities, whether being heartbroken to learn that the ballet dancer has a boyfriend or humorously replying to Edward Everett Horton's questions with a series of melodious "huh-hums," he is outstanding. Also—possibly with the assistance of James Wong Howe's lenses—he looks younger and trimmer than in his previous two pictures (though still too old to play the twenty-five-year-old archduke).

Still, even with Novarro's pleasant performance, Howe's lush cinematography, the magnificent sets and costumes, and the beautiful hit tunes "The Night Is Young" and "When I Grow Too Old to Dream," *The Night Is Young* became MGM's second-biggest money loser of the season (after Constance Bennett's *Outcast Lady*) and the third-weakest box-office performer of Novarro's career. The relatively poor showing of *The Night Is Young* overseas, where both musicals and Novarro were highly popular, is especially puzzling. Either Novarro's international appeal had finally been shattered by his series of weak vehicles, or MGM failed to publicize the picture properly—perhaps because by the time *The Night Is Young* opened abroad, neither Novarro nor Laye was any longer at the studio.

· · ·

The Night Is Young marked the end of Novarro's association with MGM. Plans to reteam him with either Jeanette MacDonald or Evelyn Laye in the operetta *Love While You May* were scrapped, as his contract was "abrogated by mutual consent" shortly after he finished work on *The Night Is Young*.

Novarro later recalled being summoned to the office of MGM general manager Eddie Mannix, who told him that his latest vehicle "wasn't very good." Novarro agreed. On January 3, 1935, upon receiving $19,000 as severance pay, he terminated his affiliation with the studio. The public learned of the rupture only on February 7, one day after Novarro's thirty-sixth birthday and four weeks after the opening of *The Night Is Young*. MGM's brief statement read, "While there was no disagreement, Mr. Novarro requested release from his contract at a time when the studio had a story in preparation for him, but not ready for production."

Contrary to the claims of some film historians, Novarro's fall from eminence was neither a matter of homophobia nor the result of a general lack of interest in exotic lovers. Because Novarro was gay, there were the inevitable rumors that he was fired after being caught in a compromising situation, though who supposedly caught Novarro doing what with whom remains a mystery. Another set of rumors had Mayer issuing Novarro an ultimatum: marriage or the door. It is as if the studio head believed that a wedding ring would magically transform the revenues of Novarro's last three films— which ultimately resulted in a $760,000 loss (approximately $10 million today)—into million-dollar profits. Similarities to William Haines's own alleged ultimatum are no coincidence.

The "decline of the exotic lover" theory is based on the false assumption that Novarro's career had been built on such characters. Surely he played numerous non-American parts throughout the years, but the vast majority of his foreign roles are mainstream heroes dressed in unusual garb. Novarro is no more exotic in *Scaramouche*, *Across to Singapore*, or *The Pagan* than Errol Flynn in *Captain Blood*, Clark Gable in *Mutiny on the Bounty*, or Jon Hall in *The Hurricane*. Nor was Novarro more of an "exotic lover" in *Ben-Hur* than Charlton Heston in the remake. Though not a blue-eyed blond, Novarro looked no more "exotic" than other dark-haired, dark-eyed performers, whether native or foreign, including fast-rising, bedroom-eyed imports Charles Boyer and Francis Lederer.

The end of Novarro's stardom was above all else the result of his own lack of professional focus coupled with Mayer and Thalberg's lack of vision.

Had Novarro been less concerned with arias and monasteries, he might have fought for better parts and better costars with the same intensity he fought for money. Another pairing with Garbo or with MacDonald, both of whom—like Novarro himself—were extremely popular overseas, would have given his mid-1930s film career the boost it so desperately needed. The role of the Spanish ambassador in *Queen Christina* would have been ideal, and since Novarro and Garbo had had such a good rapport she might have accepted him instead of demanding John Gilbert. The lead in *The Merry Widow*, which had almost been Novarro's (Maurice Chevalier landed the role), would also have been a professional coup—though not profitable, the picture brought the studio more than $2.5 million in revenues. Yet, while his MGM status dangled precariously over the box-office abyss, Novarro was touring the concert stages of Europe and South America.

Mayer and Thalberg were equally to blame, for they had often cast Novarro in roles for which he was obviously unqualified. The studio heads insisted that they "carefully" selected Novarro's vehicles, but if so, "carefully" did not mean "intelligently." Had they tried, Mayer and Thalberg could not have found a worse letdown for *Ben-Hur* than *A Certain Young Man*. *Huddle* was an equally dismal follow-up to *Mata Hari*, and the same can be said about *Laughing Boy* as a successor to *The Cat and the Fiddle*. Those and other inappropriate vehicles such as *The Son-Daughter* and *Son of India* were responsible for the erosion of Novarro's box-office allure at home and abroad. *Picture-Play* had observed in 1930 that Novarro could count on "the most loyal following of any star through good pictures and bad"; but even his "legions of fans" could withstand only so much. Had the front office understood that the appeal of their onetime top male star lay in his light romantic playing, Novarro's MGM career would not have ended in 1935.

Novarro was the last star of the old Metro Pictures to fade from the marquee and the next to last of the original MGM contract players to leave (Norma Shearer would follow seven years later). It had been nearly eleven years and twenty-two motion pictures—including one legendary superspectacle—that had brought the Culver City studio more than $31,000,000 (approximately $350 million today) in revenues, an amount second only to that amassed by Joan Crawford's thirty-six films.

Fifteen years were to pass before Novarro set foot on an MGM soundstage again.

ELEVEN

Illusion of Happiness

I have been playing the same part in different costumes, with different people, all the time!" Novarro remarked soon after leaving MGM. "I don't want to hang on to the yesterdays. I don't want to keep remaking the same stories. Viennese romances, football pictures! I left MGM amicably, but that's the reason. What was the use of making another film with the same old theme?" Novarro seemingly failed to recognize his own responsibility in the matter. Nearly three years earlier, Herbert Howe had chastised Thalberg and MGM for giving Novarro "a dirty deal," but Howe had also blamed the star for accepting stories for which he was completely unsuited. He had, after all, *willingly* accepted roles in inferior vehicles such as *Huddle*, *The Son-Daughter*, and *Laughing Boy*, and at times had even signed with the studio specifically to make those very pictures he was now criticizing.

In early 1935, besides complaining about his last MGM films, Novarro expressed immense happiness with his newfound freedom. But despite his public expressions of glee, Novarro was apprehensive about the future. After more than a decade of stardom, he now faced a professional void. He was financially secure and had fewer obligations to his now adult siblings, but he would miss the added security of a steady MGM paycheck. And whether or not he had come to terms with the unpleasant truth, his popularity had waned. At thirty-six, Novarro was a Hollywood has-been. "Friends" were no longer calling. Nor was his phone ringing with dozens of film offers—and the few that came his way he considered inappropriate. When MGM invited him back to play second fiddle to the Marx Brothers in *A Night at the Opera*, Novarro refused the offer, saying that such a part should go to a beginner—and *he* was no beginner (the role went to Allan Jones).

After more than twelve years—one-third of his life—as a major film star,

Novarro would now have to create another identity. Perhaps he believed this new endeavor would be "all for the best," but his old motto notwithstanding, Novarro was to discover that he now lacked the spirit to fulfill the task. Herbert Howe had once written that with the possible exception of Charles Chaplin, he had "never known anyone who is so wholly the performer" as Novarro. Acting in the studio during the day, he would rush home in the evening to direct and perform at his Teatro Intimo. "When Ramon isn't acting," Howe had summed up, "he is like a theater with the lights out. He really does not exist." Indeed, shortly after his departure from MGM, Novarro suffered a nervous breakdown. On doctor's orders, he temporarily closed his Valley Oak home and moved back to the Gramercy house, taking the Argentinian swimmer José Caraballo with him.

Novarro's willingness to obey his doctor and temporarily leave the Valley Oak home is understandable, but his decision to bring Caraballo to the Gramercy house is utterly incomprehensible. The kind of relationship Novarro and Caraballo shared has never been made clear, but Novarro's friends have asserted that he was seriously smitten with the good-looking swimmer. Thus, Caraballo's stay at Gramercy must have been uncomfortable for both Novarro, who now had to conceal his feelings from numerous Samaniego eyes, and for the other family members who understood that Caraballo was no mere guest. This situation was in all likelihood a first: Herbert Howe had often been present at the house, but he had never *lived* there.

By the 1930s, homosexuality, though unacknowledged by mainstream society, had become a fact of life even among the conservative Samaniegos. Rafael Gavilán, Novarro's childhood playmate, had become an effeminate hairdresser who was clearly not interested in the opposite sex—a fact that did not prevent his being welcomed at family gatherings. Novarro, for his part, was now a thirty-six-year-old bachelor with no prospective wife in sight. Yet, there is no indication that his parents tried to pressure him into marriage, for they surely knew by then that Novarro was *different*. Even Señora Samaniego, though not as well educated as her husband (after years in the United States, she remained basically monolingual), must have been aware of her son's sexual orientation. How she reconciled her strong religious convictions—which deemed "sexual inversion" a sin—with her love for her son is impossible to say, though such a subject was likely never discussed.

Even if there had ever been any hint that Novarro should find a wife, the de facto head of the Samaniego household had long since put such hopes to rest. For years he had commanded respect as the financial pillar of the family, and he did not tolerate any intrusion into his private sphere. His phone was never to be answered by anyone but him unless he had made special arrangements. His drinking was his own concern. And so were his male "friends." But despite the imposed silence on the subject, the Sama-niegos' customary circumspection, and Novarro's dominant position in the household, Caraballo's presence at Gramercy was such a blatant affront to the mores of that traditional Catholic family that it led to serious tensions. These culminated in a family quarrel that resulted in the temporary banish-ment of the Argentinian guest from Gramercy.

To prevent outside worries, such as the Caraballo episode, from further affecting his already precarious emotional balance, Novarro kept himself busy while at the family house. He began practicing yoga, dismissed his secretary Philip Moreland, redecorated his quarters, spent time writing both a play and a screenplay, and took dance lessons in preparation for a British Isles concert tour that summer. In the fall, he hoped to produce his play at London's Old Vic Theatre—a far-fetched prospect, as the Old Vic special-ized in classical plays—because he felt that the British capital had been "kindest" among the cities he had visited during his 1933 European tour.

Those myriad changes Novarro effected in his lifestyle, although signif-icant, did not go deep enough. The new identity he urgently needed to create was still too indeterminate, which helps explain his aiming in so many different professional directions. Inevitably, such haphazard career moves would lead to many more frustrations than triumphs.

Initially, Novarro's main focus was to finish his play, *It's Another Story*, a semiautobiographical piece through which the former star vented his bitter-ness toward Hollywood. The plot centered on the disillusions of a "Mexican lad who yearns for great things. He is so ambitious, so eager to make good. Finally, after many, many years of struggle, he becomes a great motion picture star. Everything is at his command; the world is his. But the young star, knowing all this, learns later that life has more to offer than just the pleasure of living. He feels that now, with wealth and power, he can do the things he always wanted to do. But the things he wanted to do become meaningless. For there is no motivation behind them; he finds himself doing them—and it is a tasteless, meaningless proceeding. And so, with all his material dreams fulfilled, the young star discovers that life is empty, hope-less."

Novarro envisioned himself as the lead and Beulah Bondi, adept at por-traying mother roles, as one of the main supporting characters. "Naturally, it is founded on my own experience of the cruelties and insincerities of the film trade," Novarro told the *New York Times*, "and my hero dies a happy, sweet death after the torments of being a star." He abstained from elabo-rating on the precise sources of the "cruelties and insincerities of the film trade," but his remarks reinforce the view that he saw himself as a victim of—and not an active participant in—the Hollywood system.

Novarro had reportedly begun working on *It's Another Story* at the stroke of midnight of January 1, 1934, but if that was true, his superstitious gesture failed to bring the play any luck. As might have been expected, the announced engagement at the Old Vic never materialized, and despite lofty plans to present *It's Another Story* in Spanish and French before producing a screen adaptation, Novarro never finished writing even the English-language version of the play.

One important reason Novarro set aside *It's Another Story* in the spring of 1935 was his shifting of focus to the production of motion pictures. He formed R.N.S. (Ramón Novarro Samaniegos) Productions to make six Spanish-language films geared to the Hispanophone market in the United States and throughout Hispano-America, with the first of these set to be *Contra la corriente* (*Against the Current*).

The story of *Contra la corriente* begins when a local society girl and an Argentinian swimming champion meet and fall in love at the 1932 Olympic Games in Los Angeles. They marry, but their different lifestyles keep them apart until the husband realizes his wife must be treated harshly to appreciate her marriage. The conventional plot may seem at first an indication of Novarro's conservative stance regarding women's role in society—excepting sophisticated female artists and raunchy aviatrixes—but it was probably no more than a calculated attempt to appeal to his target market. After all, most films of the time, whether in Spanish or in English, dealt with women in a similar manner. And most important, *Contra la corriente* would be an ideal vehicle for José Caraballo. Like Rex Ingram, Novarro was intent on introducing to the world a new male star.

On March 14, 1935, shooting began at the Talisman Studios, the former Fine Arts facilities where D. W. Griffith had filmed *Intolerance*. As with the making of *La Sevillana*, R.N.S. Productions' first project relied heavily on Novarro's family. Eduardo designed the sets; Carmen and uncle Ramón Guerrero took supporting roles; and Antonio, who had codirected the 1932 bullfight-themed short *An Old Spanish Custom* (distributed by MGM), worked as assistant director. Novarro served as writer, director, and producer but declined to appear in front of the camera. For sixteen days, he directed Caraballo and Spanish leading lady Luana Alcañiz at the studio, and then took his troupe to the streets of Los Angeles for location shooting until mid-July. According to the *Hollywood Reporter, Contra la corriente* cost a not inconsiderable $60,000 (the *New York Times* reported a cost of $200,000, but that seems much too high).

Once *Contra la corriente* was ready for release, Novarro ran into a serious obstacle: he was unable to sell his film. Increasingly frustrated with his inability to find a distributor in the weeks that followed, Novarro abruptly left for New York, from where he was to sail for England with Carmen and his assistants Jorge Gavilán and Rebecca Ravens. The head of R.N.S. Productions had just committed himself to appear in a London production of Frederick Herendeen's *All the King's Horses* and now had little time to worry about the fate of *Contra la corriente*. Thus, in order to try his luck on the British stage, he sold to RKO for a nominal fee the distribution rights of his company's first production.

Novarro's private life manifested a similar lack of constancy. In the mid-1930s, future MGM researcher George Schönbrunn asked playwright and scenarist Hans Müller if a certain wealthy New Yorker was truly the lover of Ramon Novarro. "How can you say *the* lover of Ramon Novarro?" retorted Müller. "It's like saying *the* novel of Dumas." Müller's response, despite its flippancy, was quite to the point. Whether because of his heavy drinking, his hectic work schedule, or his familial obligations—or all three, combined with a fear of emotional attachment—Novarro had been unable to settle with one partner since the acrimonious end of his relationship with Herbert Howe. In fact, when Novarro departed New York in August 1935, his liaison with Caraballo, however intimate it had been, was over. The would-be film star remained on the American side of the Atlantic while Novarro crossed the ocean toward what would prove to be the most disastrous venture of his career.

Some of Novarro's friends had expressed concern that *All the King's Horses,* which had had a successful Broadway run in 1934, would be an inadequate vehicle for his talents. Even so, Novarro was determined that his legitimate stage debut would be in this musical variation of *The Prisoner of Zenda*, in which an actor impersonating a Ruritanian prince falls in love with the prince's wife. His costars, both of whom were American and had had previous musical stage experience, were silent-film actress Doris Kenyon and vaudevillian Eddie Foy, Jr. Carmen was to have a small role as a dancer.

Rehearsals at London's 1,119-seat His Majesty's Theatre began in early October. In order to fit into the tight period uniforms, Novarro had to suffer the inconvenience of wearing a corset, though ultimately that turned out to be a minor irritant. More important, the play was constantly being rewritten to match the personality of the star, while director Tom Reynolds and some of the British cast members kept complaining that Novarro's voice was not projecting to the back rows of the theater. The star paid them little heed. After all, he was an accomplished singer with a well-trained voice, and he had successfully toured Europe and South America.

When not rehearsing for *A Royal Exchange*, as *All the King's Horses* was called in England, Novarro spent his time with twenty-three-year-old Cecil Everley, whom he had met through French actor Jaque Catelain. Everley was then working at his father's engineering company, but took time off to chaperone the visiting Hollywood celebrity. Catelain knew that Novarro would be attracted to Everley—tall, slim, blond, blue-eyed—and he may have also guessed that the young Englishman would be smitten with the Mexican movie star. If so, he was right. Novarro and Everley's friendship quickly developed into an affair.

Meanwhile, rehearsals continued—and so did Novarro's voice-projection problems. The frustrated director and British performers were now angry with the star, who refused to follow their advice for making his speech audible everywhere in the theater. Worried about the mounting tension, Carmen invited Tonio Selwart, a friend of Novarro's then appearing in a British stage production of *The Pursuit of Happiness*, to attend one of the rehearsals. "I couldn't understand [Novarro], unfortunately," the German-born Selwart recalls. " 'We both have accents,' I told him. 'You should speak up.' His response was, 'Don't talk to me now, I'm rehearsing.' "

A Royal Exchange finally opened on Friday, December 6, 1935, after a number of postponements caused by endless rewrites (eight days prior to the opening, it was decided that the production should return to the original version). Expectations were high on both sides of the stage curtain. Londoners had been lining up for hours in the cold and damp weather to buy tickets to see Ramon Novarro perform live in their city. Novarro, for his part, was hoping to return to Hollywood with a triumphant London stage appearance to his credit. The night before, he had knelt by the grave of nineteenth-century actor Sir Henry Irving at Westminster Abbey and prayed for the success of the production. Being strongly superstitious, he undoubtedly believed it a good omen that the plot of his legitimate-theater debut paralleled that of his first important motion picture. Presumably as an added good-luck charm, Novarro renamed one of his characters Carlos Gavilán (Gavilán being the second half of his mother's maiden name).

The evening started well, with Carmen dancing two lively and well-received numbers. While his sister danced, Novarro, looking elegant in an overcoat and a hat, walked onto His Majesty's stage to warm and enthusiastic applause. But as the action proceeded, it became clear that both Novarro and *A Royal Exchange* were in dire need of more than just prayers and good-luck charms.

During one of Novarro's speeches, a yell from the gallery suddenly echoed through the theater: "Speak up, we can't hear you!" Novarro paused for an instant, then continued his dialogue. More cries of "Louder! Louder!" emanated from the gallery. After some more heckling, Novarro turned to the gallery and yelled back, "Now, *I* didn't understand *you!*" Tonio Selwart, sitting in the audience, was shocked. "Novarro was like a child when he was performing," he recalled. "How can anybody get out of a play and talk with [the audience]?"

As the evening progressed, the gallery became increasingly hostile. When Novarro reappeared onstage for the sixth or seventh time wearing one more shining, tight-fitting uniform of a different color, they burst into derisive laughter. A fierce duel with the villain was received with enthusiastic applause, but later, as the star lay fully bandaged near death, the gallery let out a mocking "Uuuuhhhhhhhhhh."

The vociferous gallery notwithstanding, the actors managed to finish the performance. There were three curtain calls, during one of which the heavy curtain fell right on Novarro's neck. But despite the myriad mishaps, the star of the play thought he should make an opening-night speech. Selwart had previously advised Novarro to "make it as short as possible," but after asking the audience to "please give us a chance," Novarro babbled on about the greatness of the English theater and of the late British stage star Ellen Terry. His declarations were received with more hoots from the gallery. Finally, Novarro thanked the polite audience for keeping their composure in spite of the badly mannered people in the cheaper seats. Predictably, Novarro's remark was greeted with vicious jeers, as voices in the gallery hollered, "Go back to Hollywood!"

Few friends came backstage to compliment or express their sympathy to the stars. Selwart, who did come to pay his respects, told Novarro, "You must be happy it's over." That evening, however, happiness was an alien sentiment for the ex–Hollywood star. The next day's reviews, most of which sided with "the badly mannered people in the cheaper seats," further dampened Novarro's spirits.

"A pretty sorry mess it is, when all's done," lambasted *The Times*. "Mr. Novarro has a small, not unpleasing voice, and a certain mousy precision of manner—a certain modesty, too, which prevents him from pretending to be what he certainly is not; but as a romantic hero in glittering uniforms on the stage of His Majesty's, he is almost pathetically misplaced." Another reviewer declared, "You can lead a film star to the rarer waters of West End presentation, but it is essential that he should drink with some gusto. That was the only mistake Senor Novarro made last night."

Explaining her brother's failure on the British stage, Carmen simply remarked, "He was used to the movies." Indeed, Novarro had never been required to project his voice while on a film soundstage—the microphone had performed that task for him. Novarro could project his voice well when singing because of years of practice, but he had never trained specifically for stage dialogue delivery. "It's a different method to sing than [to use one's] speaking voice," Selwart explained. That fact had become clear to Novarro a little too late.

A Royal Exchange lasted only ten performances. The producer wanted to close the £15,000 show after the second presentation, but, in a futile attempt to keep the production going, the principals waived their salaries and Novarro put up £6,000 of his own money to ensure that the minor players earned some income after weeks of arduous rehearsals. By the time the play folded on December 14, Novarro had lost $10,000.

Upon ringing down the curtain on the last performance—after a half-hour delay due to the hysterical weeping of his female fans that kept interrupting the action—Novarro spoke to the audience. "I will not expose my company to what happened on the first night," he explained, pointing to his fellow performers, who had gathered onstage. "These people have all been thrown out of work, they have worked hard and do not deserve it. Though the play is finished I am staying here in England, and I shall appear on the London stage again before the end of the year." Cheers from the audience. "In April," Novarro continued, "I hope to put on my own play [*It's Another Story*, now retitled *The Failure of Success*]." Referring again to *A Royal Exchange*, Novarro finished with, "Our company here have been splendid, but they did not have a chance.... I have been booed, but it has not disheartened me, but given me the courage and the guts, pardon the word, to go on. When I put on my play here, I do not want you to like it because of me, but because of the entertainment I offer you."

Following his speech, Novarro retired to his dressing room, where he talked to the press and to members of the ever loyal Ramon Novarro Film Club (the "RNFC," founded in 1927, and in which he served as "honorary president"). After being told that a crowd was standing outside in the freezing cold waiting for him to leave the theater, Novarro, wrapped in a beige dressing gown, went to the window of his dressing room, leaned over the windowsill, and talked to the fans below. Snow was beginning to fall, while the chimes of a distant clock announced that it was already midnight. At that moment, a fan asked the star to sing. In reply, Novarro began crooning "The Pagan Love Song" to the crowd below. As the fans joined in, passersby stopped to stare at the peculiar scene. "Surely nothing of the kind has ever happened before outside a London theater," observed RNFC newsletter editor Audrey Homan.

With the closing of *A Royal Exchange*, news reached Hollywood that the former MGM star had been "laughed off" the London stage. Headlines such as "Ramon Novarro Flees from Boos" and "London Cold to Novarro" were not the type of reports Novarro had been expecting from his overseas venture. But in spite of such demoralizing setbacks, Carmen asserted that her brother was "not too much" disappointed by the *A Royal Exchange* disaster. Novarro's interviews also seemed to indicate that he regarded his British stage fiasco as a solid learning experience. "Heckle me? They shout right out, 'Go back to Hollywood!'" Novarro told *Modern Screen* two years later. "It was somebody in the gallery who had had too much to drink, but he started all the others. Then while I am standing on the stage trying to calm the audience, the curtain comes down on my neck. It makes us all feel very badly, but particularly it is hard on my neck! All this happening is very bad for the life of the play. Bad publicity, bad for us. We do not sell tickets, so I put my own money in for two weeks, that the people who have rehearsed so kindly with us do not lose all their wages. Then we close.... You always have to fall down, pick yourself up and start all over again."

At the time, however, Novarro's thoughts were hardly that philosophical. Cecil Everley later told George Schönbrunn that Novarro was "completely flabbergasted" by the audience's reaction on opening night. Despite the often humorous and self-deprecating observations he later made to reporters, Novarro was fully aware that *A Royal Exchange* had destroyed his chance of returning to films via the London stage. Everley recalled that Novarro "was in a dreadful state" after the production folded, and took to drinking uncontrollably. Novarro's drunken stupors during the days that followed were so severe that he was unable to control his bodily functions. Not surprisingly, soon afterward Novarro and Everley had an acrimonious split. (When Schönbrunn mentioned Everley at a Hollywood gathering in the early 1940s, Novarro's reaction was "rather disagreeable." Nor was Novarro any friendlier when he encountered Everley at another Hollywood party. Novarro did not ask for Everley's address or phone number, and refused his offer of a ride home.)

·   ·   ·

Shortly after closing *A Royal Exchange*, Novarro received an offer for a one-week performance at a Budapest music hall. This was a welcome opportunity to leave London for a few days, though this temporary escape to Central Europe was to become another professional nightmare.

"It's funny now, but it was not funny then," Novarro told *Modern Screen*. The manager of the Budapest hall had promised to pay his salary and expenses on a daily basis, but after performing for two nights without receiving any wages, Novarro demanded the money owed him. The manager assured Novarro he would get paid before his departure, "but I am not assured because I am told after I get to Budapest that this manager is crooked, and you have to get your money every day from the box office." Novarro thus refused to go onstage until he received his payment in cash. The manager remained unmoved. He not only declined to give his star performer any money, but also told theater patrons that Novarro had canceled his presentations because he was ill and had lost his voice. Upon hearing of the manager's remarks, Novarro headed to an exclusive café and, after telling the restaurateur who he was, sang four songs at the piano to prove to Budapest that his voice was just fine.

That problem behind him, Novarro had to deal with another more serious. As he was never in the habit of carrying large sums of cash, he found himself stranded in the Hungarian capital at Christmastime without any money. He wired London (probably Carmen) for funds, but it was Christmas Eve. The banks were closed and would remain so for two more days. In desperation, Novarro cabled his attorney Stanley Barnes in California and some other friends asking for money, but nothing could be immediately done during the holidays. Eventually, he was saved by his Budapest hotel manager, who loaned him enough cash for his train fare back to London.

Soon, newspapers around the world were reporting that ex–movie star Ramon Novarro was broke and reduced to singing in Hungarian barrooms. Novarro's business manager, George Ward, had to issue a statement that his client was not broke, as his assets were estimated at $50,000 (if true, a surprisingly low sum for someone who had made close to $600,000 in his last four years at MGM), and that he had needed some cash only to avoid a temporary embarrassment. Despite Ward's pronouncements, cables and letters offering or containing money poured into the Gramercy household. The donations were either returned to the various senders or, if anonymous, given to different charities.

On December 30, sixteen days after the last curtain fell on *A Royal Exchange*, Novarro and Carmen opened at the Holborn Empire in London, in a revue sketch similar to the one they had performed in South America.

This time, there were no cries of "Go back to Hollywood!" The same type of audience that had sat in the cheap gallery seats at His Majesty's awarded Novarro and Carmen an enthusiastic reception. "He was just like a child," Tonio Selwart remembered. "He was so happy they liked him that he sang and sang and sang, and it was very endearing, but not very professional." In fact, the performers who were to follow the act were left waiting in the wings while Novarro joyfully sang one encore after another. After angry complaints from the other artists, the management informed Novarro that he would never be invited back to the Holborn.

Undaunted, Novarro and Carmen left London to spend four months touring British and Irish music halls. The work was incessant and tiring, but the only major mishap during the tour occurred in Scotland, where Novarro fell seriously ill with jaundice and rheumatism (which he blamed on the arduous making of *Ben-Hur*). Confined in bed for two weeks with a high fever that prevented him from sleeping, he was cared for by Rebecca Ravens, who had some previous nursing experience. At the end of the two weeks of mandatory rest, a feeble Novarro forced himself to travel to Nottingham to carry out his engagement there.

Upon returning to London, Novarro, still quite weak, astonished most of the seventy-eight RNFC members present at a March 15, 1936, meeting by visiting their headquarters. (Audrey Homan knew Novarro was supposed to appear, but had kept mum about it.) "I have no words because words mean nothing," the club's honorary president told the enthralled fans. "It is the thought behind them, to thank you for your loyalty to me: I can only say that I would gladly go through ten times the hardships I have gone through, to have loyalty such as yours." Indeed, *loyal* is the word for the RNFC members. During Novarro's tenure at MGM, they had written letters to the studio suggesting appropriate parts for their star; they also wrote to film houses asking for revivals of Novarro's MGM films, gave donations to different charities under Novarro's name, held frequent meetings to share thoughts about their star, and sent him presents across the Atlantic. Novarro's visit that March 15 was a genuine display of his appreciation for the faithfulness of his fan club. In the years to come, he would continue to demonstrate his gratitude through letters, phone calls, and gifts—such as the bust made of him in Argentina, which he donated to the club in the late 1930s.

The British Isles music hall tour finally ended on May 1. By then, Novarro had given up on his play. He and Carmen were offered vaudeville engagements in Spain and Australia, but Novarro, at that point feeling "awfully bored" by his nightly routine, declined the offers. Even so, on the way back to Los Angeles he mustered enough stamina to perform with his sister in Toronto and in Chicago.

Novarro's successful song-and-dance presentations—in Dublin alone more than eighty thousand spectators watched the show—may have served as some consolation for his earlier London stage debacle, but he knew that recognition in mostly provincial music halls would not guarantee another starring film role next to Garbo or MacDonald. Despite his warm reception in Leeds and Portsmouth, Novarro was to return to Los Angeles as much of a has-been as when he had left.

After more than ten months away from home, Novarro and Carmen landed at the Burbank airport on June 10, 1936. Awaiting them were family members, several reporters, and Alice Terry and Rex Ingram. (Terry had moved back to Los Angeles following her mother's death in 1934, while Ingram, after two years living in Cairo and roaming throughout North Africa, had recently joined his wife because of both his failing health and the deteriorating political situation in Europe.) After being kissed for the cameras by his visibly plump former costar, Novarro tersely dismissed the unfortunate opening night of *A Royal Exchange* as the work of "radicals," and claimed that the play had closed so abruptly because the management had been threatened with a boycott. He added that he intended to rest for two months, and then prepare to either tour the Orient or return to film work.

Soon after a three-day retreat with the Jesuits at El Retiro, Novarro suffered a severe relapse of the jaundice that kept him bedridden for a week. He was nursed back to health by Rebecca Ravens at the Santa Monica house of Dolores del Río's mother, who was then visiting relatives in Mexico. Ravens's care was surely effective, since by midsummer Novarro was busy studying music and, somewhat belatedly, promoting *Contra la corriente*.

Contra la corriente had opened on March 6 at New York's Teatro Campoamor to unenthusiastic reviews. The *New York Times* referred to the picture as "a routine" effort, sardonically remarking that "when Ramon Novarro transferred his activities from acting to writing and directing, it did not signify any epoch-making changes or improvements in the world of motion pictures." Trade publications concurred, declaring that Novarro's first independent production would have no chance in the mainstream American market, even in a dubbed version.

Having missed the New York premiere, on July 25 Novarro made a personal appearance at the Los Angeles opening, posing for a photograph with fellow attendees Alice Terry and Louis B. Mayer. But despite Novarro's long overdue attempt to promote his film, *Contra la corriente* remained confined to Spanish-language movie houses in the United States. The picture was later distributed in South America by the RKO subsidiary Radio Films, S.A.E., but in spite of (unconfirmed) stories of its success abroad, Novarro's enthusiasm for producing more films on his own had by then faded. "The experiment [of *Contra la corriente*] only proved that directing was not my field," Novarro recalled years later. "I liked it, yes—but acting was my true métier. I'd long been in the game, had enjoyed the help of at least four wonderful directors, and it was not unreasonable for me to try to direct. But I saw quickly enough that what I could achieve as an actor was more satisfying than what I could do as a director." Left unsaid were his distress over distribution problems and high production costs, and the fact that his muse José Caraballo was no longer in his life. With this radical reversal of attitude about directing—Novarro had said the exact opposite in 1930 after directing *La Sevillana*—*Contra la corriente* remains the sole picture ever made by R.N.S. Productions.

Now that he had finished his European commitments and had discarded the role of film director, Novarro was unsure what to do next. Just as in the period that followed his departure from MGM, he again fell into a deep depression. Friends urged him to get back to work, for Novarro had always been able to function well when he was busy with films or music. "I have been advised to make a picture immediately, tomorrow," he told the *Los Angeles Times* in early August 1936. "They tell me it is fatal to be off the screen so long. Make anything! But I don't agree. You let your friends down when you play just any part. I'm going to wait for the right one!"

Novarro was actually eager to set foot once again in a film studio, but he seemed to be psychologically unprepared for the task. He traveled to Mexico on the advice of friends in an attempt to find film deals south of the border, but even though "everything turned out very well," he returned to Los Angeles without any commitments. In the latter part of 1936, he spent much of his time alone at the Valley Oak house, trying not "to feel that I was being a slacker, and yet [feeling] I couldn't cheapen myself by doing something that I considered unworthy." According to Novarro, his self-imposed solitude "solved my problems. . . . I had long talks with myself, honest talks. All that had to be changed was changed—in thought, speech and action. . . . By the New Year, a life with a purpose was shining brightly before me."

In early 1937, Novarro enrolled in the Olga Steeb Music School, resumed his long hours of daily music practice, and began his efforts to trade the Valley Oak house for "some income property." In letters to Audrey Homan and to his old friend and fellow devout Catholic Noël Sullivan, Novarro declared he felt happier and more contented with his newfound self. "The past has gone into oblivion," he wrote Homan. "I am grateful for everything, regretting nothing, and more grateful still for the hardships that have brought such peace and contentment to my soul, and the capacity to value them as I should."

Whether or not those expressions of inner peace reflected reality cannot be confirmed. Throughout his life, Novarro would invariably write or talk about having found inner peace, even during times when he was drinking uncontrollably. It was the old "All's for the best" routine he liked to put on. He had suffered, he had learned, he was happy. But whether he was being honest or just self-deceiving, challenges remained for the "peaceful and contented" Novarro. He had recently suffered considerable financial losses with the productions of both *Contra la corriente* and *A Royal Exchange,* and was having a difficult time finding a buyer for the Valley Oak property. He may have written Homan that he thought it "wonderful" to do his own grocery shopping and to fight with the grocer about the price of eggs, but money had become a concern.

In the spring of 1937, when third-rate Republic Pictures doubled a salary offer for him to star in three pictures, Novarro readily agreed—a decision that clearly indicates that major studios such as Paramount and Warner Bros., or even second-rate ones such as RKO and Universal, had not been competing for his talents.

Small-time actor Irving Pichel, whose few directorial credits included the unusual *She* and *The Most Dangerous Game* (with Ernest B. Schoedsack), was assigned to direct the first Novarro vehicle since his departure from MGM more than two years earlier: *She Didn't Want a Sheik,* a parody of desert movies such as Valentino's *The Sheik* and Novarro's own *The Arab* and *The Barbarian.* In this latest desert tale, Novarro was to play a singing sheik passing for a singing guide who seduces a bratty American corkscrew heiress, played by pert B movie leading lady Lola Lane. Republic's first Novarro-starring vehicle was set to be an upscale production by the studio's standards, but the former MGM star had to get used to substantially fewer perks than those he had enjoyed at his previous studio. After all, *She Didn't Want a Sheik* was a mere "quickie" by MGM standards, a fifty-three-minute picture shot in less than two weeks in the spring of 1937.

When *She Didn't Want a Sheik*—now renamed *The Sheik Steps Out*—was previewed for film critics, those present debated whether the ex-superstar would be able to recover his former popularity, with opinions ranging "from complete confidence to the other extreme." Actually, with a comeback vehicle suited to his talents, Novarro could easily have regained at least some of his former fame. At thirty-eight, he was several years younger than Ronald Colman and William Powell, and about the same age as James Cagney, Spencer Tracy, Clark Gable, Charles Boyer, Gary Cooper, and Nelson Eddy, whose operettas opposite Jeanette MacDonald were bringing huge profits to MGM.

Because of his two previous successes in roles as an Arab, Novarro believed *The Sheik Steps Out* would be the comeback vehicle he needed. "I like it," he told *Modern Screen*. "It is like one I did once for Rex Ingram that was very good for me. I do not even talk to my lawyers about it or my friends. I think I like it. I will do it. That is part of the philosophy that I have attained. It is: do the things you think best, and do not worry." Regrettably, Novarro's newfound philosophy was not foolproof. He *should* have done some worrying before accepting *The Sheik Steps Out*, or at least have had his attorney and assorted advisers do the worrying for him.

The picture, released at the Warner's Beverly Hills Theater on July 24, 1937, was greeted with notices that were undoubtedly kinder than they might have been without the presence of a well-liked old-timer. As *Variety* observed, the only point of interest about *The Sheik Steps Out* "is the reappearance of Ramon Novarro. . . . Story, dialog, and acting by the supporting players are second rate." Indeed, despite the promised thrills in the ads— "Once again he sings Pagan love songs as he woos and wins a lovely daughter of luxury"—*The Sheik Steps Out* is merely a faded carbon copy of *The Barbarian*. Lacking that earlier film's sexual tension—courtesy of the Production Code—*The Sheik Steps Out* also fails to offer even a modicum of the wit necessary for an effective parody. All that is required of Novarro, who wears a ghastly white-powder makeup, are cutesy ogles while he bares his torso, sings forgettable songs (with lyrics provided by his friend Elsie Janis), and seduces Lola Lane's spoiled heiress.

Even though exoticism was still an important part of American motion pictures—*The Hurricane*, set in the South Pacific, was one of that year's biggest hits, while the following year's *Algiers* would garner Charles Boyer an Academy Award nomination—*The Sheik Steps Out* failed to ignite the country's box office. Prior to signing his contract with Republic, Novarro should have known that a charmless, cheaply made comeback vehicle was the wrong route toward recovering his former star status.

Before his next Republic assignment, Novarro sang on several radio broadcasts, performed with Carmen in music halls in the American South and

Midwest, and spent much of his free time with his family. He continued to live at the Valley Oak home, but stayed for long stretches at the Gramercy residence. Novarro wanted to spend as much time as possible with his aging parents—his sickly father was now sixty-six years old and Señora Samaniego was sixty-five—especially since most of his siblings had by then moved elsewhere. (One temporary addition to the Gramercy household had been his sister Leonor, who several years earlier had decided against renewing her religious vows.)

During that time, Novarro continued his family life in much the same way as he had during his years of stardom. He carried on with his directorial efforts at the Teatro Intimo, went to church with his mother, and gave sumptuous parties at the family house on special occasions. Señora Samaniego's Saint's Day on July 1 and the Posadas ceremony at Christmastime were two of the family's major festivals, with rehearsals for the Teatro Intimo presentations lasting for weeks before those events. At such functions, Novarro often sang while Carmen danced classical Spanish or Mexican numbers.

Soon after the 1937 year-end celebrations, Novarro announced at a party for Republic mogul Herbert J. Yates that his next picture would be a comedy by Hans Kräly (who had previously cowritten *The Student Prince* and *Devil-May-Care*) about a temperamental Parisian artist who discovers in the flesh the ideal woman he had once painted. Filming was scheduled to begin in early spring 1938 under the direction of Hungarian-born John H. Auer and with Novarro's former leading lady Madge Evans as the girl of the painter's dreams, but numerous script rewrites delayed the production until June. As a result, Evans bowed out—much to Novarro's disappointment—and was replaced by former Warner Bros. ingenue Marian Marsh.

Filming lasted a mere twelve days. "They were very quick about it," Marian Marsh recalled; "it was 'quickly quick.'" Novarro had to cope not only with the disconcerting pace of *A Desperate Adventure*, as the picture was eventually called, but also with hassles that turned the production into a veritable ordeal. Part of the problem was the myriad script alterations that turned the story line into an incoherent jumble, but the main source of anguish for the former MGM star was his treatment by the Republic crew.

In an interview with author William Drew, Marsh stated that Novarro "was a homosexual and there was a lot of teasing ... going on at his expense on the set because the prop-men were real he-mannish. I didn't understand what it was all about and somebody had to give me an idea of what was going on." Such disrespectful and abusive behavior directed at a star would have been unthinkable at MGM, regardless of Mayer's opinions of homosexuality. MGM was supposed to be a family unit that, although dysfunctional, at least offered a veneer of professional decorum. Obviously, neither Herbert Yates nor John Auer saw Republic in the same light.

In spite of the hardships, Novarro maintained his usual professionalism. "He always was on time," Marsh remembered. "He said 'good morning' to everyone in a very nice manner. He was very polite." Still, whenever he was not working on a scene, Novarro kept a distance from everyone else. After the picture was completed, he refused the studio's next assignment, a pirate story in which he had previously expressed interest. Republic continued sending him paychecks for several weeks, as Novarro was supposed to begin work on the third picture of his contract, but the star kept objecting to the material submitted to him. Besides the grievous shooting of *A Desperate Adventure*, Novarro was reluctant to work at Republic again after the dismal August 15 opening of that picture.

The poor reception given *A Desperate Adventure*, though hardly surprising, was unfortunate. Despite its inane plot and poor direction, the picture revealed an astoundingly young, charming, and good-looking Novarro that filmgoers had not seen since the early 1930s. The source of Novarro's regained youth remains unclear. After leaving MGM, he had taken up yoga and meditation exercises, which perhaps helped to reduce his drinking abuse and its physical effects. Yet, the difference between his worn appearance in his last several pictures and his manicured youthfulness in *A Desperate Adventure* is too striking to be merely the product of either good lighting or months of sobriety. Even though there are no reports confirming that he underwent surgery at that time, a face-lift—a not uncommon procedure among film performers as early as the 1920s—was the probable cause of Novarro's sudden rejuvenation, especially considering that his improved looks lasted for the next few years in spite of recurrent drinking bouts.

One such bout occurred shortly after the opening of *A Desperate Adventure*. In September, after several drinks at a friend's house, Novarro was driving along Sunset Boulevard when he failed to yield to a pedestrian at a street crossing. That incident led to his first reported traffic violation caused by alcohol. The pedestrian was not hit, but Novarro, despite attempts to place the blame on the pedestrian, was fined $10 for his carelessness. During the next few years, such encounters with the law would become almost annual events.

By 1939, Novarro's career was at a standstill. After months of rejecting Republic properties, Novarro at last abrogated his ties to the studio since his contract had stipulated that his next picture should have started no later than January 2. This break was to be expected, for Novarro was unable to adapt to a Poverty Row studio after spending eleven years at MGM. Also, this decision to renege on his contractual obligation was a rare wise (if unethical) career move, as his connection with Republic would surely have led to more disappointments. Yates had wanted Ramon Novarro as a contract player to add prestige to his third-rate film company, but Novarro had little to gain from working in grade-C pictures. Money, which had been an issue at first, had become less of a concern, as Novarro had curtailed his expenses since moving back to the Gramercy house in late 1938. After nearly two years of trying, he had finally succeeded in trading the Valley Oak house for several lots in the San Fernando Valley.

Describing himself as "happy, wiser and free," Novarro continued reading scripts, hoping for one that would restore his faded popularity. Unrealistically, he was intent on playing the lead in Twentieth Century–Fox's *The Rains Came*, but the role went to that studio's leading male star, Tyrone Power. In a letter to Audrey Homan, Novarro stated that "nothing would please me more" than to star in a remake of *Ben-Hur*, but he must have known that in 1939 no studio would star him in a grade-A production, let alone in a costly superspectacle. In the summer, a considerably more modest but alluring project from overseas finally broke Novarro's lengthy professional recess.

For ten years, Marcel L'Herbier, the celebrated French director of the silent classic *L'Argent*, had been attempting to film his adaptation (with dialogue by Jean Cocteau) of Russian playwright Nicolas Evreinoff's *La Comédie du bonheur* (*The Play of Happiness*), a Pirandello-like tale about an insane asylum escapee who changes the lives of three dreary boardinghouse dwellers with his "Play of Happiness." Jaque Catelain, who had appeared in more than a dozen films for L'Herbier, was the likely connection between the ex–Hollywood star and the ex–avant-garde director gone mainstream since the advent of sound. Novarro was to play an important role in *La Comédie du bonheur*, though the actual lead belonged to the rotund, Swiss-born star of French films Michel Simon, one of Jean Renoir's favorite actors. Rounding out the prestigious cast were Sacha Guitry's former wife and frequent costar Jacqueline Delubac, stage star Sylvie, and newcomers Micheline Presle and Louis Jourdan.

On August 16, 1939, Novarro left New York aboard the *Normandie* for France. Five days later he arrived in Le Havre, where he was received by L'Herbier and dozens of reporters and fans. After settling in a suite at the Hôtel Lancaster on the Champs-Elysées, Novarro socialized with a few friends, met with the picture's cast at a party sponsored by the newspaper *Paris-Soir*, and gave interviews in anticipation of the production. Then, just a few days later, *La Comédie du bonheur* was thrown into disarray by the announcement of a nonaggression pact between Germany and the Soviet Union, which made war between France and Germany seem inevitable. That same day, the United States embassy in Paris issued a warning that all American citizens should leave France immediately.

With the prospects for *La Comédie du bonheur* uncertain, Novarro was not sure if he should stay in France. He contacted producing company Artis-Film, which made tentative reservations for him to leave aboard the *Champlain* in late August, as production of the film had been postponed indefinitely. While deciding on his next step, Novarro spent a quiet weekend at a friend's château in Deauville, where he was advised by friends to make use of his boat reservation. On August 29, three days before the Nazi invasion of Poland, he left on the *Champlain* as planned, though expecting to return once Artis-Film notified him of the new shooting schedule.

After seven weeks in New York without hearing from Artis, Novarro headed back to Los Angeles. While en route, he received a telegram from the French company inviting him to go to Spain, a neutral country then recovering from its devastating civil war, to make both *La Comédie du bonheur* and its newly proposed Spanish-language version. Novarro replied with a request for more details about the revamped project while he continued his trip home. After weeks without any more news from overseas, he embarked on a mini concert tour of three small California towns. The enthusiastic reception accorded his blend of Spanish- and English-language songs encouraged him to plan for performances in Texas and Louisiana in the spring of 1940, and for a more extensive tour covering Brazil, South Africa, Australia, and New Zealand later that year.

On March 2, 1940, a cable from Artis-Film forced a change in plans. Novarro was asked to leave for Europe immediately; only upon his arrival in Portugal was he to be told whether *La Comédie du bonheur* would be shot in Spain or in Italy. To waste no time, Novarro flew from Los Angeles to New York, and from there traveled to Baltimore, sailing for Lisbon on March 8. While in the Portuguese capital, he learned that Marcel L'Herbier had arranged with the assistance of the local French ambassador to produce *La Comédie du bonheur* in Italy. The picture would now be a joint Franco-Italian effort shot in French at Rome's Scalera studios.

Shooting began shortly after Novarro's arrival in Rome, but the twelve-week production bogged down in financial mismanagement. Remembering his Hungarian experience, Novarro refused to report on the set one day until he had received—and cashed—his week's paycheck. When L'Herbier was summoned back to Paris, possibly because of budgetary problems, Novarro was left in charge of the direction, though the extent of his work behind the cameras is uncertain. In a letter to Homan describing his *La Comédie du bonheur* experiences, he made no mention of any directorial duties, though he did assert that the producers liked his "work and technical knowledge so much" that they wanted him to stay in Italy. Novarro, however, wanted to leave as soon as filming was completed. As a compromise, he agreed to return at a later date to direct and star in a screenplay he had written, *Truthful Lies*, a lightweight romantic comedy about a carefree Mexicano and a wealthy American girl who find love in Acapulco.

On June 2, one hour after completing work in *La Comédie du bonheur*, Novarro left for Genoa to board the refugee liner *Manhattan*, the last ship to leave that port for the United States before Italy entered the war.

La Comédie du bonheur, dubbed in Italian, was released as *Ecco la felicità* (Here's happiness) in Rome on December 23. Nearly two years later, on July 23, 1942, that same cut, back in the original French, surfaced in Paris. The picture was considered a minor work in L'Herbier's career, but Novarro, when mentioned, was generally well received. *La Comédie du bonheur* supposedly had a brief commercial run in the United States sometime in the 1940s, but no reviews can be found to confirm its showing on American screens.

Years later, L'Herbier admitted that *La Comédie du bonheur* was "a film that I finally was able to make when I didn't believe in it at all, thanks to the war." But despite the director's lack of faith in the theme—the happiness imparted by the "play" is unreal, but "the illusion of happiness" is enough to bring bliss to all involved—*La Comédie du bonheur* is a pleasant, though highly theatrical, slice of philosophical nonsense. Once again, Novarro looks younger and more handsome than he had in his later MGM films, but his performance is disappointingly unsubtle and his mannerisms effete. Still, Novarro's participation in this film is of interest because he acts and sings in French, and because he plays an ambitious and egotistical character who resembles a side of himself that had always been carefully concealed from both the public and most of his friends.

Issuing a rare political statement, that Americans should "protect their freedom of speech and press at all costs," Novarro arrived at the Burbank airport on June 17, 1940, and rapidly began plans to jump-start his career on this side of the Atlantic. Upon learning that MGM planned to film Ethel Vance's bestseller *Escape* with Norma Shearer, Novarro asked his former costar to help him get the role of the chief villain, a tenacious Nazi officer. Shearer, still a major name at the studio despite a series of box-office disappointments, promised to recommend him. Yet, Novarro heard nothing about the role until the announcement that Conrad Veidt had been hired to play the part. Angered by the slight, Novarro never spoke to Shearer again.

But if Hollywood was not beckoning, small-town theaters were. For $200 a week, a fraction of his old MGM salary but the standard pay of stage grand dames Ethel Barrymore and Ina Claire, Novarro began getting summer stock engagements with the help of agent Alan Brock, a former stage and screen juvenile who specialized in finding theatrical work for dethroned film idols. Novarro's first such assignment was in late summer, when he started a tour of New England in an adaptation of Rudolph Lothar and Fritz Gottwald's romantic comedy *The Command to Love*. "I worked harder than ever in my life," Novarro later recalled, as he had to memorize sixty-three pages of dialogue in five days. Ultimately, however, the warm reception given his performance as a seductive French military attaché left the forty-one-year-old actor eager for more of that kind of work.

Novarro's newfound professional happiness was abruptly dampened when he received news that his father was gravely ill in Los Angeles. Following a long period of stability, Dr. Samaniego's delicate health had rapidly deteriorated in the late 1930s, when he underwent a prostatectomy and a new series of treatments for his chronic facial neuralgia. Since then, he had been spending most of his time in the Gramercy house, his meals served to him in his bedroom. On November 15, Dr. Samaniego, age sixty-nine, finally succumbed to myocardial degeneration. Novarro, still busy on the East Coast, was unable to return to Los Angeles until one day after the funeral.

Four weeks later, Novarro was involved in his most serious car accident thus far. In a letter to Audrey Homan, he recounted his version of the night of the crash: At approximately midnight on December 12, he was driving home from a birthday party for Laura Hope Crews (Aunt Pittypat in *Gone with the Wind*) when, at the intersection of Sunset Boulevard and Havenhurst Drive in West Hollywood, "a driver coming in the opposite direction led me to believe he was going to turn left, so I eased to my left in order to give him more clearance space, but he became frightened and changed his mind." The result was a violent head-on collision.

Both drivers were injured. According to Novarro, a doctor heard the crash and drove to the accident scene, where he found the unconscious actor pinned between the wheel and the seat. By the time the doctor forced the car door open, Novarro had stopped breathing and had swallowed his tongue. "The doctor decided there was no time to wait," Novarro wrote

Homan, "and he gave me an alcohol injection, poured some alcohol in my mouth, pulled my tongue out and started me breathing again. If it hadn't been for his kindness, I wouldn't be here today. God bless him."

Having suffered a concussion, two broken ribs, a badly bruised chest that made breathing difficult, a cut on his chin, and a dislocated ankle, Novarro spent two and a half weeks in a hospital (his ankle remained in a cast for six weeks). "But accepting things as I think one should," he explained to Homan, "I managed to be cheerful, happy and grateful even in the hospital. My Christmas there was the loveliest I ever spent. Yes, Audrey there is beauty in everything and it's up to us to find it."

After leaving the hospital, Novarro, who had stated his occupation as "concert singer," was charged with driving over the center line and failing to make a proper turn. At first he pleaded not guilty, but once he was ordered to stand trial he reversed his plea. Even then, he had to "appear in court like any other criminal," and was fined $25. Three days later, sporting a goatee he had grown to let the cut on his chin heal, Novarro left by train for New York via New Orleans to "quiet down my somewhat shattered nerves."

Novarro's version of the accident in his letter to Audrey Homan was clearly a fabrication. His claim that he veered to the left to give the other driver "more clearance space" was a patent excuse for reckless driving. The "doctor" who allegedly appeared on the scene to save Novarro's life by pouring alcohol into his veins and in his mouth was never heard from again. But the most curious aspect of Novarro's letter to Homan is his total disregard for the fate of the other driver. That individual, Lyle E. Willey, also suffered injuries, and could have been killed. Nowhere in the letter did Novarro express sorrow or regret for the suffering he had caused that other person. In a letter to another friend, Novarro thanked "the grace of God" for his having survived a potentially fatal car accident, but once again there was no mention of the other driver.

The man who could be so generous with his money could also be unabashedly self-centered when trying to shield himself from recriminations—whether from the law, from friends and relatives, or from within. Even so, such tactics fell far short of total effectiveness. The law would find him guilty of reckless driving a number of times; his family, according to Ferdinand Pinney Earle's son Eyvind, was "extremely embarrassed" by his drunken driving arrests; and Novarro himself was undoubtedly aware of both his culpability in the car accident and his alcoholism. Despite his attempts at self-deceit, Novarro knew he had a serious problem that he was unable to solve.

Additionally, Novarro's claim of feeling "cheerful, happy and grateful" while agonizing in the hospital seems to have been more of his ongoing "peaceful and contented" offscreen performance. According to his philosophy of life, heavily influenced by his strict Catholic background, Novarro felt it was his duty to accept and be thankful for pain. "You know, I'm not sorry for anything that has ever happened to me," he had told the press after leaving MGM. "It has all been an experience, not wasted time. The only profitable emotion is suffering, anyway. After the grief passes, you comprehend so much more."

In a letter to Homan written two months after the start of World War II, Novarro described the sea voyage aboard the *Champlain* as having been "uneventful, outside a few people who became obnoxious by complaining when there was no reason to find fault with the way God ran His world." Apparently, war and mayhem were also included in his old "All's for the best" philosophy. In that same letter, he added, "I feel there's a purpose, and a good one, behind everything that happens. Am I going to find fault with things because I don't understand them? No sir." This letter was followed six weeks later by a Christmas note reminding Homan that the "peace and happiness we reach for come from within ourselves. . . . Outward things can affect us only as much as we let them."

Though well-intentioned, Novarro's words of hope show a profound lack of sensitivity. After all, he was telling Homan in battle-torn England about God's unquestionable wisdom, from the safety and comfort of his Gramercy mansion. Yet, that was his way of expressing his self-prescribed view of reality—whether or not he fully believed it. If Novarro did have questions about "the way God ran His world," he seems to have kept them buried deep within himself.

As Novarro grew older, his philosophy of life became, like every other aspect of his existence, increasingly bound to Catholicism. But instead of leading to a stronger spiritual awareness, religion became an obsession—a substitute for alcohol during his periods of abstinence. Lacking both a solid emotional attachment and the psychological sturdiness to withstand the passing of his youth, his looks, and his stardom, Novarro seized upon his religion as an emotional crutch. Thus began his cycle of guilt for his homosexuality, for his drinking, and for any other "ungodly" thoughts or conduct, followed by periods of fervent religion-induced abstinence, followed by either a sexual encounter or more drinking, which led back to feelings of guilt. This was a cycle he would repeat for the rest of his life.

TWELVE

Comeback and Farewells

Novarro's cycle of guilt-abstinence-binge-remorse was broken only when he was busy at work. But now, in order to satisfy his yearning for artistic expression and to meet his financial needs, Novarro had to seek out acting roles himself. He expressed interest in performing in a motion picture with a "philosophical story which would help people to find themselves," but no screen stories were offered—"philosophical" or otherwise. He also hoped to appear on the New York stage in the winter of 1941, but found "nothing but trash" among the plays submitted to him. Thus, summer stock, in spite of the hard work involved, became his chief professional activity.

In April 1941, Novarro starred in *Dans l'ombre du harem* (In the shadow of the harem), his French-language stage debut with the theater group La Comédie de Montréal. In Novarro's words, this staging of Lucien Besnard's play about a vengeful sheik redeemed by mother love afforded him "the greatest acting opportunity" of his career. "It was a part . . . as cruel as Charles Laughton can be," he wrote Audrey Homan, "plus a certain lyric quality that Novarro [he sometimes wrote about himself in the third person] seems to have. I've never felt so much at home in a part in my life." He followed that assignment with a well-received production of Jacques Deval's comedy of manners *Tovarich*, which was presented in small towns across New England. To preserve his energies for the summer run, Novarro avoided socializing with the rest of the cast, retiring to his quarters as soon as the show was over. "He was very well behaved," actor William Hughes later recalled, and indeed, as was Novarro's habit while working, he refrained from drinking.

When not playing with small theater groups, Novarro participated in a few radio broadcasts and toured in a revue with Carmen in film houses across the Midwest. Besides his unflagging need for appreciation and applause, financial considerations had prompted Novarro to make those personal appearances. He had been living more modestly than in the old days, but he still needed income to avoid using up his savings. "I've never liked money matters," he wrote Homan, "but I must pay attention to those things, especially as I have so many dependents, and I feel I always will have, because my brothers as soon as they marry have other obligations to attend to. I have the whole weight of the household on me." Yet, though less comfortable than he once had been, Novarro was in a far better financial position than many silent-film stars, some of whom, like Charles Ray, Clara Kimball Young, and his former *Ben-Hur* leading lady May McAvoy, had been forced to eke out a living as extras or bit players.

When not working, Novarro continued to be a part of the Hollywood party scene, though on a distinctly lesser scale than in previous years. "It is in the company of old friends that I realize my change," Novarro wrote Noël Sullivan in 1937. "I don't seem to be very much interested in the things that concerned me in the past. Consequently, I have very little, or nothing, to say; and less patience to listen." Besides Sullivan, whom Novarro saw whenever he visited Northern California, other old friends with whom he still maintained a good rapport were Rex Ingram and Alice Terry.

Since Ingram had insisted on living in an area with trees and a river after returning to Los Angeles, he and Terry had settled on a large estate in Studio City (there were scattered trees nearby, and the Los Angeles River ran alongside their property). Ingram lived in his studio, where he kept himself busy sculpting and writing a novel, while Terry occupied the adjacent two-story main house, which she began sharing with her sister Edna in the mid-1940s. Novarro often visited with his former leading lady, who spent most of her time in town with her lover Gerald Fielding, but he saw his old mentor less frequently. Despite suffering from high blood pressure caused by a virus he had contracted in Egypt, Ingram spent much of his time traveling, now mainly to Mexico and Central America.

Additional members of Novarro's small circle of close friends were Janet Gaynor, whom he had met through F. W. Murnau, and Gaynor's husband, MGM costume designer Adrian, both of whom were Novarro's frequent bridge partners. Others who would gather for card games at the house of Gaynor's mother were real estate agent Newell Van Der Hoef, Austrian émigré and struggling actor George Schönbrunn, and art history teacher Natalie Bateson, who was to become one of Novarro's longest-lasting friends.

Schönbrunn remembered the tall, slender, dark-haired Natalie Bateson as resembling "an Egyptian statue," but her cool aristocratic poise notwithstanding, Bateson possessed a relentless inner drive. Once she set her sights on Novarro, she became determined to have him as a husband. The aging gay actor with a sizable bank account seemed ideal husband material: he could provide her with social status and financial security, and, equally important for a woman who preferred the company of her own sex, he would not make any emotional or sexual demands on her.

"She was pushy," Schönbrunn later remarked. "Everything was so overdone, all this kissing and carrying on. She *had* to be the life of the party." Nevertheless, being the life of the party was not sufficiently alluring to make Novarro abandon his convictions about the sanctity of marriage. Now semiretired from the limelight, he had no need for a marriage of convenience, nor was he willing to add another dependent to an already extensive list. After failing to walk down the aisle with Novarro, Bateson, who had also tried her luck with Adrian before losing him to Janet Gaynor, finally settled on interior decorator Paul Chamberlain—though even after her marriage she continued her dogged pursuit of the more prestigious Novarro.

Despite Bateson's unswerving perseverance, Novarro appreciated her elegance and sophistication and often visited her small Hollywood home on Highland Avenue. Although at times he could be highly chauvinistic, Novarro respected and appreciated members of the opposite sex who were attractive, cultured, and worldly, qualities he perhaps found missing in upperclass Mexican women raised in that country's strict patriarchal system. Of course, there were exceptions such as Pancho Barnes, but most of Novarro's female friends possessed at least two of those three qualities. In the Gramercy household, Señora Samaniego was held above such requisites, but two other family members met Novarro's standards in that regard. One was his assertive and independent-minded sister Luz; the other was Teresa Bracho.

No close blood ties can be confirmed, but Novarro invariably referred to the svelte, impeccably attired and bejeweled Teresa Bracho as his "cousin." (Teresa was apparently related to the Bracho family of Durango, who *were* cousins of the Samaniegos.) She had come to the United States in the mid-1930s with her Catholic priest brother, but had taken off on her own after he settled in the American Midwest. Upon her arrival in Los Angeles, she became a permanent guest of the Samaniegos.

Later in the decade, Bracho lived with Novarro at Valley Oak, handling assorted domestic chores and taking special care of Novarro's needs. She always had tea and refreshments ready for him in the evening, was always willing to play Chinese checkers with him on his free mornings, and performed little tasks she knew would please her ten-year-younger "cousin." On Novarro's thirty-ninth birthday, for example, Bracho delighted her cousin by awakening him to the tune of "Las Mañanitas," a birthday-morning Mexican song, and by carefully spelling "Happy Birthday" with small leaves of English ivy on the breakfast table. Despite once claiming that he disliked adulation, Novarro cherished the lavish attention Bracho bestowed on him, because he felt she expected nothing in return (though he also enjoyed Natalie Bateson's fawning, in spite of her very high expectations).

Bracho continued to perform household favors for Novarro even after their return to the Gramercy house in late 1938. Her source of income in those years is uncertain, but whether it came from her own funds in Mexico or from Novarro, Bracho was not officially paid for her domestic services. She was a family member, not a servant. Also, possibly more than anyone else in those days, she was Novarro's closest friend and foremost confidante—though if his lack of openness with other intimate friends is any indication, much was left unsaid between them.

During the early 1940s, Novarro was also seeing a man half his age now known as Don Atkins. Atkins has asserted that in 1940 he and Novarro began an intermittent four-year affair, during which Novarro rented a three-story house for him on North Catalina Drive in Hollywood. According to Atkins, Novarro behaved like a kinder, gentler male Norma Desmond: a man filled with generosity, but eager to recover his lost fame and forever dreaming of a spectacular comeback.

Atkins's story about the love affair cannot be confirmed. Novarro's friends and family members were unable to recall him, even though Atkins has contended that he was invited to the Gramercy house (a place he loathed) for dinner on several occasions, and that the Samaniegos often telephoned Novarro at the Catalina house. In any case, if they truly were lovers, Atkins was an odd choice for Novarro. A slight man with dyed light blond hair, he would have raised numerous eyebrows at the Samaniegos' dinner table.

Atkins has also claimed to have been at Novarro's side when the actor became embroiled in another alcohol-related traffic episode in October 1941. In this latest incident, his car stalled on Hollywood Boulevard, and Novarro was apparently too inebriated to get it started again. After spending the night in jail, he was allowed to contact his attorney, Stanley Barnes, and was released on $50 bail.

That arrest led to numerous unpleasant headlines illustrated by a photograph of the wearied-looking actor being released from his cell. "I've never felt so furious and revengeful in my life," a humiliated Novarro wrote Audrey Homan. Since some reports claimed that he had to pay a $150 fine but was unable to raise the money, Stanley Barnes had to offer a public rebuttal, stating that his client had "ample funds in trust with which he can live in comfort for the rest of his life." Novarro, for his part, publicly asserted that he had only "taken some drinks," and had pleaded guilty to drunken driving simply because it was "so much easier and quicker." This latest excuse, however, sounded too much like the old ones to be convincing. In fact, Novarro received "some nasty letters that suggested I'd given up my religion and [had] completely gone to the dogs."

But even after this major embarrassment, Novarro continued to drink and drive. In April of the following year, he was once again arrested after leaving the party at which he had refused a ride from ex-lover Cecil Everley. This time, he was fined $150, given a thirty-day suspended jail sentence, and placed on one year's probation. He also had to surrender his driver's license for six months and was told to see a psychiatrist. If Novarro was known to take a single drink during that period, he would be sent to jail.

Probably as a means of restoring his reputation—now that he was creating more headlines for his drunken driving than for his acting—Novarro declared he was ready to take up arms for his adopted country. On August 6, 1942, eight months after the Japanese attack on Pearl Harbor and four months after Novarro's latest arrest, the *Los Angeles Examiner* announced that "Ramon Novarro arose yesterday to ask for the privilege of serving America as a soldier." Since the forty-three-year-old actor was still a Mexican national, he had to telegraph an "urgent" appeal to the Mexican congress asking for permission to enlist in the United States Army. Chances that his request would be granted were minimal, as the Mexican government had already denied more than 5,000 such petitions. Nonetheless, much to Novarro's surprise, the request was approved.

Caught off guard, Novarro rapidly issued another announcement: before joining the American armed forces, he would offer his services to his native land—Mexico had declared war on the Axis powers in June. In mid-September he flew to Mexico City, where he met with Mexican president Manuel Ávila Camacho, who, according to Novarro, suggested that the film star's services would be better employed in the fledgling Mexican film industry. Thus ended Novarro's image-boosting flag-waving role. He was fortunate that the matter was quickly forgotten by the American press, for during such ardent patriotic times this failed publicity stunt might have led to even greater ridicule than his drunken-driving arrests.

Conveniently, President Ávila Camacho's suggestion that Novarro should put his talents to use in his native country coincided with the actor's first foray into the Mexican cinema. Since the late 1930s he had been toying with the idea of starring in a Mexican film, but none of his hopes had come to fruition. A concrete offer had finally materialized when director Julio Bracho, whose mother was Señora Samaniego's sister, invited him to appear in *Reina de reinas (Queen of Queens)*, a retelling of the purported sixteenth-century apparition of a brown-skinned Virgin Mary that had led to the conversion of Mexican Indians to Catholicism.

Filmmaking had emerged in Mexico soon after its appearance in Europe in the mid-1890s, but civil war, economic difficulties, and competition from Hollywood—where Spanish-language films were made until the late 1930s—had prevented the Mexican film industry from fully developing until the early 1940s. In 1942, the establishment of the Banco Cinematográfico, a government-supported credit agency that extended financing to film producers, greatly stimulated the growth of local film production and marked the beginning of the Golden Age of Mexican cinema. Dolores del Río traveled south of the border to resurrect her fading motion picture stardom, while numerous other performers, including Pedro Armendáriz, Ricardo Montalbán, and María Félix, were launched to international fame.

Julio Bracho was one of the behind-the-scenes talents who were developed during that period. Besides directing *Reina de reinas,* Bracho cowrote the screenplay with René Capistrán Garza, the fervently Catholic former leader of the League for the Defense of Religious Freedom. In fact, *Reina de reinas* was part of a Catholic revival in Mexican society that had occurred after Ávila Camacho became president in 1940. Since the revolution, the Church had been stripped of much of its power—priests had to be registered with the government, foreigners were banned from ecclesiastical posts, and the clergy was forbidden to wear religious garb in public—but Ávila Camacho, who publicly declared himself a Catholic, set the stage for a more pacific coexistence between the Church and the Mexican government.

After a two-year absence, Novarro was happy to be back in front of the cameras in a project that was heavily imbued with the Catholic faith—he had earlier asserted he was "vitally" interested in the production of religious pictures. He also enjoyed being treated as a foreign dignitary during filming, which took place in October 1942 at the CLASA studios in Mexico City. As Juan Diego, the fifty-seven-year-old Aztec peasant who witnessed the apparition, Novarro played his first Mexican character since becoming a star and his first Spanish-speaking part since *La Sevillana* twelve years earlier. He was supported by a strong cast that included Domingo Soler, a member of the "Royal Family of the Mexican Theater," and rising sex symbol Gloria Marín.

Renamed *La Virgen que forjó una patria* (The Virgin who forged a nation), Novarro's first Mexican production opened in Mexico City on December 11, the eve of the feast of the Virgin of Guadalupe. Reviews were mixed, with general praise for the performances but severe criticisms of the disjointed plot and Bracho's pedestrian direction. The box-office returns of *La Virgen que forjó una patria* are unknown, but the picture probably suffered because it was released soon after the similarly themed and better received *La Virgen morena* (*The Dark Virgin*). In May 1944, Novarro's latest vehicle surfaced at the Belmont Theater in New York City, then dedicated to Spanish-language films, but there is no indication that it was ever shown in English-language art houses. Distributors apparently agreed with *Variety*'s statement that the picture was too tedious even for the American art house circuit—though the magazine did praise Novarro's "forthright" interpretation.

An overlong and unsubtle piece of religious propaganda, described by Mexican film historian Emilio García Riera as "right-wing and reactionary," *La Virgen que forjó una patria* lacks interest except as Novarro's sole appearance in a Mexican motion picture. Despite his star billing, Novarro has what amounts to an extended cameo, though he does generally well in a role unlike any other in his twenty-year screen career. His poor, humble, and illiterate Juan Diego is appropriately unglamorous and totally unlike the Ramon Novarro of Hollywood films; but, ironically, Novarro neither looks nor sounds right for his first Mexican character: His "Indian" makeup notwithstanding, he is too European-looking to pass for an Aztec; at forty-three, he is much too young to play the part of a fifty-seven-year-old man; and his beautifully enunciated Spanish, although charming, hardly fits the part.

Still, even if *La Virgen que forjó una patria* did not turn out to be a major artistic and financial success, Novarro returned to Los Angeles fully satisfied with the experience. "I enjoyed my work there immensely," he wrote Noël Sullivan in early December, "and got what I went after, which was a Commission in the Mexican Government to supervise their War Films Propaganda. I must return by the end of January but my work will give me ample time to direct and act in pictures, and do just what I want to do and no more.... [I] feel very happy and grateful for the way things turned out, which were more than I ever dreamed, expected, or merited." Ultimately, however, Novarro was never to take part in another Mexican motion picture in any capacity. The reasons for that are unclear, especially considering that

Mexican producers tried to pair him with Dolores del Río and that his cousin Julio Bracho became one of the most important figures in the local film industry. Most probably, Novarro's failure to build a career south of the Rio Grande can be attributed to his continued lack of professional focus.

The old Coué credo, "Every day in every way I'm getting better and better," which had propelled the budding go-getter Ramón Samaniego to the uppermost heights of stardom, no longer worked for the middle-aged Ramon Novarro. Only six years older than del Río, whose Mexican screen career was to flourish for the next twenty years, Novarro could easily have restored his film prestige in his native country. Since numerous Mexican pictures were garnering wide praise around the globe, a renewed career in Mexico would likely have led to quality offers north of the border. Hollywood veteran del Río and newcomers Arturo de Córdova, Ricardo Montalbán, and Pedro Armendáriz were some of the Mexican stars who landed major roles in American motion pictures of the 1940s and 1950s.

If Novarro had truly wanted to work in Mexican films, he should have remained in Mexico—as del Río did—to actively pursue a film career. Instead, he continued traveling back and forth across the border, hoping to be offered the script that would bring him back to world fame. Unsure as to which side of the Rio Grande might revive his film stardom, Novarro ended up forgotten on both sides. *La Virgen que forjó una patria* turned out to be his last motion picture as a star.

In 1943, eight years after his departure from MGM, Novarro's film career was virtually over. Had it not been for World War II, he might have returned to Europe to appear in more local productions, such as the filming of his own *Truthful Lies* in Italy, but even world peace would not have guaranteed Novarro's commitment to his profession. Moreover, his chances of being cast in romantic leads were fading as rapidly as his rejuvenated looks. As it had in the mid-1930s, alcohol was once again ravaging his appearance.

Weeks or, at times, months of sobriety were broken by severe drinking binges. During one of his frequent trips to Mexico City, Novarro visited "Mexico's Sweetheart" Lupita Tovar on the CLASA set of *Resurrección*. Tovar, who had known Novarro for more than a decade, was shocked by his appearance. "He didn't look so good," she later recalled. "He had been drinking. It was for me very, very sad to see his condition." Novarro was so intoxicated he could barely keep himself standing.

Work had invariably kept Novarro sober, but after *La Virgen*, acting jobs, even on stage, had become markedly scarcer. His most recent good offer had been for a small role in a Broadway Theater Guild production of Leonid Andreyev's *He Who Gets Slapped*, but that was eventually canceled. "I'm willing to start at the bottom," he had written Audrey Homan about that project, "and if I make up my mind, can make myself into a real stage actor." Indeed, Novarro could have developed into an accomplished stage actor, but, as usual, he failed to make up his mind. Not surprisingly, his legitimate-stage career, like his long dreamed of operatic pursuit, was stillborn. Sporadic summer stock jobs and occasional radio appearances remained his only professional activities until the end of the decade.

"Not long ago a waitress in a Mexico City restaurant growled at a man to wait when he asked for service. Twenty years before, any waitress would have been enraptured at the opportunity to take his order." Thus began a January 1944 *Saturday Evening Post* piece, "Where is . . . Ramon Novarro?" in which the former film star discussed plans to jump-start his acting career in Mexico and to distribute Mexican films in the United States and Latin America. In the interview, Novarro added that if these prospects were to misfire he would set films aside and take a course in "plastics" (he probably meant he would study art, in Spanish, *artes plásticas*).

Since the Mexican prospects did misfire, Novarro used his time to study art, religion, and philosophy, and to go to movies or play Chinese checkers with Teresa Bracho. Though not a recluse, he had drastically reduced his socializing by the mid-1940s. He was hardly ever mentioned in Hollywood society columns and never took part in the ritzy poolside gay parties at the homes of George Cukor or Cole Porter.

Gone were the elaborate festivities and Teatro Intimo presentations at the Gramercy mansion. Since early 1944, financial pressures had led Novarro to rent out the back wing of the house. When a friend of Noël Sullivan's asked to stay at Gramercy while in Los Angeles, Novarro refused to take him in. "I like to do things well or not at all, dear Noël," he explained, "and somehow now that I am not able to do them as I used to, I would rather abstain from giving a cheap imitation of what hospitality should be." As in the early 1920s, most of his social life was confined to his family and a few close friends.

In mid-decade, that low-key lifestyle was disrupted by three major blows. On April 8, 1946, Novarro invited Teresa Bracho to come down from her bedroom for a game of Chinese checkers. After half an hour had passed, he called for her to hurry up. As there was no answer, he sent his mother up to Bracho's bedroom, where Señora Samaniego found the fifty-six-year-old Bracho lying in bed in a coma. A doctor rushed to the scene, but Bracho was beyond help. For years an angina sufferer, she had been felled by a sudden heart attack. Novarro was devastated. "Now that she's gone," he told his sister Luz, "I can't tell you how much I miss her."

The other two blows came later that year. On September 1, Señora Samaniego, whose health had been failing for several years, suffered an attack caused by an intestinal infection. It was three months before she regained some of her strength. In the meantime, Novarro discovered that Stanley Barnes, his attorney and business adviser for sixteen years, was to be sworn in as a judge of the Ninth Circuit Court of Appeals in January 1947.

Barnes did not officially terminate their relationship until the end of 1947, but he was too busy with his new position to provide Novarro with the accustomed help. Nearing fifty and without a steady paycheck, Novarro could ill afford another debacle like the Louis Samuel affair of 1930, after which Barnes's advice had been crucial in arranging a refund from the Internal Revenue Service and in securing the best possible deals with MGM. Instead of looking for another adviser, Novarro decided it was time he learned to handle his own business affairs.

With the steady rise of property values after World War II, Novarro was able to secure a loan to erect a building for JCPenney on one of his San Fernando Valley lots. His architect brother Eduardo was hired to design the project, but despite Novarro's lofty plans, numerous complications arose during the long construction process. Those further weighed on his already fragile state of mind.

"I have been quite nervous of late as everything I've planned has gone wrong," Novarro wrote Noël Sullivan in July 1947, "and although I feel we should be more patient as we grow older, just to be different I'm doing the opposite and its [sic] not doing me any good." His most recent physical exams had come out well, but Novarro could find no relief from the emotional anxieties caused by financial uncertainty, Teresa Bracho's death, his mother's ill health, professional inactivity, and the JCPenney building problems. Even though Novarro was being treated by a psychiatrist at the time—in his memoirs, he implied that he had sought psychiatric help because of his drinking—he remained in a state of depression.

Making matters worse, "after a great deal of hopeful anxiety and a lot of money spent," Novarro was denied the right to rezone the Gramercy property, which he intended to sell as a multiple-tenant dwelling. (The once exclusive West Adams district had long ceased to be a desirable residential area for wealthy families.) He had considered selling or renting out the house in the early 1940s, when the dwindling number of occupants coupled with growing financial pressures had made the upkeep of the mansion unduly burdensome, but only late in the decade did he finally decide to sell it. At that time, he began developing a property at 10938 Riverside Drive in North Hollywood, where ten bungalows, each with its own private front and back entrances, were under construction. One of the bungalows was to become Novarro's home, and another Señora Samaniego's; the others would be rented out. So that his finances would not be overextended by the construction, it was necessary to sell the Gramercy house; Novarro's inability to do so only added to his many problems.

During those stressful periods, Novarro at times expressed his frustration in excessive aggressiveness. As he had never been overly fond of children, visiting nephews and nieces had learned to steer clear of him, but even so, Novarro would occasionally punish them for mishaps they were innocent of, before getting word from Señora Samaniego that the children were not at fault. Often, his attitude was that the Gramercy house was his domain and he could do as he pleased. Whenever he failed to get his way—often through his mother's interference—he would turn sullen.

Nearly ten years after his return to Gramercy, Novarro now again felt a strong need for his own personal space, which explains another of his real estate ventures at that time: the acquisition of a forty-nine-acre property eighty miles southeast of downtown Los Angeles and three and a half miles from the Pala Asistencia, in his words, "the sweetest, poorest and smallest Mission in California." Christened El Rosario, Novarro's little ranch boasted "lovely oak and sycamore trees, fertile soil, seclusion and great beauty," and a two-room adobe structure that was to be turned into the new owner's living quarters and his own private spiritual retreat.

After the 1947 holidays at the Gramercy house, Novarro dismissed the maid and the cook, apparently for financial reasons. Now, the only residents remaining in the once vibrant Samaniego household were Novarro, Eduardo, and an increasingly fragile Señora Samaniego. With Gramercy as a tangible reminder of a glorious past that had disintegrated, Novarro began spending more of his time at El Rosario. "I can hardly believe it how I can be so happy and so uncomfortable at the same time," he wrote Sullivan after a stay of several days at the ranch in early 1948. Even so, Novarro's "happy and uncomfortable" stays at El Rosario during the late 1940s were relatively brief, as he was unable to remain in solitude for long. Throughout his life he had been surrounded by a large family, and during adulthood he had always had someone to keep him company, whether Herbert Howe, assistants Frank Hansen and Philip Moreland, or Teresa Bracho. Since idling away at Gramercy would only have deepened his gloom, Novarro had to find some form of activity to escape his personal anguish.

Since Bracho's death, Novarro had been considering another screen comeback, "not as a leading man of course," he wrote Sullivan, "but as a character actor, so I have gone back renewing important connections that I've discarded for so many years. Things look quite promising and somehow I feel that is what I need to snap out of this lethargy in which I've been submerged for such a long time." In December 1946 he had met with "a very important man at MGM," but that meeting had led nowhere. It would be another two years before a "depressed and bored" Novarro finally resumed his film acting career.

By late 1948, six years had passed since Novarro's last appearance in front of the camera, ten years since the release of his last American picture, and nearly fourteen years since his departure from MGM. The Hollywood Novarro was returning to was light-years away from the one the young Mexican hopeful had found in the late 1910s, and significantly remote from the Hollywood he had left in the late 1930s. Television was beginning to displace motion pictures as the country's foremost pastime; the federal government was in the process of forcing studios to divest their theater holdings; and anti-Communist hysteria was rampaging throughout the film capital. Novarro, of course, had also changed dramatically. He was twenty pounds heavier, his now gray hair was rapidly thinning, and his once handsome face had aged nearly beyond recognition.

The Columbia production of *Rough Sketch* was to mark Novarro's debut as a motion picture character actor, his first supporting role since *Rupert of Hentzau* twenty-seven years earlier. Directed by John Huston, fresh from the critical triumphs of *Key Largo* and *The Treasure of the Sierra Madre,* and starring Jennifer Jones, John Garfield, and Pedro Armendáriz, *Rough Sketch* was poised to become one of the most discussed motion pictures of the year. Set in Cuba during the last days of the Gerardo Machado y Morales dictatorship, the film presents as heroes a ragtag group of revolutionaries seeking to kill the dictator and his cohorts—a "subversive" plot that infuriated many conservatives during the height of the cold war.

In sharp contrast to the controversy surrounding his comeback vehicle, Novarro's return to Hollywood created little excitement. Largely forgotten by the industry that had once "belonged to him," the forty-nine-year-old former superstar was required to fill out a questionnaire stating his qualifications and professional background before Columbia would sign him. Although Novarro later joked about it in print, this demoralizing procedure must have been another unwelcome blow to his battered ego. (At least, Huston gave him the part of a revolutionary leader without requiring a test.)

The minuscule role he landed was also quite a comedown for one who had once been the top male romantic star in motion pictures. As usual, if Novarro's ego suffered, he kept his feelings to himself. At a small cocktail party, when hostess Pola Negri—who had not worked for years—inquired, "So, what have *you* been doing, Ramon?" the former Judah Ben-Hur nonchalantly replied, "Playing bit parts."

Yet, in spite of finding his name below the title and down the cast list of *We Were Strangers*, as *Rough Sketch* was finally titled, Novarro relished being back on a film set. Soon after finishing that picture he began work on another controversial thriller, *The Big Steal*, a low-budget film noir for RKO in which he had a small part as a Mexican police officer—his first role as a Mexican national in an American motion picture. This time, the controversy was unrelated to the story line, which revolves around a stolen payroll and car pursuits through the Mexican countryside. *The Big Steal* received ample press space because it was RKO's attempt to capitalize on the notoriety of Robert Mitchum's arrest for "possession and conspiracy to possess flowering tops and leaves of Indian hemp," after a police raid had caught him and three others with marijuana at a cottage in the hills above West Hollywood.

Shooting of *The Big Steal* began on the RKO lot on January 26, 1949, with Mitchum, Jane Greer (a last-minute replacement for Lizabeth Scott), and William Bendix in the leading roles. After most of the interior scenes had been completed, the company, minus Mitchum, traveled to Tehuacán in southern Mexico to film exteriors. Despite RKO's plea that a delay in filming might cause "hundreds of innocent people" to lose their jobs, three days before the unit's departure Mitchum was unexpectedly sentenced to two years' probation, sixty days of which were to be spent at the county jail. Since filming could not be delayed because of both restricted Mexican shooting permits and William Bendix's other film commitments, director Don Siegel shot around Mitchum or used a double whenever possible.

Siegel, who suffered from diabetes and at times failed to show up for work, also had to take extra care with the pregnant Jane Greer, an actress he thought inadequate for the part. Further complicating matters, most of the cast and crew fell seriously ill with Montezuma's revenge. Despite eating and drinking everything, Novarro escaped the diarrhea epidemic, though, according to Greer, he seemed nervous during filming and kept mostly to himself.

Unknown to his fellow workers, Novarro was gravely concerned for his seventy-seven-year-old mother. Señora Samaniego had been in fragile but stable health for two years, but an intestinal obstruction had led to a serious attack at Christmastime 1948. She underwent a colostomy on Christmas Day, and the following February had to endure further surgery to remove a tumor in her colon. Only Novarro, who had just turned fifty, and his sister Leonor were privy to the gravity of their mother's illness. Even then, Novarro had to temporarily abandon his mother to fulfill his *Big Steal* commitment.

On February 25, Señora Samaniego died following a stroke caused by a blood clot in her brain. Novarro, who flew the next day to Los Angeles, must have been devastated. Throughout his life, he had been fully devoted to his mother, even though their relationship had at times been marred by his drinking and, perhaps, by his sexual orientation. "He wanted to please her," Carmen later recalled, but Novarro had been both unable and unwilling to satisfy some of Señora Samaniego's wishes. He had not become the concert pianist his mother had envisioned, nor had he married and become a father the way respectable men were supposed to. Worst of all, he was an alcoholic. Señora Samaniego had abhorred her oldest son's addiction, for which she blamed the film industry, and she had fruitlessly pleaded with him to stop drinking. Once, when she expressed gratitude for the riches he had given her, she added that none of her other children had brought her the sorrow he had.

After a requiem mass at St. Agnes Church, Señora Samaniego was buried in the family plot at the Calvary Cemetery in East Los Angeles.

Shortly after the funeral, Novarro and Eduardo moved out of the Gramercy house where the Samaniego family had lived for a quarter of a century. In public, Novarro presented his usual philosophical persona in explaining his move from Gramercy. "What would my youngest brother and I do in a house of seventeen rooms?" he mused. "I would be a slave to my possessions—and I don't like that." 10938 Riverside Drive, approximately ten miles northwest of the West Adams district, became their new and much smaller home. Carmen and her husband, Novarro's former secretary Jorge Gavilán, also moved into one of the bungalows, where they were to work as property managers. The Gramercy house would finally be sold in September of that year for $3,550—approximately half the price Novarro had originally paid for it.

In mid-April 1949, soon after Robert Mitchum's release from jail, Novarro returned to Mexico for two weeks to work on the remaining scenes of *The Big Steal*. In July, he again headed south of the border, this time for Eduardo's wedding in Mexico City, at which ceremony Novarro—"miscast again!"— was best man. "And that I think relieves me of all obligation towards the family," he wrote Sullivan at that time. "I am well in health but feel very strange as if I had outlived my usefulness."

Also in April, *We Were Strangers* had opened to dismal box-office receipts. Even the continuing controversy surrounding the picture, such as the threat of a boycott by the Los Angeles Federation of Women, failed to incite the curiosity of the public. Reviews were mostly negative, with the majority of critics unfairly ignoring Novarro's brief but outstanding performance, the only redeeming element of an otherwise insufferable picture. Those who did mention him, however, usually offered enthusiastic praise for the old veteran. "[I] tried to be as different as I possibly could from Mr. Novarro—both in appearance and temperament," Novarro explained in a letter to Noël Sullivan. Indeed, he was completely unrecognizable to those who remembered him from his days as a star, or even from his last film appearance in *La Virgen que forjó una patria*. Makeup for the role surely aged him some, but alcohol and excess weight were the main causes of his haggard appearance, as he also looked older than his years in his subsequent films.

Novarro's physical deterioration is especially shocking when compared to the appearance of two of his silent era contemporaries. Both Don Alvarado (in *The Big Steal*) and Gilbert Roland (in *We Were Strangers*, and later in *Crisis*), respectively five and six years Novarro's junior, look remarkably younger and healthier than the former MGM screen idol. Gilbert Roland, in particular, looks about a generation younger than Novarro. In fact, while Novarro was by then suited to play only grandfatherly, nonromantic roles, Roland, Novarro's double in a brief sequence in *The Midshipman*, was to keep busy portraying suave and erotically charged characters well into his sixties.

In early July, almost three months after the disheartening release of *We Were Strangers*, *The Big Steal* opened to only slightly better notices, though this time Novarro's lengthier—and less effective—performance received numerous accolades. RKO was so pleased that it wanted him to star as the shrewd and humorous Mexican police officer Colonel Ortega in a series of B movies, but Novarro declined the offer. "I do not want to be typed," he told the *Los Angeles Times*. "I belong to no studio; it is better just to take the parts as they come along. I want the right to say yes or no to them all."

The next part Novarro said yes to was that of a wagon-train chief who meets death at the hands of bushwhackers in *The Outriders*, a Western directed by Roy Rowland and starring Joel McCrea. Though shot mostly on location in Kanab, Utah, Novarro's first Western—and first all-Technicolor film— brought him back to his old alma mater for the filming of interior scenes. "I know I am going to enjoy returning to MGM," Novarro declared. "I always feel so at home at that studio."

Yet, the MGM Novarro returned to in the fall of 1949 had little in common with the studio he had left fifteen years earlier. Irving Thalberg had been dead for thirteen years. Former costars Norma Shearer, Greta Garbo, Jeanette MacDonald, and Myrna Loy had been replaced by June Allyson, Jane Powell, Elizabeth Taylor, and Deborah Kerr. Among the silent era performers, only Lionel Barrymore and Lewis Stone remained. Louis B. Mayer was also still there, but his clout had become increasingly tenuous. MGM-Loew's profits for 1948 had reached their lowest level since the depths of the Depression, forcing Mayer to share some of his power with Dore Schary, fresh from a stint as chief of production at RKO. Mayer's ouster from the film empire he had ruled for over a quarter of a century was a mere two years away. Not surprisingly, no fanfare greeted the return of the actor who had once been the studio's top male star.

In January 1950, Novarro returned to MGM once again for his next picture, *Crisis*. Set in a fictitious South American country, this political melodrama concerns an American brain surgeon who must decide whether to save the life of an ailing despot, a character partly inspired by the Dominican Republic's strongman Rafael Trujillo. The distinguished cast, led by Cary Grant, José Ferrer, Paula Raymond, and Signe Hasso, also included silent era veterans Gilbert Roland, Antonio Moreno, and Pedro de Cordoba. A steely-eyed Novarro was given the small role of Colonel Adragon, the dictator's ruthless henchman—in his own words, the sole "nasty heavy" of his career.

With Cary Grant's support, *Crisis* marked screenwriter Richard Brooks's debut behind the cameras, in what turned out to be a grueling production. Uncontrollably anxious about this first assignment, Brooks was a brutal taskmaster, alienating actors and crew members, who resented not only his boorishness but also his double standard—Grant was never harassed or yelled at. The director's rudeness was especially harsh on Novarro, who knew that Brooks had wanted someone else for the part (Mexican actor Rodolfo Acosta had been first choice for the role). When the studio failed to provide the former superstar with his own cast chair, Gilbert Roland created such an uproar that it reached Mayer's office.

Novarro maintained his customary professionalism throughout filming in spite of MGM's discourtesy, Brooks's unpleasantness, and the sometimes arduous shooting schedule. But once the production was over, the severely distressed fifty-one-year-old actor checked himself into Scripps Clinic in La Jolla for tests and an extended rest.

. . .

"Ramon Novarro's emergence as a character actor continues to be one of the joys of present day filmgoing," remarked *The Hollywood Reporter* upon the release of *The Outriders* in March 1950. "To watch this veteran wrap up a scene and take it home is to observe the work of an artist who learned his celluloid ABC's the hard way." In fact, as in *We Were Strangers* and to a lesser extent in *The Big Steal*, Novarro's presence is the highlight of a routine picture. Four months later, Novarro shone one more time in *Crisis*, single-handedly creating a sense of excitement in the first third of the picture. Once the vicious Colonel Adragon is forced into the background, *Crisis* loses its sole palpable element of danger and degenerates into standard Hollywood pablum.

Despite the positive notices he received for his four film appearances as a character actor, Novarro abruptly ended his screen comeback after *Crisis*. The emotional stress during the making of that film had been too much for him. In addition, his critically acclaimed performances had been little seen, as none of his comeback films had been major box-office successes. Thus, there had been no great demand for Novarro's services among the Hollywood film studios. Finally, Novarro was no longer desperate for an income. He had made $8,000 for his work in *The Big Steal* and $7,500 for *Crisis* and probably was paid about as much for his other roles. More important, his real estate investments were now performing well, while his expenses had been considerably curtailed since his move to the more modest quarters on Riverside Drive.

Once his film work ended in early 1950, Novarro began spending more time alone at El Rosario. When he was in Los Angeles, his occasional social activities remained restricted to a handful of new friends, including RKO publicist Leonard Shannon, whom Novarro had met while working on *The Big Steal*, and to the remaining old ones such as Natalie Bateson, Gloria Swanson, Alice Terry, and an increasingly frail and reclusive Rex Ingram. By midsummer, Novarro's mentor had disappeared from that short list.

Even after suffering two heart attacks during a 1948 trip to North Africa, Rex Ingram had continued with his travels until his deteriorating health, worsened by a bout of malaria in Mexico, finally forced him to settle down in Studio City. While at home, he kept busy sculpting and painting, and dabbled with the idea of writing a script based on Ralph Korngold's *Citizen Toussaint*, the story of Haitian independence leader Toussaint-Louverture—a project that was never realized. On July 21, 1950, shortly after being admitted to the Park View Hospital for a series of tests and X-rays, the fifty-seven-year-old former director unexpectedly suffered a cerebral hemorrhage and fell into a coma. In a few hours, Ingram was dead. Novarro, Alice Terry,

Antonio Moreno, and Gilbert Roland were some of those present at the July 26 funeral service at the Forest Lawn Cemetery in Glendale.

"In my philosophy," Novarro had written Noël Sullivan in 1939, "grief for the dead doesn't exist. Not because the sun disappears from our eyes in a lovely sunset, will I grieve over its seeming disappearance or deny its existence." In the last four years, however, Novarro had lost his closest friend, his mother, his mentor, and even his house. Each had been in itself a major loss, but together they must have inflicted upon him an overwhelming emotional blow.

Teresa Bracho had nurtured and indulged Novarro as a wife might have, but without imposing any physical or emotional demands. Señora Samaniego had been Novarro's nurturer from the day he was born. Whatever their differences, they always strove to support and keep their family together through numerous crises. Though only a few years older than Novarro, Ingram had nurtured him professionally, guiding and protecting the ambitious but inexperienced young Mexican with fatherly care. Without Ingram, stardom and its riches would quite likely have forever eluded Novarro. Finally, the Gramercy house had stood as the monument to Novarro's personal and professional achievements in the United States; it was the physical representation of his accomplishments in "paradise." As 1950 came to a close, all were gone.

"Christmas was very quiet and of course very sad," Novarro wrote Noël Sullivan in early 1951. "Memories are part of us, aren't they?"

THIRTEEN

The Last Years

In the early 1950s, Novarro spent much of his time alone at El Rosario—a remarkable change for someone who had always been in constant need of company. This newly acquired habit of solitude, coupled with his frequent contact with the priests at the Pala Asistencia and regular visits to other Catholic retreats around the country, led to the reemergence of rumors that he was planning to join a monastery. In fact, those thoughts did cross Novarro's mind at that time, perhaps because he had been greatly impressed by Thomas Merton's autobiographical *The Seven Storey Mountain*, an account of the author's joining a Trappist order.

Novarro spent occasional weekends at the Trappist monastery Our Lady of the Holy Trinity in Huntsville, Utah, and visited with the abbot of the Our Lady of Guadalupe monastery near Lafayette, Oregon, but nothing came of his aspirations. Now in his early fifties, he was deemed too old to join the order. Whatever disappointment he may have felt at the time, years later Novarro could recall with wry humor his desire to become a Trappist, once remarking, "Imagine an actor taking a vow of silence."

The fading of his Trappist dream notwithstanding, Novarro's unflagging devotion grew even more ardent during the early 1950s as he continued to be overwhelmed by the closeness of death: his sister Luz had a benign brain tumor removed, and his older sister Rosa, now Mother Superior Guadalupe, developed intestinal problems that seriously hindered her digestive system. Now well into middle age, Novarro himself had been in unstable health for some time, which moved him to strive for salvation while he still could. Predictably, religion became the main focus of his increasingly obsessive nature.

During Novarro's stays at El Rosario, the austerely furnished adobe house—with a bell added to create the effect of a mission—served as a retreat for meditating, reading books on spirituality, and studying religious philosophy. He prayed constantly while at the house, and attended mass every morning and rosary prayers every evening. While at the wheel of his Chevrolet station wagon, he often frightened his passengers by paying more attention to his rosary beads than to the mountainous road—a habit somewhat akin to his drinking and driving. His letter stationery now displayed "A.M.D.G."—*Ad Majorem Dei Gloriam,* or To the Greater Glory of God— St. Ignatius of Loyola's phrase and the motto of the Society of Jesus, which expresses the overpowering desire to offer everything to God. At times, Novarro even walked around the house in a black Franciscan robe.

Much of that quasi-fanatical religiosity went no deeper than Novarro's own spiritual self-interests. Prayers and contributions to religious institutions were in good part a form of advance payment to facilitate his passage through the gates of heaven. Secular philanthropies and the plight of the world's destitute masses were of little concern to him. What truly concerned Novarro was his own salvation.

With Novarro so completely devoted to his religious observances, alcohol ceased to be a problem while he was at El Rosario. Forrest McCoy, whose in-laws worked as the ranch caretakers in the mid-1950s, does not remember ever seeing Novarro intoxicated. Even so, when away from El Rosario, Novarro continued to drink heavily, whether for relaxation at social events or to find courage to pursue his sexual urges.

By the early 1950s, Novarro's looks had long disappeared, and his name meant little or nothing to young men who had been infants at the time of *Scaramouche* and *Ben-Hur.* The youthful and attractive men who had been drawn to him when he was young and famous had become nearly unattainable. Now in his fifties—and looking considerably older—Novarro had little choice but to pay for sexual companionship. One of the young men he employed for that purpose was a Santa Barbara hustler known as Chuck, who later stated that Novarro was by then a steady client of male prostitutes, and had already begun putting both his life and his public image in danger by driving inebriated around Hollywood in search of sex. Either through sheer luck or by paying off blackmailers, Novarro never became involved in a sex scandal while he was alive.

One important reason for Novarro's unrestrained behavior during those

days was his professional inactivity. Throughout the years, whenever he concentrated his efforts on singing and acting, he was able to avoid excessive
drinking, dangerous sexual escapades, and extreme religiosity. But in spite of
asserting early in the 1950s, "I am eager to go to work and I believe this
is the thing for me to do," he undertook no film or concert work during
the decade. In 1951, Republic suggested he read Isabelle Gibson Ziegler's
novel *The Nine Days of Father Serra*, a fictionalized account of eighteenth-
century Spanish priest Junípero Serra and his nine-day wait for a sign from
God, but no film project ever came of it. Novarro also resumed his vocal
training about this time and publicly talked of several offers to appear
onstage, but nothing came of these ventures either—perhaps because he was
unsure whether he wanted to resume his show business career or retreat
behind the walls of a Trappist monastery. The little work he accepted in
those days consisted of guest appearances in a handful of television variety
shows, such as Ed Sullivan's *Toast of the Town* and *The Ken Murray Show*.

Alan Brock, Novarro's former summer-stock agent, was responsible for
his television work on the East Coast. Agent and client had never met until
Novarro came to New York for a taping of *The Ken Murray Show* in February
1952. After a meeting at the Warwick Hotel, where Brock had his offices,
they developed a steady rapport that was to last until Novarro's death. "He
appeared naïve," Brock later declared, "but underneath he was sharp and
knowing."

Although Novarro's "knowingness" did not extend to his professional
goals, which remained fuzzy, he had learned a great deal about financial
investments after the departure of his attorney, Stanley Barnes. In sharp
contrast to his economic situation in the late 1940s, Novarro found himself
on solid financial ground in the 1950s because of both his lucrative real
estate ventures and the reduction in his living expenses.

Free from hectic work schedules and with money to spare, Novarro took
lengthy trips to Europe nearly every year throughout the 1950s. These European forays usually involved a combination of leisure and religion, as
Novarro turned some of his travels into pilgrimages. In October 1950,
shortly after Rex Ingram's death, he made his first transatlantic voyage since
La Comédie du bonheur more than a decade earlier. This trip was strictly religious; Novarro sailed on the *Vulcania* for Italy to witness the pronouncement
of Pope Pius XII's encyclical *Munificentissimus Deus* (which defines the dogma
of Our Lady's assumption into heaven) and to ask the pope for a plenary
indulgence—total forgiveness for his sins—so his soul could bypass purgatory and head straight to heaven.

Novarro was a firm believer in the three traditional regions of the afterlife:

hell, purgatory, and heaven. "There is a prayer that I always say for a person at the news of their death," he wrote fellow devout Catholic Noël Sullivan in 1952. "Clement VIII conceded the release of a soul in Purgatory every time this Prayer was said. We use it in Spanish all the time and I am sending you one of the Remembrance Cards that my sister had made in Mexico.... Here is your chance to get all the English speaking people out of Purgatory." Probably because of his good deeds toward his family and friends and to his Catholic charities, Novarro believed himself safe from hell. Purgatory, however, was a distinct possibility for a vain and ambitious gay man with a drinking problem. Pope Pius XII was said to have granted the actor an audience, but whether the pope also granted him the desired plenary indulgence is not known. Whether or not fully absolved of his sins, Novarro continued his search for spiritual solace in Assisi, Lourdes, and Fátima, "all the places I should have visited long ago."

After Novarro sold a property across from the JCPenney building in early 1953, his European trips became increasingly extended. In November of that year, he sailed on the *Andrea Doria* for a four-month stay abroad that included a visit to the San Ramón Nonato holy sites in Barcelona and confession and holy communion services with Father Pio—regarded by many as a saint because of his stigmata. (Worshipers normally had to wait a month or longer to see the priest; Novarro had to wait only one day.) He had also planned to visit Israel, but gave up on the trip after being warned that the region was unsafe. The nonreligious portion of the stay abroad included visits with friends in Paris and throwing a dinner party for the Ramon Novarro Film Club members at the Hotel Savoy in London, Novarro's first visit to that city since *A Royal Exchange* eighteen years earlier.

In 1954, the RNFC was one of the oldest active film-star fan clubs in the world. Throughout the years, Novarro had developed a long-distance bond with his RNFC fans by mail, mostly through correspondence with club secretary Audrey Homan, who would then transmit the news to the other members. The dinner at the Hotel Savoy was one more gesture of appreciation for the unflagging devotion of his mostly British fans.

Eighteen club members attended—almost all females and, according to an *Evening News* reporter, "mostly Civil Service types and suburban housewives." Throughout the evening, Novarro enthralled his guests with stories about his early career and costars; served his own explosive brand of cocktail named after Mexico's most active volcano, the Popocatepetl; personally handed a corsage of flowers to each lady in attendance; posed for pictures (after losing sixteen pounds, he looked healthier than he had in years); and invited Homan and a randomly selected companion to visit him in Paris, with all expenses paid. "Of course I wish you could all come," he told the anxious ladies, each of whom had to try her luck by picking a piece of paper from a bowl—the winner was a North London secretary, Margaret Neville. Although Novarro liked to retire early, he continued to entertain his guests until after midnight.

If Novarro's charitable contributions to churches were to a certain extent a form of spiritual bribery, the Savoy dinner party and the free three-day Paris trip for two—including plane fare, accommodations, meals, and even theater tickets—were an unquestionable demonstration of unselfish generosity. He had no need for publicity at that time; those gifts to his fans were merely a demonstration of his gratitude for almost three decades of continuous loyalty.

Looking "happy, confident, prosperous," Novarro left for the French capital the next day. After visiting with Homan and Neville in Paris and hosting a cocktail party for his fifty-fifth birthday at the Café de la Régeance, he traveled to Rome for Easter and, on March 12, finally sailed back on the *Andrea Doria* from Naples. "I go back with sweet memories, and deeply grateful for them," he wrote to the RNFC. "By that I mean London. God bless you all. Ramon."

In mid-April 1954, an invigorated Novarro arrived back in California after spending two weeks in New York. A few days later, he drove down to El Rosario, finding it in complete disarray. He had wanted to sell the ranch for some time—"the deer eat all that grows above ground, and the gophers eat all below," he had complained—but finding buyers turned out to be a problem. Eventually, Novarro decided to keep El Rosario and continue using it as his retreat. He fired the old caretakers and hired an El Cajon couple whose duties consisted of caring for the main house, tending to a one-acre strawberry field, and picking the best and largest strawberries, which were then sold locally or shipped to restaurants in New York and Chicago.

Besides serving as his sanctuary, El Rosario also became Novarro's screenwriting quarters. Since buying the screen rights in 1938 to Owen Wister's novella *Padre Ignacio; or, the Song of Temptation*, Novarro had intermittently considered adapting the book into a screenplay. Set in an isolated California mission in 1855, *Padre Ignacio* is the tale of a priest who finds inner peace after encountering a young, handsome stranger with a passion for adventure and music. Novarro's interest in the story was undoubtedly a result of several similarities—whether actual or wishful—between himself and the padre: Padre Ignacio is a Spanish lover of opera who has become a priest both to redeem himself for his selfishness and to escape from the sufferings of the world. Yet, he must still struggle with his earthly desires until finally learning to find "contentment with renunciation."

Novarro planned to find independent financing for the project, which he renamed *Just Passing By*, an allusion to the fleetingness of life. His intention was to serve as producer, director, scriptwriter (with the assistance of a friend, Lou Holmes), and star—as Padre Ignacio. In April 1956, he announced that a search for the young male lead had begun. In late summer, both *The Hollywood Reporter* and *Variety* reported that Novarro was working on a deal with Rubén Calderón, head of the Azteca Studios in Mexico, to guarantee financing and distribution of the widescreen picture, which would be shot in Mexico City and California at a cost of $500,000. Production was slated to begin on October 1.

While not working on *Just Passing By*, Novarro spent his time remodeling his Riverside Drive apartment, handling his business interests, taking occasional trips, and, at times, getting drunk and looking for companionship. He also took the time to become an American citizen in late 1954—nearly forty years after his arrival in the United States. His social life remained confined to a small circle of friends, though he would sporadically take part in larger nostalgic gatherings, the most important of which took place at Mary Pickford's Beverly Hills mansion on Easter 1956.

"Do you ever realize how few people come out of that [film] business alive?" Novarro had wondered during one of his London interviews. Actually, many did. More than two hundred luminaries of the silent era were on hand at Pickfair, where Mary Pickford was now living with her husband of nineteen years, actor Charles "Buddy" Rogers. (Pickford had divorced Douglas Fairbanks in 1936; three years later, Fairbanks was dead of a heart attack.) Among those present were Novarro, Antonio Moreno, Metro Pictures' star Viola Dana, and *Ben-Hur*'s May McAvoy (still working as an extra) and Francis X. Bushman (working now and then in small roles).

Novarro was also on hand in the fall of the following year to receive a George Eastman House medal of honor "for distinguished contribution to the art of motion pictures 1926–1932." Other recipients that year included Greta Garbo, Mary Pickford, Lillian Gish, Richard Barthelmess, and Maurice Chevalier, who was delighted to meet Judah Ben-Hur for the first time. Novarro told reporters that Garbo had at first agreed to come, but had broken out in a nervous rash and had been ordered to bed. The two *Mata Hari* costars had not kept in touch throughout the years, but remained on good terms whenever they met.

· · ·

Novarro continued working on *Just Passing By* throughout 1956, though October 1, the date set to begin production, came and went without a single frame of film being shot. Despite his dealings with Rubén Calderón, the necessary financing failed to come through.

In December, Herbert Howe, after having spent eight years in Europe, made a surprising reappearance on the scene by announcing to the press that Novarro was in London to negotiate another deal for the project. *Just Passing By* was now scheduled to be shot in Paris, with Suzy Volterra, the widow of the director of the Casino de Paris, putting up the money. That deal, however, also fell through. In the next few years, after Howe had again disappeared from the scene, a similar scenario would be repeated each time Novarro, with decreasing enthusiasm, tried to find backing for his production. Things might well have turned out differently had he found a prominent actor for the role of the young stranger, but no one was ever announced for that part. Eventually, *Just Passing By* became one more of Novarro's failed efforts.

As for Herbert Howe, so far as is known he and Novarro had not seen each other for years. After their split in the late 1920s, they had kept out of each other's way until 1932, when Howe interviewed Novarro at the MGM commissary for his *New Movie Magazine* column. Novarro, at the time working on *Huddle*, had by then become a frequent partygoer and heavy drinker—a radically different man from the young ascetic Howe had met nearly a decade earlier. Besides poking fun in "The Hollywood Boulevardier" at the notion of a Novarro-Garbo romance, Howe nostalgically observed, "Lunching with Ramon Novarro in the studio commissary, I did lament that them which doth our charms alter should leave our vexing traits untouched. Ramon, once the mystically elusive Mexican (and that was no publicity), is today a forthright, regular guy in a sweat shirt learning to play football for his next picture.... Yet Ramon, dieting on tomato juice and dreamfully helping himself to sausages off my plate [an "irritating habit" Novarro had supposedly caught from Alice Terry], was the alibi-mystic I-knew-when." Still, at least one Novarro trait remained unchanged. "Though Hollywood has dimmed Ramon's Aztec glamor," Howe admitted, "it has not robbed him of his wit. Speaking of the MGM policy of all-star casts in each picture, he remarked: 'I can't understand why they didn't use us all in *Freaks*.'"

Novarro's enduring humor notwithstanding, Howe continued to avoid his former lover's company. Years passed before they (and Terry) saw each other again—in December 1937, at the funeral services for Howe's father. Novarro then wrote Audrey Homan that he "was so glad" to have seen his old friend, who had remained "just the same, just as amusing." Yet, their friendship was never rekindled. Claiming to be "worn out doing nothing," soon after the funeral Howe traveled to the Mexican seaside resort of Mazatlán for a rest. He called Novarro upon his return to Los Angeles, but that is the last time his name appears in Novarro's correspondence.

Howe's whereabouts in the 1940s and early 1950s are unknown. His influence as a Hollywood commentator had dwindled with the demise of the *New Movie Magazine* in 1935, and he seems to have finally made good on his promise to abandon the industry. In the late 1940s, author Lawrence Quirk met him at a party, and the former columnist appeared to be in ill health. Howe moved to Europe not long afterward.

On September 16, 1959, less than three years after briefly resurfacing in his old position as Novarro's publicist, Howe suffered a fall while walking on a city street, breaking his right hip. His condition quickly deteriorated because of chronic cardiovascular disease, and on October 23, at age sixty-six, Howe died of pneumonia at the Los Angeles County General Hospital. His death went unnoticed by the trade press, for which he had once been a star columnist.

Navarro's reaction to the passing of his former companion is not known.

Novarro's brief TV variety show appearances, his fruitless attempts to find backing for *Just Passing By*, and his participation in nostalgic reunions and award ceremonies resulted in scant notices in the American press. The late 1950s, however, were to unexpectedly bring him back to international attention via three disparate routes.

The first was television. In November 1958, Novarro made his television acting debut in a two-part episode of the miniseries *The Nine Lives of Elfego Baca* on *Walt Disney Presents*. He resumed his show business career after an eight-year hiatus on his physician's advice; the fifty-nine-year-old actor was found to be suffering from excessively low blood pressure, and a return to work was prescribed as a means of improving his health. "I was bored," Novarro admitted about his long stretch of professional inactivity. "I haven't felt this healthy in years."

Novarro next appeared in the news in early January 1959. On January 3, less than one month after his second *Elfego Baca* episode was aired, he was stopped by the police after running a red light at the intersection of Hollywood Boulevard and Highland Avenue. "I only had a bourbon and soda— or maybe three—at my sister's," he told the officers, who reported that Novarro had become abusive during questioning. He was arrested after failing a sobriety test, but was freed later that day on $263 bail.

That incident was Novarro's first reported scrape with the law for driving while intoxicated since the early 1940s, even though he had continued to drink heavily during the intervening years. Either his luck had come to an end, or he was finding police officers less receptive to bribes. As he had done nineteen years earlier, Novarro at first pleaded not guilty to the charge of drunken driving, only to reverse his plea and pay a fine.

Novarro made news on a lighter note when he was invited to the November 18, 1959, premiere of MGM's *Ben-Hur* remake at Loew's State Theater in New York. Starring Charlton Heston and Stephen Boyd as Judah Ben-Hur and Messala, respectively, and directed by William Wyler, one of the dozens of assistants for the chariot race sequence in the original film, the remake had cost the financially troubled studio nearly $15 million—the highest amount ever spent on a motion picture until then (without adjusting for inflation). Curiously, MGM's future once again depended on the success of a *Ben-Hur* picture shot in Italy and beset with problems. (Producer Sam Zimbalist's fatal heart attack was blamed on the stressful production.)

Novarro escorted Carmel Myers to the premiere, and later smiled at the cameras while standing next to Heston. The silent-era Judah Ben-Hur seemed to be enjoying the evening while watching someone else make a success of his most famous role, but his actual feelings may have been quite different. (The premiere took place a mere three weeks after Herbert Howe's death, which had been another reminder of the passing of time.) One strange remark Novarro made years later during an interview with DeWitt Bodeen gives a hint of professional jealousy. "A curious thing happened," he recalled about that evening; "the audience was rooting out loud for Messala to win the chariot race. The anti-hero was already in then. . . . I think, had I been Charlton Heston, I would have wanted to play Messala." Novarro also told several other interviewers that the new version was technically superior to the 1925 film, but that artistically it had missed the mark.

Even so, MGM's new three-hour-and-thirty-two-minute *Ben-Hur* (approximately one hour longer than the original) turned out to be an even bigger box-office success than its predecessor. And despite its slow pace and uninspired direction, the remake was also an outstanding critical triumph, winning eleven out of its twelve Academy Award nominations (a record tied by *Titanic* in 1998), including Best Picture and Best Actor.

The new wave of attention Novarro received from the *Ben-Hur* remake came at a propitious time, for it helped spur the resumption of his acting career: renewed public interest in Ramon Novarro meant more offers to appear onstage, on television, and on-screen. By that time, Novarro had sold El Rosario, and had settled at the 10938 Riverside Drive bungalow. He had also begun working on his first motion picture in a decade—Paramount's comic Western *Heller in Pink Tights*.

"John Barrymore once told me that if I ever got a chance to appear in a film directed by George Cukor, it would be an experience I'd value," Novarro later declared, "and I did greatly enjoy every moment working for Mr. Cukor." Indeed, *Heller in Pink Tights* must have been a unique experience for all involved, considering that this Western was an aberration in Cukor's three-decade career of mostly drawing-room comedies and romantic melodramas. In addition, the picture boasted an eclectic cast that included Sophia Loren, Anthony Quinn, Eileen Heckart, Steve Forrest, former child star Margaret O'Brien, and Novarro's silent-era contemporary Edmund Lowe.

On February 29, 1960, *Heller in Pink Tights* opened to unenthusiastic reviews and disappointing business, with Eileen Heckart's egocentric stage mother garnering most of the positive notices for acting. Novarro's corrupt businessman was generally either ignored or lumped together with the other "capable" supporting players, when in reality his brief but memorable performance is the best element of the film. While most of the cast (with the exception of Steve Forrest's sleek fast-shooter) chew on the gaudy scenery, Novarro subtly delineates his character with a slight lift of an eyebrow, a sly look to the side, or a suave smile that makes his greedy villain—like Rupert of Hentzau nearly forty years earlier—far more captivating than the nominal heroes of the picture.

Heller in Pink Tights turned out to be Novarro's last feature film. In June 1959, the *Los Angeles Times* had announced that he was to support Sal Mineo in a color remake of *The Pagan*, in which Novarro was to play the newly created role of the Pagan's father. Nothing came of that project or of the few other film roles offered to him in the next several years, either because the pictures themselves were never produced, or because the producers did not match the veteran actor's requested minimum of $3,000 a week.

When not working, Novarro continued to drink uncontrollably. In late May 1960, three months after the premiere of *Heller in Pink Tights*, he was arrested twice during a forty-eight-hour period for drunken driving. First, he rear-ended a bus on Hollywood Boulevard; two nights later, he hit a parked car while driving by the North Hollywood Park, a cruising area for gay men. He was taken into custody both times after failing a sobriety test, and later released on bail. In the first case, Novarro claimed he had "just had a glass of sherry"; in the second, he insisted that he had had only "two gin drinks." For the North Hollywood arrest, he pleaded not guilty, but admitted he had been driving while under the influence of a "nerve medicine" prescribed by his doctor.

Novarro's first-ever drunken-driving trial took place in early summer 1960. On June 9, the jury deadlocked on the misdemeanor drunken-driving charge, but the Van Nuys Municipal Court judge fined Novarro $250 for driving while under the influence of nonnarcotic drugs. Perhaps because of the notoriety surrounding his drunken-driving arrests, and also in part because of another car accident in mid-1961—he was a passenger then, and suffered a broken rib and a collapsed lung—Novarro did not work again until late 1961, and then for the small screen.

"I find that the basic art of silent pictures—pantomime—can be very helpful in television," Novarro told the *New York Times*. "Television is a very intimate medium, after all, and sometimes a look or a gesture will be more effective than speech." In fact, as with his quasi cameos in feature films, Novarro steals the few scenes in which he appears in "La Strega," an episode of the horror anthology series *Thriller* hosted by Boris Karloff and starring Jeanette Nolan (in the title role as an evil witch) and Ursula Andress. "La Strega" is also one of several *Thriller* episodes directed by former Warner Bros. star Ida Lupino, who was apparently so pleased with Novarro's performance that she decided to produce and direct a television series tailored to his talents. Yet, elaborate plans, including the shooting of a pilot named *The Green Peacock* starring Novarro and Lupino's husband Howard Duff, failed to entice prospective buyers. The series never materialized.

Two years earlier, Novarro had received an offer to appear in a Spanish adaptation of the Leslie Stevens play *The Marriage-Go-Round*, which was to be produced in Madrid with Dolores del Río as his costar. Despite the allure of the proposal, Novarro had been forced to decline it because the producers demanded two daily performances, which he felt would have been too strenuous. Even so, he did accept his next stage offer, possibly because the role was smaller and less physically demanding than that of the Spanish project: the part of Ligarios in Gene Wesson's *Infidel Caesar*, Novarro's first concrete chance to appear on Broadway. But before heading for the glamorous footlights of New York, he had to take care of a more mundane—but serious—matter.

On February 20, 1962, nearly two years after his latest drunken-driving arrest and exactly two weeks after his sixty-third birthday, Novarro hit another vehicle when he ran a red light at the intersection of Sunland Boulevard and San Fernando Road in Sun Valley, approximately seven miles north of his Riverside Drive home. After failing one more sobriety test, he was arrested for the fourth time in a little more than three years.

"I am old and I just want to die," an alleged declaration by the star of *Ben-Hur* to the arresting officers, turned this latest Novarro encounter with the law into international news. Surprisingly—for an actor whose heyday had been more than thirty years earlier—Novarro received hundreds of letters and telegrams of sympathy, some of them from places as distant as Ghana and Pakistan. Some writers chastised the former screen idol for thinking his life was nearly over, while others begged him to reconsider his death wish. Joan Crawford asked him to call on her whenever he felt down, as she had also gone through similar rough times. After pleading with him to yearn for life, one woman wrote, "But if you still decide you want to die, please do me one favor. Before you do anything about it, please call me, reversing the charges, and sing 'Pagan Love Song' once more to me."

Novarro later affirmed that he had been misquoted. "I speak with an accent still—I've never been able to lose it, and, naturally, on such an occasion, I was nervous," he told *Screen Stories*. "They must have misunderstood—or maybe it made a better story to misunderstand. I had been arrested before on the same charge and what I actually said was 'I'd sooner die than have this happen again.' I was thinking of the arrest, the notoriety, people believing that I was a common drunk. Actually—and this is very true—I haven't had more than two drinks in any one day in over twenty years."

The Van Nuys Municipal Court judge did not believe Novarro's "two drinks in any one day" story. On March 27, he was convicted of misdemeanor drunken driving. Two weeks later, he was fined $275 and sentenced to fifteen days in jail, to be served in October. He also had his driver's license revoked—from now on, Edward Weber, his secretary since 1959, would also serve as his driver. Three days after the sentencing, Novarro left for New York to begin rehearsals on *Infidel Caesar*. In the meantime, his attorney, John Frolich, filed an appeal, Novarro's only chance to avoid a jail term.

Set in Fidel Castro's Cuba, *Infidel Caesar* was former nightclub comedian Gene Wesson's adaptation of Shakespeare's *Julius Caesar*, with television actor Michael Ansara in the title role. The play, on which Wesson had worked for two years, was scheduled to have the first of two preview performances at the Music Box Theater on Friday, April 27.

Nevertheless, like some of Novarro's other long-awaited professional dreams, his Broadway debut never came to pass. After the disastrous preview performances, the producers closed the play before it officially opened. However disheartened he was by one more major professional setback—which probably reminded him of *A Royal Exchange*—Novarro presented his standard resigned persona in public. "Poor Novarro indeed," he remarked a few months later. "It would have been 'Poor Novarro' if we had opened. I'm so glad we closed when we did. . . . This way nobody knows how really bad it was except we of the company and that poor preview audience."

But if Broadway was not beckoning, regional theaters were. Shortly after the *Infidel Caesar* fiasco, Novarro received offers to appear in summer stock in three musicals—*The Desert Song, Flower Drum Song,* and *Fanny.* "I probably won't," he told *Screen Stories.* "It is such hard work and I really have nothing to prove. Many people, you know, think I am down and out. I'm not." Besides always making sure that no one thought him downcast because of professional disillusionments, Novarro consistently made a point of mentioning his solid financial standing in interviews. "I'm better off now than when I retired," he had declared during his 1954 stay in London, and since then, articles about him almost invariably emphasized his wealth and real estate investments. This was likely Novarro's way both to distance himself publicly from the many silent-era stars who had become destitute, and to ensure that producers would not offer him less money.

The financial offers Novarro received for the stage musicals undoubtedly met his expectations, for despite his initial misgivings, he finally agreed to play in both *The Desert Song* and *Flower Drum Song* (he was never to perform in *Fanny*). He traveled to Texas in late May 1962 knowing that his appeal on the drunk-driving case had been denied—which meant he would have to serve his October jail sentence. He protested to the press that his arrest and conviction had been a miscarriage of justice and a violation of his constitutional rights, and vowed that he would fight to clear his name. But in the meantime, he put on greasepaint and acted onstage at Forth Worth's 1,800-seat Casa Mañana, where Sigmund Romberg's *The Desert Song* opened on June 4 to rave reviews and an enthusiastic audience response. "Novarro was a nostalgic plus as General Birabeau," observed the *Fort Worth Telegram,* "heartwarming in his role and handling it in high fashion." Novarro himself was ecstatic about the reception, affirming that he had "enjoyed one of the three happiest weeks of my life. Nowhere, have I been treated so wonderfully as in Rio, Ireland and Fort Worth."

Two months later, his appearance as an old-fashioned Chinese patriarch in Richard Rodgers and Oscar Hammerstein II's *Flower Drum Song* was equally well received. "I am returning to the singing stage after twenty-five years, and I love it," Novarro announced at the time, even though this latest theatrical experience caused him a considerable amount of unpleasantness. Part of the problem was his *Flower Drum Song* costar, Juanita Hall, then reliving the role of Madame Liang she had made famous on Broadway and on-screen. Hall, in fact, has the dubious distinction of being the one leading lady in Novarro's career with whom he did not get along—he thought her arrogant and domineering, and resented her displays of temperament.

Making matters worse, Novarro also felt that the management of the Indianapolis theater where he first played in *Flower Drum Song* failed to treat him with the respect due the star of *Ben-Hur*, *Scaramouche*, and *The Student Prince*. Although he made clear to the management that he was Ramon Novarro, a veteran of a long and distinguished career, the managers remained unmoved. Their star was Juanita Hall, not Ramon Novarro. The public, however, felt differently. After each performance, dozens of fans waited patiently at the stage door for Ramon Novarro, not Juanita Hall. He would then sign autographs and cordially chat with those men and women, many of whom had admired him for decades. The nominal star of the show received scant notice as she passed through the crowd of Novarro fans on her way out of the theater.

Following the five-week tour with the *Flower Drum Song* company through three midwestern states—these were to be his last appearances onstage—Novarro returned to Los Angeles in late September. After a second appeal of his case was denied, he surrendered to authorities on October 3 to begin his fifteen-day jail sentence—though, ultimately, he was to spend only one day behind bars. Soon after his incarceration, John Frolich persuaded a federal court judge to hold another hearing and to apply leniency to his client, as Novarro had "solved any psychological problems he may have had and has not driven a car or taken a drink for several months."

At Novarro's new hearing, Frolich argued that authorities had violated due process of law and that Novarro had been unlawfully detained because the misdemeanor drunken-driving charge had been signed by a court bailiff instead of by the arresting officer. The judge disagreed, but in spite of this latest denial, Novarro continued fighting for vindication. Through some twisted logic, he may even have believed his own series of lies about his drinking—lies that would gain public credence if he managed to shift the blame for his arrest to the legal system. His subsequent appeal, on the grounds that his constitutional rights had been violated, was eventually taken all the way to the United States Supreme Court. The case was denied by the court in 1967, but Novarro was never to serve the rest of his sentence.

Despite announcing that he wanted to star in a repertory revival of the old George Arliss play *The Green Goddess*, Novarro abruptly ceased all his professional activities in the aftermath of his imprisonment. The demanding stage tour and the emotional strain of his jail sentence had been too much for him. Ill health had intermittently plagued him since the late 1920s, when he began complaining to friends about a whole array of ailments, whether arthritis, low blood pressure, or monthlong colds during his European travels (in London in 1960, he had come down with pneumonia). By the early 1960s, he had developed cirrhosis of the liver and a lack of blood-clotting capability—possibly caused by alcohol abuse—that resulted in black and blue marks on his skin. In mid-January 1963, Novarro, a habitual smoker for decades, discovered he was also suffering from both emphysema and a debilitated heart, and around that time he began having sporadic attacks of pleurisy that made his breathing difficult and painful. Also, he referred to the pending jail sentence as the equivalent of having the Sword of Damocles over his head, a plight that had turned him into "a nervous wreck." He still recited the old "All's for the best" to friends in trouble, but he had a difficult time believing that adage when *he* was the one in distress.

Because Novarro was now suffering from so many serious ailments, his doctor advised him to slow down. That injunction explains his professional inactivity throughout 1963 and most of 1964, a period when he resumed his long-neglected singing and yoga exercises and began taking painting lessons with Alice Terry. Novarro's vocal training, in particular, produced good results. British conductor John Lanchbery, a longtime fan and former RNFC member, later reminisced about playing the piano at a gathering at Novarro's home while the host sang "The Pagan Love Song," reaching a clear high G before an enthralled audience. Novarro also displayed an undeniable talent as a painter—whenever he mustered enough discipline to work on a canvas—as evidenced by surviving samples of his work, including a few still-life paintings, and portraits of Jesus and of a very stern-looking Señora Samaniego.

In the fall of 1963, Novarro moved into a one-story Spanish-style house he had bought at 3110 Laurel Canyon Boulevard, near the top of a hillside overlooking the San Fernando Valley. Once there, he immediately busied himself remodeling the property, including landscaping the surrounding gardens and erecting a gate to ensure privacy. ("I think they call it progress," he lamented to the *New York Times* about the construction boom around him.) Novarro also built a music-room annex on which he spent $5,000—a sum he thought so impressive that he liked telling visitors he "had $5,000 in that room." The interior decoration was eclectic: one room was filled with brocaded drapes and heavy bedspreads, while another housed plain, dark furnishings. Mexican-made hand-carved furniture and baroque religious art stood next to simple, unadorned pieces.

After moving to Laurel Canyon, Novarro spent most of his time at the new home. Much to his annoyance, to get around town he was now dependent on rides from either friends or personal assistant Edward Weber. As a result, he socialized little outside his house, except for visits with his small circle of friends. Novarro's declining health also made out-of-town traveling difficult, though he continued flying south of the border at least once a year, whether to visit family members or to look for a farm near Cuernavaca in south-central Mexico, where he intended to retire in quiet solitude. But, his severe health problems notwithstanding, Novarro continued his drinking pattern during that time of professional idleness: periods of sobriety followed by severe alcoholic binges.

In July 1964, Novarro's drinking was once again kept under control when he finally resumed his acting career with a small role in the World War II television series *Combat*. The series, which was filmed at MGM, marked Novarro's first time on a Culver City soundstage in nearly fifteen years. All the old-timers were gone by then (Mayer himself had been dead for seven years), and some of the soundstages were being used for television programming, not feature films. Nevertheless, such reminders of the passing of time did not diminish Novarro's desire to keep working in productions that would not tax his health. "When I was a star," he told the *New York Times*, "we not only worked very long hours, we had crushing responsibilities, too. In television I just go to the studio to act. I have none of the worries, and all of the fun."

Shortly after finishing the *Combat* episode, Novarro portrayed a priest for the first time in his career in the Western series *Rawhide*, then returned to MGM to appear as an Italian aristocrat dying of cancer in a three-part episode of *Dr. Kildare*, starring Richard Chamberlain. Happy with both his work and the production, Novarro offered his Laurel Canyon house for that episode's wrap-up party; but after this *Dr. Kildare* stint, Novarro's sudden burst of activity ended with equal abruptness. "I like to play fathers—preferably those who can sit down comfortably," he had recently told the *Valley Times*, but ill health made even such "comfortable" parts too much of a burden. Novarro was thus forced to retreat once more to his hillside home, finding enough stamina to attend daily mass and see a few friends but, as usual, avoiding large parties and Hollywood functions. One exception was the 1965 Academy Awards ceremony, for which Gregory Peck, then a member of the Academy Board of Governors, gathered a group of surviving silent-film stars who were shown sitting in the audience during the telecast. (Novarro had been one of the Academy's original 230 members in 1927; none of his subsequent films had garnered even a single Academy Award nomination.)

. . .

After nearly one year of professional inactivity, Novarro found his health improved sufficiently to allow him to return to work. His first role was that of a lonely old man with too much imagination in the Western series *Bonanza*, a bravura performance that ranks with Novarro's best work. Three months later, he played an elderly French count in another *Combat* episode, "Finest Hour," opposite former MGM star and two-time Academy Award winner Luise Rainer. It was a difficult production; Rainer, working in front of the cameras for the first time in more than twenty years, tried to direct both her fellow performers *and* director Don Tait. Further complicating matters, Novarro began suffering from one of his intermittent pleurisy attacks. As soon as a scene was over, he would retreat to his dressing room and remain there until called again. Instead of attending the wrap-up party at the end of filming, Novarro checked into a hospital.

In spite of those difficulties, Novarro's appearance in "Finest Hour" was a high point of his later career. The eccentric and proud Count De Roy, a character with whom Novarro shared more than a few traits, was his show-iest and possibly longest role since he had starred in *La Virgen que forjó una patria* more than twenty years earlier. Sporting a goatee, a French accent, a beret, and a cane, Novarro rises above the inane script to beautifully convey the idiosyncrasies of a man of refinement whose world is—literally—about to crumble. Whether expressing his love for the countess, effectively played by Rainer, or having a last drink with the Germans while knowing that all of them—and the concrete symbol of his vanishing world, the family château Armady—will be torn to pieces in a few seconds, Novarro gives meaning to that episode's title.

As his health continued to deteriorate—worsening arthritis affected his walking and sometimes made dressing difficult—Novarro now had little energy to do much beyond attending mass every morning, playing solitaire, and drinking. During the occasional recovery periods, quite likely when he refrained from alcohol, he would feel sufficiently invigorated to paint, sing, tend to his garden, and, following the recommendation of his friend and sometime publicist Leonard Shannon, work on his memoirs. Shannon, to whom the prospective autobiography was dedicated, was supposed to assemble and edit the manuscript after Novarro's death.

The decision to write an autobiography was a major change of heart for Novarro. During the course of the 1954 dinner at the Hotel Savoy in London, one of Novarro's fans had asked him if he would consider writing his memoirs. "No," came the reply. "I would be the only one to read it and it would bore me." Ten years later, Novarro had changed his mind, mainly because he feared that someone else might write a book about him, and he "would rather have those who read [my life story], read me and not someone else's idea of me!" He was understandably afraid that some facts might be presented inaccurately, and also, of course, that some other facts might be presented much too accurately. Novarro presumably believed that once his autobiography had been published, no one else would want to market another book about him. Consequently, *his* version of Ramon Novarro would remain the definitive one.

"Of course he won't tell <u>All</u>!" former actor David Rollins—who had known Novarro in the early 1930s—wrote to Novarro's former summer-stock agent Alan Brock. In fact, despite Novarro's avowal that the book might have to be published only after his death because it would be "very honest—and honesty can sometimes offend," his homosexuality would undoubtedly be left unmentioned. In the sections of his unfinished memoirs available for reading, which span the period from his childhood in Mexico to the early 1930s, Novarro makes absolutely no allusion to his sexual orientation, which remained a taboo subject even in his private life. The offensive "honesty" he was referring to was probably related to his alcoholism, which he—surprisingly—intended to discuss, and, according to a close friend, to ambivalent feelings about his family.

Novarro began working on his autobiography in 1965, calling it *R-3*—the laundry mark Señora Samaniego used on his shirts: "R" for Ramón, "3" because he was the third-oldest (surviving) child. Writing was a painful task, for it brought to the surface both sad and happy memories that Novarro would rather remained hidden in his subconscious. This stirring up of long-buried emotions invariably led to drinking, with the result often being a series of illegible scrawls. During the next three years, Novarro repeatedly attempted to write a coherent version of his life, but *R-3* would ultimately turn into another of his unrealized projects.

The failure of Novarro's autobiographical efforts was to be expected, as he usually found it difficult to relive the past. "Daydreaming of one's past triumphs is ridiculous," he asserted in the early 1960s. "It cheats you of the present. I live for today. It's wonderful." In reality, one of the reasons—perhaps the most important one—for his unwillingness to dwell in the past was the exact opposite of this statement. Though hardly a male version of Norma Desmond, Novarro never truly adjusted either to the loss of his stardom or to the passing of the years. A present consisting of old age, near obscurity, ill health, alcohol abuse, and relative seclusion was even more painful when contrasted with a past that had blazed with youth, fame, beauty, immense wealth, glamorous friends, and boundless aspirations. "One of the things I want to tell about in my book," he remarked with uncharacteristic bluntness a few months before his death, "is how hard it is to grow old, when you've been at the top."

When prompted to reminisce, Novarro, like many other faded stars, recalled the old Hollywood through a prism of nostalgia. "The motion picture industry of my day was a young, healthy business," he told *Screen Stories*. "Now there is too much of everything." The man who had starred in the runaway production of *Ben-Hur* went on to complain that "there is too much money spent on any one picture." Ignoring the way the antics of Clara Bow or Mae Murray had been fodder for the press, he remarked that "there is too much publicity of the wrong kind." Disregarding all-star MGM pictures such as *Grand Hotel* and *Dinner at Eight* (and his own pun about *Freaks*), he griped that "there are too many stars in one picture.... In my day, a star was *the* star and he carried a picture because he was the star." Forgetting his misadventures with Herbert Howe on the French Riviera while *Ben-Hur* was put on hold, he added, "And we took our work seriously then. People lived up to their contracts. I never held up production for a day, never cost my studio an extra cent. No star would. I wonder if the producers today wouldn't be grateful for actors who have a responsibility to their stardom, as we had."

Novarro's nostalgia—however unrealistic—was manifested in nearly every interview, whether stating to Betty Lasky, "The 1925 period, and later, were greater than the talkies," or to DeWitt Bodeen, "We of the silent screen had created a pantomimic art that had no language barriers. We were universal.... When I go to the movies nowadays, which isn't often, I get a feeling that the actors, as actors, are coasting. They're neither creating nor interpreting." In an interview for the *New York Times*, he charged that current performers concentrated on becoming "personalities" instead of good actors. "In silent pictures, individuality was all-important," the actor who was initially promoted as a Valentino clone complained; "now everyone tries to be similar."

Curiously, when discussing his own career, Novarro was highly critical. Humorously dismissing his professional accomplishments, he once wrote that the three things about his career he was proud of were: "[I] didn't play a dual role, didn't put my feet and paws in the Grauman's Theater and I didn't win an Oscar." On a more serious note, during his 1954 London visit he told a British reporter, "I never liked anything I had done. I only saw the flaws." This exaggerated statement aside—after all, Novarro did appreciate at least his achievements under Rex Ingram—he later gave a seemingly forthright assessment of his sound pictures. "With the exception of *The Pagan* in which I only sing," he told Bodeen, "and some of *Son of India* and a good part of Feyder's *Daybreak*—certainly not the ending, however—I didn't like any of the talkies in which I starred. I, too, coasted. It was, however, the vehicles themselves which were really at fault. They weren't right for me, and we were given no time to try and make them right." These and many less-than-rosy memories—his brother José's death, the betrayal by Louis Samuel, his aborted operatic career—were additional reasons for Novarro's reluctance to reminisce.

In October 1966, Novarro once again displayed his generosity toward the loyal Ramon Novarro Film Club by inviting club secretary Audrey Homan, whom he had last seen in London in 1960, to spend a week at his Laurel Canyon home with all her expenses paid, including air fare, meals, and even her taxi ride to the London airport. As a thank-you gift, Homan brought him a bedspread on which club members had embroidered all the titles of his films and plays around an inscription that read, "A Tribute to Ramon Novarro, Star of the Silver Screen from the R.N.F.C."

Always the gentleman, Novarro made Homan feel welcome with such niceties as a glass of water by her bedside every night and fresh roses in her room every day. Besides taking Homan to the usual tourist spots, Novarro introduced his guest to his family and to his old friends Frank Hansen (his personal assistant in the early 1930s) and Natalie Bateson (his infatuated friend from the 1940s). They also visited St. Anne Melkite Church in North Hollywood, a Greek Catholic church that Novarro's brother Eduardo had designed, and the old Valley Oak house in the Hollywood Hills. While Homan peered over a hedge at the pool, Novarro rang the bell, but no one was home. "Perhaps it's better so," he remarked. "It doesn't do to look back." Despite the thrill of spending a week at the home of her film idol, Homan could not help noticing Novarro's unhappiness. She later wrote him that she felt helpless as a witness to the raging battles going on inside him, and that she prayed for his victory over his inner demons.

After Homan's return to London, she described her week as Novarro's guest for the RNFC newsletter in a piece titled "Journey to a Star." Startled at how much older and frailer the former film idol looked since their last meeting, she later wrote, "Time does not stand still for any of us." In fact, Novarro, now only sixty-seven, seemed a good decade older. He dyed his hair a reddish brown tinge and had another face-lift, but he still looked bloated, tired, and haggard. "He shook my hand warmly," DeWitt Bodeen later wrote about his 1967 meeting with Novarro, "but there was little strength in his clasp. It was hard to believe that this small, frail, aging man was the same handsome, impassioned, virile hero of such film classics as *Ben-Hur*, *The Student Prince*, *Scaramouche* and *Where the Pavement Ends*. Only the eyes gave any hint of all that he had once personified."

Obviously, alcohol was the main cause of Novarro's steep physical decline. He would at times receive communion early in the morning only to return home and start drinking cocktails even before having breakfast. Some of his siblings tried to persuade him to stop drinking, but Novarro, used to being the de facto head of the family, was unwilling to heed advice. "Ramon had a problem with alcohol," his brother Angel later admitted. "He tried to lick it several times, but just couldn't do it. And Antonio said some mean things that hurt Ramon." Those "mean things" were not specified by Angel, but Novarro would not be told what to do. He and Antonio never fully mended that rift; shortly before his death, Novarro had his brother removed from a trust he had set up for his siblings.

In mid-1967, Novarro went back to work, landing guest roles in the television series *The Wild, Wild West* and *The High Chaparral*. His participation in the former show turned out to be a disaster. Novarro had received the script only one day before filming, a careless gesture on the part of the producers that made it difficult for the sixty-eight-year-old to remember his lines during production. Director Alan Crosland, Jr., demonstrated his impatience in explicit terms, making the veteran actor even more nervous and forgetful. Compounding the problem, Novarro felt uncomfortable with the series' star, Robert Conrad. The reasons for that are unclear—perhaps a mixture of desire and envy, for Novarro could not keep his eyes off of the young and beefy leading man. As soon as he finished working on *The Wild, Wild West*, Novarro went on one more drinking binge.

Around that time, Novarro was approached by Broadway producers Edward Padula and Michael Ellis, who were planning to create a play for him, but that project, too, never materialized. Thus, the *High Chaparral* episode "A Joyful Noise," first aired on March 24, 1968, turned out to be the conclusion of Novarro's acting career after more than half a century of film, stage, and television work. Going even further back in his life, his path as an actor seemed to have come full circle: his last role, like his first—when he was six years old and performing Campoamor's poem in his Durango home—was that of a priest.

Yet, the role of a cleric remained elusive in real life. "I still think about it," Novarro had admitted to *Screen Stories*. "But I'm afraid I'm too old for that now." The nearest he ever came to playing the part of a priest off camera was walking about in his Franciscan robe in El Rosario and at home in Los Angeles. He also continued to attend daily mass at St. Charles Borromeo Church in North Hollywood, though by the late 1960s he was no longer going to spiritual retreats.

Except for his continual religious activities, Novarro became increasingly reclusive, though he occasionally held small gatherings at his home and hosted Las Posadas celebrations during Christmastime. He also continued visiting with Alice Terry and playing cards with May McAvoy, Gloria Swanson, Leonard Shannon, and actress Mae Clarke, whom he had met at St. Charles. Those card games were always played for very small stakes, but even so, Novarro *hated* to lose. "No matter who else was playing," Shannon later said, "...Ramon would fan cards, cut the deck oddly, deal left or right, and sweep up hands so swiftly they could not be counted. He also kept score, in indecipherable numbers. If all else failed and he lost, he still had a few tricks"—such as paying his loss in Mexican pesos.

Having suffered from intermittent maladies for so many years, Novarro hired a live-in male nurse at the time of his television appearances. On February 18, 1968, he and the nurse left aboard the *Canberra* for Australia, Japan, and Hong Kong, a trip that was supposed to give Novarro the time and emotional strength to work on his autobiography. But after two months abroad, no progress had been made; he had spent most of his time drunk in his cabin, repeatedly making unwelcome passes at the ship's male attendants.

Shortly after returning to the United States, Novarro dismissed the nurse and reduced Edward Weber's hours, quite possibly because he wanted to save money. He had complained to Audrey Homan about his expenses, and had recently put the Laurel Canyon house up for sale because of its high upkeep. As he was tired of depending on taxicabs, Weber, or friends to chauffeur him around town, Novarro considered returning to his old bungalow on Riverside Drive, which was within walking distance of St. Charles Borromeo and other crucial venues.

Still, even while he was attempting to curtail his expenses elsewhere, Novarro continued to spend money for sexual companionship. The frequency of those encounters throughout the years is unclear, but, like everything else in Novarro's life, they probably alternated between periods of high activity and lulls of abstinence. One of those active periods took place in the summer and fall of 1968. Novarro, at times so drunk that his unsteady signature was unreadable, wrote nearly 140 checks generally ranging from $20 to $40 (approximately $125 to $250 today) to assorted "gardeners" and "masseurs," especially those of "Masseurs—The Best," at 7268½ Fountain Avenue, in Hollywood.

Although sex was the primary motive for those meetings, sexual activity did not always occur. Novarro was often too drunk to consummate any physical act; he simply walked around naked or fondled his visitors—at times there were more than one—while they watched television. He would then pass out. Partly because of his generous tips, and also because sexual acts were not always part of the deal, he became quite popular with male prostitutes. As an added enticement, Novarro would tell some of his young guests that he would try to get them started in acting careers.

Not surprisingly, most—if not all—of Novarro's friends were unaware of this habit. When he had guests over to play canasta in the afternoon, he would suggest at some point in the evening that the soirée was over. Sometimes he would simply start drinking until alcohol completely changed both his appearance and his demeanor. Leonard Shannon later stated that the eerie transformation was visible on Novarro's face: beginning at the top, it went down to the now hardened eyes until it reached the mouth, which would curl up malevolently. The sweet, courteous gentleman who liked to play card tricks was abruptly gone. Guests knew then it was time to leave without delay. At other times, Novarro would announce that other guests were expected later that night; no names were mentioned, and Novarro did not invite those already present to stay. Edward Weber would also be away on those occasions, though he must have come into contact with night visitors who overstayed their welcome after Novarro had passed out on the bed or on the sofa.

That mixture of alcohol and sex sometimes led to dangerous encounters. A friend remembered visiting Novarro one morning and finding him with a black eye. He explained that the black eye was the result of an argument with a plumber the previous day, but the friend assumed that Novarro had made an unwanted pass at the worker. In another instance, Novarro was injured during a purported dinner party when an enraged visitor—the reason for the fit of anger was never explained—hit him on the head. Though not seriously hurt, he had to check into a hospital. A third incident occurred on August 30, when he had three guests, two men and a woman. During the visit, one of the men became angry at something unspecified and threw a scotch bottle at a mirror, shattering it, and a hard object at the door of Novarro's bedroom, making a dent on it. Such episodes, coupled with Novarro's frequent drunken driving in the past, led a friend to remark that the actor for years had been living with a "death wish."

Having such a large number of strangers coming to his house also brought

Novarro another kind of trouble. The bedspread that the RNFC members had given him was stolen along with other artifacts during a burglary in the spring of 1968. Since the thieves seemed to know exactly what they were looking for—the bedspread was apparently used as a bag to carry the loot—the police assumed they had been to the house before the crime took place. Homan was heartbroken when she learned of the theft, but promised that she herself would weave another bedspread for him—one that Novarro was never to receive.

On October 19, 1968, the Ramon Novarro Film Club held its five hundredth monthly meeting. Novarro wanted to fly to London for the occasion, but ill health prevented his doing so. Instead, Homan and other club members called him on the phone. In the days that followed, Novarro attended daily mass, went to the unemployment office to collect a $65 unemployment insurance check, and worked on his garden. He also drank uncontrollably. One neighbor later asserted that Novarro—for reasons unknown—used to drink heavily around Halloween, as could be attested by his looks and behavior while distributing treats to the neighborhood children.

In the early afternoon of Wednesday, October 30, Novarro received a call from a young man he had never met. After listening to a description of the caller's physical attributes, he invited the stranger to the house "for a few drinks" later that day. Edward Weber had the day off, and Novarro would have the house to himself. The young man agreed to come as soon as he could find a ride, since he did not own a car. At 4:45 P.M., he called Novarro again to say he would be at the Laurel Canyon address in approximately forty-five minutes. He would also bring his younger brother along.

After hanging up, Novarro showered, trimmed his goatee, applied some cologne, and put on a red and blue checkered silk robe and a pair of blue canvas shoes. At 5:30 P.M., he was ready to meet his guests.

FOURTEEN

Death in the Hollywood Hills

At 8:30 A.M. on Halloween, October 31, Edward Weber arrived at 3110 Laurel Canyon to report for work. The iron gates of the main entrance were open, but since the front door was locked, Weber had to use his keys to let himself in through the kitchen.

As he walked into the living room, Weber saw that it was a shambles. Furniture was overturned. A pair of eyeglasses lay crushed on the floor. Calling "Ramon," he went into the darkened master bedroom. There was no sign of Novarro. He looked into the master bathroom. No one. Weber began searching other rooms, but Novarro was nowhere to be found. Thoroughly mystified, he returned to the master bedroom. Walking over to the window, he opened the drapes slightly. A slant of light entered the room, outlining a mass resting on the far side of the king-size bed. In the now dim light, Weber realized he was looking at Novarro's nude body, lying faceup. Only after his eyes adjusted to the dimness was he able to see how badly beaten that body was.

Futilely, he looked for life signs. Giving up all hope, he dashed back to the living room and called Novarro's brother Eduardo, the police, Novarro's priest at St. Charles Church, and Leonard Shannon.

"Len, you better come right over. This is it . . . Ramon's been murdered."

The police arrived within minutes. More than twenty officers of the Los Angeles Police Department were soon working inside the house and on the surrounding grounds. The entire property was cordoned off, and the house was ordered off-limits to everyone except immediate family members.

In the kitchen sink, the investigating officers found the remains of a dinner. A garbage can in the backyard overflowed with empty gin, vodka, and scotch bottles. They found the name "Larry" written four times on a notepad next to the living-room phone. They searched for fingerprints, found one broken tooth lying near the foot of the bed, took samples of the blood splashed on both the bedroom floor and the ceiling, and thoroughly examined Novarro's body.

Novarro's hands—the right one held an unused condom between the third and index fingers—were tied behind his back with a brown electric cord, which had also been tied around his ankles. On the right side of his neck, an initial—an "N" or a "Z"—had been carved. Lacerations and black-and-blue bruises marked his head, neck, chest, left arm, penis, and knees. A broken silver-tipped black cane, a memento from one of his films, lay on top of his right thigh. A ballpoint pen lay underneath his body, and next to it the name "Larry" had been scribbled in ink on the bedsheet. On the bedroom mirror was smeared the message "Us Girls are better than fagits[*sic*]."

Eduardo, Mariano, and Angel Samaniego arrived later that morning to identify the body. Angel, baffled by the events, told reporters now gathered outside the house that he had spoken with Novarro earlier that week. He had seemed to be doing well then. The police were equally puzzled. There was no evidence of a break-in, nor was there an apparent motive. The only clues they gathered were six pieces of bloodstained clothing: a blue jacket, a blue shirt, a large T-shirt, a Jockey undershirt, and two pairs of Jockey shorts, which a press photographer had accidentally discovered behind a fence outlining Novarro's property.

In midafternoon, agents of the coroner's office removed Novarro's body for an autopsy. His death was reported as a homicide, case 68-11032; cause of death: suffocation caused by aspiration of blood due to multiple injuries of face, nose, and mouth. If Novarro had been lying facedown or on his side, he might have survived the beating, for the blood would have dripped out instead of directly into his air passages.

Had Novarro died of natural causes, his death would have been relegated to the obituary pages of most newspapers, but the mysterious, bloody slaying of a once internationally renowned film star became front-page news the world over. That same day, the *Los Angeles Herald-Examiner* blazoned in huge letters, STAR RAMON NOVARRO MURDERED. The following morning, *The New York Times* announced on its front page, "Ramon Navarro [*sic*] Slain on Coast; Starred in Silent Film *Ben-Hur*." Other newspapers across the country and overseas devoted lengthy articles to the brutal passing of the former MGM star at the hands of an unknown killer.

Those news reports recalled Novarro's past achievements as Judah Ben-Hur and as Greta Garbo's costar. They remembered his profound faith, his desire to become a priest, and his devotion to his family, as well as his frequent arrests for drunken driving—the *Los Angeles Times* quipped that two handicaps the star had failed to cure were "an unshakable accent and an unshakable thirst." Some friends expressed horror and disbelief that so kind and distinguished a gentleman could have met such an appalling death. Others expressed positive memories of Novarro. "He never considered himself a 'has-been' because he had enough money to choose his roles," Leonard Shannon told the *Citizen News*. "He worked when he wanted and enjoyed his garden the rest of the time."

On Saturday, November 2, three days after Novarro's body had been found, the police revealed to the press the known facts of the case. The time of death was set between 9 and 9:30 P.M. on October 30. As all doors to the house were locked and there were no signs of forced entry, Novarro probably had let his killer in voluntarily. The actor had been severely beaten with a "small round striking instrument" that had been found in his bedroom. No valuables appeared to be missing.

An investigation of Novarro's bank account revealed that in the previous six months he had written more than one hundred checks to assorted gardeners and masseurs. This first evidence that Ramon Novarro was gay also marked a breakthrough in the investigation, as one of the listed "masseurs" under the escort agency's employ was named Larry Ortega.

That same day, the police questioned a county jail inmate who claimed to know a Larry Ortega who was a friend of Novarro's. The prisoner stated that he and Larry had had sex with men in exchange for money, and added that Ortega's brother-in-law, Paul Ferguson, also hustled and was known for his volatile temper. Following this lead, officers were sent to stake out the house of Ortega's parents in Los Angeles.

On Sunday, services for Novarro were held at the Cunningham and O'Connor Mortuary in downtown Los Angeles. During the six hours his body lay in state, more than a thousand mourners passed by his bier. Among those wishing to take one last look at the former film idol were a Rudolph Valentino fan and collector who wanted to pay his respects to the other major Latin Lover of the silent era; a studio worker who fondly remembered Novarro from his early days as a Metro rising star; and a female fan who cherished the actor who had corresponded with her throughout the years. At eight o'clock that night, the rosary was recited for him at St. Anne Melkite Church.

The following morning, five hundred friends and family members returned to St. Anne's for the funeral and requiem mass. Ida Lupino, Gilbert Roland, Neil Hamilton, Les Tremayne, MGM publicity director Howard Strickling, and *A Royal Exchange* costar Eddie Foy, Jr., were the only Hollywood personalities in attendance. (Weber had advised Alice Terry not to come, as she might be mobbed by reporters.) The police were also present, but failed to notice that Larry Ortega had signed the guest register of the chapel.

In his eulogy, the Very Reverend Michel Bardaquil exalted Novarro as a "good man and fine actor" and condemned the evil that had claimed his life. After the service, mourners drove to Calvary Cemetery in East Los Angeles, where Novarro was buried next to his mother in the family plot. He had wanted to be laid to rest in his Franciscan robe, but the garment was so tattered that family members decided not to abide by that wish. Novarro's grave was marked by a simple plaque bearing only the inscription "Beloved Brother," his name, and the dates of his birth and death.

Further police investigation revealed that Novarro had last been seen alive by Edward Weber between 5:30 and 5:45 P.M. on October 30. Even though it was his day off, Weber had driven up to the Laurel Canyon house after learning from the local liquor store attendant that Novarro had asked for cigarettes. Aware that his boss might have someone over—Novarro had given up smoking two years earlier, but kept cigarettes available for visitors—Weber knocked instead of using his keys. Novarro answered in his bathrobe, thanked Weber for the cigarettes, and sent him on his way. Weber also told investigators of Novarro's uncontrollable drinking, which sometimes made him lose control of his bodily functions and then completely forget his behavior by the next morning.

Meanwhile, the police were also questioning family members, friends, and neighbors. Eduardo told investigators that his brother had undergone a medical examination approximately ten days before his death, and had seemed to be in relatively stable health. A male neighbor said he had spent some time at Novarro's house, but their relationship had soured because of the older man's insistent advances toward him. Novarro's doctor reported that several of Novarro's checkups had revealed bruises in various body areas. (This assertion has been taken as proof that Novarro was into sadomasochistic sexual practices, though the reported bruises may have actually been the result of Novarro's blood-clotting malfunction.)

On Tuesday, November 5, Novarro's phone records arrived at the North Hollywood police station, showing a forty-eight-minute call to Chicago made the night of his death. That same day, the stakeout patrol brought Larry Ortega and his sister Mari Ortega Ferguson to the station for interrogation.

Mari Ferguson told the police that she had been separated from her husband, Paul, for about a week. They had been having financial problems and had recently argued violently over a can of evaporated milk. After the fight, she had left for her parents' house. She added that his younger brother, Tom, had just arrived in Los Angeles and was staying at their apartment at 13605 South Vermont in Gardena, a working-class suburb approximately fifteen miles south of Novarro's house. Mari also said she had not known Ramon Novarro and was unsure whether her husband had known him.

Larry Ortega reported that Novarro had called him on the afternoon prior to his death to inquire about a young man named Paul. Earlier that day, this young stranger had told Novarro on the phone that he had obtained his number through "Larry." Not thinking of a possible connection between his brother-in-law and the elderly actor, Ortega had replied that he did not know anyone by that name.

After discovering that the recipient of the October 30 phone call from Novarro's home was a young woman who had spoken at length to her former boyfriend Tom Ferguson in Los Angeles, the police requested the Illinois rap sheets of both Ferguson brothers. These indicated that seventeen-year-old Tom had had several previous arrests, mostly for running away from home and petty thefts. He was also wanted by the Chicago Youth Authority for having escaped from a youth home. The rap sheet of twenty-two-year-old Paul included eight months in a Wyoming jail after he was convicted of larceny, and two arrests in Chicago for brawling.

The next day, the Fergusons' fingerprints were matched to prints found at Novarro's house. The police drove to Paul Ferguson's Gardena residence but found no one. Later that day they discovered that the Fergusons were staying at the home of the brother of Paul's former employer in Bell Gardens, a suburb ten miles northeast.

At approximately five o'clock, the police arrived at the Bell Gardens house, where Tom Ferguson was passing the time watching TV. When Tom opened the door, one of the police officers told him they were searching for Paul Ferguson on a burglary charge. Tom said he did not know where his brother was, but believed he might be either at a local bar playing pool or at the neighborhood Taco Bell. Two officers were immediately sent to search the area. Presently, they returned with Paul Ferguson. Both brothers were then handcuffed, read their rights, and informed that they were being arrested for the murder of Ramon Novarro.

One hour later, Paul and Tom Ferguson arrived at the Los Angeles Police Department headquarters, where they were fingerprinted and photographed. The next day, November 7, Paul was arraigned for murder and robbery at the Van Nuys Municipal Court. He was held without bail until a preliminary hearing. Tom was sent to juvenile hall, where he bragged to cellmates of having killed Novarro.

That same day, Chicago police questioned Tom's former girlfriend. She stated that their relationship had soured after Tom had hit her during a quarrel, but on the night of October 30 he had called to say he was at a movie star's house. According to the young woman, Tom had also said that Paul was trying to find $5,000 Novarro had hidden behind a picture on the wall. The police had now found a motive for the crime.

On December 17, a Los Angeles grand jury was told that Paul and Tom Ferguson had killed Novarro during a failed attempt to rob the actor of $5,000 he had allegedly kept at his home. The brothers were indicted for first-degree murder—according to California law, a death that occurs as a result of a robbery or torture, even if accidental, is automatically first-degree murder for all participants, whether or not they were actually involved in the killing. Although a minor, Tom was to be tried as an adult.

The brothers' attorneys entered a plea of not guilty to the charge. They also moved to have the murder charge dismissed, claiming that the testimony brought before the grand jury was insufficient to sustain murder indictments, but the motion was denied. The prosecution thereupon began gathering evidence for a conviction.

Besides the shock caused by Novarro's violent slaying, friends and fans had to cope with the discovery not only that the religious Mexican gentleman had been sexually attracted to men, but also that he had frequently paid for sexual favors. Alice Terry and Novarro's gay friends dating back to the 1920s and 1930s had long been aware of his sexual orientation, though they quite likely did not know that he had patronized escort services. Others, despite years or sometimes decades of friendship, had remained unaware even that Novarro was gay.

Within the Samaniego family, the circumstances surrounding Novarro's death were simply not discussed. The Samaniegos were told that Novarro had liked to help people and had thus become involved with the young men who had killed him. In fact, some siblings refused to accept that Novarro had been gay, opting instead to believe that alcohol had made their brother act in unorthodox ways.

On November 13, Novarro's will was filed for probate in superior court. His estate, consisting primarily of stocks and real estate holdings in the San Fernando Valley, was estimated at $500,000 (approximately $2.5 million today). Novarro had also set up a trust fund for his family, excluding only his brother Antonio (a provision was made to cancel Antonio's outstanding debts to him). The largest share of the estate was given to Eduardo and Angel, for they had the largest families, but more than twenty friends and institutions were listed in the will. Novarro bequeathed some of his paintings to Alice Terry; his framed sheet music and all "remaining tangible personal property" to Edward Weber; and $15,000 to St. Anne Melkite Church—with the request that the church hold prayers for his departed soul. Novarro had always been determined not to spend any time in purgatory.

FIFTEEN

The Trial

Like Novarro, Paul Robert and Thomas Scott Ferguson came from a large Catholic family. Paul, born in Selma, Alabama, on March 25, 1946, was the oldest, and Tom, born at the Great Lakes Naval Station near Chicago on January 10, 1951, was the fourth oldest of ten children. The father, a chronic alcoholic and itinerant steeplejack, had died of spinal meningitis at the age of thirty-three, leaving his widow and children to fend for themselves.

Also like Novarro, Paul was an ardent Catholic who had at one point considered becoming a priest. By his teens, however, he had abandoned that idea and had begun earning his living in an assortment of odd jobs across the United States, including hotel handyman, steeplejack, and, as Novarro had done nearly fifty years earlier, nude model. By the time he was twenty-two, Paul was on his fourth marriage—to Mari Ortega, whom he had wed in July 1968. Tom had left home at an early age, spending much of his adolescence on the street. In his midteens, he had been sent to a reform school, reportedly for beating up an old man, but had later run away.

Since the two brothers had spent little time together throughout their adolescence, Tom was nearly a stranger to Paul when he arrived in Los Angeles on October 21, 1968—their grandmother had sent Tom west because the Chicago Youth Authority had been looking for him. The timing of his arrival could not have been worse. Paul was under great stress because he had just been laid off from Alco Engineering, and one week after Tom arrived, Mari left Paul.

Not surprisingly, Paul wanted to get rid of Tom as quickly as possible. Desperate for money, Paul also wanted to earn some quick cash. Hustling was an easy option, as that activity would earn him $20 or $25 for an evening. He might even find an older man who would be willing to take Tom in.

On October 29, the brothers visited Paul's friend Victor Nichols, a real estate investor who was familiar with the male prostitution scene. Paul asked Nichols for telephone numbers of gay men he could hustle, explaining that he was in dire need of money. Nichols consented, giving out a list of numbers including Novarro's. He recommended that when Paul called Novarro he should say that Larry Ortega had given him the actor's number, since Ortega and Novarro had developed a friendship that went beyond a mere exchange of sex for money.

After leaving Nichols's apartment, the brothers headed to a party at the residence of television producer Gene Banks. While there, Paul talked to a hustler who said he had been to the house of film actor Ramon Novarro the previous night. The hustler explained that Novarro was "a soft touch," which meant that he paid well, and that he must have had a lot of money, for he had hustlers coming over nearly every night.

The next day, October 30, Paul called Novarro at about 2:30 P.M. Following Nichols's advice, he used Ortega's name as an introduction. Novarro, pleased with Paul's description of himself, invited him to come over that same day. Two hours later, television writer Jack Marlowe, with whom Paul had lived for a short period in 1964, drove the Fergusons to 3110 Laurel Canyon.

In Paul's words, Novarro looked like a "Spanish grandee" as he opened the door and invited the brothers in. The guests were offered a variety of alcoholic beverages—gin, vodka, tequila—while they talked on Novarro's L-shaped couch. Novarro read Paul's palm, discussed the possibility of hiring Tom as his gardener, and showed Tom a film magazine with a picture of himself in *Ben-Hur*. Tom remarked that the young, handsome man in the picture did not look at all like the elderly man standing in front of him.

Tom later testified that throughout the conversation Novarro grabbed his and Paul's legs. Feeling uncomfortable, Tom moved away from the sofa, but if Novarro noticed the young man's discomfort, he was not too upset by it. Paul was the one he liked. He suggested that the good-looking, bulky twenty-two-year-old had a future in the movies and could become "a young Burt Lancaster, a superstar, another Clint Eastwood." To prove to his skeptical guest that he was serious, at about 6:30 P.M. Novarro called Leonard Shannon. Since Shannon, then a film publicist for United Artists, was still at work, Novarro spoke with his wife.

"The last phone call of his life was made from that house to us," Shannon later recalled. "And it was a strange one. . . . With hardly more than a, 'Hello, this is Ramon,' he launched into a paean of praise for 'a young man I have here. He wants to be an actor and he has star quality. I want Len to meet him. We could have lunch at the studio.' When [my wife] repeated that to me, we both agreed it did not sound like Ramon. He was not given to such corny accolades. No, it sounded as if he was calling to impress someone with words like star quality and studio, and as a person who could summon up a luncheon there with an executive." In his testimony, Paul stated that Novarro had told him to return to the house in three days to meet with Shannon. When Paul replied he had nothing to wear, Novarro assured him that from then on he "would take care of everything."

Following the phone call, the trio had dinner. As the evening progressed, they chatted about Mexico, where Paul had lived for some time, and about the music room Novarro had built for $5,000. Paul then sat at the piano and started playing "Swanee River" and "Chopsticks," being soon joined by Novarro, who tried to teach him a song he had just composed. While Paul and Novarro played, Tom sang a tune. Throughout those activities, both Paul and Novarro drank constantly. Paul later told the court that he drank more than a bottle of vodka that evening, while Novarro's autopsy revealed that his blood alcohol level was a critical 0.23.

The two brothers told the police—and later the court—radically different versions of the events on the night of October 30, 1968, from the time Paul and Novarro began playing the piano to the moment Novarro's dead body was placed on the bed.

According to Paul, while he and Novarro were playing a duet at the piano, Novarro asked which of the two brothers would stay and which would leave. Paul said he was drunk and asked if he could take a nap on the sofa before hitchhiking back home. Just before passing out, he saw his brother accompany Novarro to the patio. Sometime later, Tom woke him up with the words "The guy is dead." Paul got up and followed his brother into Novarro's bedroom, where he found the actor's nude body on the floor. "See, this guy is dead," Tom repeated. "He's turned blue." Paul touched Novarro's body; the skin felt "starchy. Like paper." After they lifted the body onto the bed, Paul saw that Novarro's hands had been tied. He put his ear on Novarro's chest and decided that his host was indeed dead. He told Tom they should call the police, but Tom suggested they should make it look like a robbery, explaining, "I didn't mean to do it." When later asked in court why he went along with Tom's idea, Paul simply replied, "Stupid-ness."

In Tom's version, Novarro agreed that both brothers could spend the night. After being shown to the guest room, Tom lay down for a few minutes, but feeling restless, he decided to call his ex-girlfriend in Chicago. On his way to the living room, he passed through Novarro's bedroom, where he saw both Paul and Novarro naked. "Get the hell out of here!" Paul yelled. Tom rapidly left, closing the door behind him. He then picked up the telephone in the dining area and dialed Chicago. Sometime during the phone conversation he heard screams coming from Novarro's bedroom. Tom said he needed to see what was happening, and hung up.

When Tom entered the bedroom, he saw Paul standing at the foot of the bed, his shorts covered in blood. Novarro was naked and sitting bent over at the edge of the bed, his gray goatee now dyed red. Obeying Paul's order, Tom helped the semiconscious Novarro to the shower. While trying to revive him, Tom twice warned Novarro not to say anything to Paul, for he might get violent again. Upon their return to the bedroom, Tom helped Novarro lie down in bed. He then noticed Paul in the adjacent bathroom, still in his blood-soaked shorts, and now wearing a felt hat and twirling a black cane while dancing in front of a large mirror.

As Paul walked back into the bedroom, he began demanding money from Novarro. At that moment, Tom walked out to urinate. A still-stunned No-varro was left sitting in bed, muttering that he had no money in the house. Shortly thereafter, Tom returned to the bedroom, where he found Paul fully dressed standing by the doorway while Novarro lay motionless on the floor. Tom knelt by Novarro's side and leaned over his chest to feel for signs of life. There were none. Paul began to sob. He had thought Novarro was going to attack him when the actor stood up from the bed and put his hand on him, saying, "Please, get out of the way." As a reaction, he had punched Novarro. The unsteady sixty-nine-year-old had been knocked off balance, and had slipped on the blood-smeared floor.

The two brothers then lifted Novarro's body onto the bed. Tom claimed that Paul tied the cord around Novarro after they had placed him on the bed, and later admitted in court that it had been his idea to make it look as if Novarro had been killed by burglars. From this point on, except for minor digressions, the two versions merged again.

The brothers began overturning furniture in the living room. Paul, still under the influence of alcohol, would turn a chair over and then put it back in its place. He then went to the kitchen and started washing dishes. Yet, he was sufficiently alert to briefly turn Novarro's body on its side and write "Larry" on the bedsheet. He also wrote "Larry" four times on a notepad in the living room and tried to wipe the blood off the floor with his clothing. In the meantime, Tom took $20 from Novarro's bathrobe pocket, scratched his neck with a knife to make it look as if a woman had clawed him, and put a condom between the fingers of his right hand. Using a makeup stick, he wrote on the bedroom mirror, "Us Girls are better than fagits." Finally, Tom closed all the drapes, locked the front door, and turned out the lights. The brothers took off their bloodied clothes and replaced them with items they had found at the house. Tom was the first to leave. Paul followed a few minutes later. After Paul threw their bloody clothes over a fence adjoining the property, the brothers fled the scene.

The pair hitchhiked downhill, arriving in Hollywood at 11:30 P.M. According to Tom, they ate at a hamburger house on Sunset Boulevard where Paul tried to arrange a date with a waitress. In Paul's version, after being dropped off on Sunset, they walked twenty minutes straight to Victor Nichols's apartment. Once there, Paul told Nichols that Tom had killed Novarro. He then asked to borrow Nichols's car, but was given instead $8 for a taxi ride to Gardena.

"I went into shock," Paul says. "When I woke up the next morning I heard what happened on the radio. [Tom and I] didn't even talk because I was walking around in shock." Once the shock passed, Paul briefly considered fleeing to Tijuana, but he and Tom did not have money for the bus fare. Hitchhiking the 120 miles to the Mexican border was a possibility, but Paul feared the police might be on the lookout for them. Afraid that they might be caught if they stayed at the Gardena apartment, the two brothers went to the Bell Gardens residence of the brother of Paul's former employer. With little money and nowhere to go, Paul spent much of his time the next few days playing pool at a local bar while Tom watched television. Paul was expecting that his former boss would soon assign him more work, but his arrest put an end to such hopes.

On July 28, 1969, nearly nine months after their arrest, the murder trial of Paul Robert and Thomas Scott Ferguson began at the Los Angeles Superior Court, with Judge Mark Brandler presiding. The brothers were to be tried individually, with a court-appointed attorney, Richard A. Walton, defending Tom, and Cletus J. Hanifin, whose services were paid for by a relative of the Fergusons, representing Paul. The prosecutor, Deputy District Attorney

James M. Ideman, was going to seek the death penalty for Paul. Tom, even though he was to be tried as an adult, could not be sentenced to death because he had been a minor at the time of the crime.

"The victim in this case, Mr. Ramon Novarro," Ideman told the seven men and five women of the jury, "... lived by himself in a large Spanish-type house and it seemed obvious that he was a man of some wealth." Ideman then attempted to play down Novarro's frequent patronizing of male hustlers, as prejudice against older men who solicited sex from younger ones could seriously damage the prosecution's case. "Now Mr. Novarro was a homosexual and probably had been one for many years," he explained. "But he was a discreet homosexual. He did not go out into the streets and try to pick up people. The young male prostitutes would come to his home and he was usually careful about who came to his home."

Ideman then recounted the events that had allegedly occurred at 3110 Laurel Canyon Boulevard on the evening of October 30, 1968. He averred that Novarro and Paul Ferguson had gone together into the bedroom, adding that Paul had believed there was a large sum of money in the house. When Novarro tried to pay for Paul's sexual services with a check, the young man demanded cash. But the actor, Ideman continued, "possibly because of his propensities," was not in the habit of keeping cash at home. Since Novarro failed to produce the money, Paul began pummeling him. Once Tom hung up with his ex-girlfriend, he joined his brother in the beating.

Ideman portrayed the twenty-two different injuries on Novarro's body as marks of torture. He contended that Novarro was first trounced with a cane—the "small round striking instrument" the police had mentioned early in the case. Once the elderly actor began to lose consciousness, Ideman continued, the brothers revived him with a cold shower. They tied his hands behind his back with an electrical cord to prevent him from warding off a series of blows to some of the most sensitive parts of his body. They then placed their victim on his back on the bed, where he lost consciousness. While Novarro was slowly drowning in his own blood, the Fergusons ransacked the house in search of the money.

"When I get through presenting the evidence," Ideman concluded, "it will show Mr. Novarro was murdered. It will show who did it. It will show that the Fergusons did it and it will show why it was done. It was done for robbery."

The defense attorneys waived the right to make an opening statement.

. . .

Tom's former girlfriend, who had been flown in from Chicago, testified that on the night of Novarro's death, Tom had told her on the phone that he and Paul would have to tie the actor to learn more rapidly where he had stashed away $5,000. When Tom put the receiver down to get cigarettes, she heard someone yell, "You're hurting me!" When she heard a body falling, Tom explained he had drunk too much and had stumbled.

Paul's landlady at 13605 South Vermont told the jury that Paul had promised to pay his late rent because he was going to receive $5,000. However, a former tenant at the building who had heard Paul's conversation with the landlady testified that Paul had made no mention of $5,000 and that the landlady was known to be untrustworthy. Further complicating matters, a police officer testified that the landlady had told him about the $5,000 at the beginning of the investigation, but no police report was made at the time to corroborate his assertion.

Several inmates who had spent time with Tom in jail stated that Tom had talked about having killed Novarro, but the testimony of one was invalidated because he had been brutally beaten by police. Another inmate said that Tom had initially claimed to have killed Novarro, but had later placed the blame on Paul.

Police investigators, several of whom sat in court despite rules that prevented witnesses from attending the trial, testified that, when questioned, Mari Ortega Ferguson had recalled Paul telling her that he was going to get $5,000. They also asserted that they had identified the fingerprints of both brothers in Novarro's bedroom and in the two adjacent bathrooms. Still, Tom's attorney, Richard Walton, noted that the drawers in many rooms had been left untouched and that none of the pictures on the walls had been out of place. There were no signs of fingerprints on any of the wall hangings, even though the Fergusons allegedly believed that Novarro had stashed the $5,000 in a wall safe behind one of the pictures.

For Paul's defense, Cletus Hanifin called a court-appointed psychiatrist, who testified that Paul suffered from a sociopathic disorder as a result of a traumatic childhood, and had a sex-identity conflict that made him exaggerate his masculinity. The psychiatrist also stated that Paul's mental capacity was seriously impaired under the influence of alcohol, making him a danger to himself and to others—though he would have been unable to form the intent to commit murder. Three doctors were called to refute the defense doctor's findings, but none of them had spent more than two hours studying Paul. They also contradicted one another on methods of diagnosing psychopathic behavior.

Victor Nichols, who had to testify in order to avoid felony charges—he had failed to notify police after learning of Novarro's death—told the court he had given Novarro's number to Paul, but asserted he knew nothing about Novarro except that Larry Ortega thought him "a very kind man." Nichols added that late on the night of October 30, while Tom rested in another room, he and Paul had a brief conversation during which Paul said, "Tom went to bed with Ramon. Ramon tried to seduce him and he hit him several times and he is dead." According to Nichols, Tom confessed to having killed Novarro. (Tom later disputed Nichols's statement in court.)

On August 25, Hanifin called Paul to the stand. Paul admitted to having worked as a hustler for "three months and one week. Two and half months in 1964, a week in 1965, and four or five days in 1968." He also stated that he had asked Nichols for the names of men he could hustle, but denied any knowledge of the $5,000. He then gave his version of the early part of the evening of October 30 at 3110 Laurel Canyon, including Novarro's mention of a music room he had built for $5,000.

Hanifin's defense focused on Novarro's offer to find Paul work as an actor, for his client would not have wanted to beat and torture someone who could have started him in a film career. Paul maintained that, later in the evening, Novarro and Tom had left for the garden while he had passed out on the couch. He had heard Tom talking on the phone, but was unable to remember in court what had been said. He was later awakened by Tom, who told him that Novarro was dead.

Paul then described the overturning of furniture and other tactics to make it seem that Novarro had been killed by burglars. When asked why he wrote the name "Larry" on the bedsheet and on a notepad, Paul denied he had been thinking of his brother-in-law. He also asserted that he had never seen Novarro's cane until the prosecution presented it as an exhibit in the court, and denied having hit Novarro in any way. He added that the actor was "a nice old guy" and had done nothing to offend him.

Next, Richard Walton asked Paul whether it had ever occurred to him that he might have killed Novarro during one of his drunken blackouts. Paul stated that he had been worried about that possibility, but that Tom had assumed responsibility for the killing. "I didn't kill him," Paul affirmed. "It was my brother." Walton then accused Paul of trying to deceive the jury because he thought they would be less severe on a minor.

In the sixth week of the trial, Walton called the Fergusons' mother to the witness stand. He quoted a letter she had written to Tom that read, "Paul Robert wrote the first trial day . . . that everyone was out to save his own skin and he is in a corner now. Tom, when you testify, think about what you are saying.... You're holding Rob's life in your hands.... You can either let him live or die." Despite the evidence, the witness denied having attempted to sway her son Tom's testimony. She also testified that Tom had written to her that both he and Paul had killed Novarro, and that Tom had stated in a letter that Novarro "deserved to be killed. He was nothing but an old faggot." She added that Tom had a bad reputation for truthfulness, and that while still in Chicago he had talked about "a queer" who had given him money for sex. Her testimony about Tom's letters could not be corroborated, because she claimed to have destroyed the letters immediately after reading them.

Tom, calm and composed—the *Los Angeles Times* referred to him as "an enigma throughout the entire trial"—took his turn on the witness stand on September 2. He told the court that he had seen Paul in bed with Novarro; had spent nearly one hour on the phone with his former girlfriend while Paul remained alone with the actor; and had found a bloodied Novarro sitting on the bed while Paul, in his blood-soaked shorts, stood near him. Finally, Tom said that while he urinated, Paul beat Novarro to death.

Tom recalled that the next day Paul had told him he had not meant to kill Novarro, but the alcohol had made him lose control. Tom also claimed that Paul had initially persuaded him to take the blame for the killing. Paul had explained that he would face the gas chamber if convicted, while Tom, as a minor, would get only six months at a juvenile facility. Tom further testified that he had at first gone along with Paul's plan, for he had been under great pressure, including pressure from his mother, to save his older brother from the death penalty. He had changed his mind after learning that Novarro had been viciously beaten with a cane. When asked if he felt "unfriendly" toward his brother, Tom replied that he felt neither friendly nor unfriendly. "Paul's mentally ill and needs help," he stated. "I'm neutral as far as Paul is concerned because I understand the situation." Tom also denied ever mentioning to his ex-girlfriend that there was $5,000 in the house.

When Tom remarked that the badly beaten Novarro had begun muttering, "Hail Mary, full of grace..." after being taken to the shower, Paul threw a pen at him, screaming, "Oh, you punk liar son of a bitch! Tell the truth!" Judge Brandler immediately sent the jury out of the courtroom and warned Paul that he would be bound and gagged if he disrupted the proceedings one more time. Upon their return, the jurors were told to disregard the incident. "That was meant to upset me," Paul later said. "We're Catholic."

When cross-examined by Ideman, Tom testified that Paul had seen a vision of his estranged wife when Novarro tried to kiss him. Paul shoved

Novarro away, causing him to fall and injure himself. When asked why he had told fellow inmates that he had been responsible for Novarro's death, Tom said, "For two reasons: One, my brother told me if I did this the D.A. would pick up on some of them and have them brought into court, and, Two, I thought it was my obligation to—you know—just take it for him." Paul had also told him that, as an accused murderer, he would gain respect at the California Youth Authority facility where he would be sent. "It's just a big thing," the now eighteen-year-old explained. "They leave murderers alone. . . . This is a highly publicized case, and it would tend to make everybody look up to you and stuff like that."

In the final arguments, each attorney offered a summation and then a rebuttal, with the prosecutor having the final word. After noting that there had been two contradictory defenses and that jurors should remember what evidence was introduced against which defendant, Paul's attorney, Cletus Hanifin, asked the jury why his client would have killed a man who could have been his benefactor and could have sponsored his entrée into Hollywood. Hanifin asserted that Paul had either been asleep during the beating or had blacked out and was not responsible for his actions, and contended that the $5,000 had been evidence manufactured by the police and the prosecutor. He added that if the brothers had gone to 3110 Laurel Canyon to rob Novarro, they would surely have found something valuable in the house to take with them and would have concocted a plan for a getaway— neither of which was done. He asked the jury to consider the fact that although Novarro had supposedly been beaten with a cane, there was no blood on the cane found next to his body. And finally, Hanifin stated that Novarro's liquor bill in the month prior to his death had been $300. "For forty years," he argued, "Novarro had been an accident walking around looking for a place to happen."

In his summation, Richard Walton contended that Paul had killed Novarro after blacking out, and that Tom had at first assumed responsibility for the slaying because of family pressure. Walton knew that if Paul was blamed for the crime, Tom's sentence could be no harsher than his brother's; if the jury deemed Paul to have been temporarily insane, he might receive a light sentence and Tom might get off with an acquittal.

Another of Walton's tactics was to shift the blame from the accused perpetrators to the victim. "Back in the days of Valentino, this man who set female hearts aflutter, was nothing but a queer," he told the jury. "There's no way of calculating how many felonies this man committed over the years, for all his piety." Walton then asked, "What would have happened that night if Paul had not gotten drunk on Novarro's booze, at Novarro's urging and at Novarro's behest? Would this have happened if Novarro had not been a seducer and a traducer of young men? The answers to those questions will determine the issue and degree of guilt of Tom Ferguson and the issue and degree of guilt of Paul Ferguson."

James Ideman observed that even though Novarro had "homosexual tendencies and drank to excess," he was well liked by his associates and had made great contributions to the entertainment industry. "I hope sincerely you will not put Mr. Novarro on trial," Ideman exhorted the jury. "He has paid for whatever he did and now it is the Fergusons' turn to pay for whatever they may have done." He claimed that the contradictions found in the testimony of Paul's former landlady were proof that she had not been rehearsed, and reminded the jury that Mari Ortega Ferguson also had told police that Paul was expecting to get $5,000.

Ideman then quipped, "[A]fter listening to the Fergusons testify, I was beginning to wonder if what we were dealing with was a suicide. Perhaps Mr. Novarro wrapped himself in that electrical wire and beat himself to death with the cane." He explained that the brothers' alleged ignorance about the $5,000 resulted from their knowing "the consequences of robbery-murder," and added, "They are hustlers—I don't know why I keep using those nice words. That means a male whore. That is what they are. They sell their bodies to other men for money. What kind of a person do you think does that?...Novarro was trussed up like an animal and beaten to death. I don't think you would treat an animal like that.... This is deliberate torture. You don't strike a man on his genitals and split his scalp with a cane unless you are torturing him."

Judge Brandler then instructed the jury on how to treat the evidence presented and on other legal technicalities, such as the definition of murder and all the possible verdicts. Since the instructions were lengthy and quite complex, Walton asked that they be given to the jurors in writing. His petition was denied.

On September 17, after eight hours of deliberating over more than two hundred exhibits, 6,500 pages of transcripts, and six weeks of testimony, the jurors returned with their verdict: Paul and Thomas Ferguson were found guilty of first-degree murder. Tom was to automatically receive the maximum penalty of life in prison, while Paul's fate—life in prison or death row—would be determined during the penalty phase of the trial, which was to be held the following week. Both defense attorneys promised to appeal the verdict, as they believed the jury could not have looked at all the evidence in such a short time.

The brothers showed no reaction the moment the verdict was read. They then turned to the spectators, lifted their eyebrows, and shrugged.

More drama ensued during the penalty phase. Mari Ortega Ferguson denied she had ever told the police that Paul had mentioned $5,000 to her. Paul's former employer asserted that Paul was a youth of good character and berated James Ideman for not letting him testify earlier. When Ideman asked Paul if he felt sorry for what he had done, the defendant lost his temper. Pointing his finger at Ideman, Paul yelled, "You're a pig, a filthy pig! Just to get a lousy murder conviction, you've kept evidence out of this trial.... You know and I know that I didn't do it!" He also accused Ideman of falsifying evidence and "having people lie," and accused a police officer of committing perjury. He then turned to the jury and cried. "Ladies and gentlemen," he said, "no matter what you believe, this is all a lie. I never hurt anybody."

The next day, Tom took the witness stand in a dramatic about-face. "I didn't kill [Novarro, though] it was my fault that he died," he asserted, adding that Paul had not in any way been responsible for Novarro's death. "Mr. Novarro came up to me when Paul was asleep on the couch," Tom told the court. "... We had a sex act—oral copulation.... He kept trying to put his fingers up my rectum.... I started hitting him." Badly beaten, Novarro staggered into the bathroom to wipe the blood off his face, while Tom urinated. "I looked at him and it made me sick," Tom explained. He then hit Novarro again. A few minutes later, Novarro dashed for the phone. "I hit him again. I was just mad. I tied him up.... I went in to wake up Paul. He came in and Mr. Novarro was on the floor—he looked dead.... I got the glove and cane out of the closet—just goofing around with it, twirling it like a baton. Then I hit him on the face with it and threw it on the floor. Just sickening he was.... Then I saw the cane on the floor and I cracked him across the head twice. He was like a sick punk."

"Are you saying these things now just to save your brother?" Ideman inquired.

"I don't want it on my shoulders if I send him to the gas chamber and I sit up there [in prison] like Mr. Cool," Tom replied.

Tom also remarked that he did not feel guilty about having committed perjury because Paul "was supposed to get manslaughter and I was supposed to get off. It's not our fault that we got a dumb jury." He alleged that he had previously petitioned to change his testimony but had been refused, and that Ideman had initially told him he was only technically guilty and could get an acquittal. When Ideman began to correct Tom's statement, Tom called him a liar. The district attorney then affirmed that there was no record of any such petition. Tom challenged him to check it.

"What did you mean, when you said that you didn't kill him but that you were responsible for his death?" Judge Brandler asked Tom.

"He wasn't killed," Tom replied. "He died of a broken nose and I'm the one who busted his nose. . . . I caused his death . . . [Novarro] caused his death . . . we caused his death. He was as much part of it as I was."

Ideman was unmoved. "I've about had it up to here with the Fergusons!" he exclaimed. He urged the jury to ignore Tom's confession and give Paul the ultimate penalty. As an additional argument in favor of execution, Ideman suggested that putting Paul in prison with other men would be like putting him in a harem.

Although Tom apparently had nothing to lose with his about-face—he had already been sentenced to life in prison, the maximum punishment for a minor—Richard Walton had advised his client not to testify during the penalty phase. He gave three reasons for that: It would hurt Tom's chances for a new trial, it could be used against him at a retrial if the conviction should be reversed, and it would hurt his chances for an early parole. Tom's testimony to save his brother's life may have also been unnecessary.

On September 25, after two and a half hours of deliberation, the jurors returned with their verdict for Paul: life in prison. They indicated that they remained unconvinced that Novarro's death had been intentional and believed it unjust to give Paul a much stiffer sentence than his younger brother's for the same crime.

"I'm glad Tom finally told the truth," Paul told the *Los Angeles Herald-Examiner*. "It sounds like Tom is really sorry for what he has done to me. And the very reason he was in Los Angeles was because I wanted to help him. I love my brother."

On October 27, 1969, Paul and Thomas Ferguson were formally sentenced to life in prison. Judge Brandler had denied a request for a retrial, ignoring Cletus Hanifin's and Richard Walton's arguments that there was not enough evidence to convict their clients and that the judge's own rulings had been inconsistent with the law. The judge recommended that the Ferguson brothers never be paroled, as the trial had "established convincingly and conclusively not only to the jury but to this court the guilt of each of the Fergusons . . . to the brutal, vicious torture-killing of Mr. Ramon Novarro."

Epilogue

In 1978, nearly ten years after the trial of the Ferguson brothers, author Joel L. Harrison published *Bloody Wednesday*, an account of the police investigation following Novarro's slaying and the ensuing murder trial. In his book, Harrison proposes that the Fergusons were guilty of manslaughter, not first-degree murder, and discusses the possibility that the $5,000 was a fabricated motive. He also asserts that Paul's defense attorney, Cletus Hanifin, had in his possession statements written by his client that incriminated him as the sole perpetrator of Novarro's death. Harrison then accuses Hanifin of suborning perjury, for, despite that knowledge, the attorney had let Paul take the stand to testify against his brother.

As reported in *Bloody Wednesday*, Paul had written:

> I remeber [*sic*] sitting next to Mr. Navarro [*sic*] and having him kiss me, I didn't care I was going to be a star. Then I remember being in the bed-room [*sic*] and having Tom come in. Some conversation was exchanged but I haven't any real notion of what was said, however I know he gave me a beer and that I was undressed. Next I was sitting on the edge of the bed and a feeling of hate engulfed me inside all over. I exploded and hit Mr. Navarro. I don't know if it was one, two, three, four, five times, but every blow I'm sure hit him in the face. I jumbed [*sic*] up and turned away "oh my God. I've hit him! I'm going to jail for no reason."

After the explosion, Harrison reports, Paul demanded to be led into Novarro's office. Novarro replied that he had no office. Badly bruised, he went to the bathroom. Upon his return to the bedroom, he reached for the phone. Paul grabbed him and pinned him on the bed. At that moment, Tom arrived and suggested that Paul tie Novarro up. Paul tried but got tangled in the cord. Tom then took Novarro to the bathroom to wash the blood off of him. As Novarro walked back into the bedroom, Paul hit him again. Novarro lost his balance and fell to the floor. He began coughing. Paul walked out of the room and started playing with a hat, putting it on and taking it off. Shortly thereafter, Tom approached him to say that Novarro was dead.

In *Bloody Wednesday*, Tom Ferguson asserts that he took no part in the killing, claiming that he accepted responsibility for it during the penalty phase of the trial because he wanted to save Paul from the gas chamber. Judge Mark Brandler remained unconvinced. During a 1998 interview, he stated that "there was no question in my mind whatsoever that both were equally guilty." Yet, even though Tom was hardly known for his honesty, this time he was apparently telling the truth.

In a November 1998 phone interview, a little more than thirty years after the October 30, 1968, events, Paul Ferguson discussed at length Novarro's death, his role in it, and what had transpired behind the scenes both before and during the trial.

> When [Novarro] kissed me, I reacted like a Catholic, what they call homosexual panic. Some old guy in the desert says, "Kill homosexuals." It's inbred.... I was too drunk to be civilized. Whatever my most primitive moral standings were, I reacted. It had nothing to do with Novarro, nothing to do with his being homosexual. It all had to do with how I saw myself. And the fact that my brother was there. And that he could see me in that homosexual act. It all had to do with my Catholic upbringing, with my five thousand years of Moses. And that's the only reason why this whole thing happened. Because that's what society teaches you.... I think after I hit Mr. Novarro...I turned around and sat down on the sofa. I got up and went to find [Novarro] in the bedroom. "This guy's dead."...We didn't go there to rob him. We had never heard of these $5,000. We didn't steal anything.... There was no robbery, no torture, no murder. The killing was manslaughter.

Since Paul had been unwilling to face the possibility of a death sentence, he had attempted to persuade his younger brother to take the blame for him.

The fact that Paul has nothing to gain from assuming responsibility for

Novarro's death gives credibility to his confession. Moreover, his assertions match what Tom had repeatedly asserted during the sentencing phase of the trial. In a November 23, 1998, letter Paul expressed his chagrin for "the shame [the events of October 30, 1968] caused the Navarro [*sic*] family, as well as my own family," and "my regret concerning the panic and cowardice shown by not calling the police on the night Mr. Navarro died and the consequences suffered by all concerned at this lapse. Especially, Tom, my brother, who has paid with his entire life for the failure of his big brother to act like a big brother."

Tom, for his part, continues to maintain his own innocence.

Throughout his life, Novarro did his utmost to keep his sexual orientation private and free from scandal, but inevitably, numerous tales—none of them accompanied by any evidence—have been disseminated since his well-publicized death. Among those are his patronizing male bordellos at the height of his fame, his making sexual advances toward male employees at MGM, his having a torrid affair with Rudolph Valentino, and, most infamous of all, his being killed by a sex toy. This well-known Novarro myth apparently originated in 1975 with the publication of Kenneth Anger's *Hollywood Babylon*, a book filled with lurid and sensational stories, one of which has Valentino giving Novarro a black art-deco dildo that is later stuck down the actor's throat by one of the Ferguson brothers, suffocating him to death. According to this tale, the dildo, before being put to such a ghastly use, had been kept in a bedroom shrine dedicated to the Italian Latin Lover, whom Novarro had idolized throughout the years.

Both Paul and Tom Ferguson angrily deny ever seeing such an object at Novarro's house. Their assertions are supported in *Madam Valentino*, Michael Morris's biography of Natacha Rambova, in which James Ideman, the prosecutor at the Fergusons' trial and now a United States district judge, avers, "With reference to the claim that Mr. Novarro was choked to death by means of an 'Art Deco dildo,' I can tell you that that did not happen.... I certainly never made any statement to the effect that such an instrument was used. I did not even know of its existence." Also, C. Robert Dambacher of the coroner's office affirmed in a letter to Michael Morris that no dildo was found at the scene of death or thrust down Novarro's throat. Dambacher concluded that the person who wrote that statement had to be either sick or trying to sensationalize the actor's death.

Subsequent versions of the sex-toy-as-a-murder-weapon story have Novarro suffocating on a gold-plated, diamond-encrusted, or lead dildo, but whatever its substance, and whether or not it was an actual replica of Valentino's penis as some have claimed, the dildo—more than *Ben-Hur, Scaramouche,* or *The Student Prince*—has been associated with the name Ramon Novarro for over a quarter of a century. This has marked a radical shift in Novarro's public image, one that stands in sharp contrast to that of his heyday, when he was sold as the sensitive, philosophical, quasi-mystical film star.

The best example of that mystical image appeared in a piece written by his companion Herbert Howe. In one of the "On the Road with Ramon" installments for *Motion Picture,* Howe recalled that shortly after their return to the United States from location shooting of *The Arab* in the spring of 1924, Novarro presented him with a rare copy of *The Meditations of Marcus Aurelius* in which he had inscribed, "This is the book that I wrote in one of my past incarnations.... I dare you to make me out a liar." Howe recalled "with guilt my superior air toward [Novarro's] childish philosophy recurrently expressed in 'All's for the best'...but as phrased by Ramon in a previous incarnation, it is a staff for life":

> When the sovereign power within is true to nature, it stands to adjust itself to every possibility and every chance that may befall...All that happens, happens aright. Watch closely, you will find it so. Not merely in the order of events, but by scale of right, as tho some power apportions all according to worth....

"True to the god within," Howe concluded, "not caring what others may say, Ramon Novarro today is the living line of the Emperor Antoninus."

Surely, Howe's articles were thinly veiled promotional pieces for his client-lover, but even then, the "mystically elusive Mexican" image was more true to the actual Novarro than the current public perception of him. Publicity aside, until personal crises and the pressures of stardom gradually eroded his capacity to cope with the disparate elements within, Novarro *did* believe that his "sovereign power" was capable of adjusting itself "to every possibility and every chance that might befall." After all, he had survived a revolution and serious economic privations to become the protégé of one of the top directors in the industry and a film star of the first magnitude.

Even after the old adage "All's for the best" had become a hollow phrase repeated by force of habit, Novarro's quest for inner peace continued. If happy moments were fleeting, he at least endeavored to experience them during his religious retreats, while alone at El Rosario, in the company of his few close friends, and perhaps even when together with some of the young men he paid for sex and companionship.

More than a pretty face heavily promoted by one of the top directors and by one of the top columnists of the era, the young Novarro was an ambitious and highly capable performer who created some of the most indelible characterizations of the silent and early sound era. More than merely a compulsive drinker and patron of young hustlers, the older Novarro was a troubled Catholic who, setting aside his "god within," struggled to suppress his nature and to conform to outside religious and cultural norms. For him to be chiefly remembered today as a perverted elderly homosexual killed by a sex toy that never existed is an injustice to both the complex individual and to the accomplished—and historically important—actor that was Ramon Novarro.

Afterword

In 1975, nearly six years after his conviction, Tom Ferguson petitioned the presiding judge of San Joaquin County to appoint an attorney to file an appeal or reopen his case. Tom's petition was largely based on Joel Harrison's investigation, including his discovery of the written statements by Paul. As a result, Tom was released from prison on probation and was placed on a work furlough program the following year. After violating the terms of his probation, he was returned to prison, but was paroled on June 15, 1977.

After his release, Tom worked in a board and care home in Grand Rapids, Michigan, and later at the Sonoma State Hospital in California. In the 1980s, he was accused of raping a middle-aged woman. He avows his innocence, but pleaded no contest at the time in a deal with prosecutors. He was sentenced to eight years in jail, and was paroled in 1990. Seven years later, he was sent back to prison after failing to register as a sex offender within the allotted time required by California law. Tom Ferguson, now fifty-one years old, is serving a six-year sentence at the California Medical Facility in Vacaville.

Upon his arrival at San Quentin, Paul Ferguson felt, in his own words, "extremely angry and bitter." After months of despondence, Paul began dividing his time between the prison's firehouse and writing courses, graduating in 1974 with an associate of arts degree in epistemology (a branch of philosophy dealing with the origin, nature, and limits of knowledge). The following year, he won $100 as first prize for fiction from the P.E.N. Prison Writing Committee for "Dream No Dreams," a short story about a peace-loving hippie arrested in Cook County, Illinois. He also taught creative writing courses to fellow inmates and was praised by wardens and civic groups for his efforts in stilling racial violence among prisoners.

Paul was paroled one year after Tom, on July 17, 1978, after serving nearly nine years of his life sentence for first-degree murder. He was discharged in 1981. Paul continued writing sporadically and developed his own construction business, working as a steeplejack and builder throughout the United States, and also in Mexico and Ecuador. He eventually settled in Poplar Bluff, Missouri, where he owned a nightclub and served as a rodeo promoter.

In March 1989 Paul was arrested on charges of first-degree rape and sodomy. He affirms his innocence, asserting that he has the necessary documentation to support his claim, and blames local politics and a corrupt legal system for his conviction. During the trial, the prosecutor mentioned an earlier murder charge against Paul, though apparently neither names nor details were given to the court. Paul was sentenced to sixty years in prison, but had his time cut in half through an appeal. Now fifty-six years old, he has served ten years of his thirty-year sentence. While in jail, he has written numerous short stories and articles, an unpublished novel about "a half-blood Indian in today's America," and his version of this latest arrest and conviction. In the manuscript, "The Rape of the Red Ryder" (Paul was known as "the Red Ryder" while at San Quentin), he angrily attacks the Missouri legal system.

"Mr. Novarro's death still affects me," Paul Ferguson says, "both personally and in society. It pretty much crashed my world and the dust has never settled."

Sister Guadalupe, who lived in a convent in Coyoacán, near Mexico City, died in 1973. Rosa, who had adopted her older sister Guadalupe's name when she became a nun, died in 1978. Leonor, who had renounced her vows in the 1930s, married in the early 1940s and later moved with her husband to Coyoacán. Maintaining her religious ties, she managed the finances of Sister Guadalupe's convent. Leonor and her husband retired to Chula Vista, California, just north of the Mexican border, where she died in 1990.

Antonio tried his hand at a variety of projects, from writing short stories to promoting three-dimensional motion pictures, but finally settled at the Twentieth Century–Fox sound department. He died in 1988, after suffering a heart attack in the parking lot of a Los Angeles restaurant.

Luz, the sister with whom Novarro had danced as extras in *The Four Horsemen of the Apocalypse,* died in 1991 after a long illness.

Mariano, the brother with whom Novarro had traveled north in 1916, initially practiced dentistry in Tampico, Mexico, but later returned to Los Angeles, where he opened an office in the downtown district. An aviation fanatic, he was for a time nicknamed "the Flying Dentist." He died in 1993.

Eduardo was involved in numerous architecture projects, including the Screen Actor's Guild building in Hollywood. He eventually retired to the San Diego area, where he died in early 1999 following a stroke.

Carmen, Novarro's dancing partner in the 1930s and early 1940s, abandoned her show business aspirations as she approached middle age. Like her brother Ramón, she developed an alcohol problem. She died in 2000 in a San Diego suburb.

At the time of this writing, Angel, now in his early nineties, lives in the San Diego area.

Marion Morgan's pantomimic style of dancing faded from popularity with the coming of sound in the late 1920s. Morgan, however, continued working, and is credited for the dance sequences in the films directed by her lover Dorothy Arzner. The couple also coauthored the stories on which the Mae West vehicles *Goin' to Town* and *Klondike Annie* are based. Morgan died in 1971 in the California desert resort of La Quinta, where she had lived with Arzner for twenty years.

After antagonizing Irving Thalberg, Cedric Gibbons, and Louis B. Mayer during the making of *Ben-Hur,* Ferdinand Pinney Earle never worked for a Hollywood studio again. In the late 1920s, Earle kidnapped his ten-year-old son Eyvind from his estranged wife and moved to Europe, where he conceived Charles Boyer's ascension to heaven in Fritz Lang's *Liliom* in 1934 and the panoramic views of Jerusalem in Julien Duvivier's 1935 biblical film *Golgotha.* The Nazi invasion of France abruptly ended Earle's European career. In later years, Earle worked as a portrait artist until his death of a heart attack on July 13, 1951.

In 1945, nearly two decades after his last important film role, Malcolm McGregor, Novarro's early rival at Metro Pictures, died at age fifty-two of burns suffered after falling asleep with a lit cigarette.

. . .

Despite having his career revived by *Ben-Hur*, Francis X. Bushman suffered another professional downturn in the late 1920s. He was also wiped out by the 1929 stock market crash, which left him more than $100,000 in debt. A Chicago newspaper reported at the time that Bushman "would marry any woman who could support him in the manner to which he was accustomed." There were no takers.

In later years, Bushman played small roles in numerous pictures, including *David and Bathsheba*, *Sabrina*, and *The Story of Mankind*. His last film appearance was in *The Ghost in the Invisible Bikini* in 1966. He died on August 23 of that year, after a fall in his Pacific Palisades home.

George Walsh retired from films in 1936. In later years he became a horse trainer at the ranch of his brother, film director Raoul Walsh. In 1981, he died of pneumonia at the age of ninety-two in the Los Angeles suburb of Pomona. According to his son, George Walsh II, Walsh never blamed Novarro for the *Ben-Hur* fiasco, though he believed the Mexican actor was ill-suited for the part because of his slight physique. Throughout Walsh's life, *Ben-Hur* remained a painful topic.

Following *Ben-Hur*, Fred Niblo directed several important productions, including *The Temptress* and *The Mysterious Lady* with Greta Garbo, *Camille* with Norma Talmadge, and the *The Enemy* with Lillian Gish. The coming of sound, however, ended his Hollywood career. He left MGM in 1930, and later attempted to revive his prestige in England. That venture was a complete failure. Niblo died of pneumonia at the age of seventy-four in 1948. Enid Bennett, his widow and Novarro's leading lady in *The Red Lily*, died in 1969.

In the mid-1930s, not long after transferring the Valley Oak house to Novarro, Louis Samuel moved into another house designed by Lloyd Wright, at 579 Bundy Drive. In the mid-1960s, Samuel once again contracted with Wright to build a house for him and his second wife, but ill health forced him to cancel the plans. He died in 1975.

. . .

Noël Sullivan, Novarro's ardently Catholic friend and fellow lover of music, died of a heart attack on September 15, 1956, at the age of sixty-five. He was buried at the Carmel of the Infant Jesus at Santa Clara monastery.

After a handful of appearances in German films and a brief marriage to actress Camilla Horn (rumor had it that the couple only lived together), Novarro's singing teacher Louis Graveure left Germany in 1938. In a 1939 letter to Madame Clara Novello Davies, his former singing teacher in England, the "Belgian" Louis Graveure finally confessed that he was indeed the Englishman Wilfred Douthitt, and begged her forgiveness. She responded with an invitation for Graveure to sit at her box in the Drury Lane Theatre to watch a performance of her son Ivor's latest musical, *The Dancing Years*.

Graveure died in Los Angeles in 1965 at the age of seventy-seven.

William Haines quit films in the mid-1930s after starring in two pictures for Poverty Row studio Mascot Pictures. Haines later became a well-known interior designer. He died of cancer in December 1973. Jimmie Shields, Haines's companion for nearly half a century, committed suicide the following March.

Cecil Everley, Novarro's companion during the *Royal Exchange* ordeal, developed into a successful painter. He died of cancer in 1989.

Florence "Pancho" Barnes, four times married and four times divorced, died of cancer in 1975. She was portrayed by Kim Stanley in the 1983 motion picture *The Right Stuff*.

As the years passed, Novarro and Elsie Janis saw each other with decreasing frequency, but they remained on friendly terms until her death in 1956.

In March 1939, Richard Halliburton and his ten-man crew, including his lover Paul Mooney, disappeared in the Pacific Ocean after encountering rough weather during a voyage on a Chinese junk from Hong Kong to the Golden Gate International Exposition in San Francisco.

.   .   .

Unlike numerous Hollywood personalities of the silent era, Rex Ingram—at least in part because of his wife's business acumen—died a wealthy man. Alice Terry inherited his vast art collection, their San Fernando Valley estate, and $200,000 (nearly $1.5 million today). One year after Ingram's death, Terry sued Columbia Pictures for $750,000 on the grounds that the studio's fictionalized motion picture *Valentino* showed a character representing her having an affair with Rudolph Valentino both before and after her marriage to Ingram. She won a six-figure out-of-court settlement.

With the passing of the years, Terry, considerably heavier than in her youth, became increasingly reclusive. After the death of Gerald Fielding, her lover of many years, in 1956 (he was forty-six years old), Terry spent much of her time painting and reading film magazines and books about old Hollywood. Novarro was one of the few friends with whom she socialized.

Shortly after her sister Edna died in 1984, Terry's mind began to falter. Nearly senile, she died of pneumonia on December 22, 1987, at the age of eighty-eight. *Mare Nostrum*, in which she plays a mysterious Mata Hari–like spy, remained Terry's favorite film, for she thought it the only picture that gave her a chance to act.

With the exception of Anita Page (*The Flying Fleet*), who lives in the Los Angeles area; Dorothy Janis (*The Pagan*), who until recently divided her time between Colorado and Arizona; Conchita Montenegro (*La Sevillana*), who resides in Paris; and Marian Marsh (*A Desperate Adventure*), who lives in Palm Desert, California, all of Novarro's leading ladies have passed on.

Novarro's longtime friend and literary executor Leonard Shannon lives in Goleta, California.

Novarro's former secretary Edward Weber resides in Massachusetts.

The Ramon Novarro Film Club in England continued to meet and publish its newsletter until 1984, when the dwindling number of members made the club impractical. Club secretary Audrey Homan died on July 24, 1992.

. . .

In 1944, Leonard Bernstein, Jerome Robbins, Betty Comden, and Adolph Green rented Novarro's former house at 5609 Valley Oak Drive, where they worked on the Broadway musical *On the Town*. Thirty years later, on July 17, 1974, the Los Angeles Cultural Heritage Board declared the Valley Oak house a historic-cultural monument, becoming officially known as the Samuel-Novarro House.

Other former residents at 5609 Valley Oak include restaurateur Michael Chow, film producer Charles D. Kasher, and actress Diane Keaton, who bought the house for $1.5 million in November 1988. Following extensive renovation work, she sold it in the mid-1990s.

The Laurel Canyon residence, valued at $150,000, was sold on July 26, 1969, for $76,908 to screenwriter Clifford Newton Gould (*Krakatoa, East of Java*). The house has changed hands several times in the last three decades, and has since been extensively remodeled.

In August 1971, Novarro's family sold his apartment building at 10938 Riverside Drive for $111,400 to a savings and loan institution. The building was later torn down, and the site has been turned into a car lot. The JCPenney building at 6454 Van Nuys Boulevard was sold in February 1977 for $275,000. It is now an office building.

In January 1984, the Novarro estate was discharged and the proceedings were divided among his surviving brothers and sisters and Edward Weber.

After Novarro sold the family mansion at 2265 West Twenty-second Street and Gramercy Place, the new owners emptied the pool, left the yard un-kempt, and stripped the house to pay the mortgage. The main building and adjacent structures, including Novarro's cherished Teatro Intimo, were razed in the mid–1960s to clear a path for the Santa Monica Freeway. Drivers heading east toward downtown Los Angeles pass over what once was the Samaniego estate.

As the years passed, *Ben-Hur*, the motion picture that would "remain, as the Bible remains," became but a distant memory of another era. Prior to the release of the 1959 *Ben-Hur* remake, MGM tried to ensure that no prints of the 1925 version were in circulation to avoid comparisons to the new product. Thus, Novarro's *Ben-Hur* remained a shadow of its former self for another thirty years, until Turner Entertainment and Britain's Thames Television sponsored the picture's restoration under the aegis of film historians Kevin Brownlow and David Gill. Missing footage was found, and the original color tints and the Technicolor sequences were restored with the help of a German collector and the Czechoslovakian Film Archive. With a new orchestral score by Carl Davis, the rejuvenated epic was shown to considerable acclaim at the 31st London Film Festival in 1988.

Abbreviations

AFI31–40. *American Film Institute Catalogue, 1931–1940*. Ed. Patricia King Hanson and Alan Gevinson (Berkeley: University of California Press, 1993).

AMPAS. Margaret Herrick Library, Academy of Motion Picture Arts and Sciences.

AT. Interview with author.

BRN. DeWitt Bodeen's "Ramon Novarro." *Films in Review*, November 1967.

CULS. Herbert Howe's "Close-Ups and Long-Shots" *Photoplay* column.

Ettinger. Margaret Ettinger's "To the Ladies—Ramon Novarro." *Picture-Play*, June 1922.

HHF. Herbert Howe's article "Hollywood's Hall of Fame." *The New Movie Magazine*, August 1931.

Homan. Novarro's correspondence with Audrey Homan, courtesy of Isabel Turner and Matias Bombal.

HR. *The Hollywood Reporter*.

HRR. *Harrison's Report*.

LAE. *Los Angeles Examiner*.

LAH. *Los Angeles Herald*.

LAHE. *Los Angeles Herald Examiner*.

LAT. *Los Angeles Times*.

LT. Letter to author.

MGM-USC. MGM collection at the University of Southern California Cinema-Television Library.

MP. *Motion Picture*.

MPAA. Motion Pictures Association of America, Production Code Administration files at AMPAS.

MS. *Modern Screen*.

NMM. *The New Movie Magazine*.

NP. Novarro's proposal for his autobiography, courtesy of his literary executor, Leonard Shannon.

NYHT. *New York Herald Tribune*.

NYMT. *New York Morning Telegraph*.

NYT. *New York Times*.

O'Leary. Liam O'Leary's *Rex Ingram: Master of the Silent Cinema* (Dublin: The Academic Press, 1980).

OTRWR. Herbert Howe's "On the Road with Ramon," *Motion Picture*, February–June 1927.

Parade. Kevin Brownlow's *The Parade's Gone By* (New York: Knopf, 1968).

PIC. *Picture-Play*.

PP. *Photoplay*.

Pratt. George C. Pratt interview dated April 17, 1958.

RNFC. Ramon Novarro Film Club Newsletter.

Seitz. Cinematographer John F. Seitz's oral history transcript by James Ursini, from May 1971 through May 1972.

SL. *Screenland*.

Sullivan. Noël Sullivan Papers.

VT. *Variety*.

All box-office, cost, and profit or loss information about MGM films comes from the Eddie Mannix ledger, found in the Howard Strickling Collection at AMPAS, unless otherwise noted. Cost information for the Metro films (pre-MGM) is from the Metro Pictures Corporation cost records in the special collections at AMPAS, unless otherwise noted.

The information about Novarro's wages and contracts with Metro/MGM is from the actual contracts, courtesy of Turner Entertainment Group, and from the Eddie Mannix ledger, found at AMPAS. Wage information of other Metro and MGM players from mid-1921 to mid-1926 is also from the ledger.

OTRWR: A Roman numeral representing each installment will follow the abbreviation, e.g., OTRWR-II is Part II of the series, published in March 1927.

Pratt is found in the Richard and Ronay Menschel Library at the George Eastman House. Most of the interview was published in the December 1974 issue of *Image*, the magazine of the International Museum of Photography, as " 'It's Just Wonderful How Fate Works': Ramon Novarro on His Film Career" (pp. 187–194).

Seitz is found at the Louis B. Mayer Library, American Film Institute.

Sullivan is found at the Bancroft Library at the University of California at Berkeley.

Paul R. Ferguson's letters are quoted with permission from Mr. Ferguson.

Novarro's punctuation in both his manuscript and letters was inconsistent and erratic. It has been silently corrected throughout. Quotes from Novarro's unpublished materials are reproduced with permission from Novarro's literary executor, Leonard Shannon.

Interviews with the author are referred to as AT, and are preceded by the interviewee's name and the year the interview took place. Letters to the author are referred to as LT, and are preceded by the sender's name and the date.

Preface

xiv "one mistake I did not make" William Krehm's "Where Is ... Ramon Novarro?" *Saturday Evening Post*, January 15, 1944.

xiv "gentle, gentlemanly version" Novarro's obituary notice. *VT* (Weekly), November 6, 1968.

xiv "one of the most charming..." Richard Watts, Jr.'s review of *In Gay Madrid*. *NYHT*, June 7, 1930.

I: Mexican Roots

Unless otherwise noted, quotes and general information on the background of the Samaniego family are from a series of interviews conducted in 1998 and 1999 with several family members, including Carmen Gavilán and Father Eddie Samaniego, S. J., and from Eduardo Samaniego's memoirs, courtesy of his son, Father Samaniego.

The information about the origin of the Samaniegos in Spain is from Alberto and Arturo García Carrafa's *Diccionario Heráldico y Genealógico de Apellidos Españoles y Americanos* (Madrid: Hauser y Menet, 1959) and their *El Solar Vasco Navarro*, volume 6 (San Sebastian, Spain: Librería Internacional, 1967).

Nicolas Cheetham's *New Spain, the Birth of Modern Mexico* (London: Victor Gollancz, 1974) provided a comprehensive historical background of the colonization of Mexico, while John Mason Hart's *Revolutionary Mexico: The Coming and Process of the Mexican Revolution* (Berkeley: University of California Press, 1987) was an excellent source of information about the Mexican Revolution, and Gustavo Casasola's *Historia Gráfica de la Revolución Mexicana* (Mexico City: Editorial F. Trillas, 1960) was equally helpful for its description of Durango's siege.

1 "Get Out Your Maps!..." *PP,* January 1923, p. 77.

1 The half-Moorish prince was one of the sons of King Fortun Garces and his wife, Aurea. The prince founded the Casa Solar San Meder, or House (Dynasty) of San Emeterio, near the village of Samaniego. The name "Samaniego" is said to be a corruption of the Latin "Samaniacum," or "Place belonging to Saman." The Gaelic noun "Saman" (Celts inhabited the Iberian Peninsula prior to the arrival of the Romans) can be translated as "summer's end" or "last harvest." Herbert Howe's assertion in OTRWR-I that the name Samaniego is of Greek origin seems baseless.

1 Eduardo Samaniego states in his memoirs that his ancestors received the title of Counts of the Sierra Gorda. One problem with this tale is that the Count of the Sierra Gorda was a Spaniard named Juan José de Escandón, who received that title from King Fernando VI of Spain in 1749 for his role in the colonization of Nuevo Santander (today's Mexican state of Tamaulipas). Perhaps there had been other Counts of the Sierra Gorda, or perhaps Eduardo meant another count: Manuel Samaniego, made a count by the Spanish crown in the mid-1600s and granted a *condado,* or county, in an area that encompassed sections of what are today the Mexican states of Sonora and Chihuahua. An article by fine arts professor and Universidad del Valle de México researcher David Charles Wright Carr, found on the Web site *México Desconocido,* offers detailed information about Juan José de Escandón.

2 María Josefa's mother was Ana María Ortíz. Her father was Fernando de Delgado.

2 The information about Father Ramón Ortíz comes mainly from Samuel E. Sisneros's article "El Paseño, Padre Ramón Ortíz: 1814–1896," found in the fall 1999 issue of *Password,* and from Dr. Frank Halla's dissertation "El Paso, Texas, and Juárez, Mexico: A Study of a Bi-Ethnic Community, 1846–1881" (Austin: University of Texas, 1978).

Father Ortíz's actions against the United States armies led to his arrest by the American forces and his eventual removal to the city of Chihuahua. During the trek, he witnessed the catastrophic defeat of several Mexican armies, which induced the activist and well-connected padre to leave the Church in order to run for the Mexican congress. He eventually won a seat in Mexico City and voted against the peace treaty with the United States (which nevertheless was approved). After a few more political disillusions, Father Ortíz returned to his religious work in El Paso del Norte, where he died of cancer in 1896 at the age of eighty-two. His funeral, attended by thousands, was reportedly the largest in the city's history.

2 The Samaniego land was located in an area known as "Chamizal." According to an undated clipping from the Mexican newspaper *Ultimas Noticias* (author's collection), in 1966 Novarro and two siblings entered a claim for $57 million against

the United States government, as money owed them for the decades during which the Samaniego land had remained in American hands. This report, which gave erroneous names for both of Novarro's siblings, could not be confirmed.

3 Dr. Mariano Samaniego Delgado died of cancer in 1905. He was seventy-three.

4 Legend has it that throughout Durango's history, many buildings were destroyed and left in ruins for years. These sites became breeding grounds for poisonous scorpions, which multiplied so rapidly that they became a deadly threat to the local population. Thus Durango's other nickname, *la ciudad de los alacráns*, the city of scorpions.

4–5 The information about the Samaniegos' house and Novarro's childhood. OTRWR-I, p. 21.

4 The information about Señora Samaniego's "tithes." NP, p. 1.

5 Novarro's birth certificate, dated February 6, 1899, can be found at the Church of Jesus Christ of Latter Day Saints' Los Angeles Family History Center. Several sources, as early as a *Hollywood Blue Book* of the 1920s, strangely cite Novarro's birth date as September 20, 1901.

5 "wonderful summers..." BRN, p. 528.

6 "You're the first of your race..." Lenore Coffee's *Storyline: Reflections of a Hollywood Screenwriter* (London: Cassel & Company, 1973), p. 70.

6–7 The information about the Samaniegos' family and religious rituals. OTRWR-I, p. 105.

6 "Compliments were never paid..." OTRWR-II.

8 The description of Novarro's activities at Mascarones. OTRWR-I, p. 104.

8 "questionable ideas" Ruth Biery's "Why Ramon Novarro Decided to Remain in the Movies." *PP*, ca. 1929.

8 "to die a martyr and be canonized." Allan Ellenberger's *Ramon Novarro* (Jefferson, N.C.: McFarland, 1999), p. 9.

9 "but I was rapt to Heaven and did not mind." OTRWR-I, p. 105.

9 "In Mexico City the Opera..." Bradford Nelson's "The Grand (Opera) Young Man." *SL*, July 1929, p. 54.

9 "Perhaps it was the devil..." OTRWR-I, p. 105.

10 The information about Novarro's train ride to the United States. OTRWR-I, p. 106, and Pratt.

10 "Maybe he was just testing us." Pratt, p. 188.

2: Arrival in Paradise

The information about the Samaniegos' early years in the United States comes from a series of 1998 interviews with several family members, including Novarro's sister Carmen Gavilán. Details about the house fire are from Eduardo Samaniego's memoirs.

General references to Los Angeles history and the city's Mexican community come from numerous sources, mainly a series of 1998 interviews with Father Michael Engh, S. J., professor of history at Loyola Marymount University; Antonio Ríos-Bustamante and Pedro Castillo's *An Illustrated History of Mexican Los Angeles*

(Berkeley: University of California Press, 1986); and Rodolfo Acuña's *Occupied America: A History of Chicanos* (New York: HarperCollins, 1988).

The information about Mexican immigration in the 1910s is chiefly derived from the following sources: *Mexicans in California. Report of Governor C. C. Young's Mexican Fact-Finding Committee* (R and E Research Associates, Publishers and Distributors of Ethnic Studies, 1930); *Mexican Immigration to the United States* by Manuel Gamio (Chicago: The University of Chicago Press, 1930); and Rodolfo Acuña's *Occupied America: A History of Chicanos.*

The description of Los Angeles in the late 1910s is from Thoreau Cronyn's series of articles titled "The Truth About Hollywood," which appeared in the *New York Herald* from March 19 to April 2, 1922. Thoreau's articles can also be found in Bruce Long's *Taylorology* Web site.

Much of the information about the shooting of *The Rubaiyat of Omar Khayyam* comes from several issues—from the fall of 1919 to the summer of 1921—of *Camera* magazine, a Los Angeles–based film magazine of the 1910s and early 1920s in the style of *Variety.* Courtesy of Anthony Slide.

12 "My mother thought..." Carmen Gavilán, 1998 AT.

13 Different sources give dates ranging from 1914 to 1917 for Novarro's arrival in Los Angeles, partly because of widespread confusion about his first screen appearance that apparently began with DeWitt Bodeen's *Films in Review* article about Novarro. Bodeen erroneously states that the Christmas Day, 1916, release *Joan the Woman* was Novarro's first film appearance—an impossibility, as Novarro had arrived in town a mere four weeks earlier. Actually, Bodeen meant the October 1917 release *The Woman God Forgot,* which has the same director (Cecil B. DeMille) and stars (Geraldine Farrar and Wallace Reid) as *Joan the Woman.* (In Pratt, Novarro named *The Jaguar's Claws,* released in June 1917, as his first film appearance.)

In OTRWR-III, Herbert Howe has Novarro recalling his Los Angeles arrival nine years prior to his 1924 Roman Thanksgiving during the making of *Ben-Hur.* Howe should have reported *eight* years.

13 The information about Dr. José Samaniego. Los Angeles city directories of the 1910s and the 1920 census.

14 "my motto was..." OTRWR-II. Novarro's being expelled from the set by Neilan is from Pratt.

14 Recent publications have erroneously credited Novarro as playing an injured French soldier in *The Little American,* even though there is little resemblance between the two actors. According to OTRWR-II, Novarro played a German soldier in that picture. Novarro's piano playing for Geraldine Farrar is from HHF.

14–15 Among the artists Ramón modeled for was future art director and costume designer Harold Grieve, with whom he would cross paths shortly after finishing his test for *The Prisoner of Zenda.* According to Grieve, who had been hired by Ingram as one of *Zenda*'s set designers, the young hopeful approached him and said, "Hello." Grieve, perhaps because his former nude model had his clothes on, failed to recognize him. Despite this halting start, Ramón and Grieve eventually became good friends. Grieve's meeting with Novarro is from Grieve's unpublished memoirs, courtesy of Anthony Slide.

15 Novarro's belief in Coué. Herbert Howe's "What Are Matinee Idols Made Of?" *PP,* April 1923, p. 41.

15 The story about Novarro's approaching Farrar, Mary Garden, and others is from HHF and BRN. In OTRWR-II, Novarro is quoted as saying that he also sang at a restaurant, passing out from hunger at one point.

15 The remark about Novarro not wanting acting training. Betty Lasky's "Yesterday's Star." *The Player's Showcase,* vol. I, no. 4 (summer 1965).

Edward Everett Horton was known for befriending struggling young actors. "Before Clark Gable got a break in *The Last Mile,* he used to hang around the Majestic," Horton told Hedda Hopper in later years. "I remember coming in for a matinee one time and this tall, handsome guy was asleep in my dressing room. 'I hope you don't mind, Mr. Horton,' he said. 'They told me it was all right to come in here when you aren't using the room.'" From "Hedda Hopper's Hollywood." *Chicago Tribune–N.Y. News Syndicate,* May 30, 1965.

16 "doing each one with equal skill." Louella Parsons's "Ramon Novarro." *NYMT,* January 28, 1923.

16–17 The information about Marion Morgan and *Attila and the Huns* is from NP, Pratt, and Judith Mayne's *Directed by Dorothy Arzner* (Bloomington: Indiana University Press, 1994). In OTRWR-I, Herbert Howe says that Novarro was found by Morgan while he was working as an extra in a film, but other sources have Morgan first seeing Novarro at the Majestic.

16 "quite the most beautiful thing of the year." Mayne's *Directed by Dorothy Arzner,* p. 40.

17 Ernest Belcher also taught Shirley Temple, Loretta Young, John Gilbert, and Gower Champion. He directed prologues for films and became the first choreographer to have his work presented at the Hollywood Bowl.

18 "I didn't take the work seriously..." Herbert Howe's "What Are Matinee Idols Made Of?" *PP,* April 1923, p. 104.

18 The quotes by Lina Basquette, unless otherwise noted, are from her autobiography, *Lina: DeMille's Godless Girl,* edited by Mary Garland Jonas (Fairfax, Va.: Denlinger's Publishers, 1990).

18 Basquette's mother remark about Ramon being a "sissy," and Basquette's n "insanely jealous of man..." are from Allan R. Ellenberger's *Ramon Novarro* (Jefferson, N.C.: McFarland, 1999). Besides daydreaming about Novarro, Basquette also danced with him at several functions. According to Basquette's recollections, one of these was a performance of *Carmen* at the July 8, 1922, opening of the Hollywood Bowl. Novarro's appearance seems highly doubtful, however, as his name is not listed in the show's credits and he was by then already working for Rex Ingram.

18 "When D. W. used to come in..." *LAHE,* October 31, 1968, pp. A-I, 3.

19 The information about Novarro's test for Griffith is from OTRWR-II. In this article, Herbert Howe also claims that five years after the test Griffith invited Novarro to appear in one of his "greatest productions," but Novarro refused because of his contract with Ingram. In *Los Angeles: City of Dreams* (New York: Grosset & Dunlap, 1935), author Harry Carr does Howe one better by claiming that Griffith saw Novarro perform a piece of his own authorship in which he played

all the parts, including the girl in the balcony, her ardent lover down below, and both parties to a duel, one of whom gets killed.

19 "I sometimes wonder..." DeWitt Bodeen's "Ramon Novarro." *The Silent Picture*, no. 3 (summer 1969), p. 4.

19 Derisive quotes from the press about Valentino are from Michael Morris's *Madam Valentino: The Many Lives of Natacha Rambova* (New York: Abbeville Press, 1991). Although Novarro never became friends with Valentino, he did befriend Natacha Rambova.

20 Some sources state that Novarro was Valentino's stand-in at one point, but this is untrue. Valentino had only one major starring part before Novarro landed important roles in *The Rubaiyat of Omar Khayyam* and *The Prisoner of Zenda*. This story was apparently the result of a Latin Lover identity switch, for Valentino did have Don Alvarado as his stand-in during the making of *Cobra*.

20 The "woman in black" story. Leonard Shannon, 2001 phone AT.

20–21 Dr. Samaniego appears in the city directory with the occupation "dentist" next to his name, but he never actually practiced in the United States.

21 "a first-class nut in the family..." NP, p. 5.

22 "No one seemed especially interested." DeWitt Bodeen's *From Hollywood* (New York: A. S. Barnes and Company, 1976). After Goldwyn's refusal, Richard Dix, while working in *The Wall Flower*, sneaked Novarro into the studio and shot a test of him. He tried to get Goldwyn interested once again, but to no avail. After turning down the lead as a Jewish Russian immigrant in *Hungry Hearts*, Dix suggested Novarro for the part, but the producer, probably unable to imagine the slight Mexican in a role tailored for the big and rugged Dix, hired the beefier Bryant Washburn instead. (The studio mentioned in *From Hollywood* is Paramount, not Goldwyn. This is inaccurate, as both *Hungry Hearts* and *The Wall Flower* were Goldwyn productions. Dix only became a Paramount star nearly three years after his involvement with Novarro is supposed to have occurred.)

Another story has Antonio Moreno sneaking Novarro into the Vitagraph lot to get him work as an extra. That seems improbable. Moreno was a serial star then. If he wanted to help anyone get a job, he would have done so openly.

22 For his appearance in *Man—Woman—Marriage*, Ramón was also provided with his own dressing room and had meals served to him.

23 The addition of an *s* to Samaniego is discussed in several sources, including Novarro's memoirs and OTRWR-II.

23 The explanation for Ferdinand Earle's "Affinity Earle" nickname. Fay Wray's autobiography, *On the Other Hand: A Life Story by Fay Wray* (New York: St. Martin's Press, 1989), and Eyvind Earle's *Horizon Bound on a Bicycle* (Los Angeles: Earle and Bane, 1990).

Ferdinand Earle was the brother of well-known film director William P. S. Earle. Among William Earle's most elaborate pictures is the 1923 production *The Dancer of the Nile*, with Malcolm McGregor and Carmel Myers.

24 Ferdinand Earle's quotes about *The Rubaiyat*, unless otherwise noted, are from the January 14, 1922, issue of *Camera*.

24 "Ramón came to the front door..." Eyvind Earle, 1999 phone AT.

24 "My object has been to create a dream world..." and "The privilege of enjoying beauty..." *NYMT*, February 26, 1922.

24 "just thought I was terrible." Pratt.

24 Earle bitterly complained about "the taint of commercialism" that was infecting the arts. "In the seven years I have devoted to the screen," he asserted, "I have witnessed many splendid photodramas ruined by intruding upstarts and stubborn imbeciles." Whether Ahrens was a "stubborn imbecile" or not, the law determined that irrespective of Earle's contractual agreement, The Rubaiyat Co. was the real owner of the film and could edit and release it at will. In order to press the lawsuit, Earle had to resort to a technicality. Since he had never transferred the rights to his script to the producing company, he tried to prevent Ahrens from releasing *The Rubaiyat of Omar Khayyam* with such titles as "That bird is getting to talk too much!" In protest of the disregard for Earle's artistic integrity, composer Charles Wakefield Cadman refused to turn over to the production company the music he had created especially for *The Rubaiyat*.

24 "there was too much artistic aroma." *NYMT*, undated, found in Earle's file at AMPAS.

24 The $65,000 amount is from a December 18, 1925, letter from Earle to Irving G. Thalberg, found at MGM-USC.

24 "It may never be shown to the public..." Ettinger.

24 "Two solid hours vanished as but a minute..." William E. Wing review found in *Camera*, September 9, 1922.

The Rubaiyat remained shelved until a "friendly agreement" was reached between Earle and his backers in September 1922. Earle signed a new contract, which gave him—once again—complete control over the final cut. It was then announced that Earle's "motion painting" was finally to be released (at a now undetermined date) as *Omar*, but that did not come to pass.

25 Eyvind Earle discusses the similarities between the effects and decor of *The Thief of Bagdad* and those of *The Rubaiyat* in his *Horizon Bound on a Bicycle*.

25 "Khayyam" translates into English as "Tentmaker."

25 Novarro's story about *Monte Cristo* is from Pratt and from his memoirs. He doesn't mention the name of the director who saw him in *The Rubaiyat*, but J. Emmett Flynn directed *Monte Cristo*. There is a possibility, however, that Flynn's assistant director, Robert Florey, was the "director" Novarro was talking about.

25 The information about the Hollywood Community Theater is mainly from the March 1920 issue of *Theatre Magazine*.

3: Ramon's Columbus

26 "will be hailed..." Robert Sherwood review found in the March 24, 1921, issue of *Life* (a magazine somewhat in the style of *The New Yorker*, not to be confused with the "new" *Life*).

26–27 While working as an extra in *The Four Horsemen*, Novarro's sister Luz initially thought that the handsome Rex Ingram—not Valentino—was the star of the picture.

27–28 Information about Rex Ingram. O'Leary, unless otherwise noted.

27 "The world's greatest director." Kevin Brownlow's *Hollywood, the Pioneers* (New York: Alfred A. Knopf, 1979), p. 205.

Rex Ingram was one of the editors of Stroheim's *Greed*. After reducing the film's initial forty-two reels to twenty-four, Stroheim refused to cut the picture any further and asked Ingram to continue the job. Ingram had his trusted editor, Grant Why-tock, who had already worked with Stroheim, handle the task. Whytock reduced *Greed*'s length to eighteen reels, though Joseph Farnham was responsible for the final ten-reel version and received sole credit as editor. The information on the editing of *Greed* can be found in O'Leary and in Richard Koszarski's *The Man You Love to Hate: Erich von Stroheim in Hollywood* (Oxford, U.K.: Oxford University Press, 1983).

29 The story about Mathis's resentment of Ingram. Seitz, p. 182.

According to Seitz, Valentino left Metro because of his fights with Ingram. On the last shooting day of *The Conquering Power*, Valentino wanted extra time for dinner because it was his birthday, but Ingram refused his request, saying, "He's no better than the rest of us." Valentino is said to have signed with Famous Players–Lasky the next day. (Famous Players–Lasky distributed its pictures through Paramount. Later in the decade, Paramount became the official name of the producing company as well.)

31–33 The information about the making of *The Prisoner of Zenda* comes mainly from O'Leary, and from AMPAS files on Ingram, Novarro, Alice Terry, and *The Prisoner of Zenda*. Both Novarro and Ingram discuss the picture in their respective memoirs.

The Prisoner of Zenda had already been (cheaply) filmed twice in the 1910s. Since film techniques were being developed at breakneck speed, Metro's version of Hope's novel would be remarkably more sophisticated than its predecessors.

29 The story about Ingram picking Novarro out of the ranks of extras. "The Man in the Mob," *PP*, February 1924.

29 "That was studio publicity—the usual bunk..." BRN, p. 530. Novarro, however, did perform in a live prologue for *The Conquering Power* at a Miami theater during the making of *Where the Pavement Ends*. In the prologue, he played the Valentino role, entering a dark room and rescuing Alice Terry from her father while proclaiming that love conquers all.

30 "Ingram was impressed with the boy..." O'Leary, p. 96.

30 "Mr. Ingram was looking for a 'Rupert'..." Ettinger.

30 "so prettily, all shining white..." Adela Rogers St. Johns's "The Haunted Studio." *PP*, December 1927, p. 31.

30 "When I went to the Metro casting office and asked to see Mr. Ingram..." BRN, p. 530.

30 "My dear Mr. Ingram..." is from Novarro's memoirs. This letter of intro-duction was one of the few mementos from those days that Novarro kept. A photograph of the letter can be found at AMPAS. In BRN, Novarro says that Mary O'Hara was the one who suggested that Earle write the letter.

Earle's letter was rewritten—probably by Metro's publicity department—when published in fan magazines. That version reads: "Dear Mr. Ingram: Columbus made a great discovery on this day. I believe you will too. Here is an artist." This "Earle letter" first surfaced in "The Man from the Mob."

30 "I had my make-up kit with me ..." BRN, p. 531.

31 "When Mr. Ingram ran that [third] test off ..." Ibid.

In later years, Novarro asserted that Ingram had signed him to a personal contract at $125 a week, but he is listed in the Metro payroll ledger during the shooting of *Zenda* as a studio employee at a salary of $100 week. However, Ingram theoretically could have given him an extra $25 each week.

31 "It's just wonderful how fate works." Pratt.

31 Lewis Stone had already played the dual roles in a stage version of *The Prisoner of Zenda.*

31 "a lot of fencing, a lot of hard work, very happy." Pratt.

31–32 The information about Alice Terry comes from a variety of sources, including O'Leary, film magazines of the 1920s, and a June 3, 1973, taped interview with Liam O'Leary found in the Liam O'Leary Archive at the National Library of Ireland. During a 1998 phone interview, New York Public Library video and film historian Joseph Yranski recalled conversations with actor-agent Alan Brock about Terry's immediate rapport with Novarro.

32–33 The Novarro-McGregor incident. Anthony Slide, 1998 AT.

33 "murdered by the front office ..." and "twice as erotic." Michael Powell's *A Life in Movies* (London: Heinemann, 1986).

33–34 Much of the information about Barbara La Marr's life is from Adela Rogers St. Johns's "The Girl Who Was Too Beautiful" (*PP,* June 1922) and from a series of interviews with La Marr researcher James Bangley. In the late 1910s, La Marr was often credited as Barbara La Marr Deely. Years later, Louis B. Mayer named another dark-haired beauty after her, Austrian-born Hedwig Kiesler, who was transformed into Hedy Lamarr.

34 The story about Paul Bern's suicide attempt. Adela Rogers St. Johns's *Love, Laughter and Tears: My Hollywood Story* (Garden City, N.Y.: Doubleday and Company, 1978), p. 150.

34 "Her radiance is that of moonlight ..." O'Leary, p. 113.

34 "It took three of us ..." Michael Powell's *A Life in Movies.*

35 "Very soon you will be seeing in print ..." Novarro's memoirs. Howe mentions Novarro's chubbiness and acne problem in HHF. Novarro discusses Ingram's initial desire to mold him as a new Valentino in Pratt.

35 "Alice really was remarkable ..." Pratt.

35–36 Ingram's resentment toward Valentino was returned. In a 1923 article for *Movie Weekly,* "The Romance of Rodolf [another temporary alternate spelling] Valentino's Amorous Life," Valentino says that Paul Powell was the director from whom "I learned more of the technique of the screen than from anyone else." Ingram is completely ignored in the piece.

36 "the few who could pronounce it ..." "Get Out Your Maps!" *PP,* January 1923, p. 77.

36 Novarro's official name change. "Meet Mr. Novarro," *LAT,* April 26, 1924.

36 Ramón Samaniego's transformation into Ramon Novarro. OTRWR-II and Novarro's memoirs.

36 While Metro's program for *The Prisoner of Zenda* and studio stills of *Where the Pavement Ends* announced "Ramon Navarro" as the lead, the program for *Trifling Women* heralded "Ramon Novarro."

36–37 *The Prisoner of Zenda* reviews: *Moving Picture World*, May 6, 1922; *PP,* June 1922.

Several critics who saw *The Prisoner of Zenda* before Novarro's name change identified him as "Samanyagos" in their reviews.

38 "I want to tell you that..." Ettinger.

39 The story about Griffith's refusal to use Valentino in *Scarlet Days*. Richard Schickel's *D. W. Griffith: An American Life* (New York: Simon and Schuster, 1984).

39 "black-eyed brigade." B. W. Sayres's *Who's Whose in Hollywood: A sorta Saga of Screenland* (no publisher named, 1926), p. 23. B. W. Sayres was probably a pseudonym used by an industry insider. The book can be found at AMPAS.

39 In his autobiography, *The Public Is Never Wrong* (New York: G. P. Putnam's Sons, 1953), Paramount head Adolph Zukor states that Valentino's "acting was largely confined to protruding his large, almost occult, eyes until vast areas of white were visible, drawing back the lips of his wide, sensuous mouth to bare his gleaming teeth, and flaring his nostrils."

4: Ascendant Star

41 *Trifling Women* reviews: *HRR*, October 14, 1922; *NYT*, October 4, 1922; and *VT*, October 6, 1922.

41 "Moonlight on tiger skins..." Michael Powell's *A Life in Movies* (London: Heinemann, 1986).

42 "was the finest thing he had seen." Pratt. According to Novarro, Goldwyn had been particularly impressed by a scene in which Rupert of Hentzau uses only his eyes in an attempt to seduce Antoinette de Mauban.

42 "he looked very sad..." BRN, p. 532.

42 "Mr. Ingram is the one that believed in me..." Pratt. Novarro's agent—who had done nothing to help the actor find work—was so desperate to have his client sign with Goldwyn that he tried to get Novarro's parents involved in the deal, much to the actor's dismay. Although Novarro does not explicitly state so in Pratt, he seems to have severed ties with the agent (whose identity is unknown) at that time.

42 "You have no business being grateful in this business..." Ibid.

42 "You are capable of doing the work..." Ibid.

In later years, Ingram complained that he found little appreciation from those whose careers he advanced. The three exceptions were Novarro, Willis Goldbeck, and John F. Seitz.

43 "If Goldwyn didn't have anything for me..." BRN, p. 532.

43 The *NYMT* article about the Goldwyn offer appeared on January 7, 1923.

Goldwyn conceivably offered Novarro a contract that at the *end* of two years would give the actor $2,500 a week. His initial salary, however, would have been considerably lower.

43 Marshall Neilan's and Paul Bern's remarks. Pratt.

43 In OTRWR-III, Ingram is quoted as saying that Novarro was "Michelan-

gelo's David with the face of an El Greco Don" (p. 86), to which Novarro quipped, "That proves what Mary Pickford once said—my face and my body do not match" (BRN, p. 532).

44 Ingram at first wanted ex–matinee idol Maurice Costello, known at the height of his fame as "the Dimpled Darling," to play the heavy in *Where the Pavement Ends.* "But it was the villain's role," Ingram later remarked, "and Costello would have everybody liking him better than they did the hero" (O'Leary, p. 117). The director thus settled for Vitagraph player Harry T. Morey.

44 "I worshiped the man" and assorted mishaps during the production of *Where the Pavement Ends* are from Pratt.

44 The information about the alternate endings of *Where the Pavement Ends. PIC,* February 1923.

45 "if it is the logical thing" and "making a mistake in trying..." "Novarro Sees What's Wrong." *LAT,* April 1, 1923.

45 *Where the Pavement Ends* reviews: *NYT,* April 2, 1923; *PP,* May 1923; and *VT,* April 5, 1923.

In the March 1932 issue of *New Movie Magazine,* Herbert Howe stated that *Where the Pavement Ends* was his favorite Ingram picture.

45 "I say to a man who criticizes Mr. Ingram..." and other quotes and information in this section provided by Louella Parsons are from "Ramon Novarro." *NYMT,* January 28, 1923.

47 According to the September 1922 issue of *Photoplay,* Valentino's fan mail slumped 50 percent after he was accused of bigamy.

47 Thoreau Cronyn's remarks are from "The Truth About Hollywood." *New York Herald,* March 19 to April 2, 1922. The text can also be found in Bruce Long's *Taylorology* Web site.

A February 19, 1922, letter to the editor of the *Louisville Courier-Journal* exemplifies the public sentiment at the time. The writer asserts that "the present abnormal prevalence of juvenile delinquency, together with the unusual 'crime wave' in general," is attributable to the movie screen, which, "through its various forms of heroized criminality and its exaltation of the salacious vampistic heroine is no small factor as an influence for crime and immorality." The letter can be found in Bruce Long's *Taylorology #11* Web site.

48 Although the Hays Office had the semblance of a governing body, its rules were frequently ignored by the studios. Consequently, states and counties still found it necessary to rely on their own censors.

48 "Members of the Paramount Stock Company..." Harry Carr's column "The Hollywood Boulevardier Chats." *Classic,* September 1922.

48 "chum and most intimate friend." *PP,* October 1923.

49 "crowded with Hollywood ingenues." Gavin Lambert's *Nazimova* (New York: Alfred A. Knopf, 1997), p. 249.

49 "They don't like me to say it..." Herbert Howe's "What Are Matinee Idols Made Of?" *PP,* April 1923, p. 104.

49 "it doesn't seem quite fair to me..." J. Warren Kerrigan's *How I Became a Successful Moving Picture Star* (Los Angeles, 1914. No publisher identified, apparently self-published).

50 "the screen's perennial bachelor." *PP*, January 1926. In "The Life of Eugene O'Brien," found in a *Movie Weekly* issue circa 1922, O'Brien says that he will not marry until he finds another woman as nice as his mother.

50 "Ramon Novarro has made a personal friend..." S. R. Mook's "Public Enemies of Hollywood." *Screen Book*, July 1934.

50–51 Metro won the rights to film *Scaramouche* through an arrangement with Charles L. Wagner, who owned the theatrical rights to the story. The Broadway presentation of *Scaramouche*, which opened in New York at the Morosco Theater on October 24, 1923, had Sidney Blackmer as André-Louis Moreau and Margalo Gilmore as Aline. Owing to stage fright, Alice Terry had refused to play opposite Blackmer.

51 Because of their resemblance to the actual historical figures, future montage expert Slavko Vorkapich was picked as Napoleon, while three of the picture's fifteen hundred extras were chosen to play Robespierre, Marie Antoinette, and Louis XVI.

51 The story about Ingram's unending celebration at the start of *Scaramouche* is from Seitz (p. 131). While filming the Parisian mob on their way to the Tuileries, instead of "La Marseillaise," the director had the studio orchestra strike up "Back to Erin," "The Wearing of the Green," and other patriotic Irish songs.

51 On September 15, 1923, shortly after the final cut was assembled, *Scaramouche* had a special premiere at the Belasco Theater in Washington, D.C., under the auspices of the Red Cross's relief fund for Japan's catastrophic Kanto earthquake. There is no mention of Novarro's being present, but Ingram was there to thank the audience for their enthusiastic reception.

51 The *Scaramouche* reviews: *NYT*, October 12, 1923; *VT*, September 20, 1923; and *LAT*, undated issue.

51 According to Cobbett S. Steinberg's *Film Facts* (New York: Facts on File, 1980), cinema attendance in 1924—forty-three million filmgoers a week—was 10 percent higher than in 1922, while film production had been reduced by nearly 25 percent during that same period. Both eventualities helped to propel *Scaramouche* to box-office heights not achieved by *The Prisoner of Zenda*, for the French Revolution epic had a potentially larger audience and fewer competitors.

52 Novarro's choice of *Scaramouche* as his favorite picture. *MP*, September 1926.

53 "Ingram felt a strange affinity..." O'Leary, p. 129. Other information about the making of *The Arab* is from O'Leary, Pratt, and OTRWR-II.

54 "The world to Ramon Novarro..." Louella Parsons's "Ramon Novarro." *NYMT*, January 28, 1923.

55 Novarro's "romance" with Edith Allen. *PP*, September 1923, p. 93.

55 "touched a secret spring to [Ramon's] confidence..." OTRWR-I, p. 20.

55 Herbert Howe's family history is from the 1900 census for Minnehaha County, South Dakota, and from Dana R. Bailey's *History of Minnehaha County, SD* (Sioux Falls, S.D.: Brown & Saenger, 1899). The information about Howe's early career is chiefly from the July 10, 1921, issue of the *New York Morning Telegraph* and from Adela Rogers St. Johns's "Our Herb," found in the November 1923 issue of *Photoplay*.

55 "trying to see France..." CULS, *PP*, February 1926.

56 "the most polished form of wit." St. Johns's "Our Herb," p. 54.

56 "The secret of Herbert Howe's success..." Ibid, p. 124.

56 "It seems that no one..." *PP*, June 1924, p. 58.

56 Howe's "An Evolution Trial at the Zoo." *PP*, October 1925.

56 "My advice concerning your daughter is..." Howe's "Suppose It Were Your Daughter?" *PP*, February 1926.

56 Howe's quip regarding Fitzgerald's *The Vegetable*. CULS, *PP*, August 1923.

56 The Anna Q. Nilsson article. *PP*, April 1929.

56 The "Mr. Dante's Hollywood." CULS, *PP*, February 1929, p. 127.

56 "Enlarged Cabinet of Dr. Caligari." CULS, *PP*, November 1925, p. 54.

56 Howe's reading interests. "The Answer Man" column. *PP*, April 1925, p. 111.

57 In the October 1923 issue of *Photoplay*, Howe wrote in his column, "I would like to know just who it was that started the pretty young man vogue in the films? Whom shall we blame—Rex Ingram? Then lead him on for the slaughter."

57 "a pallid personality..." HHF, p. 62.

In OTRWR-I, Howe stated that his only impression when he first met Novarro was "youth," adding, "I don't think I'd ever met anyone so young." (Howe's first interview with Novarro was published as "What Are Matinee Idols Made Of?" in the April 1923 issue of *Photoplay*.)

57 "At first thought..." OTRWR-III, p. 36.

Howe liked to say that he was a descendant of Sitting Bull. He explains in OTRWR-III that after his "ancestor" took down with a cold, he had to drink in one sitting a bottle of whiskey given him by Irish settlers, "thus getting the name of Sitting Bull—his ensuing conversation supplying the idea for the last name."

57 "He made me think of one of those bounding bright-eyed fox terriers..." HHF, p. 62.

57 "a predilection for the gents of sepia finish." *PP*, February 1925.

57 "Tony introduced me to Hollywood..." *PP*, February 1925. Howe's association with Antonio Moreno is discussed in Howe's "The Untouched Portraiture." *MP*, February 1921.

57–58 Lawrence Quirk's remarks about Howe, 1998 AT.

58 "Herb Howe is Ramon Novarro's best friend..." *PP*, April 1926.

58 "no one outside of [Novarro's] family..." OTRWR-III, p. 37.

58 "Imagine more my surprise..." *PP*, August 1929, p. 44.

58 "eyes so mesmerize a mood..." OTRWR-I, p. 20.

60 "virtual slavery." CULS, *PP*, February 1926, p. 53.

60 "The desert—also the South Sea islands..." and "disgusted." Pratt.

60 "carelessness at times was exasperating..." OTRWR-II. Once, Ingram became so irate that he forbade Novarro to sing or play his piano. According to Howe, the star spent his daily singing-practice hour softly touching the piano keys and singing silently, with a handkerchief in his mouth. "I don't think I've felt any scene quite so much," Howe wrote, "for I understood instinctively: His devout respect for Rex, to whom he felt he owed everything, at war with his sacred love for music, which is his very life."

60 "For God's sake, try to look interested!" Herbert Howe's "Secrets of Hol-

lywood's Happy Divorces," *NMM*, November 1933, p. 97. Howe does not say he is referring to Novarro and *The Arab*, but the subject of his story is clear.

60 "He was embarrassed by direct demonstrations." OTRWR-II.

60–61 *Thy Name Is Woman* reviews: *Life*, March 7, 1924; *NYT*, March 4, 1924; *VT*, March 5, 1924.

61 Adela Rogers St. Johns's remark about Mathis's love for Ingram is from an unsourced clipping found in the June Mathis file at AMPAS.

62 "a sudden change..." *Parade*, p. 447.

62 Much of the information about the merger of Metro, Goldwyn, and Mayer companies is from Bosley Crowther's *The Lion's Share* (New York: E. P. Dutton, 1957) and John Douglas Eames's *The MGM Story: The Complete History of Fifty-four Roaring Years* (London: Octopus Books Limited, 1979).

62 "My sympathies are all..." *PP*, August 1921, p. 54.

62 Ingram's intense dislike for Louis B. Mayer. O'Leary, and Alice Terry's friend, film historian Anthony Slide, 1998 AT.

63 *The Arab* reviews: *NYT*, July 14, 1924; *VT*, July 16, 1924.

63 "youth and personal magnetism." *HRR*, July 19, 1924.

63 The details of Ingram's acquisition of the Victorine studios near Nice can be found in O'Leary, p. 166.

63 Ingram's nervous breakdown. *Movie Weekly*, June 1925.

64 The information about Alice Terry's affair with Gerald Fielding and the Ingram-Terry living arrangements is from a 1998 interview with Anthony Slide. Slide and Alan Brock's friend Joseph Yranski were the sources for stories about Ingram's relentless curiosity about sexual matters. In the March 1932 issue of *The New Movie Magazine*, Herbert Howe wrote, "Rex talks Oriental philosophy—but Alice has it. She's a buddha for non-attachment. Even in human relationships she is not possessive. That is the secret of her marital continuity." Terry's longtime friend Jack Hewson told the author about Ingram's affairs with several women, including García. Hewson recalled a woman asking Terry at a party in the early 1950s, "How could you have Rex's last four mistresses at your party?" "Oh, simple," Terry replied. "*I* ended up Mrs. Rex Ingram."

64 The information about Ingram's male live-in companion. A close friend of Novarro, 1999, AT.

64 "Isn't that boy a wonder?..." *PP*, November 1923.

64 "Rex had an eliciting faith in Ramon..." OTRWR-V, p. 95.

65 The introduction to *Contra la corriente* can be found in Juan B. Heinink and Robert G. Dickson's *Cita en Hollywood* (Bilbao, Spain: Ediciones Mensajero, 1990), p. 306.

65 Ingram's remark to Novarro that he work with well-established directors is from BRN, p. 533.

5: "How Fate Works"

Most of the information about the making of *Ben-Hur* comes from the *Ben-Hur* files at MGM-USC (including salary information); the *Ben-Hur* files at AMPAS; the Ruth Waterbury article "A Modern Miracle Film," found in the March 1926 issue of *Photoplay*; the article "The *Ben-Hur* Fiasco" (attributed to A. Chester Keel—

possibly a pseudonym), found in the November 1924 issue of *Photoplay*; Bosley Crowther's *The Lion's Share* (New York: E. P. Dutton, 1957); and *Parade. Ben-Hur* historian T. Gene Hatcher was another invaluable aid.

66 The information about the West Twenty-second Street residence is from interviews with several family members, including Carmen Gavilán, and from OTRWR-IV. The price Novarro paid for the house can be found in the Los Angeles County Hall of Records.

The West Adams district was first developed at the end of the nineteenth century. Architectural styles varied from Victorian and California Craftsman to Colonial revival and Mission revival. By 1910, West Adams had become the most desired Los Angeles neighborhood. (Theda Bara and Fatty Arbuckle were two of the area's residents later in the decade.) With the advent of the automobile, neighbors began complaining about noise and traffic, which led many of the original residents to move farther west to the Hancock Park district. After World War I, several apartment buildings were built and some of the old mansions were torn down.

67 Novarro mentions his family's inability to understand his film stardom in his memoirs. The fur coat example is from a 1998 interview with Carmen Gavilán. Dr. Samaniego's morphine problem is mentioned in Eduardo Samaniego's memoirs.

67 The story about Dr. Samaniego's blindness. Madeline Glass's "What Is His Mystic Power." *PIC*, August 1930, p. 43.

68 "They shall go to school." Herbert Howe's "What Are Matinee Idols Made Of?" *PP*, April 1923, p. 104.

68 Novarro asserted in a May 4, 1967, letter to DeWitt Bodeen (found at AMPAS) that Mariano "didn't have the talent or desire for an acting career." Yet, Mariano worked as an extra in several films, is supposed to have appeared as Mariano Novarro in the 1923 Constance Talmadge picture *The Dangerous Maid*, and kept himself busy with evening acting classes. Ultimately, that minor role in the Talmadge picture was as far as Mariano's film career ever got.

68–69 *The Red Lily* reviews: *NYT*, September 29, 1924; "sordid" is from *PP*, October 1924; "hackneyed" and "prime specimens of degraded humanity" are from *VT*, October 1, 1924; and "revolting" is from *HRR*, August 9, 1924.

68 "quite a good picture." Novarro's memoirs, p. 12.

69 In another instance, exhibitors picked Tom Mix as the country's number one male box-office draw of 1926 and 1927, the years when John Gilbert was breaking box-office records with *The Big Parade, La Bohème*, and *Flesh and the Devil*. Mix (also possibly Haines) was popular in small-town theaters, where admission prices were low and the number of seats was small. However, most of the studios' money was made in the larger and pricier, though considerably less numerous, urban movie palaces.

69–70 Lewis Wallace had final approval over the stage production. That was one crucial condition for his selling the dramatics rights to his book to Klaw and Erlanger. Following Wallace's demand, Jesus was implied in the theater production by a shaft of light. Wallace's contract also stipulated that Klaw and Erlanger's rights to the story would lapse if the play was not performed on a yearly basis.

Besides the sources mentioned at the beginning of this chapter, general information about Wallace comes from the 1914 *Green Book* written by Glenmore Davis.

70 Kalem, which released its brief version of *Ben-Hur* as *The Chariot Race*, was forced to pay $25,000 in damages.

70 According to *Ben-Hur* historian T. Gene Hatcher, after Klaw dissolved his partnership with Erlanger because of a series of financial disputes, Erlanger bought the film rights to the theatrical version of *Ben-Hur* from his former partner. Erlanger then sold these rights to his own Classical Cinematograph Corporation.

71 "She fairly lives and breathes motion pictures..." *NYMT,* February 10, 1924.

71 Mathis's salary. *LAT,* June 3, 1923.

71 "Success for *Ben-Hur* is already written..." *Camera,* June 16, 1923, p. 11.

71 Since Erlanger was in agreement with the proposal, in the summer of 1923, future radio program host Major Edward Bowes, then a vice-president of Goldwyn Pictures, and studio account executive J. J. Cohn sailed for Europe to appraise Italian film production facilities and personnel. The promise of financial cooperation from an Italian film company helped convince Godsol to set up production in that country.

71 "The questions of the hour are..." *NYMT,* January 7, 1923.

72 "we wouldn't be surprised if..." *PP,* September 1923, p. 27.

72 As late as September 1923, there were rumors that an agreement for Valentino's services between Goldwyn and Famous Players was pending.

72 "I want you to know if I am fortunate..." and "Ben-Hur, the most coveted of all..." Ettinger.

73 "the best picture of 1940." *PP,* May 1923, p. 57.

73 It has been said that Brabin was selected after the independent-minded Marshall Neilan refused Goldwyn's offer because he did not want to remain abroad for a whole year. However, Goldwyn's internal correspondence, found at MGM-USC, indicates that Brabin had been for weeks the clear favorite for the directorial post. According to those studio files, Brabin was to be paid $27,500 (approximately $282,000 today) for his work.

73 "has been a student of Bible history..." *NYMT,* September 30, 1923.

73 James Quirk asserted in the September 1923 issue of *Photoplay* that after Brabin had requested a mere $80,000 to make a picture at Goldwyn, the studio "where dollars are spent like [then nearly valueless] marks" said "not enough" and ordered him to spend $200,000. P. 27.

74 "was the only one of the screen players..." *NYMT,* January 6, 1924.

In the early 1920s, Francis X. Bushman participated in a successful vaudeville tour with Beverly Bayne, his lover both on- and offscreen in his heyday and at that time his wife, but film offers had been scarce.

One actor June Mathis was unable to secure was *The Cabinet of Dr. Caligari*'s Conrad Veidt, whom she wanted for the part of Simonides. (Nigel de Brulier eventually played that role.)

74 "not only because of his ability as an actor..." An unidentified and undated clipping, possibly from the *NYMT,* found in the *Ben-Hur* AMPAS files.

74 "The cast would discourage me..." *PP,* March 1924, p. 76.

74 "the best goddamned part in the picture." *Parade,* p. 447. In Ruth Biery's "What Killed Francis X. Bushman?," a 1928 article for *Photoplay,* Bushman told a different story. He stated that when he heard there was a chance for him to play

Messala, he said to June Mathis, "June, I'm not Jesus Christ, and I can't walk on water, but I would if I can get a chance to play that role of Messala."

74 The information about Seena Owen's divorce suit is from *PIC*, July 1922. Her alleged attempt on Walsh's life is from a June 13, 1972, interview with Walsh conducted by Anthony Slide.

75 "It was no doubt Mr. Walsh's work..." *NYMT*, December 30, 1923.

75 "immediately converted us..." *NYMT*, ca. 1923, found in the *Ben-Hur* files at AMPAS.

75 "Many thanks..." February 7, 1924, wire, MGM-USC.

76 Mussolini as a "great assistance" to George Fitzmaurice. *NYT*, April 6, 1924.

Mussolini became furious when he discovered that Goldwyn was paying the Italian workers considerably less than their American peers, while other Italian high government officials were angered by the studio's decision to buy the costumes for the film in Berlin.

76 Francis X. Bushman arrived in mid-March. He later recalled being told by Brabin that his scenes would not be shot until August and so using the opportunity to tour with his sister in a vaudeville act in several countries.

77 "The worst Erlanger could do..." May 2, 1924, cable, MGM-USC.

77 "Personally I will be more than pleased..." May 20, 1924, letter, MGM-USC.

77 "million-dollar girl." *PP*, October 1923.

77 Mathis's unsuccessful collaboration with Niblo. *PP*, October 1926.

77–78 DeWitt Bodeen's affirmation that Mayer preferred Novarro to Gilbert is from his introduction to James Robert Parish and Gregory W. Mank's (with Richard Picchiarini) *The Best of MGM, the Golden Years: 1928–1959* (Westport, Conn.: Arlington House Publishers, 1981).

78 "You'll make the test in a hurry..." and other information about the encounter with Thalberg are from Pratt and from Novarro's memoirs. If Novarro had really been tested for the role of Ben-Hur as some historians have claimed, he would have told Thalberg to look at that test instead of at *Where the Pavement Ends*.

Years later, Novarro stated that Thalberg was the one responsible for his getting the role. "I was only 25 at the time," he recalled, "and Irving was three months younger than I. It was a case of youth seeing eye-to-eye" (*LAT*, September 28, 1965). Thalberg's influence may have been somewhat exaggerated in Novarro's recollections; the real decision makers in those early days were Louis B. Mayer and Marcus Loew. Furthermore, with John Gilbert unavailable, MGM's sole real option was their Mexican star.

79 Bodeen's story about Rex Ingram and *Ben-Hur* is from *The Best of MGM*, while Whytock's is from Michael Powell's *A Life in Movies* (London: Heinemann, 1986).

79 "I do not mean to deprecate Mr. Niblo..." DeWitt Bodeen's "Ramon Novarro." *The Silent Picture*, no. 3 (summer 1969).

80 "a very attractive man" and "never was much good." Pratt.

80 "Not for one tiny instant..." and the vision story are from Gladys Hall's "The Actor Who Knows That He Died." *MP*, January 1930, p. 40.

Novarro later wrote in his memoirs that he knew he was going to play Ben-

Hur because Rex Ingram had told him the role was his—if Ingram was to direct. Even after Ingram was passed over for the job, Novarro still believed he was going to play the Jewish prince, because "Mr. Ingram could never be wrong" (p. 12). Novarro made no mention of his "vision" then.

80 In Pratt, Novarro remarked that "*Ben-Hur,* without a spiritual message, would be just another spectacle." He added that at the time of the 1959 remake, he told producer Sam Zimbalist, "There's no reason why you shouldn't make a better picture the second time than [we] did the first." Yet, Novarro also believed that the technical advances of motion pictures notwithstanding, the new version would lose "the suggestion of the presence of divinity," an element essential to the success of the 1925 version.

80 "Success does not rest with us . . ." RNFC, January-February 1937.

6: Harrowing Triumph

As in the previous chapter, most of the information about the making of *Ben-Hur* comes from the *Ben-Hur* files at MGM-USC (including salary information); the *Ben-Hur* files at AMPAS; the Ruth Waterbury article "A Modern Miracle Film," found in the March 1926 issue of *Photoplay;* the article "The *Ben-Hur* Fiasco" (attributed to A. Chester Keel—possibly a pseudonym), found in the November 1924 issue of *Photoplay;* Bosley Crowther's *The Lion's Share* (New York: E. P. Dutton, 1957); *Parade;* and the generous help offered by *Ben-Hur* historian T. Gene Hatcher.

81 "The *Ben-Hur* expeditions . . ." *LAT,* June 22, 1924.

According to film historian Kevin Brownlow, June Mathis did struggle to keep the production afloat by offering Charles Brabin's job to several other directors—each of whom turned her down. By then, Mathis had lost her power and was thus unable to hold *Ben-Hur* together.

81 "The great injury I incurred . . ." March 1966 letter Walsh wrote to Brownlow. *Parade,* p. 452.

81 "If a bad beginning . . ." A. Chester Keel's "The *Ben-Hur* Fiasco." *PP,* November 1924, p. 32.

82 "Mr. Loew explains why they . . ." *PP,* January 1925, p. 92.

82 "Despite my own disappointment . . ." *PP,* October 1924.

Mathis asserted that Charles Brabin was supposed to direct only the intimate scenes, while an Italian or German director was to handle the crowd scenes. That plan had been altered after Brabin arrived in Rome and peremptorily seized control of the production.

82 "happier than she has been . . ." *NYMT,* August 3, 1924.

83 Cines became Cinecittà after extensive renovations in the 1930s.

83 "Niblo now has everything in hand . . ." June 30, 1924, telegram, MGM-USC.

83 "Condition serious . . ." July 4, 1924, telegram, MGM-USC.

83 "I inwardly breathe a prayer of relief . . ." September 23, 1924, letter, MGM-USC.

83 "Think of any great role . . ." *PP,* May 1924, p. 52.

83 "more enthusiastic than ever." July 14, 1924, letter, MGM-USC.

84 "Hollywood is still juggling . . ." *NYMT,* September 28, 1924.

The Circus Maximus set, for one, took so long to build that winter came and the lighting became unsuitable for filming.

84 "The Italians are the hardest-working people..." *Parade*, p. 126.

85 "Ramon Novarro wasn't any taller..." a July 10, 1973, interview conducted by Anthony Slide. *Films in Review*, May 1975, p. 318.

Carmel Myers, upon her June 9, 1924, arrival in Cherbourg, was detained by French police on suspicion of smuggling. After clarifying matters, she went to Germany to appear in *Garragon*, and only after that picture was finished did she go to Rome. Niblo had by then taken over the production, but Myers had so little to do at the Italian capital that she kept busy with other activities, such as posing for publicity pictures next to Roman ruins and presiding over a baby show. Claire McDowell, who was to play Ben-Hur's mother, and Frank Currier, the studio's choice to portray the kind Roman Quintus Arrius, arrived in Rome in late summer. The studio had come close to sending Wallace Beery over to play Sheik Ilderim, but besides being difficult to handle, Beery had become unavailable after signing with Famous Players–Lasky. MGM hired Anders Randolf instead, but Randolf proved inadequate and was replaced by Mitchell Lewis.

85 The March 1926 issue of *Science and Invention* provided additional details about the naval battle scene. According to *Parade*, shortly before filming Niblo discovered sharpened swords hidden on the deck of one of the galleys; the casting director had divided the extras into Fascists and anti-Fascists, with the hope of creating a more realistic battle. Someone thought the sharpened swords would make the battle even more realistic.

85 "It was a scary journey..." *Parade*, p. 459.

85 Tales that numerous extras drowned are likely false. Novarro, who was beside Niblo during the shoot, firmly asserted that there were no fatalities. The three extras rumored to be missing reportedly turned up a few days later farther down the coast, after having been rescued by a fishing boat. A miniature sea battle was later shot, with fewer contretemps, inside a studio tank and later edited into the life-size battle scene. Most of what is seen on-screen is the sea battle Niblo filmed in Italy.

85–86 Shortly after arriving in Rome, Mayer fell seriously ill with a tooth abscess and had to leave the Italian capital. Since production supervisor Harry Edington had also fallen ill, Alexander Aronson was called from Paris.

Once freed from the constraints of Mayer's close supervision, Niblo reacted to Aronson's presence like the independent-minded Rex Ingram would have. "[Niblo's] first statement to me in connection with [the production]," Aronson later complained in a December 26, 1924, letter to Mayer, "was that never in his career had he permitted anyone to make out a schedule for him." Niblo seized control of the production just as Brabin had done before him, and was reluctant to delegate any duties to assistant directors Christy Cabanne and Al Raboch (a holdover from the Goldwyn unit). The Aronson letter can be found at MGM-USC.

In Scott Eyman's *Five American Cinematographers* (Metuchen, N.J.: Scarecrow Press, 1987), cinematographer Karl Struss claims that MGM at one point thought of firing Niblo and replacing him with Cabanne.

86 Francis X. Bushman's chariot trampling Novarro's is from *Parade*, p. 464.

Bushman recalled seeing another incident at the Roman racetrack, when a driver flew through the air onto a pile of lumber after a wheel broke during practice (the driver later died of internal injuries). According to Bushman, horses were being sacrificed at an alarming rate. Whenever horses were hurt, he remarked, instead of calling a veterinarian, the production had them shot. This story cannot be confirmed. Somehow, Bushman's recollections of the making of *Ben-Hur* were considerably starker and bloodier than anyone else's.

86 Doubling for the doubles on the raft. "Novarro Used No Double in Raft Sequence." *LAT*, September 8, 1926. Novarro also mentioned that incident on a September 10, 1961, public service television spot, "Social Security in Action." In the 1959 remake, the raft scene was filmed inside a studio tank.

86–87 Novarro's collodion problems. OTRWR-III, p. 88.

87 "Sometimes when I cracked the stuff..." RNFC, March-April 1936.

87 "Nothing doing..." Pratt. Novarro says Raboch shot that sequence thirty-six times because MGM wanted three perfect takes for each scene instead of the usual two (one for the domestic and one for the foreign version). The third take was in color, for studio executives were unsure which kind of film they would use.

87 "Have definitely decided..." December 17, 1924, cable, MGM-USC.

87 "Great danger. Cast, organization..." December 22, 1924, wire, MGM-USC.

87 Howe's demand that he and Novarro stay at a different hotel is from Novarro's memoirs.

87 "or somewhere spelled something like that..." Herbert Howe's "How to Be Merry on Christmas Day." *PP*, January 1926.

87–88 Novarro and Howe's adventures in the south of France. Howe's "Ramon Novarro in Europe." *PP*, April 1925.

88 "He [Niblo] has met his Waterloo..." January 2, 1925, cable, MGM-USC.

88 "It was the coldest day..." *Parade*, p. 465.

89 "considerable temperament..." and "faithful cooperation..." January 17, 1925, letter from Aronson to J. Robert Rubin, MGM-USC.

In the March 1980 issue of *Films in Review*, Carmel Myers remembered Novarro as "perfectly charming and a perfect gentleman and absolutely wonderful to work with." After Novarro chastised her for saying "damn" on the set, she made sure never to utter that word again in his presence.

89 "Although I rebelled..." January 17, 1925, letter, MGM-USC.

89–90 "Whether he has a girl in Nice..." Ibid.

90 "Man after man came to me..." December 26, 1924, letter, MGM-USC.

90 "repeatedly stated to me..." January 17, 1925, letter, MGM-USC.

90 "He has not been the only one..." Ibid.

90 "It seems to me..." Ibid.

A holdover from the Brabin company, Bushman had been resentful of Mayer's involvement in the making of *Ben-Hur*. According to Gary Carey's biography of Mayer, *All the Stars in Heaven* (New York: E. P. Dutton, 1981), Bushman had never forgiven the studio head for persuading him and Beverly Bayne to appear in Mayer's second-rate serial *The Great Secret* back in 1917, when he was still an important star. Bushman also claimed that Mayer accused him of trying to steal scenes from

Novarro. To make matters worse for Bushman, he and Bayne separated in early 1925, and his previous wife began demanding higher alimony payments. When Bushman threatened to quit the production to travel to Egypt, an angry Mayer cabled Aronson, "If he quits *Ben-Hur*, that is finish of him in theatrical world, theater as well as pictures" (dated January 19, 1925, MGM-USC).

90 The *Paris Herald* article appeared on January 23, 1925.

90–91 Novarro and Howe in their *La France* cabin. OTRWR-III, p. 88.

91 "after having made scandalous tests..." *Scranton Republican*, March 2, 1925.

91 "everything we set out to do..." and "charming." *NYMT*, February 6, 1925.

91 "most cordial." *LAE*, February 10, 1925.

91 The arrival in Culver City was greeted with general enthusiasm and a sense of vindication by those who felt the *Ben-Hur* company should never have left California. The March 25, 1925, issue of *Preview* stated that the return of *Ben-Hur* "is the best proof in the world, too, for the fact that Hollywood is the place to make pictures" (p. 8).

91–92 Thalberg assigned art directors Cedric Gibbons and A. Arnold Gillespie to build the Circus Maximus in Culver City.

92 Novarro mentioned the doped lab technicians in a letter to columnist Jack Gordon, found in Gordon's column in the August 8, 1962, issue of the *Fort Worth Press*.

92 "After carefully working with Niblo..." March 22, 1925, cable from Mayer to Schenck and J. Robert Rubin, MGM-USC.

Lubitsch was between films at the time, and Warner's West Coast executives had green-lighted his loan to MGM. Perhaps either Nicholas Schenck or Marcus Loew vetoed Mayer's proposal, or Harry Warner was reluctant to loan out the studio's top director—whom he disliked. Or Lubitsch himself decided not to tackle a production that had brought down two respected directors, opting instead to direct an adaptation of Oscar Wilde's *Lady Windermere's Fan*.

93 In the *Midshipman* graduation ceremony, Novarro, who according to studio publicity was chosen for the part by "the officers of Annapolis" (OTRWR-III, p. 38), receives an (unsigned) diploma from the secretary of the navy.

93 Gilbert Roland's name change. *Los Angeles Daily News*, July 24, 1951. Despite his Spanish-sounding name, Duncan Renaldo was born in Romania. Don Alvarado was born José Paige in New Mexico. One side of his family was of Spanish ancestry.

94 *The Midshipman* review: HRR, October 17, 1925.

94 The navy's use of Novarro's likeness in posters. *VT*, October 24, 1925.

94 The information about Astor's tactics to enlarge Novarro's role in *A Lover's Oath* is from Pratt. In Pratt, Novarro also asserted that Astor hired another actor to play his part in newly filmed scenes. If that was true, it would have worked only in long shots.

94 *A Lover's Oath* review: *VT*, October 7, 1925.

95 The Nativity sequence, which was shot in two-strip Technicolor, required an actress capable of portraying purity and virtue as the Virgin Mary. Greta Garbo, who had been hired by Louis B. Mayer during his *Ben-Hur* foray in Europe, was reportedly considered for the virginal part, but instead landed the role of a vamp in *The Torrent*. Niblo wanted Lillian Gish, who had recently joined the

MGM star stable, but was not able to get her. Cabanne tested bit player Myrna Loy, but despite a blond wig and, in her own words, "a *fabulous* test," she did not get the part. The studio ultimately opted for Betty Bronson, fresh from her squeaky-clean Paramount success *Peter Pan*. (Myrna Loy was eventually cast as an extra in the Circus Maximus sequence.) According to *Parade*, Niblo was so displeased with Bronson's choice, even though in makeup she at least *looked* like Lillian Gish, that he refused to direct the scene. "A *fabulous* test" is from Loy and James Kotsilibas-Davis's *Myrna Loy: Being and Becoming* (New York: Alfred A. Knopf, 1987), p. 40.

95–96 Additional details about the shooting of the chariot race are from the March 1926 issue of *Science and Invention*. In an interview with Philip Jenkinson in the late 1960s, Novarro stated that he did not ride a chariot on the big racing day.

In spite of the star-studded attendance and the three thousand extras on hand, Thalberg wanted a larger crowd in the stands. So three hundred additional extras were pulled off the neighboring streets to fill in the empty spaces in the lower half of the Circus. The upper half, as seen on film, was actually a hanging miniature model with thousands of tiny puppets that, by means of levers, could sit, stand, and wave. Matching the contours of the life-size Circus to perfection, the miniature was shot simultaneously with the live action. On-screen, the dividing line between the actual set and the matte composition is impossible to discern.

Adding excitement to the proceedings, bonuses of $150, $100, and $50 were reportedly promised to the stuntmen who finished in first, second, and third place. (In *Hollywood*, a 1980 documentary by Kevin Brownlow and David Gill, Henry Hathaway says that studio comptroller Eddie Mannix offered $5,000 to the winner.) Ultimately, the actual winner that day made no difference for the picture, since close-ups of a victorious Novarro/Ben-Hur would be edited in later.

95 Novarro's $3 million insurance policy. *PP,* November 1925, p. 41.

96 "Through a miracle..." *VT,* November 18, 1959.

In the February 11, 1926, issue of the *New York Times,* Niblo said, "And some people will think that this scene is cruel to the animals. To blot out that idea, let me say that every horse and every man who figured in this accident was employed fifteen minutes later." In an interview for the *Indianapolis Times* published on August 8, 1962, Novarro stated that seven horses were killed.

96 "All of a sudden, smoke bombs went off..." *Parade,* p. 469. During a 1961 filmed interview for the Social Security Administration, "Social Security in Action," Novarro stated that his participation in *Ben-Hur* ended on December 25. A strange remark, considering that he already had left for New York on December 18.

96 "Things can be a little too long..." Pratt.

96 William Axt and David Mendoza composed a score for orchestras and organists to perform as accompaniment to the picture. According to T. Gene Hatcher, Axt and Mendoza worked on the score without having seen the assembled picture. They used existing operatic scores, including Jules Massenet's *Herodiade* and Jean Nougues's *Quo Vadis* to create a pastiche score of "respectable" music to match MGM's superspectacle.

Abraham Erlanger wanted changes made to the final edit, such as adding a beam of light to represent Christ, but Thalberg fought to maintain the picture as it was.

Thus, audiences were able to see Jesus' arms and hands, courtesy of New Zealand–born aspiring actress Nola Luxford.

97 Howard Hughes claimed that his troubled 1930 World War I aviation epic *Hell's Angels* was the most expensive motion picture ever, but its actual price was a relatively unimpressive $1.3 million (source: United Artists records in the Wisconsin Center for Film and Theater Research at the University of Wisconsin, courtesy of film historian David Pierce).

97 "Not only every Christian..." Quirk's "Speaking of Pictures." *PP*, April 1925, p. 27.

97 "Well kid..." December 31, 1925, cable, MGM-USC.

98 "We are an illusion..." Allan R. Ellenberger's *Ramon Novarro* (Jefferson, N.C.: McFarland, 1999), p. 93. Strangely, Novarro states in his memoirs that he *did* attend the New York premiere of *Ben-Hur*. Reports of the time say otherwise, and Howe, who was there, makes no mention of Novarro's presence in his description of that evening for *Photoplay*.

Another example of Novarro's reticence to appear at premieres: he did not show up at the November 1924 *Where the Pavement Ends* premiere in Italy, which was attended by Mussolini and other Italian high officials.

98–99 All *Ben-Hur* New York reviews appeared on December 31, 1925. Other reviews: *PP*, March 1926; *VT*, January 6, 1926. "[M]anly, handsome, heroic" is from the *New York World*; "the maturity and authority..." is from an unidentified, undated publication found at MGM-USC; and "strikingly vivid" is from the *New York Journal*.

98 The enthusiasm for Niblo's direction rested mainly on two scenes: the sea battle and, especially, the chariot race—which he did not direct. Even though Niblo received full credit for *Ben-Hur*, Eason went on to make a name for himself in the industry. Among other extraordinary action sequences he was responsible for are the land rush stampede in *Cimarron*, the burning of Atlanta in *Gone with the Wind*, and the train crash in *Duel in the Sun*.

99 "I have employed a dozen or more..." "Experiences with *Ben-Hur*." *NYT*, February 11, 1926.

99 "You give a great performance..." OTRWR-V, p. 118.

99 "reverent rendering of History's mightiest events..." and other information about the advertising for *Ben-Hur* is from that picture's file at AMPAS.

99 Although more prestigious than a regular motion picture house, the Biltmore lacked the appropriate equipment for showing films. A projector had to be hung on the second-floor balcony at an angle that sometimes gave the impression that the performers' neck and heads were unduly elongated.

99–100 "will, without doubt or reservation..." *LAT*, undated clipping, ca. August 3, 1926.

100 "the epic *par excellence*" is from a Cocteau essay in the July 26, 1938, issue of *Ce Soir*, found in *Jean Cocteau: The Art of Cinema*, edited by André Bernard and Claude Gauteur (London: Marion Boyars, 1992).

Francis X. Bushman claimed that *Ben-Hur* was banned in Italy once Mussolini discovered that the story's hero was not the Roman Messala, but a Jew. In reality, the picture played in that country, despite minor confrontations with local censors. A scene showing two Roman legionnaires losing their grip on Ben-Hur and another depicting the collapse of the Senatus Populesque Romanus had to be deleted. China, on the other hand, was a real trouble spot: *Ben-Hur* was interdicted on the grounds that the story promoted "Christian superstition." (This information is from the *Ben-Hur* file in the MPAA collection at AMPAS and from Wilbur Burton's "Chinese reaction to the Cinema," found in the October 1934 issue of *Asia* and cited in Kerry Segrave's *American Films Abroad* [Jefferson, N.C.: McFarland, 1997]).

100 The cost of the sequences filmed in Culver City was $1,861,326 (courtesy of Karl Thiede).

100 Critics' polls are from the 1926, 1927, and 1928 editions of the *Film Year Book*, edited by Joseph Dannenberg (New York: Film Daily, 1926–28).

98 The seductress Iras, described by Lewis Wallace as "a wonderfully beautiful woman . . . wanting nothing but a fitting mind to make her terrible as an army" (*NYMT*, December 30, 1923), has precious little time on screen. As played by Carmel Myers, she is not the least bit tantalizing.

101 "A less experienced actor . . ." Louella Parsons's "Famed Drama of *Ben-Hur* Wins Acclaim." *LAT*, August 3, 1926.

102 "As I sat there . . ." OTRWR-I, p. 107.

7: A Certain Young Man

103 After leaving the Hollywood Hills house he shared with his brother Milton, Herbert Howe moved to 513 Roxbury Drive.

103 "There's no better way of learning a fellow's character . . ." CULS. *PP,* February 1925.

103 Herbert Howe's "How to Be Merry on Christmas Day." *PP,* January 1926.

104 "gentle courtly mien you soon strike bronze . . ." OTRWR-IV, p. 114.

104 More than forty thousand mourners viewed Barbara La Marr's body during the three days it lay in state. The service at the Walter C. Blue Undertaking Chapel in Culver City was attended by thousands of mourners and stargazers. A riot ensued when the crowd broke through the police line and bolted toward the hearse in which the famous corpse was being laid. Five women fainted and had to be rescued by police to prevent their getting trampled in the melee. It took fifteen minutes for order to be restored so that the funeral procession could make its way to the Hollywood Memorial Park Cemetery.

The information about Barbara La Marr's illness, death, and funeral is chiefly from the articles "Barbara to Lie in State This Week" and "Women Riot at Star's Funeral," found, respectively, in the February 1 and 6 issues of the *Los Angeles Times;* the April 1926 issue of *Photoplay;* O'Leary; and a 1998 interview with La Marr researcher James Bangley.

104 Novarro and Howe's trip to Quebec. OTRWR-V.

105 The other nine in Adela Rogers St. Johns's list of the most handsome men on-screen were Lewis Stone, George O'Brien, Ben Lyon, John Gilbert, Richard Barthelmess, Reginald Denny, John Barrymore, Ronald Colman, and Richard Dix.

105–106 The information about John Gilbert is chiefly from Leatrice Gilbert Fountain's *Dark Star* (New York: St. Martin's Press, 1985) and Gilbert's series of articles, "Jack Gilbert Writes His Own Story," found in the June–September 1928 issues of *Photoplay.*

105 "When I kissed a lady..." Vincent X. Flaherty's "High-Powered Palpitations." *LAH,* September 4, 1949.

107 "more real American blood than..." Unidentified magazine article, ca. 1925.

107 "Ramon's Ancestors Greeted the Mayflower." *PP,* October 1925, pp. 46–47.

108 "don't ask him if he's Spanish..." *Beverly Hills Script,* June 7, 1930.

108 The information about *Patria* is from David Nasaw's *The Chief: The Life of William Randolph Hearst* (Boston: Houghton Mifflin, 2000). Shortly after the United States declared war against Germany, President Woodrow Wilson wrote to the serial's backer, William Randolph Hearst, asking that it be withdrawn, as Japan was then an American ally against Germany. Instead, the tycoon simply eliminated scenes showing the Japanese and Mexican flags.

108 In *The Memoirs of Will H. Hays* (New York: Doubleday, 1955), Hays states that the Mexican film ban, which had begun in mid-1922, was lifted in October through the interference of an envoy from the MPPDA. This incident led to the Production Code provision that "the history, institutions, prominent people, and citizenry of all nations shall be presented fairly" (p. 334). According to Kerry Segrave's *American Films Abroad* (Jefferson, N.C.: McFarland, 1997), Mexico also banned a number of American films in 1924 and 1927.

108 "any greaser that had insulted a white woman." Tom Mix's (probably ghostwritten) "Tom Mix's Own Story." *PP,* March 1925.

108 "Japs" and "colored folk." Herbert Howe's "How to Be Merry on Christmas Day." *PP,* January 1926.

108 "I would like to play in stories concerning my native people..." Gordon R. Silver's "Their Secret Ambitions." *The Film-Lovers' Annual 1932* (London: Dean and Son, 1932), p. 48.

109 "He keeps as aloof as Pola Negri..." Herbert Howe article, probably CULS. *PP,* May 1924.

109 "It is hard to write about..." Herbert Howe's "What Are Matinee Idols Made Of?" *PP,* April 1923, p. 104.

110 The information about *Bellamy the Magnificent/A Certain Young Man* is from that film's production files at MGM-USC and at AMPAS. In Pratt, Novarro states that *Bellamy* had been bought for John Gilbert. Since one major problem with the film was Novarro's obvious lack of "Englishness," one script version had him as a young man raised in Argentina and called back to England by an aunt. To solve another problem, Bellamy's unsympathetic nature, several new drafts had the warm and carefree Argentinian pressured into acting like the womanizing, foppish lord his father had been. The Argentinian nationality was later dropped.

110 "somehow seemed to be unconsciously conscious..." Memo (ca. 1926) found in the *A Certain Young Man* script files at MGM-USC.

110 To differentiate Novarro's picture from the John Gilbert vehicle *Bardelys the Magnificent,* *Bellamy the Magnificent* was initially retitled *The Heartbreaker* and later *The Man from London.*

III "artist who would one day..." CULS. *PP,* May 1926, p. 46.

III "robbed art of a true son..." Ben-Allah's *Rudolph Valentino: His Romantic Life and Death* (Los Angeles: Ben-Allah Company, 1926).

III "pink powder puff" and "Why didn't someone quietly drown..." *Chicago Tribune,* July 18, 1926.

III "Something has happened to the Valentino..." James R. Quirk's "Speaking of Pictures." *PP,* September 1924, p. 27.

112 "As Mark Twain once said..." "Studio News and Gossip" section, *PP,* July 1926, p. 109. According to the *Oxford Dictionary of Quotations,* Mark Twain actually said, "The report of my death is exaggerated."

112 "We must admit the seductive sway of perfume..." Advertisement found in undated issue of *Photoplay.*

112 "I cannot resist any one whose eyes..." *PP,* March 1925, p. 133.

112 "The stars of my day enjoyed a certain privacy..." BRN, p. 536.

113 "I know that not until late in my MGM career..." Ibid. Bodeen also quotes Novarro as saying that "the interior of my home was not photographed, and certainly not my bedroom or bathroom." Actually, his bedroom at the Gramercy house was photographed for publication, and so were numerous rooms in his Hollywood Hills home in the early 1930s.

113 "knock a fellow in the general direction of Heaven..." OTRWR-III, p. 87.

113 "one of the future Messrs. La Marr." *PP,* June 1924.

113 "the *Galahad* of pictures, but alas..." B. W. Sayres's *Who's Whose in Hollywood: A Sorta Saga of Screenland* (no publisher specified, 1926), p. 43.

113–114 "Sir Galahad's admiring audience and Greek chorus..." Ibid, p. 30.

114 "As for your other hero, yes, dear, it is indeed true..." Ibid, p. 57.

Among the dozens of film personalities B. W. Sayres discusses in *Who's Whose in Hollywood* are Cecil B. DeMille ("known also as God, and to the boys and girls as YES, MISTER"); Alice Terry and Enid Bennett ("Nothing, blonde, with influential meal tickets [Rex Ingram and Fred Niblo, respectively])"; and Marion Davies ("has splendid publicity man [lover William Randolph Hearst])."

114 "As a little boy, I used to envision myself..." Bradford Nelson's "The Grand (Opera) Young Man." *SL,* July 1929, p. 54.

114 "the glamour of costumes..." Ibid, p. 55.

115 "over there I will be judged..." "From Screen to Concert Stage." *Theatre Magazine,* January 1928.

115 "In addition to possessing a tenore robusto voice..." OTRWR-V, p. 118.

In 1911, Wilfred Douthitt suddenly disappeared after a performance at the Royal Albert Hall in London. During World War I, his music teacher, Madame Clara Novello Davies (Ivor Novello's mother), heard that he had joined the Canadian army and had been killed in action in Flanders. Years later, "the New Belgian Baritone," Louis Graveure, was announced at a concert at the Aeolian Hall in New York. Madame Davies was in attendance, and recognized him as her pupil Douthitt with a beard. Graveure, however, denied that he was Douthitt and that he owed Madame Davies money for unpaid singing lessons. This information is from Sandy Wilson's *Ivor* (London: Michael Joseph, 1975), courtesy of T. Gene Hatcher.

115 "It is so easy..." *LAH,* January 26, 1930.

115 "We worked six days a week..." BRN, p. 536.

116 The Spanish text of the Teatro Intimo opening invitation comes courtesy of T. Gene Hatcher.

116 "The direction was too good..." OTRWR-IV, p. 119.

116 "cling to the adage that there are no friends like the old friends..." OTRWR-IV, p. 117.

116–117 "never enter this theater." "From Screen to Concert Stage." *Theatre Magazine*, January 1928.

117 "Out of the darkness came the glory chant..." and following quotes in that paragraph. *PP*, October 1927, p. 81.

117 "When any of my family like my pictures..." Margaret Reid's "Directed by Ramon Novarro." *MS*, April 1931.

118 "it looks as though Alice..." "Studio News and Gossip—East and West" section, *PP*, October 1926, p. 94.

118–119 John Stahl's shooting methods. *Parade*.

Sylvia Thalberg, Irving's sister, cowrote the screen adaptation of *Lovers?* with Douglas Furber.

119 Details of Novarro's illness during the making of *Lovers?* "Ramon Novarro Is Seriously Ill with Influenza." *LAT*, October 6, 1926.

119 "I'd as soon have a chair as the typical man" and "the best actor of all..." O'Leary (p. 110) and the June 3, 1973, taped interview with Liam O'Leary found in the Liam O'Leary Archive at the National Library of Ireland.

In Pratt, Novarro says that Alice Terry wanted $25,000 to work in *Lovers?*, but Irving Thalberg told her she was not worth it. She agreed, but demanded the money anyway. Thalberg said he would give her $3,000 a week. She accepted the offer, as long as the studio also paid for her apartment, car, chauffeur, and maid. Thalberg agreed. Since Stahl rewrote much of the script, which led to several delays, Terry ultimately made $48,000 for her appearance in *Lovers?* "Irving, you're the best agent," she later told Thalberg. "From now on, you'll just work for me."

119–120 Novarro as Romeo, Faust, and Jesus comes from *PP*, August 1925 and September 1926, and from "MGM to film *Romeo and Juliet*," *LAT*, September 16, 1926. In 1936, an MGM rendering of *Romeo and Juliet* reached the screen starring Norma Shearer, then in her mid-thirties, and forty-three-year-old Leslie Howard as Romeo.

120 "The [MGM] Eastern office had to be consulted..." OTRWR-IV, p. 116.

120 *The Student Prince* ran for 608 performances after opening on December 2, 1924, at Jolson's Fifty-ninth Street Theater in New York. Romberg wrote the music; Dorothy Donnelly was responsible for the libretto, which she adapted from Aubrey Boucicault's adaptation of Wilhelm Meyer-Förster's play *Alt Heidelberg*. Although the motion picture was officially based on Meyer-Förster's novel, ads and some reviews understandably associated the MGM film with the Romberg musical.

120 Gavin Lambert mentions Stroheim as first choice for *The Student Prince* in *Norma Shearer*. Stroheim had doubled as assistant director and supporting player in a 1915 version starring Wallace Reid and Dorothy Gish, while two of his previous films, *The Merry Widow* and *Merry-Go-Round*, also had a theme similar to that of *The Student Prince*.

120–121 The information about Ernst Lubitsch, Norma Shearer, and the making of *The Student Prince in Old Heidelberg* is from the picture's files at AMPAS and at USC; Joanne D'Antonio's *Andrew Marton* (Metuchen, N.J.: Directors Guild of America and Scarecrow Press, 1991); Scott Eyman's *Ernst Lubitsch: Laughter in Paradise* (New York: Simon and Schuster, 1993); Herman Weinberg's *The Lubitsch Touch: A Critical Study* (New York: Dover Publications, 1968); Robert Carringer and Barry Sabath's *Ernst Lubitsch: A Guide to References and Resources* (Boston: G. K. Hall, 1978); Gavin Lambert's *Norma Shearer* (New York: Alfred A. Knopf, 1990); and Lawrence Quirk's *Norma: The Story of Norma Shearer* (New York: St. Martin's Press, 1988), unless otherwise noted.

120–121 Lubitsch was described by Robert Sherwood as "an extremely short, dark, thickset man, with ponderous shoulders and huge twinkling eyes...[resembling] a combination of Napoleon and Punchinello" (*The Lubitsch Touch: A Critical Study*, p. 103). In 1923, Mary Pickford imported him to the United States to direct her in the period melodrama *Dorothy Vernon of Haddon Hall*. Since he was unhappy with the screenplay, the director and his producer-star settled on another project, *Rosita*, an experience that, in spite of its financial success, proved so miserable for Pickford that she abruptly ended her association with Lubitsch. He then moved to Warner Bros.

120–121 "earnest ambition to work..." "Novarro Captivates Italy." *LAT*, January 11, 1925, p. III 34:2.

121 "never thought that Ramon Novarro..." D'Antonio's *Andrew Marton*, p. 36. In Pratt, Novarro, perhaps once again coloring his memories somewhat, says that Lubitsch was another director who "was very happy with me."

121 Norma Shearer had previously appeared in two pictures supervised by Thalberg, *He Who Gets Slapped* and *The Tower of Lies*. Their romance, however, had not yet begun flourishing.

121 "I'll do it again—and again." Philip K. Scheuer's "Novarro at 50 'Steals' Picture in Comeback." *LAT*, June 19, 1949.

122 "Frustrated actor." *Parade*.

122 Cost of *Three Women*. Eyman's *Ernst Lubitsch: Laughter in Paradise*.

122 "It was not one of my favorite films..." Quirk's *Norma*, p. 96. In Pratt, Novarro remarked that Lubitsch "had a very uncanny way of not telling you what to do, but of showing you... it was disturbing for an actor." But however "disturbed" he may have been, Novarro appreciated the nuances the director gave him about the appropriate Teutonic behavior the role required.

122 *Lovers?* reviews: *Motion Picture News*, June 10, 1927; *NYT*, April 19, 1927; and *VT*, April 20, 1927.

123 The information about the making of *The Road to Romance* is from the picture's files at MGM-USC and at AMPAS, including those in the MGM script collection and pressbook releases.

123 "it has been difficult for the adapter..." Farnum's treatment for *The Road to Romance*, MGM script collection at AMPAS.

123 The impressive 1926 Wampas Baby Star roster also included Mary Astor, Dolores Costello, Joan Crawford, Dolores del Río, Janet Gaynor, and Fay Wray.

123–124 The *Student Prince* reviews: *Life*, October 13, 1927; *NYHT*, ca. September

1927; *NYT*, September 22, 1927; *PP*, November 1927; and *VT*, September 28, 1927. Possibly because of copyright issues, *The Student Prince in Old Heidelberg* had a new score composed by William Axt and David Mendoza for cinema orchestras and organists.

124 Lubitsch's July 10, 1947, letter can be found in Weinberg's *The Lubitsch Touch: A Critical Study*, p. 286. The 1954 MGM remake was directed by Richard Thorpe and starred Edmund Purdom (whose singing was dubbed by Mario Lanza) and Ann Blyth.

124 The *Road to Romance* review, including "neat bit as a nance." *VT*, October 12, 1927.

124 "inconsequential." Pratt.

8: Crossroads

126 "Disappointments only came after..." OTRWR-IV, p. 116.

126 "I am grateful to motion pictures..." *Vanity Fair*, ca. 1927.

127 The title *China Bound* was allotted to one of the studio's low-budget comedy-adventure programmers with the duo of Karl Dane and George K. Arthur.

127 "very endearing, sincere, buoyant." Pratt.

127 George O'Hara had a small role in the 1921 release *A Small Town Idol*, one of the pictures in which Novarro danced with Marion Morgan's troupe.

128 "On a few occasions..." BRN, p. 537.

128 "What Bernhardt is to the stage..." *VT*, September 22, 1922.

128 "There are Elsie Janises born every day..." Anthony Slide's *The Encyclopedia of Vaudeville* (Westport, Conn.: Greenwood Press, 1994), p. 269.

128 "It was Elsie Janis..." BRN, p. 537.

129 "one of the world's ideal women." Undated clipping found at Novarro's files at AMPAS.

129 "always suited [Janis] better than girls'" and "was always romantically involved..." Anita Loos's *A Girl Like I* (New York: Viking Press, 1966), pp. 163–164.

129 "did everything but take..." Helen Hayes and Sandford Dody's *On Reflection, an Autobiography* (New York: M. Evans and Company, 1968).

130 "a favorite of the fair..." Howe's "The Hollywood Boulevardier" column. *NMM*, September 1930, p. 54.

130 "the finest write up a star could have had." January 3, 1938, letter, Homan.

130 "cool, detached, unsentimental" and other quotes in that paragraph. HHF, pp. 62–63.

131 José's illness. Eduardo Samaniego's memoirs and *LAT* and *LAH* press reports found in Novarro's AMPAS file.

131 With Novarro unavailable, Ingram used three other Mediterranean-looking actors in his latter pictures: Antonio Moreno in *Mare Nostrum*; Serbian-born Iván Petrovich in *The Magician, The Garden of Allah*, and *The Three Passions*; and Novarro look-alike Pierre Batcheff in *Baroud*. In its February 17, 1926, review of *Mare Nostrum*, *Variety* snidely remarked that Ingram had been "away from these shores a long time. It wouldn't do him any harm to take a jaunt back here if for nothing else than to sit around, talk with the boys, and glance over what they're doing in

picture work." The observation that *Mare Nostrum* was relegated to the side by MGM is from the October 1926 issue of *Photoplay*. After MGM declined to renew Ingram's contract, former Ingram fan Louella Parsons observed in the July 23, 1927, issue of the *New York American*, "My only surprise is that MGM did not take this stand a long time ago."

132 *Across to Singapore* reviews: *Film Daily*, May 6, 1928; *NYT*, April 28, 1928; and *VT*, May 2, 1928.

132–133 *A Certain Young Man* reviews: *NYT*, June 11, 1928; *VT*, June 13, 1928.

133 "In acting, in directing..." Margaret Reid's "Directed by Ramon Novarro." *MS*, April 1931.

133–134 *Forbidden Hours* reviews: *Film Daily*, July 29, 1928; *NYHT* (review by M.T. instead of the usual Richard Watts, Jr.), July 23, 1928; *NYMT*, July 22, 1928; *NYT*, July 23, 1928; *New York World*, July 23, 1928.

134 "for a long while been seen as a good little boy..." Regina Cannon, *New York American*, July 23, 1928.

134 "They made me play two or three characters..." Unsourced clipping, author's collection.

135 The information about Novarro's intention to join El Retiro comes from several sources, including Carmen Gavilán, 1998 AT; Ruth Biery's "Why Novarro Decided to Remain in the Movies," *PP*, October 28; and *LAHE*, October 31, 1968.

135 "I have a theory of my own about Novarro..." Harry Carr's "What Is the Mystery of Ramon Novarro?" *Motion Picture Classic*, October 1925.

135 "One can perceive about this dark..." Gladys Hall's "The Actor Who Knows That He Died." *Motion Picture*, January 1930, p. 40. The title relates to Novarro's alleged out-of-body experience while training with Marion Morgan.

135 "Oh, that place up there..." "The Gay Cavalier." *Screen Play*, June 1931.

135 "Ramón was a very complicated person..." Carmen Gavilán, 1998 AT.

135 "After all, life is nothing without religion..." Ruth Biery's "Why Novarro Decided to Remain in the Movies." *PP*, October 28, p. 102.

136 "A priest went to the Sacred Heart..." Ibid.

136 "about himself and God..." and "joyful illusioned." HHF, p. 62.

137 "I am very proud of the industry..." "Ramon May Sing in Films." *LAT*, August 5, 1928.

137–138 The information about the making of *The Flying Fleet* comes from numerous sources, including news clippings at the Novarro, George W. Hill, and *The Flying Fleet* files at AMPAS; the picture's production file at MGM-USC; and numerous undated and unidentified clippings found in film historian Joseph Yranski's *Flying Fleet* scrapbook.

Novarro's friend Pancho Barnes was one of the fliers used in *The Flying Fleet*.

137–138 The information about Anita Page is from the author's 1998 interview with Page and Randal Malone; Allan Ellenberger's *Ramon Novarro* (Jefferson, N.C.: McFarland, 1999); William J. Mann's *Wisecracker: The Life and Times of William Haines, Hollywood's First Openly Gay Star* (New York: Viking, 1998); Michael Ankerich's *The Sound of Silence* (Jefferson, N.C.: McFarland, 1998); and Page's file at AMPAS.

Page remembered almost losing her part in *The Flying Fleet* because she was too tall for Novarro. Yet, press reports of the time stated that fellow MGM starlet

Josephine Dunn was the one who ultimately lost the role because of her height. In fact, the five-foot two-inch Page was clearly shorter than Novarro, as can be attested in their full-body shots in a beach scene. If Novarro had to wear heels for the role, he wore them so as not to be dwarfed by the much taller Ralph Graves.

138 "the most beautiful girl in the world" and the Page-Novarro extended kissing story. Ellenberger's *Ramon Novarro*, pp. 91–92.

138 "We had this scene coming up..." Ankerich's *The Sound of Silence*, p. 187.

138 "standing outside when all of a sudden..." Mann's *Wisecracker*, p. 202.

138 "it's quite possible, perhaps even likely." Ibid., p. 203.

138–139 The information about William Haines is from Mann's *Wisecracker*; Haines's ("as told to" [columnist] Marquis Busby) "The Wisecracker Reveals Himself," found in the September and October 1929 issues of *Photoplay*; and the Haines file at AMPAS, unless otherwise noted.

Novarro's overall box-office pull remained stronger than Haines's in 1927— largely because of the overseas market and *Ben-Hur*—but the profit margin of Novarro's films was smaller because of their higher costs. In the following year, however, Haines's box-office earnings actually surpassed Novarro's.

139 "Billy Haines' best friend." *PP,* November 1928, p. 114. In a sly allusion to Haines's wisecracks about Polly Moran, in the March 1932 issue of *New Movie Magazine*, the article "Leap Year Valentine" thus described Haines's chief interest: "Likes antiques (not referring to his women companions)."

140 The bordello incident is mentioned in several publications, including Lawrence Quirk's *Norma*, William J. Mann's *Wisecracker*, and Allan Ellenberger's *Ramon Novarro*. Even if Anita Loos ever alluded to the bordello story elsewhere, one should be cautious about accepting it as fact. Loos often told droll tales that appear to be contrivances of the talented screenwriter and playwright that she was. In *A Girl Like I*, she has Elsie Janis saying "Hello, Mother dear!" to a butterfly she believed to be her deceased mother reincarnated, while in *The Talmadge Girls*, Loos describes an outlandish Talmadge family reunion, wherein Mama Talmadge, riding in a car with superstar daughters Norma and Constance, sees a man huddled on an icy bench and then yells at her daughters, "Will you girls take a look at that bum back there? It's your father." While the two superstars gasp, Mama tells the chauffeur, "Just buzz off before that barfly spots us" (p. 118). Amusing, surely. Factual, not necessarily.

140 Haines and Novarro's lack of rapport. Frank Lieberman, 2000 phone AT. The only photograph found showing Haines and Novarro together (with Polly Moran) was taken at MGM in 1929. Stars often posed together with other stars at the studio for publicity purposes.

140–141 The information and quotes about Novarro's meeting with Thalberg and Mayer during contract negotiations are from NP.

142 W. S. Van Dyke was born Woodbridge Strong Van Dyke II in San Diego.

142 Novarro's treatment for *The Pagan*. MGM script collection at AMPAS.

142 "Give him any sort of stringed instrument..." *Picturegoer*, November 26, 1939.

143 "It was quite a pleasant trip..." Unidentified publication, December 24, 1928, Novarro's AMPAS file.

143 "Injuries suffered in a football game ..." Unidentified publication, February 24, 1929, Novarro's AMPAS file. José's illness and death accelerated the demise of Pan Pacific Products, a small import company sponsored by Novarro, for which José had worked as a sales representative. Mariano, Antonio (who left his chemistry studies to join the company), and two family friends were also involved, but failed to keep Pan Pacific afloat.

143 *The Flying Fleet* reviews: *Chicago Tribune,* January 7, 1929; *MP,* March 1929; *NYT,* February 11, 1929; *PP,* February 1929; and *VT,* February 13, 1929. The "male Follies" quote is from *SL,* March 1929.

Director George Hill was found dead at his beach house, an apparent suicide, in August 1934.

144 "I was absorbed by my work ..." Unidentified publication ca. 1935, author's collection.

144 "Now I fear life more than death!" Undated letter ca. 1928, Sullivan.

144 "I'm just standing on the threshold of a new venture ..." Bradford Nelson's "The Grand (Opera) Young Man." *SL,* July 1929, pp. 54–55.

144 "My trip to Europe started to be ..." A July 27, 1929, letter, Sullivan.

144 "Hoping that hard work and the change of environment ..." Ibid.

144 "A boy in his early 20s was the artist ..." *The Film-Lovers' Annual 1933.*

145 "that Ramon had just been educated ..." Howe's "In Defense of Garbo." *NMM,* July 1932, p. 93.

9: The Singer of Durango

146 *The Pagan* reviews: *NYT,* May 14, 1929; *PP,* April 1929; and *VT,* May 15, 1929.

146 MGM's dislike for "The Pagan Love Song." Bosley Crowther's *The Lion's Share* (New York: E. P. Dutton, 1957). According to *Photoplay,* Dorothy Janis, whose "voice" is also heard singing "The Pagan Love Song" in the sound track, was dubbed. In the current print of *The Pagan* shown on cable television, Novarro's lips on-screen are not matched by his singing voice in the sound track, possibly the result of a poorly synchronized transfer to the video master used for broadcast.

147 "No other man of thirty-one ..." and "joyful, childlike, primitive ..." HHF, p. 63.

147 "worth going to Europe ..." *LAH,* June 22, 1929.

147–148 "I enjoyed it more than ever ..." A July 27, 1929, letter, Sullivan.

148 The information about the making of *Devil-May-Care* is from the film's file at AMPAS and from production files at MGM-USC.

148 Novarro had the right to choose which of his pictures would be published, but sometimes the studio would either forget or ignore his requests, and a picture he had nixed would appear in the press. (Ingram had advised him that if he did not want a picture to be published he should tear up the negative.) In Pratt, Novarro stated that the studio's disregard for his photo requests was the reason for his going to Hurrell. The photographer, however, later said that Novarro wanted photographs for his upcoming European opera debut (the photos were probably taken in early 1929) and did not want MGM to know about them—a strange assertion, considering that Novarro's opera debut had been widely discussed in the press.

148–149 Later in 1929, Novarro introduced George Hurrell to Norma Shearer. The actress wanted to play the title role in *The Divorcee*, but Irving Thalberg felt she lacked the seductiveness the part required. Hurrell's shots of an unusually sensual Shearer convinced her husband otherwise. She won both the role and an Academy Award, while Hurrell won an MGM contract that launched his career as one of Hollywood's foremost photographers. Mark A. Vieira's *Hurrell's Hollywood Portraits* (New York: Harry N. Abrams, 1997) and Whitney Stine and George Hurrell's *The Hurrell Style: 50 Years of Photographing Hollywood* (New York: John Day, 1976) were the main sources on Hurrell.

149 The information about Pancho Barnes's background comes from numerous sources, especially Lauren Kessler's *The Happy Bottom Riding Club: The Life and Times of Pancho Barnes* (New York: Random House, 2000).

149 "She would never use a five- or six-letter word..." Chuck Yeager and Leo Janos's *Yeager: An Autobiography* (New York: Bantam, 1985), p. 173.

149 "Ramon Novarro was a real Latin heartbreaker..." Grover Ted Tate's *The Lady Who Tamed Pegasus: The Story of Pancho Barnes* (Bend, Ore.: Maverick, 1984), pp. 56–57.

149–150 The information about the making of *In Gay Madrid* is from the picture's files at MGM-USC. The original title, *The House of Troy*, referred to the student quarters on Santiago de Compostella's *Calle la Troya*, or Troy Street.

150 MGM's foreign stars were an exception to the transition-to-sound exodus, partly because the studio was the slowest among the majors to fully switch to sound. MGM's first film with a synchronized score and sound effects was *White Shadows in the South Seas*, which had premiered on July 31, 1928, three days after the release of Warner Bros.' all-talking *Lights of New York*. In early 1929, while Paramount and Warners were already fully geared for talkies, the MGM backstage musical *The Broadway Melody* and the Norma Shearer vehicle *The Trial of Mary Dugan* had to share the same soundstage because that was the only stage at the studio equipped for sound. MGM's slowness to embrace sound was in part a result of the higher costs imposed by the new technology, which was swelling the already higher than average budgets of MGM films, and also due to the front office's mistrust of sound.

Thalberg and Mayer tried to protect their stars, whether foreign or native, by choosing what they believed were the most appropriate talking vehicles for each of them: for Lon Chaney, it was a remake of his earlier success *The Unholy Three*, in which he could make good use of different voice disguises to match different characterizations (Chaney had earlier rejected a project called *The Bugle Sounds*); for John Gilbert, it was *His Glorious Night*, a lighthearted period piece not unlike others in which the actor had excelled (the gloomy melodrama *Redemption* had been shot earlier, but was put on hold due to its poor commercial prospects); for Garbo, it was *Anna Christie*, whose central character was a Swede like the star; for Norma Shearer, it was the popular Broadway melodrama *The Trial of Mary Dugan*; and for Novarro, it was *Devil-May-Care*.

150 Film fan magazines of the time revealed that stars Richard Barthelmess, Alice White, and others had their singing voices dubbed.

151 "My dear..." Al Cohn's "How Talkies Are Made." *PP*, April 1929, p. 30.

151 Rose Hobart and Charles Farrell story. Hobart's friend Anthony Slide, 1999 AT.

151 May McAvoy did not have a lisp, as can be attested on her audiotape for USC.

151 John Gilbert's appearance in *His Glorious Night* was a complete fiasco. Many in the audience hollered at his over-the-top lovemaking. "All the fine salary, all the publicity puffs, all the paid reviews, can never undo that laugh," wrote the *Film Spectator* in its November 14, 1929, issue. Gilbert's salary and reference to problems with MGM are from the February 1929 issue of *Photoplay*.

152 *Devil-May-Care* reviews: *Film Daily*, December 29, 1929; *NYHT*, *the New York Telegram* the *New York Sun*, and the *New York Mirror*, December 23, 1929; *PP*, February 1930; and *VT*, December 25, 1929. The *Mirror* review was probably referring to French entertainer Maurice Chevalier and Irish tenor John McCormack, both recent Hollywood imports.

152 "In comparing the Novarro screen technique . . ." *Life*, January 31, 1930.

152 "He is hardly a Chevalier in quality . . ." *Devil-May-Care* review. *NYHT*, December 23, 1929.

153 Dorothy Jordan replaced original choice Raquel Torres in *Call of the Flesh*.

153 "The success of sound experiments . . ." *Call of the Flesh* press release, at AMPAS. Quotes in press releases were often either written by publicists and then approved by the star, or spoken by the star and then embellished by publicists.

153–154 The extent of Novarro's input in the creation of "Lonely" is unclear, but whether he merely suggested a couple of measures or contributed more substantially to the song, he was in all likelihood responsible for *something*. Music had always been a part of his life and would remain so—throughout the years, he would compose several pieces of music for his own enjoyment, including a simply arranged waltz. If Novarro felt like demanding credit for a song he did not compose just to acquire music royalties, his name would undoubtedly have appeared on sheet music more frequently. ("Not terribly good" is how conductor John Lanchbery described Novarro's waltz, "Tempo di valzer." Lanchbery added that the waltz had been harmonized by a "musical hack.")

154 Novarro directing most of *Call of the Flesh* is from his memoirs.

154 Novarro's request to have Renée Adorée relieved of duty and Stromberg's reaction. NP.

Adorée's health had been an intermittent problem for years. In 1923, she was involved in a car accident that left her incapacitated for a long period. In 1927, she was hospitalized because of a severe bout with the flu. That same year, a blizzard left her stranded for three weeks with the company of *Back to God's Country*. She was probably discovered to be suffering from tuberculosis in late 1929. (The preceding information is from *Parade*; news clippings found in Adorée's files at AMPAS; and *PP*, July 1927.)

154–155 Novarro's temporary move to 130 Adelaide Drive. *LAT*, April 17, 1930.

155–156 The information about Louis Samuel's embezzlement comes from interviews with several Samaniego family members, including Novarro's sister Carmen Gavilán, and from a 1999 phone interview with Eyvind Earle. The IRS report and "overassessment of income tax and interest" is from an unidentified clipping dated March 24, 1932, found in the Novarro file at AMPAS. (Coincidentally, the August 1929 issue of *Photoplay* carried an article about the embezzling schemes of the stars' business managers, "The Racketeers of Hollywood.")

156 *In Gay Madrid* reviews: *NYHT* and the *New York Sun*, June 7, 1930; the *New York Post*, June 9, 1930; *VT*, June 11, 1930; and an unidentified news clipping, possibly from the *Wall Street Journal*, June 12, 1930.

156 Novarro's opinion of Dorothy Jordan. William Hughes, an actor who appeared with Novarro in the 1941 summer-stock production of *Tovarich*, 2001 phone AT.

157 *The Broadway Melody* earned MGM more than $4 million in worldwide rentals, while the all-star extravaganza *The Hollywood Revue of 1929* brought in almost $2.5 million.

157 "Today, in the midst of the microphone panic..." *PP*, April 1929, p. 21.

157 *The King of Jazz*'s financial loss. Joel W. Finler's *The Hollywood Story* (New York: Crown Publishers, 1988).

157–158 The information about *The March of Time* is from that picture's production files at MGM-USC and from notes by film historian Miles Kreuger.

158 Shot in September 1930 by actor-director Frank Reicher, *Wir schalten um auf Hollywood* starred Austrian comedian Paul Morgan (killed in 1939 in a Nazi concentration camp) as the inventor of a pocket radio-transmitter. He ends up in Hollywood, where he meets an eclectic mix of talent, including Adolphe Menjou, Oscar Straus, Buster Keaton, Sergei Eisenstein (then in Hollywood attempting to film *An American Tragedy*), the Dodge Sisters, and Ramon Novarro. Sequences from both *The March of Time* and *The Hollywood Revue of 1929* were interspersed within the flimsy story line. *Wir schalten um auf Hollywood* opened in Berlin on June 10, 1931. Production files at MGM-USC describe "Long Ago in Alcala" as "a clever tropical number with a wharf background, sung by Novarro in a French sailor's suit, ending with him dancing the hornpipe."

158 Anita Page and Novarro's last date. Allan R. Ellenberger's *Ramon Novarro*.

158 Novarro's alcohol-induced car sickness. George Schönbrunn, a friend of Queenie Kent (Crauford's wife), 1998 AT.

159 "Old MGM training." New York Public Library video and film historian Joseph Yranski, relating a story told him by Novarro's East Coast agent, Alan Brock, 1998 phone AT.

159 Novarro's frequenting gay bars. Anthony Slide, relating information told him by Alice Terry, 1998 AT.

159 "someone made out of common clay." *Call of the Flesh* pressbook, AMPAS.

159 "woman-proof." Dorothy Calhoun's "The Man No Woman Can Vamp." *MP*, February 1929, p. 105.

159 "It seems that the most popular portrait of me..." Ibid.

159 "To her Ramon is not a star..." Katharine Albert's "The Volunteer Grandma." *PP*, April 1930, p. 35.

160 *Call of the Flesh* reviews: *NYHT*, *NYMT*, and *NYT*, September 13, 1930; and *VT*, September 17, 1930.

160 A plot contrivance similar to the one in *Call of the Flesh* is used in *Forbidden Hours*, but in that picture the roles are reversed: Renée Adorée's commoner pretends to be involved with another man so that Novarro's king Michael will return to the throne.

161 "Being identified with dramatic roles..." Bradford Nelson's "The Grand (Opera) Young Man." *SL*, July 1929, p. 55.

161 "to be operatic..." Howe's "In Defense of Garbo." *NMM*, July 1932, p. 55.

161 *Trader Horn*, *Min and Bill*, and *The Big House* were the only 1930 MGM releases with higher worldwide earnings than *Call of the Flesh*.

161–162 Juan B. Heinink and Robert G. Dickson's *Cita en Hollywood* (Bilbao, Spain: Ediciones Mensajero, 1990) and Carl J. Mora's *Mexican Cinema—Reflections of a Society 1896–1980* (Berkeley: University of California Press, 1982) were excellent sources of information about the production of Spanish-language pictures in Hollywood.

161 The unspecified uncomfortable actor in the Spanish-language version of *Mr. Wu—Wu Li Chang*—was either Ernesto Vilches or José Crespo.

162 "I want to work in a medium..." Margaret Reid's "Directed by Ramon Novarro." *MS*, April 1931.

162 Production information on *La Sevillana* comes from the picture's files at MGM-USC and at AMPAS, from *Cita en Hollywood*, and from Reid's "Directed by Ramon Novarro."

162 "At last I am doing..." Reid's "Directed by Ramon Novarro."

162 The information about Señora Samaniego's churchgoing habit is from interviews with several family members, including Carmen Gavilán. Novarro later recalled in "Directed by Ramon Novarro" that his mother played her part "so exquisitely that I was amazed. I don't say this because she is my mother—but because it is true. I didn't need to direct her—she played with utter simplicity and her lovely wisdom and tenderness and strength made the part radiant!"

162 "a spontaneous, lively, impulsive creature." *Screen Play*, June 1931.

162 Production information about *Le Chanteur de Séville* comes from that picture's files at MGM-USC.

162–163 *Variety*'s review of *Le Chanteur de Séville* appeared in the February 21, 1931, issue.

163 "I want to do simple stories..." Reid's "Directed by Ramon Novarro."

163 Michael Blankenship's article "A Fellow Traveler," found in the July 18, 1989, issue of *The Advocate*, was an excellent source of information on Richard Halliburton. Many of Halliburton's letters can be found at Sullivan. The alleged romance between Novarro and Halliburton has been mentioned in Ellenberger's *Ramon Novarro* and in the gay press.

164 "I've <u>tested</u> it already..." an undated letter, probably late December 1932 or early January 1933, Sullivan. The Underlining is Novarro's.

164–165 The information about the making of *Daybreak* is from that picture's files at MGM-USC and at AMPAS, and from Dorothy Spensley's article "Is Novarro Through?" found in *Classic*, ca. summer 1931. Numerous writers, including top MGM scenarist Frances Marion and Hungarian import Endre Bohem, meddled in the scenario, though Ruth Cummings received final credit for the adaptation, Cyril Hume (leading lady Helen Chandler's husband) for the dialogue, and Zelda Sears for melding the two into the picture's continuity.

164–165 The information about Jacques Feyder is from *Jacques Feyder*, edited by Charles Ford (Paris: Editions Seghers, 1973). A censored version of *Les Nouveaux Messieurs* opened a year after its ban by the French parliament. In Pratt, Novarro recalled that Feyder's directorial style often included visual evocations—such as telling the actor to imagine snow slowly melting in the Alps—to bring out the desired performance.

165 After Marcus Loew's death of heart failure in September 1927, William Fox, sanctioned by Loew's second-in-command Nicholas Schenck, acquired a controlling interest in Loew's Inc.—which meant the eventual absorption of MGM by Fox Studios. Antitrust laws, William Fox's involvement in a serious car accident, and the Wall Street crash ultimately prevented the takeover.

165 In Pratt, Novarro called Murnau "the greatest. He knew his camera better than anybody else." Novarro also affirmed that the German director taught Janet Gaynor all she knew, including how to fight for better contracts.

165 "proved to me . . ." BRN, p. 537. As an illustration, Murnau recounted how in *The Last Laugh* he wanted Emil Jannings not to show any emotion after a disastrous day, whereas Jannings was eager to display a no-holds-barred emotional outburst. After the scene was shot both ways and Jannings was shown the results, he finally agreed that letting the audience project their own feelings onto his expressionless face was considerably more effective than hammering them with tears, exaggerated motions, and facial contortions.

165 "was an admirer of mine." Pratt.

165 "Lubitsch and a certain group of those people . . ." Ibid. But even if Novarro harbored anti-Jewish prejudices, that did not prevent him from having several Jewish friends.

166 Most of the information and all quotes about Frank Hansen are from Pratt. The information about Hansen's political views is from a close friend of Novarro's.

166 "plastic." Howe's "In Defense of Garbo." *NMM*, July 1932, p. 93.

165–166 Certain stories have both Murnau and Novarro as compulsive sexual predators on their respective sets, with Murnau making passes at young, good-looking crew members, and Novarro inviting groups of three or four handsome studio workers for soirées at his private bungalow at a Hollywood hotel. According to such tales, Novarro "eventually got around to everyone" at MGM. Actually, if the circumspect Novarro ever proposed to anyone at the studio, which is not inconceivable, he must have acted with extreme caution. ("[E]ventually got around to everyone" is a quote found in William J. Mann's *Wisecracker: The Life and Times of William Haines, Hollywood's First Openly Gay Star* [New York: Viking, 1998.])

166–167 The information about the making of *Son of India* is from the picture's MPAA file at AMPAS and at MGM-USC, from Novarro's and Madge Evans's files at AMPAS, and from Dorothy Spensley's "Is Novarro through?"

167 The Trump murder case. Unidentified clippings in Novarro's file, AMPAS; "Novarro Sought on Subpoena," *LAH*, August 15, 1931; and "Police Solve Two-Year-Old Murder," *LAT*, August 4, 1930.

167–168 *Daybreak* reviews: *NYHT, NYMT, NYT,* and the *New York Post,* June 1, 1931. *Daybreak* boasts gorgeous cinematography—courtesy of Merritt B. Gerstad in his seventh and last picture with Novarro—which was reportedly made sharper by a new Eastman film stock that improved the look of dimly lit scenes.

Novarro looks the part of a Central European officer as convincingly as he did in *The Prisoner of Zenda.* Willi's appearance—monocle, rounder chin, thin mustache, higher forehead, huge black eyebrows (which, *Variety* observed, "looked suited to make tails for two black cats")—is remarkably similar to Rupert's (minus the goatee).

168 *Son of India* reviews: the *New York Sun,* July 27, 1931; and *VT,* July 28, 1931. In BRN, DeWitt Bodeen states that Mayer had *Son of India* recalled after its initial release and added a happy ending to it, but no records can be found to confirm that assertion.

168 "happy, charming, carefree..." *Le Cinéma notre métier* (Geneva, Switzerland: Editions D'Art Albert Skira, 1944). This is apparently a booklet written, at least in part, by Jacques Feyder and his wife, Françoise Rosay.

168–169 Novarro names Jacques Feyder as one of his favorite directors in Pratt. Feyder returned to MGM in 1932, lured by the chance to direct Garbo in *As You Desire Me* (he had already directed her in *The Kiss* in 1929), John Gilbert (later replaced by Clark Gable) in *Red Dust,* and Novarro in *The Son-Daughter.* After these three deals fell through, Feyder left Hollywood for good.

169–170 In his book proposal, Novarro states that it was Irving Thalberg's idea that he be paired with Garbo. Reports of the period state that Novarro himself had insisted on working with the prestigious and highly successful actress.

In the 1931 ads for *Mata Hari,* Garbo's and Novarro's names are of equal size and both appear above the title. In the 1940 reissue, Novarro's name appears at the bottom of ads in much smaller print than Garbo's. At that time, Garbo was still an MGM star; Novarro had left the studio five years earlier.

170–171 The information about the making of *Mata Hari* comes from the following sources, unless otherwise stated: the picture's files at AMPAS and at MGM-USC; the MPAA files at AMPAS; *AFI31–40;* Norman Zierold's *Garbo* (New York: Stein and Day, 1969); Barry Paris's *Garbo, a Biography* (New York: Alfred A. Knopf, 1995); Regina Cannon's "The Most Eligible Couple Will Never Marry," *NMM,* May 1932; "When Nordic Met Latin," *PP,* February 1932; and NP.

171 "Bedroom situations." *AFI31–40.*

171 "I felt very strange..." and "just as it will be..." "When Nordic Met Latin."

171 "In a way, it was a test..." Ibid.

171 "offstandish [*sic*]" and Novarro's remark about Garbo's opening up to him are from Pratt. Garbo "missing" her Mexican costar is from NP.

171 "She smiled graciously..." "When Nordic Met Latin." Garbo's staying late and then arriving late the next day is from NP and Pratt.

171 "It was not in the script..." *LAHE,* October 31, 1968, pp. A-1, 3.

171–172 Scenes deleted from *Mata Hari*—and from many other reissued pictures after the Production Code gained full force in the mid-1930s—were cut directly from the original negative.

172 The information about Novarro's car crash and the quotes "it is apparent the plaintiff..." and "only one drink with friends." Unidentified clippings, November 14 and 17, 1931, found at Novarro's AMPAS file, and *Movie Classic*, February 1932. Novarro would also be named a codefendant in a lawsuit against his cousin Jorge Gavilán, who had been driving Novarro's car when he crashed into another vehicle in September 1934.

173 "Oh, my heart stopped..." Pratt.

173 The *New York Times* review of *Mata Hari* appeared on January 1, 1932.

173–174 The warning against Garbo's paralyzing allure. *PP*, December 1931.

174 Magnifying *Mata Hari's* problems, the cuts for the 1940 reissue make the picture seem disjointed when watched today. When Rosanoff reminds Mata Hari in one heavily dramatic moment that she had expressed her love for him the night before, audiences are left wondering *which* night before, as she never mentions such feelings in the currently available prints.

174 "I wish this picture could be destroyed..." *AFI31–40*, pp. 1339–1340.

174–175 In regard to rumors about Garbo's lesbianism: "Incidentally, Garbo has a new girl friend—Fifi D'Orsay, the Parisian paprika," remarked "Cal York" in the "News! Views! Gossip!" section of the May 1930 issue of *Photoplay*. "Fifi is Greta's first girl pal since she and [well-known lesbian] Lilyan Tashman grew less friendly, some time back." P. 49. ("Cal York" was a pseudonym used by different writers who contributed to that section.)

174 "Garbo was magnificent..." Undated cable (ca. early 1932), Sullivan.

175–176 In 1930 none of Novarro's three pictures surpassed Lon Chaney's *The Unholy Three* at the domestic box office, and he still trailed William Haines's domestic average by $5,000. But once overseas rentals were added (usually with a delay of months after the domestic run), Novarro's pictures averaged an astounding $500,000 more in revenues than Haines's, over $350,000 more than Chaney's, and more than twice Gilbert's amount.

176 "This is magnificent!..." Ray Milland's *Wide-Eyed in Babylon* (New York: William Morrow, 1974), p. 117.

10: Fade-Out

177 Colleen Moore's salary. *Silver Screen*, December 1933.

178–179 The making of *Huddle*. *AFI31–40*, and the picture's files at AMPAS and at MGM-USC. *Huddle* was previewed with an alternate title, *For Glory and a Girl*, in 1932.

178 "A singing star..." *Terre Haute Tribune*, January 31, 1932.

178 "Oh, they'll never learn." Pratt.

179 "I am working so very hard..." February 19, 1932, letter, Sullivan.

179 "*Huddle* seems interminable." March 26, 1932, letter, Sullivan. Novarro was paid $833.33 for the soccer scenes added to the foreign version of *Huddle*.

179 "Cast as a shy, gentle..." *Providence-Journal*, May 15, 1932.

Tough guys were in vogue in the early 1930s, as exemplified by Clark Gable at MGM; Edward G. Robinson, Paul Muni, and James Cagney at Warners; and Spencer Tracy at Fox. Nonetheless, the studio's unwise decision to give their top male star a radical makeover ignored the success of more amicable performers such as William Powell (and later Dick Powell) at Warners, and MGM's own fast-ascending Robert Montgomery, who was more often than not seen making love to Norma Shearer or wisecracking in a tuxedo.

180 The information about Novarro's Valley Oak house comes from several sources, including A. B. Cutts, Jr.'s "The Hillside Home of Ramon Novarro," *California Arts & Architecture*, July 1933, and the Lloyd Wright Collection in the Arts Library at the University of California at Los Angeles.

180 "during his spare moments..." MGM photo collection at AMPAS.

181 "I had to get away from home..." "I'll Never Fall in Love Predicts Ramon Novarro," an undated clipping from an unidentified fan magazine, ca. 1933.

181 "You will never know..." August 26, 1932, letter, MGM Legal Department Records, AMPAS.

182–183 The making of *The Son-Daughter*. *AF131–40*, and the picture's files at AMPAS and at MGM-USC.

183 "the opposite of Garbo..." Pratt. Novarro lowered his voice when dismissing Hayes, before letting the sentence trail off.

183 *The Son-Daughter* reviews: *NYHT* and the *New York Sun*, December 31, 1932; *NYMT*, January 1, 1933; *VT*, January 3, 1933.

183 "I've often complained..." *Script*, December 17, 1932.

184–185 The making of *The Barbarian*. *AF131–40*; the picture's files at AMPAS and at MGM-USC; "Watching over Hollywood," *Silver Screen*, May 1933, p. 64; and Myrna Loy and James Kotsilibas-Davis's *Myrna Loy: Being and Becoming* (New York: Alfred A. Knopf, 1987).

184 "Every woman's dream..." *Being and Becoming*, p. 80.

185 "was still a big star..." and "gentle, quiet men." Ibid, p. 80.

185 "Chatter in Hollywood..." Unidentified clipping, March 21, 1933, in Novarro's file at AMPAS.

186 "Torrid romance" and other quotes in that paragraph. *Being and Becoming*, p. 80.

186 In his memoirs, Eduardo Samaniego states that Novarro eventually realized that Graveure was a charlatan who had ruined his voice. In a 1999 phone interview, Eyvind Earle also asserted that Graveure's voice exercises put too much of a strain on Novarro's vocal chords.

186–187 Novarro's remarks about the concert stage. Bradford Nelson's "The Grand (Opera) Young Man." *SL*, July 1929, pp. 54–55. During the 1933 European tour, Robert Ritchie told the press that after Novarro finished his concert stage commitments, he would star in an English film version of a French play to be shot in Paris. Novarro's contract, however, prohibited him from appearing in films outside of MGM. This announcement was clearly one of Ritchie's self-promotional tactics.

187 Ingram's alleged conversion to Islam. O'Leary and a March 1932 article in *NMM* by Herbert Howe.

187 "Rex Ingram remains in Europe..." *PP*, April 1929, p. 54.

187 Rex Ingram's problems with the Nice studios and about the making of *Baroud*. O'Leary. Ingram reportedly wanted Alice Terry as his leading lady in *Baroud*, but she had grown too overweight. Thus, he picked Rosita García, whom he had

discovered during the shooting of *Where the Pavement Ends*. According to Herbert Howe, Terry directed Ingram's scenes in *Baroud*, while Ingram directed the rest.

187 "became very angry." Betty Lasky, 1999 phone AT.

188 *The Barbarian* reviews: *NYMT*, May 14, 1933; *NYT*, May 13, 1933; and the *New York World Telegraph*, May 18.

188 "a wild, crazy picture." *Being and Becoming*, p. 80.

188 For those too slow to get the obvious, the picture provides two other hints about Loy's rape, the last of which is as clearly spelled out as 1933 would allow. Immediately before Loy's soon to be interrupted marriage to Reginald Denny, her companion, played by stage veteran Louise Closser Hale, tearfully exclaims, "This is your last virgin moment." Hale then turns her face away from Loy and toward the audience. Realizing her faux pas, she mouths in embarrassment, "VIRGIN."

189 Novarro could be found between Boris Karloff and Joan Blondell as number 64 among the top box-office attractions in the country in the *1933 Motion Picture Almanac* (covering 1932). Even then, he was still ahead of William Powell, Kay Francis, Jean Harlow, Loretta Young, and several other major stars of the 1930s.

188–190 John Gilbert's salary. Leatrice Gilbert Fountain and John R. Maxim's *Dark Star* (New York: St. Martin's Press, 1985), and several film magazines of the early 1930s. Gilbert's most successful silent pictures had starred him opposite name actresses such as Greta Garbo, Lillian Gish, Mae Murray, and Renée Adorée, and had been directed by major talents such as King Vidor and Clarence Brown. In the talkies, the best leading ladies Gilbert could get were Madge Evans, Anita Page, and Leila Hyams, and his top directors were the likes of Harry Beaumont and Sam Wood. Compounding the problem, Gilbert's acting style, which had been highly effective in silent films, rang false in the more realistic world of sound—a condition not helped by the star's voice, more high-pitched than filmgoers would have imagined.

190 Since William Haines's persona failed to evolve, most of his films became predictable and repetitious (in its December 27, 1932, review of Haines's last MGM picture, *Fast Life*, *Variety* called his shtick "stale stuff"). Likewise, what seemed fresh in 1926, when Haines starred in *Tell It to the Marines* and stole the show in *Brown in Harvard*, had become commonplace in the early 1930s with the ascendance of fellow celluloid wisecrackers Jack Oakie, Lee Tracy, and, to some extent, Robert Montgomery.

190–191 The importance of the international market to MGM and Warners can be clearly seen in the accounting ledgers of those studios. The MGM "Eddie Mannix ledger" can be found at AMPAS; Warners' "William Schaefer ledger" is at the University of Southern California Cinema-Television Library. A third ledger, RKO's "C. J. Tevlin ledger," is now located at the Turner Entertainment Group offices. The significance of the figures contained in those ledgers was discussed in the following issues of the *Historical Journal of Film, Radio and Television*: vol. 12, no. 2, 1992 (H. Mark Glancy's "MGM Film Grosses, 1924–1948: The Eddie Mannix Ledger"); vol. 14, no. 1, 1994 (Richard B. Jewell's "RKO Film Grosses, 1929–1951; the C. J. Tevlin Ledger"); and vol. 15, no. 1, 1995 (H. Mark Glancy's "Warner Bros. Film Grosses, 1921–1951: the William Schaefer Ledger").

191 "You're either to give up..." Anita Loos's *The Talmadge Girls* (New York: Viking, 1978), p. 70.

Mayer allegedly vowed to destroy Gilbert after the star punched him because of a disparaging remark about Greta Garbo. In revenge, Mayer sabotaged the recording of Gilbert's voice for his first released talkie, *His Glorious Night,* and then cast the irascible star in a succession of inferior vehicles. According to stories about Haines's dismissal, his relatively open liaison with Jimmie Shields and rumored arrests for procuring sex horrified Mayer's sense of decorum. Thus, Haines also had to leave before his behavior contaminated the rest of the MGM family. One major problem with those tales is that even if Mayer was happy to see Gilbert and Haines go—and he surely was—he would have been unable to single-handedly ruin two of the studio's major box-office attractions, while Thalberg and Nicholas Schenck, neither of whom was on good terms with Mayer, did nothing to stop him.

192 "Women—phooey!..." *LAH,* February 20, 1934.

192–193 The making of *The Cat and the Fiddle. AFI31–40;* the picture's files at AMPAS; and Edward Baron Turk's *Hollywood Diva: A Biography of Jeanette MacDonald* (Berkeley: University of California Press, 1998). The expensive price tag for *The Cat and the Fiddle* was partly a result of extensive retakes of the Technicolor finale, which cost $135,000. Additionally, Novarro had been getting paid $1,000 a week since signing a contract to appear in the picture on March 16, 1933. A new contract was written on July 11, 1933, which stipulated an added $100,000 for twenty weeks of work on both *The Cat and the Fiddle* and *Laughing Boy.*

192 "friend, counselor, and guide." *Hollywood Diva.*

192 "a wonderful director." *Being and Becoming,* p. 63.

193 Vivienne Segal's remarks about Jeanette MacDonald can be found in Anthony Slide's "Vivienne Segal." *Film Fan.*

193–194 The making of *Laughing Boy.* The picture's files at AMPAS and at MGM-USC; the MPAA files at AMPAS; the W. S. Van Dyke files, AMPAS; *AFI31–40;* and John Huston's *John Huston: An Open Book* (New York: Alfred E. Knopf, 1980).

Then-screenwriter John Huston and director William Wyler had persuaded Universal to buy the property in 1932, but that studio had scrapped the project because they had been unable to find a suitable lead. (Huston had suggested a real Native American, but the studio wanted Lew Ayres or Richard Arlen.)

193 "be foolish." Al Sherman's "Ramon Novarro to Desert the Screen." *Screen Book,* July 1934.

193 One year earlier, Novarro had expressed interest in starring opposite Lupe Velez in his own Mexican version of *The Champ,* in which he would have played a bullfighter, and Velez his adoring sister.

193 "fidelity to detail..." Undated note, MGM-USC.

194 "it was really disconcerting..." Pratt. In Pratt, Novarro says that "everything was horrible" about *Laughing Boy,* except for Lupe Velez.

194 *The Cat and the Fiddle* reviews. *NYT,* February 17, 1934: *VT,* February 20, 1934.

194 Novarro as a "safe" partner is from *Hollywood Diva.*

195–196 The Una Merkel party. "More Topics for Gossip," *Silver Screen,* May

1933, p. 46; and Allan Ellenberger's *Ramon Novarro* (Jefferson, N.C.: McFarland, 1999), p. 271.

196 "Douglass, Kay Johnson and I..." Michael G. Ankerich's *The Sound of Silence* (Jefferson, N.C.: McFarland, 1998), p. 26.

196 "a sordid, vile and dirty story..." A December 4, 1933, memo from Joseph Breen to James Wingate, MPAA files at AMPAS. *Laughing Boy* was deemed "immoral and indecent" by the Legion of Decency (*NYT*, July 7, 1935). In his autobiography, *John Huston: An Open Book*, Huston recalled *Laughing Boy* as "a wretched, vulgar picture" (p. 60).

197 Oliver La Farge throwing a glass at John Lee Mahin is from "John Lee Mahin: Team Player," an interview conducted by Todd McCarthy and Joseph McBride found in *Backstory*, edited by Pat McGilligan (Berkeley: University of California Press, 1986, pp. 241–265), p. 257.

197 "Ramon Novarro as Laughing Boy!..." Ibid., p. 257.

197 "Novarro, keenly sensitive..." Al Sherman's "Ramon Novarro to Desert the Screen," *Screen Book*, July 1934.

198 Guests at the Teatro Intimo *(left to right)*, September 1933. Note: In the late 1940s, Novarro identified some of the guests by name, without explaining who they were; others he himself failed to identify: FIRST ROW: Mindred (singer Marguerite Namara's husband), singer Marguerite Namara, Ray Milland, Tillie Chatterton (mother of actress Ruth Chatterton), unidentified, actor Louis Jean Heydt (unconfirmed). SECOND ROW: Adrian, Gloria Swanson, Michael Farmer (Swanson's husband), actress Lois Wilson, producer Bernard Hyman, unidentified, unidentified, director Tod Browning (unconfirmed). THIRD ROW: unidentified, Myrna Loy, Bob Norman, Alice Terry, Irving Thalberg, Norma Shearer, Harry Rapf, Mrs. Rapf. FOURTH ROW: MGM publicist Howard Strickling, producer Jack Chertok, unidentified, Jack Kapp, Robert Ritchie (Jeanette MacDonald's fiancé), Jeanette MacDonald, Dolores del Río, Cedric Gibbons. FIFTH ROW: Randolph Scott, unidentified, Cary Grant, unidentified, actress Virginia Bruce (Mrs. John Gilbert), John Gilbert. SIXTH ROW: Gilbert Wilson (Elsie Janis's husband), producer David Lewis (director James Whale's companion), unidentified, art director Howard Grieve, actress Jetta Goudal (Mrs. Grieve), unidentified, unidentified, Mrs. Mojica (mother of José Mojica), Mexican actor-singer (and future priest) José Mojica. SEVENTH ROW: unidentified, Charlotte Earle (Ferdinand's former wife), Novarro's attorney Stanley Barnes, Mrs. Barnes, unidentified, actress Mae Busch, unidentified. EIGHTH ROW: James Whale (by the wall), Raquel Torres, Elsie Janis, Mrs. Jaime Gurza (Gurza was a renowned Mexican newspaperman), Luz Samaniego, actress-singer Alma Real, Ms. Prado (Myrna Loy's secretary), former nun Leonor Samaniego, Señora Samaniego. Eduardo Samaniego can be seen in the lighting booth.

198 "There is nothing more difficult..." January 3, 1940, letter, Homan.

198 "sang with new surety..." *San Francisco Chronicle*, September 22, 1933.

198 Novarro had previously appeared at the Philharmonic in February 1931, in a benefit for the victims of an earthquake in Oaxaca, Mexico.

198 The information about Novarro's *The Cat and the Fiddle* concert is from the February 7, 1934, issue of the *Los Angeles Times*. His salary comes from his contractual agreements with Loew's.

198–199 Commentary and quotes about the South American trip. RNFC, November-December 1934, unless otherwise stated. Additional details were provided by Carmen Gavilán during a 1998 interview. Other sources: *LAH*, April 25, 1934; *LAT*, April 25 and September 1, 1934; and the *Courier News*, April 26, 1934. Novarro also sang at the Brazilian port city of Santos and in Rosario, two hundred miles northwest of Buenos Aires.

199 "no romance with [Myrna Loy]..." *LAT*, April 21, 1934.

200 Rodolfo Acuña's *Occupied America: A History of Chicanos* (New York: HarperCollins, 1988) provided excellent insights into the California labor movement of the 1930s.

200 "any subversive policy..." "State Radical Quiz Spurred Against Stars." *LAH*, August 19, 1934.

200 "investigate and control..." Arthur W. Sjoquist's *Los Angeles Police Department: 1869–1984* (Los Angeles: Los Angeles Police Revolver and Athletic Club, 1972).

200 "a quiet investigation into reports..." "Four Film Stars' Names Drawn into Red Inquiry." *LAT*, August 19, 1934.

200 "I deny ever giving Communists any aid..." Ibid. James Cagney had reportedly been cited because his name had appeared in letters sent to Caroline Decker by Australian journalist Ella Winter, future wife of screenwriter Donald Ogden Stewart and author of *Red Virtue*, a book about women in post-Revolution Russia. Two years later, Caroline Decker would be portrayed in fictionalized form in John Steinbeck's novel *In Dubious Battle*.

200–201 "Me a Communist?..." Ibid.

201 "It's ridiculous..." Ibid. Twenty years later, Dolores del Río would find herself facing similar charges. In 1954, she was denied an American visa to appear in *Broken Lance* because of her alleged association with Communists. Katy Jurado landed the role and an Academy Award nomination.

201 "emphatically denied" and "I belong to no Communistic organization..." "Action Nearing in Cagney's Case." *LAT*, August 20, 1934.

203 The making of *The Night Is Young*. AFI31–40; the picture's files at AMPAS and at MGM-USC; and the Evelyn Laye file at AMPAS.

202 "so completely wedded to the music..." *HR*, unspecified issue. Found in *AFI31–40*, p. 1508. In *Getting to Know Him: A Biography of Oscar Hammerstein II* (Cambridge, Mass.: Da Capo Press, 1995), author Hugh Fordin describes Hammerstein's reaction to the final adaptation of his original book: "In making *The Night Is Young*, Oscar received a discouraging lesson in film-making when the producer called in two screenwriters, who completely changed the story and characters, although they retained much of the score. So much for the organic musical, not one of Hollywood's priorities in the mid-thirties. The dismay with which he viewed a rough cut of *The Night Is Young* in early December didn't help him face the horrendous family Christmas that year."

203 "I loved Ramon..." *The Silent Picture*, summer 1969, no. 3, p. 2.

204 *The Night Is Young* reviews: *NYT*, January 14, 1935; *London Sunday Times*, March 10, 1935; and *VT*, January 15, 1935.

205 *Love While You May* was an original operetta written by Edgar Selwyn (alternate title, *New York to Paris*). Earlier in the year, Novarro had also been mentioned

as a possibility for the role of Tom-Tom in the Hal Roach production of *Babes in Toyland*, which was distributed by MGM in 1934. Tom-Tom was eventually played by Felix Knight. There was also talk in late 1934 that John Russell was writing a musical version of *The Pagan* for Novarro. That never came to pass. Also at that time, the producers of the Broadway musical *Revenge with Music* reportedly wanted Novarro to star in their show, but he was committed to MGM and *The Night Is Young*.

205 "abrogated by mutual consent." *AFI31–40*, p. 1508.

205 "wasn't very good." "Lonely Voyage of a Silent Star." *San Francisco Chronicle*, April 20, 1968.

205 "While there was no disagreement..." "Novarro Leaves MGM to Make Own Pictures." *Illustrated Daily News*, February 8, 1935.

205–206 The rumors about Novarro's departure from MGM can be found in Allan Ellenberger's *Ramon Novarro*.

206 "carefully." *LAH*, November 28, 1930.

206 "the most loyal following of any star..." and "legions of fans." Madeline Glass's "What Is His Mystic Power." *PIC*, August 1930, p. 43.

11: Illusion of Happiness

207 "I have been playing the same part..." "Extra! Novarro Quits!" Unidentified publication, ca. 1935.

207 "a dirty deal." Howe's "In Defense of Garbo." *NMM*, July 1932, p. 55. Howe also chastised Novarro for accepting the role of Lieutenant Alexis in *Mata Hari*, referring to it as "that sap part." Howe was unquestionably right in his assessment of the role, but however sappy Lieutenant Alexis was, *Mata Hari* remained Novarro's biggest box-office hit of the 1930s.

208 "never known anyone who is..." HHF, p. 63.

208 The information about the Samaniegos is from several interviews with family members, including Carmen Gavilán.

208 The José Caraballo incident at Gramercy is from an interview with two of Novarro's close friends, who have requested anonymity.

209 "kindest." Al Sherman's "Ramon Novarro to Desert the Screen," *Screen Book*, July 1934.

209 "Mexican lad who yearns for great things..." Al Sherman's "Ramon Novarro to Desert the Screen," *Screen Book*, July 1934. In this instance, Novarro stated that the hero was a composite of four famous stars, two of them dead. He refused to give their names. Some press reports at the time speculated that the two deceased stars were Wallace Reid and Rudolph Valentino.

209 "Naturally, it is founded on my own experience..." "Novarro Explains Dislike for Films." *NYT*, July 7, 1935.

210 The making of *Contra la corriente. HR*, August 3, 1935; *AFI31–40*; Eduardo Samaniego memoirs; and Juan B. Heinink and Robert G. Dickson's *Cita en Hollywood* (Bilbao, Spain: Ediciones Mensajero, 1990). The old Talisman Studios is now a shopping center.

211 "How can you say *the* lover..." George Schönbrunn, 1998 AT.

212–214 The information about *A Royal Exchange* is from the following sources:

Carmen Gavilán (1998), Tonio Selwart (1999, phone), George Schönbrunn (1998), and John Lanchbery (2000, phone), AT; RNFC, January-February 1936; *LAH*, December 14, 1935; *London Daily Express*, December 14, 1935; and several unidentified and undated clippings in Novarro's AMPAS files.

According to the January-February 1936 RNFC newsletter, Novarro had the weakest lines in the play. The wittiest lines belonged to Eddie Foy, Jr. Also, humorous sequences alternated with dramatic ones—the latter usually with Novarro—which broke the emotional continuity of the play. There were reports that Novarro paid £2,000 to keep the show going, but Audrey Homan later stated that Novarro had told her he had put up £6,000 of his money.

212 Novarro–Cecil Everley romance. George Schönbrunn, 1998 AT.

213 "A pretty sorry mess it is, when all's done..." *London Times*, December 7, 1935.

214 "You can lead a film star to the..." Unidentified London newspaper, December 7, 1935, Matias Bombal Collection.

214 "I will not expose my company..." RNFC, January-February 1936.

215 "Surely nothing of the kind..." Ibid.

215 "Heckle me?..." Mary Parkes's "A Night with Novarro." *MS*, November 1937. In Pratt, Novarro remarked with his usual coloring of the past, "I knew it was going to be a failure, so it wasn't a surprise. I was rather grateful because I got rid of all the contracts."

215 "completely flabbergasted" and other quotes in that paragraph. George Schönbrunn, 1998 AT.

216 "It's funny now..." and other quotes in that paragraph. Mary Parkes's "A Night with Novarro." *MS*, November 1937, p. 88. Other information about the Budapest engagement is from RNFC, January-February 1936; *LAT*, December 29, 1935; and *LAH*, December 28, 1935.

217 "He was just like a child..." Tonio Selwart. 1999, phone AT.

217 Novarro's illness during his British tour. Carmen Gavilán, 1998 AT; RNFC, March-April 1936. Rebecca Ravens, the woman who took care of Novarro during his illness, had also taken care of him when he had his nervous breakdown after leaving MGM. Ravens is said to have known him since he was seven years old.

217 "I have no words..." RNFC, March-April 1936.

217 "awfully bored." Pratt.

218 "radicals." Unidentified clipping, Novarro's AMPAS file.

218 The *Contra la corriente* review. *NYT*, March 10, 1936.

219 "The experiment [of *Contra la corriente*] only proved..." BRN, p. 540.

219 "I have been advised to make a picture..." *LAT*, August 2, 1936. Novarro's English RNFC members agreed that the star should wait for an appropriate role, with one of them writing him, "Resist All Movie Offers Not Noteworthy. Only Vivid Acting Roles Retain Originality." (The first letters of the words spell out RAMON NOVARRO.) This is from a cable sent to Novarro by Richard Mason, found in the January-February 1937 issue of the RNFC newsletter.

219 "everything turned out very well" and other quotes in that paragraph. An early 1937 letter to Audrey Homan, RNFC, March-April 1937.

220 "The past has gone into oblivion..." Ibid.

220 "wonderful." Ibid.

220 "from complete confidence..." *Motion Picture Herald*, August 5, 1937.

221 "I like it..." Mary Parkes's "A Night with Novarro." *MS*, November 1937, p. 88.

221 *The Sheik Steps Out* review: *VT*, July 28, 1937.

222 The information about Novarro's family life comes from interviews with several family members, including Carmen Gavilán. Herbert Howe hilariously describes a Posada in the January 1926 issue of *Photoplay*.

222 In *A Desperate Adventure*, director William Wyler's future wife Margaret Tallichet, a lovely brunette who had recently been tested for the part of Scarlett O'Hara, plays Marian Marsh's sister—and the woman who eventually wins the painter's heart.

222–223 The making of *A Desperate Adventure*. The picture's AMPAS files and Homan.

222 "They were very quick about it..." Marian Marsh, 1999 phone AT.

222 "was a homosexual..." William Drew's *At the Center of the Frame: Leading Ladies of the Twenties and Thirties* (Lanham, Md.: Vestal Press, 1999). Marian Marsh was more circumspect when discussing Novarro's *Desperate Adventure* experience with the author during a 1999 phone interview. "I paid very little attention to [the comments], because I didn't really understand what they were getting at," Marsh recalled. "Maybe it had to do with the part he was playing—and he had been Ben-Hur—maybe that's what they had been making fun of."

223 "He always was on time..." Marian Marsh, 1999 phone AT.

223 Novarro's traffic violation. *LAH*, September 22, 1938.

224 "happy, wiser and free." April 26, 1939, letter, Homan.

224 "nothing would please me more" and *The Rains Came*. December 10, 1937, letter, Homan.

224–226 The information about *La Comédie du bonheur* and Novarro's 1939–40 European sojourn are from Noël Burch's *Marcel L'Herbier*, edited by Pierre Lherminier (Paris: Editions Seghers, 1973); August 1, 1939, November 10, 1939, and October 10, 1940, letters, Homan; and BRN. Novarro had been invited to appear in the picture as early as 1937, but negotiations with the Paris-based production company Artis-Film kept being postponed because of financing problems.

226 "work and technical knowledge so much." October 10, 1940, letter, Homan.

226 "a film that I finally was able to make..." Noël Burch's *Marcel L'Herbier*, p. 127.

226 "protect their freedom of speech..." *LAH*, June 18, 1940.

272 The Novarro-Shearer rift is from Allan Ellenberger's *Ramon Novarro* (Jefferson, N.C.: McFarland, 1999). The original source for this information was Novarro's former secretary Edward Weber. Strangely, in Pratt, recorded in the late 1950s, Novarro says, "I love [Shearer] very much, she was very sweet."

227 "I worked harder than ever in my life." October 10, 1940, letter, Homan.

227 The information about Dr. Samaniego is from Eduardo Samaniego's memoirs and from interviews with several family members, including Carmen Gavilán. Dr. Samaniego's death was the second passing of a close family member Novarro

had to cope with in less than one year. His uncle Ramón Guerrero had died of pneumonia in March while Novarro was in Europe.

227–228 Novarro's car accident. *LAH*, December 18, 1940, and March 4, 1941; and a March 5, 1941, letter, Homan. All quotes in this section are from this letter, unless otherwise noted.

228 "the grace of God." January 25, 1941, letter to Minnie Fisher. Allan Ellenberger's *Ramon Novarro*, p. 145.

228 "extremely embarrassed." Eyvind Earle, 1999 phone AT.

229 "You know, I'm not sorry for anything..." "Extra! Novarro Quits!" Unidentified publication, ca. 1935, author's collection.

229 "uneventful, outside a few people..." November 10, 1939, letter, Homan.

229 "peace and happiness we reach for..." December 25(?), 1939, letter, Homan.

229 In *Homosexuality: Protestant, Catholic and Jewish Issues: A Fishbone Tale* (Binghamton, N.Y.: Haworth Press, 1989), the Reverend Robert Nugent and Sister Jeannine Gramick state that according to Roman Catholic teachings, sexuality "is good and moral only within a heterosexual, monogamous union at least potentially biologically procreative, based on mutual love and fidelity and sanctioned by some kind of covenanted marriage commitment." As recently as 1986, Vatican authorities characterized the homosexual "condition" as "objectively disordered" because it leads to nonprocreative genital acts (p. 9).

12: Comeback and Farewells

230 "philosophical story which would..." Marjory Adams's "Novarro Gets Chance to Play Part He Likes." Unidentified Cohasset, Massachusetts, publication, August 16, 1940.

230 "nothing but trash." October 10, 1940, letter, Homan.

230 "the greatest acting opportunity." Undated letter, ca. spring 1941, Homan.

230 "It was a part...as cruel as Charles Laughton..." Ibid.

230 "He was very well behaved..." William Hughes, 2001 phone AT.

231 "I've never liked money matters..." October 10, 1940, letter, Homan.

231 "It is in the company of old friends..." April 14, 1937, letter, Sullivan.

231 Information about Rex Ingram and Alice Terry. O'Leary and film historian Anthony Slide, 1998 AT.

Director Robert Florey told Slide that Kada-Abd-el-Kader, the North African boy the Ingrams had adopted in the mid-1920s, grew into a juvenile delinquent and by the mid-1940s had either voluntarily or forcibly gone back across the ocean. During a November 2000 phone interview, Terry's assistant Paul Cuva recalled hearing stories that el-Kader had become a tour guide in a North African country.

231–232 Information about Natalie Bateson. George Schönbrunn, 1999 AT, and interviews with Novarro family members.

232–233 Information about Teresa Bracho. Homan and interviews with Novarro family members.

233–234 During several phone interviews with the author, Atkins said that Novarro was attracted to him because he dominated the star intellectually. He disliked going to the Gramercy house because the Samaniegos spoke only in Spanish to make him aware of his outsider status. Strangely, Atkins was unaware of important people in Novarro's life, including Rex Ingram, Alice Terry, and Teresa Bracho. Reports about Novarro's October 1941 car accident do not name Atkins as his passenger. Atkins later said that he gave the police a fictitious name. He also claimed to possess photographs and letters proving his relationship with Novarro, but these are unavailable for viewing.

233 "I've never felt so furious..." December 17, 1941, letter, Homan.

234 "ample funds in trust," "taken some drinks," and "so much easier and quicker." "Novarro Pays Liquor Fine." *LAT*, October 30, 1941.

234 "some nasty letters that suggested..." December 17, 1941, letter, Homan.

234 "Ramon Novarro arose yesterday..." *LAE*, August 6, 1942.

234–235 Camacho's alleged suggestion that Novarro work in Mexican films. *Motion Picture Herald*, November 7, 1942.

235 René Capistrán Garza was one of the leaders of the Cristero Rebellion of 1927, which had pitted certain segments of the Catholic Mexican population against the rigidly anticlerical Mexican government.

235 "vitally." April 14, 1937, letter, Sullivan.

236 *La Virgen que forjó una patria* review: *VT*, June 7, 1944. *Variety* reviewed the picture at the Belmont, where it was shown with English subtitles. Other Spanish-language films shown at that theater in the spring of 1944 had no subtitles.

236 "right-wing and reactionary." Evalia Reyes Díaz's "La Década de oro del cine mexicano." Web site www.crisolags.com/paginas/cinefilia/eve/0001.htm.

236 "I enjoyed my work there immensely..." December 16, 1942, letter, Sullivan.

237 "He didn't look so good..." Lupita Tovar, 1998 phone AT.

237–238 "I'm willing to start at the bottom..." September 8, 1941, letter, Homan.

238 "Not long ago a waitress..." William Krehm's "Where is... Roman Novarro?" *Saturday Evening Post*, January 15, 1944.

238 "I like to do things well..." January 11, 1947, letter, Sullivan.

239 "Now that she's gone..." and the information about Teresa Bracho's death are from interviews with Novarro's relatives.

239 In 1946, Novarro filed a lawsuit against former friend Pancho Barnes, claiming she owed him $8,540 (approximately $78,000 today). The suit, one of the many in which Pancho was involved in the 1940s, was apparently settled out of court for an unreported sum. The lawsuit was reported in the March 6, 1946, issue of the *Los Angeles Times*.

239 The information about the JCPenney building. *Courier News*, November 5, 1945.

239 "I have been quite nervous of late..." July 29, 1947, letter, Sullivan.

239 "after a great deal of hopeful anxiety..." Ibid. The depression of the 1930s had given the West Adams area a mortal blow, as many houses were lost to foreclosure, while others had to add boarders. By the end of World War II, many of the largest mansions had been subdivided into apartments.

240 Novarro's attitude when distressed and his need for company. Interviews with several of his family members, including Carmen Gavilán.

240 "the sweetest, poorest..." January 22, 1948, letter, Sullivan.

240 "lovely oak and sycamore trees..." Ibid.

240 "I can hardly believe it..." April 10, 1948, letter, Sullivan.

241 "not as a leading man of course..." December 12, 1946, letter, Sullivan.

241 "a very important man at MGM." December 12, 1946, letter, Sullivan.

241 "depressed and bored." Philip K. Scheuer's "Novarro at 50 'Steals' Picture in Comeback." *LAT*, June 19, 1949.

241–242 The Columbia questionnaire. Ibid.

242 "So, what have *you* been doing, Ramon?" and Novarro's reply. George Schönbrunn, 1999 AT.

242 Producer David O. Selznick, Jennifer Jones's husband, wanted *Rough Sketch* to be retitled *The Sharks Were Hungry in Havana Bay*. As was his custom, Selznick flooded Columbia and John Huston with memos suggesting ways to make Jones's participation in the picture more effective.

242 The making of *The Big Steal*. Jane Greer, 1998 phone AT; Leonard Shannon, 2001 phone AT; Don Siegel's *A Siegel Film: An Autobiography* (London: Faber and Faber, 1993); Lee Server's *Robert Mitchum* (New York: St. Martin's Press, 2001); *NYT*, February 20, 1949.

Lizabeth Scott was withdrawn from the film by her boss, producer Hal B. Wallis, after Mitchum's conviction in early January 1949.

242 "possession and conspiracy..." Lee Server's *Robert Mitchum* (New York: St. Martin's Press, 2001), p. 176.

242 "hundreds of innocent people." *Motion Picture Herald*, February 19, 1949.

243 Details about Señora Samaniego's death. December 16, 1946, letter, Sullivan; and several interviews with Novarro's family members, including Carmen Gavilán.

243 "He wanted to please her." Carmen Gavilán, 1998 AT.

243 "What would my youngest brother..." Scheuer's "Novarro at 50 'Steals' Picture in Comeback." LAT, June 19, 1949.

244 "miscast again!" May 30, 1949, letter, Sullivan.

244 "And that I think relieves me..." Ibid.

244 The Los Angeles Federation of Women accused *We Were Strangers* of being "cleverly disguised propaganda to advance the Communist Party line." *LAH*, May 12, 1949.

244 José Yglesias of the left-wing newspaper *Daily Worker* complained that the accented English spoken in *We Were Strangers* had a Mexican—not Cuban—lilt, and that the calypso rhythms found in the picture were not real Cuban music.

244 Gavin Lambert's review of Novarro's *We Were Strangers* performance in the fall 1949 issue of *Film Quarterly* was an exception to the actor's generally positive notices. "One regrets only a minor performance of Ramon Novarro," Lambert wrote, "who, as the leader of the movement, returns to overplay emphatically."

244 "[I] tried to be as different..." November 3, 1948, letter, Sullivan.

244 Gilbert Roland doubled for Novarro in *The Midshipman* in the scene when Novarro's Cadet Randall is thrown into the ocean.

244 "I do not want to be typed..." Scheuer's "Novarro at 50..."

245 "I know I am going to enjoy returning to MGM..." *LAH*, undated clipping.

245 "nasty heavy." January 10, 1950, letter, Sullivan.

245–246 The making of *Crisis*. Paula Raymond, 1998 phone AT; and the Arthur Freed Collection at MGM-USC (including salary information). Raymond remembered Novarro as "a charming gentleman."

245–246 Novarro's feeling uncomfortable with Richard Brooks is from BRN. Gilbert Roland's interference on Novarro's behalf is from an interview author Allan R. Ellenberger conducted with J. J. Cohn. *Ramon Novarro* (Jefferson, N.C.: McFarland, 1999).

246 "Ramon Novarro's emergence as a character actor..." *HR*, March 6, 1950.

246–247 Information about Rex Ingram's last years. O'Leary.

247 "In my philosophy, grief for the dead..." February 23, 1939, letter, Sullivan.

247 "Christmas was very quiet..." March 15, 1951, letter, Sullivan.

13: The Last Years

248 Novarro's interest in *The Seven Storey Mountain*. April 18, 1949, letter, Sullivan. Novarro was also deeply impressed by Merton's *Seeds of Contemplation*.

248 In an e-mail to the author dated September 29, 2001, Friar Dismas Gannon recalled that Novarro visited the Our Lady of Guadalupe monastery twice, once while it was still located in New Mexico, and the second time after the move to Oregon. At that time, Novarro made a gift to that Trappist community of $17,000, having to sell some of his stocks to raise that sum. The reaction of the monastery's abbot, Dom Columban Hawkins, was, "He's a prince."

248 "Imagine an actor..." Bill Slocum column. *New York Mirror*, April 15, 1962.

248 Information about the illnesses of Novarro's sisters. Sullivan and interviews with family members.

249 Information about El Rosario. Forrest McCoy, March 4, 2001, LT; and Sullivan. Novarro also mentioned his activities at the ranch in several interviews, including Philip K. Scheuer's "Novarro at 50 'Steals' Picture in Comeback." *LAT*, June 19, 1949.

249 Novarro's name is listed in second place on an April 26, 1959, plaque dedicated to those who assisted in the restoration of the Pala Mission.

249 A close friend recalled Novarro's lack of interest in the suffering of the world's destitute masses. In Novarro's view, all was well with the world regardless of how horrible things seemed to be, because God knew what he was doing. Eternal damnation, however, was a major concern.

249 The information about Chuck. Wes Muchmore, 1998 phone AT.

250 "I am eager to go to work..." *LAH*, November 8, 1951.

250 "He appeared naive..." Alan Brock's "My Friend Ramon." *Classic Film Collector*, fall-winter 1968.

251 "There is a prayer that I always say..." June 3, 1952, letter, Sullivan.

251 "all the places I should have visited long ago." September 23, 1950, letter, Sullivan. Other information about Novarro's European trips in the 1950s comes from Sullivan and from *The Passionate South: Latin Lover*, edited by Giannino Malossi (Milan: Edizioni Charta, 1996).

251 "mostly Civil Service types..." and the description of Novarro's Savoy dinner party. Jympson Harman article, *[London] Evening News*, January 21, 1954; RNFC, summer 1954.

252 "Of course I wish you could all come." *[London] Evening News*, January 21, 1954.

252 "happy, confident, prosperous." William Hickey's column. *[London] Daily Express*, January 19, 1954.

252 "I go back with sweet memories..." April 13, 1954, letter to the Ramon Novarro Film Club, RNFC, summer 1954.

252 "the deer eat all that grows..." *Irish Evening Herald*, January 21, 1954.

253–254 The information about *Just Passing By* comes from numerous sources, including *HR*, April 5 and August 30, 1956; *LAH*, December 1, 1956; *Los Angeles Mirror*, January 17, 1956; and *VT*, September 7 and October 30, 1956.

253 Novarro's American citizenship. December 3, 1954, letter, Sullivan.

253 "Do you ever realize how few people..." *Irish Evening Herald*, January 21, 1954.

253–254 According to an undated article (circa 1964) in the film magazine *Estrellas de ayer*, Novarro's last meeting with Garbo occurred in the early 1960s when he was in New York City. He was walking down Fifth Avenue when he saw a newspaper photograph that reminded him of his *Mata Hari* costar. Suddenly he turned, and Garbo was standing behind him, hiding under a wide-brimmed hat and sunglasses. She said, "Hello, baby," and disappeared into the crowd.

255 Herbert Howe's reappearance in Novarro's life. Unidentified clipping, author's collection.

254 "Lunching with Ramon Novarro..." *NMM*, May 1932, p. 110.

255 "was so glad." January 3, 1938, letter, Homan.

255 "just the same, just as amusing." Ibid.

255 "worn out doing nothing." Ibid.

255 Lawrence Quirk's meeting with Howe. Lawrence Quirk, 1998 AT.

255 Howe's death. Certificate of death from the State of California Department of Health Services.

255 "I was bored..." and information about his low blood pressure. The Ramon Novarro Studio Biography for Walt Disney Productions, September 15, 1958, at AMPAS.

256 "I only had a bourbon and soda..." *Los Angeles Mirror*, February 3, 1959. In Allan Ellenberger's *Ramon Novarro* (Jefferson, N.C.: McFarland, 1999), Don Atkins states that Novarro bribed a police officer at least once in the 1940s after being stopped for erratic driving.

256 In *Charlton Heston: In the Arena* (New York: Simon and Schuster, 1995), Heston recalls William Wyler exclaiming, "I wonder which one of these guys [*Ben-Hur* assistant directors] will direct the next remake" (p. 189).

256 When asked about the elimination of the seductress Iras from the new version, Carmel Myers replied, "It must be because they couldn't find anyone in Hollywood as sexy as I am" (BRN, p. 535).

256 "A curious thing happened..." BRN, p. 535. Ironically, Francis X. Bush-

man claimed that at the Broadway premiere of the 1925 *Ben-Hur*, the audience cheered for *him* during the chariot race ("Francis X. Bushman: Hollywood's First Star Talks about His Life & Times," interview copyrighted by George Garabedian in 1975. Made available to the author by T. Gene Hatcher). Bushman was a master teller of outlandish stories.

256 In his autobiography *In the Arena*, Charlton Heston states that Cecil B. DeMille exhorted him to take the role of the Jewish prince by remarking that Novarro had been "dead wrong" for the part (p. 178). In view of the overwhelmingly positive notices Novarro received at the time, DeMille's observation was at best a gross misstatement. Although considerably smaller and less brawny than Heston, Novarro looks more convincing than Heston both as a Middle Easterner and as a young man in the picture's early scenes. Comparisons are difficult in terms of acting because of the two virtually different media, silent and sound film, but while Heston's long-suffering Jewish prince relies less on pantomime than Novarro's, he also lacks the inner fire and charisma his predecessor had brought to the role a quarter of a century earlier.

257 "John Barrymore once told me..." BRN, p. 542. *Heller in Pink Tights* was a problematic production. According to Patrick McGilligan's *George Cukor: A Double Life* (St. Martin's Press, 1991), the cast would often receive new pages to memorize on the day the scenes were to be shot. Once the picture was finished, Paramount drastically recut it.

257 A sample of *Heller in Pink Tights* reviews: HR, March 12, 1960; NYT, March 17, 1960; VT, March 9, 1960.

257 Novarro's minimum of $3,000 a week. Letter to Alan Brock, ca. 1963, author's collection.

258 "just had a glass of sherry." "Novarro Faces 2 Drunken Charges." Unidentified Los Angeles newspaper, June 2, 1960, Novarro's file at AMPAS.

258 "two gin drinks." Ibid.

258 "nerve medicine." *LAH*, July 13, 1960.

258 "I find that the basic art..." Joanne Stang's "Novarro Rides Without Chariot." *NYT*, November 15, 1964.

258 *The Green Peacock* information. Novarro's publicity document, author's collection.

259 "I am old and I just want to die." John Springer's "Great Movie Stars: Where Are They Now?" *Screen Stories*, November 1962, p. 67.

259 "But if you still decide you want to die..." Ibid., p. 68.

259 "I speak with an accent still..." Ibid., p. 67.

260 "Poor Novarro indeed..." Ibid., pp. 49, 67.

260 "I probably won't..." Ibid., p. 67.

260 "I'm better off now..." William Hickey's column. *[London] Daily Express*, January 19, 1954.

260 "Novarro was a nostalgic..." HR, August 5, 1962.

260 "enjoyed one of the three..." Jack Gordon's column. *Fort Worth Press*, June 8, 1962.

261 "I am returning to the singing stage..." "Whatever Happened to Ramon Novarro." *Movie Illustrated*, June 1965.

261 Novarro's *Flower Drum Song* tour and problems with Juanita Hall. Interviews with Novarro family members, including Carmen Gavilán; several letters Novarro wrote to Leonard Shannon, courtesy of Mr. Shannon.

261 "solved any psychological problems..." *Sunday News,* January 6, 1969.

261–262 Novarro's several pleas following his arrest. *LAT,* October 5, 1962.

262 The information about Novarro's illnesses throughout the years. Sullivan, Homan, and a series of letters to Cecil Brock.

262 "a nervous wreck" and the information about Novarro's feelings in regard to his pending sentence and his trust that "All's for the best." NP, pp. 14–15.

262 "The Pagan Love Song" in high G. John Lanchbery, 2000 phone AT.

262 "I think they call it progress." Joanne Stang's "Novarro Rides Without Chariot."

263 "had $5,000 in that room." Leonard Shannon, 2001 phone AT.

263 "When I was a star..." Joanne Stang's "Novarro Rides Without Chariot."

263 "I like to play fathers..." Allen Rich's "Matinee Idol Ramon Novarro Plays TV Role." *Valley Times,* August 15, 1964.

264 The shooting of "Finest Hour." George Schönbrunn, then working at the MGM research department, 1999 phone AT.

265 "No, I would be the only one..." *Irish Evening Journal,* January 21, 1954.

265 "would rather have those who read it..." NP, p. I.

265 "Of course he won't tell All!" February 15, 1968, letter, courtesy of Joseph Yranski. Underlining is David Rollins's.

265 "very honest..." BRN, p. 543.

265 Novarro stated in his book proposal his intention to write about his bouts with alcohol. While interviewed by Philip Jenkinson in the late 1960s, Novarro mentioned that drinking affected *everyone* to one degree or another.

265 The information about Novarro's problems writing his memoirs is from a close friend of Novarro's.

265–266 "Daydreaming of one's past triumphs..." Jack Gordon's column. *Fort Worth Press,* June 8, 1962.

266 "One of the things I want to tell..." "Lonely Voyage of a Silent Star." *San Francisco Chronicle,* April 20, 1968.

266 "The motion picture industry..." John Springer's "Great Movie Stars: Where Are They Now?" p. 68.

266 "The 1925 period, and later..." Betty Lasky's "Yesterday's Star." *The Player's Showcase,* vol. I, no. 4 (summer 1965), p. 42.

266 "We of the silent screen..." BRN, p. 537.

266 "In silent pictures, individuality was all-important..." Joanne Stang's "Novarro Rides Without Chariot." In an unidentified clipping dated June 16, 1931, found in the Novarro file at AMPAS, Novarro himself had complained, "We are much handicapped in this country by the producers' ideals of beauty at the cost of everything. That is the reason that, despite their many faults, we find German and other foreign pictures a rest. Attitudes and gestures of players are natural and individual—not all set in a common mold."

267 "[I] didn't play a dual role..." Novarro's personal papers, courtesy of Leonard Shannon.

267 "I never liked anything I had done..." William Hickey's column. *[London] Daily Express,* January 19, 1954.

267 "With the exception of *The Pagan...*" BRN, p. 537.

267 "Perhaps it's better so..." and the information about Homan's visit. Several letters in Homan; "Journey to a Star," RNFC, autumn 1966. Novarro's inner demons are mentioned in a November 6, 1966, letter.

268 "Time does not stand still for any of us. Audrey Homan's autobiographical *1901 and All This* (Suffolk, U.K.: Yarrow Press, 1993).

268 "He shook my hand warmly..." DeWitt Bodeen's "Ramon Novarro." *Silent Picture,* summer 1969, no. 3.

268 "Ramon had a problem with alcohol..." Allan Ellenberger's *Raman Novarro,* p. 175.

268 The codicil that removed Antonio from the will was signed and witnessed on October 9, 1968.

268 The difficult filming of *The Wild, Wild West.* John Lanchbery, 2001 phone AT. The information about Novarro's feelings regarding Robert Conrad is from a Novarro friend.

269 "I still think about it..." John Springer's "Great Movie Stars: Where Are They Now?" p. 68.

269 "No matter who else was playing..." Leonard Shannon, August 27, 2001, LT.

269 Novarro's ill-fated trip aboard the *Canberra.* Information conveyed to the author by a passenger on the same late winter 1968 voyage. In a 1991 article for the *Hollywood Magazine,* Patrick Brock states that in 1967 he found a critically ill Novarro at his London hotel room and rushed him to a hospital. Brock also recounted having met Novarro several times during the actor's trips to England. Yet, although Novarro wrote letters to a Cecil Brock in England, no correspondence or mention of Patrick Brock could be found in his personal documents. Additionally, there is no indication that Novarro visited England after 1960.

269 Novarro's decision to sell the Laurel Canyon home. Homan, ca. summer 1968.

270 The information about Novarro's hiring male prostitutes and the problems that would at times occur comes from several sources, including close friends of the actor; the Jim Kepner files at the ONE Institute and Archives in Los Angeles; Joel Harrison's *Bloody Wednesday* (Canoga Park, Calif.: Major Books, 1978); and correspondence with Paul Ferguson.

270 The transformation in Novarro's face. Leonard Shannon, 2001 phone AT.

271 "death wish." A close friend of Novarro's, 2000 AT.

271 The bedspread theft. Homan, May 30, 1968.

271 Novarro's actions in the week prior to his death. Numerous newspaper accounts following his death, including *LAT, NYT,* and *LAHE,* November 1, 1968. A neighbor recalled Novarro's drinking binges around Halloween during a 1999 telephone interview.

271 "for a few drinks." Jim Kepner files.

14: Death in the Hollywood Hills

The court records of *People of the State of California* versus *Paul Robert Ferguson and Thomas Scott Ferguson* for the murder of Ramon Novarro, July 28 to October 27, 1969, have been either lost or misplaced. The trial transcripts, if they do exist, are unavailable for researchers. The chief sources used for the information contained in this chapter comes from the following: Jim Kepner files at the ONE Institute and Archives (Kepner accompanied and transcribed the Fergusons' trial for a series of articles in *The Advocate* and for a future book project that never materialized); several newspaper accounts—*LAT, NYT, LAHE*, et cetera—mostly in the week following Novarro's death and during the course of the trial, which received wide coverage in the Los Angeles press; correspondence with both Paul and Thomas Ferguson; and Joel Harrison's *Bloody Wednesday* (Canoga Park, Calif.: Major Books, 1978).

272 "Len, you better come right over..." Leonard Shannon, August 27, 2001, LT.

272–273 The police assumed that there had been a party the previous night—which would explain so many bottles of alcoholic beverages in the garbage Dumpster. However, those bottles had been there for several days, as Novarro had hosted a family party the week before. The garbage had not yet been picked up.

273 Description of Novarro's bruises and lacerations and cause of death come from the coroner's report by J. Wallace Graham, M.D., deputy medical examiner.

274 "an unshakable accent..." Jerry Cohen and Dial Torgerson's "Ramon Novarro, Star of Silent Films, Slain." *LAT*, November 1, 1968.

274 "He never considered himself a 'has-been'..." "Life Unrolled Like Film Legend." *Hollywood Citizen News*, November 1, 1968.

274 "small round striking instrument." "Novarro Death Instrument Found." *LAHE*, November 2, 1968.

275 "good man and fine actor." "500 Attend Final Rites for Novarro." *LAHE*, November 4, 1968.

276 The Ferguson brothers had told the Bell Gardens resident that they had been locked out of Paul's apartment after Mari left.

278 Novarro's will. Probate records, Los Angeles County.

15: The Trial

As in the previous chapter, unless otherwise noted, the information and quotes contained in this chapter come from the following: Jim Kepner files at the ONE Institute and Archives (Kepner accompanied and transcribed the Fergusons' trial for a series of articles in *The Advocate* and for a future book project that never materialized); several newspaper accounts—*LAT, NYT, LAHE*, et cetera—mostly in the week following Novarro's death and during the course of the trial, which received wide coverage in the Los Angeles press; correspondence with both Paul and Thomas Ferguson; and Joel Harrison's *Bloody Wednesday* (Canoga Park, Calif.: Major Books, 1978).

279 Tom's beating up an old man. Henry Lee's "Finis for a Faded Star." *Sunday News*, January 6, 1969.

280 "Spanish grandee." Paul Ferguson, 1999 phone AT.

280 "The last phone call of his life..." Leonard Shannon, September 3, 2001, LT.

282 "Please, get out of the way." Harrison's *Bloody Wednesday*, p. 190.

283 "I went into shock..." Paul Ferguson, 1999 phone AT.

286–287 In a September 7, 1969, interview with the *Los Angeles Times* under the title "A View of 2 Sons As Seen Through a Mother's Eyes," the Fergusons' mother asserted that she believed both brothers were involved. "But there's something wrong there," she added. "I know Tom and his stories. I know he's told lies." When asked why she had not visited her sons while they awaited trial, the mother, who lived in Chicago, replied, "I have wanted to see them all along, but, you know, money doesn't grow on trees."

287 "an enigma throughout the entire trial." Ron Einstoss's "He's Responsible for Novarro's Death, Young Ferguson Says." *LAT*, undated issue ca. September 1969.

287 "That was meant to upset me..." is from an unidentified news clipping, ca. September 1969.

291 "I'm glad Tom finally told the truth..." *LAHE*, September 25, 1969.

Epilogue

293 "I remeber [*sic*] sitting next..." Harrison's *Bloody Wednesday*, p. 289.

294 "There was no question in my mind..." Judge Mark Brandler, 1998 AT.

294 "When [Novarro] kissed me..." Paul Ferguson, 1998 phone AT.

295 "the shame [the events of October 30, 1968]..." Paul Ferguson, November 23, 1998, LT.

295 "With reference to the claim that..." Michael Morris's *Madam Valentino: The Many Lives of Natacha Rambova* (New York: Abbeville Press, 1991).

295 C. Robert Dambacher wrote about his findings in an August 28, 1990, letter to Michael Morris.

296 Novarro, Herbert Howe, and Marcus Aurelius. OTRWR-II.

Afterword

298 Tom's petition for a retrial and subsequent events. Tom Ferguson, a series of 1998 letters to the author; and Joel Harrison's *Bloody Wednesday* (Canoga Park, Calif.: Major Books, 1978).

298–299 Paul's years in San Quentin. Paul Ferguson, a series of 1998–2002 letters to the author; and Randy Shilts's "Paul Ferguson Remembers the Ramon Navarro [*sic*] Murder," *The Advocate*, October 5, 1977.

298 "extremely angry and bitter." "Actor's Killer Wins Award for Fiction." *LAHE*, June 30, 1975.

299 "a half-blood Indian in today's America." Paul Ferguson. May 30, 2001, LT.

299 "Mr. Novarro's death still affects me..." Paul Ferguson. May 30, 2001, LT.

299–300 The information about the Samaniego siblings comes from interviews with several family members, including Carmen Gavilán and Father Eddie Samaniego, S. J.

300 Information about Marion Morgan. Judith Mayne's *Directed by Dorothy Arzner* (Bloomington: Indiana University Press, 1994).

300 Information about Ferdinand Pinney Earle. Eyvind Earle's *Horizon Bound on a Bicycle* (Los Angeles: Earle and Bane, 1990).

301 "would marry any woman . . ." Richard J. and Mary Buckingham Maturi's *Francis X. Bushman: A Biography and Filmography* (Jefferson, N.C.: McFarland, 1998).

301 George Walsh's assertion that Novarro lacked the required physique to play Ben-Hur. George Walsh II, 2000 phone AT.

301 Louis Samuel's request that Lloyd Wright build another house for him is found in the Lloyd Wright collection in the Arts Library at the University of California at Los Angeles.

302 Louis Graveure and Mme. Clara Novello Davies's encounter. Sandy Wilson's *Ivor* (London: Michael Joseph, 1975).

303 Alice Terry's later years. Anthony Slide, 1998 AT; and Jack Hewson, 2000 AT.

304 "remain, as the Bible remains." *VT* review of *Ben-Hur*, January 6, 1926. In Pratt, Novarro says that in the mid-1940s he was told by a studio operator that a note on the *Ben-Hur* print stated, "To be shown to no one under any circumstances." The studio had been thinking of remaking *Ben-Hur* since the mid-1930s.

In BRN, DeWitt Bodeen states that Novarro appeared as an extra and bit player in more than one hundred films before his big break in *The Prisoner of Zenda*. However, Novarro says in Pratt that he worked in only a handful of pictures during those early years. Below is a list of his known film appearances as an extra or bit player. In addition to those titles, he also played a bit part in an unidentified Mabel Normand vehicle (probably for Goldwyn, ca. 1920) and danced with Derelys Perdue in an unidentified Robertson-Cole production starring Sessue Hayakawa. Apart from the story that has Rex Ingram picking the young Ramón Samaniego from the ranks of extras to replace Valentino, a tale that Novarro himself has rebuffed, there is no indication that he actually appeared in Ingram's *The Conquering Power*.

Figures for *The Prisoner of Zenda* and *Trifling Women* are from the Metro Pictures Corporation cost records in the special collections at AMPAS. Figures for *Scaramouche*, *Thy Name Is Woman*, *Wir schalten um auf Hollywood*, *La Sevillana*, and *Le Chanteur de Séville* are courtesy of Karl Thiede. All other box-office, cost, and profit or loss information about MGM films is from the Eddie Mannix ledger, found in the Howard Strickling Collection at AMPAS. The cost of *We Were Strangers* is from Stuart Kaminsky's *John Huston: Maker of Magic* (Boston: Houghton Mifflin, 1978). Figures for *The Big Steal* are courtesy of Dr. Richard Jewell, associate dean and professor, University of Southern California School of Cinema-Television.

Abbreviations

Pr: Producer Dir: Director Scr: Screenwriter Ph: Cinematographer
Ed: Editor AD: Art Director Sp: Special effects Tt: Intertitles
Mus: Music B&W: Black and white

Extra/Bit Parts

The Jaguar's Claws (1917) Lasky/Paramount. Dir: Marshall Neilan. Starring Sessue Hayakawa.
The Woman God Forgot (1917) Artcraft/Paramount. Dir: Cecil B. DeMille. Starring Geraldine Farrar and Wallace Reid.
The Little American (1917) Artcraft/Paramount. Dir: Cecil B. DeMille. Starring Mary Pickford and Jack Holt.
The Hostage (1917) Lasky/Paramount. Dir: Robert Thornby. Starring Wallace Reid.
The Goat (1918) Famous Players–Lasky/Paramount. Dir: Donald Crisp. Starring Fred Stone.

The Four Horsemen of the Apocalypse (1921) Metro. Dir: Rex Ingram. Starring Rudolph Valentino and Alice Terry.

A Small Town Idol (1921) Mack Sennett Comedies Corp. Dir: Erle C. Kenton. Starring Ben Turpin, Phyllis Haver, and James Finlayson.

Man—Woman—Marriage (1921) Universal. Dir: Allen Holubar. Starring Dorothy Phillips and James Kirkwood.

The Concert (1921). Metro. Dir: Victor Schertzinger. Starring Lewis Stone and Myrtle Stedman.

Featured and Starring Roles

Mr. Barnes of New York, Goldwyn Pictures Corporation. Opened on May 22, 1922. Pr: Samuel Goldwyn. Dir: Victor Schertzinger. Scr: Gerald Duffy and J. E. Nash, from the novel by Archibald Clavering Gunter. Ph: George Brewster. Silent. B&W. Running time: 5 reels (approx. 60 min.).

Cast: Tom Moore (Mr. Barnes), Anna Lehr (Marina Paoli), Naomi Childers (Enid Anstruther), Lewis Willoughby (Gerard Anstruther), Ramon Samaniego (Antonio Paoli), Otto Hoffman (Tomasso), Sidney Ainsworth (Danella).

The Prisoner of Zenda, Metro. Premiered at the Astor Theater, New York City, on July 31, 1922 (general release on September 11, 1922). Pr & Dir: Rex Ingram. Scr: Mary O'Hara, from the 1897 play by Edward Rose and from the novel by Anthony Hope. Ph: John F. Seitz. Ed: Grant Whytock. AD: Anton Myers. Silent. B&W. Running time: 9 reels (approx. 110 min.). Cost: $323,062 (no other financial information is available).

Cast: Lewis Stone (Rudolf Rassendyll/King Rudolf), Alice Terry (Princess Flavia), Robert Edeson (Colonel Sapt), Stuart Holmes (Grand Duke "Black" Michael), Ramon Novarro (Rupert of Hentzau), Malcolm McGregor (Count von Tarlenheim), Barbara La Marr (Antoinette de Mauban), Edward Connelly (Marshall Von Strakencz), Lois Lee (Countess Helga), John George (the Lizard).

Trifling Women (working title: *Black Orchids/The Black Orchid*), Metro. Premiered at the Astor Theater, New York City, on October 2, 1922 (general release on November 6, 1922). Pr & Dir: Rex Ingram. Scr: Rex Ingram, from his screenplay for the 1917 motion picture *Black Orchids* (although not credited, the story was inspired by Marie Corelli's *Vendetta*). Ph: John F. Seitz. Ed: Grant Whytock. AD: Leo E. Kuter. Silent. B&W. Running time: 9 reels (approx 110 min.). Cost: $273,449 (no other financial information is available). NOTE: *Trifling Women* is now lost.

Cast: Lewis Stone (Marquis Ferroni), Barbara La Marr (Jacqueline de Séverac/Zareda), Ramon Novarro (Henri Batiste/Ivan de Maupin), Edward Connelly (Baron François de Maupin), Pomeroy Cannon (Léon de Séverac), Hughie Mack (Père Alphonse Bidondeau), Gene Pouyet (Colonel Roybet), John George (Achmet), Joe Martin (Hatim-Tai, the orangutan).

Where the Pavement Ends (working title: *The Passion Vine*), Metro. Opened at the Capitol Theater, New York City, on April 1, 1923. Pr & Dir: Rex Ingram. Scr: Rex Ingram, from the short story "The Passion Vine" found in John Russell's book *The Red Mark and Other Stories.* Ph: John F. Seitz. Ed: Grant Whytock. Silent.

B&W. Running time: 8 reels (approx. 95 min.). NOTE: *Where the Pavement Ends* is now lost.

Cast: Edward Connelly (Pastor Spener), Alice Terry (Matilda Spener), Ramon Novarro (Motauri), Harry T. Morey (Captain Hull Gregson), John George (Napuka Joe).

Scaramouche, Metro. Special premiere at the Belasco Theater, Washington, D.C., on September 15, 1923. New York City premiere held at the Forty-fourth Street Theater on September 30, 1923 (general release in February 1924). Pr & Dir: Rex Ingram. Scr: Willis Goldbeck, from the novel *Scaramouche: A Romance of the French Revolution* by Rafael Sabatini. Ph: John F. Seitz. Ed: Grant Whytock. Silent. B&W. Running time: 10 reels (approx. 120 min.). Cost: $858,723 (no other financial information is available).

Cast: Alice Terry (Aline de Kercadiou), Ramon Novarro (André-Louis Moreau), Lewis Stone (Marquis de la Tour d'Azyr), Edith Allen (Climène Binet), Lloyd Ingraham (Quinton de Kercadiou), Julia Swayne Gordon (Countess Thérèse de Plougastel), William Humphrey (Chevalier de Chabrillane), Otto Matiesen (Philippe de Vilmorin), George Siegmann (Georges Jacques Danton), Bowditch Turner (Le Chapelier), James A. Marcus (Challefau Binet), Lydia Yeamans Titus (Madame Binet), John George (Polichinelle), Edward Connelly (Minister to the King), Slavko Vorkapitch (Napoléon Bonaparte).

Thy Name Is Woman, a Louis B. Mayer Production distributed by Metro. Premiered at the Mission Theater, Los Angeles, on February 4, 1924. Pr: Louis B. Mayer. Dir: Fred Niblo. Scr: Bess Meredyth, from the 1915 play *Der Weibsteufel/The She-Devil* by Karl Schönherr, translated by Benjamin Glazer. Ph: Victor Milner. Ed: Lloyd Nosler. Silent. B&W. Running time: 9 reels (approx. 110 min.). Domestic rentals: $388,000 (no other financial information is available).

Cast: Ramon Novarro (Juan Ricardo), Barbara La Marr (Guerita), William V. Mong (Pedro, the Fox), Wallace MacDonald (Captain Rodrigo de Castelar), Robert Edeson (Comandante), Claire McDowell (Juan's mother), Edith Roberts (Dolores).

The Arab, Metro-Goldwyn. Opened on July 13, 1924. Pr & Dir: Rex Ingram. Scr: Rex Ingram, from the 1911 play *The Arab* by Edgar Selwyn. Ph: John F. Seitz. Ed: Grant Whytock. Silent. B&W. Running time: 7 reels (approx. 85 min.).

Cast: Ramon Novarro (Jamil Abdullah Azam), Alice Terry (Mary Hilbert), Jerrold Robertshaw (Dr. Hilbert), Maxudian (Governor), Jean de Limur (Hossein, his aide).

The Red Lily, Metro-Goldwyn. Opened at the Capitol Theater, New York City, on September 28, 1924. Pr: Louis B. Mayer and Irving G. Thalberg. Dir: Fred Niblo. Scr: Bess Meredyth, from an original story by Fred Niblo. Ph: Victor Milner. Ed: Lloyd Nosler. Silent. B&W. Running time: 7 reels (approx. 85 min.).

Cast: Enid Bennett (Marise La Noue), Ramon Novarro (Jean Leonnec), Wallace Beery (Bobo), Frank Currier (Hugo Leonnec), Rosemary Theby (Nana), Mitchell Lewis (D'Agut), Emily Fitzroy (Mama Bouchard), Georges Periolat (Papa Bouchard), Dick Sutherland (Toad), Gibson Gowland (Le Turc), George Nichols (Concierge).

A Lover's Oath (aka *The Rubaiyat of Omar Khayyam/A Son of Omar*), Astor Distribution Corporation. Opened at Loew's New York on September 29, 1925 (filmed in

1921). Pr & Dir: Ferdinand Pinney Earle. Scr: Ferdinand Pinney Earle, from Edward Fitzgerald's 1859 English-language translation of Omar Khayyam's collection of poems, *The Rubaiyat* (ca. 1120). Ph: Georges Benoit. Ed: Milton Sills. Sp: Gordon Bishop Pollock. Silent. B&W. Running time: 6 reels (approx. 70 min.). Cost: $65,000 (according to Earle in a December 18, 1925, letter to Irving Thalberg). NOTE: *A Lover's Oath* is now lost.

Cast: Ramon Novarro (Ben Ali), Kathleen Key (Sherin), Frederick Warde (Omar Khayyam), Edwin Stevens (Hassan Ben Sabbath), Hedwiga Reicher (Hassan's wife), Snitz Edwards (Omar's servant), Charles A. Post (Commander of the Faithful), Arthur Edmund Carewe (Prince Yussuf), Paul Weigel (Sheik Rustum), Philippe de Lacy (his son), Fay Wray (extra).

The Midshipman (working title: *Midshipman Sterling*), MGM. Opened at the Capitol Theater, New York City, on October 11, 1925. Pr: Bernard Hyman. Dir: Christy Cabanne. Scr: F. McGrew Willis and Christy Cabanne, from a story by Carey Wilson. Ph: Oliver Marsh. Ed: Harold Young. Silent. B&W. Running time: 8 reels (approx. 95 min.). Cost: $175,000. Domestic rentals: $460,000. Foreign: $490,000. Profit: $455,000.

Cast: Ramon Novarro (Dick Randall), Harriet Hammond (Patricia Lawrence), Wesley Barry (Ted Lawrence), Margaret Seddon (Mrs. Randall), Crauford Kent (Basil Courtney), Maurice Ryan (Fat), Harold Goodwin (Tex), William Boyd (Spud), Kathleen Key (Rita), Joan Crawford (girl on the park bench), Gilbert Roland (bit as Novarro's double).

Ben-Hur, MGM. Premiered at the George M. Cohan Theater, New York City, on December 30, 1925. Pr: Irving Thalberg and Louis B. Mayer by special arrangement with A. L. Erlanger, Charles B. Dillingham, and Florenz Ziegfeld, Jr. Dir: Fred Niblo. Directorial Associates: Alfred L. Raboch and B. Reeves Eason (and Christy Cabanne, uncredited). Scr: Carey Wilson and Bess Meredyth, based on June Mathis's adaptation of General Lew Wallace's 1880 novel. Tt: Katherine Hilliker and H. H. Caldwell. Ph: Karl Struss, Percy Hilburn, René Guissart, and Clyde De Vinna. Ed: Lloyd Nosler (chief editor). AD: Cedric Gibbons, Horace Jackson and others. Sp: Ferdinand Pinney Earle, Kenneth Gordon Maclean, and others. Silent. B&W with two-strip Technicolor sequences. Running time: 12 reels (approx. 145 min.). Cost: $3,967,000. Domestic rentals: $4,359,000. Foreign: $5,027,000. Loss: $698,000. 1931 reissue: Cost: $36,000. Domestic rentals: $199,000. Foreign: $1,153,000. Profit: $779,000. Total cost: $4,003,000. Domestic rentals: $4,558,000. Foreign: $6,180,000. Profit: $81,000.

Cast: Ramon Novarro (Ben-Hur), May McAvoy (Esther), Francis X. Bushman (Messala), Carmel Myers (Iras), Betty Bronson (Mary), Claire McDowell (Princess of Hur), Kathleen Key (Tirzah), Nigel de Brulier (Simonides) Mitchell Lewis (Sheik Ilderim), Leo White (Sanballat), Frank Currier (Quintus Arrius), Charles Belcher (Balthasar), Dale Fuller (Amrah), Winter Hall (Joseph), Myrna Loy (extra).

Lovers? (working title: *The Great Galeoto*), MGM. Opened at the Capitol Theater, New York City, on April 9, 1927. Pr: Irving Thalberg. Dir: John M. Stahl. Scr: Douglas Furber and Sylvia Thalberg (Novarro has asserted that Stahl rewrote much of the script), from *The World and His Wife* by Frederic Nordlinger, an English-language adaptation of *El Gran Galeoto, drama en tres actos y en verso* by José Echegaray y Eizaguirre. Tt: Marion Ainslee and Ruth Cummings. Ph: Max Fabian. Ed: Margaret Booth. Silent. B&W. Running time: 6 reels (approx. 70 min.). Cost: $347,000. Domestic rentals: $368,000. Foreign: $268,000. Profit: $104,000. NOTE: *Lovers?* is now lost.

Cast: Ramon Novarro (Ernesto), Alice Terry (Teodora), Edward Martindel (Don Julian), Edward Connelly (Don Severo), George K. Arthur (Pepito), Lillian Leighton (Doña Mercedes), Holmes Herbert (Milton), John Miljan (Alvarez), Roy D'Arcy (Señor Galdos).

The Student Prince in Old Heidelberg (working title/aka: *Old Heidelberg*), MGM. Opened at the Astor Theater, New York City, on September 21, 1927 (general release on January 30, 1928). Pr: Irving Thalberg. Dir: Ernst Lubitsch. Scr: Hans Kräly, from the novel *Karl Heinrich* by Wilhelm Meyer-Förster. Tt: Marion Ainslee and Ruth Cummings. Ph: John Mescall. Ed: Andrew Marton. AD: Cedric Gibbons and Richard Day. Silent. B&W. Running time: 10 reels (approx. 120 min.). Cost: $1,205,000. Domestic rentals: $894,000. Foreign: $662,000. Loss: $307,000. NOTE: The picture was copyrighted as *The Student Prince in Old Heidelberg* and was often referred to in the press by that name, but, strangely, the on-screen credits read only *Old Heidelberg*.

Cast: Ramon Novarro (Prince Karl Heinrich), Norma Shearer (Kathi), Jean Hersholt (Dr. Friedrich Jüttner), Gustav Von Seyffertitz (King Karl VII), Philippe de Lacy (Young Karl, the heir apparent), Edgar Norton (Lutz), Bobby Mack (Johann Kellerman), Edward Connelly (Court Marshal), Otis Harlan (Old Ruder), John S. Peters, George K. Arthur, Lincoln Stedman, Lionel Belmore (students), Edythe Chapman (Young Karl's Nanny).

The Road to Romance (working title: *Romance*), MGM. Opened at the Capitol Theater, New York City, on October 8, 1927. Pr: Hunt Stromberg. Dir: John S. Robertson. Scr: Josephine Lovett, from the 1903 novel *Romance* by Joseph Conrad and Ford Maddox Hueffer (aka Ford Maddox Ford). Tt: Joseph Farnham. Ph: Oliver Marsh. Ed: William Hamilton. Silent. B&W. Running time: 7 reels (approx. 85 min.). Cost: $280,000. Domestic rentals: $425,000. Foreign: $298,000. Profit: $202,000. NOTE: *The Road to Romance* is now lost.

Cast: Ramon Novarro (José Armando), Marceline Day (Serafina), Marc MacDermott (Pópolo), Roy D'Arcy (Don Balthasar), Cesare Gravina (Castro), Bobby Mack (drunkard), Otto Matiesen (Don Carlos), Jules Cowles (Smoky Beard).

Across to Singapore (working title: *China Bound*), MGM. Opened at the Capitol Theater, New York City, on April 29, 1928. Pr: Eddie Mannix. Dir: William Nigh. Scr: adaptation by Ted Shane, from the novel *All the Brothers Were Valiant* by Ben Ames Williams; continuity by Richard Schayer. Tt: Joseph Farnham. Ph: John F. Seitz. Ed: Ben Lewis. Silent. B&W. Running time: 7 reels (approx. 85 min.). Cost: $290,000. Domestic rentals: $548,000. Foreign: $333,000. Profit: $306,000.

Cast: Ramon Novarro (Joel Shore), Joan Crawford (Priscilla Crowninshield), Ernest Torrence (Captain Mark Shore), Frank Currier (Jeremiah Shore), Dan Wolheim (Noah Shore), Duke Martin (Matthew Shore), Edward Connelly (Joshua Crowninshield), James Mason (Finch), Anna May Wong (Bailarina).

A Certain Young Man (working titles: *Bellamy the Magnificent*, *The Heartbreaker*, *The Man* *from London, Fashions in Love*), MGM. Opened at the Capitol Theater, New York City, on June 9, 1928. Pr: Bernard Hyman. Dir: Hobart Henley (and George O'Hara, uncredited). Scr: Doris Bureel, with continuity by Donna Barrell (inspired by Roy Horniman's novel *Bellamy the Magnificent*). Tt: Marion Ainslee and Ruth Cummings. Ph: Merritt B. Gerstad. Ed: Basil Wrangell. Silent. B&W. Running time: 6 reels (approx. 70 min.). Cost: $363,000. Domestic rentals: $263,000. Foreign: $237,000. Loss: $50,000. NOTE: *A Certain Young Man* is now lost.

   Cast: Ramon Novarro (Lord Gerald Brinsley), Renée Adorée (Henriette), Marceline Day (Phyllis), Carmel Myers (Mrs. Crutchley), Bert Roach (Mr. Crutchley), Huntley Gordon (Mr. Hammond), Ernest Wood (Hubert).

Forbidden Hours (working titles: *The Sun King, The Loves of Louis, His Night*), MGM. Opened at the Capitol Theater, New York City, on July 22, 1928. Pr: Bernard Hyman. Dir: Harry Beaumont. Scr: A. P. Younger. Tt: John Colton. Ph: Merritt B. Gerstad. Ed: William Hamilton. AD: Cedric Gibbons and Richard Day. Silent. B&W. Running time: 6 reels (approx. 70 min.). Cost: $293,000. Domestic rentals: $401,000. Foreign: $198,000. Profit: $109,000.

   Cast: Ramon Novarro (His Majesty, Michael IV), Renée Adorée (Marie de Floriet), Dorothy Cumming (Queen Alexia), Edward Connelly (Prime Minister), Roy D'Arcy (Duke Nicky), Mitzi Cummings (Princess Ena), Alberta Vaughn (Nina).

The Flying Fleet (working titles: *The Ensign, Eagles of the Fleet, Gold Braid, The Flying Ensign*), MGM. Opened at the Capitol Theater, New York City, on February 9, 1929. Pr: Bernard Hyman. Dir: George W. Hill. Scr: Richard Schayer, from an original story by Lt. Comdr. Frank Wead, USN, and Byron Morgan. Tt: Joseph Farnham. Ph: Ira Morgan, with special air photography by Charles A. Marshall. Ed: Blanche Sewell. With synchronized music and sound effects (no dialogue). B&W. Running time: 86 min. Cost: $385,000. Domestic rentals: $658,000. Foreign: $628,000. Profit: $443,000.

   Cast: Ramon Novarro (Tommy Winslow), Ralph Graves (Steve Randall), Anita Page (Anita Hastings), Edward Nugent (Dizzy), Carroll Nye (Tex), Summer Getchell (Kewpie), Gardner James (Specs), Alfred Allen (Admiral), Claire McDowell (Mrs. Hastings).

The Pagan, MGM. Opened at the Capitol Theater, New York City, on May 11, 1929. Pr: Irving Thalberg. Dir: W. S. Van Dyke. Scr: Dorothy Farnum, from a story by John Russell. Tt: John Howard Lawson. Ph: Clyde de Vinna. Ed: Ben Lewis. With synchronized music and sound effects (no dialogue). Song: "The Pagan Love Song," lyrics by Arthur Freed; music by Nacio Herb Brown. B&W. Running time: 77 min. Cost: $293,000. Domestic rentals: $639,000. Foreign: $713,000. Profit: $562,000.

   Cast: Ramon Novarro (Henry Shoesmith, Jr.), Dorothy Janis (Tito), Renée Adorée (Madge), Donald Crisp (Mr. Slater).

Devil-May-Care (working title: *The Battle of the Ladies*), MGM. Opened at the Astor Theater, New York City, on December 22, 1929. Pr: Albert Lewin. Dir: Sidney Franklin. Scr: Hans Kräly; adaptation by Richard Schayer, from the 1851 French play *La Bataille des dames* by Ernest Legouvé and Eugène Scribe; and dialogue by Zelda Sears. Ph: Merritt B. Gerstad. Ed: Conrad A. Nervig. AD: Cedric Gibbons.

Ballet Dir: Albertina Rasch. Ballet Mus: Dimitri Tiomkin. Songs: lyrics by Clifford Grey, music by Herbert Stothart. Sound. B&W with a two-strip Technicolor sequence. Running time: 96 min. Cost: $487,000. Domestic rentals: $713,000. Foreign: $703,000. Profit: $357,000.

Cast: Ramon Novarro (Armand), Marion Harris (Louise), Dorothy Jordan (Leonie), John Miljan (De Grignon), William Humphrey (Napoleon), George Davis (Groom), Clifford Bruce/Brooke (Gaston).

In Gay Madrid (working title: *The House of Troy*), MGM. Opened at the Capitol Theater, New York City, on June 7, 1930. Pr: Paul Bern. Dir: Robert Z. Leonard. Scr: Bess Meredyth, Salisbury Field, and Edwin Justus Mayer, from the novel *La Casa de la Troya* by Alejandro Pérez Lugin. Ph: Oliver T. Marsh. Ed: William S. Gray. Mus: Fred E. Ahlert, Xavier Cugat, and Herbert Stothart; song lyrics by Clifford Grey and Roy Turk. Sound. B&W. Running time: 81 min. Cost: $467,000. Domestic rentals: $551,000. Foreign: $398,000. Profit: $122,000.

Cast: Ramon Novarro (Ricardo), Dorothy Jordan (Carmina), Lottice Howell (La Goyita), Claude King (Marques de Castelar), Eugenie Besserer (Doña Generosa), William V. Mong (Rivas), Beryl Mercer (Doña Concha), Nanci Price (Jacinta), Herbert Clark (Octavio), David Scott (Ernesto), George Chandler (Enrique), Bruce Coleman (Corpulento), Nicholas Caruso (Carlos).

The March of Time (working titles: *Hollywood Revue of 1930, Show World*), MGM. Unreleased. Pr: Harry Rapf. Dir: Charles Reisner. Novarro's Song: "Long Ago in Alcala," words and music by André Messager. Sound. B&W with Technicolor sequences.

Cast: Joe Weber, Lew Fields, Ramon Novarro, Marie Dressler, Fay Templeton, Josephine Sabel, Bing Crosby, Karl Dane, Louis Mann, Barney Fagan, William Collier, Sr., DeWolf Hopper, Benny Rubin, Raquel Torres, Vivian and Rosetta Duncan, the Albertina Rasch Ballet Corps.

NOTE: The MGM-produced German-language picture *Wir schalten um auf Hollywood* (*We Tune In to Hollywood*) features musical numbers from *The March of Time*, including Novarro's "Long Ago in Alcala." Distributed by Parufamet (Paramount-Ufa-Metro). Opened at the Capitol, Berlin, on June 10, 1931. Dir: Frank Reicher. Scr: Paul Morgan. Ph: Ray Binger, John Arnold, and Irving Ries. Ed: Adrienne Fazan. AD: Cedric Gibbons. Songs: Oscar Straus and Christian Sinding. Sound. B&W with two-strip Technicolor sequences. Running time: 70 min. Cost: $83,281 (no other financial information is available).

Cast: Paul Morgan (as himself), Egon von Jordan (Karl Peter Ferdinand). As themselves: Buster Keaton, Ramon Novarro, Nora Gregor, Oscar Straus, Adolphe Menjou, Heinrich George, John Gilbert, Joan Crawford, Dita Parlo, Norma Shearer, Sergei Eisenstein, Wallace Beery, the Dodge Sisters, the Albertina Rasch Ballet Corps.

Call of the Flesh (working titles: *The Singer of Seville, The Dancer of Seville*), MGM. Opened at the Capitol Theater, New York City, on September 12, 1930. Pr: Hunt Stromberg. Dir: Charles Brabin (Novarro claims he directed most of the picture himself). Scr: Story by Dorothy Farnum, dialogue by John Colton. Ph: Merritt B. Gerstad. Ed: Conrad A. Nervig. Songs: lyrics by Clifford Grey, music by Herbert Stothart. Although not credited in the picture, Novarro's name is on the "Lonely" sheet music as a co-composer. Sound. B&W, originally with a two-strip Technicolor sequence. Running time: 100 min. Cost: $464,000. Domestic rentals: $619,000. Foreign: $1,003,000. Profit: $285,000.

Cast: Ramon Novarro (Juan de Dios), Dorothy Jordan (María Consuelo Vargas), Renée Adorée (Lola), Nance O'Neil (Mother Superior), Ernest Torrence (Esteban), Mathilde Comont (La Rumbarita), Russell Hopton (Captain Enrique Vargas).

La Sevillana (aka *Sevilla de mis amores/El Cantante de Sevilla*). MGM. Opened at the Teatro Califórnia Internacional, Los Angeles, on December 5, 1930. Pr: Irving Thalberg. Dir: Ramon Novarro. Scr: Spanish-language adaptation of *Call of the Flesh* by Ramón Guerrero. Assistant Director: Carlos F. Borcosque. Ph: Merritt B. Gerstad. Ed: Tom Held. Songs: Ramon Novarro (Spanish-language lyrics) and Herbert Stothart. Sound. B&W. Running time: 102 min. Cost: $103,437. (No other financial information is available. Both its cost and rentals were probably included in the *Call of the Flesh* figures.)

Cast: Ramon Novarro (Juan de Dios), Conchita Montenegro (María Consuelo Vargas), Rosita Ballesteros (Lola), José Soriano Viosca (Tío Esteban), Sra. L. G. de Samaniego (Madre Superior), Martín Garralaga (Capitán Enrique Varga), Sra. María Calvo (Lulu Lapenco), Michael Vavitch (Empresario).

Le Chanteur de Séville (aka *Séville de mes amours*), MGM. Opened at the Madeleine Theater, Paris, on February 21, 1931. Pr: Hunt Stromberg. Dir: Ramon Novarro. Scr: French-language adaptation of *Call of the Flesh* by Yvan Noé and Anne Mauclair. Ph: Merritt B. Gerstad. Ed: Tom Held. Songs: Ramon Novarro and Herbert Stothart. Sound. B&W. Running time: 105 min. Cost: $96,598. (No other financial information is available. Both its cost and rentals were probably included in the *Call of the Flesh* figures.)

Cast: Ramon Novarro (Juan de Dios), Suzy Vernon (María Consuelo Vargas), Pierrette Caillol (Lola), Georges Mauloy (Esteban), Mathilde Comont (La Rumbarita), Marcel de la Brosse (Enrique Vargas).

Daybreak, MGM. Opened at the Capitol Theater, New York City, on May 29, 1931. Pr: Bernard Hyman. Dir: Jacques Feyder. Scr: Zelda Sears, from Ruth Cummings's adaptation of Arthur Schnitzler's 1926 novel *Spiel im Morgengrauen*; dialogue by Cyril Hume. Ph: Merritt B. Gerstad. Ed: Tom Held. AD: Cedric Gibbons. Sound. B&W. Running time: 76 min. Cost: $515,000. Domestic rentals: $418,000. Foreign: $223,000. Loss: $126,000.

Cast: Ramon Novarro (Willi Kasda), Helen Chandler (Laura Taub), Jean Hersholt (Herr Schnabel), C. Aubrey Smith (General von Hertz), William Bakewell (Otto), Karen Morley (Emily Kessner), Kent Douglass/Douglass Montgomery (Erich Von Lear), Glenn Tryon (Franz), Clyde Cook (Josef), Sumner Getchall (Emil), Clara Blandick (Frau Hoffman), Edwin Maxwell (Herr Hoffman), Jackie Searle (August).

Son of India (working title: *The Son of the Rajah*), MGM. Opened at the Capitol Theater, New York City, on July 24, 1931. Pr: Hunt Stromberg. Dir: Jacques Feyder. Scr: Ernest Vajda, from the novel *Mr. Isaacs* by F. Marion Crawford, with additional dialogue by John Meehan and Claudine West. Ph: Harold Rosson. Ed: Conrad A. Nervig. Sound. B&W. Running time: 72 min. Cost: $503,000. Domestic rentals: $491,000. Foreign: $490,000. Profit: $84,000.

Cast: Ramon Novarro (Karim), Conrad Nagel (William Darsay), Marjorie Rambeau (Mrs. Darsay), Madge Evans (Janice Darsay), C. Aubrey Smith (Dr. Wallace), Mitchell Lewis (Hamid), John Miljan (Juggat), Nigel de Brulier (Rao Rama).

Mata Hari, MGM. Opened at the Capitol Theater, New York City, on December 31, 1931. Pr: Bernard Fineman. Dir: George Fitzmaurice. Scr: Story by Benjamin Glazer and Leo Birinski, dialogue by Doris Anderson and Gilbert Emery. Ph: William Daniels. Ed: Frank Sullivan. Sound. B&W. Running time: 103 min. Cost: $558,000. Domestic rentals: $931,000. Foreign: $1,296,000. Profit: $879,000. 1940 reissue: Domestic rentals: $81,000. Foreign: $81,000. Profit: $27,000.

Cast: Greta Garbo (Mata Hari), Ramon Novarro (Lt. Alexis Rosanoff), Lionel Barrymore (General Shubin), Lewis Stone (Andriani), C. Henry Gordon (Dubois), Karen Morley (Carlotta), Alex B. Francis (Caron), Blanche Frederici (Sister Angelica), Edmund Breese (Warden), Helen Jerome Eddy (Sister Genevieve), Frank Reicher (cook/spy), Lennox Pawle (DiSignac), Mischa Auer (man executed), Cecil Cunningham (gambler), Michael Visaroff (Jacques), Sarah Padden (Sister Teresa).

Huddle (alternate title: *For Glory and a Girl*), MGM. Opened at the Capitol Theater, New York City, on June 16, 1932. Pr: Bernard Hyman. Dir: Sam Wood. Scr: Robert Lee Johnson and Arthur S. Hyman, from the story by Francis Wallace; dialogue by Walton Hall Smith and C. Gardner Sullivan. Ph: Harold Wenstrom. Ed: Hugh Wynn. Sound. B&W. Running time: 104 min. Cost: $514,000. Domestic rentals: $476,000. Foreign: $333,000. Loss: $28,000.

Cast: Ramon Novarro (Tony Amatto), Madge Evans (Rosalie Stone), Una Merkel (Thelma), Ralph Graves (Coach Malcolm Gale), John Arledge (Jim "Pidge" Pidgeon), Frank Albertson (Larry Wilson), Kane Richmond (Tom Stone), Martha Sleeper (Barbara Winston), Henry Armetta (Mr. Amatto), Ferike Boros (Mrs. Amatto), Rockliffe Fellows (Mr. Stone), Joe Sauers (Orville Slater).

The Son-Daughter, MGM. Opened at the Capitol Theater, New York City, on December 30, 1932. Pr: Hunt Stromberg. Dir: Clarence Brown. Scr: John Goodrich and Claudine West, from the 1919 play by George M. Scarborough and David Belasco; dialogue by Leon Gordon. Ph: Oliver T. Marsh. Ed: Margaret Booth. AD: Cedric Gibbons. Sound. B&W. Running time: 86 min. Cost: $423,000. Domestic rentals: $379,000. Foreign: $313,000. Profit: $6,000.

Cast: Helen Hayes (Lien Wha), Ramon Novarro (Tom Lee/Prince Chun), Lewis Stone (Dr. Dong Tong), Warner Oland (Fen Sha), Ralph Morgan (Fang Fou Hy), Louise Closser Hale (Toy Yah), H. B. Warner (Sin Kai).

The Barbarian (working title: *Man of the Nile*), MGM. Opened at the Capitol Theater, New York City, on May 12, 1933. Pr: Bernard Hyman. Dir: Sam Wood. Scr: Anita Loos and Elmer Harris, from a story by Edgar Selwyn. Ph: Harold Rosson. Ed: Tom Held. AD: Cedric Gibbons. Mus: Herbert Stothart. Song: "Love Songs of the Nile," lyrics by Arthur Freed, music by Nacio Herb Brown. Sound. B&W. Running time: 83 min. Cost:$447,000. Domestic rentals: $337,000. Foreign: $506,000. Profit: $100,000.

Cast: Ramon Novarro (Jamil El Shehab), Myrna Loy (Diana Standing), Reginald Denny (Gerald Hume), Louise Closser Hale (Powers), C. Aubrey Smith (Cecil Harwood), Edward Arnold (Pasha Achmed), Blanche Frederici (Mrs. Hume), Marcelle Corday (Marthe), Hedda Hopper (American tourist), Leni Stengel (German tourist), Akim Tamiroff (Colonel).

The Cat and the Fiddle, MGM. Opened at the Capitol Theater, New York City, on February 16, 1934. Pr: Bernard Hyman. Dir: William K. Howard (additional scenes by Sam Wood, uncredited). Scr: Bella and Sam Spewack, from the play by Jerome Kern and Otto Harbach. Ph: Harold Rosson and Charles Clarke (B&W); Ray Rennahan (color). Ed: Frank E. Hull. AD: Alexander Toluboff (B&W) and Natalie Kalmus (color); interior decoration by Edwin B. Willis. Mus. Dir: Herbert Stothart. Songs: Music by Jerome Kern, lyrics by Otto Harbach. Sound. B&W with Technicolor sequence. Running time: 88 min. Cost: $843,000. Domestic rentals: $455,000. Foreign: $644,000. Loss $142,000.

Cast: Ramon Novarro (Victor Florescu), Jeanette MacDonald (Shirley Sheridan), Frank Morgan (Jules Daudet), Charles Butterworth (Charles), Jean Hersholt (Professor Bertier), Vivienne Segal (Odette Brieux), Frank Conroy (theater owner), Henry Armetta (taxi driver), Adrienne D'Ambricourt (concierge), Joseph Cawthorn (Rudy Brieux).

Laughing Boy, MGM. Opened at the Metropolitan Theater, Brooklyn, New York, on May 11, 1934. Pr: Hunt Stromberg. Dir: W. S. Van Dyke. Scr: John Colton and John Lee Mahin, from the 1929 novel by Oliver La Farge. Ph: Lester White. Ed: Blanche Sewell. Mus: Herbert Stothart. Song: "Call of Love," lyrics by Gus Kahn, music by Herbert Stothart. Sound. B&W. Running time: 79 min. Cost: $518,000. Domestic rentals: $180,000. Foreign: $84,000. Loss: $383,000.

Cast: Ramon Novarro (Laughing Boy), Lupe Velez (Slim Girl/Lily), William Dickenson (George Hartshone), Chief Thunderbird (Laughing Boy's father), Catalina Rambula (Laughing Boy's mother), Tall Man's Boy (Wounded Face), F. A. Armenta (Yellow Singer), Deer Spring (Jesting Squaw's son), Pellicana (Red Man).

The Night Is Young, MGM. Opened at the Capitol Theater, New York City, on January 11, 1935. Pr: Harry Rapf. Dir: Dudley Murphy. Scr: Edgar Allan Woolf and Franz Schulz, from a story by Vicki Baum. Ph: James Wong Howe. Ed: Conrad A. Nervig. AD: Cedric Gibbons, Frederic Hope, and Edwin B. Willis. Mus: Sigmund Romberg; libretto by Oscar Hammerstein II. Mus Dir: Herbert Stothart. Sound. B&W. Running time: 80 min. Cost: $573,000. Domestic rentals: $268,000. Foreign: $299,000. Loss: $234,000.

Cast: Ramon Novarro (Paul Gustave), Evelyn Laye (Lisl Gluck), Charles Butterworth (Willy Fitch), Una Merkel (Fanni), Edward Everett Horton (Szereny), Donald Cook (Toni), Henry Stephenson (Emperor), Rosalind Russell (Countess Rafay), Herman Bing (Nepomuk), Albert Conti (Moehler), Elspeth Dudgeon (Duchess), Charles Judels (Riccardi), Christian Rub (cafe proprietor), Gustav von Seyffertitz (Ambassador), Snub Pollard (drummer), Billy Gilbert, Cecilia Parker.

The Sheik Steps Out (working title: *She Didn't Want a Sheik*), Republic. Premiered at Warner's Beverly Hills Theater, Beverly Hills, on July 24, 1937 (released on September 6, 1937). Pr (associate): Herman Schlom. Dir: Irving Pichel. Scr: Adele Buffington; additional dialogue by Gordon Kahn. Ph: Jack Marta. Ed: Ernest Nims and Murray Seldeen. Mus Dir: Alberto Colombo. Songs: Felix Bernard, Winston Tharp, Alberto Colombo, and Elsie Janis. Sound. B&W. Running time: 55 min.

Cast: Ramon Novarro (Ahmed Ben Nesib), Lola Lane (Phyllis "Flip" Murdock), Gene Lockhart (Samuel P. Murdock), Kathleen Burke (Gloria Parker), Stanley Fields (Abu Saal), Billy Bevan (Munson), Charlotte Treadway (Polly Parker), Robert Coote (Lord Eustace Byington), Leonard Kinskey (Allusa Ali), Georges Benazent (Count Mario), Jamiel Hasson (Kisub), C. Montague Shaw (Dr. Peabody), George Sorel (Bordeaux), Martin Garralaga (hotel clerk), Josef Swickard (Muslim priest).

A Desperate Adventure (working titles: *It Happened in Paris, As You Are*), Republic. Opened on August 15, 1938. Pr (associate) and Dir: John H. Auer. Scr: Barry Travers, from an original story by Hans Kräly and M. Coates Webster. Ph: Jack Marta. Ed: Ernest Nims and Murray Seldeen. Sound. B&W. Running time: 65 min.

Cast: Ramon Novarro (André Friezan), Marian Marsh (Ann Carrington), Margaret Tallichet (Betty Carrington), Eric Blore (Trump), Andrew Tombes (Cosmo Carrington), Tom Rutherford (Gerald Richards), Maurice Cass (Dornay), Erno Verebes (Marcel), Michael Kent (Maurice), Cliff Nazarro (Tipo), Rolfe Sedan (prefect of police), Gloria Rich (Mimi), Lois Collier (Angela).

La Comédie du bonheur (*The Play of Happiness*), Artis-Film/Discina. Opened in Rome on December 23, 1940. Pr: André Paulvé. Dir: Marcel L'Herbier. Scr: Marcel L'Herbier, from the play by Nicolas Evreinoff; dialogue by Jean Cocteau. Ph: Massimo Terzano. Mus: Jacques Ibert. Sound. B&W. Running time: 108 min.

Cast: Michel Simon (Monsieur Jourdain), Ramon Novarro (Félix), Jacqueline Delubac (Anita/Annette), Micheline Presle (Lydia), Sylvie (Madame Maria), Louis Jourdan (Fédor), André Alerme (Déribin), Marcel Vallée (Dr. Acario), Jaque Catelain (director of Radio Azur).

La Virgen que forjó una patria (*The Virgin Who Forged a Nation*), Films Mundiales. Opened at the Palacio Chino in Mexico City on December 11, 1942. Opened in the U.S. at the Belmont Theater, New York City, on May 19, 1944. Pr: Agustín J. Fink. Dir: Julio Bracho. Scr: Julio Bracho and René Capistrán Garza. Sound. Ph: Gabriel Figueroa. Ed: Jorge Bustos. Mus: Miguel Bernal Jiménez. B&W. Running time: 106 min.

Cast: Ramon Novarro (Juan Diego), Domingo Soler (Friar Martín), Gloria Marín (Aztec slave), Julio Villareal (Don Miguel Hidalgo), Ernesto Alonso (Captain Ignacio Allende), Victor Urruchua (Captain Juan Aldama), Fanny Schiller (Josefa Ortíz), Paco Fuentes (Pedro de Alonso).

We Were Strangers (working title: *Rough Sketch*), Horizon/Columbia. Opened at the Astor Theater in New York City, on April 27, 1949. Pr: Sam Spiegel (as S. P. Eagle). Dir: John Huston. Scr: Peter Viertel and John Huston, from the "China Valdez" episode in Robert Sylvester's novel *Rough Sketch*. Ph: Russell Metty. Ed: Al Clark. Mus: George Antheil. Mus Dir: Morris Stoloff. Sound. B&W. Running time: 105 min. Cost: $900,000.

Cast: Jennifer Jones (China Valdes), John Garfield (Tony Fenner), Pedro Armendáriz (Armando Ariete), Gilbert Roland (Guillermo), Ramon Novarro (Chief), Wally Cassell (Miguel), David Bond (Ramón), José Pérez (Toto), Morris Ankrum (bank manager), Tito Rinaldo (Manolo), Paul Monte (Roberto).

The Big Steal, RKO. Opened at the Mayfair Theater, New York City, on July 9, 1949. Pr: Jack J. Gross. Dir: Don Siegel. Scr: Geoffrey Homes and Gerald Drayson

Adams, from Richard Wormser's story "The Road to Carmichael's." Ph: Harry J. Wild. Ed: Samuel E. Beetley. Mus: Leigh Harline. Sound. B&W. Running time: 71 min. Cost: $922,000. Domestic rentals: $1,425,000. Foreign: $425,000. Profit: $180,000.

Cast: Robert Mitchum (Lt. Duke Halliday), Jane Greer (Joan Graham), William Bendix (Capt. Vincent Blake), Patric Knowles (Jim Fiske), Ramon Novarro (Col. Ortega), Don Alvarado (Lt. Ruiz), John Qualen (Julius Seton), Pascual Garcia Pena (Manuel).

The Outriders, MGM. Opened at the Loew's State Theater in New York City on March 1, 1950. Pr: Richard Goldstone. Dir: Roy Rowland. Scr: Irving Ravetch. Ph: Charles Schoenbaum. Ed: Robert J. Kern. Mus: André Previn. Sound. Color. Running time: 93 min. Cost: $1,621,000. Domestic rentals: $1,540,000. Foreign: $639,000. Loss: $497,000.

Cast: Joel McCrea (Will Owen), Arlene Dahl (Jen Gort), Barry Sullivan (Jesse Wallace), Claude Jarman, Jr. (Roy Gort), James Whitmore (Clint Priest), Ramon Novarro (Don Antonio Chaves), Jeff Corey (Keeley), Ted de Corsia (Bye), Martin Garralaga (Father Damasco).

Crisis (working titles: *Basra, Visitor for Basra*). MGM. Opened at the Capitol Theater, New York City, on July 3, 1950. Pr: Arthur Freed. Dir: Richard Brooks. Scr: Richard Brooks, from the story "Basra" by George Tabori. Ph: Ray June. Ed: Robert J. Kern. Mus: Miklos Rozsa. Sound. B&W. Running time: 95 min. Cost: $1,581,000. Domestic rentals: $891,000. Foreign: $512,000. Loss: $723,000.

Cast: Cary Grant (Dr. Eugene Ferguson), José Ferrer (Raoul Farrago), Paula Raymond (Helen Ferguson), Signe Hasso (Isabel Farrago), Ramon Novarro (Col. Adragon), Antonio Moreno (Dr. Nierra), Teresa Celli (Rosa), Leon Ames (Sam Proctor), Gilbert Roland (Gonzales), Pedro de Cordoba (Father del Puento), Robert Cabal (Vyman).

Heller in Pink Tights (working title: *Heller with a Gun*), Paramount. Opened on February 29, 1960. Pr: Carlo Ponti and Marcello Girosi. Dir: George Cukor. Scr: Dudley Nichols and Walter Bernstein, from the novel *Heller with a Gun* by Louis L'Amour (with additions from nineteenth-century actor Joseph Jefferson's autobiography *Good Troupers All* and from a 1940s treatment written by D. W. Griffith partly based on Jefferson's book). Ph: Harold Lipstein. Ed: Howard Smith. Mus: Daniele Amfitheatrof. Sound. Color. Running time: 100 min.

Cast: Sophia Loren (Angela Rossinni), Anthony Quinn (Tom Healy), Margaret O'Brien (Della), Steve Forrest (Maybrey), Eileen Heckart (Lorna Hathaway), Ramon Novarro (De Leon), Edmund Lowe (Manfred Montague).

As Director/Producer/Writer
Contra la corriente (Against the current), an R.N.S. production distributed by RKO. Opened at the Teatro Campoamor, New York City, on March 6, 1936. Pr, Dir and Scr: Ramon Novarro. Assistant Dir: Antonio Samaniego. Ph: Edward Snyder and Jerry Ash. Ed: Ethel Davey. AD: Eduardo Samaniego (assisted by Stephen Stepanian). Mus: Professor Juan Aguilar. Sound. B&W. Running time: 89 min.

Cast: José Caraballo (Alberto Dortel), Luana Alcañiz (Rosalie Martín), Alma Real (Dolores Palacios de Martín), Ramón Guerrero (Frank Martín), Marina Ortíz

(Tía Pascuas), Luís Diaz Flores (Carlos Marco), Nena Sandoval (Juana), Carmen Samaniego (Maruca), Luz F. Moran (Sra. Torres), John Pérez (Ricardo Gavilán).

Short Film
The Christmas Party, MGM. Released during the 1931 Christmas season. Dir: Charles Reisner. Scr: Robert E. Hopkins. Sound. B&W. Running time: 9 min.

Cast (as themselves): Jackie Cooper, Lionel Barrymore, Wallace Beery, Marion Davies, Marie Dressler, Jimmy Durante, Cliff Edwards, Clark Gable, Charlotte Greenwood, Jerry Madden, Polly Moran, Ramon Novarro, Anita Page, Norma Shearer.

SELECT TV APPEARANCES

The Ken Murray Show (CBS), on February 6, 1952. Host: Ken Murray. Guests: Adolph Zukor, Buster Keaton, Ramon Novarro, Ruby Keeler.
Ed Sullivan's Toast of the Town (CBS), on December 23, 1951. Host: Ed Sullivan. Guests: Julie Harris, Gloria Swanson, Ramon Novarro, Billy DeWolf, Roger Price, St. Vincent Ferrer Boys Choir.
Walt Disney Presents: The Nine Lives of Elfego Baca (ABC). "Elfego—Lawman or Gunman," on November 28, 1958, and "Law and Order, Inc." on December 12, 1958. Cast: Robert Loggia (Elfego Baca), James Dunn (J. Henry Newman), Ramon Novarro (Don Esteban Miranda), Skip Homeier (Ross Mantee), Valerie Allen (Lucita Miranda), Carl Benton Reid (Judge Hargraves), Clegg Hoyt (Bruiser), Joe Maross (Towne), Raymond Bailey (Arnold Bixby).
Hedda Hopper's Hollywood (NBC), January 9, 1960. Host: Hedda Hopper. Guests: Lucille Ball, Robert Cummings, Anthony Perkins, Gary Cooper, Stephen Boyd, Ramon Novarro, Francis X. Bushman, Don Murray, Marion Davies, John Cassavetes, King Vidor, Gloria Swanson, Debbie Reynolds, Judy Garland, Janet Gaynor, Bob Hope, and others.
Thriller (NBC). "La Strega," on January 15, 1962. Pr: William Frye. Dir: Ida Lupino. Scr: Alan Caillou. Presenter: Boris Karloff. Cast: Ursula Andress (Luana), Alejandro Rey (Tonio Bellini), Jeanette Nolan (La Strega), Ramon Novarro (Maestro Giuliano), Frank De Kova (Lt. Vincoli), Ernest Sarracino (Padre Lupari).
Combat (ABC). "Silver Service," on October 13, 1964. Pr: Gene Levitt. Dir: Sutton Roley. Scr: Kay Lenard and Jess Carneol. Cast: Jack Hogan (William G. Kirby), Mickey Rooney (Harry White), Ramon Novarro (Charles Gireaux), Claudine Longet (Claudette).
Rawhide (CBS). "Canliss," on October 30, 1964. Pr: Bruce Geller and Bernard L. Kowalski. Dir: Jack Arnold. Scr: Stirling Silliphant. Cast: Eric Fleming (Gil Favor), Dean Martin (Gurd Canliss), Laura Devon (Augusta Canliss), Michael Ansara

(Don Miguel), Ramon Novarro (Father Tasso), Theodore Bikel (Pence), Jack Kruschen (Barkeep), Scott Marlowe (Tate).

Dr. Kildare (NBC). "Rome Will Never Leave You," aired in three parts on November 12, 19, and 26, 1964. Pr: David Victor. Dir: John Newland. Scr: Sally Benson, from a story by Jane and Ira Avery. Cast: Richard Chamberlain (Dr. Kildare), Alida Valli (Contessa Luisa Brabante), Daniela Bianchi (Francesca Paolini), Mercedes McCambridge (Sister Teresa), Ramon Novarro (Gaspero Paolini), Paul Stewart (Dr. Giuseppe Murtelli).

Bonanza (NBC). "The Brass Box," on September 26, 1965. Dir: William F. Claxton. Scr: Paul Schneider. Cast: Lorne Greene (Ben), Michael Landon (Little Joe), Ramon Novarro (José Ortega), Michael Dante (Miguel).

Combat (ABC). "Finest Hour," on December 21, 1965. Pr: Gene Levitt. Dir: Don Tait. Scr: Sutton Roley. Cast: Rick Jason (Lieutenant Hanley), Luise Rainer (Countess De Roy), Ramon Novarro (Count De Roy), Pierre Jalbert (Caje), Maurice Marsac (Claude), Kurt Kreuger (Major Werner), James Dobson (Lieutenant Schaefer).

The Wild, Wild West (CBS). "The Night of the Assassin," on September 22, 1967. Dir: Alan Crosland, Jr. Scr: Robert Dennis and Earl C. Barret. Cast: Robert Conrad (West), Ross Martin (Artemis), Robert Loggia (Colonel Barbossa), Ramon Novarro (Don Tomás), Donald Woods (Griswold), Nina Roman (Lupita), Conlon Carter (Halvorsen), Nate Esformes (Perrico), Carlos Romero (Lieutenant).

The High Chaparral (NBC). "A Joyful Noise," on March 24, 1968. Pr: William F. Claxton. Dir: Richard Benedict. Scr: William Blinn. Cast: Leif Ericson (John), Linda Cristal (Victoria), Cameron Mitchell (Buck), Henry Darrow (Manolito), Mark Slade (Blue), Ramon Novarro (Padre Guillermo), Laurie Mock (Maria), Robert Yuro (Ramon), Penny Stanton (Sister Angelica), Angela Clarke (Sister Luke).

SELECT STAGE APPEARANCES

At the Hollywood Community Theater

Salomé, by Oscar Wilde. February/March 1921. Dance Dir: Marion Morgan. With Betty Blythe (Herodias), Ramon Samaniegos (Herod).

The Royal Fandango, by Gustavo Morales. Opened on September 26, 1921. With Margaret Loomis. Ramon Samaniegos, Starke Patterson, Manuel Pérez.

Enter Madame, by Gilda Varesi and Dolly Byrne. February 1922. With Henrietta Crossman (as Madame), Ramsey Wallace, Helen Raymond, Ramon Samaniegos (as the Italian doctor).

In London
A Royal Exchange. Presented by J. L. Sacks. Book and lyrics by Frederick Herendeen from the original play by Lawrence Clarke (in the United States, the musical was called *All the King's Horses*). Adapted by Archibald Menzies. Dir: Tom Reynolds. Mus: Edward Horan. Dances and ensembles by Max Rivers. Opened on December 6, 1935, at His Majesty's Theater, London. Closed on December 14, 1935, after ten performances.
Cast: Ramon Novarro (Carlos Gavilán), Doris Kenyon (Princess Sylvia), Eddie Foy, Jr. (Con Conley), Hugh Wakefield (Baron Martínez), Doris Carson (Countess Eloise), Max Turganoff (Andre Kessel), Charles Walenn (José), Karl Melene (Pedro Cortez), Barrie Livesey (Baron Bathy), Julie Nash (Sherry Shannon), George Bryan (Waiter), Carmen Samaniego (Dancer), Leslie Bannister (Attendant).

In Summer Stock
The Command to Love, by Herman Bernstein and Brian Marlow, from the German play *Liebe auf Befehl* by Rudolph Lothar and Fritz Gottwald. Summer 1940 in New England. Novarro played Gaston, the Marquis de Saint Lac.
Dans l'Ombre du harem, by Lucien Besnard. April 1941 in Canada.
Tovarich, by Jacques Deval, adapted by Robert E. Sherwood. Summer 1941 in New England. Novarro played Prince Ouratieff.
Noah, by André Obey. Fall 1959 at St. Andrew's Priory, Valyermo, California. Novarro played Noah.
The Desert Song, by Otto Harbach, Oscar Hammerstein II, and Frank Mandel. Mus: Sigmund Romberg. Opened on June 4, 1962, at the Casa Mañana, Fort Worth. With Ramon Novarro (General Birabeau), Linda Loftis (Margot Bonvalet), and Nolan Van Way (the Red Shadow).
Flower Drum Song, by Oscar Hammerstein II and Joseph A. Fields, from the novel by C. Y. Lee. Mus: Richard Rodgers; lyrics by Oscar Hammerstein II. August/ September 1962 in Ohio, Indiana, and Michigan. With Juanita Hall (Madame Liang), Ramon Novarro (Wang Chi-Yang), and Michi Kobi (Linda Low).

On Broadway
Infidel Caesar. Presented by Ray Shaw in association with J. and M. Mitchell, Bernard A. Lang, and Peter Petrello. Adaptation and direction: Gene Wesson. Mus: Joe Reisman. Two preview performances on April 27 and 28, 1962, at the Music Box, New York City.
Cast: Michael Ansara (Cesar), Marta Pérez (Calpurnia), Gene Wesson (Antonio), Albert Popwell (Soothsayer), John Cullum (Cassios), Mark Margolis (Casca), Armand Alzamora (Metellos Cimber), James Earl Jones (Cinna), Shelby Taylor (Octavios), Frank Ferrer (Lepidos), Agustin Mayor (Antonio's servant), John Ireland (Brutos), Rafael Campos (Lucios), Maria Brenes (Portia), Ramon Novarro (Ligarios).

Acuña, Rodolfo. *Occupied America: A History of Chicanos*. New York: HarperCollins, 1988.

Affron, Charles. *Lillian Gish: Her Legend, Her Life*. New York: Scribner's, 2001.

Ankerich, Michael G. *Broken Silence: Conversations with 23 Silent Film Stars*. Jefferson, N.C.: McFarland, 1993.

———. *The Sound of Silence*. Jefferson, N.C.: McFarland, 1998.

Barraclough, David. *Movie Record Breakers*. Secaucus, N.J.: Quintet Publishing, 1992.

Basquette, Lina. *Lina: DeMille's Godless Girl*. Ed. Mary Garland Jonas. Fairfax, Va.: Denlinger's Publishers, 1990.

Ben-Allah. *Rudolph Valentino: His Romantic Life and Death*. Los Angeles: Ben-Allah Company, 1926.

Bernard, André, and Claude Gauteur, eds. *Jean Cocteau: The Art of Cinema*. Translated from the French by Robin Buss. London: Marion Boyars, 1992.

Bernard, Emily, ed. *Remember Me to Harlem*. New York: Alfred A. Knopf, 2001.

Berry, Faith. *Langston Hughes: Before and Beyond Harlem*. Westport, Conn.: L. Hill, 1983.

Bodeen, DeWitt. *From Hollywood*. New York: A. S. Barnes and Company, 1976.

———. *More from Hollywood: The Careers of 15 Great American Stars*. New York: A. S. Barnes, 1977.

Brownlow, Kevin. *Hollywood, the Pioneers*. New York: Alfred A. Knopf, 1979.

———. *The Parade's Gone By*. New York: Alfred A. Knopf, 1960.

Burch, Noël. *Marcel L'Herbier*. Edited by Pierre Lherminier. Paris: Editions Seghers, 1973.

Burton, Humphrey. *Leonard Bernstein*. New York: Doubleday, 1994.

Carey, Gary. *All the Stars in Heaven*. New York: E. P. Dutton, 1981.

Carr, Harry. *Los Angeles: City of Dreams*. New York: Grosset and Dunlap, 1935.

Carrafa, Alberto, y Arturo García. *Diccionario heráldico y genealógico de apellidos españoles y americanos*. Madrid: Hauser y Menet, 1959.

———. *El Solar Vasco Navarro*. Volume VI. San Sebastian, Spain: Librería Internacional, 1967.

Carringer, Robert, and Barry Sabath. *Ernst Lubitsch: A Guide to References and Resources*. Boston: G. K. Hall, 1978.

Carroll, David. *The Matinee Idols*. New York: Arbor House, 1972.

Carter, Gaylord. "Silents Were Never Silent." In *Films of the 1920s*, edited by Richard Dyer MacCann, 25–31. Lanham, Md.: Scarecrow Press, 1996.

Casasola, Gustavo. *Historia gráfica de la revolución mexicana*. Mexico City: Editorial F. Trillas, 1960.

Chauncey, George. *Gay New York: Gender, Urban Culture, and the Making of the Gay Male World, 1890–1940*. New York: HarperCollins, BasicBooks, 1994.

Cheetham, Nicolas. *New Spain, the Birth of Modern Mexico*. London: Victor Gollancz, 1974.

Coffee, Lenore. *Storyline: Reflections of a Hollywood Screenwriter*. London: Cassel, 1973.

Cooper, Miriam, and Bonnie Herndon. *Dark Lady of the Silents: My Life in Early Hollywood*. Indianapolis: Bobbs-Merrill, 1973.

Crawford, Joan, and Jane Kesner Ardmore. *A Portrait of Joan*. Garden City, N.Y.: Doubleday, 1962.

Crowther, Bosley. *Hollywood Rajah: The Life and Times of Louis B. Mayer*. New York: Henry Holt, 1960.

———. *The Lion's Share*. New York: E. P. Dutton, 1957.

Dannenberg, Joseph, ed. *Film Year Book*. New York: Film Daily, 1920–1933.

D'Antonio, Joanne. *Andrew Marton*. Metuchen, N.J.: Directors Guild of America; Scarecrow Press, 1991.

Dowd, Nancy, and David Shepard. *King Vidor*. Metuchen, N.J.: Directors Guild of America; Scarecrow Press, 1988.

Drew, William. *At the Center of the Frame: Leading Ladies of the Twenties and Thirties*. Lanham, Md.: Vestal Press, 1999.

Eames, John Douglas. *The MGM Story: The Complete History of Fifty-four Roaring Years*. London: Octopus Books, 1979.

Earle, Eyvind. *Horizon Bound on a Bicycle*. Los Angeles: Earle and Bane, 1990.

Eisner, Lotte H. *Murnau*. Berkeley: University of California Press, 1973.

Ellenberger, Allan R. *Ramon Novarro*. Jefferson, N.C.: McFarland, 1999.

Eyman, Scott. *Ernst Lubitsch: Laughter in Paradise*. New York: Simon and Schuster, 1993.

———. *Five American Cinematographers*. Metuchen, N.J.: Scarecrow Press, 1987.

Finler, Joel W. *The Hollywood Story*. New York: Crown, 1988.

———. *The Movie Directors Story*. New York: Crescent Books, 1985.

Ford, Charles, ed. *Jacques Feyder*. Paris: Editions Seghers, 1973.

Fordin, Hugh. *Getting to Know Him: A Biography of Oscar Hammerstein II*. Cambridge, Mass.: Da Capo Press, 1995.

Fountain, Leatrice Gilbert, and John R. Maxim. *Dark Star*. New York: St. Martin's Press, 1985.

Franklin, Joe. *Classics of the Silent Screen*. New York: Bramhall House, 1959.

Gamio, Manuel. *Mexican Immigration to the United States*. Chicago: University of Chicago Press, 1930.

Gelman, Barbara, ed. *Photoplay Treasury*. New York: Crown, 1972.

Goldwyn, Samuel. *Behind the Screen*. New York: George H. Doran, 1923.

Harrison, Joel L. *Bloody Wednesday*. Canoga Park, Calif.: Major Books, 1978.

Hart, John Mason. *Revolutionary Mexico: The Coming and Process of the Mexican Revolution*. Berkeley: University of California, 1987.

Hayes, Helen, and Sandford Dody. *On Reflection, an Autobiography*. New York: M. Evans, 1968.

Hays, Will H. *The Memoirs of Will H. Hays*. New York: Doubleday, 1955.

Heinink, Juan B., and Robert G. Dickson. *Cita en Hollywood.* Bilbao, Spain: Ediciones Mensajero, 1990.

Herman, Hal C., ed. *How I Broke into Movies.* Los Angeles: Hal C. Herman, 1929.

Heston, Charlton. *Charlton Heston: In the Arena.* New York: Simon and Schuster, 1995.

Higham, Charles. *Merchant of Dreams: Louis B. Mayer, M.G.M. and the Secret Hollywood.* New York: Donald I. Fine, 1993.

Hoffman, Abraham. *Unwanted Mexican Americans in the Great Depression: Repatriation Pressures, 1929–1939.* Tucson: University of Arizona Press, 1974.

Jacobson, Laurie. *Hollywood Heartbreaks.* New York: Simon and Schuster, 1984.

Janis, Elsie. *So Far So Good!* New York: E. P. Dutton, 1932.

Kaminsky, Stuart. *John Huston: Maker of Magic.* Boston: Houghton Mifflin, 1978.

Katz, Ephraim. *The Film Encyclopedia.* 2nd ed. New York: HarperCollins, 1994.

Katz, Friedrich. *The Life and Times of Pancho Villa.* Stanford, Calif.: Stanford University Press, 1998.

Kerrigan, J. Warren. *How I Became a Successful Moving Picture Star.* Los Angeles: No publisher identified, apparently self-published, 1914.

Kessler, Lauren. *The Happy Bottom Riding Club: The Life and Times of Pancho Barnes.* New York: Random House, 2000.

Koszarski, Richard. *The Man You Love to Hate: Erich von Stroheim in Hollywood.* Oxford, U.K.: Oxford University Press, 1983.

Lambert, Gavin. *Nazimova.* New York: Alfred A. Knopf, 1997.

———. *Norma Shearer.* New York: Alfred A. Knopf, 1990.

Lennig, Arthur. *Stroheim.* Lexington: University Press of Kentucky, 2000.

Lloyd, Ann, ed. *Movies of the Silent Years.* London: Orbis Publishing, 1984.

Loos, Anita. *A Girl Like I.* New York: Viking, 1966.

———. *The Talmadge Girls.* New York: Viking, 1978.

Loy, Myrna, and James Kotsilibas-Davis. *Myrna Loy: Being and Becoming.* New York: Alfred A. Knopf, 1987.

Maas, Frederica Sagor. *The Shocking Miss Pilgrim.* Lexington: University Press of Kentucky, 1999.

MacCann, Richard Dyer. *The Stars Appear.* Metuchen, N.J.: Scarecrow Press, 1992.

Malossi, Giannino, ed. *The Passionate South: Latin Lover.* Milan: Edizioni Charta, 1996.

Mann, William J. *Behind the Screen: How Gays and Lesbians Shaped Hollywood, 1910–1969.* New York: Viking, 2001.

———. *Wisecracker: The Life and Times of William Haines, Hollywood's First Openly Gay Star.* New York: Viking, 1998.

Marion, Frances. *Off with Their Heads.* New York: MacMillan, 1972.

Marx, Samuel. *Mayer and Thalberg: The Make-Believe Saints.* New York: Random House, 1975.

Mayne, Judith. *Directed by Dorothy Arzner.* Bloomington: Indiana University Press, 1994.

McGilligan, Pat, ed. *Backstory.* Berkeley: University of California Press, 1986.

Meier, Matt S., and Feliciano Rivera. *The Chicanos: A History of Mexican Americans.* New York: Hill and Wang, 1972.

Meyer, Eugenia, ed. *Cuadernos de la Cineteca Nacional: Testimonios para la historia del cine mexicano*. Mexico City: Dirección de Cinematografía de la Secretaria de Gobernación, 1976.

Milland, Ray. *Wide-Eyed in Babylon*. New York: William Morrow, 1974.

Mitchell, Greg. *The Campaign of the Century*. New York: Random House, 1992.

Monroy, Douglas. *Rebirth: Mexican Los Angeles from the Great Migration to the Great Depression*. Berkeley: University of California Press, 1999.

Mora, Carl J. *Mexican Cinema—Reflections of a Society, 1896–1980*. Berkeley: University of California Press, 1982.

Morris, Michael. *Madam Valentino: The Many Lives of Natacha Rambova*. New York: Abbeville Press, 1991.

Munn, Michael. *The Hollywood Case Murderbook*. New York: St. Martin's Press, 1987.

Nasaw, David. *The Chief: The Life of William Randolph Hearst*. Boston: Houghton Mifflin, 2000.

Nash, Jay Robert. *Murder Among the Mighty*. New York: Delacorte Press, 1983.

The New York Times Film Reviews, 1913–1968. New York: New York Times; Arno Press, 1970.

Nugent, Robert, and Jeannine Gramick. *Homosexuality: Protestant, Catholic and Jewish Issues: A Fishbone Tale*. Binghamton, N.Y.: Haworth Press, 1989.

O'Leary, Liam. *Rex Ingram: Master of the Silent Cinema*. Dublin: The Academic Press, 1980.

Osborne, Robert. *65 Years of the Oscar: The Official History of the Academy Awards*. New York: Abbeville Press, 1994.

Paris, Barry. *Garbo, a Biography*. New York: Alfred A. Knopf, 1995.

Parish, James Robert. *The Hollywood Deathbook*. Las Vegas: Pioneer Books, 1992.

———. *The Jeanette MacDonald Story*. New York: Mason/Charter, 1976.

Parish, James Robert, and William T. Leonard. *Hollywood Players: The Thirties*. New Rochelle, N.Y.: Arlington House, 1976.

Parish, James Robert, and Gregory Mank, with Richard Picchiarini. *The Best of MGM: The Golden Years, 1928–1959*. Westport, Conn.: Arlington House, 1981.

Parsons, Louella. *The Gay Illiterate*. New York: Doubleday, Doran, 1944.

Powell, Michael. *Million Dollar Movie*. New York: Random House, 1992.

Quinlan, David. *The Illustrated Guide to Film Directors*. Totowa, N.J.: Barnes and Noble Books, 1983.

Quirk, Lawrence. *Norma: The Biography of Norma Shearer*. New York: St. Martin's Press, 1988.

Ramón, David. *Dolores del Río*. Volumes I and II. Mexico City: Editorial Clio, Libros y Videos, 1997.

Ríos-Bustamante, Antonio, and Pedro Castillo. *An Illustrated History of Mexican Los Angeles*. Berkeley: University of California Press, 1986.

Sayres, B. W. *Who's Whose in Hollywood: A Sorta Saga of Screenland*. Los Angeles: No publisher identified, ca. 1926.

Schickel, Richard. *D. W. Griffith: An American Life*. New York: Simon and Schuster, 1984.

Schulberg, Budd. *Moving Pictures: Memories of a Hollywood Prince*. New York: Stein and Day, 1981.

Segrave, Kerry. *American Films Abroad*. Jefferson, N.C.: McFarland, 1997.

Server, Lee. *Robert Mitchum*. New York: St. Martin's Press, 2001.

Shipman, David. *The Great Movie Stars: The Golden Years*. New York: Hill and Wang, 1979.

Shulman, Irving. *Valentino*. New York: Trident Press, 1967.

Siegel, Don. *A Siegel Film: An Autobiography*. London: Faber and Faber, 1993.

Slide, Anthony. *Eccentrics of Comedy*. Lanham, Md.: Scarecrow Press, 1998.

————. *The Encyclopedia of Vaudeville*. Westport, Conn.: Greenwood Press, 1994.

————. *The Idols of Silence*. New York: A. S. Barnes, 1976.

St. Johns, Adela Rogers. *Love, Laughter and Tears: My Hollywood Story*. Garden City, N.Y.: Doubleday, 1978.

Starr, Kevin. *Material Dreams: Southern California through the 1920s*. Oxford, U.K.: Oxford University Press, 1990.

Steinberg, Cobbett S. *Film Facts*. New York: Facts on File, 1980.

Stine, Whitney, and George Hurrell. *The Hurrell Style: 50 Years of Photographing Hollywood*. New York: John Day, 1976.

Tate, Grover Ted. *The Lady Who Tamed Pegasus: The Story of Pancho Barnes*. Bend, Ore.: Maverick, 1984.

Thompson, Frank, ed. *Henry King, Director: From Silents to 'Scope*. Based on interviews by David Shepard and Ted Perry. Los Angeles: Directors Guild of America, 1995.

Tornabene, Lyn. *Long Live the King*. New York: G. P. Putnam's Sons, 1976.

Turk, Edward Baron. *Hollywood Diva: A Biography of Jeanette MacDonald*. Berkeley: University of California Press, 1998.

Ullback, Sylvia. *Hollywood Undressed: Observations of Sylvia Ullback as Noted by Her Secretary*. New York: Brentano's, 1931.

Variety Film Reviews. New York: Garland Publishing, 1983.

Vieira, Mark A. *Hurrell's Hollywood Portraits*. New York: Harry N. Abrams, 1997.

————. *Sin in Soft Focus: Pre-Code Hollywood*, New York: Harry N. Abrams, 1999.

Viñas, Moisés. *Indice cronologico del cine mexicano (1896–1992)*. Mexico City: Universidad Nacional Autónoma de México, 1992.

Weinberg, Herman. *The Lubitsch Touch: A Critical Study*. New York: Dover Publications, 1968.

West, Dennis. "Mexico: from the Golden Age to the Present." In *World Cinema Since 1945*, edited by William Luhr, 447–65. New York: Ungar, 1987.

Wilson, Sandy. *Ivor*. London: Michael Joseph, 1975.

Wister, Owen. *Padre Ignacio*. New York: Harper and Brothers, 1925.

Yeager, Chuck, and Leo Janos. *Yeager: An Autobiography*. New York: Bantam, 1985.

Zierold, Norman. *Garbo*. New York: Stein and Day, 1969.

ACKNOWLEDGMENTS

I first heard of Ramon Novarro about ten years after his death. I was in my early teens and still living with my family in Rio de Janeiro when I saw his name in an English-language film book whose title has long vanished from my memory. Not surprisingly, the first thing I learned about this screen idol was his murder at the hands of two hustlers. I did not know the exact meaning of the word "hustler," but soon enough it became clear that the author was referring to male prostitutes.

Fully aware of my own sexual orientation, I felt a morbid curiosity. I was ignorant of Novarro's appearance, but I assumed that this film actor must have been both handsome and masculine—an alluring image for a thirteen-year-old gay kid desperately looking for others like himself. Additionally, I wanted to find out more about Ramon Novarro's life in order to understand how such a tragedy could have befallen a man who had once been a major Hollywood star.

The rudimentary research I did at the time failed to yield any significant discoveries. Very little printed material about Novarro and only a few photographs were readily available. In those pre-VCR and pre–cable television days, the films that show Novarro at his best were nearly impossible to find in the United States, let alone in Brazil. As a result, my interest in Novarro waned until the mid-1990s, when I finally saw some of his early work at the Silent Movie Theater in West Hollywood. I tried to learn more about him at that time, but the new sources I found were superficial and inconsistent. Current criticism of his work is rare, and most recent articles about him deal mainly—and often only—with his death. Thus the decision to write a comprehensive account of Ramon Novarro's life and career.

In order to complete this five-year-long project, I have relied on the cooperation of dozens of individuals on four different continents.

Beyond Paradise would never have gotten off the ground without the assistance of the following individuals: Matias Bombal, a generous friend and a faithful Ramon Novarro admirer, spent time and effort finding Novarro treasure troves and then unselfishly shared them with me—without him, much of the information contained in this book would have remained beyond my reach; Dr. Frank Carothers, a friend for many years, an unremitting source of support from the earliest stages of this project, and always patient and ready to help when I called him to ask about uncertain prepositions and overlong sentences—Frank was an indispensable help in the shaping of this manuscript; T. Gene Hatcher, currently working on a *Ben-Hur* project, is another generous friend who shared whatever Novarro information and material he had, and whose thorough, detailed, and thoughtful editorial comments also played a key role in the final text; James Robert Parish was always supportive and took time off from his myriad projects to provide helpful suggestions and comments for *Beyond Paradise*; Novarro's literary executor Leonard Shannon trusted me and my book—and I am as thankful for that as for the priceless box of Novarro memorabilia he kindly gave me; and finally, film historian and author Anthony Slide guided me through every stage of the manuscript— besides helping me find contacts and information, Tony, as importantly, challenged my viewpoints and biases and helped me ask the right questions during my research.

I also want to express my sincere thanks to those who have spent time (sometimes long hours) reminiscing about Ramon Novarro or helping me find pertinent information about Novarro and/or the Hollywood of the 1920s–1960s: Don Atkins, James Bacon, Michael Bailey, Larry Billman, Michael Blankenship, James Campbell, Charles Clark, Kevin Crease, Constance Cummings, Critt Davis, Sandy DeKay, Richard DeNeut, the late Ken DuMain, the late Eyvind Earle, the late Douglas Fairbanks, Jr., Tucker Fleming, Leatrice Gilbert Fountain, Michael Frankovich, Jr., Friar Dismas Gannon, Pieter Gerits, the late Jane Greer, Charlton Heston, the late Rose Hobart, William Hughes, Claude Jarman, Jr., Jerry Jensik, Tom Koch, Lupita Tovar Kohner, Lyn Larsen, Betty Lasky, Frank Lieberman, Forrest McCoy, Randal Malone, the late J. J. Maloney, Marian Marsh, Wes Muchmore, the late Joseph J. O'Donohue IV, Anita Page, Thea Paul, Lois Peyton, Len Power, David Price, Paula Raymond, Seth Riggs, Jessica Rosner, Tonio Selwart, John Siglow, Eliya Silverstein, the late Mary Anne Styburski, Scott Tobin, George Walsh II, Edward Weber, Alan Weiss, the late Ted Wick, Charles Williamson, and others who have requested anonymity. Finally, I would also like to thank Ramon Novarro's family members who have helped me in this endeavor, including Novarro's nephew Father Eddie Samaniego, S.J., who allowed me to read his father Eduardo Samaniego's memoirs, and the late Carmen (Samaniego) Gavilán.

My deepest thanks to George Schönbrunn for his hospitality and the long hours he spent with me reminiscing about Novarro, Natalie Bateson, Cecil Everley—and Pola Negri; to Jack Hewson for his candidness when discussing Alice Terry; to Paul Cuva for generously providing me with photographs he inherited from the Alice Terry estate; and to John Lanchbery, for his reminiscences and for a copy of Novarro's "Tempo di valzer."

I must also thank the following film historians, scholars, and writers who have provided essential information and support for *Beyond Paradise:* Michael Ankerich, James Bangley, Janet Bergstroem, Robert Birchard, Kevin Brownlow, William Drew, Robert Gitt, Eve Golden, Juan B. Heinink, Dr. Richard Jewell, Matthew Kennedy, Miles Kreuger, Gavin Lambert, Emily Leider, Bruce Long, William J. Mann, Jon Mirsalis, David Pierce, Lawrence Quirk, Karl Thiede, Bob Thomas, Edward Baron Turk, the late Gene Vazzana, and Mark A. Vieira.

My heartfelt gratitude to Allan R. Ellenberger, who so generously provided me with information and materials he had amassed while researching Novarro's life; to Robert G. Dickson, who helped me find contacts in Mexico and presented me with material about Novarro's Spanish-language film and tapes of some of Novarro's television appearances, and who even found me a print of *La Virgen que forjó una patria*; to Father Michael Morris, S.J., who put me in touch with Father Eddie Samaniego; to Philip Jenkinson, for sending me a videotape of his late-1960s interview with Novarro; to Jeffrey Vance, for loaning me original photographs from his *Ben-Hur* and *Trifling Women* collections; to New York Public Library Film and Video librarian Joseph Yranski, for long and informative telephone conversations, and for trusting me with his collection of Ramon Novarro photographs and scrapbooks; and to the Silent Society's Randy Haberkamp, for loaning me his rare collection of film fan magazines of the 1920s and 1930s—without ever asking when I would bring them back.

Miren Jasone Amurrio, Fernando de Juana, Joaquín Polo, and Amos Samaniego helped me trace the origins of the name Samaniego; Frank Lopez gave me information about Novarro's alleged ancestor, Juan José de Escandón; Antonio DuBois, Walter Matsuura, and Martin Wile talked to me about the history of the West Adams district; Father Michael Engh, S.J., of Loyola Marymount University, discussed the reality of Mexican immigrants in the Los Angeles of the 1910s and 1920s; Jeffrey Balkin kindly allowed me to photocopy sections of Rex Ingram's memoirs and several letters from the Alice Terry estate; and Daniel Schwarz provided me with videotapes featuring Ramon Novarro.

I also thank Richard May, vice-president of film preservation for Warner Bros., for allowing me to watch prints of two extremely rare Novarro pictures, *The Midshipman* and *Forbidden Hours*; Roger Mayer, president and chief operating officer at Turner Entertainment Group, who permitted me to have copies of Novarro's MGM contracts—thus proving wrong everyone who told me I would *never* be able to get those copies; and to Kathleen S. Newberry, who actually made the copies and sent them my way.

I would also like to thank the following people and institutions: the staff of the Academy of Motion Picture Arts and Sciences Margaret Herrick Library, with special thanks to Don Li, Tony Guzman, and Sandra Archer at the information desk, and Barbara Hall of special collections; the Bancroft Library, University of California at Berkeley; the British Film Institute; the Charles E. Young Research Library and the Arts Library, University of California at Los Angeles; the staff of the Church of Latter-Day Saints Family History Center in Los Angeles; Ned Comstock of the University of Southern California Cinema-Television Library; Eliane Perez of the Biblioteca Nacional do Rio de Janeiro; Jean Fickett, James Forger, and Shawn Myrda of the Michigan State University School of Music; the George Eastman House; Karen Krebs-Wellerstein of the School of Dental Medicine at the University of Pennsylvania; the Los Angeles Public Library; the National Library of Ireland; Pedro Raigoza of the Museo Regional de Durango; the Samuel Paley Library, Temple University; Mischa Schutt of the ONE Institute and Archives in Los Angeles; and Dace Taub of the University of Southern California Regional History Center.

Judge Mark Brandler, Paul Robert Ferguson, and Thomas Scott Ferguson candidly discussed the most difficult section of the book for me: the events on October 30, 1968, and the ensuing trial of the Ferguson brothers. I am deeply grateful for their trust, especially for Tom Ferguson's consent that I meet with him at the California State Prison in Lancaster, and for Paul Ferguson's lengthy letters and his allowing me to read his as yet unpublished manuscript, "The Rape of the Red Ryder."

Isabel Turner, a member of the Ramon Novarro Film Club, contributed to this project with priceless and unique materials, including Audrey Homan's collection of letters, photographs, news clippings, and dozens of RNFC newsletters. I also thank Ms. Turner for her perceptive notes and suggestions in regard to my manuscript. Others I would like to thank for their editorial comments are Randy Davidson, Brad Owen, and Lew Williams.

Finally, I thank my agent Malaga Baldi for her steady support, and, at St. Martin's Press, my editor, Keith Kahla, for his incisive comments, Teresa Theophano for her patience when replying to my myriad questions, and production editor Robert Cloud and copy editor Adam Goldberger for their careful attention to my manuscript. Others who contributed to this project with their moral support (and, in some cases, also with their time and money) were Dr. Susan Barber and Dr. Sue Scheibler of Loyola Marymount University, Jerome Braun, Simon Davis, Mathias Frischmuth, André Loureiro, and my father and my late mother. My sincerest thanks to all of you.

INDEX